PRACTICAL ASPECTS OF MEMORY

Proceedings of the International Conference on Practical Aspects of Memory, held under the auspices of the Welsh branch of the British Psychological Society, in Cardiff from September 4–8, 1978.

PRACTICAL ASPECTS OF MEMORY

Edited by

M. M. Gruneberg

Psychology Department
University College
Swansea, Wales

P. E. Morris

Department of Psychology
University of Lancaster
England

R. N. Sykes

Psychology Department
University College
Swansea, Wales

1978

ACADEMIC PRESS
London · New York · San Francisco

A Subsidiary of Harcourt Brace Jovanovich, Publishers

ACADEMIC PRESS INC. (LONDON) LTD.
24/28 Oval Road,
London NW1

United States Edition published by
ACADEMIC PRESS INC.
111 Fifth Avenue
New York, New York 10003

Library of Congress Catalog Card Number: 78-73453
ISBN: 0-12-305050-2

Printed in Great Britain by
Galliard (Printers) Ltd, Great Yarmouth, Norfolk

PREFACE

This book consists of papers presented at the International Conference on Practical Aspects of Memory, held under the auspices of the Welsh Branch of the British Psychological Society, in Cardiff, from the 4th-8th September 1978. The objectives of the Conference, which as far as we are aware was the first of its kind, were to examine ways in which the considerable advances recently made in our theoretical understanding of memory could be applied to 'real-life' memory problems, and to examine ways in which an attack on real life problems could throw light on aspects of theoretical interest and importance. In no way was the aim of the Conference to drive a wedge between theoretical and practical aspects of memory, in a fashionable search for relevance. Nevertheless, it is our view that the practical significance of memory research has been largely ignored by psychologists, and it is this gap that the Conference sought to stimulate psychologists to fill.

Five years ago, a conference on practical aspects of memory would probably have been impossible, so the success of the Conference, as measured by the large number of distinguished academic psychologists from all over the world who attended, is some measure of the sympathy which our aims attracted. Yet given the relatively short time that psychologists have been interested in some of the problems discussed at the Conference, too much should not be expected in the way of ready solutions. Rather the importance of the Conference should be seen in terms of the questions which psychologists are now willing to ask, and the Conference should be judged in terms of the whole, rather than on the strengths or weaknesses of any individual paper.

Because we feel the importance of the Conference lies as much in terms of the questions posed as of the answers given, and because we feel the Conference proceedings would benefit from publication as soon after the Conference as possible, editing and indexing have been kept to a minimum, although a few papers have had to be omitted for a variety of reasons. The book has been organised into a number of sections. After the opening address, the first part consists of papers of general interest. The second part consists of papers relevant to educational psychology, and the final part consists of papers of interest to clinical psychologists. The first section contains symposia on *Memory and Everyday Life*, *Eye-Witnessing*, *Facial Recognition*, *Stress and Arousal*, and *Individual Differences*. Included in the second section are symposia on *Memory in Children*, *Reading and Memory*, *Memory and Dyslexia*, *Memory Strategies*, *Memory in the Deaf*, and *General Educational Problems*. In the third section are symposia on *Brain Damage*, *Measurement in Clinical Populations* and *Drugs*. In organising the presentation of the book we are aware that some symposia, such as Dyslexia, could have been placed in either the Clinical or Educational section, and the allocation to the Educational section was therefore somewhat arbitrary. Furthermore, the papers presented in symposia at the Conference have been added to by other papers presented elsewhere in the Conference, where such papers seemed appropriate to the subject matter of the symposia.

No conference of this kind could be organised without the help of a large number of people. We should therefore like to thank Mr. John Castell and Dr. Tony Chapman, Chairman and Secretary of the Welsh Branch of the B.P.S., the stewards who ensured the smooth running of the Conference, and our highly competent secretarial help from Miss Jackie Scholz and Mrs. Maureen Rogers. We should also like to thank Professor Neisser for his stimulating and beautifully presented opening address, and all the delegates, for the way they came to the Conference determined to make it a success.

Michael M. Gruneberg
Peter Morris
Robert N. Sykes.

CONTENTS

CONTENTS

CONTENTS

CONTENTS

PART II: PRACTICAL ASPECTS OF MEMORY - EDUCATIONAL IMPLICATIONS

Memory in Children

Memory and Reading

CONTENTS

CONTENTS

CONTENTS

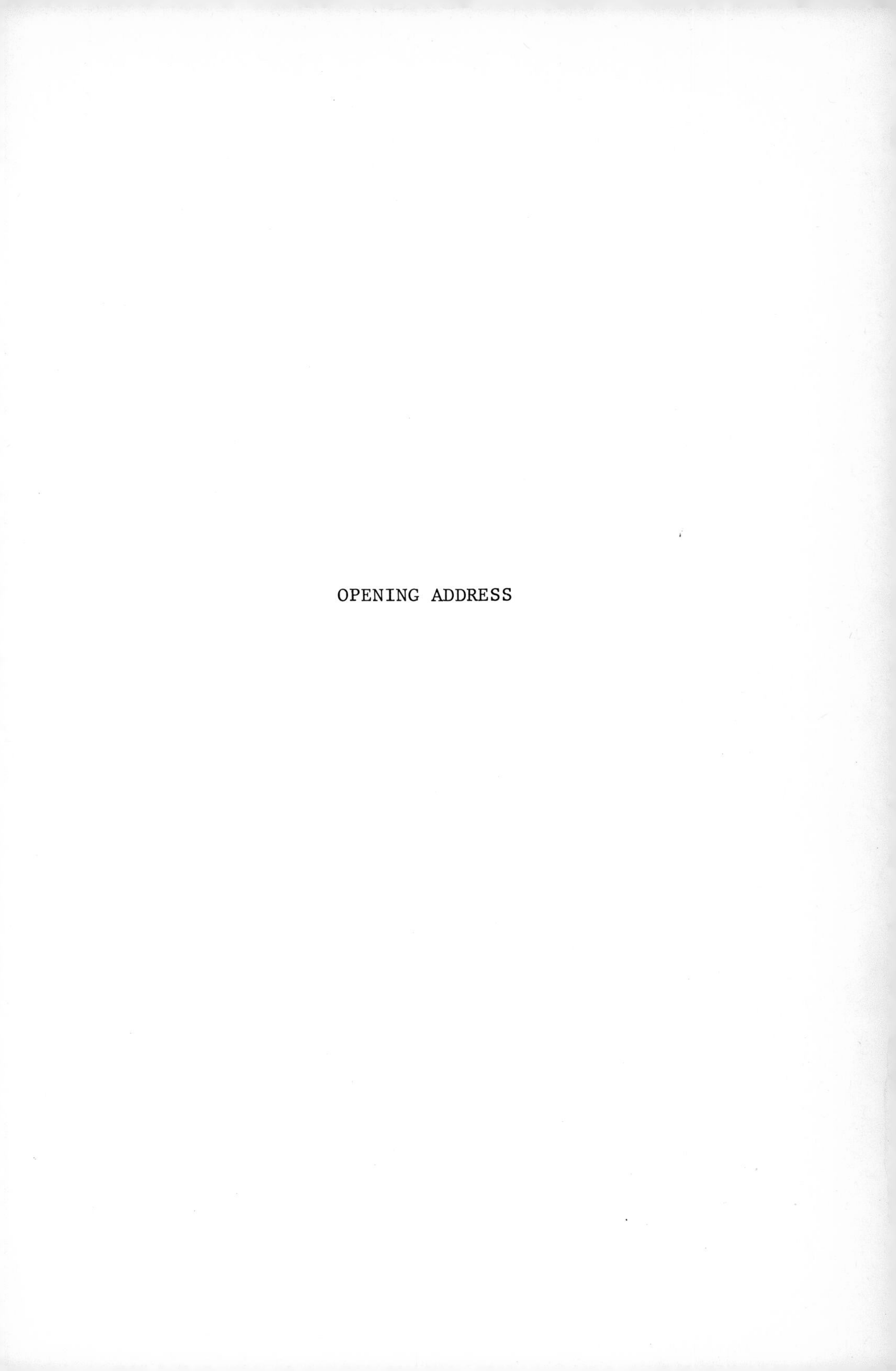

OPENING ADDRESS

MEMORY: WHAT ARE THE IMPORTANT QUESTIONS?

Ulric Neisser
Cornell University
Ithaca, N. Y. 14853

It is a distinct honor to open a conference on practical aspects of memory, and an unusual one. So far as I know, there has never been such a conference before. Perhaps it seems especially remarkable to me because I am an American, and therefore have relatively little experience of fruitful interchange between theoretical and applied psychology. British experimental psychologists have a long tradition of benefitting from that interchange, but we are less used to it in the United States. Unfortunately, the naturalistic tradition has been weaker in the study of memory than in many other areas, even in Britain. Nevertheless, it has not been entirely lacking: it was from Cambridge that Bartlett launched his quixotic challenge to the memory establishment of the 1920s and 1930s. He was convinced that his contemporaries understood neither the purpose nor the nature of memory, and that standard laboratory procedures just obscured its real characteristics. His challenge went almost unheard for 40 years, from the publication of Remembering (1932) until this decade, but it is unheard no longer. There is suddenly a host of theorists talking about "schemata" (e. g., Rumelhart, 1975; Anderson, 1977), and a host of experimenters studying memory for stories (e. g., Bransford & Johnson, 1973; Mandler & Johnson, 1977). In my view this work is still somewhat deficient in ecological validity--hardly anyone memorizes one-page stories except in the course of psychological experiments--but it is still a great step forward (cf. Neisser & Hupcey, 1974). Perhaps, as someone once said of something else, the naturalistic study of memory is an idea whose time has come.

I am slightly embarrassed that I cannot remember the source of that particular expression, but not surprised. It is a frequent experience for me. I am often unable to recall the authors of phrases that I would like to quote, and have equal difficulty in remembering who told me things. These retrieval failures pose some interesting questions. Why do they occur? Do other people have less trouble recalling sources than I do? Is my difficulty in remembering the source of a written quotation related to other types of memory failure, or are they independent? In fact, how does one go about remembering sources, or arguments, or material appropriate to one's train of thought? What makes for skill in such activities?

These questions may not be the "important" ones that my title has promised, but they are interesting nevertheless. They involve real uses of memory in humanly understandable situations. It is therefore discouraging to find that nothing in the extensive literature of the psychology of memory sheds much light on them, so that anyone who wishes to study such problems must start from scratch. Unfortunately, this is not an isolated instance. It is an example of a principle that is nearly as valid in 1978 as it was in 1878: If _X_ is an interesting or socially significant aspect of memory, then psychologists have hardly ever studied _X_.

Let me give another example of that principle, again drawn from my own immediate experience. In giving this address, I naturally hope that I will make some impression on you: that you will remember at least part of what I say. But what _do_ people remember of speeches that they hear, or arguments made to them? Who remembers what, and why? The social psychologists have touched lightly on these issues in their examination of persuasion, but they have been interested in opinion change rather than in memory. Apart from their work, the effect of lectures on listeners has hardly been studied at all. A couple of recent exploratory experiments--one by Kintsch & Bates (1977) and the other by Keenan, McWhinney & Mayhew (1977)--suggest that such studies might yield intriguing results: listeners seem to remember the lecturer's irrelevant asides better than his text, for example.

This is part of a larger question. Most experimental psychologists of memory are also teachers. We earn our living by presenting information to students, often by lecturing, and at the end of the term we set examinations to see if they remember any of it. But what happens after that? Students attend universities partly because they hope to acquire knowledge that will be valuable to them afterwards; that is, they expect to remember some of it. We certainly share their hope. Despite the old saying that "education is what is left over when you have forgotten what you learned," (which I also cannot reference properly), we would be dismayed if a kind of educational Korsakov amnesia regularly wiped out all trace of our teachings. How much, then, do students retain? This really _is_ an important question. Higher education has become a central feature of Western culture, involving millions of people every year, and it depends heavily on the assumption that students remember something valuable from their educational experience. One might expect psychologists to leap at the opportunity to study a critical memory problem so close at hand, but they never do. It is difficult to find even a single study, ancient or modern, of what is retained from academic instruction. Given our expertise and the way we earn our livings, this omission can only be described as scandalous.

Other illustrations of the general principle are readily available. You need only tell any friend, not himself a psychologist, that you study memory. Given even a little encouragement, your friend will describe all kinds of interesting phenomena: the limitations of his memory for early childhood, his inability to remember appointments, his aunt who could recite poems from memory by the hour, the regrettable recent decline in his ability to recall people's names, how well he could find his way around his home town after a thirty years' absence, the differences between his memory and someone else's. Our research, of course, has virtually nothing to say about any of these topics.

Psychology's thundering silence on such questions might be excused if the study of memory had only just begun. One cannot do everything right away. The fact is, however, that we have been studying memory, and doing memory experiments, for nearly a hundred years. Research on the topic went on continuously even during the dreary decades of behaviorist domination, and has recently reached almost frenzied proportions. This research was not carried out by uneducated or incompetent people; some of the best minds in psychology have worked, and are presently working, in the area of memory. Why, then, have they not turned their attention to practical problems and natural settings?

The answer is not far to seek. Psychologists are not interested in such questions primarily because they believe they are doing something more important. They are working toward a general theory of memory, a scientific understanding of its underlying mechanisms, more fundamental and far-reaching than any research on worldly questions could possibly be. They can claim that their work has already established broad generalizations and led to new discoveries; it is even now converging on specific and powerful theories. If these claims were valid, they might justify neglecting problems that seem more obvious and interesting to our non-psychologist friends. Therefore I will examine each of them briefly: the established principles, the new discoveries, and the theories themselves. As you may already suspect, the results of my survey will not be encouraging.

Let us take the empirical generalizations first. No one could deny that many of them are solid and well-established; so solid that occasional exceptions may be intriguing but cannot undermine their validity. Consider, for example, mnemonic interference and its dependence on similarity, the superiority of meaningful material (stories) over meaningless material (lists), the positive effect of increasing study time, or the savings that appear when once-familiar material is relearned. Such enduring principles comfort those of us who teach courses in memory, because they provide a refuge from the undecided quarrels of the theoreticians. Besides, they are true. Unfortunately they rarely make much impression on our students, perhaps because they are so unsurprising. Students know them long before they hear our lectures. This has been made embarrassingly obvious by the results of Kreutzer, Leonard, and Flavell's (1975) interview study of children's knowledge about memory. Every one of the generalizations I have mentioned is familiar to the average middle-class third-grader in America from his own experience! Indeed, most of them are known to kindergarteners. If the psychology of memory must rest its case on accomplishments like these, it has little to boast of.

In teaching these familiar generalizations, of course, we do not confine ourselves to simply stating the naked facts. We emphasize method as well as content: appropriate experimental conditions, suitable control groups, well-defined terms, limiting cases. Most of all we emphasize theoretical explanations, of which there are never less than two for any phenomenon. In this way we always have a good deal to talk about, and there are many fine points by which the better students can be separated from the poorer ones. It is doubtful, however, whether the experimental details add anything to the power of the principles themselves. The opposite is more often the case. When a particular experimental result seems to contradict an established principle, a dozen psychologists leap into the breach to restore it. A case in point occurred when Tulving (1966) apparently showed that prior study of a list of words does not improve performance if that list appears later as part of a longer one. Tulving's finding seemed to undermine one of the commonplace principles, but it was an empty threat. The flaws in the experiment were soon revealed (e. g., Novinski, 1969; Slamecka, Moore, and Carey, 1972) and the status quo restored. The only long-run effect of the controversy was to provide another theoretical complication that students can be required to master.

Let me leave the familiar generalizations now, and turn to the genuine discoveries. There certainly have been some, although perhaps no list of them could command universal agreement. One important cluster of discoveries concerns the various kinds of immediate and short-term memories. We _do_ know more about these now than third-graders, and for that matter more than William James or Ebbinghaus did. Although we are not yet entirely clear about the details of the iconic and post-iconic mechanisms in vision, for example, a good deal of progress has been made. Similarly, we have begun to unravel the tangle of echoic stores, articulatory loops, and working memories that are related to hearing and to speech. This is an important area, and I would not deny that the work has added to our understanding of cognition. Nevertheless, it stretches a point to call such mechanisms "memories." They fit the formal definition, but what most people mean by "memory" is quite different. It is disconcerting to find that contemporary textbooks of memory devote a quarter or a third of their pages to "memories" that last less than a minute. Shouldn't memory have something to do with the past?

If the work on short-term memory seems to be leading to significant progress, other discoveries have fared less well. A particularly discouraging example is Sternberg's (1966) discovery that what may be called "memory search time" increases linearly with the number of alternatives that must be searched, at least in many situations. This phenomenon seemed important when it was first reported, but by now it has almost become a bore. It has been so thoroughly investigated and described that everything is known except what it means. We have found out too much about it, and yet not enough. Psychology seems to exploit its experimental effects somewhat in the way that the mass media exploit public figures. It is as difficult for a phenomenon to remain interesting as for a statesman to remain impressive and admirable, given the relentless scrutiny of television and the press. In that case, too, the details with which we are bombarded never add up to a genuine understanding of the subject himself. Instead, we are presented with a continuous stream of reactions, elaborations, and details that ends by putting us to sleep. The linear search function has suffered a similar fate. It may even be at a greater disadvantage than the politicians, whose power over us makes them intrinsically interesting. We return to the television set again and again in the faint hope of understanding Jimmy Carter: his decisions are significant for us. Once we have become disenchanted with Sternberg's linear function, however, why should we ever go back to it?

Another important discovery on my short list is the possibility of deliberately rotating mental images, established by Roger Shepard and his colleagues (Shepard & Metzler, 1971; Cooper & Shepard, 1973; etc.) It has not yet been over-exploited, and there are tantalizing promises of more discoveries to come. Recent work by Lynn Cooper (1976), for example, suggests that there may be fundamental individual differences in how people make the visual comparisons that such experiments require. Unfortunately, little work is being done to follow up her finding. Instead, everyone's attention is riveted on much weightier theoretical issues. Does the existence of mental rotation force us to assume that there are "analogue" representations in memory, or can the phenomenon be reconciled with the hypothesis that all mental structures are "propositional"? This is just the sort of question that psychologists love; the kind that has kept us busy for a hundred years. After an overall theory of forgetting or storage or remembering is established, the effort to bring every new experimental result under its umbrella can occupy an army of researchers for a decade at a time. Has it been an effective way to study memory? Let's look at the record.

Before the current crop of theories--EPAM, HAM, ACT, ELINOR, and their highly capitalized competitors--there were others. For example, there was the interference theory of forgetting (McGeoch, 1972; Postman & Underwood, 1973). Interference theorists believed (some still believe) that all forgetting is due to interference from irrelevant associations, and have occasionally tried to demonstrate it directly. More often, they have tried to settle questions about the nature and origin of the interference: response competition, unlearning, intra-experimental interference, extra-experimental interference, and so on. Like almost all theorists in experimental psychology, they supposed that they were uncovering the general principles of mental life. Applications would follow in due course. Like almost all theorists, they took certain assumptions for granted (motives as drives, spontaneous recovery of extinction over time) while they treated others as taboo (repression, decay of memories). Now that their approach has gone out of fashion, we can see that this selection of assumptions was questionable. Why should we take some motivational effects as fundamental and treat others as epiphenomena, or accept time as an independent variable for spontaneous recovery but not for spontaneous decay? That particular pattern of assumptions appeared because interference theory was an offshoot of a more general stimulus-response psychology, or "learning theory," of whose decline and fall I shall have more to say shortly. With learning theory out of fashion, the experiments of the interference theorists seem like empty exercises to most of us. Were they ever anything else?

To me, the very notion of uncovering the "cause of forgetting" seems rather strange. It is a little like trying to establish the cause of juvenile delinquency or crime. Such studies are no longer popular, because both "crime" and "cause" turned out to be much richer notions than had been supposed. There are white-collar crimes and violent crimes, premeditated crimes and crimes of passion, crimes committed by the poor and by the rich, undiscovered crimes and crimes leading to conviction, crimes that are part of an accepted cultural pattern and crimes committed by lonely and desperate individuals. There are causes of crime like racism and capitalism, like ignorance and folly, like opportunity and lack of opportunity, like an impoverished childhood or a spoiled one, like inadequate law enforcement or the enactment of absurd laws, like criminal organizations, like lust and greed and the other five sins but also like the demands of conscience and the clear-eyed perception of all the alternatives. Most of all, there is the complexly intertwined history of a particular individual who encounters particular situations. How, then, can one hope to discover the cause of crime?

Forgetting is an equally incoherent notion. Perhaps you fail to retrieve a piece of information that, by some standard, should have been available: you can't think of my name. At the same time, though, there is a lot that you _are_ thinking of. What you do and what you think in every human situation has many causes at many levels, ranging from social convention to unconscious drive. What you do _not_ do (i. e., think of my name) is an aspect of what you are doing, and has just as many causes. A great deal is going on. To point this out is not to argue that forgetting is due only to interference and not to decay. The matter is equally complex if the necessary information has decayed simply because you and I were introduced too long ago. Even then, its non-existence would be a cause of remembering just as much as of forgetting: of what you do as well as of what you don't do. What is needed to understand such failures is a detailed examination of what actually happens in them, rather then the theoretical manipulation of abstract and _a priori_ concepts. But I am getting ahead of my story.

Today the interference theory of forgetting has few supporters. It has been replaced by new theories, mostly models of information storage and retrieval systems with various subdivisions and properties. Before considering their importance and probable fate, I would like to review another part of the history of psychology. It offers an analogy that can teach us a great deal, and perhaps help us to avoid some unnecessary labor. As someone (whom I again cannot remember) once put it, those who do not study history are condemned to repeat it. The history I have in mind is that of learning theory and behaviorism.

Not long ago, learning theory dominated almost the whole of experimental psychology (at least in America). It set the problems, prescribed the methods, defined the range of permissible hypotheses, and seemed generalizable to every aspect of life. Its intellectual leaders wrote books with titles like _Principles of Behavior_ and _The Behavior of Organisms_, and their broad claims were backed up by hundreds of experiments. To be sure, the experimental subjects were almost always white rats; a few skeptics wondered whether it was quite safe to generalize from "animals" to humans, but hardly any one doubted that at least animal behavior was being investigated in a scientifically fruitful way. The most influential philosophers of the time produced accounts of scientific method - hypothesis testing, manipulation of variables, and the like - that justified the learning theorists at every step. There was dispute about whether Hull, Spence, Skinner, or (as an outside possibility) Tolman was closest to ultimate truth, but not much about the merit of their common enterprise.

Today, learning theory has been almost completely swept away. Not entirely, perhaps: with the mainland of animal behavior lost to their foes, a behaviorist remnant is holding out on well-defended islands like "behavior modification" or "behavior therapy." They still sound confident, but they are watching the straits with an anxious eye. There are even a few stalwarts fighting rearguard actions in the rat laboratories, putting out research reports that the triumphant majority don't bother to read. Nevertheless the battle is essentially over, and it was surprisingly brief. What happened?

The fundamental blow was struck by a small group of scientists who called themselves "ethologists," not psychologists, and were not concerned with learning theory at all. They wanted to know how animals really behaved in natural environments. They were not so much interested in hypotheses as in the animals themselves. Wasps, herring gulls, ducklings and jackdaws are a curious base on which to build a scientific revolution, but one occurrred. The work of the ethologists showed that the concepts and methods of learning theory were simply irrelevant to the understanding of natural behavior. Every species seems to have a different set of learning abilities, and to respond to different sorts of variables. Even in a single species or a single organisms, patterns of behavior vary drastically with changes in the gross environment, with fluctuations in hormone levels, with stages of maturation. Given these facts, notions like "conditioning," "reinforcement," "extinction," and "generalization" require constant reinterpretation if they are to survive at all. The very distinction between what is learned and what is innate has become uncertain. Even the laboratory rat has turned on his old friends (rats are apparently treacherous after all) by exhibiting a kind of learning that none of the old models could accommodate: a food aversion acquired on a single trial with a reinforcement delay of many hours.

This new wave of research has not resulted in universal agreement on theoretical issues. The disputes among "behavioral biologists," as these investigators are now often called, are just as vigorous as the arguments between learning theorists once were. Many of them will surely seem just as pointless to the eye of the historian. But whatever the ultimate fate of the theories may be, the observations of animal behavior that are now being made can never become irrelevant or uninteresting. We are finding out what really happens in the world around us, and that will be worth knowing in any imaginable future.

I have dwelt on this bit of psychological history at some length because I believe it has a clear application to the subject at hand. Theories of memory are invariably based on the performance of experimental subjects in specialized laboratory tasks. So, too, were the learning theories of the 1930s and 1940s. The tasks themselves are ingeniously designed to shed light on the experimenter's hypothesis, or to decide among competing theories. So, too, were the procedures of the behaviorists. The most widely acclaimed memory theories are those which seem most far-reaching, and explain many experimental results on the basis of relatively few assumptions. This, too, characterized the glory days of stimulus-response psychology. A plausible and explicit set of methodological assumptions justifies current research practices. The same thing was true in the case of learning theory, although the old reliance on the hypothetico-deductive method has been replaced by a new attachment to computer simulation. Finally, modern theories of memory have as little relevance to everyday memory as learning theory had to what is usually called "learning." The sentences and brief "stories" which are popular in research laboratories today are an improvement on the nonsense syllable, but they are far from representative of what ordinary people remember and forget.

In short, the results of a hundred years of the psychological study of memory are somewhat discouraging. We have established firm empirical generalizations, but most of them are so obvious that every ten-year-old knows them anyway. We have made discoveries, but they are only marginally about memory; in many cases we don't know what to do with them, and wear them out with endless experimental variations. We have an intellectually impressive group of theories, but history offers little confidence that they will provide any meaningful insight into natural behavior. Of course, I could be wrong: perhaps this is the exceptional case where the lessons of history do not apply, and the new theories will stand the test of time better than the old ones did. Let me be frank: I have not pinpointed any fatal flaw in Hunt's distributed memory model (Hunt, 1971), Tulving's conception of encoding specificity (Tulving, 1974), Anderson's ACT (1976), or the others. I cannot prove that they are misguided. But because they say so little about the everyday uses of memory, they seem ripe for the same fate that overtook learning theory not long ago.

The psychologists who have spent a century studying esoteric forms of memory in the laboratory are not really uninterested in its more ordinary manifestations, and have always hoped that their work would have wide applicability sooner or later. Their preference for artificial tasks has a rational basis: one can control variables and manipulate conditions more easily in the lab than in natural settings. Why not work under the best possible conditions? Memory is memory, or so it would seem. This methodological assumption resembles the assumptions made by the learning theorists in their study of "learning." Unfortunately, it turned out that "learning" in general does not exist: wasps and songbirds and rats integrate past experiences into their lives in very different ways. I think that "memory" in general does not exist either. It is a concept left over from a medieval psychology that partitioned the mind into independent faculties: "thought" and "will" and "emotion" and many others, with "memory" among them. Let's give it up, and begin to ask our questions in different ways. Those questions need not be uninformed by theory, or by a vision of human nature, but perhaps they can be more closely driven by the characteristics of ordinary human experience.

What we want to know, I think, is how people use their own past experiences in meeting the present and the future. We would like to understand how this happens under natural conditions: the circumstances in which it occurs, the forms it takes, the variables on which it depends, the differences between individuals in their uses of the past. "Natural conditions" does not mean in the jungle or in the desert, unless that happens to be where our subjects live. It means in school and at home, on the job and in the course of thought, as carefree children and as reflective old men and women. Because changes in the social and cultural environment can change the uses of the past, we will have to study many settings. The psychological laboratory is the easiest of these settings in which to work, but it is also among the least interesting; we ourselves are the only people who spend much time there voluntarily.

The task before us is much harder than that which confronted the ethologists. They had several great advantages. For one thing, it is easier to observe animals than people. Animals don't mind it as much (if you are quiet) and are not so aware of what you are up to. Their habitats are more limited, in many cases, and their behaviors more stereotyped. Moreover, the time-dependence of their behavior is much shorter: you rarely have to consider events of twenty years ago to understand what an animal is doing today. They do not have language to help them control the application of the past to the present, and seem to spend more of their time in action as opposed to thought.

One difference between our task and that of the ethologists deserves special mention. They began with a ready-made categorization of their subject-matter, whereas we have none. It is obvious that there are many different kinds of animals--species--which can be studied separately. In setting out to do a field study of animal behavior, one usually need not worry about how to distinguish the robins from the herring gulls. In studying memory, however, we do not know how to separate different kinds of cases. Indeed, we cannot even be sure whether any natural lines of demarcation exist. This is a genuinely important question, and one of the first things we should be trying to find out. Are there functionally different types of memory in everyday life? If so, what are they?

Although I am far from sure how to classify the phenomena of memory, I must put them in some kind of order to discuss them at all. Science cannot proceed without some way of defining things so we can set out to study them. The organization I will use is based on the functions of memory. What do we use the past *for*? Happily, when the question is put in this way, it turns out that the sum total of relevant psychological work is not zero after all.

There has been some valuable research and thinking about the natural uses of memory, usually by individuals outside the mainstream of contemporary theory. These beginnings offer promising leads for further work; I will mention some of them below.

First of all, everyone uses the past to define themselves. Who am I? I have a name, a family, a home, a job. I know a great deal about myself: what I have done, how I have felt, where I have been, whom I have known, how I have been treated. My past defines me, together with my present and the future that the past leads me to expect. What would I be without it? Much of that formative past is now tacit rather than explicit knowledge: I do not dwell on it, and I cannot recall it as such. The specifics are beyond recall, although their resultant is here in person. Some things, however, I can remember very explicitly when I choose. I think back on my childhood, or my youth, or on something that happened this morning. Typically I do this alone, silently, without telling anybody. I often do it deliberately and voluntarily, but memories may also come unbidden--"involuntary memories," as Salaman (1970) calls them--either in waking life or in sleep. All these are cases where the past becomes present to me, and to me alone.

Many questions suggest themselves about such personal evocations. Some were asked long ago by Freud and the psychoanalysts. Why do just these memories come, and not others? When are they trustworthy, and when fabricated? Why do I have so few from my very early childhood? Do some people have more of them than others, and if so why? What function do they serve? How does the nature and incidence of personal recollection vary with age, culture, sex, and situation? What happens when whole sections of the past become inaccessible, as in functional amnesias?

Work has been done on some of these questions, but not much. Freud (1905) drew attention to the phenomenon of infantile amnesia and tried to explain it by repression; Schachtel (1947) later proposed a cognitive account which seems more plausible (cf. Neisser, 1962). Freud also wrote two papers on early memories (1899, 1917), a topic which has been studied sporadically over the years by many psychologists (Dudycha & Dudycha, 1941) recently including Douglas Herrmann and me. As you will learn from his presentation (Herrmann & Neisser, 1979), women college students report better memory of childhood experiences than men do. Others have noticed the same sex difference in early memories; I wish I understood it. We still know very little about these questions, and what we do know mostly concerns deliberate, voluntary remembering. Spontaneous recall may be quite a different matter. Esther Salaman's fascinating autobiographical book A Collection of Moments (1970), which describes many images of early childhood that came to her unbidden and unexpected, may be a useful source of hypotheses about spontaneous memory.

One frequently recalls past experiences in search of some sort of self-improvement. Where did I go wrong? Could I have done things differently? What were my alternatives? How did all this start? These questions can be asked privately or with a listener. "Going public," even to a single individual, makes a difference. Both private and shared recollection can have profound consequences for that sense of self which is so dependent on what one remembers. Psychoanalysis and psychotherapy are obvious examples of this use of the past, but they are by no means the only ones. Something similar probably happens in the Catholic confessional, of which I know very little. Some Communist countries have institutionalized confession as a way of strengthening social unity and reforming individual behavior. To be sure, those who confess in political settings must be quite careful about what they say. Is that selectivity exhibited only in their public statements, or does it extend to what they remember privately? According to recent experimental evidence, people's memory of their own prior attitudes can change dramatically when the attitudes themselves have shifted (Goethals & Reckman, 1973).

There are other occasions when one's personal memories achieve a kind of public importance. A familiar example occurs in legal testimony, where an exact account of the past can be critical in determining a defendant's future. Psychologists have been interested in this issue for many years. At the beginning of the century William Stern published several volumes of a scholarly journal devoted exclusively to the psychology of testimony (Beiträge zur Psychologie der Aussage), and Münsterburg wrote a widely-cited book about it called On the Witness Stand (1909). Unfortunately, this early work produced few insights except that the testimony of eyewitnesses is often inaccurate. A series of ingenious experiments by Elizabeth Loftus

(Loftus & Palmer, 1974; Loftus, 1975) has revived interest in the problem, and begun to define the kinds of distortions that can occur as well as their sources.

One does not remember only events that one has personally experienced, but also those known at second-hand: things that have happened to other people. We learn from the experiences of our friends and acquaintances, and also from historical figures whose lives are somehow relevant to our own. In a literate society, we do not often think of history as something remembered; it is usually something written down. In many parts of the world, however, history has long been the responsibility of memory specialists, or oral historians, whose knowledge of ancient deeds and agreements exerts a controlling influence on contemporary events. D'Azevedo (1962) has described the role of oral historians among one African tribe, the Gola; it seems clear that this cultural practice is widespread in Africa and elsewhere. The history that is passed on through generations in this way is surprisingly accurate. The historians do not learn it by rote, but in an integrated and intelligent way. Whether this requires special gifts and special training, or whether anyone could remember any amount of oral history if it were appropriate to do so, is an open question.

In general, the relation between literacy and memory is poorly understood. It is one of those issues where every possible position can be and has been plausibly argued. Perhaps unschooled individuals from traditional societies have particularly _good_ memories, because they must rely on those memories so heavily where nothing can be written down (Riesman, 1956). Perhaps, however, they have relatively _poor_ memories because they lack the general mnemonic skills and strategies that come with literacy and schooling (Scribner & Cole, 1973). Certainly they perform badly in standard psychological memory experiments (Cole, Gay, Glick, and Sharp, 1971). Or maybe they are just like us: good at remembering what interests them. That is what Bartlett (1932) thought, though he could not resist endowing nonliterate Africans with a special facility for low-level "rote recapitulation" as well. In my own view, it may be a mistake to treat culture and literacy as overriding variables: individual differences and individual experience are more important. If the experimental task is remembering oral stories, then experience in listening to stories will make a big difference. That is probably why E. F. Dube (1977) recently found that both schooled and unschooled young people from Botswana were far better at story recall than American school children of the same age. However, he also found enormous individual differences correlated with estimates of the subjects' intelligence, made by tribal elders for the non-literate children and on the basis of school grades for the others. The best of the unschooled subjects exhibited remarkably high levels of recall.

Memory is also involved in many activities of daily life. We make a plan and have to remember to carry it out, put something down and have to recall where it is, are given directions and must remember them if we are to reach our destination, encounter a prior acquaintance and want to pick up the relationship where it left off. Our access to the past is probably better when remembering is embedded in these natural activities than when it occurs in isolation. At least this is true for young children, as Istomina (1948) has shown in an elegant series of experiments. Different individuals are unequally skilled in different kinds of everyday memory, according to questionnaire data that Herrmann and I have recently collected (Herrmann & Neisser, 1979). But we still know almost nothing about these practical uses of memory, important as they are.

In most instances of daily remembering, it is meanings and not surface details that we must recall. Just as the oral historian remembers what happened instead of memorizing some formula of words that describes it, so too we recall the substance of what we heard or read rather than its verbatim form. This is now generally acknowledged, even in laboratory research. The new wave of enthusiasm for Bartlett's ideas and for the use of stories as memory materials has led us to devalue the study of rote emorization almost completely. This is entirely appropriate, if "rote memory" means the learning of arbitrary lists of words or syllables for experimental pruposes. The fact is, however, that many cultural institutions depend heavily on exact and literal recall. When we speak of remembering a song or a poem, for example, we do not mean that we have the gist of it but that we know the words. Rubin (1977) has recently shown that literal memory for the National Anthem, the Lord's Prayer, and similar texts is widespread among Americans. Verbatim memory is even more important in other societies, I think; some memorize the Koran where others study the Bible and still others learn long speeches from Shakespeare.

This happens whenever it is the text itself, and not just its meaning, that is important. A text can be important for many reasons: patriotic, religious, esthetic, or personal. For singers and actors, the reason can even be professional. Whatever the reason, people's ability to recite appropriate texts verbatim at appropriate times ought to be deeply interesting to the psychology of memory. The fact that we have not studied it is another particularly striking example of my original proposition: if X is an interesting memory phenomenon, psychologists avoid it like the plague. Hundreds of experimentalists have spent their lives working on rote memory, without ever examining the rote memorization that goes on around them every day.

The last use of the past that I will discuss concerns intellectual activity itself. Although I have little talent for recalling the sources of quotations, I am not too bad at remembering experiments; if it were otherwise, I could not have prepared this address. However, this ability certainly does not make me unique. Everybody who is skilled at anything necessarily has a good memory for whatever information that activity demands. Physicists can remember what they need to know to do physics, and fishermen what they need for fishing; musicians remember music, art critics recall paintings, historians know history. Every person is a prodigy to his neighbors, remembering so much that other people do not know. We should be careful in what we say about memory in general until we know more about these many memories in particular.

These are some of the important questions, and we must seek the answers as best we can. Our search need not be entirely haphazard; I am not recommending an aimless accumulation of ecological minutiae. We will surely be guided by our general conceptions of human nature and human social life, as well as by more particular hypotheses about the phenomena we study. Without such conceptions and hypotheses, we can make little progress. The challenge will be to shift from testing hypotheses for their own sake to using them as tools for the exploration of reality.

It is a challenge that will not be easy to meet. The realistic study of memory is much harder than the work we have been accustomed to: so much harder that one can easily forgive those who have been reluctant to undertake it. After all, we bear no malice toward that legendary drunk who kept looking for his money under the streetlamp although he had dropped it ten yards away in the dark. As he correctly pointed out, the light was better where he was looking. But what we want to find *is* in the dark, out there where real people make use of their pasts in complicated ways. If we are to find it, we must look there. The convening of this conference may suggest that we are finally heading in that direction. Perhaps the next few days will reveal that the light is not so dim after all.

REFERENCES

Anderson, J. R. (1976). *Language, Memory, and Thought.* Lawrence Erlbaum, Hillsdale, N. J.

Anderson, R. C. (1977). The notion of schemata and the educational enterprise. In: *Schooling and the Acquisition of Knowledge.* (R. C. Anderson, R. T. Spiro, and W. E. Montague, eds). Lawrence Erlbaum, Hillsdale, N. J.

Bartlett, F. C. (1932). *Remembering.* Cambridge University Press.

Bransford, J. D. and Johnson, M. K. (1973). Consideration of some problems of comprehension. In: *Visual Information Processing.* (W. G. Chase, ed). Academic Press, New York.

Cole, M., Gay, J., Glick, J. A., and Sharp, D. W. (1971). *The Cultural Context of Learning and Thinking.* Basic Books, New York.

Cooper, L. A. (1976). Individual differences in visual comparison processes. *Perception and Psychophysics.* 19, 433-444.

Cooper, L. A. and Shepard, R. N. (1973). Chronometric studies of the rotation of mental images. In: *Visual Information Processing.* (W. G. Chase, ed). Academic Press, New York.

D'Azevedo, W. L. (1962). Uses of the past in Gola discourse. *Journal of African History.* 3, 11-34.

Dube, E. F. (1977). *A Cross-cultural Study of the Relationship Between "Intelligence" Level and Story Recall.* Doctoral Dissertation, Cornell University, Ithaca, N. Y.

Dudycha, G. and Dudycha, M. (1941). Childhood memories: A review of the literature. *Psychological Bulletin.* 38, 668-682.

Freud, S. (1905; republished 1938). Three contributions to the theory of sex. In: *The Basic Writings of Sigmund Freud.* (A. A. Brill, ed). Random House, New York.

Freud, S. (1899; republished 1956). Screen memories. In: *Collected Papers of Sigmund Freud*. Vol. 5. (J. Strachey, ed). Hogarth Press, London.

Freud, S. (1917; republished 1956). A childhood recollection from "*Dichtung und Wahrheit.*" In: *Collected Papers of Sigmund Freud*. Vol. 4. (J. Strachey, ed). Hogarth Press, London.

Goethals, G. R. and Reckman, R. F. (1973). The perception of consistency in attitudes. *Journal of experimental social psychology*. 9, 491-501.

Herrmann, D. J. and Neisser, U. (1979). An inventory of everyday memory experiences. *In this volume.*

Hunt, E. (1971). What kind of a computer in man? *Cognitive Psychology*. 2, 57-98.

Istomina, Z. M. (1948; republished 1975). The development of voluntary memory in preschool-age children. *Soviet Psychology*. 13, 5-64.

Keenan, J. M., MacWhinney, B., and Mayhew, D. (1977). Pragmatics in memory: A study of natural conversation. *Journal of Verbal Learning and Verbal Behavior*. 16, 549-560.

Kintsch, W. and Bates, E. (1977). Recognition memory for statements from a classroom lecture. *Journal of Experimental Psychology: Human Learning and Memory*. 3, 150-159.

Kreutzer, M. A., Leonard, C., and Flavell, J. H. (1975). An interview study of children's knowledge about memory. *Monographs of the Society for Research in Child Development*. 40, Serial No. 159.

Loftus, E. G. (1975). Leading questions and the eyewitness report. *Cognitive Psychology*. 7, 560-572.

Loftus, E. G. and Palmer, J. C. (1974). Reconstruction of automobile destruction: An example of the interaction between language and memory. *Journal of Verbal Learning and Verbal Behavior*. 13, 585-589.

Mandler, J. M. and Johnson, N. S. (1977). Remembrance of things parsed: Story structure and recall. *Cognitive Psychology*. 9, 111-151.

McGeoch, J. A. (1942). *The Psychology of Human Learning*. Longmans, Green, New York.

Munsterburg, H. (1909). *On the Witness Stand*. Doubleday. Page, New York.

Neisser, U. (1962). Cultural and cognitive discontinuity. In: *Anthropology and Human Behavior*. (T. E. Gladwin and W. Sturtevant, eds). Anthropological Society of Washington D. C.

Neisser, U. and Hupcey, J. (1974). A Sherlockian experiment. *Cognition*. 3, 307-311.

Novinski, L. S. (1969). Part-whole and whole-part free recall learning. *Journal of Verbal Learning and Verbal Behavior*. 8, 152-154.

Postman, L. and Underwood, B. J. (1973). Critical issues in interference theory. *Memory and Cognition*. 1, 19-40.

Riesman, D. (1956). *The Oral Tradition, the Written Word, the Screen Image*. Antioch Press: Yellow Springs, Ohio.

Rubin, D. C. (1977). Very long-term memory for prose and verse. *Journal of Verbal Learning and Verbal Behavior*. 16, 611-622.

Rumelhart, D. E. (1975). Notes on a schema for stories. In: *Representation and Understanding*. (D. G. Bobrow and A. Collins, eds). Academic Press, N. Y.

Salaman, E. (1970). *A Collection of Moments*. Longman Group, London.

Schachtel, E. G. (1947). On memory and childhood amnesia. *Psychiatry*. 10, 1-26.

Scribner, S. and Cole, M. (1973). Cognitive consequences of formal and informal education. *Science*. 182, 553-559.

Shepard, R. N. and Metzler, J. (1971). Mental rotation of three-dimensional objects. *Science*. 171, 701-703.

Slamecka, N. J., Moore, T., and Carey, S. (1972). Part-to-whole transfer and its relation to organization theory. *Journal of Verbal Learning and Verbal Behavior*. 11, 73-82.

Sternberg, S. (1966). High-speed scanning in human memory. *Science*. 153, 652-654.

Tulving, E. (1966). Subjective organization and effects of repetition in multi-trial free-recall learning. *Journal of Verbal Learning and Verbal Behavior*. 5, 193-197.

Tulving, E. (1974). Recall and recognition of semantically encoded words. *Journal of Experimental Psychology*. 102, 778-787.

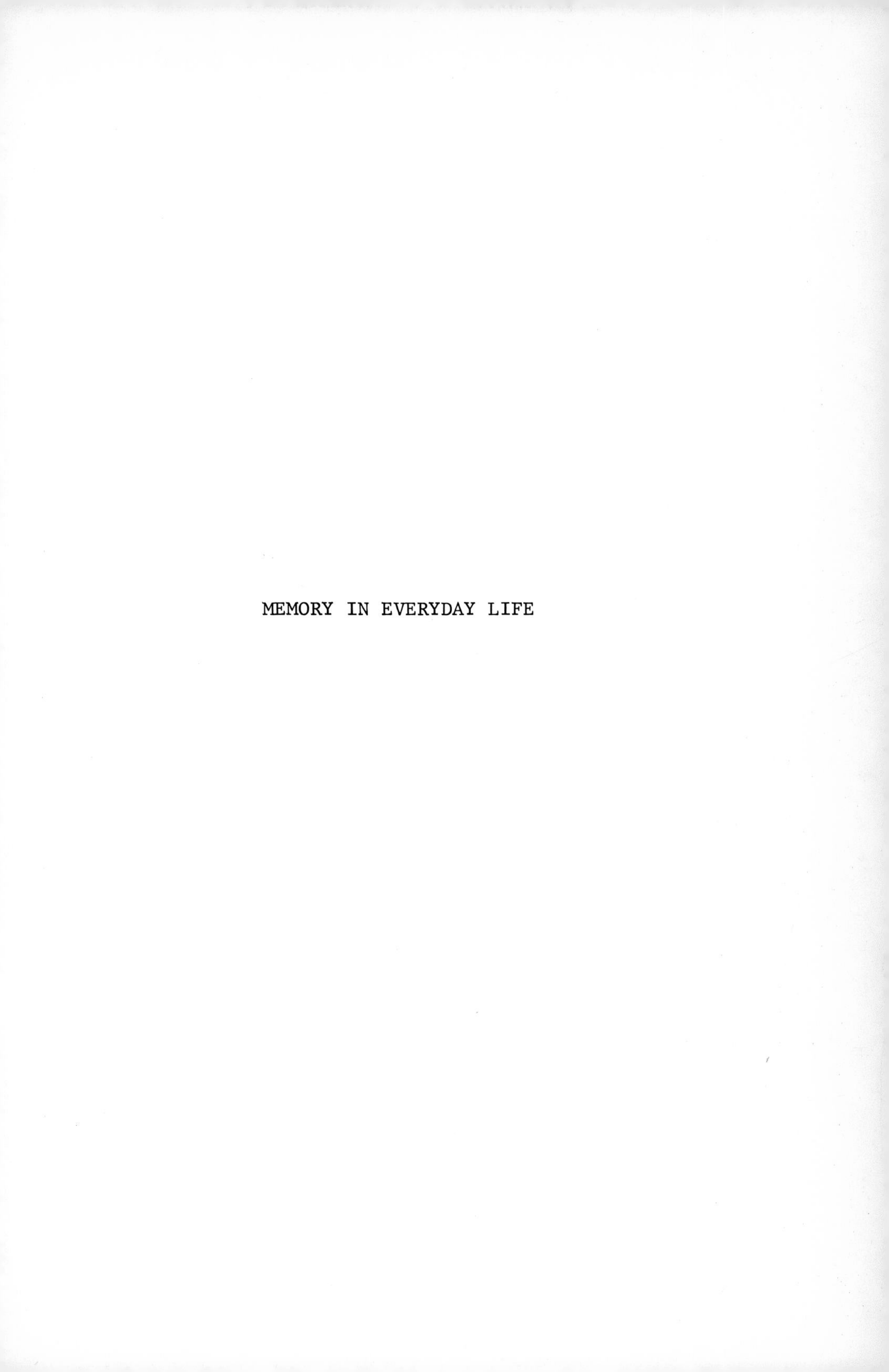

MEMORY IN EVERYDAY LIFE

REMEMBERING TO RECALL IN EVERYDAY LIFE: AN APPROACH TO ABSENT-MINDEDNESS

A. J. Wilkins and A. D. Baddeley
MRC Applied Psychology Unit, 15 Chaucer Road, Cambridge, England

ABSTRACT

Two groups of subjects, one with high and one with low free recall scores, were instructed to operate a miniature print-out clock at pre-arranged times, four times a day for a week. Their accuracy at operating the clock was inversely related to their free recall scores. If subjects operated the clock they remembered that they had done so, whereas if they forgot to operate it they often appeared to be unaware of their omission.

INTRODUCTION

Ebbinghaus, one of the pioneers in the study of human memory, required his subject first to learn artificial material, and afterwards to recall that material at some specific time. Subsequent work has shown a trend away from the artificiality of this approach. This trend has involved not only changes in the materials that are learned (words instead of nonsense syllables) but also the means whereby they are learned. The studies of incidental learning (Hyde and Jenkins, 1969), semantic memory (Collins and Quillian, 1969) and memory for newsworthy events (Warrington and Sanders, 1971) provide examples of this trend. In the case of semantic memory research, for instance, naturalistic information is learned in the real world and the experimenter has no control over its acquisition. Instead it is the processes of recall that are of paramount interest. In the present study, which is also concerned with the processes of recall, the break with the Ebbinghaus tradition has been carried one stage further.

Most, if not all, studies of memory have in common with the work by Ebbinghaus the fact that the experimenter has had control over the subject's recall; the subject has been required to recall at the experimenter's request rather than at a time when he would normally do so.

This "prompted recall" rarely occurs in everyday memory which, as the work by Harris (this volume) has shown, usually involves the person remembering to do something at a particular time, or at some particular point in the sequence of everyday events. Consider, for example, the task of taking medication at scheduled times each day. This task is typical of many everyday memory tasks in that a person has to provide his own cues for recall. It is also simpler than most memory tasks in that the person has nothing to recall other than that he must take his medication. The recalled information is minimal - it is the time of recall that is critical. The task therefore seemed an appropriate one with which to begin a study of self-cued memory.

We used an analogue of a pill-taking task in which, rather than taking pills, subjects were required to operate a miniature print-out clock at pre-arranged times. We gave the task to two groups of subjects, one with high scores on a test of free recall and the other with low, in order to see whether subject-cued recall was related in any way to memory as measured in the laboratory. We chose free recall of lists of words because (1) this is a very widely used laboratory test of memory, (2) its theoretical basis has received considerable study, (3) the task is a sensitive indicator of disorders of memory such as amnesia (Baddeley and Warrington, 1970), and (4) performance of other tests of memory correlates with performance at free recall (unpublished data).

METHOD

Subjects. Thirty-one female volunteers from the Applied Psychology Unit subject panel aged between 35 and 49, who had taken part in a study of individual differences in memory, were selected on the basis of their scores on a test of free recall of lists of words. The test consisted of 10 lists, each of 16 two-syllable words presented visually for one second with a one-second interval between words. Subjects were instructed to write down the last few words first but recall order was otherwise unrestricted. Recall was immediate. The recall scores ranged from 29/160 to 98/160 in the sample of 100 subjects tested, with a mean of 62.2 and a standard deviation of 12.5. Of those subjects in the sample who were available for subsequent testing, the 16 with the highest scores comprised a high free recall group with percentile scores in the range 72-99 (mean percent correct = 49%); the 15 subjects with the lowest scores formed a low free recall group with percentile scores from 4 - 40 (mean percent correct = 31%).

Apparatus. A circuit board from an electronic wrist-watch with light-emitting diode display (CBM Business Machines Ltd.) was mounted in a fibreglass block moulded to fit between the spools of a Kodak "Instamatic" cartridge so as to prevent light reaching the surface of the film. Sandwiched between the surface of the light-emitting diodes and the surface of the film was a filter with a neutral density of about 3.0. The ensemble fitted within a plastic box measuring 11 x 6 x 3 cm and weighing 150 gm. In one of the 11 x 3 cm sides of the box were mounted side by side a knob which could be used to advance the film from one spool to the other, and a push-button switch which activated the watch circuit thereby exposing the film and creating a photographic record of the time of day at which the button was pushed. A label beneath the controls bore instructions as to how and when to operate the machine. Another label attached to the 11 x 6 cm side of the box carried the request "Please record omissions" and had three vertical columns headed "date", "time" and "comment" in that order.

Procedure. The subject was given the print-out clock and shown how to operate it by turning the knob and pushing the button. She was asked to operate the clock at 8.30 a.m., 1.00 p.m., 5.30 p.m. and 10.00 p.m. (the times shown on the label attached to the clock) each day for seven days. The subject was instructed that if she forgot to push the button at the target time she should push it as soon as she remembered. If she failed to remember before the next response was due she should make a note of this "omission" on the label attached to the clock and respond to the subsequent target as normal. She was then given concrete examples to clarify these instructions. Nine subjects in the high free recall group and eight in the low began the task on a Monday. The remaining subjects began on a Friday. All subjects started between 8.30 a.m. and 5.30 p.m.

RESULTS

From the sequence of response times recorded by the clock there was, of course, no way of telling to which target time a response should be allocated, other than that (1) the response occurred at a time similar to that of the target, and (2) the putative responses to neighbouring targets also occurred at appropriate times. Fortunately, the histogram of response densities as a function of time showed four distributions with virtually no overlap, and with peaks $4\frac{1}{2}$ hours apart corresponding to the target times. The distributions were therefore superimposed, and the resulting distribution is shown in Fig. 1. Responses occurring from $2\frac{1}{4}$ hours before to $2\frac{1}{4}$ hours after a target time were allocated to that target time unless this allocation conflicted

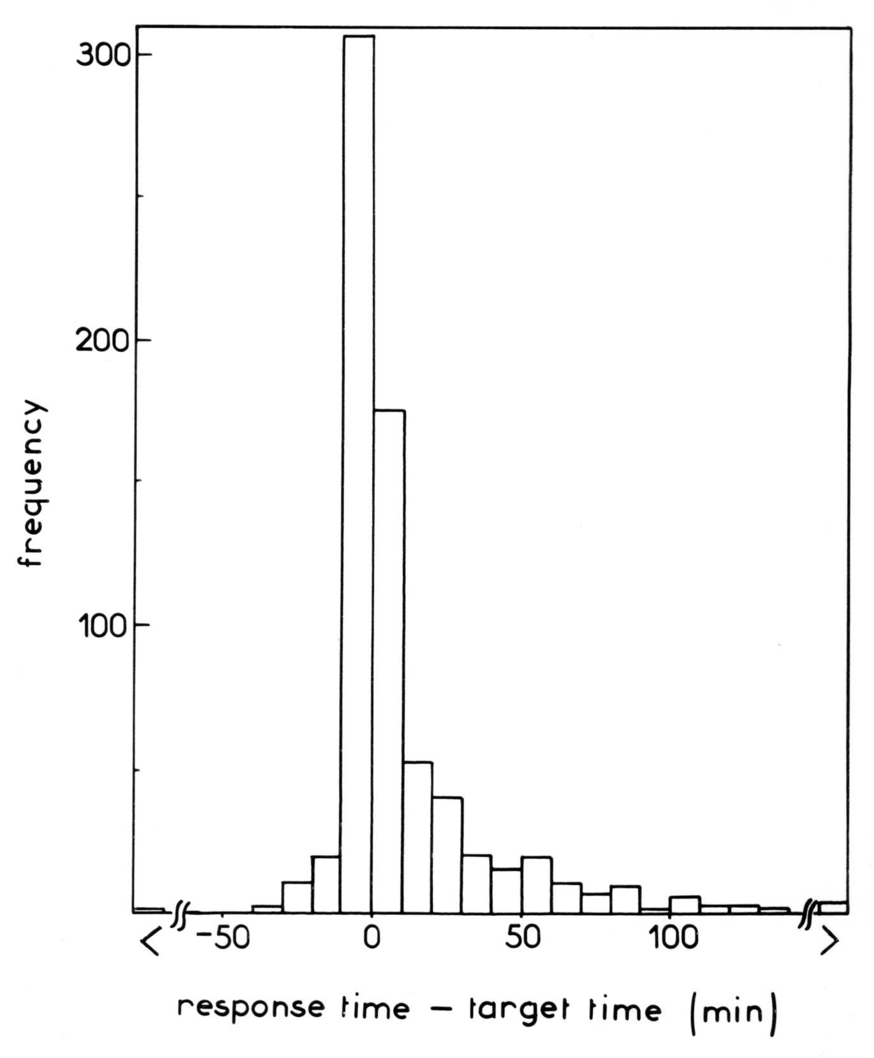

Fig. 1 Distribution of the differences between response times and target times.

with that based on the ordinal position of the response with respect to neighbouring targets (which it did in only two instances). The above treatment of the data begs the question as to whether on some occasions subjects responded more than once to a target. However, no subject ever responded more than four times in one day, so that if multiple responses did in fact occur, they would have had to have been only on those occasions when subjects omitted a subsequent response. Given that omissions (as attested by responses to neighbouring targets) comprised only 3.6% of observations, it may reasonably be assumed that there were few, if any, multiple responses to a single target.

There was some difficulty in selecting the measure most suitable as an index of subjects' performance of the task. Late responses may well have been the direct result of absent-mindedness, whereas early responses are unlikely to have been so. Given that there is such a functional dichotomy it would have made sense to attempt to analyse early responses separately from late ones. Unfortunately, what was "early" or "late" *for the subject* depended on the time-check the subject used: whether she wore a watch at the time, and if so, whether it happened to be running fast or slow, for example. In other words, there was no criterion on the basis of which to distinguish early responses from late ones, except, perhaps in the more extreme cases. Given that any separation of extreme cases would have been arbitrary, it made more sense to treat all responses on a single continuum: that which forms the basis of the distribution shown in Fig. 1.

An analysis of variance of the differences between target and response time was performed with the following factors: subject group (high or low free recall), target time (8.30 a.m., 1.00 p.m., 5.30 p.m. and 10.00 p.m.), day of task (1st - 7th) and day of commencement (Monday, Friday). The analysis revealed a significant effect of subject group, $F(1,26) = 5.88$, $p < 0.05$, a significant effect of target time $F(3,78) = 3.23$, $p < 0.05$, and a significant effect of day of task, $F(6,154) = 2.56$, $p < 0.05$. The effect of day of commencement and the interaction terms were not significant.

The absence of a significant interaction between day of task and day of commencement indicated that there was no effect of the day of the week (e.g. weekdays vs. weekends). Newman-Keuls tests of the scores for the four target times revealed that subjects were more accurate at 8.30 a.m. than they were at 1.00 p.m. and 5.30 p.m. (The accuracy of performance at 10.00 p.m. did not differ from that for the other three target times). Newman-Keuls tests for performance on the seven days of the task failed to reveal any significant differences between days despite the significant F-ratio in the analysis of variance.

Table 1

Mean differences between response time and target time (in minutes late).

Subject group	Target time			
	8.30 am	1.00 pm	5.30 pm	10.00 pm
High free recall	6.2	16.0	19.5	11.1
Low free recall	4.4	10.3	8.1	8.7

Table 1 shows the relevant means and it will be noted that the effect of subject group arose because subjects with high free recall scores performed more poorly than those with low.

There were a total of 30 failures to respond to a target, and 15 of the 31 subjects failed to respond at least once during the week. Only 19 of the 30 failures were acknowledged and nine of the 15 subjects failed to acknowledge an omission on one or more occasions. There was no significant difference between subject groups in the number or type of omissions.

DISCUSSION

Subjects with high free recall scores responded less accurately at the pre-arranged times than those with lower scores. This result was not anticipated. It was thought that performance would be more likely to be related to motivational factors; obsessional subjects who frequently looked at their watches tending to perform more accurately. Given the likely contribution of such factors to experimental noise no effect of free recall ability had been anticipated. Indeed this was why the groups were formed from the extremes of the distribution of free recall scores so as to maximise the likelihood of revealing any effect. The fact than an effect occurred and that it was in the direction opposite to that which might be expected from a simple notion of memory ability is open to many competing speculative interpretations. One possibility is that a subject's life-style provided cues for recall; subjects with high free recall scores tending to have a higher educational level and to lead more varied lives. This interpretation is consistent with the fact that performance was best at 8.30 a.m. when people tend to do fairly humdrum things that are similar from one day to the next. To see whether life-style was a contributory factor, subjects were asked to keep a diary for a period of a week about six months after they had taken part in the first experiment. The 23 subjects who were available for testing were issued with a sheet of paper bearing labelled sections for the four target times for each of the seven days of the week, starting on a Monday or a Friday, as appropriate to the conditions of the first experiment. The subjects were asked to note down at the end of each day, in the space provided, the activity in which they had been engaged at these particular times. The diaries were scored by (1) noting the number of activities repeatedly performed at similar times, and (2) noting for each target time the number of occasions during the week that the subject was away from home. These measures were used as covariates in analyses of covariance of the data from the earlier experiment with target time and subject group as separate factors. The effect of time of day was significant for both covariates but using these to adjust the original analysis did not affect the overall picture. Evidently if life-style is an important factor in self-cued recall, more sensitive measures are needed to pick up its effects. At this stage further speculation as to the reason for the difference between the two subject groups is unlikely to be productive. The only firm conclusion that can be made is the rather obvious one that far more factors are involved in everyday memory than those measured in the laboratory. It is nevertheless rather intriguing that the present results seem to support the myth that absent-minded persons tend to be those with high educational level.

An aspect of the data that is perhaps more interesting is the fact that 30% of the subjects forgot to push the button on one or more occasions *of which they were apparently unaware*. As many as 36% of all omissions were not acknowledged by subjects. This result might be readily interpretable as a lack of motivation in reporting failures, rather than an unawareness of these failures, were it not for the fact that subjects appeared to be quite diligent about reporting any responses that they deemed inappropriate. Many late responses were acknowledged as being late, despite the instruction only to record omissions. Apparently subjects simply forgot they had omitted a response. This forgetting was obtained despite the fact that subjects rarely, if ever, forgot that they had pushed the button if they had in fact done so:

there were very few (if any) multiple responses to a single target, and subjects never acknowledged an omission when one had not in fact occurred. The data seem to suggest that if a subject responded she remembered that she had done so, whereas if she forgot to do so she often failed to remember her omission. This bias, if it is real, is difficult to explain in terms of proactive interference between traces of earlier responses. Whatever its explanation, the bias has obvious relevance for the everyday task of taking a pill, in that it stresses the importance of pill boxes which enable a day's or a week's dose to be placed in labelled compartments so that a patient can easily tell whether or not a pill has been taken (cf. the packaging of the contraceptive pill).

The findings of the present experiments have two implications for the study of memory. First, laboratory tasks may generalise rather poorly to the real world because of the way in which the experimenter cues recall. Second, studies of memory that rely on subjects reporting their failures to recall (e.g. Reason, 1976) may miss a substantial proportion of failures of which subjects are apparently unaware.

ACKNOWLEDGEMENTS

The authors are grateful to Dr. I. Nimmo-Smith for assistance with the statistical analysis and to Dr. G. Hitch for his critical comments on an earlier version of this manuscript.

REFERENCES

Baddeley, A.D. and Warrington, E.K. (1970). Amnesia and the distinction between long- and short-term memory. *Journal of Verbal Learning and Verbal Behaviour*. 9, 176-189.

Collins, A.M. and Quillian, M.R. (1969). Retrieval time from semantic memory. *Journal of Verbal Learning and Verbal Behaviour*. 8, 240-247.

Hyde, T.S. and Jenkins, J.J. (1969). The differential effects of incidental tasks on the organisation of recall of a list of highly associated words. *Journal of Experimental Psychology*. 82, 472-481.

Reason, J. (1976). Absent minds. *New Society*, 38, 244-245.

Warrington, E.K. and Sanders, H.I. (1971). The fate of old memories. *Quarterly Journal of Experimental Psychology*. 23, 432-442.

AN INVENTORY OF EVERYDAY MEMORY EXPERIENCES

Douglas J. Herrmann
Hamilton College
Clinton, New York 13323
Ulric Neisser
Cornell University
Ithaca, New York 14850

ABSTRACT

The *Inventory of Memory Experiences (IME)* includes 48 questions about how often the respondent experiences various kinds of everyday forgetting (Part F) and 24 questions about how well he remembers certain things from early childhood and daily life (Part R). It was administered to 205 college students; 41 of them took it twice. Analysis of Part F in-indicated the existence of about 8 specific memory abilities (for names, conversations, errands, etc.) as well as a general factor. Part F had a reliability of .68. Results for Part R included a significant sex difference in recall of childhood experiences and a solid relation between the rated quality of memories and their ages. Overall, it is clear that everyday memory is not a unidimensional trait.

INTRODUCTION

All contemporary theories of memory are based on the results of specialized laboratory experiments. However,so little is known about the use of memory in everyday life that we cannot tell whether these theories apply outside the laboratory. We also know very little about individual differences in remembering and forgetting except for the special case of mental imagery. Yet, as Underwood (1975) has pointed out, individual differences can provide crucial tests of theories in this area. Moreover, it is just these neglected aspects of memory that are of the most interest to the man in the street, who may remark that he has a poor memory for jokes but never forgets a face.

The present study is the first phase of a research program aimed at developing basic information in these areas. We have begun by devising a 72-item questionnaire called the

Inventory of Memory Experiences (IME). This questionnaire, which was developed on the basis of *a priori* reasoning, personal intuitions, and a little data from an earlier pilot study, asks respondents how often they forget various kinds of things and how well they remember certain others.

The use of a questionnaire to obtain data like these presents certain problems. Many of those problems can be addressed by a detailed examination of the data themselves. In our case that examination is encouraging, as will appear below. The subjects took their task seriously and responded discriminatively. One problem of validity deserves special consideration, however. Technically speaking, responses on the *IME* represent what Flavell (1977) has called "metamemory": people's beliefs about their own mnemonic abilities. Without field studies of actual memory performance, we cannot be sure whether these beliefs are accurate. Nevertheless there are reasons for being optimistic in the meantime.There is considerable evidence that self-reports can be accurate predictors of cognitive performance. Hart's (1965) work on "feeling of knowing" showed that people can tell whether they are going to recognize items that they are unable to recall. Flavell and his collaborators have shown that school age children can predict several aspects of their own memory performance rather well. Kozlowski and Bryant (1977) found that subjects' reports about their"sense of direction" were strongly related to performance on appropriate objective tests. Finally, Schmeck, Ribich, and Ramanaiah (1977) have demonstrated that various kinds of self reports of learning in academic settings correlate with recognition and recall scores. It is reasonable to believe, therefore, that responses people give on the *IME* may also be good indicators of their actual behavior.

The *IME* comes in two sections. The one in which we have the most confidence is Part F, which includes 48 questions about forgetting. Each asks the respondent to estimate how often he experiences a particular kind of forgetting, using a seven-point scale whose extremes are labelled "never" and "always," with intermediate steps labelled "once in a while, now and then, about half the time," and"very often." A typical item (the most typical, in terms of its many high correlations with other items) is "How often do you find, at the end of a conversation, that you forgot to bring up some point or some question that you had intended to mention?" On its face at least, this question deals with memory for intentions. The entire set of questions was designed *a priori* to sample eight more or less separate types of experiences: forgetting of intentions (I), people (P), names (N), geographical information (G), conversations (C), and things learned by rote (RT): absentmindedness (A); failure to retrieve something one knows (RF). Only 47 of the items actually deal with forgetting; the remaining one (#12) concerns the experiences of *deja vu:* "Sometimes people find that a place looks strangely familiar even though they know they have never been there before. How often does this happen to you?" Part F consists of six pages, with one item from each of the eight *a priori* categories on each page; in other respects the items are randomly ordered. The categories themselves were not intended to carry much theoretical weight, but merely to ensure an adequate sampling of memory experiences. Table 1 of the Appendix exhibits the 48 items arranged according to the factors that emerged from the analysis; the *a priori* category that gave rise to each question is indicated by an appropriate code letter.

The other part of the *IME*, Part R, consists of three sections of eight questions each. Part R followed Part F for half the subjects and preceded it for the other half. All the questions ask how well the respondent remembers something, on a seven-point scale that goes from "perfectly" to "not at all" with a midpoint at "fairly well." Section R-1 is about recall of early childhood, defined as the time before the respondent entered school or turned six years old; it includes such questions as "Do you remember any time that you were sick or hurt as a young child? Think of whatever time you remember best. How well do you remember it?" Section R-2 asks about various specific events: "The last time you bought a pair of shoes," "The first long trip you ever took by yourself," etc. The respondent must indicate how long ago the event took place as well as how well he remembers it; analysis of the relationship between the elapsed time and the rated quality of the memory enables us to plot crude "forgetting functions." Section R-3 concerns people's use of memory in conversations. A typical item is "When you and your friends have seen the same movie or TV show,do you ever talk about it afterwards?" If so, how well do you usually remember the show? The items included in Sections R-1, R-2, and R-3 appear in Tables 3, 4, and 2 respectively. (Only 7 of the 8 items in R-1 and R-3 were analyzed; the last questions, which asked the subject to choose the memory he would rate, were included for exploratory purposes only.)

The *IME* was administered to 205 Cornell undergraduates (93 males and 112 females) who had volunteered to participate in a study of everyday memory. Four or five months later, 41 of them were persuaded to return and take the *IME* a second time. They were instructed not to try to recall their earlier responses, but to answer each question in terms of their present judgment. The results presented here refer to the 205 original Inventories unless otherwise noted.

RESULTS

Part F - Means

The forgetting ratings for each question were converted to a numerical 7-point scale and averaged (see Table 1). Only 5 of the 48 items were reported as forgotten more than "half the time" (on the average): They concern the names of TV or movie actors, the names of people one has just met, maps, long distance telephone numbers, and dreams. At the other extreme, only three types of forgetting were reported as almost "never" happening, with scale scores greater than 6.0: finding a place totally unfamiliar though one has been there before, forgetting to button or zip up one's clothing, and failing to recognize people as familiar a few days after meeting them. The average for all 47 items (excluding the *deja vu* question) was 4.86, almost a third of the way from forgetting "half the time" toward "never" forgetting. There were considerable differences among subjects in the amounts of forgetting they reported. The person who reported the most forgetting across all 47 items had a mean of 2.94; she forgot things "fairly often." The one (also a female) who reported the least forgetting had a mean of 6.36, between "once in a while" and "never." The mean for males, 4.93, did not differ significantly from that for females, 4.79.

Part F - Reliability

Test-retest reliabilities were calculated from the data of the 41 subjects who took the *IME* twice. The reliability of the total Part F score was .68, which compares favorably with that of many psychometric instruments. As Table 1 shows, the individual items had reliabilities ranging from .15 to .74; the median was .49 (with an n of 41, correlations higher than .30 are significant at the .05 level). The only two items with individual reliabilities above .70 refer to being unable to find something you just put down and forgetting the name of someone to whom you have just been introduced.

Part F - Factor structure

Correlations were computed between all pairs of questions in Part F. (n was 205 except where an occasional subject had omitted an item.) In the resulting matrix of 1128 correlations, only 9 were negative and none significantly so. (Three of these 9, including the most negative at 0.12, involved the *deja vu* item, justifying our decision to regard it as unique.) Thus the responses form a positive manifold, just as the tests of mental ability invariably do: people who report one kind of everyday forgetting tend to report other kinds also. Question #41, forgetting to bring up an intended point in a conversation, had the largest number of high correlations with other items and is thus the "most typical" item. Its reliability of .58 is also high.

A series of factor analytic procedures were carried out to clarify the structure of the data. A principal components analysis was conducted first, and revealed a strong first principal component with an eigenvalue of 12.2, accounting for about 25% of the variance in the scores. (This is another expression of the fact that most of the correlations are positive). Our subjects varied along a general dimension of everyday forgetting, or at least of willingness to report it. As one might expect, item #41, the most typical question, had the highest loading on the first principal component; item #12, concerning *deja vu* had the lowest.

In addition to the first component, the principal components analysis produced 12 other factors with eigenvalues greater than 1.0. Subsequently, a principal factor analysis was applied to the 13 factors above this cutoff. Although all 13 factors seem to be interpretable after rotation, we decided to adopt the more conservative procedure recommended by Montanelli and Humphreys (1976), which compares obtained eigenvalues to randomly generated ones. Only eight of our 13 eigenvalues substantially exceeded the cutoff provided by this procedure, so further analysis was based on eight factors. To facilitate interpretation, the data were subjected to a number of eight-factor analyses with orthogonal and oblique rotations. Since all of them produced roughly the same patterns of factor loadings, and since the varimax orthogonal solution exhibited slightly better simple structure, we have chosen it as the best representation of the data.

Table 1 exhibits the eight rotated factors as defined by the items that load heavily on them. (Two items that do not load appreciably on any factor appear at the end of the table.) Judging by the content of the heavily-loading items, the factors can be described as follows:

1. A *rote memory* factor involves forgetting things like numbers and addresses, and having to check them.
2. An *absentmindedness* factor involves forgetting what one has just done, or intended to do.
3. A *name* factor involves inability to recall people's names.
4. A *people* factor involves recognizing individuals by their appearance.
5. A *conversation* factor involves remembering jokes, stories, and conversations.
6. An *errand* factor involves remembering a list of things to do.
7. A *retrieval* factor involves an inability to recall why something seems familiar.
8. A *place* factor involves remembering where things are.

To determine the relative memorability and forgettability of particular factors, we averaged the mean ratings of the items that loaded over .500 on them (see Table 1). By this index *rote memory* and *names* give people the most trouble while *people* and *conversations* are remembered best.

PART R

In the analysis below, the three sections of Part R are treated separately. Although we undertook factor analyses of each section, their results were not particularly illuminating and will not be presented; the discussion will be based on simpler statistics. Section R-3 will be considered first because its subject matter is most similar to that of Part F.

Section R-3

Section R-3 asks how well the respondent remembers various things in discussions with friends. Mean ratings for the various items were all quite similar; on the seven-point scale they ranged from a low of 4.29 for news items to a high of 5.55 for what people were wearing, (see Table 2). The inter-correlations among the items were not high: only 2 of 21 exceeded .40. When we averaged the 7 ratings for each subject into a total score, the mean for males, 4.90, did not differ significantly from that for females, 4.97. The reliability of the total score was only .47, substantially lower than for Part F. (The median reliability of individual items is only slightly less in R-3 than in F; the lower reliability of the total score is probably due to the smaller number of items involved.) Overall, scores in R-3 correlated .38 with both the total scores on F and the first principal component of F. A modest positive correlation of this sort is not unexpected, since both sections deal with remembering recent and contemporary things. Correlations of R-3 with the individual factors of Part F were all appreciably lower and do not deserve detailed consideration.

Section R-1

Section R-1 asks how well the respondents remember various things from early childhood. The mean ratings ranged from a low of 3.71 for remembering any adult outside their own family to a high of 5.01 for remembering any toy they had played with (see Table 3). The intercorrelations among the individual items were again low, with only two over .40. When the ratings were averaged, a striking sex difference emerged. Females' ratings of the quality of their childhood recollections averaged 4.38, more than a third of a scale step higher than the males' average of 3.89. The difference is significant at the .001 level by a t-test. Other evidence also suggests that R-1 measures something different from the other sections: it correlated only .26 with the total F-score, .25 with the first principal component of F, and .29 with R-3. Presumably these values are lower than R-3's correlations with F because R-1 deals with early childhood. The reliability of R-1 was .46.

Section R-2

Because Section R-2 (Table 4) asks about such a wide range of recent and remote events, we do not attach much importance to subjects' average scores or to their correlation with other parts of the *IME*. Since the subjects were asked to indicate how long ago a given event had occurred as well as to rate their memory of it, however, we were able to plot a crude "forgetting curve" for each item. As Table 5 shows, six of the questions exhibited a significant negative regression of the quality of memories on their ages. Moreover, not all the "forgetting curves" had the same slope. Relatively recent events like buying shoes and having a birthday lost memory quality at a rate of more than a full scale step a year; those like meeting one's best friend or taking one's first trip alone, which have a much wider range of remoteness, had smaller slopes. The naturalness of this result bolsters our confidence in the construct validity of the *IME*.

CONCLUSIONS

We think we have shown that people can give meaningful and discriminating reports of their everyday memory experiences. While the validity of these reports remains to be fully established, a number of important conclusions have already emerged. First, the common idea that one's overall memory is "good" or "bad" requires revision. While our results do indicate the presence of a general factor (the first principal component of Part F), they also show that there are specific memory abilities for various kinds of experience. There are indeed people who appear to have poor memory for jokes and a good memory for faces! The existence of at least eight different memory factors means that future theories will have to distinguish among different types of content in their explanations of everyday memory phenomena.

ACKNOWLEDGMENTS

We are deeply grateful for the help of Sanford Gottlieb, who collaborated with us in all phases of developing the *IME*; of Gary Weiss and Alan Gold, who administered it to 205 people; of Sally Sellers, who administered the reliability test and other questionnaires;and of the subjects themselves who worked honestly and seriously at the relatively tedious task we set for them.

REFERENCES

Flavell, J.H.(1977) *Cognitive Development*, Prentice-Hall, Englewood Cliffs.

Hart, J.T.(1965) Memory and the feeling of knowing experience. *Journal of Educational Psychology*, 56, 205-216.

Kozlowski, L.T. & Bryant,K.J.(1977) Sense of Direction, spatial orientation, and cognitive maps. *Journal of Experimental Psychology: Human Perception and Performance*, 3, 590-598.

Montanelli, R.G.Jr. & Humphreys,L.G.(1976). Latent roots of random data correlation matrices with squared multiple correlations on the diagonal: A Monte Carlo study. *Psychometrika*, 41, 341-348.

Schmeck, R.R., Ribich,F., & Ramanaiah,N. (1977).Development of a self-report inventory for assessing individual differences in learning processes. *Applied Psychological Measurement*, 1, 413-431.

Underwood, B.J. (1975). Individual differences as a crucible in theory construction. *American Psychologist*, 30, 128-134.

APPENDIX

Table 1. Items of Part F arranged by factors

Factor 1 ("Rote Memory") MN=4.36

#33 (RT) Think of times when you have made a long distance call, with the area code and number (like "607-555-6815," for example) written down on a piece of paper in front of you. Some people begin to dial the number, and then must look back at it again in order to finish dialing all ten digits. How often does this happen to you? FL=.663*, MN=3.69, R=.469.
#45 (RT) Think of times when you have called somebody on the phone, using a phone number that you had called several times before. How often do you find that you must look the number up again because you don't remember it? FL=.596*, MN=4.82, R=.471.
#23 (RT) Think of times when you have addressed a letter to someone, at an address that you had used several times before. How often do you find that you must look up the address again because you don't remember it? FL=.576*, MN=4.78, R=.395.
#14 (RT) Think of times when you have looked up a local number in the phone book. Some people begin to dial the number and then must look back at it again in order to finish dialing. How often does this happen to you? FL=.570*, MN=4.25, R=.465.

Note: All items loading ≥ .300 on a factor are listed with it, in order from highest to lowest loadings, though typically only the higher loadings were used to identify the factors. Unique items (which do not load ≥ .300 on any other factor) are starred*. FL: loading on the listed factor; MN: mean self rating, with higher values indicating less forgetting (for factors, MN is the average of the means for items with FL ≥ .500); R: reliability. The # indicates the number of the item on the *IME* itself; the code in parentheses is the *a priori* category it was intended to represent.

#38 (G) Think of times when you have had a map or directions to help you find some unfamiliar place. In this situation people may look at the map or directions when they start out, <u>and then have to look again later</u> because they have forgotten part of the route. How often does this happen to you? FL=.568*, MN=3.61, R=.330.
#17 (G) Think of times when someone has given directions to get to some unfamiliar place. How often do you forget the directions before you get there?FL=.517,MN=5.00, R=.523.
#8 (G) Suppose you were going back to some place (such as a friend's house) where you had been only once before. Would you have to ask for directions? FL=.366, MN=4.69, R=.546.
#26 (RT) When you go out to run a few errands (and don't have them written down on a list), how often do you forget to do at least one of them? FL=.325, MN=4.68, R=.336.
#41 (I) How often do you find, at the end of a conversation, that you forget to bring up some point or some question that you had intended to mention? FL=.309, MN=4.36, R=.583.

<u>Factor 2</u> ("Absentmindedness") MN=4.73

#18 (A) How often are you unable to find something that you put down only a few minutes before?FL=.660*, MN=4.69, R=.738.
#22 (I) Think of times when you have gone to a room to do something or get something. How often do you get there and find that you can't remember why you went? FL=.623*, MN=4.76 R=.461.
#41 (I) How often do you find, at the end of a conversation, that you forgot to bring up some point or some question that you had intended to mention? FL=.496, MN=4.36, R=.583.
#4 (I) How often do you discover, when you have just gone out, that you must return for something you had intended to bring but accidentally left behind? FL=.423, MN=4.56,R=.489.
#24 (C) When someone says he has told you something already (at some earlier time), how often do you find that you have no recollection of his telling you any such thing? FL=.403, MN=5.36, R=.541.
#6 (A) When you put something away and then look for it a week or so later, how often do you forget where you had put it? FL=.387, MN=4.68, R=.635.
#35 (I) When someone asks you to give a message to a friend, how often do you forget to do so? FL=.344*, MN=5.16, R=.447.

<u>Factor 3</u> ("Names") MN=4.57

#7 (N) How often do you find that just when you want to introduce someone you know to someone else, you can't think of their name? FL=.642*, MN=5.29, R=.561.

#25 (N) Think of times when you have met people at a social gathering (a party, a meeting, etc.) and happened to see them on the street a few days later. How often are you unable to remember their names although you know perfectly well when and where you met them? FL=.630*, MN=4.68, R=.510.
#44 (N) Think of times when you have been introduced to people at a social gathering (a party, a meeting, etc.) and have wanted to call them by name a few minutes later, how often do you find that you have already forgotten their name? FL=.598*, MN=3.67, R=.715.
#40 (N) Think of times when you have run into somebody whom you once knew, but haven't seen for a couple of years. How often are you unable to remember their name, even though you know perfectly well who they are? FL=555*, MN=4.62, R=.456.
#10 (N) When you are talking about a person (a casual friend, a political figure, etc.) how often do you find that you cannot recall the person's name just when you need it? FL=.431*, MN=5.26, R=.479.
#21 (N) Think of times when you have recognized an actor (in a movie or TV show) as one whom you have seen in other shows before. When this happens, how often do you fail to remember the actor's name? FL=.364, MN=3.52, R=.633.
#16 (I) How often do you forget birthdays or anniversaries when you had intended to do something special (send a greeting, bring a gift, etc.)? FL=.344*, MN=5.40, R=.618.
#1 (P) Think of times when you have run into people whom you once knew, but haven't seen for a couple of years. How often do you fail to recognize them, so that they don't even look familiar to you? FL=.339*, MN=5.87, R=.630.
#19 (RF) People may be asked about something(such as a brand name or an address of an item in the news) that they are sure they know, and yet be unable to remember it just when they are asked. How often does this happen to you?FL=.326*, MN=5.10, R=.378.
#46 (C) When you want to remember an experience, a joke, or a story, how often do you find that you cannot do so? FL=.315, MN=4.99, R=.680.

Factor 4 ("People") MN=5.71

#39 (P) When you are in a restaurant and want to speak to your waiter or waitress, how often do you forget what he or she looked like (so you don't know which waiter or waitress to call)? FL=.620*, MN=5.32, R=.489.
#42 (P) Think of times when you have met people at a social gathering (a party, a meeting, etc.) and happened to see

them on the street a few days later. How often do you fail to recognize them, so that they don't even seem familiar to you? FL=.540*, MN=6.10, R=.218.
#24 (C) When someone says he has told you something already (at some earlier time),how often do you find that you have no recollection of his telling you any such thing? FL=.352, MN=5.36, R=.541.
#43 (A) When you need to know what the date is, how often do you find that you must look it up (or ask someone) because you don't know it? FL=.331*, MN=4.19, R=.598.
#30 (P) Think of times when you have recognized an actor (in a movie or TV show) as one whom you have seen in other shows before. How often are you unable to remember where, or in what show, you saw the actor before?FL=.313, MN=4.52,R=.333.
#20 (P) Think of times when you have met people at a social gathering (a party, a meeting, etc.) and happened to see them on the street a few days later. How often do you find that although they seem familiar to you, you can't remember where you met them before? FL=.300, MN=5.45, R=.148.

Factor 5 ("Conversations") MN=5.71

#28 (C) When you are telling someone a joke or a story, how often do you forget the punch line or ending before you get to it? FL=.615*, MN=5.71, R=.571.
#46 (C) When you want to remember an experience, a joke, or a story, how often do you find that you cannot do so? FL=.457, MN=4.99, R=.680.
#24 (C) When someone says he has told you something already (at some earlier time), how often do you find that you have no recollection of his telling you any such thing? FL=.451, MN=5.36, R=.541.
#11 (C) Think of times when you have wanted to tell a friend about a conversation that you had with another person. How often do you find that you have forgotten part of what you wanted to tell? FL=.448*, MN=5.17, R=.296.
#2 (C) How often do you remember something that somebody said to you, but forgot just who said it? FL=.440*,MN=4.81, R=.503.
#29 (I) How often do you forget to keep appointments if you don't write them down? FL=.436*, MN=5.43, R=.602.
#34 (RF) When you have just asked a question, how often do you realize that you already knew the answer yourself? FL=.426*, MN=5.00, R=.565.
#31 (RF) People may be asked about something (such as a brand name or an address or an item in the news) and think that they don't know the answer; but when someone else gives

the answer they realize that they knew it after all. How often does this happen to you? FL=.402, MN=4.34, R=.667.
#37 (C) How often do you start to tell someone a piece of information, a joke, or a story, only to discover that you have told that very item to the same person before?FL=.339*, MN=4.67, R=.625.
#5 (RF) Think of times when you have awakened in the morning sure that you have just been dreaming. How often do you find that you can't remember any details of the dream at all? FL=.334*, MN=3.99, R=.362.
#19 (RF) People may be asked about something (such as a brand name or an address or an item in the news) that they are sure they know and yet be unable to remember it just when they are asked. How often does this happen to you? FL=.303, MN=5.10, R=.378.

Factor 6 ("Errands") MN=4.73

#3 (R) If you go to the supermarket to buy four or five things (without a written shopping list), how often do you forget at least one of them? FL=.746*, MN=4.79, R=.509.
#26 (R) When you go out to run a few errands (and don't have them written down on a list), how often do you forget to do at least one of them? FL=.533, MN=4.68, R=.336.
#4 (I) How often do you discover, when you have just gone out, that you must return for something you had intended to bring but accidentally left behind?FL=.340, MN=4.56, R=.489.
#12 (G) Sometimes people find that a place looks strangely familiar even though they have never been there before. How often does this happen to you? FL=.328*,MN=4.79, R=.406.

Factor 7 ("Retrieval") MN=4.77

#48 (RF) How often when someone mentions a name that sounds familiar to you (it "rings a bell"), do you find that you cannot identify it: that is, you can't say who the name belongs to, or why it seems familiar?FL=.522*,MN=4.66, R=.316.
#13 (P) Think of times when you have run into people whom you once knew, but hadn't seen for a couple of years. How often do you find that although they seem familiar to you, you can't remember where you met them before? FL=.513*, MN=4.87, R=.148.
#21 (N) Think of times when you have recognized an actor (in a movie or TV show) as one whom you have seen in other shows before. When this happens, how often do you fail to remember the actor's name? FL=.468, MN=3.52, R=.633.
#30 (P) Think of times when you have recognized an actor (in a movie or TV show) as one whom you have seen in other shows

before. How often are you unable to remember where, or in what show, you saw the actor before?FL=.467,MN=4.52, R=.333.
#31 (RF) People may be asked about something (such as a brand name or an address or an item in the news) and think they don't know the answer; but when someone else gives the answer they realize that they knew it after all. How often does this happen to you? FL=.370, MN=4.34, R=.667.
#47 (G) Think of times when you have taken a new shortcut or a new street in a town that you otherwise know fairly well. How often are you surprised to see where the shortcut had led you? FL=.358*,MN=4.70, R=.597.
#20 (P) Think of times when you have met people at a social gathering (a party, a meeting, etc.) and happened to see them on the street a few days later. How often do you find that although they seem familiar to you, you can't remember where you met them before? FL=.332, MN=5.45, R=.148.
#19 (RF) People may be asked about something (such as a brand name or an address or an item in the news) that they are sure they know, and yet be unable to remember it just when they are asked. How often does this happen to you? FL=.307, MN=5.10, R=.378.

Factor 8 ("Places") MN=4.69

#8 (G) Suppose you were going back to some place (such as a friend's house) where you had been only once before. Would you have to ask for directions? FL=.513, MN=4.69, R=.546.
#6 (A) When you put something away and then look for it a week or so later, how often do you forget where you had put it? FL=.483, MN=4.68, R=.635.
#32 (A) How often do you find that you have forgotten to button or zip up some part of your clothing? FL=.418*, MN=6.20, R=.206.
#17 (G) Think of times when someone has given you directions to get to some unfamiliar place. How often do you forget the directions before getting there? FL=.406,MN=5.00,R=.523.
#27 (G) Sometimes people find that a place looks completely unfamiliar even though they know they have been there before. How often does this happen to you? FL=.379*, MN=6.29,R=.266.
#9 (RF) How often, when you have confidently answered a question, do you realize later that the answer you gave was wrong? FL=.330*, MN=5.46, R=.286.

VARIABLES NOT LOADING ≥ .300 ON ANY FACTOR

#15 (A) How often do you forget that you have just done something, and start to do it over again? (For example, open a soda for yourself and discover that you already had one open, or go to set your alarm clock and find that you had

already done so.) FL=--, MN=5.87, R=.354.
#36 (A) How often do you have to check more than one pocket (or more than one section of your purse or wallet) to find something you want? FL=--, MN=4.07, R=.498.

Table 2: Section R-3

#17 Did you ever visit someplace with friends and afterwards talk about the furniture or the decorations or other objects that were there? If so, how well did you remember(IS,HWDYR) the show? MN=4.72, R=.456.
#18 When you and your friends have seen the same movie or TV show, do you ever talk about it afterwards? IS,HWDYR the show? MN=5.23, R=.581.
#19 When you have eaten a meal in a restaurant, do you ever talk about it with friends later? IS,HWDYR the different things that you ate? MN=5.55, R=.274.
#20 When you and your friends have been with some other person, do you or they ever talk afterwards about the clothes that person was wearing? IS,HWDYR those clothes? MN=4.59, R=.391.
#21 When you have seen something happen, (an accident, an unusual event, etc.), do you ever talk about it with friends later? IS, HWDYR what you have seen? MN=4.29, R=.287.
#22 Do you ever watch a sporting event, and talk about it with friends later? IS, HWDYR it? MN=5.30, R=.549.
#23 Do you ever watch a TV news report, or read about something in the newspaper, and afterwards talk about it with friends? IS, HWDYR it? MN=4.66, R=.496.
#24 Is there any other kind of experience, besides those mentioned so far, that you often talk about? IS, HWDYR those experiences? MN=--, R=--.

Table 3: Section R-1

#1 Do you remember any <u>toys</u> that you had as a young child? (Don't count any toys you have kept until now.) Think of whatever toy you remember best. HWDYR what it was like? MN=5.01, R=.328.
#2 Do you remember any <u>piece of clothing</u> that you had as a young child? (Don't count any clothing you have kept until now.) Think of whatever piece of clothing you remember? HWDYR what it was like? MN=4.37, R=.536.
#3 Do you remember any <u>trip</u> that you took as a young child? Think of whatever trip you remember best. HWDYR it? MN=3.74, R=.506.
#4 Do you remember any time that your <u>parents punished you</u> as a young child? Think of what ever time you remember best. HWDYR it? MN=3.84, R=.637.

#5 Do you remember any time that you were sick or hurt as a young child? Think of whatever time you remember best. HWDYR it? MN=4.29, R=.566.
#6 Do you remember any child you used to play with when you were a young child? (Don't count brothers or sisters, or people you still know.) Think of whatever playmate you remember best. HWDYR them? MN=4.12, R=.388.
#7 Do you remember any adult, outside your own family, that you knew as a young child? (Don't count people that you still know.) Think of whatever adult you remember best. HWDYR them? MN=3.72, R=.374.
#8 Do you remember any other object or experience from the time when you were a young child, besides those mentioned so far? Think of whatever other experience you remember best. HWDYR it? MN=--, R=--.

Table 4: Section R-2

#9 Do you remember the last time you went to see a doctor? About how long ago was it (AHLAWI)? HWDYR that time? MN=6.13, R=.413.
#10 Do you remember the last time you bought a pair of shoes? AHLAWI? HWDYR buying the shoes? MN=6.28, R=.303.
#11 Do you remember what you did on your last birthday? AHLWI? HWDYR your birthday? MN=5.21, R=.283.
#12 Think of your closest friend (if you are married, think of your husband or wife). Do you remember the day that you first met him or her? AHLAWI? HWDYR the day you met them? MN=3.93, R=.467.
#13 Do you remember the first long trip that you ever took by yourself? AHLAWI? HWDYR the trip? MN=4.97, R=.651.
#14 Do you remember the first time you earned any money yourself (outside of what your parents may have given you)? AHLAWI? HWDYR the time you earned the money?MN=3.96,R=.416.
#15 Do you remember the first day you went to school (in first grade or in kindergarten)? AHLAWI? HWDYR that day? MN=2.68, R=.152.
#16 Do you remember any dream you had more than a year ago? About how long ago did you have the dream?HWDYR the dream? MN=4.39, R=.584.

Note: the questions in the above tables were drawn from the *Inventory of Memory Experiences (IME)*

Table 5: Section R-2 Regression Analysis of Ratings and Ages of Rated Memories.

No.	Item[1]	Range of Reported Ages (years)	Correlation[2]	Slope (Rating Steps per year)	Intercept (Rating)
9.	Doctor visit	0-3	-.380**	- .722	6.486
10.	Shoes purchase	0-3	-.452**	-1.209	6.658
11.	Last birthday	0-3	-.279**	-1.540	6.042
12.	Day met friend	0.1-20	-.464**	- .270	5.332
13.	First trip	0.1-17	-.406**	- .196	5.917
14.	First earnings	0.2-14	-.283**	- .182	5.541
15.	First day at school	10-19	.157*	.192	.044
16.	Memorable dream	1-17	.010	.003	5.038

[1]See Table 4 for exact wording.
[2]Significance Levels: **p < .01 *p < .05.

ON KEEPING TRACK OF THE PRESENT STATUS OF PEOPLE AND THINGS

R. A. Bjork

University of California
Los Angeles, California, U.S.A.

T. K. Landauer

Bell Laboratories
Murray Hill, New Jersey, U.S.A.

ABSTRACT

In order to function with reasonable efficiency in everyday life, one needs to differentiate current information from out-of-date information in one's memory. In the present paper, we first illustrate the importance of such updating processes in everyday and applied contexts. We then show that encoding processes that are effective in terms of the long-term accumulation of information in memory are not necessarily effective in keeping one's memory current. Finally, we report an experiment on "mate updating"--that is, on keeping track of who is currently married to whom--designed to explore several aspects of the updating process.

INTRODUCTION

The common-sense measure of human memory ability seems to be based on a kind of accumulation notion. People with good memories are people who retain or accumulate more information in memory than do other people. Many of the memory tasks we face, however, require not that we remember everything, but, rather, that we remember only the current or most recent exemplar of information of a certain type. We need to remember our *current* phone number, we need to remember where we left the car *today*, we need to remember what the trump suit is on the *current* hand, we need to remember who is *now* in charge of some administrative function, we need to remember where the emergency brake is on our *present* automobile, we need to remember the name of a friend's *current* spouse, we need to remember the *new* procedure for accomplishing something on a computer, and so on. There is no particular value in remembering our old phone number, for example, or where we left the car yesterday, or what the trump suit was on the preceding hand. In fact, accumulating such out-of-date information in memory creates the potential for errors and confusion.

In a number of applied job contexts as well, efficient updating is far more important than (maybe even inconsistent with) the long-term accumulation of information. Short-order cooks, air-traffic controllers, intelligence analysts, people in various command and management positions who need to keep track of the present status of personnel, supplies, or equipment, and many others must not get confused between current and out-of-date information.

It is important to distinguish between the ability to remember the most recent of a series of inputs to memory and the ability to remember as much of the total input series (not necessarily in the right order) as possible. For one thing, people who are good at keeping current may not be so good at total recall, and vice-versa. Similarly, encoding processes that are efficient in updating one's memory may not yield good total recall, and vice versa.

To illustrate the latter point, consider the results of an experiment by Bjork and McClure (1974). In Bjork and McClure's experiment, subjects were required to keep track of the current response word associated with each of four different stimulus words. On each trial of the experiment, one of the four stimulus words was presented and subjects were asked to give the last response word that had been paired with that stimulus. As soon as the subjects responded, they were shown a new response word for that stimulus. Thus, subjects went through a long series of trials on each of which one of the four stimulus words was first presented as a probe-test of the subject's memory for the most recent response word paired with that stimulus and then a new response word was presented together with the stimulus. This task, which is sometimes referred to as the maximal PI (proactive interference) task, goes back at least as far as a study by Yntema and Mueser (1960) and has been used by a number of investigators.

Bjork and McClure (1974) added two new wrinkles to the basic task. First, each subject was asked to use one of several different encoding strategies during the series of trials. Second, at the end of the experiment, without forewarning, subjects were asked to recall as many of the response words presented during the experiment as possible.

Two of the three encoding strategies used by Bjork and McClure (1974) yielded an instructive interaction. One of the strategies (Ordered Rehearsal) consisted of trying to keep the current four response words available in an active rehearsal set. When the response word paired with a given stimulus was replaced by a new response word, the new word was to be inserted into the rehearsal set in place of the old (out-of-date) word. The other strategy (Image Replacement) consisted of forming a new interactive image incorporating a given stimulus word and any new response word paired with that stimulus.

It is certainly no surprise to students of human memory that Bjork and McClure (1974) found that final-recall performance in the Image-Replacement Condition was a great deal better than final-recall in the Ordered-Rehearsal Condition. In terms of keeping track of the current response associated with a given stimulus, however, the Ordered-Rehearsal Condition was considerably better than the Image-Replacement Condition. It appears that the Image-Replacement Condition resulted in a much stronger representation in long-term memory of the responses paired with a given stimulus than did the Ordered-Rehearsal Condition, but in terms of giving the current response at any one point in time, that advantage was more than offset by the difficulty in discriminating which of the responses paired with a given stimulus was the most recent response.

Bjork and McClure (1974) contend that the Ordered-Rehearsal Condition more closely approximates a "destructive" updating process than do conditions such as the Image-Replacement Condition. Destructive updating is a process where the act of storing new information destroys or makes inaccessible the old information. A good example of purely destructive updating is the way the memory in a computer is updated: When new-information is stored at a given location, the old information at that location is obliterated. Another example of destructive updating is the displacement notion of how items are lost from short-term memory.

In terms of effective updating, a destructive updating process clearly has the advantage that out-of-date information is no longer around to compete with current information. It should be pointed out, however, that good long-term retention of all of a series of inputs to memory is not necessarily inconsistent with remembering well which of those inputs is the most recent. Provided that there is some underlying structure that orders the inputs ("structural" updating in Bjork and McClure's, 1974, terms), both updating and total recall can be very good indeed. In fact, the third encoding strategy used by Bjork and McClure (1974), Story Construction, which was designed to be such a structural updating condition, yielded updating and total-recall performance levels that were higher than the best of the other two conditions. In the Story-Construction Condition, subjects were asked to develop a simple story corresponding to each stimulus word in which each new response word would provide the basis for extending the story; the story narrative, then, is the structure that orders the successive response words in memory.

The principal goal of the present study was to ascertain whether there is any evidence that people can actually destroy or erase information in updating their memories. The Ordered-Rehearsal Condition in Bjork and McClure's (1974) experiment may not demonstrate destructive updating, but, rather, that such rote rehearsal can keep items available in short-term memory indefinitely with little or no increment in the representation of those items in long-term memory (see, e.g., Craik & Watkins, 1973; Woodward, Bjork, & Jongeward, 1973).

The task employed in the present experiment is formally similar to that used by Bjork and McClure (1974), but has a somewhat different flavor. Using common male and female first names, subjects were asked to keep track of who a given hypothetical person was married to, if anybody.

The destructive updating question was approached in two ways. One way was to see whether subjects could take advantage of negative information. For example, if subjects are first told that persons A and B are married, and are later told that A is now married to C, does an intervening statement that A and B are divorced help subjects' delayed retention of the fact that A is now married to C?

The other approach to the destructive updating question was via a spacing manipulation. One might expect that "destruction" of the memory trace corresponding to the fact that A is married to B would be easier to accomplish the "fresher" or less consolidated that trace. For example, when subjects are first told that A and B are married and then, after a variable interval, are told that A and C are married, destructive updating would be expected to yield better long-term retention of the A-C pairing the shorter the interval between the A-B pairing and the A-C pairing. Given that updating is not destructive in nature, one might expect the opposite result since, from the standpoint of the final test, the closer in time the original A-B and A-C pairings, the more difficult they would be to distinguish from each other.

METHOD

Subjects, Apparatus, and Procedure

The subjects were 335 undergraduates at Bowling Green State University in Bowling Green, Ohio. They participated in the experiment as one part of a demonstration lecture given by a visiting lecturer (experimenter) to two different classes.

Each subject was given a deck of computer cards. The experiment consisted of three phases. During the first (practice) phase, the experimenter explained the mate updating task and had subjects turn over the first few cards in the deck, which were practice cards involving the marriages or divorces of well-known celebrities. Subjects turned over one card every 9 sec in response to a buzz from a metronome. After subjects were familiarized with the task and the procedure, they went through the second (study) phase. Each card during the study phase said either "A and B are married" or "A and B are divorced," where A and B were the first names of a hypothetical man (woman) and woman (man), respectively. The study phase consisted of 23 cards, two cards that served as a primacy buffer, 18 cards that comprised the experimental conditions of interest, and 3 recency cards. At the end of the study phase, subjects were asked to put away their decks, and the experimenter gave a 30 min demonstration lecture on another topic.

Finally, in the third (test) phase, the subjects were tested for their memory of the final marital status of every stimulus (left-hand) name presented during the study phase. On each test card a given stimulus name was shown together with a horizontal line to its right for the subject's response. If, in the subject's judgement, that person ended up divorced, the subject was to write "divorced." If, on the other hand, the subject thought that person ended up married, the subject was asked to try to write down the first name of that person's current (i.e., final) spouse. Subjects were not, however, required to guess if they did not know.

Design

The study phase contained exactly one stimulus person corresponding to each of the following eight conditions.

(1) Control: A + B. This condition consisted of one study card stating that "A and B are married."

(2) Massed Updating: A + B, A + C. This condition consisted of two study cards, the first stating "A and B are mar-

ried," the second (presented after only two intervening cards) stating "A and C are married."

(3) Spaced Updating: A + B, ---, A + C. This condition is the same as Massed Updating, except that five cards intervened between the A + B and A + C study cards.

(4) Multiple Updating: A + B, A + C, A + D. This condition consisted of three study cards stating that A is married to B, then C, and finally D. Two cards intervened between both the A + B and A + C cards and the A + C and A + D cards.

(5) Positive Repetition: A + B, A + B. Similar to the Control Condition except that the statement "A and B are married" was repeated on two cards, with two cards intervening.

(6) Negated Repetition: A + B, A - B. The same as the Positive Repetition Condition, except that the second card stated "A and B are divorced."

(7) Repeated Competition: A + B, A + B, A + C. The same as the Multiple Updating Condition except that the first and second study cards both state that "A and B are married."

(8) Negated Competition: A + B, A - B, A + C. The same as the Repeated Competition Condition, except that the second study card states "A and B are divorced."

Complex counterbalancing procedures insured that, across subjects, particular name pairs occurred approximately equally often in the different conditions, that the average serial input position of the final card in a given condition during the study phase was roughly equal for all conditions, and that a given name was used approximately equally often as a stimulus name and as a response name. In a given deck, for a given subject, half the pairs shown during the study phase were male, female pairs and half were female, male pairs. Finally, four non-overlapping sets of names were used for different subjects.

RESULTS

The results of the mate updating experiment are shown in Table 1. The proportions of all responses that were correct, that were intrusions of the name of a former spouse (updating intrusions), that were intrusions of some other name (other intrusions), that were incorrect "divorced" responses (erroneous divorce), and that were omitted (omissions) are shown for each of the eight conditions. The results are marred somewhat by a low rate of correct responding coupled with a high rate of omissions. The correct response proportions are generally well above chance, however, and updating intrusions, which are also clearly above chance, also demonstrate retention of study-phase information on the subjects' part.

Table 1

Proportions of All Responses that were of Certain Types

Condition	Response Type				
	Correct	Updating Intrusion	Other Intrusion	Erroneous Divorce	Omission
Control A+B	.126	----	.356	.015	.503
Massed Updating A+B,A+C	.093	.101	.346	.024	.436
Spaced Updating A+B,--,A+C	.116	.110	.391	.033	.349
Multiple Updating A+B,A+C,A+D	.096	.126[a]	.395	.030	.353
Positive Repetition A+B,A+B	.283	----	.319	.012	.386
Negated Repetition A+B,A-B	.084	.176	.349	----	.391
Repeated Competition A+B,A+B,A+C	.054	.140	.394	.045	.367
Negated Competition A+B,A-B,A+C	.097	.164	.382	.066	.290

[a]The proportions of all responses that were intrusions of the B and C responses were .060 and .066, respectively.

The Multiple Updating, Positive Repetition, and Repeated Competition Conditions, though not of primary interest, were included in the design to check whether certain sensible results obtained. As one would expect, there was a substantial repetition effect. Compared to the Control Condition, repeating the A + B pairing (the Positive Repetition Condition) more than doubled the proportion of correct responses, and repeating the pairing of A with a former spouse (the Repeated Competition Condition) decreased the proportion of correct responses to less than half the proportion in the Control Condition. Increasing the number of former spouses from one to two (A + B, A + C, A + D vs. A + B, A + C) did not, however, decrease the proportion of correct responses.

The comparisons of principal interest are between the Massed Updating and Spaced Updating Conditions, and between the Negated Competition and the Spaced Updating Conditions. Neither comparison supports the notion that subjects' updating processes are destructive in nature. To the degree that subjects were able to update destructively, one might have expected better performance in the Massed Updating Condition than in the Spaced Updating Condition. In fact, the proportion correct is higher in the Spaced Updating Condition, though that difference is not significant. Subjects were also not able to take advantage of the "cancellation" information in the Negative Competition Condition (A+B,A-B,A+C) in contrast to an apparent implication of the destructive updating notion. The Negated Competition Condition in fact yielded slightly worse performance than the Spaced Updating Condition, though again the difference was not significant.

In general, consistent with the comparison of the Spaced Updating and Negated Competition Conditions, it appears from the data in Table 1 that the A-B divorce event in the Negated Repetition and Negated Competition Conditions did more to reinstate the A + B pairing than to cancel that pairing. Looking at the Updating Intrusion column in Table 1, the frequency with which B was given as an intrusion in the Negated Repetition and Negated Competition Conditions is as high as the frequency with which B is given as an intrusion in the Repeated Competition Condition, and all three conditions yield a higher proportion of updating intrusions than the conditions (Massed Updating, Spaced Updating, and Multiple Updating) in which the name of a former spouse is not repeated.

DISCUSSION

Taken at face value, the present results suggest that human updating is not destructive in nature. We certainly do not contend, however, that the present results are conclusive. With a higher rate of correct responding, for example, or with a greater range of intervals in the massed versus spaced updating question, the results might well have been different. It is even possible that changing the divorce statement in the Negated Competition Condition from "A and B are divorced" to

"A is divorced" might have improved performance substantially in that condition, since such a statement would not reinstate the A, B pairing. In short, the present study was intended as an initial exploration of an important component of the updating problem. For a discussion of other aspects of the updating problem, see Bjork (1978).

ACKNOWLEDGEMENTS

The research reported herein was carried out while the first author was a Visiting Consultant in the Human Information-Processing Research Department, Bell Laboratories, Murray Hill, New Jersey. We appreciate the cooperation of Professor Kirk Smith at Bowling Green State University and we thank Karl Gutschera and Ann Boscardin for their assistance in this research.

REFERENCES

Bjork, R. A. (1978). The updating of human memory. In: *The Psychology of Learning and Motivation*. Vol 12. (G. H. Bower, ed). Academic Press, New York.

Bjork, R. A. and McClure, P. (1974). Encoding to update one's memory. Invited paper, Meetings of the Midwestern Psychological Association, Chicago, Illinois.

Craik, F. I. M. and Watkins, M. J. (1973). The role of rehearsal in short-term memory. *Journal of Verbal Learning and Verbal Behavior*. 12, 599-607.

Woodward, A. E., Bjork, R. A. and Jongeward, R. H. (1973). Recall and recognition as a function of primary rehearsal. *Journal of Verbal Learning and Verbal Behavior*. 12, 608-617.

Yntema, D. B. and Meuser, G. E. (1960). Remembering the present states of a number of variables. *Journal of Experimental Psychology*. 60, 18-22.

INCIDENTAL RETRIEVAL AND MEMORY FOR COINCIDENCES

D.L. Hintzman, S.J. Asher, and L.D. Stern
Department of Psychology
University of Oregon
Eugene, Oregon 97403

Memory retrieval is frequently triggered by chance encounters with effective retrieval cues. It is hypothesized that such "incidental retrieval" could account for the common belief that coincidences (e.g. "precognitive" dreams) occur too often to attribute to chance. Cue-related memories may tend to be selectively retained, and their relative rate of occurrence therefore overestimated. Such selective remembering is demonstrated in the laboratory, in free recall of incidentally learned words. Three experiments are reported and their theoretical implications are discussed.

One practical use of science is to give the layman rational explanations of everyday events that would otherwise inspire awe and superstition. Few educated people these days would pray for rain, cast a spell to start a stalled vehicle, or sacrifice a virgin to appease a rumbling volcano. The physical sciences have been notably successful in providing convincing accounts for such phenomena which leave little room for occult beliefs.

Psychology has had less success. Dreams, hallucinations, drug states, and hypnosis are not well understood. Many educated laymen--and, a few psychologists--believe in extrasensory perception, telepathy, precognition, and even communication with the dead. The roots of belief in such psychic phenomena seem to lie in striking personal experiences. Arthur Koestler says:

> It seems that the majority of serious people engaged in parapsychological research--even of the dreariest card-guessing kind--derive their motivation from such spontaneous, quasi-traumatic experiences, which are subjectively more convincing to them than the best-designed laboratory experiment. (Hardy, Harvie, and Koestler, 1975, p. 170)

The kinds of experiences to which Koestler refers can all be referred to as coincidences. Let us define a coincidence as the occurrence, within a relatively short time, of two events which could not be causally related, but which have similar or related meanings. The vagueness of the phrase "relatively short time" allows us to include among coincidences not just related events that are temporally contiguous, but also dreams that foretell the future, answered prayers, premonitions, and fulfilled wishes and prophesies.

The rational argument has always been that coincidences are simply due to chance. But many persons are convinced that they occur with too great a frequency to be explained in this way, and must therefore have some special significance. In order to determine their significance, some people have collected coincidences, in an attempt to discern an underlying pattern.

One such collector was Paul Kammerer, an Austrian biologist who committed suicide in 1926, at the age of forty-five, amidst charges that one of his experiments supporting Lamarckism had been faked (see Koestler, 1971). In 1919, Kammerer published a book which described 100 coincidences (or "series," as he called them), and proposed that they be classified according to an elaborate taxonomy. Coincidences were categorized not only by subject matter, but also according to properties Kammerer called order, power, and parameters. He also distinguished homologous and analogous series, pure and hybrid series, inverted series, alternating, cyclic, and phasic series, and so on (Koestler, 1971, 1972).

Kammerer saw in coincidences the operation of what he called the "law of seriality"--a universal principle independent of, but equal in importance to, causality. The law stated that events of the same or related meaning tend to come in series --that is, to be clustered together in time--even though there is no way they could be causally connected.

The psychologist Carl Jung was greatly influenced by Kammerer's book. Jung proposed to account for coincidences with an "acausal principle" which he called "synchronicity"-- really little more than a restatement of Kammerer's law. The essence of both Kammerer's and Jung's views, it is important to note, was that events tend to cluster together in time on the basis of their *meanings*, even when no causal relationship exists.

Now according to modern science and philosophy, meanings exist not in external events themselves, but in the subjective interpretation of those events. Jung clearly saw that this view was incompatible with the principle of synchronicity, and therefore proposed that modern science and philosophy were wrong. He advocated a return to the pre-scientific view that events have a "self-subsistent meaning," and argued further that these meanings make contact with the mind through the "collective unconscious," which somehow is able to transcend the physical framework of space and time.

Jung was led to this radical-but-vague hypothesis primarily by two kinds of evidence: first, reports of ESP experiments conducted by J.B. Rhine and others; and second, experiences of strange coincidences in everyday life. But the hypothesis that is most consistent with the "ESP" data, as Hansel (1966) has shown, is simply that experimental control has been incredibly lax, and that given incentive and opportunity, subjects (and experimenters) sometimes cheat. When control is tightened, non-chance scoring goes away; and attempts to replicate the few positive results that have been obtained almost invariably fail.

Regarding everyday coincidences, Jung gave special emphasis to those concerning dreams:

> We often dream about people from whom we receive a letter by the next post. I have ascertained on several occasions that at the moment when the dream occurred the letter was already lying in the post-office of the addressee. (Jung, 1955, p. 39)

Why do such events make a convincing case for synchronicity?

> Meaningful coincidences are thinkable as pure chance. But the more they multiply and the greater and more exact the correspondence is, the more their probability sinks and their unthinkability increases, until they can no longer be regarded as pure chance but, for lack of a causal explanation, have to be thought of as meaningful arrangements. (Jung, 1955, pp. 142-143)

Jung's observation about "unthinkability" is one that could have led him in a very different direction. Unthinkability is a subjective judgment; and as a psychologist, Jung might well have sought to explain the judgment, rather than accepting its validity. That is, he might have asked not why coincidences occur too often to attribute to chance, but why we <u>feel</u> that they occur too often to attribute to chance. This approach to the problem admits of a solution which, unlike those offered by Kammerer and Jung, does not deny causality, and is completely consistent with accepted psychological theory.

Suppose that the "unthinkability" of pure chance as an account of coincidences is represented by a ratio: the number of events that enter into coincidences, divided by the total number of events (those that enter into coincidences plus those that do not). The hypothesis is that this ratio seems much larger than it actually is, because we underestimate the magnitude of the denominator. This occurs because of selective remembering--events that do *not* enter into coincidences are more likely to be forgotten than are events that do. Since memory is notoriously faulty, such selection would have a wide range in which to operate, and could have a powerful effect. Furthermore, it is not necessary that the person experiencing the events be especially attuned to coincidences or believe in their significance; there are theoretical reasons to expect such selective remembering in everyone.

Most memory retrieval is not deliberate or intentional, but is "incidental"--that is, it is triggered automatically by encounters with appropriate retrieval cues. (Experimental evidence for incidental retrieval comes from several sources--see Hintzman, 1976). Dreams provide an excellent example of how incidental retrieval could exaggerate the "unthinkability ratio. Sleep researchers tell us that the average person dreams between 10 and 20 episodes each night. That comes to some 5,000 dreams per person per year. Nearly all of these dreams are promptly forgotten--in fact, some people incorrectly believe that they do not dream at all (Goodenough, Shapiro, Holden, and Steinschriber, 1959). Introspection suggests that when we do recall a dream it is frequently because of a chance encounter with an appropriate retrieval cue the following day (e.g. a letter from someone who figured prominently in the dream). If the only dreams we remembered were those followed by appropriate retrieval cues, then the "unthinkability ratio," regarding dreams, would equal one, since no dreams would be remembered other than those related to later cues. It is perhaps surprising that the belief in precognitive dreams is not even more widespread than it is.

There are at least two ways that incidental retrieval could lead to selective retention later on: first, retrieving the dream constitutes an opportunity for rehearsal of the dream itself; and second, if the correspondence between dream and retrieval cue is especially striking, the relationship itself is likely to receive special attention. In either case, the assumption is that retrieval provides an additional opportunity for learning. Where dreams are concerned, this effect would be exaggerated, since the retrieval takes place in the waking state, which is far more conducive to learning than is sleep. The general argument, however, is not restricted to dreams. Selective retrieval would also contribute to the "unthinkability ratios" for trivial everyday coincidences, premonitions, fulfilled wishes, and so on.

A priori, this hypothesis is more plausible than Jung's in three ways: First, it does not deny causality--indeed, the crucial assumption is that the retrieval cue *causes* one to remember the earlier, related event. Second, it does not assume self-subsistent meaning. Incidental retrieval occurs only because the second event has been assigned, subjectively, a meaning similar to that of the first. Third, it deals with coincidences in which the two events do not temporally coincide (e.g. precognitive dreams) without stepping outside the framework of space and time. The retrieval cue and the arousal of the earlier memory trace *are* temporally contiguous--this is how awareness of the coincidence occurs.

It may be worth adding that, in collections of anecdotes, e.g. Hardy *et al* (1975), selective remembering is operating on another, higher level, as well. Each individual picks only his most noteworthy coincidences to relate to others (perhaps with some distortion), and the collector chooses only the most remarkable of those to publish. The pool of original events from which published coincidences are sampled must be astronomically large--so large that even the most improbable kinds of coincidences are almost certain to occur. And because of the various sources of selective bias operating, it is just the most improbable coincidences that become circulating or published anecdotes. The "unthinkability ratio" is thus raised to the n*th* power.

But the faults of the anecdotal method are well known. Let us return specifically to the problem of selective remembering. We have done three memory experiments to simulate selective remembering in the laboratory and to determine something of the nature of the underlying processes (the first two are also described briefly in Hintzman, 1976). In each experiment, subjects dealt with stimuli while engaged in orienting tasks not requiring memorization (incidental learning tasks), and certain "coincidences"--carefully arranged by the experimenter--occurred. Each coincidence was a meaningful relationship between one event (E_1) and another (E_2) occurring later during the session. Still later, a recall test was given. Our primary interest was in the effects of coincidences on performance on this test.

A description of the first experiment will illustrate the method and the basic result. The experiment consisted of five stages. In stage 1, 50 subjects each rated 21 concrete nouns on two semantic scales: small-large, and ugly-beautiful. Stage 2 consisted of an unrelated filler task lasting about nine min. In stage 3, the subjects were shown 18 pictures of objects (e.g. pocket knife, shoe) and were asked to estimate how often they came into contact with or used each type of object. Although the subjects were not told this, 7 of the 18 pictures corresponded to words that had been rated in stage 1. Stage 4 was another filler task, lasting about six min. Finally, in stage 5, the subjects were unexpectedly asked to write down as many of the words from stage 1 as they could recall.

In this experiment, the word constitutes E_1 and the corresponding picture constitutes E_2. Let us call the 7 words which corresponded to pictures and the 14 words which did not Related and Unrelated words, respectively. Free recall of Related words was 63%; while that of Unrelated words was 47%, a highly significant difference. One might suspect that the inflated recall of Related words was due to confusion between the word list and the picture list; but the number of names of unrelated pictures appearing as intrusions in recall of the words was very small. On the average, only 3% of unrelated pictures were incorrectly recalled as words. The experiment thus confirmed our expectation: an event that bears a meaningful relationship to a later event is more likely to be remembered than one that does not.

At the end of the experiment, we administered a questionnaire. On it, we asked the subjects whether they had noticed that some of the pictures corresponded to previously rated words, and 58% responded in the affirmative. This is evidence that incidental retrieval occurred, as our hypothesis predicts. Even subjects who responded "no," however, recalled more Related than Unrelated words. This may mean that conscious retrieval is not necessary to produce facilitation, or that these subjects had simply forgotten noticing the coincidences by the time they were given the questionnaire.

The technical name for the phenomenon demonstrated in the first experiment is *retroactive facilitation*, since memory for E_1 was enhanced by the interpolation of the related E_2. A natural question that arises is whether *proactive facilitation*--enhanced memory of E_2, due to a prior E_1--can be demonstrated in a similar manner. There is at least one explanation of the preceding result which suggests that the effect should be unidirectional, and that proactive facilitation should not occur. This hypothesis attributes the facilitation shown in the first experiment solely to rehearsal of E_1, when it is retrieved by E_2. E_1 does not provide a similar rehearsal opportunity for E_2; thus such rehearsal would benefit only memory for E_1.

The second experiment was done to determine whether proactive facilitation would occur. The design of the experiment differed from that of the first in only one respect: the stage 1 and stage 3 tasks were interchanged. Thirty-four subjects rated the pictures (E_1) in stage 1 and the words (E_2) in stage 3, and were asked in stage 5 to recall the stage-3 words. As in the first experiment, intrusion of picture names in word recall was rare (4% including two aberrant subjects, 2% excluding them). Recall of Related words averaged 62%, significantly greater than that of Unrelated words, at 49%. Thus, a coincidence enhances later recall of both E_1 and E_2; both retroactive and proactive facilitation occur.

The third experiment reverted to the retroactive facilitation design of the first--that is, the pictures were presented after the words. The retention interval for the words was 24 hours, and within this interval some words corresponded to an early E_2 picture, some to a late E_2 picture, and some to neither. We hoped to determine, from this design, whether the facilitative effect depends on the point of interpolation of E_2. The notion of incidental retrieval suggests that it should. The more recent an event is, the more easily its trace is retrieved. Assuming that this is true of incidental as well as intentional retrieval, one might expect E_2 to enhance E_1 recall less and less, the longer it is delayed. Running counter to such a tendency, however, may be the recency of E_2 at the time of the test. The longer E_2 is delayed, the closer it occurs to the recall attempt. If an early E_2 is more effective than a late E_2, the hypothesized role of incidental retrieval will receive strong support. If a late E_2 is more effective, the implications are not so clear. One possibility is that E_2 provides a boost in "activation" of the concept common to E_1 and E_2, thus making E_1 more accessible to recall.

The experiment had 7 stages. In stage 1, the 81 subjects rated 25 concrete nouns on the same scales that had been used before. Stage 2 was a filler task taking about 10 min. In stage 3, the subjects rated 30 drawings of objects on a frequency-of-encounter scale. Five of these corresponded to words from stage 1 (the Related Early words). Stage 4 was a 24-hr. interval; subjects were dismissed and told to return the next day. Stage 5 again required 30 drawings to be rated for frequency of encounter. Five of these were drawings that had been used in stage 3. Of the rest, five corresponded to stage-1 words (Related Late words) and 20 did not. Stage 6 was another filler task lasting about 6 min.; and this was followed by free recall of the words, in stage 7.

Recall performance on Related Early words and Related Late words was 33% and 38%, respectively, a non-significant difference. Both, however, were recalled significantly better than Unrelated words, at 25%. (Intrusions of picture names from the early and late picture sets were about equally likely--3% and 4%, respectively--and the intrusion rate for the five pictures that occurred in both sets was 8%).

Thus, our third experiment replicated the basic finding, but was not very informative about underlying processes. The fact that an E_2 delayed 24 hours was so effective, however, suggests that incidental retrieval may not be the only process underlying the facilitative effect.

In retrospect, it seems that the selective remembering we have shown here may be "over-determined." By this, we mean that there are several plausible mechanisms, consistent with current memory theory, all of which may be contributing to the result. First, there is incidental retrieval, by E_2, of the trace of E_1. This provides an opportunity for rehearsal of E_1 and for special attention to the coincidental relationship between the two events. Second, one does not have to become aware of the coincidence when E_2 occurs--it can be discovered at a later time, since retrieval of either E_1 or E_2, on the retention test, will aid retrieval of the other. Some of our subjects' retrospective reports suggested that this had occurred. Still another mechanism that could contribute to selective remembering is "activation" of the concept common to E_1 and E_2. A temporary boost in such activation by E_2 would temporarily make it easier to remember both E_1 and E_2.

We have argued that the "unthinkability" of chance as an explanation of meaningful coincidences may be a *memory illusion*, due to the selective remembering of meaningfully related events. Other events, which do not contribute to coincidences, tend to be quickly forgotten, and their rate of occurrence is thus greatly underestimated. Our experiments show that, in free recall, such selective remembering does occur, and suggest that more than one underlying process may contribute to this selective bias. These observations support a conclusion that others, working in the area of human judgment, have drawn (e.g. Tversky and Kahneman, 1974)--namely, that one's intuitions about the relative likelihoods of events are not to be trusted. Psychologists, parapsychologists, physicists, and popes--we are all human, and we are all subject to the same errors of judgment. Degree of conviction, particularly if it is based on memory, is a poor guide to the truth.

REFERENCES

Goodenough, D., Shapiro, A., Holden, M., and Steinschriber, L. (1959). A comparison of "dreamers" and "nondreamers": eye movements, electroencephalograms, and the recall of dreams. *Journal of Abnormal and Social Psychology*. 59, 295-302.

Hansel, C.E.M. (1966). *ESP: A scientific evaluation*. Charles Scribner's Sons, New York.

Hardy, A., Harvie, R., and Koestler, A. (1973). *The challenge of chance*. Hutchinson and Co. Ltd., London.

Hintzman, D.L. (1976). Repetition and memory. In: *The Psychology of Learning and Motivation*, Vol 10. (G.H. Bower ed), pp. 47-91. Academic Press, New York.

Jung, C.G. and Pauli, W. (1955). *The interpretation of nature and the psyche*. Pantheon Books, Inc., New York.

Kammerer, P. (1919). *Das Gesetz der Serie*. Deutsch Verlags-Astalt, Stuttgart und Berlin.

Koestler, A. (1971). *The case of the midwife toad*. Hutchinson and Co. Ltd., London.

Koestler, A. (1972). *The roots of coincidence*. Hutchinson and Co. Ltd., London.

Tversky, A. and Kahneman, D. (1974). Judgment under uncertainty: Heuristics and biases. *Science*. 185, 1124-1131.

REAL WORLD MEMORY AFTER SIX YEARS: AN *IN VIVO* STUDY OF VERY LONG TERM MEMORY

M. Linton
University of Utah
Salt Lake City, Utah 84112

Typical research does not reflect memory's richness, but our experience suggests that memory is highly interactive and, for some materials at least, remarkably durable. The present study examines retention of episodic events from the life of a single individual over a six year period. During this time approximately 5500 events were recorded and 11,000 tests of these items occurred. Preliminary analyses suggest that forgetting occurred at a fairly constant rate over much of the six-year course of the study.

INTRODUCTION

How long will I remember a paté I've relished, a passionate kiss, a tennis match with my Sunday foursome, or an article on intellective functioning read for a class? Or, more generally, how long do I remember events stored in my personal real-world episodic memory? How much can we infer about this highly complex, intricate and interactive memory system from studies which focus on materials deliberately selected to interact minimally with this system? It seems likely that a discontinuity exists between arbitrary items and personal events and that we will understand the latter only by studying them. Major problems arise, however, when we attempt to generate an adequate unit of analysis with which to examine real world memories. A brief recapitulation of my efforts to deal with these difficulties appears in Linton (1975). In 1972 I initiated an exploration of long term memory that avoided many problems and seemed capable of answering some questions about retention of events. Although the detailed procedures of this study have been presented elsewhere (Linton, 1975), the general method is summarized here.

METHOD

In brief, the plan was to use a single subject, and employing the "event" as a memory unit, to generate items and provide periodic tests for a number of years. The experimenter, serving as subject, wrote 5500 items (complete with salience ratings) during the six year study. The "events" were based on naturally occurring incidences in my own life (at least two items were written each day). A semirandom subset of items was tested each month. Approximately 11,000 tests or retests of items occurred during the six years.

What is an Event?

Let me now consider the definition of an event. Because I could see no compelling argument for any specific narrow definition of an event (there were then and are now surprisingly few hints from the research literature on the nature of events) only two constraints were placed on the items developed: length (they could not exceed three 62-character lines) and uniqueness (they must be distinguishable from all other events when they were written). Events could otherwise be any episode or action that occupied some brief period of time. Style of specifying the event was permitted to vary freely. The size of the event, that is, the level of generality of the item also varied.

Salient portions of the test are as follows: randomly selected items were drawn, in pairs. They were read, their order judged, then for each item a probable date of occurrence (day, month and year) was determined. Items forgotten or not distinguishable from other items were withdrawn from the file. Items were then rated on a number of scales, and the memory-search strategy was categorized.

Problems with the Items

One question that haunts this study is item comparability from beginning to end of the study. It is a nontrivial task to create two uniquely specified events, 365 days a year for six years. Did the items change systematically during the course of the study? Although the required analyses have not been done (in fact, the optimal analysis is not clear) an informed guess is that at least two classes of changes have taken place: 1) Originally five and then later two items were written each day. The requirement for five novel items often meant that relatively trivial items or "composite" items were generated. If, in fact, less memorable items were produced during this early period then forgetting of early (1972) items should be greater than for later years. Inspection of the data presented later does not confirm this intuition. 2) Some learning has probably occurred with respect to event representations that are particularly suitable for long term recall. For example, routine descriptions of racquet matches are rarely included. Despite the enthusiasm of these moments, the distinguishing features of the approximately 1500 matches I've played during this six year period are lost within a matter of days or weeks. Such "unsuitable" items probably became progressively less frequent over the course of the study. There is, however, little evidence of the shifts in recall probability over time that would be expected if changes in discriminability were a major factor.

What is Forgetting?

In recognition studies problems of the subject's criterion (criterion shifting, yea-saying biases, etc.) always exist and the present study shares these difficulties. Most problematic is the choice made early in the study not to include control items, that is, not to include descriptions of "events" similar to bonafide descriptions to serve as a control for potential biases. The rationale for that decision is discussed at length elsewhere (Linton, 1975) and may be summarized as being due to the difficulty of designing adequate control items and the disadvantages associated with the concommitant increase in the size of the item pool. Furthermore, since the study's primary dependent variable was to be accuracy of dating of remembered items, there seemed little risk of making at least one error, that is, claiming to remember an item when indeed it was forgotten. It should be explicitly noted, however, that the present analyses are based only on forgetting data and hence, in isolation, lack this control.

When an item was read, the first judgment made was the global one of whether the event was recalled. Determining whether an event is "remembered" requires a surprisingly complex judgment. A few of the troublesome kinds of cases are described. 1) Perhaps the most ambiguous form of forgetting involves an item that a) must have happened, b) is logically implied by events that are remembered, or c) is totally plausible and compelling, but cannot be recalled. "I receive a call from Maureen, Strassberger's secretary, indicating that she will make the travel arrangements to Washington." No matter that Maureen herself is long forgotten, is this representation somewhere within my memory? I do remember this trip, at least vaguely, and can, even at present, date the five-year-old item within 25 days by a set of inferences. However, this item was judged to be forgotten. 2) Other items are lost because the descriptions are too superficial or because, with time, once adequate descriptions no longer discriminate between events in memory. Often several events in memory may fit the description. It is also possible to read a true event that has no specific associated memory. "I narrowly beat HEO at tennis today." It is possible for me to know that I have occasionally beaten HEO at tennis without recalling any specific instance. 3) A more complete kind of forgetting occurs when a clearly understandable item does not find a match in memory. I simply "don't recall" the item. 4) A final form, and the most complete form of forgetting, occurs when an item becomes incomprehensible. The description seems to refer to nothing presently in memory. Might such occurrences simply reflect badly written items? Indeed they might, but two pieces of evidence argue against this interpretation. First, this phenomenon *begins* to occur only 3-4 years after the items are written, and follows long periods without rehearsal. Second, early tests of these items are fairly typical, with no evidence of item incomprehensibility.

RESULTS AND DISCUSSION

When an item was read, an effort was made to date the item as precisely as possible. If the item could not be recalled or could not be distinguished from other related items it was appropriately marked and removed from the study. Originally no analyses were intended for these discarded items, however, examining them provides a preliminary answer to questions of changing availability of items in memory over time and the present report focuses on these data.

Why is Forgetting So Slow?

The Nature of the Items. The original expectation was that forgetting would be relatively rapid and would resemble the typical Ebbinghaus forgetting curve. However, this expectation was not met. For one thing, forgetting was much *less* rapid in this study than was anticipated. Plausible explanations for this result include: 1) memories are more accessible with cued-recall than with free recall tasks; 2) the easily encoded items had received a relatively permanent representation. Thus, the task was a simple one, and the salient materials must be judged quite memorable.

A Forgetting Function? There is little in the foregoing to suggest a dramatic change in the shape of the function from that predicted by Ebbinghaus. I was surprised, therefore, by the outcome of the series of analyses to be reported.

I began by considering all 1345 items written in 1972. Only 0.7% of the items written in 1972 were forgotten in the same calendar year. During 1973, 1974, 1975, and 1976 the percent of 1972 items forgotten varied from 5-6% with an increase to 9.3% for 1977. These data appear in Figure 1. The points on this curve (which excludes 0 years) lie close to a straight line. Similar curves were developed for the data for the later years of the study. The general shape of these curves were closely analogous and a composite curve representing performance for years 1-6 of the study is shown in Figure 1. For this composite (all items), year 1 comprised all 1972 items forgotten in 1972, all 1973 items forgotten in 1973, etc. Year 2 comprised all 1972 items forgotten in 1973, all 1973 items forgotten in 1974, etc. This composite curve closely resembles the 1972 data. At the end of six years, about 32% of the material had been forgotten. Moreover, forgetting has occurred at a relatively even rate over this period of time.

A second way of summarizing these *same data* is simply to take the successive years of the study and ask how much has been forgotten from these successive years. These values represent the total amount lost (the cumulative forgotten values) from successive years' memories. These data are presented in Figure 1 (number forgotten from calendar year).

These analyses, however, relate forgetting only to the total number of items originally written. This estimate is low because many items haven't received a contemporary test and hence have not been identified as "forgotten" even if that is their present status. Therefore, an additional analysis examined the frequency of forgetting as a function of the frequency with which items of a particular age were tested. For example, in 1977, 193 of the 1345 items written in 1972 (six-year-old items) were tested. At that time 58, or 30.1%, were "forgotten." Comparable values were obtained from all 48 tests occurring from 1974 to 1977. These results also appear in Figure 1. The close resemblance of this function to the earlier functions indicates that the shape of the function does not depend on the opportunity of the items to be tested.

The analyses described avoid a number of kinds of confounding. For example, the similarity of the individual yearly curves argues that the shape of the composite curve cannot be attributed to differences among items written at different times in the study. However, other possibilities of confounding remain: for example, items may vary with some easily forgotten and others progressively resistant to forgetting. If the number of each type varies in a systematic but unknown way, the shape of the obtained curve would not directly reflect the basic forgetting function. (There is, incidentally, no reason to assume that materials in other studies may not suffer from this same difficulty.)

Number of Rehearsals. In addition, the preceding analyses did not control for the number of rehearsals (tests) an item has received nor for the spacing of the rehearsals which may differ throughout the course of the study. Rehearsals should

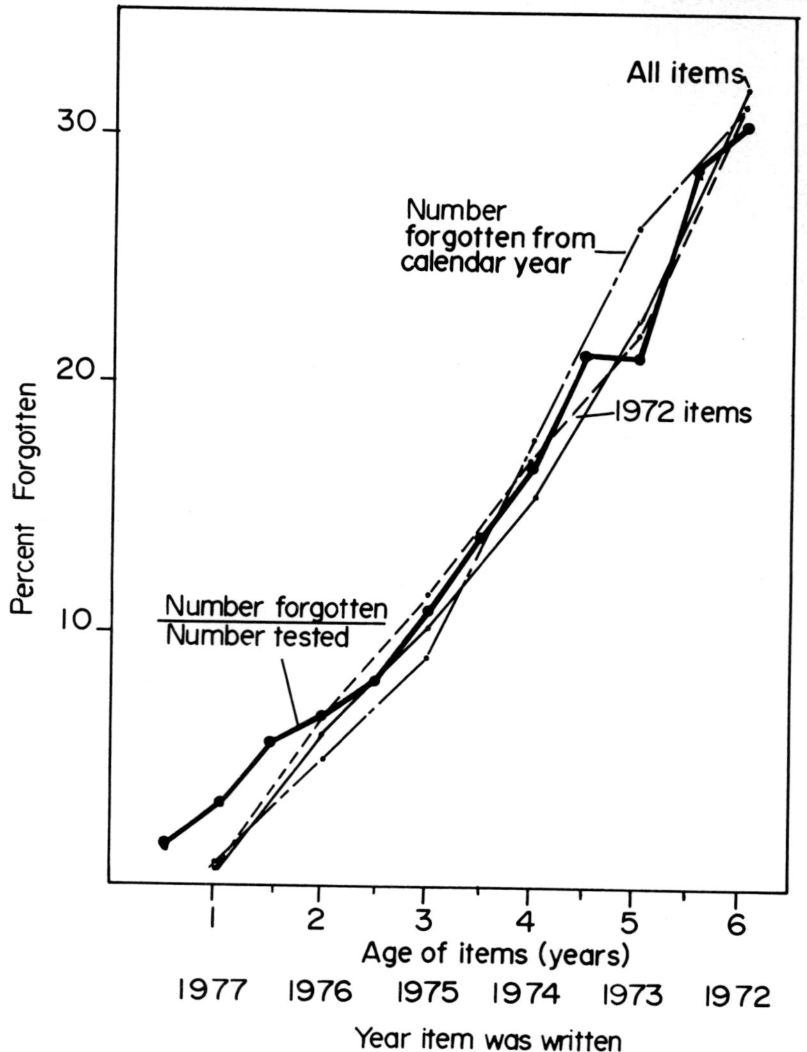

Fig. 1 Percent of items forgotten during six years as a function of number of items written or number of items tested.

make material more resistant to forgetting. On the average, older items have received more rehearsals than younger ones, hence unequal rehearsal opportunity should *underestimate* the probability of forgetting older items. Intervals between rehearsals, too, are likely to be correlated wtih item age and the effect would be to yield an *overestimate* of rate of forgetting older items.

Does the number of rehearsals change the slope of the forgetting function? The probability of an item being forgotten

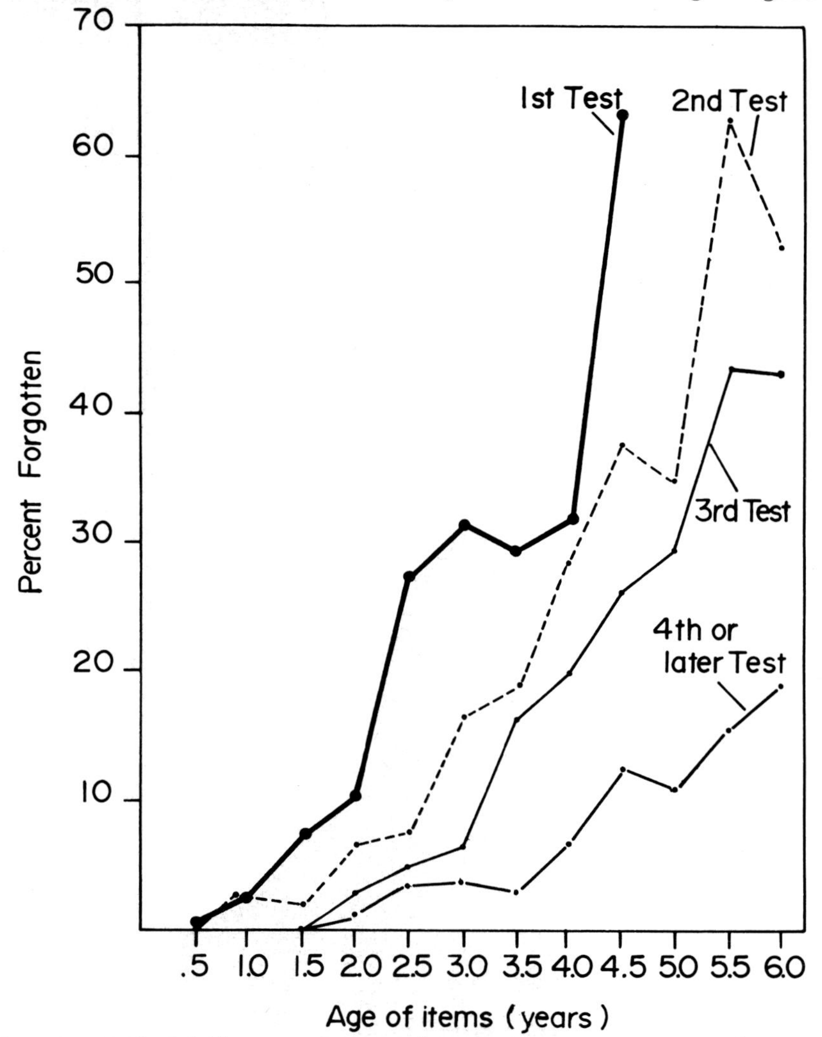

Fig. 2 Probability of forgetting an item as a function of age and number of tests (rehearsals).

was computed as a percentage of total items similar in age and rehearsal history tested at that time. Figure 2 shows that the larger the number of rehearsals the flatter the slope relating age at terminal test and probability of forgetting. In this task, rehearsals have little effect during the earliest year or so of the study, however, over time the effect of rehearsals increases. For example, at the end of 4½ years (the last date at which items receive an inaugural test) items tested for the first time are forgotten 63.6% of the time in comparison with 12.5% probability for items tested more than three times. The effectiveness of rehearsals in reducing forgetting may be seen even more clearly at six years.

It is notable that a few widely spaced rehearsals have such a dramatic effect on retention. In examining real world events, however, two kinds of rehearsal must be considered--the formal rehearsal imposed by tests, and informal, nonlaboratory rehearsal when these memories are in daily life. The formal rehearsals can be precisely pinpointed in time and numbered accurately. The depth of processing of the memory cannot be assessed nearly so accurately, however, but an average of only 2½ minutes is spent on each item. The effect of test rehearsals seems remarkably large considering the small amount of time spent on these formal rehearsals. Perhaps the several minutes of intense thought are adequate to maintain memories for many years. Informal rehearsal, on the other hand, is far more difficult to assess accurately and a full consideration of this topic with the associated analyses is beyond the scope of this paper.

Conclusion. Most satisfying, perhaps, for this innovative methodology is the observation that the data are orderly. The analyses provide some hints about durability of real-world episodic memories. The slope of the forgetting functions look linear, although, the present curve would presumably become negatively accelerated over time. The initial positive acceleration (evident when 0 years is included in the graph) is probably best explained in terms of encodability of materials. Taken by themselves these analyses are incomplete, focusing as they do on a narrow set of variables taken out of the context of the larger study. It is my hope that comprehensive analyses of these data will provide a better explanation of how episodic memories are embedded in the complex fabric of our minds.

REFERENCE

Linton, M. (1975) Memory for real-world events. In: *Explorations in Cognition*. Chapter 14. (D.A. Norman and D.E. Rumelhart, eds), pp 376-404. Freeman, San Francisco.

WHEN DID YOU LAST . . . . ?

A.D. Baddeley, V. Lewis and I. Nimmo-Smith
MRC Applied Psychology Unit, 15 Chaucer Road, Cambridge, England

ABSTRACT

We studied the recall by members of our subject panel of their previous visit to the Applied Psychology Unit. We found clear forgetting over a six month period of information on the approximate date of the visit and of details of experimenters and tasks involved, but little forgetting of other features such as time and length of test session. A range of recall strategies were reported, the most effective being to use some other life event as a cue to the date of the visit.

INTRODUCTION

A few months ago we were asked to talk about the implications of forgetting for retrospective survey methodology. There is clearly no shortage of laboratory work on forgetting, but survey designers might very reasonably have doubts about extrapolating from highly artificial laboratory studies, typically using intentionally learnt unrelated words or CVCs retained over periods of 24 hours or less, to the field situation where subjects are asked about highly meaningful but incidentally acquired information which may be tested anything up to years after the event. Fortunately it proved possible in the case of most phenomena to find at least one experiment indicating whether it was replicable outside the laboratory. Although the amount of such evidence was embarrassingly sparse, the general picture was reassuring in indicating that there is at least broad comparability between forgetting studied in the laboratory and in the outside world (Baddeley, in press). For example Warrington and Sanders (1971) have shown that both recall and recognition of newsworthy events show a forgetting curve extending over many years which is at least broadly comparable to the classic Ebbinghaus function. Retroactive interference effects have been shown by Baddeley and Hitch (1977) who studied the ability of rugby players to remember the names of opposing teams they had played. Since most players missed a number of games it proved possible to separate out elapsed time and number of intervening games; when this was done it became clear that forgetting was related to intervening events rather than time, indicating a phenomenon somewhat like retroactive interference (RI). This result suggests that information is likely to be more accurately retained if the subject is questioned only about the *last* occurrence of a particular event. Indeed, if forgetting is entirely due to RI then one might expect that the classical Ebbinghaus forgetting function would not occur under these circumstances. While proactive interference (PI) might be present, the results of Underwood and Ekstrand (1966) suggest that events learned under distributed practice do not lead to PI. While it is unclear as to what would constitute distributed practice under real life conditions, it is at least possible that PI will only be found under conditions as artificial as those associated with massed practice verbal learning in the laboratory. We decided therefore that there was need to study the question of whether the forgetting of real life events could be demonstrated under conditions where only the last occurrence of a given event is tested.

METHOD

In order to study this question, we required some event which could be clearly specified, which occurred at varying intervals before test, and which involved events of which we had objective and reliable information against which to compare our subjects' recall. The recall by our subject panel of their last visit to the APU offered just such a situation. Our subjects are volunteers who come along to the Unit to be tested, typically three or four times a year, but with a considerable range of frequency. We have accurate records of each visit, including the date, time and length of the visit, together with information on experimenters and what type of task they were using. We therefore produced a questionnaire (reproduced in Baddeley, in press) which tested the subject's ability to recall such information, and asked the subject about any strategies or cues that were used. It was given to a total of 88 members of the Unit's panel, about two-thirds of whom completed the questionnaire while taking part in group testing, while the remainder completed it after individual testing. The interval since the last visit ranged from 2 to 540 days, with 16, 17, 22, 20 and 13 subjects falling into the 0-60, 61-120,

121-180, 181-240 and >240 day ranges respectively.

RESULTS

1. *Date of last visit.* Subjects were asked to indicate the date of their last visit by circling the year and month and indicating the approximate date by putting a mark on a 10 cm line representing a month. They were invited to report the actual date if remembered.

The discrepancy between actual date and date recalled increased with delay ($r = 0.57$ $p < .001$) indicating clear forgetting. The size of the error increased by about 19 days for every 100 days that elapsed. There was a tendency for underestimation at longer delays, the correlation between the error and the actual date of the prior visit being -0.33 ($p < .01$).

2. *Recall strategies.* Subjects were asked how they had arrived at their estimate of the date of their last visit. Reported strategies were sorted into the following post-hoc categories.

(a) *Time of day or day of week cues:* These typically related the visit to some regular routine e.g. "It was definitely a Friday because I remember collecting fish and chips for tea" or "I knew it was in the afternoon because I skipped work between giving an anaesthetic to a sheep and preparing another for surgery. We only operate afternoons".

(b) *Time of year cues:* These included weather, "It snowed in the morning"; plants, "The garden flowers were in bloom" and seasonal variations in life-style such as school holidays or the cricket season.

(c) *Specific events:* These relate the visit to some more striking or easily dated event such as a wedding anniversary, visits from relatives, the start of a new job or some more unusual event e.g. "It was the morning of the Jubilee barbecue".

(d) *Unit routine:* Some subjects based their estimate on generalizations about the frequency with which they are invited to act as subjects e.g. "I come about every two months".

(e) *No strategy reported.*

Table 1 shows the number of reports of each of the above strategies. The total exceeds 88 since some subjects reported using more than one strategy. Analysis of variance indicated overall differences among the strategies in mean accuracy ($F_{4,87} = 2.44$, $p < .05$). However, it is clear from Table 1, that subjects using different strategies tended to differ

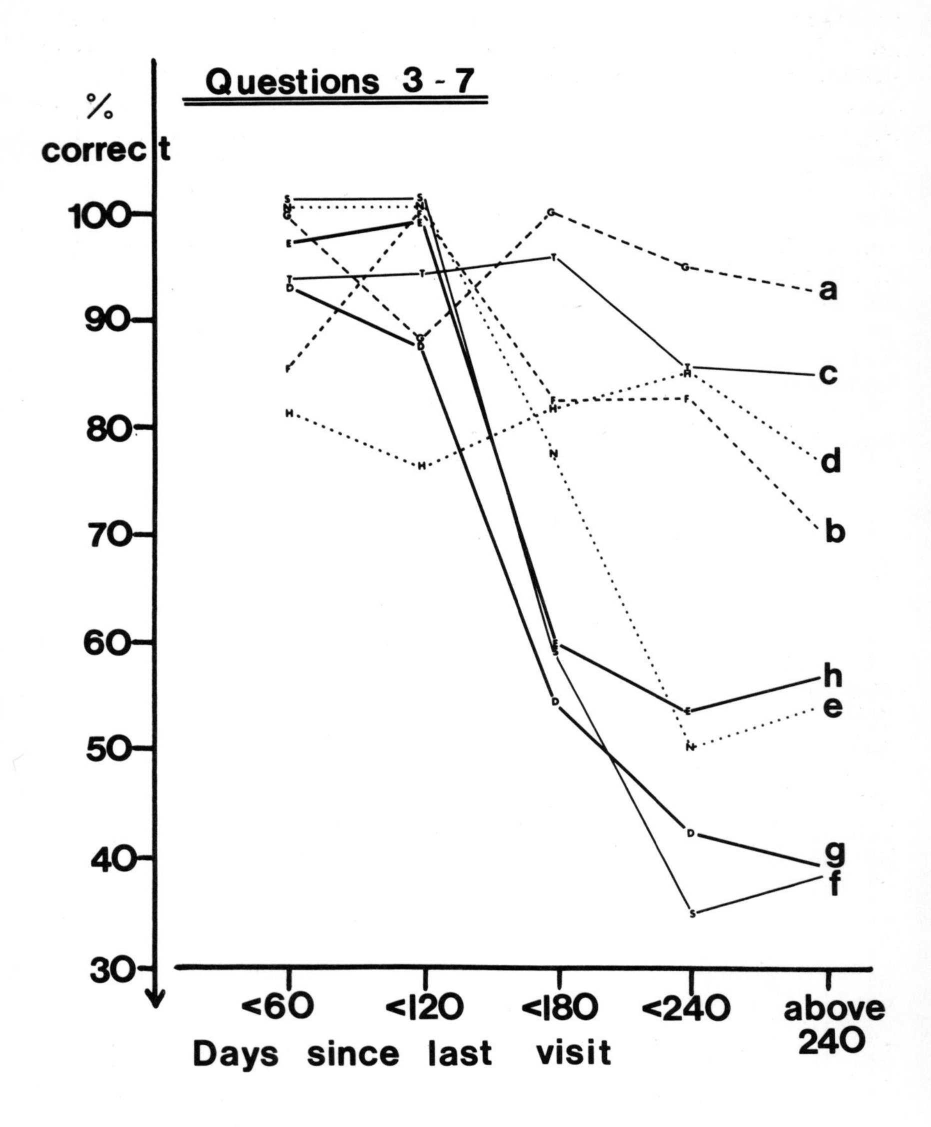

Fig. 1 Rate of forgetting as a function of question. (for details see text)

in their length of retention interval. Although there was no significant relationship between strategy used and retention interval, delay is clearly a potentially confounding factor. It was therefore included in a covariance analysis. When adjusted for delay, the difference in accuracy across strategies remained ($F_{4,86} = 3.16$, $p < .01$). Comparison between conditions indicated that the personal event strategy was significantly better than any other ($p < .05$); the only difference among the remaining strategies was that the time of day and time of year strategies were better than the Unit routine strategy ($p < .05$).

Table 1

Frequency and effectiveness of strategies used to recall the date and time of the last visit.

	Strategy				
	1	2	3	4	5
No. of Reports	7	29	19	6	31
Mean Error of Date Recall (Days)	16.4	42.6	21.5	64.7	43.9
Mean Elapsed Time (Days)	74.6	203.3	175.3	177.5	146.5
Mean Adjusted Error (Days)	33.6	35.8	20.0	62.7	47.7

Key: 1 Time of Day or Week; 2 Time of Year; 3 Personal Event; 4 Unit Routine; 5 None

3. *Retention of information about the test session.* Fig.1 shows the mean percentage of correct recall for questions about the test session. In each case a rough indication of whether or not forgetting had occurred was obtained by splitting subjects into two equal groups, the 44 subjects tested at less than 160 days interval and the 44 tested after more than 160 days and recording the number of subjects making one or more errors on the item in question. Forgetting was then assessed using the χ^2 test, with 1 degree of freedom to compare the performance of the two delay groups.

a. *Group or Individual testing:* No forgetting, $\chi^2 = 2.2$, $p > .05$.

b. *Type of Subject (Male, Female or Mixed Group):* No forgetting, $\chi^2 = 2.1$, $p > .05$.

c. *Time of Test:* No forgetting, $\chi^2 = 2.2$, $p > .05$.

d. *Length of Session:* No forgetting, $\chi^2 < 1$, $p > .05$.

e. *Number of Experimenters:* Clear evidence of forgetting, $\chi^2 = 20.55$, $p < .001$.

f. *Sex of Experimenter:* Clear evidence of forgetting, $\chi^2 = 27.2$, $p < .001$.

g. *Description of Experimenters:* Performance was initially very good with only 5 of the 44 short delay subjects failing to provide a recognizable broad characterization of the experimenters, whereas 17 subjects failed to do so after the longer delay ($\chi^2 = 12.18$, $p < .001$).

h. *Description of the Experiments:* This behaved in the same way as information about the experimenters, $\chi^2 = 7.26$, $p < .01$.

Overall Performance: There were considerable individual differences, with some subjects being consistently accurate. As might be expected, subjects making no errors at all on questions a - h were more frequent in the group tested after the shorter delay (20 out of 44) than after the longer delay (7 out of 44), $\chi^2 = 9.02$, $p < .01$.

DISCUSSION

Our results indicate that forgetting does occur, even if RI is minimized by testing only the last occurrence of a clearly specified event. This is particularly clear in the case of recalling the date. Subjects use a range of recall strategies of which the most effective appears to be reliance on some "land mark" event which is easier to date than the visit to the APU. The least effective strategy is that based on assumptions about the regularity of visits, perhaps because there is no regular pattern.

Clear forgetting occurs for some features of the experimental session but not others. What distinguishes these two types of question? Neither number of alternative answers nor initial level of performance allows a clear separation. Perhaps the most plausible difference is between those features that characterize the whole session (size and type of groups, length of session) which were well retained, and those which changed during the session (experimenters and tests performed) which showed forgetting.

Should the forgetting we found be attributed to PI? If so, subjects who were remembering their first visit should show less forgetting than the rest. Unfortunately we had too few subjects of this kind to allow a valid comparison. As far as they go however our results do add to the small but growing evidence suggesting that forgetting in everyday life is not too dramatically different from that observed within the artificial confines of the laboratory.

ACKNOWLEDGEMENTS

We are grateful to R.S. Edwards for assistance in data collection and analysis.

REFERENCES

Baddeley, A.D. The limitations of human memory: Implications for the design of retrospective surveys. In: *The recall method in social surveys.* (H. Goldstein and L. Moss, eds), University of London Institute of Education 'Studies in Education Series', London, (in press).

Baddeley, A.D. and Hitch, G.J. (1977). Recency Re-examined. In: *Attention and Performance IV.* (S. Dornic, ed), pp 647-667, Lawrence Erlbaum Associates, Hillsdale, N.J.

Underwood, B.J. and Ekstrand, B.R. (1966). An analysis of some shortcomings in the interference theory of forgetting. *Psychological Review.* 73, 540-549.

Warrington, E.K. and Sanders, H.I. (1971). The fate of old memories. *Quarterly Journal of Experimental Psychology.* 23, 432-442.

HUMOROUS PRESENTATIONS OF MATERIAL AND PRESENTATIONS OF HUMOROUS MATERIAL: A REVIEW OF THE HUMOUR AND MEMORY LITERATURE AND TWO EXPERIMENTAL STUDIES

A. J. Chapman and P. Crompton
University of Wales Institute of Science and Technology
Cardiff

INTRODUCTION

Judging by mass media presentations there is a widespread belief that the use of humour in advertisements benefits the sales of a vast variety of products. In television, some children's education programmes have introduced humour as a major ingredient - *Sesame Street* is the prime example. Presumably advertizers and educators are working on the premise that humour facilitates the reception and retention of a message. However, relatively few researchers have succeeded in their attempts at demonstrating either that humour does facilitate learning or that humour is useful in effecting attitude changes. The majority of empirical studies report nonsignificant trends, while a few even suggest that humour can be detrimental to learning. In the first part of the present paper we review the literature appertaining to humour and memory, and in the second part we report two new experiments.

HUMOUR AND MEMORY: A BRIEF REVIEW OF THE LITERATURE

Taken together, published studies are fragmented and, taken individually, one can seriously contest whether any one study has made an important contribution to theory - either humour or memory theory. Nevertheless, there are several areas of humour theory which could provide useful bases for empirical research. The four most substantial of these have been identified by McGhee (1979) in an analysis of television humour. First, from Berlyne's (1972) *arousal theory*, McGhee notes that the reward value of humour should promote interest when added to items of information; also, by inducing arousal fluctuations, it may help to maintain arousal within a range conducive to learning. Second, central to *psychoanalytic theory* is the notion that humour alleviates stress and tension (Freud, 1960). The mechanisms involved have not been specified precisely but if humour is therapeutic and does diminish debilitating and unpleasant tension, then a plausible hypothesis is that, under some circumstances at least, people become more receptive to information when it is blended with humour.

The third and fourth lines of theory would predict impairments in learning and memory. The third gives emphasis to the *playful state* emanating from humour and/or promoted by humour (cf. McGhee, 1977): it is to be expected that there is some incompatibility between a playful frame of mind and an efficient cognitive processing of information. None of these first three lines of theory has inspired any published research on learning or memory although there have been unsuccessful attempts to show that forgetting of jokes is a function of repression (Lee and Griffith, 1960, 1963).

The fourth line of theoretical analysis has had a rather more direct bearing on the empirical literature. Nevertheless it has served as a platform for just a small number of studies and these studies do not constitute anything approaching a unified group. Schramm (1973) and others have emphasized the *inhibiting and distracting* effects of humour. One's enjoyment of humour and one's reflections upon humour may extend into periods when important information is being presented; thus some information may never be received and other information may not be adequately rehearsed. Also the contrast between enjoyment derived from humorous and nonhumorous items can be such as to create dissatisfaction with the latter.

Other writers have suggested that humour may be beneficial to learning as long as it relates directly to the information to be retained (e.g. Lesser, 1972, 1974). In other words, there is an important distinction to be drawn between, on the one hand, interlacing a message with humour items which are not intrinsic to that message and, on the other hand, allowing salient and distinctive aspects of the message to determine the permissible content and style of the humour. In the former, gaps are rendered in the material to allow the presentation to be made humorous (e.g. by inserting jokes) while, in the latter, the material itself may be made the subject of fun in a more integrated presentation.

We shall return shortly to this distinction between humorous presentations and presentations of humour. But let us first examine the empirical literature. Two features are immediately conspicuous. One is that a high proportion of studies have been conducted on large classes of college students whose stimulus material has usually been contained within lectures: perhaps not surprisingly, these studies have characteristically been poorly controlled. The second is that most of the humour studies which embody tests of recall have been concerned primarily with investigating attitude changes in persuasive messages; this group of communication studies has been reviewed in detail by Gruner (1976) and, as far as memory is concerned, he concludes that there is little or no evidence of humour being of benefit.

A string of studies has failed to yield any effect of humour on memory. Most of these studies have been detailed in unpublished conference papers and in dissertations submitted for research degrees (Curran, 1972; Gruner, 1967, 1970; Kennedy, 1972; Kilpela, 1961; Neumann, 1972; Taylor, 1964, 1971; Youngman, 1966). In two experiments, Markiewicz (1972, 1973) found that memory for arguments contained in a humorous message is significantly poorer than for those in a serious message; but she noted in a subsequent review paper (Markiewicz, 1974) that she had failed in her empirical research to distinguish between retention and initial comprehension. Some hint as to the probable complex nature of humour's influence is provided in an unpublished dissertation by Weinberg (1973) in which an interaction is reported between humour, anxiety and intelligence. The principal finding was that when learning psychology in class, low anxious college students of high intelligence benefitted from the interjection of humorous examples, whereas high anxious students of lower intelligence were penalized by them. Previously, Smith, Ascough, Ettinger and Nelson (1971) had reported that it was high anxiety students who benefitted from humour: those who were moderately anxious found humour to be distracting.

Otherwise, there appear to be just three studies suggesting that learning can be improved through the introduction of humour: these are studies by Davies and Apter (1979), Hauck and Thomas (1972) and Kaplan and Pascoe (1977). Additionally, there are several 'memory for jokes' studies which are united in indicating that it is the jokes which are perceived as the most humorous which are the most readily recalled (Chapman, 1973; Heim, 1936; Lee and Griffith, 1963; O'Connell and Peterson, 1964).

The experimental research of Hauck and Thomas (1972) led them to conclude that humour facilitates retention of information acquired incidentally but not of information acquired intentionally. Children were presented with drawings of sets of three everyday objects (e.g. shoe, hat and glove) and they were invited to write a few sentences associating any two from the three. Instructions were varied systematically so that some subjects were required to think of humorous uses, while others thought of uses which were unusual but which were not humorous, and a third group thought of common uses. From a test one day later, correctly recalled objects from pairs were assumed to have been intentionally learned and the third objects, when recalled, were assumed to have been incidentally learned. However, as Davies and Apter (1979) have already noted, there are no data to justify the view that any 'intentional learning' took place. It is probably safe to assume that humour's facilitative effect arose with items in the triples to which least attention was paid (since the effect was for nonpaired items), but this may be explicable in terms of subjects in the humour condition simply taking longer to choose their pairings.

The most extensive empirical research to date has been reported recently by Davies and Apter (1979). They tested children (N=285) aged between eight and eleven years. Half the children were shown humorous versions of tape-slide teaching programmes, and the others saw equivalent nonhumorous versions. Four topics were covered and each programme lasted approximately twenty minutes. They were presented to children in their classes during school hours, and retention tests were administered on three occasions: the same day, after one month, and after nine months. The recall data collected on the day of the tape-slide presentation strongly supported the view that humour aids learning; after one month the beneficial effect of humour remained marked; but after nine months the effect was no longer statistically significant. While acknowledging that contaminating factors may have intervened Davies and Apter point to the possibility that the facilitative effects of humour may be limited to the relative short-term.

A second important piece of research is that of Kaplan and Pascoe (1977). University students (N=580) either attended a lecture presented seriously throughout or they attended one of three presented with humour. In one of those three the humour was related closely to the concepts in the lecture material; in the second, the humour was unrelated to the lecture concepts; and in the third there was a mixture of 'concept-related' and 'concept-unrelated' humour. A post-lecture test indicated that students' levels of comprehension in the four lectures were approximately equal. However, in a recall test six weeks later it was found that students who had attended the lectures with concept-related humour remembered more of the examples than did those who had attended the serious version. Like Kaplan and Pascoe, Lesser (1972, 1974) and others have given emphasis to the importance of humour being truly integrated with the learning material.

TWO EXPERIMENTAL STUDIES

This section of the paper reports some of our own preliminary research. We are seeking ways of circumventing and/or overcoming the major problems highlighted by early studies. In particular, some attention is paid in this research to the validation of humour and to presenting the humour in a cohesive and integrated package with the material to be remembered. The research was in three phases and these phases shared several methodological features. The subjects were boys and girls aged five and six years. They were selected on the basis of age alone from infants schools in Cardiff; and testing took place inside those schools. With the experimenter (PC) present, the children were tested individuall once only, and they were randomly assigned to treatment groups. The stimulus material was specially prepared for this research and it comprised two matched sets of ten animal paintings/ pictures (tiger, rhinoceros, elephant, giraffe, hippopotamus, zebra, lion, donkey, camel and monkey). Colour slides of the pictures were displayed for equal lengths of time on a Caramate slide-tape projector, giving automatic cueing of slides to commentary on the auditory tape. Instructions to subjects were recorded on the same tape.

Phase I: Humour validation

In the first phase of the research, subjects were shown all twenty slides so as to determine whether a five/six-year-old subject-population agreed with the experimenters'/artist's distinction between 'funny' and 'serious' caricatures of animals. The slides were presented to ten boys and ten girls and each child saw them in a different order. Individual pictures were rated on a four-point funniness scale by subjects pointing to one of four line-drawings: these were of a face with the curvature of the mouth arranged to show level of amusement. The results strongly confirmed expectations. Each drawing within the set which was intended to be funny was rated significantly funnier than its serious counterpart; and comparing scores for the sets as a whole there was a highly significant difference in mean ratings (Means = 3.6 and 2.0 respectively; $p<.001$).

Phase II: Experiment I

Children were played a story (*Topsy and Tim at the Zoo*) which had been modified slightly so that only the ten animals depicted in the slides were featured in the story and each was mentioned three times in quick succession. (In fact, the story had largely determined the choice of stimulus pictures). One group of subjects (n=15) was shown the set of funny pictures, and the other group of subjects (n=15) was shown the serious pictures. Immediately after the story, each child was asked ten questions in the form of a quiz-game. Only the first question was directly related to the humour/serious pictures *per se*: "First; of all the animals that Topsy and Tim saw at the zoo which ones can you remember?" The subsequent questions were all related to the story-line and, since no child had heard the story before, no question could be answered from prior knowledge. For example, one question was, "What animal was next to the donkeys' field?"

From Kaplan and Pascoe's (1977) work it was expected that humour would not produce any improvement on items tested in Questions 2 to 10 but it was expected that there might be an improvement on Question 1 because the humour was of some relevance. As anticipated, humour did not affect answers to Questions 2 to 10, but nor did it facilitate recall of the animals for Question 1. However, informal observations and pilot work suggested that an experimental effect might have been manifested using a cued recall task, and this was introduced in the experiment following.

Phase III: Experiment II

Rather than accompanying a story, the slides immediately followed simple statements about spelling: "t is for tiger", "c is for camel" etc.. By this means, it was intended that the humour be better integrated with the material to be retained and, also, a cued recall task could be introduced which seemed sensible to the children. There were two treatment groups, corresponding to the funny and serious pictures, with fifteen orders of slide presentation, balanced as far as possible. For recall, subjects were given the first letter of the animal name as a cue: for example, "What was the letter t for?" The recall quiz immediately followed the presentation of the set of slides. As predicted, humour did facilitate recall (F=5.72;df=1,25;p<.05), the mean number of correct responses being 4.9 for funny pictures and 3.6 for serious pictures. (This finding has been substantiated in a similar experiment, the mean scores then being 5.3 and 3.4 respectively; and there is some suggestion in that experiment that the beneficial effect of humour is sometimes greater for boys).

CLOSING REMARKS

Empirical studies showing that humour can aid recall are swamped in number by the studies which suggest either that humour has no effect or that it has a negative effect. However, most of the studies cited above have referred to memory as a secondary issue and, partly as a consequence, they are methodologically poor. Important control groups have sometimes been omitted (cf. Gruner, 1976; Markiewicz, 1974); and subjects have often assigned themselves to conditions. Stimulus materials have almost certainly varied, not just with respect to humour, but on other dimensions too; lectures, for instance, have varied by several minutes in duration. One cannot even be sure that subjects have considered the researchers' materials to be funny. Perhaps most important of all, however, is the point already made, that to aid memory humour probably has to be directly related to, and integrated with, the items to be remembered.

It should also be borne in mind that students behind desks and subjects behind sets of apparatus can usually be relied upon to attend to a presentation. Unlike most teachers and researchers, those who operate through the mass media must normally compete for one's attention at times when one is free to switch activities at any moment. The advertizer's audience, for example, has to be enticed from other activities, and humour may be invaluable in helping to secure a relaxed and contented audience. It may be rather surprising to find that some of the limited data on humour and advertizing suggest that introducing humour can sometimes decrease sales (cf. McGhee, 1979), but presumably there can come a point when one is presented with too much humour and then none of the message is taken seriously.

One may speculate that the teacher, the advertizer and other might use humour to best advantage if the messages themselves can be produced in a humorous fashion (without, of course, denigrating the product). Further, one may speculate that to encase with humour, or to interrupt with humour, a message which is otherwise presented seriously, is a poor strategy; it is one which can impair retention of the message. In other words, to reflect upon a joke or a humorous incident in an advertisement or in a lecture, should necessitate the recipient rehearsing aspects of the message: if not, humour may be detrimental to memory. Nevertheless, studies of speaker ethos and course evaluation indicate that employment of humour is likely to guarantee relatively high attendance at lectures (cf. Gruner, 1976): therefore, there are always likely to be some 'exposure' benefits deriving from *humorous presentations* of material as well as from presentations of *humorous material*.

ACKNOWLEDGEMENTS

We are grateful for the kind hospitality given by Miss I. M. Roberts, Mrs. M. C. M. Taylor and their teaching staffs at Lakeside Infants School and Llanedeyrn Infants School, Cardiff.

REFERENCES

Berlyne, D. E. (1972). Humor and its kin. In: *The Psychology of Humor*. (J. H. Goldstein and P. E. McGhee, eds), pp 43-60. Academic Press, New York.

Chapman, A. J. (1973). Funniness of jokes, canned laughter and recall performance. *Sociometry, 36*, 569-578.

Curran, F. W. (1972). A developmental study of cartoon humor and its use in facilitating learning. Unpublished Doctoral Dissertation, Catholic University of America.

Davies, A. P. and Apter, M. J. (1979). Humour and its effects on learning in children. In: *Children's Humour*. (P.E. McGhee and A. J. Chapman, eds), in press. Wiley: Chichester.

Freud, S. (1960). *Jokes and Their Relation to the Unconscious*. Norton, New York.

Gruner, C. R. (1967). Effect of humor on speaker ethos and audience information gain. *Journal of Communication, 17*, 228-233.

Gruner, C. R. (1970). The effect of humor in dull and interesting informative speeches. *Central States Speech Journal, 21*, 160-166.

Gruner, C. R. (1976). Wit and humour in mass communication. In: *Humour and Laughter: Theory, Research and Applications*. (A. J. Chapman and H. C. Foot, eds), pp 287-311.

Hauck, W. E. and Thomas, J. W. (1972). The relationship of humor to intelligence, creativity, and intentional and incidental learning. *Journal of Experimental Education, 40*, 52-55.

Heim, A. (1936). An experiment on humour. *British Journal of Psychology, 27*, 148-161.

Kaplan, R. M. and Pascoe, G. C. (1977). Humorous lectures and humorous examples: some effects upon comprehension and retention. *Journal of Educational Psychology, 69*, 61-65.

Kennedy, A. J. (1972). An experimental study of the effect of humorous message content upon ethos and persuasiveness. Unpublished Doctoral Dissertation, University of Michigan.

Kilpela, D. E. (1961). An experimental study of the effects of humor on persuasion. Unpublished Master's Thesis, Wayne State University.

Lee, J. C. and Griffith, R. M. (1960). Forgetting of humor: repression? *American Psychologist, 15*, 436.

Lee, J. C. and Griffith, R. M. (1963). Forgetting of jokes: a function of repression? *Journal of Individual Psychology, 19*, 213-215.

Lesser, G. (1972). Assumptions behind the production and writing methods in "Sesame Street". In: *Quality Instructiona Television*. (W. Schramm, ed). University of Hawaii Press.

Lesser, G. (1974). *Children and Television: Lessons from Sesame Street*. Random House, New York.

Markiewicz, D. (1972). The effects of humor on persuasion. Unpublished Doctoral Dissertation, Ohio State University.

Markiewicz, D. (1973). Persuasion as a function of humorous vs. serious messages or contexts. Unpublished manuscript.

Markiewicz, D. (1974). Effects of humor on persuasion. *Sociometry, 37*, 407-422.

McGhee, P. E. (1977). A model of the origins and early development of incongruity-based humour. In: *It's a Funny Thing, Humour*. (A. J. Chapman and H. C. Foot, eds). pp 27-36. Pergamon Press, Oxford.

McGhee, P. E. (1979). Toward the integration of entertainment and educational functions of television: the role of humor. In: *The Entertainment Functions of Television*. (P. H. Tannenbaum, ed). Lawrence Erlbaum, New York.

Neumann, L. E. (1972). Humor in classroom instruction. Unpublished Doctoral Dissertation, St. Louis University.

O'Connell, W. E. and Peterson, P. (1964). Humor and repression *Journal of Existential Psychology, 4*, 309-316.

Schramm, W. (1973). *Men, Messages and Media: A Look at Human Communication*. Harper and Row, New York.

Smith, R. E., Ascough, J. C., Ettinger, R. F. and Nelson, D. A (1971). Humor, anxiety and task performance. *Journal of Personality and Social Psychology, 19*, 243-246.

Taylor, P. M. (1964). The effectiveness of humor in informative speeches. *Central States Speech Journal, 5*, 295-296.

Weinberg, M. D. (1973). The interactional effect of humor and anxiety on academic performance. Unpublished Doctoral Dissertation, Yeshiva University.

Youngman, R. C. (1966). An experimental investigation of the effect of germane humor versus nongermane humor in an informative communication. Unpublished Master's Thesis, Ohio University.

PLANS AND ERRORS IN MEMORY FOR URBAN GEOGRAPHY

R.W. Byrne

University of St. Andrews,
St Andrews,
Fife, Scotland

ABSTRACT

Even subjects who know a town well make striking and consistent patterns of errors when they are asked to estimate road distances and angles. These errors give information about the way in which subjects remember the information, and in the present study support a model in which routes are encoded as "plans", consisting of strings of locations connected by motor programs, and a spatial area is represented by a network of such strings.

INTRODUCTION

Every day, most of us find our way about in a complicated maze of streets, paths and buildings, and do so in an automatic fashion without any impression of mental effort. However, it can readily be seen that our knowledge of urban geography is incomplete, error-prone and idiosyncratic, simply by trying to draw an accurate plan of a town which we know well. Typically we begin at a single point or distinctive shape of roads (perhaps a cross or a square in the town centre) and trace out along linear routes and branches until a network is formed. Soon, we encounter evidence of error: parallel straight roads which ought to intersect, small areas seeming magnified out of proportion, and so on. Unfortunately, although widely used, map-drawing has at least two disadvantages as a technique for the study of geographical knowledge. It is entirely limited by the technical drawing skill of the subject, so there is no way of separating errors of knowledge from lack of skill. Secondly, a commonsense knowledge of geometry allows construction of forms and patterns which are not "known" (explicitly represented in memory), so we cannot separate direct knowledge from deduced and constructed facts. Furthermore, if maps are drawn by tracing along linear paths, any error will be cumulative and the final products will differ radically if different starting points are chosen. Thus, although interesting in themselves, subjects' attempts at map-drawing give us a poor idea of their mental data-base of information, and we must turn to other, more indirect, manifestations of their knowledge.

In the current study, interest centred on the possibility that much geographical information is encoded in a form which preserves only topological connectedness: the ROUTE-MAP hypothesis (the terms "route-map" and "survey-map" follow Shemyakin, 1962). A town encoded as a route-map can be viewed as a network of strings, each branch-point corresponding to a road junction. The strings themselves can equally well be thought of as descriptions of routes, or plans of how to traverse them. In either case, particular locations are the "nodes" and the "links" are statements or motor programs. Neither the distances between locations nor the precise angles at which routes join need to be encoded in a route-map: the order of locations and branches is sufficient for navigation. This is contrasted with a representation which does preserve horizontal vector distance: the SURVEY-MAP hypothesis. Here the shapes and relative lengths of routes and the angles at which they join are essential for the representation to be self-consistent. It is, of course, possible to construct intermediates between these extreme hypotheses, with portions of survey-map and portions of route-map representation. These hybrid forms cannot in general be mapped on to a plane surface.

To test between these possibilities, in experiments 1 and 2, estimates were collected of distances between pairs of locations and angles between pairs of intersecting roads. The survey-map hypothesis predicts simply that these estimates should be distributed about the true values. To make estimates at all, a system equipped only with a route-map must make additional assumptions about the world. The simplest assumptions would seem to be that roads are *straight* between junctions, that angles at junctions are *equal* (and therefore, when the majority of junctions tend to involve four roads, each angle is ninety degrees), and that the more locations there are on a route the longer, on the whole, the route will be. Distances should therefore be estimated as longer if they lie in complex areas like town centres (as there are more known locations on the route) or if they involve many changes of direction at intersections (as any location where a turn is necessary is obligatorily represented on a description or program of the route). On some interpretations, a survey-map would predict *under-estimation* of routes involving many turns, as in such a case the "crow flight" distance will usually be shorter than if the route were direct. Angles between roads will, on a route-map hypothesis, tend to be estimated as nearer to a multiple of 90° or 45° than is really the case (unless the town-plan is based on a hexagonal block, like a honeycomb, when 120° multiples are possible).

EXPERIMENT 1

The purpose of this experiment was to ascertain the effect (if any) on subjects' estimates of walking distance of varying the number of turns in the route and the amount of complexity of its surroundings (routes in a town centre *versus* routes in outlying streets). A third variable, actual length of route, was also introduced, but was not relevant to the main hypothesis.

Method

Eighty undergraduates, selected on the criterion of at least one year's residence in St. Andrews, used a ratio scaling procedure to estimate walking distances between pairs of prominent locations in the town. Routes between these pairs independently varied length, the number of major bends, and the location - whether in the central shopping district or the residential outskirts. The order of presentation of the locations, and the sex of subjects were both balanced, and random presentation orders were used.

Results

Analysis of variance showed that neither of the between-subject variables, sex and order of presentation, approached significance, so the data were pooled for further analysis.

All three independent variables had highly significant effects:-

1. Routes are judged longer if they lie within the town centre ($F(1,76) = 26.0$, $p<0.001$)

2. Routes are judged longer if they include several bends compared with predominantly straight routes ($F(1,76) = 34.8$,

p<0.001).

3. Shorter routes are proportionate overestimated compared with longer ones ($F(2,152) = 57.9$, $p<0.001$). This effect of length had a highly significant linear trend ($F(1,76) = 120.7$, $p<0.005$).

In addition three significant interactions were found, linearity x location ($F(1,76) = 19.1$, $p<0.001$), linearity x length ($F(2,152) = 11.8$, $p<0.001$) and location x length ($F(2,152) = 9.9$, $p<0.001$). t-tests indicated that the effect of non-linearity of route was significant for routes in the town centre ($t(239) = -7.4$, $p<0.001$) but not for those outside the centre ($t(239) = -1.7$, $p = 0.098$); that the effect of non-linearity of route was significant on 300m and 500m routes ($t(159) = -4.9$ and -5.4, $p<0.001$ in each case) but not for the 750m routes ($t(159) = -0.06$, $p<0.9$); and that the effect of location was significant on 300m and 500m routes (t(159 = 5.4 and 2.5, $p<0.001$ and 0.05) but not on the 750m routes ($t(159) = 1.9$, $p = 0.06$). No other interactions reached significance.

It was suspected that the effect of length might be some form of experimental artifact, since the middle category of length estimations had a percentage error close to zero. An unequal groups analysis of variance was therefore performed using data from only the *first* estimation of each subject, but the effect of length was still significant ($p<0.05$) despite the much smaller pool of data. This rules out one possible range effect (Poulton 1975) from the range of distances presented. However, another possible form of range effect comes from the use of the ratio scaling technique. If subjects are biased towards the use of middle of scale values (which here are close to the longest distance used) this would clearly produce a greater over-esimtation of short distances, and an effect visible on the very first trial.

Discussion

The location of a route, its linearity and its absolute length all have effects on subjects' estimations of its length. The effect of length, both in this and previous studies can be plausibly interpreted as a range effect (Poulton, 1975) resulting in relative overestimation of short distances and underestimation of longer ones. The other two effects are in the directions predicted by the original hypothesis. Routes with more bends and routes within the central shopping area are relatively overestimated in length, and both of these effects would result from the heuristic that the more locations there are recalled to be along a route, the longer it is likely to be judged. The number of locations remembered will on average be proportional to the length, but points where a change of bearing is needed will always be recalled, and segments of route with many memorable locations will tend to be over-represented.

EXPERIMENT 2

This experiment investigated the extent to which subjects' estimates of road angles are veridical or heavily biased by simplifying assumptions. In particular the assumption that "roads intersect at right angles" was postulated, but this is clearly *too* much of a simplification since it is so easy to produce counterexamples from memory. In order to select experimental materials, it was instead assumed that if road configurations could be loosely described as "turn left", "straight on" or "turn right", then the angles would be remembered as multiples of 90°: cases where "fork left/right" or "slightly left/right" would be appropriate are then excluded. Thus angles within a range of 60° to 120° were investigated, excluding angles which in fact did closely correspond to 90° since they are irrelevant to the hypothesis.

Method

Thirty members of the M.R.C. Applied Psychology Unit subject panel were asked to draw plans of ten familiar Cambridge road junctions, paying particular attention to the angles at which roads met. It was stressed that accuracy of angular configurations was essential. Pairs of roads were selected so that in half the cases they met at 60° - 70° and in half at 110° - 120°.

Results

For each angle t-tests were used to find the probability that the distribution of estimates could have resulted either from the true angle or ninety degrees. The results show that in all cases there are significant differences from the angle (in nine cases $p<0.001$, in one $p<0.02$). In all but one case the estimates are closer to ninety degrees, and in eight out of ten cases there is no significant difference from this value. Even in the single case where t-tests suggest closer affinity to the real angle than a right angle, this is due to two extreme values and the distribution of estimates peaks in the 85-94° range.

Discussion

Road angles in the range of 60° to 120° are all remembered as if they were right angles. This quantization cannot be the rule, as in fact the true angles can readily be perceived by anyone who stops to consider at the junctions and so, with sufficient practice, must be learnable: one could not expect such a drastic effect on road angle close to a subject's home. However, most of our knowledge of urban geography is of the kind tested here, derived from prolonged experience of complex road networks, in circumstances which do not permit careful deliberation at every junction.

GENERAL DISCUSSION

The results of both experiments point to the conclusion that an important mental representation of large-scale spatial information does not encode vector information. Rather than a "survey-map" (isomorphic to a two-dimensional conventional map), subjects in these tasks use a "route-map" (in the sense of Shemyakin, 1962). Topological connectedness of routes (including the order of locations along the routes) and quantized directions for changes of bearing are represented accurately, as we know that the representation is fully adequate for urban navigation. Its weaknesses are evident in the experiments reported here, and also when one attempts to draw an accurate map from memory but finds gross distortions and impossibilities in the result produced.

We suggest that the most economical form for a route-map is as a *plan* (Miller, Galanter and Pribram, 1960). Route-maps govern large-scale locomotion, and therefore ultimately result in the execution of motor programs. At the same time, they are not stereotyped sequences, so that a high-level program or plan seems a plausible format. We propose that in a route-map a linear or branching series of location-descriptions are used as the criteria for operations which result in changes of directions. For example, a route-map might resemble:-

AT (*start of journey*)	:	*command*
AT (*location*)	:	*command*
AT (*destination*)	:	STOP

eg

AT (home)	:	TURN LEFT
AT (tee junction with Bridge Street)	:	TURN RIGHT
AT (Student Union)	:	CONTINUE
AT (cross road with High Street)	:	TURN LEFT
AT (Woolworths)	:	STOP

This kind of representation appears adequate for all the experimental data known at present and meshes well with everyday phenomena, but some details are unspecified. For example, if a town is represented by route-maps they must form a *net* not just a linear or branched string: how is a net of plans indexed, and how are shortest paths computed? One simple possibility is by "spreading activation search" (Collins and Loftus, 1975) in which the two nodes to be connected (ie the start and end of a route) are accessed directly and some form of activation spreads out along arcs from each. When the two areas of activation first meet at a node, a pathway through the network is available which is the shortest in the network's metric. Since the actual distance between nodes is not represented, this will not necessarily be the shortest route in reality: systematic errors are to be expected.

Route-maps are undoubtedly laid down in memory prior to survey-maps under normal circumstances. They are isomorphic with the experience of route travel by which the information is learnt, while survey-maps require rotation to a vertical perspective. Children show evidence of route-map representation considerably before survey-maps (eg Piaget, Inhelder and Szeminska, 1960; Shemyakin, 1962). In a study carried out in Cuidad,Guyana before any town-plans were publicly available, route-map drawings of adults were general while spatially-dominant drawings only appeared in those with greatest familiarity of the area (Appleyard, 1970). Both these approaches rely on map-drawing as the experimental task and it is therefore difficult to be sure whether a spatially-dominant result comes from a survey-map representation or simply a route-map with the use of geometrical commonsense knowledge.

Is there, then, any clear evidence that mental representation of the form of survey-maps exist at all? One observation which suggests that they do is that one can sometimes describe the *shapes and configurations* which routes would form when viewed from above, even when one has not viewed them with this perspective (either in reality or as a conventional map). Another intriguing phenomenon is that there is a *preferred orientation* for drawing a sketch-map of a town. This is not constant across subjects (though North at the top is much the commonest orientation), but a subject will find it harder to construct a map in an orientation different from his or her preferred one. Related to this is the observation that it is possible to use a conventional map without rotating it when one changes direction, although it is easier and more reliable to rotate it so that its orientation matches that of the land.

It seems probable, therefore, that survey-maps *can* exist in our repertoire of mental representations, but that they are by no means the universal format for large-scale spatial information, and their structure and function is a target for future research.

REFERENCES

Appleyard, D. (1970). Styles and methods of structuring a city. *Environment and Behaviour*. 2, 100-117.

Collins, A.M. and Loftus, M.R. (1972) A spreading activation theory of semantic processing. *Psychological Review*. 82, 407-428.

Piaget, J., Inhelder, B. and Szeminska, A. (1960). *The child's conception of geometry*. New York: Basic Books.

Poulton, E.C. (1975). Observer bias. *Applied Ergonomics*. 6, 3-8.

Shemyakin, F.N. (1962). Orientation in space. In *Psychological Science in the U.S.S.R. Vol. 1, Part 1*. (B.G. Anan'yet et al., eds.), (Rep. No. 11466), Washington, D.C.: U.S. Office of Technical Reports.

MAKING SOMETHING STAND OUT: THE ISOLATION EFFECT IN MEMORY PERFORMANCE

Richard S. Cimbalo

Daemen College
Buffalo, New York 14226, USA

Cermak (1975), in his book entitled *Improving Your Memory*, notes that "...advertisers use bright colors, catchy phrases, loud noises, movement, or flashing lights in their displays; anything to catch your attention" (p.27). An experimental operationalization of this process in the area of verbal learning and memory is the von Restorff or isolation effect (IE) wherein a different item is introduced into a set of common items. The IE refers to the fact that the different item displays better retention than a comparable item in a homogeneous list. It is a very robust effect spanning some 80 years (Calkins, 1894) and numerous variations and replications (Wallace, 1965).

One need only examine the structure of this paper, and most other papers and books, and note their use of italicizing, indenting, etc., to realize the assumed importance of such procedures. Superimposed on used, preorganized texts in a college bookstore, Fowler and Barker (1974) found that 92% contained significant applications of further emphasizing techniques. It is surprising to note the scarcity of quality research surrounding such a prevalent phenomenon.

Both the modal model (Waugh and Norman, 1965) and the levels of processing approach (Craik and Lockhart, 1972) to memory, currently the two most prominent approaches to human information processing, are in agreement on the importance of selection. They differ primarily in the emphasis placed on the structural versus process results of selection. Items selected by the subject in the modal model pass to different, more permanent stores whereas with the process approach more developmentally sophisticated, time consuming strategies assure the selected item of a greater resistance to forgetting.

In this paper two basic issues will be considered which clearly emerge from research with isolation and which possess both theoretical and practical significance. The first involves the conditions necessary to achieve the enhanced memory performance for the isolate and the second concerns itself with memory performance for the surround or context. As will be shown these two issues are seldom independent of both organismic and task variables.

ISOLATED ITEM PERFORMANCE (MEMORY FOR THE PART)

Achieving isolation

Color, size, shape, electric shock, digits in lists of letters and vice versa, voice, meaningfulness, noise, intensity, spacing, underlining, borders and nudes have all been used to assess the effects of introducing differences in a task of memory performance. There are few studies which have not found evidence for the IE when a clearly presented and perceived item occurs in a list. Its robustness in the verbal learning literature would seem to rival the serial position effect.

Factors affecting the IE

If more than a single item is made different in the list, the IE may not occur (Newman and Jennette, 1975). Evidence also suggests that the IE can habituate (Morton, 1941). The background items can exert an influence on the IE. The IE is stronger when less meaningful items surround it (Rosen, Richardson and Saltz, 1962).

How different can one make the isolate? Gumenik and Levitt (1968) found that the larger (or smaller) one made the isolate the greater the IE. Cimbalo, Capria, Neider, and Wilkins (1977) in a multidimensional attempt at establishing differences found the following order of effectiveness with college students: size, color, and spacing. Detterman (1975) also presents evidence for free recall and recognition tasks that very intense stimuli (120 db vs 60 db) may result in the absence of the IE. Detterman's findings, however, may be the result of distortion.

A simultaneously-presented list of items in a short-term memory (STM) paradigm yields a stronger IE (Cimbalo et al., 1977). In a free recall task, which can be categorized as a long-term memory (LTM) paradigm because of its multi-trial nature, Einstein, Pellegrino, Mondani, and Battig (1974) found the reverse to be true i.e., a stronger IE with a successively presented list. It should be noted here that the STM-LTM distinction will be used throughout the paper despite the obvious limitations (Houston, 1976). The dichotomy seems to be useful in making some sense out of otherwise confusing data. The use of modal model nomenclature is not viewed as precluding a level of processing approach but the two are viewed as quite similar for the level of resolution attempted in this paper. The STM paradigm is usually used to refer to a single presentation of unrelated items which exceeds the memory span and is only presented for a few seconds per item. The LTM paradigm refers to multiple presentations of unrelated items which exceeds the memory span and is presented for many seconds or even minutes per item.

Age differences are present for the IE. Younger children (5-6 years) have a more pronounced IE and actually display better performance than older children (9-11 years), and older subjects (over 60 years) do not display the IE at all (Cimbalo, Brink, Nowak and Soderstrom, 1978). Acredolo, Pick and Olsen (1975) found that landmarks in an open-field situation removed any differences in memory for spatial location between preschool and eight-year-old children. The young preoperational child seems to benefit most from the landmark and Acredolo et al. (1975) report that "Without an understanding of metric distance, these children relied on topological relations and were therefore quite dependent on the presence of landmarks to help them code location." (p.501)

If one tries to make different an item at or near the beginning of a list in a STM paradigm it does not produce the IE but an isolate in the middle or end will (Cimbalo, 1970). In a LTM task some evidence for an IE in beginning list items exists (Bone and Goulet, 1968).

In a task involving memory for textual materials it was found that highlighting (coloring words in a transparent ink) improves retention of selected material and that active highlighting is better than a passive reading of already highlighted material (Fowler et al. 1974). Smart and Bruning (1973) found an interesting interaction for the learning of prose material between the source of isolation and the relevancy of isolation such that when subjects underlined their own material and it was irrelevant the poorest performance was achieved. However, when irrelevant was underlined by the experimenter a decrement in performance with respect to the unisolated control was not obtained and was therefore contrary to the results cited earlier by Fowler et al. (1974) Active isolation was not necessarily superior but it depended to a large extent upon whether the material highlighted was relevant or not. Klare, Mabry, and Gustafson (1954) have shown that is a subject has a high aptitude for material there was no difference between selective and random underlining, but if he had a low aptitude there was poorer performance in the random condition.

Practical implications

If our goal is to enhance memory for a particular item in a simultaneously-presented array, then a clearly perceived size and/or color variation introduced into the middle of a string would seem to be most effective. In this central position one would take full advantage of sameness or homogeneity of the surround which should result in better isolated item recall performance. Care must be taken not to emphasize too many items (probably no more than one), to present the same type of isolation too many times or to alter the item to the point of producing distortion. For repeated presentations of a list (LTM) a successive presentation would seem to produce a stronger IE. If the person is allowed to respond freely, i.e. without order contraints an isolated item toward the end of the list produces an IE at least as strong as the middle position.

It would seem that isolating an item is a very useful technique with children but at first blush appears useless in communicating the target item with older persons. The abundance of literature with college-age subjects supports the effectiveness of isolation as a memory aid in this group.

Allowing individuals to perform their own highlighting with connected discourse where one is reading for meaning, enhances the memory for such emphasized information as long as they have a high aptitude for the to-be-learned material. For connected discourse the role played by position of isolation, part of speech isolated, etc. is currently unexplored.

UNISOLATED ITEM PERFORMANCE IN ISOLATED LISTS (MEMORY FOR THE WHOLE)

The consistency of the IE is in stark contrast to the findings with regard to the performance on the more similar items in the list with an isolate. The effect of the isolate on the immediately adjacent items (spread of effect) and on list performance as a whole is replete with seeming contradictions. The spread of effect is so sensitive to task variables such as rate of presentation, list length, strategy employed, instructions (e.g. Cimbalo et al., 1977) that it will not be considered separately here but only as a part of the larger effect of overall list performance.

Overall list null effect (OLNE)

Wallace (1965), in a review article dealing with the IE, marshalls convincing evidence to support a 'rob Peter to pay Paul' explanation. Accordingly, the IE results from increased processing of the isolate which in the fixed time frames employed can only be obtained from a reduction in the processing of the other items in the list. Wallace (1965) writes: "There has been no consistent finding, dealing directly or indirectly with the von Restorff phenomenon, which would suggest that isolation enhances overall list learning" (p.413). The great bulk of the literature supports this argument. Cimbalo (1970, 1971) found this effect with different rates of presentation, list lengths, methods of presentation, serial positions and methods of recall. Similar results are reported by Fowler et al. (1974) for connected discourse, i.e., overall performance for isolated passages did not differ from the unisolated control. There are many more articles which support the total time hypothesis.

Overall list facilitation effect (OLFE)

More recently a dozen studies have been cited which indicate that isolating an item does help in learning the whole list (Paul helps Peter) (Cimbalo et al., 1977). The conditions necessary and/or sufficient for producing and/or enhancing the OLFE have been argued to be: (a) a serial memory task wherein a repetition strategy is employed, (b) an isolated item centrally located in the list, and (c) a simultaneous presentation of list items (Cimbalo et al., 1977). Under these conditions it appears that an organizational process is operative which breaks up complex, confusing masses of material into a more easily learned structure wherein the parts fit more easily together and the whole is more effectively recalled.

Although the isolated item itself is not remembered better in older persons the isolated list is remembered better as a whole and the young children behave much as our college-age population in that under the conditions previously specified they too demonstrate the OLFE (Cimbalo et al., 1978).

Cashen and Leicht (1970) report finding both the IE and the OLFE with connected discourse in a formal educational setting. They tested college freshmen on the contents of three articles from *Scientific American* dealing with various areas of psychology.

Overall list debilitation effect (OLDE)

Cimbalo and Mahoney (1970) presented data which indicated significant decrements in performance for unisolated items in an isolated list in direct relation to the ease of encoding and performance superiority for the isolated unit. The more meaningful or more easily pronounceable was the isolated trigram, the worse was the performance on the remaining list items. A similar effect was reported by Detterman and Ellis (1972). They used male and female nudes with exposed genitalia as the isolated item. They found significant performance decrements on items preceding and succeeding the isolate which they equated with retrograde and anterograde amnesia effects respectively. This effect seems much more difficult to reliably replicate and extend (Cimbalo, Nowak and Stringfield, in press).

Practical Implications

Textbooks often use headings in darkened print, key words in italics, color, etc. to supposedly serve as learning aids. The basic research would indicate some cautionary notes in this regard. The highlighted or emphasized element can help the person to organize the total message more effectively. However, emphasis alone does not guarantee enhanced performance but can also result in interfering distortions or the setting up of competitors for the individual's processing mechanism. The most effective techniques for isolating can probably be gleaned from a closer investigation of our own students and their highlighting behavior (Fowler et al., 1974).

Isolation techniques appear to be useful in enhancing information transfer in the young and old as well as the college-age people who predominate in the literature. Although the research predicting overall performance is becoming clearer for lists of items or for episodic memory (Cimbalo et al., 1977) the picture for connected discourse or semantic memory remains confusing.

GENERAL DISCUSSION

A problem for the very young of our species in their attempt to handle incoming information is the existence of but a few simple strategies or plans (Flavell, 1970). For those labelled as schizophrenics the problem is to distinguish the target item from a background of noise (McGhie, 1969). For the older members the strategies and plans developed over the years seem to become prepotent over the stimulus configurations of the surround (Cimbalo et al., 1978; Talland, 1968). Research with the retarded has stressed the inability to properly sequence the various memory strategies even though each separate strategy can be used competently (Butterfield, Wambold and Belmont, 1973). For the young, old, schizophrenic and retarded the use of an appropriate isolate would help to either draw attention to the relevant structures or processes and/or help to divide confusing arrays into more easily manageable units. However, a point that clearly emerges from the research to this point is that a mere blob of color or streak of highlighter introduced at random into an array of information will not assure improved overall performance. Both organismic and task variables will have to be examined carefully before a prediction of enhanced performance can be made.

The macrotheories of psychology's past which sought to account for all human behavior have proved inefficient in dealing with the emerging data base and microtheories appear much more effective (Chaplin and Krawiec, 1976). But as humans with inquiring minds there is a continual struggle to put it all together i.e., the sensory store, STM, LTM and the various processes correlated with each to understand what we do when we read, learn or understand. In this particular attempt to deal with the actual implications of a memory phenomenon it is both humbling and exciting to try to cope with the entire domain of cognitive psychology from simple perceptions to the comprehension of connected discourse. In many instances the distilled experiments of the laboratory have had to be strained to handle the complexities of life. It is when trying to deal with the complex practicalities that some reassurance may be derived from Harlow's (1972) reasoning that "...one cannot generalize, but one must. If the competent do not wish to generalize the incompetent will fill the field." (p.716) An interesting line of development, which promises to help reduce strained generalizations, is the use of more realistic stimulus arrays and situations (e.g. Acredolo et al., 1975). However caution must be exercised that one does not sacrifice internal for external validity (Neale and Liebert, 1973). Also with the increase in stimulus complexity we often lack the ability to resolve conflicting results. As reported earlier Fowler et al., (1974) did not find the OLFE with connected discourse whereas Cashen and Leicht (1970) did. The reason for the discrepancy is not at all clear and although Fowler et al., (1974) cite the earlier article they avoid any attempt at resolution. Details of the two studies (parts of speech isolated, position of isolation, study time, meaningfulness, concreteness, etc.) are either omitted entirely or are wholly incomparable. Caution must be used in interpreting studies which achieve realism at the cost of control but the situation here seems comparable to the experimental and correlational approaches to research. Each approach has its function and its limits and they can be mutually beneficial.

REFERENCES

Acredolo, L.P., Pick, H.L.Jr. and Olsen, M.G. (1975). Environmental differentiation and familiarity as determinants of children's memory for spatial location. *Developmental Psychology*, 11, 495-501.

Bone, R.N. and Goulet, L.R. (1968). Serial position and the von Restorff isolation effect. *Journal of Experimental Psychology*. 76, 494-496.

Butterfield, E.C., Wambold, C. and Belmont, J.M. (1973). On the theory and practice of improving short-term memory. *American Journal of Mental Deficiency*. 77, 654-669.

Calkins, M.W. (1894). Association. *Psychological Review*. 1, 476-483.

Cashen, V.M. and Leicht, K.L. (1970). Role of isolation effect in a formal educational setting. *Journal of Educational Psychology*. 61, 484-486.

Cermak, L.S. (1975). *Improving your memory*. Mc-Graw-Hill, New York.

Chapin, J.P. and Krawiec, T.S. (1974). *Systems and theories of psychology*. Holt, Rinehart and Winston, New York.

Cimbalo, R.S. (1971). Short-term memory: list length and the isolation effect. *Proceedings of the 79th Annual Convention of the American Psychological Association*, 6, 35-36.

Cimbalo, R.S., Brink, L., Nowak, B.I. and Soderstrom, J.A. (1978). Children and the aged are humans too!: the isolation effect and implications for a theory of human information processing. Unpublished manuscript, Daemen College, Buffalo, N.Y., 1978.

Cimbalo, R.S., Capria, R.A., Neider, L.L. and Wilkins, M.C. (1977). Isolation effect: overall list facilitation in short-term memory. *Acta Psychological*, 41, 419-432.

Cimbalo, R.S. and Mahoney, M.S. (1970). Short-term memory: effects of type of trigram isolated and position of isolation. *Psychonomic Science*. 18, 77-78.

Cimbalo, R.S., Nowak, B.I. and Stringfield, C. (in press). Isolation effect: overall list facilitation and debilitation in short-term memory. *Journal of General Psychology.*

Craik, F.I. and Lockhart, R.S. (1972). Levels of processing: A framework for memory research. *Journal of Verbal Learning and Verbal Behavior.* 11, 671-684.

Detterman, D.K. (1975). The von Restorff effect and induced amnesia: production by manipulation of sound intensity. *Journal of Experimental Psychology: Human Learning and Memory.* 1, 614-628.

Detterman, D.K. and Ellis, N.R. (1972). Determinants of induced amnesia in short-term memory. *Journal of Experimental Psychology.* 95, 308-316.

Einstein, G.O., Pellegrino, J.W., Mondani, M.S. and Battig, W.F. (1974). Free-recall performance as a function of overt rehearsal frequency. *Journal of Experimental Psychology.* 103, 440-449.

Flavell, J.H. Friedricks, A.G. and Hoyt, J.D. (1970). Developmental changes in memorization processes. *Cognitive Psychology.* 1, 324-340.

Fowler, R.L. and Barker, A.S. (1974). Effectiveness of highlighting for retention of text material. *Journal of Applied Psychology.* 59, 358-364.

Gumenik, W.E. and Levitt, J. (1968). The von Restorff effect as a function of difference of the isolated item. *American Journal of Psychology.* 81, 247-252.

Harlow, H.F., Gluck, J.P. and Suomi, S.J. (1972). Generalization of behavioral data between nonhuman and human animals. *American Psychologist.* 27, 709-716.

Huston, J.P. (1976). *Fundamentals of learning.* Academic Press, New York.

Klare, G.R., Mabry, J.E. and Gustafson, L.M. (1955). The relationship of patterning (underlining) to immediate retention and to acceptability of technical material. *Journal of Applied Psychology.* 39, 40-42.

McGhie, A. (1969). *Pathology of attention.* Penguin, Baltimore, Maryland.

Morton, N.W. (1941). The reciprocity of visual clearness and the span of apprehension. *American Journal of Psychology.* 54, 553-558.

Neale, J.M. and Liebert, R.M. (1973). *Science and behavior: an introduction to methods of research.* Prentice Hall, Englewood Cliffs, New Jersey.

Newman, S.E. and Jennette, A.D. (1975). The effects of set size on learning an item in the set. *American Journal of Psychology.* 88, 117-124.

Rosen, H., Richardson, D.H. and Saltz, E. (1962). Supplementary report: meaningfulness as a differentiation variable in the von Restorff effect. *Journal of Experimental Psychology*. 64, 327-328.

Smart, K.L. and Bruning, J.L. (1973). An examination of the practical import of the von Restorff effect. *Proceedings of the 81st Annual Convention of the American Psychological Assocation*. 8, 623-624.

Talland, G.A. (1968). Age and the span of immediate recall. In: *Human Aging and Behavior*. (G.A. Talland, ed.), pp.93-129. Academic Press, New York.

Wallace, W.P. (1965). Review of the historical, empirical, and theoretical status of the von Restorff phenomenon. *Psychological Bulletin*. 63, 410-424.

Waugh, N.C. and Norman, D.A. (1965). Primary memory. *Psychology Review*. 72, 89-104.

THE CHALLENGE OF PROBABILISTIC REASONING

John Fox
University of Sheffield.

Much of the reasoning that we engage in is about events that have not yet happened. Indeed the aim of our mental reasoning is often to reveal a probable future, or the most likely state of some corner of the world that we cannot directly observe. For example "will the shops be open later?" Memory has a direct role in such matters because it often throws up relevant, helpful information in a very timely way. How often have we answered our own questions, like the example of the shops, with some thought like "No, its Thursday afternoon"? The mystery of how knowledge appears so appropriately, like that of the English custom of half-day closing, is a current preoccupation of Cognitive Science. We want to be able to say something about the remarkable coordination that is achieved between these processes of "reasoning" and "recall".

How reasoners almost invariably recover relevant rather than irrelevant material from memory is a well-recognised theoretical problem. A second problem is less often aired. Consider the question "will the hardware store carry furniture polish?". One approach to explaining how we resolve this kind of uncertainty is to emphasise its problem-solving aspects - we "figure out" whether we are likely to find furniture polish by considering what hardware is, whether polish is hardware, and so on. But another common enough kind of strategy is to recall instances (of hardware stores) and to try to determine whether they had had things like polish. If most of them did, then it is likely that this particular store will also; if one can't think of ever seeing any, then it is unlikely that hardware stores carry furniture polish. If you accept my examples then it will be clear that our imaginary thinker is edging towards making "probability" assessments, in the sense that frequencies can be equated with probabilities. At any rate conclusions are being formed that might be described as probabilistic in nature - some hardware stores do stock polish, some don't, so we could say there is a *probability* that this particular store will have it. The curious thing is that as soon as you start talking about probability you find yourself in a quite different part of psychology, where your colleagues are preoccupied with things like data sampling, and "conservatism" and difficult mathematical formulae. Here no-one seems terribly interested in memory, networks, propositions about hardware stores, or how relationships are represented (probabilistic or otherwise) It doesn't seem obvious how these two equally important strands of the subject may be brought together.

A field of applied research where there is a considerable need to bring theories of memory and notions of probabilistic information processing together is the field of clinical reasoning. Our own area of interest is in trying to match computer-based decision aids to the cognitive faculties of clinicians, and we are committed to the view that a prerequisite of this is some understanding of those cognitive faculties. Clinical reasoning is deeply influenced by uncertainty - diseases don't always present the same symptoms, and patterns of symptoms don't always indicate the same disease. But when he is presented with a case history the clinician is usually successful in recalling, or at least figuring out, a sensible spectrum of diagnostic hypotheses, and some symptom or sign to distinguish the hypotheses will be recalled. Yet we know nothing of how probabilistic relationships are encoded or retrieved; all our models are for the deterministic case. Are reliable relationships recalled more quickly or more easily than unreliable ones? Doctors speak constantly of the "sensitivity" of a test (how often a positive result is produced given an underlying pathology) and the "specificity" of a symptom (how unique it is to a particular condition). These relationships clearly influence clinical judgement and thus must have some representation in clinical knowledge, but which of our theories tell us anything of the character of such representations? These questions are a serious challenge to our conceptions of memory.

PROBABILITY, AND SOME ASPECTS OF MEMORY

One of the classical interpretations of "probability" of course is that it is the formal equivalent of a generalisation from past events. If 70% of duodenal ulcer patients have complained of pains in the early morning then we may say that, if a patient has this sort of ulcer, the probability of such pains is 0.7. The clinician takes inductive steps of this kind, and he will predict that most duodenal ulcer patients will report this complaint. Indeed it is a clinical sign that he will set much store by in making his diagnoses; that is to say he knows that such pains are common after the condition is established (the sign is sensitive) and that they are much less likely with other conditions (the sign is quite specific to this condition).

How can we interpret these observations theoretically? One obvious approach is to think of clinical knowledge as essentially a prodigious collection of relationships between clinical entities - "network" theorists are beginning to acquire a substantial array of tools for the representation of such complex data-structures. It would seem rather natural to think of the knowledge of diseases and symptoms as "disease nodes" superordinate to "symptom nodes". (The symptoms in this case being those typical of the clinical picture of duodenal ulcer.) Even though clinical knowledge is vast and heterogeneous - it seems unlikely that everything clinical is reduceable to a simple hierarchy - the network theorist is untroubled. He will argue that the simple relational triple

(DUODENAL-ULCER associated-with NIGHT-WAKING)

is indeed simplistic, but that much more complex structures could be added if necessary without changing the basic approach. Such structures might elaborate this relationship in detail, implicating causal rather than mere assocation relationships, perhaps even specifying the reasons for pain as diurnal variation in acid secretion etc,. but the network character of the formalism is not altered. Where elaborations are needed in our model we simply replace the association link with a sub-network that expresses the clinical knowledge we need to capture. The network theorist can also cope with quantification of relationships ("*Most* cases of duodenal ulcer ...") by "labelling" his network. At least one recent theorist (Anderson, 1976) has added the concept of trace-strength to a network theory. Commonly traversed links, it is suggested, are strengthened by use. Thus the link specifying the relationship between duodenal ulcer and night-waking will be "stronger" than links to symptoms that are uncommon with this condition. Once this has been added to the model then we can give a theoretical account of one of our clinical concepts, sensitivity. We may predict that common symptoms will be recalled more quickly than rare ones (and that common diseases will come to mind more quickly than rare ones) and if we have some way of introspecting upon the strength of these relationships then we are within striking distance of understanding the cognitive basis of judgements of frequency and probability. So far, the theory fares well.

A theorist in another tradition, however, will observe that doctors do not merely make quantified comments about the frequencies of symptoms in patient populations, or the mechanisms of disease. With very little prodding he will tell you, in great detail, about his most "puzzling cases". His narratives are about individuals, not distilled descriptions summarising the statistical characteristics of patient populations; his clinical knowledge appears to record large amounts of information about particular patients. (Information about a patient may be recalled when the doctor is thinking of the patient himself, another member of his family, a patient with similar clinical problems and so on.) Clearly, then, an episodic aspect of memory is showing through; the doctor can recall *instances* as well as summary statistics, though with few exceptions our theories can tell us little about this ability. One exception is the "memory without organisation" proposed by Landauer (1975). Landauer describes a model of memory in which recall does not rely upon a tightly controlled search through a highly organised data-structure. Rather, a probe is broadcast through the memory, which consists of a relatively random collection of instances or events, in response to which data sufficiently like the probe will be returned. The formal property of this model, of course, is that it copes well with the ability to recall instances, but in making quantified statements like "most duodenal ulcer patients suffer from night-waking" the model is more unwieldy - it must rely heavily on separate cognitive processes. To judge that night-waking is more probable with duodenal ulcer than gastric ulcer for example, the judge would have to recall some instances of each kind of patient and then do something akin to counting. The cognitive processes would also have to ensure adequate control so that too many instances were not recalled, which would tend to make the count impossibly complex. On the other hand the network theorist has the advantage that he merely has to suppose that the strengths of the network links can be compared directly; the cognitive processes required are much less unwieldy.

Such judgements of relative probability are often central to clinical reasoning - about one third of patients with gall-bladder disease, for example, will report some symptom of jaundice, though this would be rare for patients with an ulcer condition, while in other respects the clinical pictures can be quite similar. To use the earlier term the symptom is very specific, and it is clear that doctors make use of the fact that jaundice is more probable for some conditions in making their differential diagnoses. How do the theories cope with this observation? I think the answer is that they do not cope with it directly but rely again on processes of inference, not memory processes, to give an account of the origin of the concept of specificity. Remember that current network models can directly express the relationships between diseases and symptoms, and the strengths of those relationships, but it is not clear how they would express differences between relationships, such as differences in the strengths of disease-symptom associations. Nor is it clear how emphasising the instance aspects of memory (or perhaps we might call it the "episodic" aspect) could easily capture such information. On this view even simple relationships between instances are not recorded in the memory but must be obtained via inference processes (a problem that is redoubled when we must derive relationships-between-relationships). To express the idea of specificity, then, the network and instance models resolve the difficulty most naturally by appealing to reasoning processes that *figure out* relationships-between-relationships; they are not encoded automatically in the memory.

Such views of memory are not fundamentally incompatible with the ability to express higher-order relationships. If one supposes that a particular relationship is brought to the attention of a doctor, just as medical text-books bring clinical knowledge to students' attention, then this can presumably be encoded as a network (or episode). We now know a new "fact" which is no different in principle from any other fact. The thing is that these relationships must be inferred, they do not, on these models, get picked up automatically by the memory encoding process. However one could conceive of a memory process in which such relationships *were* encoded automatically. On such a model, I shall call it an enhancement model, salient relationships, not merely common ones, would be enhanced. Taking our jaundice example, the overall probability of jaundice with gall-bladder disease is not great (asking about the symptom is not a very sensitive test for the disease) but if it should occur it is very significant. Many relationships in the world are like this so could we not expect our memory processes to emphasise salient features? Early writers on memory (e.g. Woodworth and Schosberg 1955 p.774) mentioned the phenomenon of "sharpening" of distinctive features of a stimulus in memory; superficially at least sharpening is a process that resembles the preferential encoding of salient relationships of an enhancement mechanism. The question is do we need such a mechanism for a complete view of memory, or can the identification and representation of salient relationships be left to other cognitive processes?

AN EMPIRICAL ANALYSIS OF SENSITIVITY AND SPECIFICITY

Some work we have done on simulated diagnosis has provided

data that can be turned onto this point. My hypothesis is that memory processes ensure that important information comes to mind more quickly than unimportant information. An obvious way of ensuring this is to arrange that material that is strongly associated, or is particularly pertinent or salient, is given priority during recall. Perhaps then some information about the representation of sensitivity and specificity can be obtained by asking people to retrieve clinical facts that differ on these dimensions.

In a recent study I asked a number of medical students to spend some time making simple differential diagnoses. There were five diseases and five symptoms that could be asked about. The relationships between the symptoms and the diseases were probabilistic - when a particular disease was present each symptom would be present on some proportion of occasions, but absent on others. The proportions were different for different dieseases and quite characteristic. A computer played the part of each "patient", decided for each problem what "disease" it was going to have, and answered questions about its symptoms on the basis of the probabilities in its database. Over a period of about one-two hours the medical students had considerable experience of the symptoms and diseases by carrying out 75 diagnostic problems. What I hoped to do, in part, was to encourage the students to build up a comprehensive and intimate knowledge of the relationships between the diseases and symptoms, by active use of the information during extensive problem-solving. A second part of the experiment probed this knowledge. The technique used for this was the well-known one of confirming or disconfirming facts (e.g. Anderson, 1974) where the facts in our case were of the form TONSILLITIS GOES WITH EARACHE (or randomly in the reverse order). Whether the subject agreed or disagreed with each proposition was recorded with a button-press, together with the time he took to make the decision. I was interested in how the strength of a disease-symptom association (sensitivity) affects speed of recall of that association, and how the salience of associations (the specificity or characteristicness of the symptoms) affects it, if at all. For example one symptom included in the task was vomiting, which was strongly associated with Hepatitis, moderately associated with Meningitis, and associated with nothing else. We might say, then, that vomiting is a symptom that is rather specific in this database - it is characteristic of Hepatitis and little else. On the other hand, a raised temperature could occur with all of the diseases (though it was more likely with some) so the symptom "raised temperature" may be said to be much less specific than the symptom "vomiting".

An analysis of variance of the response times for confirming and disconfirming the disease-symptom relationships showed a number of significant results, the most important being highly significant effects associated with the disease mentioned in the proposition and a highly significant interaction between the disease mentioned and the symptom mentioned. Curiously there was absolutely no effect associated with which symptom was probed in the proposition. This was in sharp contrast with the very considerable disease effect.

The first aspect of the data to be examined in detail is associated with the concept of sensitivity. Table 1 presents the mean decision times for the disease-symptom propositions (where these could be obtained) as a function of the strength of the relationship between the two. It can be seen from the table that as the probability of the symptom occurring becomes more extreme, the time for the subjects to confirm or disconfirm the proposition falls. This effect is quite dramatic, as it is of the order of half a second. The finding has two interpretations. The first interpretation is simply that as the strength of the link between the disease node and the symptom-present (or symptom-absent) node increases the link is more easily traversed, and retrieval of the association is achieved more quickly. Alternatively, we might interpret the finding as reflecting less conflict on the subject's part. If, on reading the proposition, the subject recalls both positive and negative instances of the symptom occurring with the disease then he may take some time deciding whether he should regard the symptom as "typical" or not. On the other hand if the symptom always occurs with the disease then all the instances will be alike and the cognitive decision process should find it easier to select the appropriate response. That is, both the "network" and the "instance" models are consistent with this finding. The main effect of disease is also consistent with both views; looked at as a network we simply assume that access to the "nodes" representing familiar diseases is easier, or on the instance view there would be more instances of familiar diseases (by definition) so on average an instance would be recovered more quickly from the memory.

Probability	0-.1	.2	.3	.4	.5	.6	.7	.8	.9	1.0
Decision time	91	114	-	129	123	123	-	116	101	84

Table 1: Mean times (cSecs) to confirm/disconfirm propositions as a function of strength of association of disease and symptom (Fox 1978).

Apparently then the probability of an association, whether high or low, has a substantial effect on the time to confirm the association; as we shall discuss in a moment this may have a significant effect on the nature of clinical reasoning.

The evidence for an effect of symptom *specificity* consistent with an enhancement component to the memory process is, on the other hand, poor. Firstly it was demonstrated that the choice of symptom mentioned in each probe proposition had *no* effect on speed of response, even though the task was designed in such a way that the specificity of the symptoms varied considerably. To return to our example, responses to propositions about the association of "elevated temperature" and the five diseases were not significantly slower than responses to propositions about relationships between the symptom "vomiting" and the five diseases - though the specificity of the latter symptom is much greater. Analysis of the salience of *individual* disease-symptom relationships, over and above the overall specificity of each symptom, also failed to show any relationship with decision-time (Table 2).

$\sum_{i=1}^{i=n} (P_a - P_i)^2 / n$	0-.1	.1-.2	.2-.3	.3-.4	.4-.5	.5-.6
Decision time	123	90	103	100	109	86

Table 2: Mean times (cSecs) to confirm/disconfirm propositions as a function of the salience of the disease-symptom association, measured by the function at top-left (P_a = association probability, p_i=the probability of the symptom occurring with each of the other n diseases. A detailed correlation (Kendall) of the two parameters was insignificant.

The original focus of the study was not memory as such but processes of decision-making under the influence of memory - that is how does the recall of material relevant to a decision influence the decision that is made? The aim was to model the diagnostic decision processes using rules specifying what the reasoner concluded under what conditions. As discussed earlier, thought processes reflect a fluent synchrony of processes of inference and the timely recall of relevant information, so how should we conceive of the recall process that supports the use of these rules? This turned out to be quite critical. If we took a model resembling Landauer's, in which a recall probe is broadcast throughout a loosely organised set of instances of disease-symptom associations we obtained a highly satisfactory account of the subjects' decision behaviour in the diagnostic task. If on the other hand we assumed a tightly controlled search through a complex data-structure such as a disease-symptom hierarchy, the performance of the decision model collapsed. The critical difference between the two approaches was that to treat the data as a hierarchy demanded a rigid scheme of retrieving disease data, viz disease by disease. That is to say all the knowledge relevant to one disease hypothesis would "come to mind" before any knowledge of other hypotheses, while the looser organisation could return a rich mixture of relevant facts about disease-symptom associations, in response to a globally broadcast probe. To summarize, the model took the times to confirm or disconfirm disease-symptom associations in the memory study as a direct measure of the *availability* of the knowledge of these relationships. Under such an assumption simple, non-probabilistic rules gave a very satisfactory model of the subjects' decision behaviour. Substituting more complex retrieval assumptions (or classical probabilistic schemes) only served to degrade the effectiveness of the model.

For this task then, and this method of probing the medical students' knowledge, the evidence seems to support the idea that the clinical notion of "sensitivity" of a symptom is reflected in speed of recall, but that the notion of "specificity" is not. A tentative conclusion from this is that the concept of specificity of a symptom is not one that derives from some enhancement mechanism embodied in the memory system, but from the cognitive reasoning processes that make use of this system. In addition the findings from the decision study suggest that the decision processes are greatly influenced by the speed with which the relevant information is recalled, and that recall of this type of data more strongly reflects a loose collection of instances than the tight relational structure that is evident in the deterministic tasks that are more commonly used in the laboratory. How these different aspects of memory interact with other tasks, deterministic or probabilistic, is a topic worthy of further investigation.

ACKNOWLEDGEMENTS

Thanks to Vicki G. Bruce and Rod Nicholson for their comments on earlier drafts.

REFERENCES

Anderson, J.R. (1974). "Retrieval of propositional information from long-term memory", *Cognitive Psychology*, 6, 451-74.

Anderson, J.R. (1976). *Language, Memory and Thought*, Hillsdale, New Jersey: Lawrence Erlbaum Associates.

Fox, J. (1978). "Making decisions under the influence of memory", *MRC Social and Applied Psychology Unit, Sheffield University, Memo 177*.

Landauer, T.K. (1975). "Memory without organization: some properties of a model with random storage and undirected retrieval", *Cognitive Psychology*, 7, 495-531.

Woodworth, R.S. and Schlosberg, H., (1935). *Experimental Psychology, (Third Edition)*, London: Methuen.

MEMORY FOR MEDICAL INFORMATION

Philip Ley
Plymouth Polytechnic
Plymouth Devon

PATIENTS' FORGETTING AND ITS CORRELATES

Studies of the amount of information given to them that is not recalled by patients are summarized in Table 1.

TABLE 1

Patients' recall of information presented by doctors

Investigation	Type of Patient	% recalled
1. Ley & Spelman (1965)	47 medical out-patients	63
2. Ley & Spelman (1967)	a) 22 medical out-patients	61
	b) 22 medical out-patients	59
3. Joyce *et al*. (1969)	a) 30 out-patients	48
	b) 24 out-patients	46
4. Ley, Bradshaw *et al*.(1973)	20 general practice patients	50
5. Ley, Whitworth *et al*.(1976)	157 general practice patients	56

Attempts to discover individual difference correlates of forgetting have investigated age, intelligence, anxiety and medical knowledge. Ley and Spelman (1967) found no consistent relationship between age and recall, but Ley, Whitworth *et al*.(1976) and Joyce *et al*.(1969) did find significantly less recall by older patients. While intelligence does not seem to be related to recall, patients with more medical knowledge recall more of what the doctor says than those with less, and there appears to be a curvilinear relationship of the Yerkes-Dodson type between anxiety level and forgetting (Ley and Spelman 1967). Amount of information presented is related to recall. In the four samples of patients studied by Ley and Spelman (1965, 1967) and Ley, Bradshaw et al.(1973) a significant linear relationship was found between number of statements presented and number of statements not recalled. This is also true of the analogue experiments reported by Ley and Spelman (1967) and Ley (1972). For the patient samples the linear regression equation to predict forgetting is: $Y=0.56X-0.94$, where X is the number of statements made by the doctor, and Y is the number forgotten by the patient.

The type of medical statement also appears to be related to its probability of recall. Ley and Spelman (1965) found that diagnostic statements tended to be best recalled and that statements concerned with instructions and advice were worst recalled. Significantly poorer recall of instructions and advice was also found by Ley, Whitworth et al.(1976), but not by Ley, Bradshaw et al.(1973), although in this last study the differences were in the right direction but not significantly so. The finding is not a universal one, e.g. Joyce et al.(1969), and in any case seems to be due largely to a primacy and/or "importance" effect. It was noticed that the clinician involved in the Ley and Spelman (1965) study tended to present the diagnosis first to his patients, then to present other information, and then to give his advice. This suggested that the poor recall of instructions and advice might be due to a primacy effect. Analogue experiments with volunteer subjects confirmed the existence of a primacy effect in recall of medical information (Ley, 1972).

The "importance" hypothesis was a common sense one. It seemed likely that given that patients received more information than they could recall they would best recall what they considered to be most important. It followed from this and the findings on differential forgetting of the various types of medical information, that (1) there should be differences in perceived importance of medical statements and (2) their perceived importance should be correlated with the probability of their being recalled. Ley (1969) showed that laymen considered diagnostic statements, instruction-advice statements and other statements to differ significantly in importance; with the diagnostic statements being regarded as the most, and instructions-advice as the least important, and Ley (1972) showed that rated importance was correlated with probability of recall.

CONTROL OF FORGETTING I: CONTENT OF FORGETTING

Given that statements presented first, and that statements considered more important were better recalled, it was possible to control forgetting of instructions and advice. Recall of these statements should be increased either by presenting them before other information or by stressing their importance. Ley (1972) investigated these possibilities in an out-patient setting with the result summarized in Table 2, both placing instructions first and stressing their importance led to significant increases in recall.

TABLE 2

Recall of instructions and advice according to the method of presenting them

Method	*Mean % Recalled*
1. Usual	50.3
2. Instructions and advice prescribed first	87.3
3. Importance of instructions and advice stressed	68.8

CONTROL OF FORGETTING II: AMOUNT OF INFORMATION RECALLED

Although the use of the primacy effect, and stressing their importance, increased recall of instructions and advice it made no difference to the overall amount recalled by patients. Fortunately four methods for increasing total recall have been discovered to be effective. These are (1) the use of shorter words and sentences, (2) explicit categorisation, (3) repetition and (4) the use of concrete-specific rather than general-abstract statements.

The first of these methods derived from the evidence produced by Korsch and her colleagues (Korsch et al.,1971), and Ley, Goldman et al.(1973) that information presented to patients is likely to be too difficult for them to understand. Ley, Goldman et al.(1973) had used Flesch's Reading Ease Formula to estimate the difficulty level of x-ray leaflets issued to patients. The Flesch Formula implicates word and sentence lengths as the chief predictors of the proportion of the population who will understand presented material. In view of this and the known relationship between meaningfulness and recall it seemed reasonable to assess the effects of the use of shorter words and shorter sentences on recall of medical information. Results of experiments on this topic by Ley, Goldman et al.(1973) and Bradshaw et al.(1975) are summarized in Table 3.

TABLE 3

Recall of medical information varying in comprehensibility as measured by the Flesch Formula

Investigation	Material	% Recalled	p
Ley, Goldman et al.(1973)	a) barium meal leaflet	Easy 73 Hard 78	ns
	b) cholecystrogram leaflet	Easy 79 Hard 59	<.01
Bradshaw et al. (1975)	a) diet instructions	Easy 31 Hard 24	<.25
	b) diet instructions	Easy 43 Hard 25	<.05
	c) diet instructions	Easy 40 Hard 27	<.01

The second technique-explicit categorization - was based loosely, (perhaps over-inclusively), on research findings concerning the effects of organizational factors on recall. The technique consists of the clinician presenting the information to patients in categories, which he has announced in advance. For example he might say:

"I am going to tell you:
What is wrong with you;
What tests we are going to carry out;
What I think will happen to you;
What treatment you will need;
What you must do to help yourself;
First what is wrong with you...........................
Second what tests we are going to carry out.............
Thirdly what I think will happen to you.................
Fourthly what treatment you will need...................
Fifthly what you must do to help yourself..............

Explicit categorization is contrasted with implicit categorization, where the material is organized in the same way as in explicit categorization, but the doctor does not announce the categories. Results obtained by Ley, Bradshaw, Eaves and Walker (1973) (see Table 4) and several unpublished analogue studies show that use of explicit categorization usually leads to increased recall of medical information.

TABLE 4

The effects of their Doctors' Use of Explicit Categorization on Patients' Recall of Medical Information

Technique used by Doctor	Percent recalled of: Diagnostic statements	Instructions and advice	Other Statements
Normal	61	28	46
Explicit categorization	67	65	70

Repeating things seemed to be another possible way of increasing recall of medical information. Surprisingly the effects of repetition on recall were not nearly as consistent as might have been expected. In studying recall of x-ray leaflets Ley, Goldman et al.(1973) found no better recall after two or three repetitions than after one, and analogue experiments also show a lack of consistent large effects.

Serendipity was responsible for the fourth method. In the study by Ley (1969) of rated importance of different categories of medical information, it was noticed that some apparently similar advice statements received very different importance ratings. Closer inspection showed that the statement receiving the higher rating was in all cases a more definite, concrete, specific version of the other. For example the general version might be: "You must lose weight, and the specific "You must lose 7 lbs. in weight"; or the general version might be "You need regular holidays"; and the specific "Take two full weeks holiday a year."

This suggested that specificity might be correlated with perceived importance, and thus with the probability of recall. To test the hypothesis that specific statements would be better recalled than general ones Bradshaw et al. (1975) performed three experiments on recall of dietary instructions for the obese. Their results are shown in Table 5.

TABLE 5

Recall of specifically and generally phrased instructions about dieting

Subjects	Mean % Recalled General	Mean % Recalled Specific	p
1. 40 volunteers given *both* general and specific statements	10.3	45.0	$<.001$
2. 32 volunteers given *either* general *or* specific statements	19.0	49.0	$<.001$
3. 44 obese females given *either* general *or* specific statements	16.0	51.0	$<.001$

More indirect proof that these methods can increase recall of medical information is provided by Ley, Whitworth *et al* .(1976). A manual containing suggestions for improving communication in ways likely to increase patients' recall was prepared. In essence it was based on the findings outlined above and made six suggestions:

(1) Give instructions and advice before other information
(2) Stress the importance of the instructions and advice you give
(3) Use short words and short sentences
(4) Use explicit categorization where possible
(5) Repeat information
(6) Give specific detailed advice rather than general rules

Recall of information by patients of four general practitioners was monitored for a period before the doctors had read the manual, and then for a period after they had read it and tried to put its suggestions into effect. Significant differences in the amounts recalled by patients were found, and are shown in Table 6.

TABLE 6

Patients' recall of information presented by G.P.s (1) before and (2) after the doctors had started to use procedures designed to increase recall

Doctor	Mean proportion recalled by patients (1) Before	(2) After
A	.52	.61
B	.56	.70
C	.57	.73
D	.59	.80
Type of Patient		
Child	.62	.73
Adult	.58	.70
Elderly	.42	.64

Finally, it is worth mentioning that these techniques may have an effect on patients' compliance. Ley, Jain and Skilbeck (1976) found that leaflets using short words and sentences were very effective in reducing patients' medication errors, and Ley (1977) reports an experiment in which a booklet on weight loss using short words and sentences; explicit categorization and repetition led to a mean weight loss of 15 lbs. in a group of obese women as opposed to the mean weight loss of 8 lbs. in a group who read an ordinary booklet, (but see Ley, 1978 for some less encouraging results).

REFERENCES

Bradshaw, P.W., Ley, P., Kincey, J.A., and Bradshaw, J. (1975). Recall of medical advice: comprehensibility and specificity. *British Journal of Social and Clinical Psychology*, 14, 55-62.

Joyce, C.R.B., Caple, G., Mason, M., Reynolds, E., and Matthews, J.A. (1969). Quantitative study of doctor-patient communication. *Quarterly Journal of Medicine*, 38, 193-194.

Korsch, B., Freeman, B., and Negrete, V. (1971). Practical implications of doctor-patient interactions: analysis for pediatric practice. *American Journal of Diseases of Children*, 121, 110-114.

Ley, P. (1969). *Memory aspects of doctor-patient communication*. University of Liverpool: Unpublished Ph.D. thesis.

Ley, P. (1972). Primacy, rated importance and recall of medical information. *Journal of Health and Social Behaviour*, 13, 311-317.

Ley, P. (1977). Psychological studies of doctor-patient communication. In S. Rachman (Ed) *Contributions to Medical Psychology, I*. Oxford: Pergamon Press.

Ley, P. (1978) Psychological and behavioural factors in weight loss. In G.A. Bray (Ed.) *Recent advances in obesity research, II*. London: Newman Publishing.

Ley, P., Bradshaw, P.W., Eaves, D.E., and Walker, C.M. (1973). A method for increasing patients recall of information presented to them. *Psychological Medicine*, 3, 217-220.

Ley, P., Goldman, M., Bradshaw, P.W., Kincey, J.A., and Walker, C.M. (1973). The comprehensibility of some x-ray leaflets. *Journal of the Institute of Health Education*, 10, 47-55.

Ley, P., Jain, V.K., and Skilbeck, C.E. (1976). A method for decreasing patients medication errors. *Psychological Medicine*, 6, 599-601.

Ley, P., and Spelman, M.S. (1965) Communications in an out-patient setting. *British Journal of Social and Clinical Psychology*, 4, 114-116.

Ley, P., and Spelman, M.S. (1967). *Communicating with the patient*. London: Staples Press.

Ley, P., Whitworth, M.A., Skilbeck, C.E., Woodwarward, R., Pinsent, R.J.F.H., Pike, L.A., Clarkson, M.E., and Clark, P.B. (1976). Improving doctor-patient communication in general practice. *Journal of the Royal College of General Practitioners*, 26, 720-724.

ACKNOWLEDGEMENTS

The research described in this paper was made possible by research grants from the Department of Health and Social Security and the Health Education Council. This financial assistance is gratefully acknowledged.

RECALLING MESSAGES BROADCAST TO THE GENERAL PUBLIC

W.A. Wagenaar
Institute for Perception TNO
Soesterberg, The Netherlands

1. ABSTRACT

Messages broadcast to the general public, such as weather forecasts or traffic reports, are poorly recalled even shortly after presentation. It is shown that this problem arises from the typical composition of such messages which forces the listener to store and reproduce the message just as a list of nonsense material. In such cases no more then ten idea units can be reproduced, and these may even be quite meaningless, out of their proper context. Some practical suggestions are made for the improvement of this situation.

2. INTRODUCTION

When you ring the bell of any Dutch home at 8.30 p.m. the odds are ten to one that the person opening the door will have just heard the weather forecast. Ninety percent of the people thus interrogated will tell you that they could not miss the weather forecast, that it is clear and not too short nor too long. However, when asked what the forecast was they stand dumbfounded; they either do not give you any answer at all, or they give you a highly inaccurate or even completely erroneous representation.

Here we clearly have a practical problem: people cannot reproduce a message broadcast for their use. It is questionable whether this practical problem is related to memory. It is not unlikely that for some people the weather forecast is just entertainment; such people would not even attempt to process and store the information presented. This explanation does not fit in with the observation that 62% of the population attach a more than average importance to the weather forecast. Another explanation for the low reproducibility of weather forecasts would be that listeners translate the information into actions to be taken, such as watering the garden, and subsequently forget the original information. This explanation is incompatible with two observations. One is that only 6% of the people indicate that they sometimes listen in to the broadcast for any special reason; the remaining listeners hear the forecast just because they consider weather information very interesting in itself. The second observation is that many recollections are essentially unrelated to the original message, thus indicating that the verbal response is not a reconstruction based on specific actions stored in memory. A third explanation would state that people generally have insufficient intelligence to understand the forecast. This is in part true, as appeared from the extremely low familiarity with the Weather Bureau's jargon, but this explanation is invalidated by the observation that even highly intelligent people have great trouble when they try to recall the weather forecast.

I will not go on offering all sorts of explanations for the fact that people cannot remember what the weather forecast is; rather I will propose one explanation and give some reasons why I feel this explanation is valid. My arguments are based on two types of broadcastings, viz. the weather forecast and the radio traffic report. Let me first give examples of both.

Forecast for tonight and tomorrow. In the evening in the southern part of the country a good deal of cloud, with in the southeastern region some temporary rain, otherwise some cloudless periods but tomorrow in the afternoon some local showers, especially in the northern and western regions. Wind moderate to strong, along the coast occasionally high to stormy, earlier from the southwest, later veering to the northwest. Minimum temperatures about 10⁰ C, on the Wadden Shallows a few degrees higher. Maximum temperatures from 16⁰ C in the northwest to 22⁰ C in the southeastern regions.

Note a few details. The message looks a bit like normal prose, but the sentences do not contain verbs. No references are made to present weather conditions. Points of the compass are used to indicate wind directions and regions of the country. Some statements are extremely complicated; e.g. the phrase beginning with 'otherwise' indicates that there are no clouds tonight in any region except the south and southeast nor tomorrow in any region except the north and west. The message contains 32 idea units (Bransford & Johnson, 1972) which is not unusual.

On the following roads traffic jams are reported. A2 Den Bosch in the direction of Utrecht, between Culemborg and Vianen, a jam of 6 km. A27 Gorkum in the direction of Vianen, between Lexmond and Vianen, a jam of 3 km. A29 Hellegatsplein

in the direction of Rotterdam, at the entrance of Heinenoord-tunnel, a jam of 2 km. (Another five of such messages).
On the highway Boskoop-Bleiswijk-Rotterdam slow-downs are to be expected in both directions; the road is blocked at Bleiswijk till 9 p.m.; drivers are advised to use the alternative route via Zoetermeer if necessary. Traffic on the A27 should allow for some delays in both directions due to repair works at Keizersveer Bridge. In the northern regions slippery roads are to be expected.

Note that this message is extremely long (70 idea units); also that the information covers the whole country and that a correct understanding depends on a quite detailed geographical knowledge.

The history of memory research has shown two quite distinct traditions: memory for nonsense material, as it was started by Ebbinghaus (1885), and memory for meaningful prose, first studied in detail by Bartlett (1932). These two traditions remained separated mainly because the processes involved were thought to differ widely. Retrieval of nonsense material was described as a *reproduction* of lists as they are stored, whereas the recall of prose was thought to involve *reconstruction* on the basis of a 'schema' and some abstracted details (Hasher & Griffin, 1978). One of the objections against Ebbinghaus' procedures was that nonsense material does not allow reconstruction processes, that therefore the material has no ecological validity and that the picture of memory thus obtained must be quite unrealistic. I will argue that messages as shown above are processed by the receivers very much in the same way as lists of nonsense material, that the body of knowledge obtained in this tradition is quite relevant for my practical problem and that, in fact, the low reproducibility of these messages is to be attributed to the limitations of memory for nonsense material.

As all experiments discussed in this paper are published separately in full detail (Wagenaar & Visser, 1977, 1978 and *in press*) and in order to save considerable space the method and results sections will be kept rather short and informal.

3. METHOD

(a) *Subjects*

The subjects were male and female students from the State University of Utrecht, and employees of the Institute for Perception. Specific characteristics such as level of education and driving experience are indicated in the results section, when appropriate.

(b) *Material*

The messages consisted of normal forecasts as they are issued by the Dutch Weather Bureau, and traffic reports as they are provided by the Police Office. The length of the messages was varied from 12 to 32 idea units (weather forecasts) and 15 to 70 idea units (traffic reports). These ranges are representative of message length encountered in reality. The traffic reports were constructed in such a way as to always contain 12 idea units relevant to a particular route (say from Amsterdam to Eindhoven).

(c) *Apparatus*

The messages were read into a tape recorder by a professional newscaster. The presentation of the messages to subjects occurred in a normal office room; ambient noise was kept at a low level, but was not completely excluded. The subjects responded by writing on a response sheet containing category tags *clouds, precipitation, wind direction, wind force, minimum temperature, maximum temperature* in case of weather forecasts, and *road nr, cities bordering the stretch of road, location of the jam, length of the jam, messages on delays, obstructions, works carried out, messages on road conditions* in the case of traffic reports. Thus the recall was cued rather than free, which may have had some facilitating effects (Mandler, 1967).

(d) *Procedure*

Specific procedural variables are discussed in the results section,

(e) *Statistical analysis*

No statistical test will be mentioned in the results section, but all differences mentioned were statistically significant, as is shown in the separate reports of the experiments. All differences were tested by means of various ANOVA designs.

4. RESULTS

(a) *Effects of message length*

These results are based on 75 subjects, employees of the Institute, each presented with one message only (weather forecasts) and 50 subjects, students, each presented with one message only (traffic reports).

Effects of message length, as shown in Table 1, seem to be quite different in weather forecasts and traffic reports. In weather forecasts we observed a ceiling of about eight units

Table 1. Effects of message length

Weather forecasts			Traffic reports		
Message length	Idea units reproduced		Message length	Idea units reproduced	
	raw	%		raw	%
12	5.4	45	15	8.4	56
17	6.8	40	25	8.5	34
22	9.4	43	40	10.6	26
27	8.1	30	55	13.6	25
32	8.2	26	70	17.0	24

reproduced when lists length increased, whereas of the traffic reports up to 17 items can be reproduced. In the weather forecast experiment Miller's magical number 7 ± 2 seems to apply nicely (Miller, 1956) whereas this is definitely not the case in the traffic report experiment. Still it should be emphasized that the higher scores occurred only with extremely long messages, and that the scores are quite poor percentagewise: after an initial 50% the scores drop to about 25% with list length 70. The percentage scores are far below scores normally obtained in recall of prose studies. Bartlett obtained a fair 60% in first reproductions of the 'war of ghosts' story; Crouse (1971) and Anderson & Bower (1973) report 60% performance with biographical stories.

(b) *Effect of level of education*

In the weather forecast experiments two types of subjects were employed: with and without academic background. In fact the occupational level ranged from department heads to cleaning ladies. The overall scores for the two groups were 8.4 and 6.9 respectively; Miller's magical margins were not surpassed by the sophisticated subjects.

In the traffic information experiments subjects with and without a driving licence were used. Their overall scores were 13.6 and 9.9 respectively. This difference, which was quite significant, shows that the scores above 7 + 2 were largely due to subjects with a driving licence.

(c) *Which information is not reproduced?*

The idea units in the weather forecasts can be divided into two categories: primary information, such as *rain, sunny spells, storm*, and secondary information such as *possibly, along the coast, during the night*. The reproduction scores reached an average 46% for primary units and 18% for secondary units, and this difference was independent of message length. The longer messages contained a larger portion of secondary units and that is why the scores did not increase in proportion with list length.

The information contained in the traffic reports can be roughly subdivided as is shown in Table 2. This table shows

Table 2. Scores for four categories of information in the traffic reports experiment.

Categories	Scores for subjects with driving licence	Scores for subjects without driving licence
Road nr.	35%	34%
Cities	51%	34%
Location of jam	61%	30%
Length of jam	29%	22%

that the subjects with a driving licence derived their higher score from a better reproduction of locations and city names. Road numbers and lengths of jams were discarded as secondary information.

(d) *Effects of selectivity*

Sometimes people are not interested in all of the weather forecast, or all of the nationwide traffic report, and it could indeed be argued that a 'total recall' instruction is quite unrealistic. Therefore it was asked whether instructions to select certain parts of the message would improve the performance. The results are based on 75 subjects, employees of the Institute, each presented with one message (weather forecasts) and 50 subjects, students, each presented with four messages (traffic reports).

In the weather forecast experiment subjects were instructed before presentation of the message to reproduce only information relevant for the central regions of the country (where they were all living). The results show that the performance drops to an average of 5.4 units. Expressed as percentages of the total number of relevant units presented we find no positive effects of selective listening: 52% for primary units and 19% for secondary units.

In the traffic report experiment subjects were instructed to reproduce information relevant for a certain route. This instruction was given either before or after the presentation of the message. Out of 12 relevant units per message 6.6 were reproduced by subjects with a driving licence, when they received the instruction prior to presentation of the message.

When the instruction was given after presentation of the message the score dropped to 3.9 units.

5. DISCUSSION

What is the general picture emerging from these data? First it should be noted that the two types of messages were not always processed in the same manner. Whereas the raw scores never surpassed 7 + 2 in the weather forecast experiments, this cannot be said about the scores for traffic reports: subjects with a driving licence obtained quite high scores. Presumably these scores were obtained by using a background familiarity with places where traffic jams are likely to occur, and by employing the redundancy in the message: an experienced driver will know that there is always a jam at Vianen Bridge, that Vianen is situated along a motorway (A) with a specific number (2) and that the stretch of this motorway is between Utrecht and Den Bosch. Thus he could get five idea units correct by a mere guess. A similar effect of guessing is not easily envisaged for weather reports: there is no 'schema' that, if stored, permits a reasonable reconstruction. Thus weather forecasts are a bit like nonsense material, while traffic reports are more like meaningful prose, allowing a fair amount of reconstruction activity.

In both types of messages listeners are forced to store only some hightlights. These highlights are locations of jams in the traffic reports and primary units in weather forecasts. The latter choice can be quite detrimental to the understanding of the message. Although 'rain' is mentioned in 70% of the forecasts in Holland, there is no place where rain will fall on more than 30% of the days. Therefore 'rain' is always accompanied by limiting modifiers such as *possibly, now and then, in some places*. The listener, not storing these modifiers, will find that the Weather Bureau erroneously predicted rain in the majority of cases!

Another difference between weather forecasts and traffic reports becomes evident from the results of the selectivity experiments. Recall of the weather forecast is not improved by paying attention to relevant parts of the message. The reason why must be that the weather forecasts are phrased in such a complicated manner that selective storage can occur only after a thorough analysis of the text. There is no time for such an analysis during presentation; the listener is forced to store the whole message and do the selection afterwards. Then he will find that some of the units stored were in fact irrelevant, and the number of units reproduced will fall below 7.

The effect of selection was much better in the traffic report experiment. The performance at about 30% when no selection instruction was given (Table 1) was increased to over 50% when selection instructions were given prior to presentation. This improvement could occur because the traffic report is phrased in a simple manner, enabling a quick distinction between relevant and irrelevant units. Together with the observation that it is quite sufficient to store the location of a jam, it is no surprise that experienced drivers were relatively good at recalling relevant parts of the traffic report.

The main conclusion must be that recall of messages is generally poor when the message is processed just like nonsense material. Recall is much better when the material allows for such processes as selection prior to storage and reconstruction in the recall stage.

6. PRACTICAL CONSEQUENCES

From the foregoing it is clear that messages broadcast to the general public should be composed in such a way as to promote selection and reconstruction processes. Therefore it is recommended to provide a general schema that can be easily remembered. The forecast presented in section 2 has a schema that could be phrased like this: *the present wind will bring some cloudless periods, but tomorrow the situation will change when a strong northwestern wind will bring rain and lower temperatures.* Further details can be easily attached to this structure. If such schemata cannot be found it should not be attempted to present the whole bulk of information, since the listener will not store more than a few highlights. The Weather Bureau should rather itself select these highlights in such a way that the information presented is, although not so detailed, essentially correct. In a similar way it could prove quite effective not to include road numbers and lengths of jams in traffic reports. Also long messages should be constructed in such a way that selection of relevant clauses is facilitated. In the case of the weather forecast this could be effectuated by splitting up the message into regional forecasts. The example in the introduction could easily be divided into one forecast for the northern and western regions, and one for the remaining parts of the country. Lists of traffic jams could be ordered according to regions, instead of the haphazard ordering used at the moment.

A large number of further recommendations has been made to the authorities sponsoring this research. They are of minor importance, however, compared to the general lesson to be learned: messages presented to the public should be composed such that they can be more sophisticatedly processed than nonsense material.

7. REFERENCES

Anderson, J.R. and Bower, G.H. (1973). *Human associative memory*. Winston, Washington D.C.

Bartlett, F.C. (1932). *Remembering: A study in experimental and social psychology*. Cambridge University Press, Cambridge, U.K.

Bransford, J.D. and Johnson, M.K. (1972). Contextual prerequisites for understanding: Some investigations of comprehension and recall. *Journal of Verbal Learning and Verbal Behavior*, 11, 717-726.

Crouse, J.H. (1971). Retroactive interference in reading prose materials. *Journal of Educational Psychology*, 62, 39-44.

Ebbinghaus, H.E. (1885). *Memory: A contribution to experimental psychology*. Dover, New York. (Translated in 1913)

Hasher, L. and Griffin, M. (1978). Reconstructive and Reproductive Processes in Memory. *Journal of Experimental Psychology: Human Learning and Memory*, 4, 318-330.

Mandler, G. (1967). Organization and memory. In: *The psychology of learning and motivation*. Vol. 1 (K.W. Spence and J.T. Spence, eds) pp327-372. Academic Press, New York.

Miller, G.A. (1956). The magical number seven, plus or minus two: some limits on our capacity for processing information. *Psychological Review*, 63, 81-97.

Wagenaar, W.A. and Visser, J.G. (1977). Recalling the weather report. *Institute for Perception, Report nr.* 1977-C10.

Wagenaar, W.A. and Visser, J.G. (1978). Distilling information from broadcast road information reports. *Institute for Perception, Report nr.* 1978-C5.

Wagenaar, W.A. and Visser, J.G. (in press). The weather report under the weather. Accepted for publication by *Ergonomics*.

INFLUENCE OF SCROLLING UP ON THE RECALL OF TEXTS

G. Oléron and H. Tardieu
Ecole Pratique des Hautes Etudes
Université René Descartes, Paris, France

1. ABSTRACT

To test the influence of scrolling up on the recall of seven sentences forming or not a text, three modalities of presentation (constant duration 21s) were used : one sentence after the other, at a time on a line, is scrolled up upon the screen ; the seven sentences are presented simultaneously and immediately scrolled up ; in the third condition (control) all the sentences were non-moving.

The influence of scrolling up is independent of the level of abstraction of the sentences (three levels). There is an interaction between the modalities of scrolling up and the three levels of organization of the sentences, when the number of sentences correctly recalled is considered.

2. INTRODUCTION

Immediate recall of sentences of an abstract text is harder than of sentences of a concrete text. The way these sentences are organized affects the recall of the two types of texts.

What happens when the information-gathering process is made more difficult when, for example, the sentences are scrolled on a screen from the bottom up ?

On the one hand, obliging the eyes to read both horizontally and vertically at the same time disturbs the act of gathering information. It has been shown how isolated words are less well recalled when scrolled from the bottom up (Oléron, Rossi, Tardieu, 1977).

On the other hand, the very fact of complicating the gathering of information can induce an added effort on the reader's part, thereby facilitating recall : is there, then, a certain compensation to be found ?

It can be hypothethized that in the case of very simple sentences (none longer than one line on a screen) with a constant presentation time, recall will be less with scrolling up than with a non-moving text. Presumably, too, the more organized the text, the more scrolling up will disturb immediate recall.

For this experiment we studied two modalities of scrolling up, each with a constant presentation time. In the first, each sentence is presented singly, moving across the screen ; the next sentence does not appear until the last one has disappeared. In the second modality, the whole text is scrolled at once.

We used three kinds of text, which can be fitted on an abstract-concrete axis: abstract, descriptive, narrative. All are composed of seven direct transitive (Subject, Verb, Object) "kernel" sentences. These texts present three levels of organization : sentences with no relation between one another ; sentences based on a theme ; sentences which tell a story with a logical-temporal connection.

It is hypothetized that on account of the scrolling there will be an interaction between the effect of the modality of scrolling and the type of organization of the text : the higher the degree of textual organization, the more scrolling will disturb recall.

The index for describing the extent of the recall will be the exactness of the sentences recalled. This extent obtained during scrolling, will be compared to the extent of recall of a non-moving text. This will be the control situation.

3. EXPERIMENT CONDITIONS

(a) *Presentation technique*

The non-moving or scrolled sentences printed in lower case, appear on demand on the Velec monitor screen with the aid of a T1600 computer. Constant contrast between text and background was selected and maintained. This, the preference of several judges as being most pleasing to the eye, was a white text on a dark gray background. The subject is 1.50 m from the screen. Each line of text is centered on the screen.

Presentation time, for each of the three conditions, is 21 seconds per text.

The first scrolled presentation is a quasi-scrolling : each sentence stays motionless for a duration which varies according to the conditions, then moves to the next line.

The screen scanning employs a 24 line displacement from bottom to top.

For the scrolling of the text as a whole, the sentences are shown on the bottom seven lines of the screen, beneath a frame and immediately begin to scroll upwards over the next 17 lines, each line lasting 813 ms.

For the sentence by sentence scrolling, each sentence stays on the bottom line for 150 ms, and scrolls up the next 23 lines. Then it is replaced by the next sentence.

And last, for the non-moving presentation, the text remains motionless for 21 seconds.

(b) *The material : the texts*

There are nine texts of seven sentences. Each sentence has a subject, a verb and an object, with the necessary articles before the two nouns. These sentences have the following characteristics :

(i) *variable organization.*
- no semantic or phonetic relation between the sentence : Ø
- all the sentences relate to the same semantic theme : $\overline{0}$
- each of the seven sentences depends on the preceding sentence in the semantic development of the text : 0

(ii) *variable of abstraction.* There are three levels of abstraction chosen : the texts are either Narrative (N), Descriptive (D) or Abstract (A).

(iii) *examples of sentences.*
- AØ : war fosters hatred
  the world wants justice
- D$\overline{0}$: the waterfall wears away the rock
  the rain soaks the sidewalk
- N0 : the plough digs the furrow
  the farmer sows seed-corn

(c) *The experiment*

The subject first undergoes a training session with a text in the condition of the experiment. This text will always be the same. The subject himself triggers the appearance of the text.

The subject is instructed to remember as many complete sentences as he can. Later he indicates the isolated lexical elements he can recall.

The nine texts are presented in different order, counterbalanced for all of the 18 subjects for an experimental condition.

There are three groups of subjects for the three experimental conditions : GI is for the text with non-moving presentation (I), GII has the text with sentence by sentence scrolling (Pd) and GIII has the scrolled up text (Td).

Recall is made by the subject orally. In the analysis of the results we noted the number of correct sentences recalled exactly, word for word, and the number of correct sentences in which certain words were replaced by synonyms.

(d) *Analysis of the forms of procedure for subjects*

The average number of sentences recalled per text (a maximum of seven) are compared in the different experimental conditions, utilizing a method of analysis of comparisons perfected by Lépine, Rouanet and Lebeau (1976). We note the number of sentences where the exact words are recalled in their totality, and the sentences in which they are replaced by synonyms, conserving the general meaning of the sentence.

4. RESULTS

The principal variables studied : modality of "Presentation" (non-moving text I, sentence scrolling up one by one Pd, and text scrolling as a whole Td), the degree of "abstraction-concreteness" of the text (three levels A, D, N), the mode of organization of the sentences (three levels : Ø, $\overline{O}$, O), all have significant influences on the extent of the recall. The results are particularly examined as a function of the influence of scrolling, and certain comparison findings will not be presented. After studying the global influence of the variables, we will study the interactions of these variables two by two. We will only examine the influence of the "abstraction" and of the "organization" within the different conditions of presentation. (cf. Table I).

TABLE I

Mean for exact sentences (a and b) and synonyms sentences (c and d)

a	Ø	$\overline{O}$	O		b	A	D	N	
I	3,2	2,7	3,1	3	I	2,7	3	3,3	3
Pd	3,1	2,7	2,2	2,7	Pd	2,4	2,6	3	2,7
Td	3,6	3,2	2,8	3,2	Td	2,7	3,2	3,6	3,2
	3,3	2,9	2,7			2,6	2,9	3,3	

c	Ø	$\overline{O}$	O		d	A	D	N	
I	3,6	3,1	3,8	3,5	I	3,1	3,5	3,8	3,5
Pd	3,5	3,2	3,1	3,3	Pd	2,9	3,2	3,7	3,3
Td	4	3,6	3,4	3,7	Td	3,2	3,7	4,1	3,7
	3,7	3,3	3,4			3,1	3,5	3,9	

(a) *Presentation*

The comparison of the recall of the texts presented motionlessly (I = 3) with the two other modalities of scrolling (Td + Pd = 2.95) is not significant $F(1,51) = 0.33$. On the other hand, the comparison Td = 3.2 and Pd = 2.7 is very significant($F(1,34) = 15.72$; $p < .0005$). It does not then seem that the scrolling up of a text presented as a whole hinders its recall. And yet the scrolling up of sentences one by one does impoverish recall. There is strong interaction between the modality of presentation and the other variables ($F(16,408) = 4.94$; $p < .0005$). We will study these effects later (same results with synonyms)(cf. Table I).

(b) *Organization*

As numerous studies have shown, especially the work of Katona (1940), Ehrlich (1972), Tulving and Donaldson (1972), Oléron, Koskas and Eugène (1973), Oléron and Tardieu (1978), the possibility of organizing the elements of a series improves the extent of recall. In the particular case of a single presentation, the effect is clear if the organization can be rapidly discovered. In our results we find a rate of recall $\emptyset = 3.3$ for the non-related sentences, $\overline{O} = 2.9$ for sentences centered on a theme, $O = 2.7$ for narrative sentences. The comparison between $\emptyset$ and $\overline{O} + O$ shows itself to be significant ($F(1,51) = 19.32$; $p < .0005$). Here the most organized sentences are the least well retained. The result is the same with synonyms and also significant : $\emptyset = 3.7$, $\overline{O} = 3.25$, $O = 3.43$ ($F(1,51) = 29.89$; $p < .0005$). Thus the diversity of sentences presented once favors discriminating between them, whereas the single presentation of sentences on a theme causes confusion among them. Narrative provokes condensed evocations.

(c) *Abstraction*

As the preceding work made it possible to predict (Moeser, 1974 ; Pezdek and Royer, 1974 ; Marschark and Paivio, 1977), the abstract elements are the least well retained. The comparison ($A = 2.6$) with descriptive sentences ($D = 2.9$) and narrative sentences ($N = 3.3$) is significant ($F(1,51) = 125.98$; $p < .0005$). This result is equally clear in the case of synonyms : $A = 3.1$, $D = 3.5$, $N = 3.9$ ($F(1,51) = 34.74$; $p < .0005$). Texts telling a story or *relating an action* (for the independent sentences) are the best recalled. If we compare the descriptive sentences with these latter we do indeed find significant differences with exact sentences ($F(1,51) = 50.19$; $p < .0005$) and the same holds considering the case with synonyms ($F(1,51) = 14.40$; $p < .005$).

(d) *Interactions of the "organization" and "abstraction" variables with the mode of "presentation"*

Tables II and III present these interactions.

The interaction between the mode of Presentation and the mode of Organization (see Table II) is only partially significant when texts with non-related sentences are excluded. The comparison of interaction between I, Pd, Td, O, $\overline{O}$, shows clearly that scrolling up hinders the recall of organized elements and would tend to favor the recall of different sentences centered on a theme ($F(1,51) = 25.6$; $p < .0005$).

TABLE II

Mean for exact sentences

	$\overline{O}$	O
I	2.7	3.1
Pd Td	2.95	2.5

This result is the same when synonymous sentences are taken into account ($F(1,51) = 18.85$; $p < .0005$).

The interactions between the modes of Presentation and the modalities of Abstraction are never significant. The same hierarchies are found in all lines and in all columns of Table I. Sentences having to do with an action are the best recalled in scrolling up.

In each of the Pd and Td scrolling conditions there is to be found a significant interaction between the variables of Organization and Abstraction if Abstract sentences are not considered.

TABLE III

Mean for synonymous sentences and exact sentences in Pd condition

	Ø	$\overline{O}$	O		Ø	$\overline{O}$	O
D	4	2.7	2.8	D	3.6	2.5	1.6
N	3.3	3.8	4	N	2.7	3.3	3.1
	synonymous sentences				exact sentences		

The comparison is very significant ($F(1,17) = 38.09$; $p < .0005$) for the exact sentences.

The values presented are those corresponding to the sentences scrolling up one by one. It can be seen that the fluctuations of the extent of recall vary greatly; the descriptive organized texts DO are particularly badly recalled, even more so for exact sentences. This interaction also exists for sentences with synonyms ($F(1,17) = 21.39$; $p < .0005$).

5. CONCLUSION

On the whole, in the temporal conditions of our experiment, the scrolling up of the text tends to favor the recall of the sentences. But as we have seen, it hinders the retention of the organization of the text with respect to a non-moving presentation which makes possible a better placing of the different elements into a relationship. On the other hand, the scrolling is in this case a stimulant when it comes to a narrative. The scrolling up of sentences one by one always decreases the recall, though less, however, when they have no relationship between one another.

REFERENCES

Ehrlich, S. (1972). *La capacité d'appréhension verbale*. PUF, Paris.

Katona, G. (1940). *Organizing and memorizing. Studies in the psychology of learning and teaching*. Columbia University Press, New York : Monningside Heights.

Lépine, D., Rouanet, H. and Lebeaux, M.O. (1976). L'analyse des comparaisons systématiques dans un plan à un facteur aléatoire. *Document roneotypé*.

Marschark, M. and Paivio, A. (1977). Integrative processing of concrete and abstract sentences. *Journal of Verbal Learning and Verbal Behavior*, 16, 217-231.

Moejer, S. (1974). Memory for meaning and wording in concrete and abstract sentences. *Journal of Verbal Learning and Verbal Behavior*, 13, 682-697.

Oléron, G., Koskas, E. and Eugène, N. (1973). Nature et place d'une erreur dans la rétention immédiate d'un texte bref. *Bulletin de Psychologie*, 26, 448-457.

Oléron, G., Rossi, J.P. and Tardieu, H. (1977). Défilement sur écran et perception de mots. *Document ronéotypé*.

Oléron, G. and Tardieu, H. (1978). Efficacité de l'évocation de textes perçus en déplacement : utilisation des synonymes. *(à paraître)*.

Pezdek, K. and Royer, J. (1974). The role of comprehension in learning concrete and abstract sentences. *Journal of Verbal Learning and Verbal Behavior*, 13, 551-558.

Tulving, E. and Donaldson, W. (1972). *Organization of memory*. Academic Press, New York, Londres.

MEMORY AIDS

SOME PSEUDO-LIMITATIONS OF MNEMONICS

K. L. Higbee
Brigham Young University
Provo, Utah U.S.A.

Mnemonics generally refers to rather unusual, "artificial," memory aids, such as narrative stories, acronyms, rhymes, verbal mediators, and visual imagery. This article emphasizes visual imagery because it is the most thoroughly researched and most unusual mnemonic technique, and because it underlies virtually all mnemonic systems.

While mnemonics do have limitations (see Higbee, 1977; Hunter, 1977b; Morris, 1977), there are also pseudo-limitations of mnemonics--criticisms that are not completely valid, or that are based on limitations that may not be as serious as some critics suggest. This article discusses four pseudo-limitations and describes what is "pseudo" about them (why they are not completely valid): (1) Mnemonics are not practical. (2) They do not help with understanding. (3) They are crutches. (4) They are tricks.

IT'S NOT PRACTICAL

Both the kinds of memory tasks studied in the research laboratory and the kinds of memory demonstrations done by performers can contribute to the impression that visual imagery mnemonics are not practical. In the research laboratory, most research on visual imagery in verbal learning and memory has concentrated on paired-associate and serial learning of unrelated nouns. Although these paradigms are convenient for psychological researchers, many people's practical memory problems do not fit well within either paradigm.

People sometimes tell me after a lecture and demonstration in which I have memorized a list of 20 words called out by the audience, or have been tested on a magazine I memorized, that they do not have much use for remembering a long list of unrelated nouns, or for memorizing a magazine. After all, they are not planning to go on tour giving memory shows. Many of them applaud the demonstration as if they were watching a magic show rather than an exhibition of applied psychology.

If, in fact, the memory tasks in research studies and in demonstrations were all that mnemonics were good for, people might have a good case for claiming that the practical value of mnemonic systems is not worth the effort it takes to learn them. After all, how often do you need to memorize a list of pairs of nouns, or a list of unrelated words, or a magazine?

I anticipate such objections in my teaching and emphasize that mnemonic systems are not just for research or for show. I point out to the audience that they may not *want* to do some of the kinds of feats I do in my demonstrations, but the important point is that they *can* do them; such feats are not beyond the capacity of the normal memory. And if they can do these things, that also means that they can do other things with their memories that they *do* want to do, but may have also thought were beyond their abilities.

What are some of these "other things?" Practical uses of mnemonic techniques and systems for such memory tasks as foreign languages, absent-mindedness, people's names, and numbers have been described by psychologists (e.g., Cermak, 1976; Higbee, 1977; Morris, 1977). Recent research has continued to indicate that visual mnemonics can help in such areas as memory for advertisements (Lutz and Lutz, 1977), learning foreign languages (e.g., Delaney, 1978; Ott, Blake, and Butler, 1976; Pressley, 1977), and schoolwork (see Higbee, 1978).

The potential applicability of mnemonics beyond the research lab and the mnemonists' demonstrations is also suggested by the wide range of people that have been found to use mnemonics effectively. Mnemonic elaboration has been found to improve memory in preschool children (see Levin, 1976) and in the elderly (e.g., Treat, Poon, Fozard, and Popkin, 1977). It has also been used by mentally-retarded children (see Martin, in press), and even by brain-damaged patients (e.g., Crovitz, in press).

As a final comment on practical uses of mnemonics, it should be noted that what is "practical" depends on individual needs. For example, one person may see no practical need for memorizing dozens of people's names, while a teacher may find that ability very useful; one person may see the ability to memorize numbers as impractical, while another who works with measurements, prices, or schedules may find it very useful. Even the educational uses of mnemonics may not seem as practical to someone who is not in school. Thus, what is practical to one person may not be practical to another.

WHAT ABOUT UNDERSTANDING?

Some people (and some textbooks) dismiss mnemonic systems with the comment that they are effective for certain kinds of rote memory tasks, but that many learning tasks involve understanding and reasoning more than straight memory for facts. The implication is that the systems are not worth learning because they do not help with understanding and reasoning.

There are two ways of responding to this criticism. First, the statement that mnemonics do not help with understanding may not be entirely accurate. There is evidence that pictures and visual imagery can help in understanding concepts and sentences (e.g., Davidson, 1976; Dyer and Meyer, 1976; Honeck, Sowry, and Voegtle, 1978), and prose reading material (e.g., Davidson, 1976; Levin, 1976; Peng and Levin, 1978).

But let us suppose that the statement is true that mnemonics do not help with understanding. In fact, it is probably true that mnemonics are not as useful for such tasks as they are for straight memory. A second response to the criticism then is, so what? Mnemonics are not *intended* for such tasks as reasoning, understanding, and problem-solving. They were not developed for that purpose. They are intended to aid learning and memory. Should we discard something if it does not do what it is *not* intended to do as effectively as it does what it *is* intended to do?

To say that mnemonic systems are not worth using because many learning tasks do not involve straight memory is somewhat like saying that the multiplication tables are not worth learning because many math problems do not involve multiplication. There are also many math problems that *do* involve multiplication. Likewise, it is true that many tasks are not straight memory, but it is also true that many tasks *are* straight memory. Whether we like it or not, most of us have many things to remember--names, phone numbers, things to do, things to buy, addresses, dates, errands, etc. And, despite the lofty goals espoused by teachers--such as insight, creative thinking, and critical analysis--much of schoolwork also involves straight memory (see Bower, 1973, p. 70; Rohwer and Dempster, 1977, p. 407).

Thus, even if mnemonics did help only remembering and not understanding, many people may still have enough to remember in school and elsewhere to make the use of memory aids worthwhile. In addition, people who are more concerned with understanding and reasoning than with memorizing can still benefit in at least two ways by using mnemonics: First, they can memorize the necessary routine things more efficiently, and thus free their minds to spend more time on tasks that involve understanding and reasoning. Second, they can better remember the facts that they use for understanding and reasoning; even tasks that involve reasoning and understanding require that you remember the facts in order to reason with them and understand them (see Trabasso, 1977).

IT'S A CRUTCH

Some people have criticized mnemonic techniques or systems on the basis that a person may become dependent on them, and use them as memory crutches. (In fact, Hunter, 1977b, p. 65, refers to a mnemonic as an "artificial memory-crutch.") Thus, a person who memorizes material with a mnemonic may not be able to remember the material without the mnemonic. He will become dependent on the mnemonic to remember the material. A common example is the difficulty most people have remembering the numbers of days in November without going through the rhyme, "30 days has September, April, June, and November . . ." The critic says, "What happens when you forget the crutch?"

There are at least three responses to this question. First, the "crutch" is frequently not forgotten as easily as the items would be without the crutch (Cermak, 1972). One may remember some mnemonics long after he has forgotten the material. For example, some people can remember the sentence they used to memorize the names of the cranial nerves ("On Old Olympus' Towering Tops . . . ") long after they have forgotten the names of the nerves. However, remembering the mnemonic is not responsible for their having forgotten the material.

Second, such dependency frequently does not happen. It is possible that this can occur with some material that one does not learn very thoroughly and/or use very often. However, especially if the material is something that a person will be using regularly, he will find that he no longer needs to recall the original mnemonic association in order to recall the material. The material may come automatically. I can recall material that I learned years ago using mnemonics, but cannot remember some of the associations I originally used to learn the material.

A third response to the crutch criticism is that even if a person did become dependent on a mnemonic to remember certain material, is that bad? Is it undesirable for a person with poor eyesight to become dependent on eyeglasses to help him see better? Even a person with good eyesight may need a telescope to see distant objects clearly. Is it worse for a person to depend on mnemonic associations to remember the names of everyone he meets than to forget everyone's name? I used a mnemonic system to memorize the telephone numbers of more than 100 people in a group to which I belong. I must refer to my associations to remember all of the numbers, but is this worse than not remembering the numbers? I do not think so. Even if the crutch criticism of dependency were true, it may be better to remember material using a mnemonic than to not remember the material.

An irony of the crutch criticism is that it serves as the basis for two conflicting criticisms. On one hand, the critic says that you cannot remember the material without the crutch (meaning that you are lost if you forget the crutch). On the other hand, the critic says that you become too dependent on the crutch for remembering the material (meaning that you cannot forget the crutch).

IT'S A TRICK

For some people, understanding the principles of memory and applying them via mnemonic techniques is not really memorizing. Some researchers have even referred to mnemonics as "artificial memory" (e.g., Crovitz, 1971), and I have at least four 1977-1978 general psychology textbooks that refer to mnemonics as "tricks." In doing memory demonstrations, I have observed that people are impressed by my amazing memory until I explain a little about the mnemonic systems used, at which time I no longer have an amazing memory, but am just a faker. (Perhaps this is why some memory "experts" do not divulge their secrets.)

Viewing mnemonics as tricks and gimmicks probably contributed to the hesitancy of many psychologists to accept mnemonics as a legitimate area of investigation before the 1960s, and contributes to people's applauding a memory demonstration as if it were a magic show (after all, magicians do tricks), rather than a demonstration of applied psychology. In fact, one commercial memory course is entitled, "Memory Magic," and another course, using parts of an automobile as loci, is entitled, "Auto-magic."

However, mnemonics do not *replace* the basic psychological principles of learning; they *use* them. Such principles of learning as association, organization, meaningfulness, attention, retrieval cues, deep encoding, and visual imagery are incorporated in the use of mnemonic systems (see Higbee, 1977; Morris, 1977). Several researchers have suggested that a study of mnemonics can help us understand the functioning of normal memory, and provide a way of testing the generality of theories of memory (see Baddeley, 1976, p. 357; Norman, 1976, p. 130; Peterson, 1977, p. 393), and there is recent research evidence to support these contentions (Begg, 1978; Bellezza and Reddy, 1978).

Even the well-known examples of exceptional memories such as Luria's S. (1968), V.P. (Hunt and Love, 1972), and Aitken (Hunter, 1977a), are not complete exceptions to the processes of natural memory. Baddeley (1976) notes that the two major factors underlying the performance of such people--imagery and a rich network of meaningful associations--are also important in normal memory, and thus such people may be extremes of normal memory rather than something qualitatively different.

SUMMARY

Pseudo-limitations of mnemonics are criticisms that are not completely valid or are not as serious as some critics suggest. This article, which is condensed from a much more complete discussion in the conference paper, discusses four pseudo-limitations and describes what is "pseudo" about them: (1) Mnemonics are not practical. (2) Mnemonics do not help with understanding. (3) Mnemonics are crutches leading to dependence on them. (4) Mnemonics are just tricks, not really memorizing.

REFERENCES

Baddeley, A. (1976). *The Psychology of Memory.* Basic Books, New York.

Begg, I. (1978). Imagery and organization in memory. *Memory and Cognition*, 6, 174-183.

Bellezza, F.S. and Reddy, G. (1978). Mnemonic devices and natural memory. *Bulletin of the Psychonomic Society*, 11, 277-280.

Bower, G. H. (1973). Educational applications of mnemonic devices. In: *Interaction: Readings in Human Psychology.* (K. O. Dole, ed.), pp. 201-210. D. C. Heath, Lexington, Mass.

Cermak, L. S. (1972). *Human Memory: Research and Theory*. Ronald Press, New York.
Cermak, L. S. (1976). *Improving Your Memory*. McGraw-Hill, New York.
Crovitz, H. F. (1971). The capacity of memory loci in artificial memory. *Psychonomic Science*, 24, 187-188.
Crovitz, H. F. (in press). Memory retraining in brain-damaged patients: The airplane list. *Cortex*, in press.
Davidson, R. E. (1976). The role of metaphor and analogy in learning. In: *Cognitive Learning in Children*. (J. R. Levin and V. L. Allen, eds.), pp. 135-162. Academic Press, New York.
Delaney, H. D. (1978). Interaction of individual differences with visual and verbal elaboration instructions. *Journal of Educational Psychology*, 70, 306-318.
Dyer, J. C. and Meyer, P. A. (1976). Facilitation of simple concept identification through mnemonic instruction. *Journal of Experimental Psychology: Human Learning and Memory*, 2, 767-773.
Higbee, K. L. (1977). *Your Memory: How it Works and How to Improve it*. Prentice-Hall, Englewood Cliffs, NJ.
Higbee, K. L. (1978). Recent research on mnemonics: Historical roots and educational fruits. Manuscript submitted for publication.
Honeck, R. P., Sowry, B. M., and Voegtle, K. (1978). Proverbial understanding in a pictorial context. *Child Development*, 49, 22-28.
Hunt, E. and Love, T. (1972). How good can memory be? In: *Coding Processes in Human Memory*. (A. W. Melton and E. Martin, eds.), pp. 237-260. V. H. Winston and Sons, Washington, D.C.
Hunter, I. M. L. (1977a). An exceptional memory. *British Journal of Psychology*, 68, 155-164.
Hunter, I. M. L. (1977b). Imagery, comprehension, and mnemonics. *Journal of Mental Imagery*, 1, 65-72.
Levin, J. R. (1976). What have we learned about maximizing what children learn? In: *Cognitive Learning in Children*. (J. R. Levin and V. L. Allen, eds.), pp. 105-134, Academic Press, New York.
Luria, A. R. (1968). *The Mind of a Mnemonist*. Basic Books, New York.
Lutz, K. A. and Lutz, R. J. (1977). Effects of interactive imagery on learning: Application to advertising. *Journal of Applied Psychology*, 62, 493-498.

Martin, C. J. (in press). Mediational processes in the retarded: Implications for teaching reading. *International Review of Research in Mental Retardation*. Vol. 9. (N. R. Ellis, ed.), pp. 61-64. Academic Press, New York.

Morris, P. (1977). Practical strategies for human learning and remembering. In: *Adult Learning: Psychological Research and Applications*. (M. Howe, ed.), pp. 125-144. John Wiley and Sons, London.

Norman, D. A. (1976). *Memory and Attention*. 2nd ed., John Wiley and Sons, New York.

Ott, C. E., Blake, R. S., and Butler, D. C. (1976). Implications of mental elaboration for the acquisition of foreign language vocabulary. *International Review of Applied Linguistics in Language Teaching*, 14, 37-48.

Peng, C. and Levin, J. R. (1978). Strategies in reading comprehension: IX. Durability of picture effects in children's story recall. Paper presented at the meeting of the American Educational Research Association, Toronto, March.

Peterson, L. R. (1977). Verbal learning and memory. In: *Annual Review of Psychology*. Vol. 28. (M. R. Rosenzweig and L. W. Porter, eds.), pp. 393-415. Annual Reviews, Palo Alto, CA.

Pressley, M. (1977). Children's use of the keyword method to learn simple Spanish vocabulary words. *Journal of Educational Psychology*, 69, 465-472.

Rohwer, W. D., Jr. and Dempster, F. N. (1977). Memory development and educational processes. In: *Perspectives on the Development of Memory and Cognition* (R. V. Kail, Jr. and J. W. Hagen, eds.), pp. 407-435. Lawrence Erlbaum Associates, Hillsdale, N.J.

Trabasso, T. (1977). The role of memory as a system in making transitive inferences. In: *Perspectives on the Development of Memory and Cognition* (R. V. Kail, Jr. and J. W. Hagen, eds.), pp. 333-366. Lawrence Erlbaum Associates, Hillsdale, N.J.

Treat, N. J., Poon, L. W., Fozard, J. L., and Popkin, S. J. (1977). Toward applying cognitive skill training to memory problems. Paper presented at the meeting of the American Psychological Association, San Francisco, August.

SENSE AND NONSENSE IN TRADITIONAL MNEMONICS

P. E. Morris
Department of Psychology
University of Lancaster
Lancaster, England

ABSTRACT

Research on imagery and a mnemonic for learning names reviewed in the first section illustrates the effectiveness of several of the mnemonic techniques recommended in memory improvement systems. However, in the second section limitations on the effectiveness of some common mnemonic techniques are demonstrated. Bizarre images do not lead to better recall than images of ordinary situations, and first letter mnemonics only improve the retention of order, they do not help the learning of unrelated items. In the third section an analysis of memory problems reveals severe limitations in our knowledge of strategies to aid recall. We can give little advice on improving retrieval or remembering future intentions.

INTRODUCTION

For centuries many mnemonic techniques have been known and advocated by authors of texts promising to improve memory. In the first section of this paper I will illustrate how experimental support has accumulated for many of these techniques. However, not all the advice which has been offered in memory improvement systems actually leads to better recall. In the second section I will discuss two such cases. Finally, even with a knowledge of successful mnemonic techniques one is left with a feeling of dissatisfaction. In the third section I offer an analysis of memory problems which indicates the relatively few situations in which mnemonics can be of assistance. This taxonomy of memory problems reveals many conditions in which we are almost totally ignorant of appropriate strategies to aid recall.

EFFECTIVE MNEMONIC TECHNIQUES

Memory experts such as Bruno Furst (1944) and Harry Lorayne (1957) emphasise the importance of attention, observation and concentration upon what is to be remembered. Few would question the importance of these. However, beyond this reminder that many apparent cases of *forgetting* are really failures to *get* in the first place, they offer techniques which can be summarised as ways of organising the disconnected, of providing appropriate, specific cues and of making the meaningless meaningful. I have reviewed these techniques more fully elsewhere (Morris, 1977, 1979). Since my interest in this paper is to illustrate the limitations of the mnemonic methods I will confine discussion of their effectiveness to two experimental demonstrations.

The importance of association, of linking together the items to be remembered, has been a central theme of the memory improvers. Many of their mnemonics provide ways of linking the apparently disconnected. One way of doing this is to form mental images which interconnect the items to be remembered in some integrated way. The use of mental imagery opens up the possibility of spatial association. It may, for example, be difficult to find much to connect a cat and a table, but a cat can always be imagined *on* a table.

A study of mine with Ralph Stevens (Morris and Stevens, 1974) illustrates that the value of forming images as a mnemonic aid is not that imaging as such improves recall but that imagery provides an opportunity for associating apparently disconnected items. The Table shows the mean recall from lists of twenty-four concrete words in Experiment I by Morris and Stevens (1974).

TABLE I

Linking images	Single images	Control	
20	13.6	14.1	(max 24)

One group of subjects was told to form images integrating the first three items, the next three items, and so on into imaginal scenes. The second group imaged each item separately. The third group were given no specific mnemonic instructions. As can be seen, while images integrating the items improved recall, the imaging of individual items had no effect.

An experiment by Sue Jones, Peter Hampson and myself (Morris, Jones and Hampson 1978) gives a further illustration of the success of the mnemonic methods of the memory experts. We tested a technique for learning people's names recommended by Lorayne (1957). Three stages are involved. The name is converted to some imagable substitute, then a prominent feature of the person is chosen, and finally an image formed linking the substitute for the name to this feature. Thus, Mr. Gorden may be converted to 'garden' and, if he has a long nose, a garden imagined growing over his nose.

We had 40 subjects learn randomly chosen names to randomly selected photographs of faces. After an initial test on 13 face-name pairs half of the subjects spent about ten minutes being trained in the technique while the control subjects took part in an unrelated experiment. When tested on a new set of face-name pairs, while control subjects showed no significant change, the mnemonic group improved their performance by almost 80%.

There have been similar demonstrations of the effectiveness of many of the mnemonic methods recommended by the memory experts. Fuller reviews will be found in Morris (1977, 1979).

INEFFECTIVE MNEMONIC TECHNIQUES

Research which merely confirms what the memory improvement systems have always taught may add confidence in the systems but can also bring into question the need for experimental tests of the mnemonics. If we keep finding that the memory improvement systems work why not stop doing experiments and accept the advice that they give? However not all the advice has been found to be sound nor all currently used mnemonics successful.

There is general agreement within the memory improvement systems that when images are formed they should be as bizarre as possible. Bizarre images should lead to better recall than images of conventional, ordinary scenes. However at least 13 experiments have failed to find better recall when subjects form bizarre as compared with ordinary images. (References to most of these will be found in Higbee, 1977 and Paivio, 1971.)

Several possible explanations for the lack of difference between bizarre and ordinary images have been suggested. Some of the experiments may have failed to allow subjects sufficient time to form bizarre images. Also, the value of bizarre images may increase with the frequency of use of the imagery mnemonic as interference increases. In an unpublished study by Alison Prentice and myself we found that subjects averaged two seconds to report the formation of an ordinary image linking two concrete nouns but took four seconds to report forming bizarre images to the same pairs. Twenty pairs were presented, one pair at a time, to ten subjects in each of the two groups. On four occasions the subject was asked to describe the images formed to check that they were following the instructions. Several of the earlier studies of bizarre imagery used a 5 sec/pair rate of presentation which could have overwhelmed subjects trying to comply with the bizarre imagery instructions. However where, as in the present experiment subjects have been allowed enough time to form bizarre images no evidence of better recall than with ordinary images has been found. Often, as in our experiment, there has been an insignificant tendency for ordinary images to lead to better recall.

In a second experiment we followed up the possibility that the advantage of bizarre images develops when imagery mnemonics are used repeatedly, perhaps frequently involving the same pegs or loci (see Morris 1977, 1979). We attempted to increase interference by pairing five different responses with the same fifteen stimuli in a paired-associate task. The seventy-five pairs, all composed of common concrete nouns were randomly ordered and presented to each subject at a rate of ten seconds per pair. The subjects were then tested by being asked to write the five correct response words against the appropriate stimuli. Ten subjects were given instructions to form bizarre images, ten instructions to form 'common' images of the most natural situation that occurred to them. Mean correct recall was 33.8 responses by bizarre imagers and 37.2 by common imagers, an insignificant difference, but again in the direction of ordinary images.

It may be that the frequency of use of the imagery mnemonics by the stage memory experts, and the practice in imaging that they have received may result in bizarre images being beneficial to them. Such images do encourage the formation of unique, integrated images. However, for those of us who use imagery mnemonics relatively rarely there is no evidence that we need to take the time and effort to form bizarre images.

Some of the most popular memory aids are first letter mnemonics, for example, ROY G BIV and 'Richard Of York Gave Battle In Vain' for the colours of the rainbow.

While there is no doubt about the *popularity* of these

mnemonics the evidence for their *effectiveness* does raise doubts (see Gruneberg, 1978). While two studies have found the mnemonics to aid recall, three report no effect and another found only an 18% improvement in recall of order and none in overall recall.

With Neil Cook (Morris and Cook, 1978) I tried to locate the reason for the poor showing of the mnemonic. In our first experiment we compared experimenter and subject generated mnemonics, and, where mnemonics were provided, manipulated the concreteness of the mnemonic words. Subjects learned six lists of five words, all of which began with consonants so that meaningful mnemonic words could be formed by inserting vowels appropriately. An example list is "hammer, slipper, peach, trunk, leopard" with the mnemonic word HOSPITAL.

We found no signs of benefit from the mnemonics. We began to believe that the general confidence in the first letter mnemonic was an enormous delusion. However, when we reconsidered the situations in which first letter mnemonics are commonly used we realised that they tend to involve problems of ordering items. We speculated, therefore, that in the experimental tests of the mnemonic where new lists of items had to be learned, the first letter mnemonics may not be very effective retrieval cues. However, where the items are either well known, or easily generated and where their order is important, but there is no logical sequence to the items, then the mnemonic may show its effectiveness.

We used the days of the week as a well known set of items. Thirty-four subjects had to learn three random orderings with one minute to study each. Phrases such as "FeaST WaS MeaT" and "SMiTe ThiS WiFe" were provided as first letter mnemonics to half the subjects, the capital letters indicating the order of the days. Recall was tested by giving the first day in each ordering, and, to control for guessing, making subjects fill in a response for each of the remaining six days. Tested after two minutes of unrelated activity the subjects who had been given the mnemonic phrases were able to recall in the correct positions, on average 14.5 of the 18 possible items while the control subjects recalled only 9.7. After 30 minutes neither group showed any loss in performance. Thus, where the items were well known but the order needed to be retained the first letter mnemonics contributed to a dramatic improvement in performance. The mnemonic does not help, however, in the learning of new, unrelated lists of items.

AN ANALYSIS OF MEMORY PROBLEMS

If we are seriously concerned about practical memory problems we need to know what these problems are. When the types of memory problems that can arise are examined it rapidly becomes clear that mnemonic techniques will help in only a limited number of situations. Figure 1 is an algorithm which classifies memory problems. This is, of course, my own analysis, and others are possible, but this will illustrate the range of situations in which someone with a memory problem may find himself.

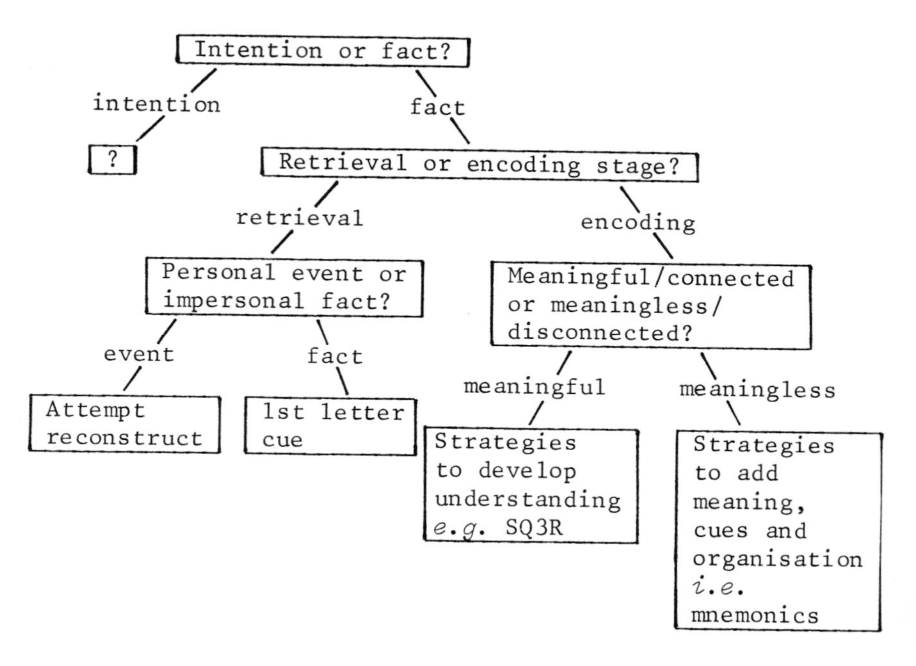

Fig. 1 *An analysis of memory problems and possible strategies to overcome them.*

The first question is whether in the specific instance it is a case of remembering an intention or a fact. An intention here means something that has to be done in the future such as buy a present or keep an appointment. Facts are things like names, telephone numbers, where we left the car keys and so on. This initial distinction is important. Forgetting intentions can be very embarrassing and it is not surprising that the popular external memory aids described by

John Harris (this volume) are mainly to cue our memory for future actions. However, our knowledge of how we remember what we intend doing is virtually non-existent. It is obvious that we plan our lives, that these plans guide what we do and that the plans must be set up, modified, consulted and sometimes forgotten. To understand why sometimes we fail to carry out our intentions we need to know how our plans are constructed and how they influence our behaviour. We know so little about this whole aspect of our cognitive functioning that no advice, other than to suggest the use of some of the external memory aids described by Harris, can be offered to the person who wishes to remember to do something. Hence the question mark in the algorithm. Further discussion of memory for intentions will be found in Morris (1979).

If the memory problem involves a fact then the next question is whether the fact has already been encoded and the problem is one of retrieval, or whether one is deciding how best to encode the fact for future recall. If retrieval is being attempted then is the memory one of a personal event such as a visit to a friend, or is it of an impersonal fact such as the date of the battle of Waterloo? This is, of course, Tulving's (1972) episodic/semantic distinction.

Many memory problems are retrieval problems. At the time that encoding took place either there seemed to be no reason for special encoding strategies, or there was no time, or we were confident that our memories would not let us down. There has been almost no research on practical strategies to aid retrieval. Where a personal event is involved an attempt to reproduce the original situation either by returning there in real life or by imaginary reconstruction probably helps recall, but there has been no attempt to study how this reconstruction can be maximised nor whether other strategies may be equally valuable. Recall from semantic memory can be aided by self cuing with the first letters of the alphabet (see Gruneberg and Sykes, this volume). Beyond this we know little about ways of improving retrieval.

Where control of encoding is still possible a range of techniques are available. The task is easier, since while retrieval strategies can only exploit whatever encoding occurred initially, it is possible at the encoding stage to direct one's activities to make the best use of the memory system and produce the highest probability of future recall (see Morris, 1978 and 1979). The next question is whether the material to be remembered is meaningful and well integrated or meaningless and/or disconnected. If the material is essentially meaningful and well organised then the learner can be directed to study strategies which are designed to develop his understanding of the material. One such method which is often recommended to students is the Survey, Question, Read, Recite, Review (SQ3R) technique of study (Morris, 1979).

It is only when we reach the final condition of needing to learn meaningless or disconnected information that the mnemonic techniques are of value. They supply meaning, organisation and specific retrieval cues to situations where such information is inherently sparce or absent (see Morris 1977 and 1979 for discussion). There are many such situations, and the mnemonics should be a useful tool in the equipment of the technologist of memory improvement. Unfortunately, while we can recommend many different, effective mnemonics we can give little helpful advice for anyone struggling with one of the other types of memory problem that I have described above. Until we can suggest useful strategies in these important situations where intentions have to be remembered or retrieval elicited we will be a long way from a practical technology of memory. When non-psychologists ask us how to improve their memories it is usually the very aspects of memory about which we are most ignorant that cause them the greatest problems. Hopefully, by the next conference on Practical Aspects of Memory we will be nearer to giving them useful advice.

REFERENCES

Furst, B. (1944). *How to Remember*. Greenberg, New York.

Gruneberg, M.M. (1978). The feeling of knowing, memory blocks and memory aids. In: *Aspects of Memory*. (M.M. Gruneberg and P. Morris eds). Methuen, London.

Higbee, K.L. (1977). *Your Memory: How it Works and How to Improve it*. Prentice-Hall, New Jersey.

Lorayne, H. (1957). *How to Develop a Super-power Memory*. Frederick Fell, New York.

Morris, P.E. (1977). Practical strategies for human learning and remembering. In: *Adult Learning: Psychological Research and Applications*. (M.J.A. Howe ed). Wiley, London.

Morris, P. (1978). Encoding and retrieval. In: *Aspects of Memory*. (M.M. Gruneberg and P. Morris eds). Methuen, London.

Morris, P.E. (1979). Strategies for learning and recall. In: *Applied Problems in Memory*. (M.M. Gruneberg and P.E. Morris eds). Academic, London.

Morris, P.E. and Cook, N. (1978). When do first letter

mnemonics aid recall? *British Journal of Educational Psychology*. 48, 22-28.
Morris, P.E., Jones, S. and Hampson, P.J. (1978). An imagery mnemonic for the learning of people's names. *British Journal of Psychology*. 69, 335-336.
Morris, P.E. and Stevens, R. (1974). Linking images and free recall. *Journal of Verbal Learning and Verbal Behavior*. 13, 310-315.
Paivio, A. (1971). *Imagery and Verbal Processes*. Holt, Rinehart and Winston, New York.
Tulving, E. (1972). Episodic and semantic memory. In: *Organisation of Memory*. (E. Tulving and W. Donaldson eds). Academic, New York.

THE PAST AND PRESENT OF MNEMOTECHNY

R.E. Rawles
University College London

Beginning with the Ancient Greeks and ending with present-day students, the development of mnemotechny is traced through the Renaissance, the Middle Ages and Victorian times. The techniques practised by mnemonists and members of the acting profession involving 'Photographic' memory and visual imagery are also discussed. A survey of revision methods for examinations indicates that an impoverished form of the 'Place Method' is currently much used in various disciplines at University level.

EVOLUTION OF THE PLACE METHOD

This paper considers the development of mnemotechny - the skill of assisting the memory, especially by the employment of artificial aids; and how its secrets are used by contemporary students.

The origins of the art lie deep in antiquity and have been meticulously recovered by the Renaissance scholar Frances Yates (1966) in her beautiful book. A text which introduced literate psychologists to, or at least reminded those with a classical background oppressed by an hegemonic Behaviourism of, Simonides' successful post-mortem identifications, recall of the names of guests by the positions in which they have been seated, at a banquet in 477 BC. Cicero recorded the 'Place Method' in *De Oratore II* and Paivo (1971) included it in an influential account of mnemonics.

Cicero exhorted students of Rhetoric to apply *memoria technica*, for in the social formation of that time power was knowledge and knowledge was memory. But as Sorabji (1972) has made clear Aristotle was also interested in these crafts and advocated them for participants in Dialectic. Indeed, he urged the use of a testicular image to represent the witnesses *(testes)* in a lawsuit.

The advent of Christianity created Saint Augustine (354-430) who in his *Confessions* (translated by the memorable Pine-Coffin, 1961) dwells upon a memory image of Carthage, and the Middle Ages produced Petrus Ravennas (ca.1448-1508) inventor of a truly inimitable scheme comprising 100,000 different loci. Later, Robert Fludd (1574-1637) developed a less elaborate arrangement called 'The Memory Theatre'. Fludd was a Rosicrucian and the occult philosopher is often concerned with memory. See the Key written by Saralden (1934) for this Ancient Order.

With Victoria on the throne Stokes (1868) contrived a Mnemonical Globe, coloured, twenty-four inches in circumference and now on display in the British Museum (Hill,1978). The Globe is possessed of a face and the Greenwich Meridian runs straight down the nose. Countries are to be recalled by their position in relation to the visage, although there is much space on the back of the head. Verbal mnemonics are also recommended, e.g. 'EUROPE' becomes'YOU'RE UP', and this provides a cue to scrutinize some others below.

A FEW VERBAL MNEMONICS

Both Morris (1977) and Higbee (1977) have reviewed the'Peg or Hook', 'First Letter', 'Rhymes' and 'Phonetic' mnemonic systems. They do actually work and the 'First Letter' method facilitates the retrieval of lists of names. One just has to store: 'F. CHOW W(i)L J(u)MP' to instantly emit some surnames which probably correspond to real people viz. Foley, Conway, Howard, O'Connor, Watson, Wheeler, Lewis, John, Molteno, Pelling.

Although Atkinson (1975) has remarked on the paucity of instructional situations in which such aids are useful, the first of the few mnemonics were verbal, as outlined by Sir John Hammerton (1941). 'T.M.P.' and 'Flaps' was a general catchword to remember the drill of vital actions in RAF flying procedure and prevented accidents due to lapses of memory.

MNEMONISTS IN FACT AND FICTION

Of course, some people have trained their mnemonic skills to a high level and others have been born with rare memorial powers, sometimes seeming to impede other cognitive abilities as in the case of idiots savants (Lester, 1977).

For example, Jedidiah Buxton (1707-1772) was a poor labourer from Derbyshire who performed difficult problems in arithmetic by the strength of his memory and refused to be interfered with. Neither noise, nor conversation would interrupt him and he could leave off in the midst of calculations and return to them years afterwards. Ogden (1929) points out that though he did little else in his whole life but multiplication, he singularly failed to realize that the simplest way to multiply a number by 100 is to add on '00'.

There are similarities here to Shereshevskii (Luria, 1969).

The possession of an exceptional memory has often led to the stage, and the demonstration of phenomenal recall to a captive audience. W.J. Bottell (1875-1956) known on the Halls as 'Datas' stoked the ovens at a Gas Works in South London before turning professional and writing about his system (Datas, 1904). 'Memory', played by Wylie Watson, in Hitchcock's film version of John Buchan's *The Thirty-Nine Steps* (Bennett and Reville, 1935) is a depiction of 'Datas', for Watson utters the catchphrase 'Am I right, Sir? on revealing the steps in the secret design.

Datas utilized visual imagery powers as does Leslie Welch, Britain's most famous memory man. His knowledge of all the major sporting events of the last half century is classified in files for each year. He has literally internalized this information and when asked a question imagines himself inspecting the relevant file and seeing the answer (Kendall, 1971).

ACTING AND PHOTOGRAPHIC MEMORY

Thespians need to memorize and they too might use visual imagery to store a representation of a part. Harry Edwards in a letter to Osborn (1902) discloses an ability to recall the handwriting of a script and the position of each speech upon a page. The Shakesperian actor, Michael Hordern has recently described the same strategem (Chaillet, 1978), and argues that the book is not in his hand but in his head.

Naturally, there are alternative methods and the school of acting influences the choice of technique. Members of the Moscow Arts Theatre learn actions rather than words (Smirnov, 1973). They never suffer from Edwards' fate of knowing the words but not understanding the meaning of a character. Once he took the part of Falstaff at twelve noon and played it perfectly at night. A remarkable feat marred only by a total failure to interpret such a rumbustious personage.

Cutts and Moseley (1969) concluded that there is no such thing as Photographic memory in the strong sense of taking a snapshot of a page and filing it in the mind like a photoprint which can be scanned at will. Nevertheless, the people mentioned above demonstrate just such a faculty. If encoding time is not required to be instantaneous, and the gist of the processes is remembering where the information has been seen, then many more people can claim 'Photographic' memory in this weaker sense.

THE PLACE ON THE PAGE METHOD

Returning to the 'Place Method' *per se*, a simple version

of 'The Memory Theatre' was devised by The Rev.Bacon (1889). A 3x3 matrix provided locations on the floor of a room with an additional place above the middle cell. Thus, ten loci could be used in which to imagine common objects, exemplars being *davenport, whatnot, piano,* with a *chandelier* suspended from the ceiling over the centre of the floor. Material to be remembered is pictured in association with these objects and recalled via the places which act as prompters. An ordered sequence of events like the succession of the Kings of England is preserved using each cell in turn. Strings greater than ten are handled by re-starting from the first cell.

David Naismith, Q.C., simplified this method still further and suggested that the student of History visualizes an array for every ten-year period. The 0's always appear in the top bar, the 1's in the upper left-hand corner, the 9's in the lowest right-hand corner; and so on. Events in each decade are placed in the appropriate space. Meiklejohn (1907) put the system into a textbook which was widely read in L.C.C. Secondary Schools, and hoped that it would make the getting up of History as easy as remembering the situation of a street or square.

The ultimate simplification of the method is to image merely the place on the page where details have been printed or written. Recall of the general location may then lead to recall of the particulars. Rothkopf (1971) was the first to show experimentally that incidental memory for location of information in a text is truly possible, and later the tetrad Zechmeister, McKillip, Pasko and Bespalec (1975) found that both item and spatial recall increased directly with degree of visual memory for position.

So, psychology rediscovered, and made scientifically respectable, a practice investigated by Galton with his questionary on visualizing, to which Darwin answered 'I cannot remember a single sentence, but I remember the place of the sentence and the kind of type'. (Francis Darwin, 1887).

REVISING FOR EXAMINATIONS

The advice

There exists a plethora of books on this subject. Most commend the use of mnemonics or at least do not despise them (Mace, 1962); unlike Colvin and Bagley (1913) who warn that they are dangerous and should only be employed when all other methods fail. Perhaps an overly frequent indulgence leads to mental blindness.

The visual 'Place on Page' method is not treated in many

contemporary guides. Lorayne and Lucas (1976) reduce it to an associative routine. However, Dineen (1977) and Brown (1977) do favour visualization. The latter supporting the diagrammatic key word note-taking technique of Buzan (1974), although ideas laid out in this way might be less susceptible to the 'Page' method than orthodox notes.

Earlier writers were more positive. Pear (1930) prescribed concentration on the notebook just before the examination. Several books would destroy the advantage to visual memory of the paragraphs in constant spatial relation thus found. Sir Josiah Stamp (1935) recommended students to memorize in their dominant imagery mode and he himself liked to see the matter in black and white, often remembering the exact place on the page where the vital fact lay. Similarly, Burt (1950) was committed to exploitation of the strongest imagery.

What students do.

Blick and Waite (1971) discovered that 34% of a college student sample would use the 'First Letter' method to learn words in a free-recall task. Concerning the use of mnemonics in examinations, Gruneberg (1973) ascertained that 53% of 141 psychology graduates had at times applied such devices to their preparation for Finals, the most popular ruse again being the 'First Letter' procedure. A few students reported employing other methods (unspecified), but apparently nobody had used the 'Page' system. Gruneberg does not find this surprising and argues that techniques involving imagery cannot normally be applied to the retention of abstract material. Likewise, Bugelski (1971) in defining an image, reasons that because mathematical formulae have no concrete objects as referents, any attempt to use imagery in their manipulation or retention will prove nugatory. Nonetheless, $E=mc^2$ can be visualized on the page, and this application of 'Formal' or 'Meta' imagery cuts across simple-minded verbal/imaginal, abstract/concrete distinctions. Admitting this function of imagery by no means insinuates an acceptance of a picture-theory of meaning, it just implies that representations of abstract concepts can be retrieved from memory. In passing, it is worth noting that Einstein was a visually mediated thinker (Patten, 1973).

Therefore, it is surely quite likely that even students of mathematics may make use of the 'Page' method. To check this, and to determine how often the technique is employed in revision a short questionnaire was constructed. It contained four statements: 'Learn information by repeating it over to yourself', 'Make sure that you understand the material', 'Remember the information by seeing in your mind's eye where it is written on a page in your notes or textbook', and 'Visualize diagrams or tables'. The subject was required to indicate on four-point scales ('Never', 'Rarely', 'Often', 'Very Often') the frequencies with which any of these methods were used. A question asking for details of additional techniques practised was also included.

Two different samples of paid volunteers, University of London students from diverse departments, completed the questionnaire either at the start of the Autumn Term or towards the end of the Summer Term before examinations began.

A full analysis of the data obtained and a comparison with Gruneberg's findings will be presented elsewhere. For the moment, Table 1 below suffices to show that 49% of the total sample often used the 'Page' method in revision.

TABLE 1

'Place on the Page': Frequency of Usage

Group	Never	Rarely	Often	Very Often
Autumn (N=104)	16	36	30	22
Summer (N=87)	20	26	26	15

Only one of the eleven mathematicians questioned never used the procedure. This signifies that imagery can be put to service in the learning of abstract symbols. The Summer group were more forthcoming about other methods of preparing for examinations which were looming up on their horizons. Many continuously re-wrote notes, boiling them down each time to a tractable residue. Others tried mnemonics. One person repeated lectures to himself in bed before an imaginary audience.

CONCLUSION

The past of mnemotechny is rooted in the intricate memory systems of the Ancient Greeks, the complicated 'Memory Theatres' of the Middle Ages and the bizarre skills of Victorian mnemonists.

Its present is revealed on the stage and in the university. The contemporary student's remembering of the place on the page is but a shadow of the older mnemonic arts.

REFERENCES

Atkinson, R.C. (1975). Mnemotechnics in Second-Language Learning, *American Psychologist*, 30, 821-88.

Bacon, J.H. (1889). *A Complete Guide to the Improvement of Memory*. Second Edition. Isaac Pitman, London.

Bennett, C. And Reville, A. (1935). *The Thirty-Nine Steps*. (Screenplay). Gaumont British, London.

Brown, M. (1977). *Memory Matters*. David and Charles, Newton Abbot.

Bugelski, B.R. (1971). The Definition of the Image, In: *Imagery: Current Cognitive Approaches*. (S.J. Segal, ed.) pp.49-68. Academic Press, New York.

Burt, C. (1950). Can Our Memory Be Improved? *The Listener*. 45, 675-76.

Buzan, T. (1974). *Use Your Head*. B.B.C. London.

Chaillet, N. (1978). Michael Hordern: The Loner, *The Times*. 13 May, p7.

Colvin, S.S. and Bagley, W.C. (1913). *Human Behaviour. A First Book in Psychology for Teachers*. Macmillan, New York.

Cutts, N.E. and Moseley, N. (1969). Notes on Photographic Memory. *Journal of Psychology*, 71, 3-15.

Darwin, F. (1887). *The Life and Letters of Charles Darwin*. Volume III. Third Edition. John Murray, London.

Datas (1904). *A Simple System of Memory Training*. Gale and Polden, London.

Dineen, J. (1977). *Remembering Made Easy*. Thorsons, Wellingborough.

Gruneberg, M.M. (1973). The Role of Memorization Techniques in Finals Examination Preparation - A Study of Psychology Students, *Educational Research*, 15, 134-39.

Hammerton, J. (1941). *ABC of the RAF*. Amalgamated Press, London.

Higbee, K.L. (1977). *Your Memory How it Works and How to Improve it*. Prentice-Hall International, London.

Hill, G. (1978). *Cartographical Curiosities*. British Museum Publications, London.

Kendall, E. (1971). For Some Memory Lane is Endless..... *The Observer Magazine*, 21 March, 12-13.

Lester, D. (1977). Idiots Savants: a Review. *Psychology*. 14, 20-23.

Lorayne, H. and Lucas, J. (1976). *The Memory Book*. A Star Book, W.H. Allen, London.

Luria, A.R. (1969). *The Mind of a Mnemonist*. Cape, London.

Mace, C.A. (1962). *The Psychology of Study*. Revised edition Penguin Books, Harmondsworth.

Meiklejohn, J.M.D. (1907). *A New History of England and Great Britain*. Eleventh Edition, Meiklejohn and Holden, London.
Morris, P. (1977). Practical Strategies for Human Learning and Remembering. In: *Adult Learning. Psychological Research and Applications*. (M.J.A. Howe, ed.) pp.125-44. John Wiley & Sons, London.
Ogden, C.K.(1929). *The ABC of Psychology*. Kegan Paul, Trench Trubner, London.
Osborn, H.F. (1902). Rapid Memorizing, 'Winging a Part", as a Lost Faculty, *Psychological Review*, 9, 183-84.
Paivio, A. (1971). *Imagery and Verbal Processes*, Holt, Rinehart and Winston, New York.
Patten, B.M. (1973). Visually Mediated Thinking: A Report of the Case of Albert Einstein. *Journal of Learning Disabilities*, 6, 415-20.
Pear, T.H. (1930). *The Art of Study*. Kegan Paul, Trench Trubner, London.
Pine-Coffin, R.S. (1961). Saint Augustine *Confessions*. Penguin Books, Harmondsworth.
Rothkopf, E.Z. (1971). Incidental Memory for Location of Information in Text. *Journal of Verbal Learning & Verbal Behavior*, 10, 608-13.
Saralden, (1934). *The Key to the Art of Concentration and Memorizing. Book Two. Memorizing*. Supreme Grand Lodge of A.M.O.R.C., San Jose, California.
Smirnov, A.A. (1973). *Problems of the Psychology of Memory*. Plenum Press, New York & London.
Sorabji, R. (1972). *Aristotle on Memory*. Duckworth, London.
Stamp, J. (1935). The Management of Mind. *University of London University College Annual Report*, 122-40.
Stokes, W. (1868). *Stokes's Capital Mnemonical Globe*. William Stokes, London.
Yates, F.A. (1966). *The Art of Memory*. Routledge and Kegal Paul, London.
Zechmeister, E.B., McKillip, J., Pasko, S., & Bespalec, D. (1975). Visual Memory for Place on the Page. *Journal of General Psychology*, 92, 43-52.

EXTERNAL MEMORY AIDS

John E. Harris
MRC Applied Psychology Unit,
15 Chaucer Road, Cambridge, England

ABSTRACT

In investigating memory aids psychologists have concentrated on testing the effectiveness of certain mnemonic skills which can be learned and applied to specific memory tasks. Despite the sometimes dramatic results of using these techniques in contrived situations, they may be of little use in everyday life. On the other hand, external memory aids such as shopping lists, diaries and cooking timers are frequently used in our everyday lives. It is argued, with supporting data coming from interview studies, that these form an important but neglected practical aspect of memory. Some effectiveness criteria and possible classifications are suggested.

FREQUENCY OF USE OF EXTERNAL AND INTERNAL AIDS

When I recently became interested in methods of aiding memory, I found that most of the psychological investigation was concerned with what may be called *internal aids*. Typical experiments (e.g. Bower and Clark, 1969) compared the performance of two groups of subjects at a memory task, where one group is given a hint as to how to perform the task, for example, "In order to remember these words, make up a story connecting them", while the other group is given no hints as to how to remember the words.

While internal memory aids of this type have attracted most attention from experimental psychologists, it is worth considering just how widely and how often they are used in comparison with such common external aids as diaries, memos and shopping lists.

This was investigated in a study in which I interviewed 30 students at Southampton University. The interview included questions about which memory aids the students used and how often. Each memory aid I asked about was described in sufficient detail to ensure that the student would recognize any aid he or she might use.

The external aids I asked about were (a) shopping lists, (b) diaries, (c) writing on the hand, (d) alarm clocks, watches and timers - three questions on different uses, (e) writing paper memos to oneself, (f) writing on or marking calendars, year planners etc., (g) asking someone else to give a reminder, and (h) leaving something in a special place where it will be encountered at the time it needs to be remembered. I also asked whether the students used any other external aids and gave as examples knotted handkerchiefs, changing rings to unfamiliar positions on fingers, and turning wristwatch to underside of wrist.

As far as internal aids were concerned it was more difficult to know what to include. Some schemes, such as that which leads to clustering in free recall of categorized lists, appear to be widely used, to be effective, and psychologists have studied their results. However, such schemes represent normal memory operations and are not usually referred to as "mnemonics" or "memory aids". They are also automatic in the sense that they are not taught and that in many instances the user is probably not aware of using them. At the other extreme there are the techniques which often have to be consciously learned and used, such as the "peg" and "loci" methods. Indeed it is probably the time and effort involved in learning and employing this type of aid which limits the amount they are used. Unfortunately, there seems to be no clear cut off point between these internal memory aids and what one might call normal remembering schemes.

Therefore, the way I chose which internal aids to ask about was by including those which I had come across in the memory aid literature as having been investigated, plus some others which were merely mentioned. Those chosen were (a) first letter mnemonics, (b) rhymes, (c) the method of loci, (d) the story method, (e) mentally retracing a sequence of events or actions, (f) the peg method, (g) turning numbers into letters, (h) face-name association, and (i) searching through the alphabet to find the initial letter of a forgotten name or word. With the exception of (g), these are all described by Morris (1977). In addition the students were asked if they used any other method of committing things to memory or for retrieving them from memory.

The students rated how often they had used these aids, both external and internal, on a seven point scale which is given in the lower part of Fig.1. The points on the scale may appear to be strange choices. However, I needed to use the same scale for all the aids whether they were hardly ever

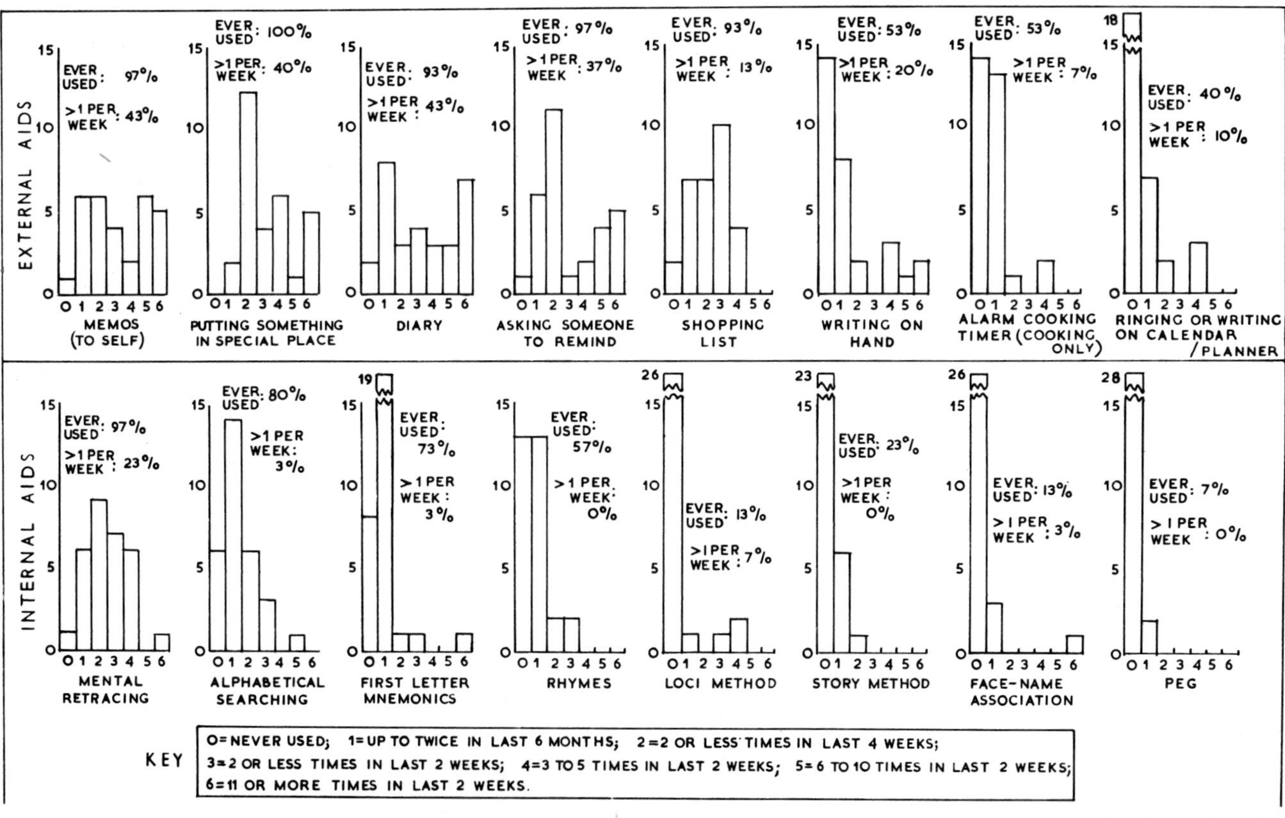

Fig. 1 *Reported frequency of use of memory aids by students (N=30). The vertical scale is the number of students in each category 0 to 6.*

or very frequently used, and an alternative scale I had used in a pilot questionnaire had proved inadequate.

The bar charts in Fig.1 show the reported frequencies of use of some of the memory aids. The abscissa represents the level of use of a memory aid, while the ordinate represents the number of students, out of a total of 30 who claimed to use it at a particular level. The top row shows the eight reportedly most used external aids, and the bottom row shows the equivalent internal aids. Both rows have the more frequently used aids on the left, though the categories used and distributions found do not allow perfect ordering.

The most apparent observation is how few of the internal aids are reported to be in frequent use, despite the fact that one might expect students to be among the most frequent users of these mnemonics.

Interestingly the two internal aids reported to be most used, mental retracing of events or actions and alphabetical searching, are rather different from the rest of the internal aids in the study. They are both pure *retrieval* strategies, in that no special encoding effort needs to have been made in order to use them. The other internal aids I asked about provide schemes for *encoding* or *learning*. It is mainly these which have been investigated and yet they are seldom used.

A comparable though more extreme pattern emerged from a similar study of 30 female members of the Cambridge Applied Psychology Unit subject panel, whose mean age was 46 years, (against a mean of 21 years for the student sample), and consisted mainly of housewives some having part-time jobs. The main difference was far greater reported use of certain external aids by this group, particularly of diaries and writing on calendars/year planners.

Before concluding this section on frequency of use, some additional points should be made. First, investigators of internal mnemonics would not necessarily claim that they are investigating frequently used aids. For example, Morris (1977) admits that even he, with his unusual knowledge of these techniques, makes little use of them in everyday life. There may also be theoretical rather than practical reasons to find out which of them are effective in the laboratory.

Second, some memory aids may be considered important in that they are used on a high proportion of possible occasions, even when the rarity of such possible occasions keeps the absolute frequency of use at a low level.

Third, both the interview studies described in this section were performed with samples from mainly middle-class, high ability populations. A less privileged sample might be expected to use less memory aids, both internal and external. Different occupations and living conditions produce varying memory loads as well as different types of memory problems, possibly calling for the use of different aids. While these considerations limit what generalizations can be made from the data presented above to other groups, it is not unreasonable to assume that students' use of internal memory aids is, at least, above average in frequency.

Fourth, mention should be made of the possible divergence between reported frequency of use and actual frequency of use. There does not seem to be much in the memory literature that suggests what this relationship might be. Flavell and Wellman (1977) differentiate four categories of memory phenomena, one of which is *metamemory*. Metamemory refers to an "individual's knowledge of and awareness of memory, or of anything pertinent to information storage and retrieval" (p.4). From their review it seems that the metamemory literature is developmentally orientated and does not contain a great deal of information about the knowledge of adults about their memories and the way they use them, let alone the aids they use. What information is given appears optimistic, for example, "It seems to us that the adults..... demonstrated an impressive amount of metamemory. They could predict their memory spans accurately; they were sensibly uncertain about their ability to predict them, in view of the novelty of the task situation; they believed that information about peers' performance on a novel memory task might provide a useful clue" (p.12).

On the other hand Wilkins and Baddeley (see this volume) have found that when people forgot to push a button, which they had been instructed to push at four specific times each day, they often failed to record this forgetting, though they had been instructed to make a note of it when they realized they had forgotten.

Certainly, (from my own questionnaire and interview studies), people appear to have difficulty in *recalling* (without being prompted by examples) what memory aids they use. However, once a particular aid is mentioned, and if necessary described in detail, my interviewees seemed quite ready to tell me how often they had used them, it sometimes being difficult to stop the flow of examples this elicited! The three open-ended questions about any other external and internal aids which they had used, but about which there had been no specific question, produced disappointing results. This is the basis for the above claim that people have difficulty in unprompted recall of the aids they use. This conclusion is dramatically confirmed by data from a later part of the interview, (not so far reported here), from which it was apparent that the Cambridge subjects made extensive use of address books, telephone number books and birthday books. These were rarely mentioned in response to the earlier open ended questions.

While these were all external aids, there were also indications that there may be internal aids which are more used than those specifically mentioned in the interview. For example, two Cambridge subjects mentioned internal mnemonics used when shopping without a written list. One of these aids was to remember the total number of items to be bought as well as what they are. This ensures that one does not terminate the shopping trip too early leaving some items unbought, and also allows one to make a confident decision to go home when the right number of items has been bought. The second shopping mnemonic is a pure retrieval one. It consists of imagining the contents of the bread-bin, the larder, the fridge, etc. as last seen, in order to remember how empty they were. This can then be used as a basis for what needs buying. It is clearly related to the method of loci, though that involves encoding by imagining things in places where they have never been and so is not a pure retrieval method.

There is not space here to report or discuss other results of the interview studies, such as greater reported use of external aids by female than by male students. It is hoped to present the studies in full elsewhere. However, some more general observations about external memory aids are included below.

TYPES OF EXTERNAL AID AND SOME CRITERIA GOVERNING THEIR EFFECTIVENESS

As well as distinguishing between internal and external aids these categories can be further sub-divided. Some distinctions among internal aids have already been mentioned. External aids may be separated into two groups. One group includes those whose function is merely external storage of information, either because it may be more accurate or complete than internal storage, or because internal storage mechanisms may be overloaded, (e.g. jotting down intermediate results during mental calculations). The second group of external memory aids are those that act as cues for action. For example, the words "wedding anniversary" in a diary are usually sufficient (if read at the appropriate time), because the user is quite capable of retrieving from his own memory the information that he should buy some flowers or take whatever is appropriate action. What he needs is a cue for a particular action, not a detailed description of the action.

Further classification of cueing devices can be made according to the type of cue which they provide. For example, an alarm cooking timer provides an *active* reminder, while a shopping list provides *specific* information about which items to buy. This type of classification leads one to look at the criteria for the effectiveness of external aids and of the cues which they provide.

For a cue to be maximally effective it should (a) be given as close as possible before the time when the action is required - it may be no good reminding someone as he leaves home in the morning to buy some bread on his way home from work, (b) be *active* rather than *passive* - a passive reminder in a diary may fail if the user forgets to consult it, and (c) be a specific reminder for the particular action that is required - a knotted handkerchief may only remind its user that something must be remembered but not what that something is.

While some currently available memory aids provide cues which rate well on one of the above criteria, few rate well on all three. In certain situations a cooking timer with a bell or buzzer rates particularly well. As regards temporal proximity, it is set to ring at the time when the action, (such as taking a cake out of the oven), is required. As regards being active, the bell rings so that the user does not need to remember independently that he must consult it. As regards specificity, the cooking timer's bell is usually distinct from the door bell or that of the telephone. However, it is not perfect in this respect as the user may often cook more than one thing at a time. An absent-minded person might well interpret the timer's bell as relevant to the saucepan which is visible rather than to the cake in the oven which is not.

Because they provide active, temporally proximate cues, some people use portable alarm cooking timers for other purposes, such as to remind them to turn on the TV for a certain programme. However, the more situations for which a bell-timer is used the less specific is the cue provided by the bell. This is also true for alarm watches which are now on the market, though they do have two distinct advantages over the cooking timer; a) the alarm watch is portable, and

b) it has another use, (it tells the time). As a result it is normally carried around and the user does not have to remember specially to take it with him.

So in addition to the three above mentioned criteria by which the effectiveness of cues for action can be judged, there are further criteria which apply to the instruments which provide the cues; a) such an instrument should be as portable as possible; b) it should be of use in as wide a range of situations as possible - so that the user bothers to carry it around and also so that he developes a habit of using it every time he wants to remember something he would otherwise forget; c) it should be able to store as many cues as possible for as long as possible - often cooking timers can only be set to ring at one particular time so that a further time can only be set after the first has been reached; also they often can only be set up to one hour at a time; and d) it should be easy to use and not require the use of a pencil or stylus.

While the total of seven criteria are not always mutually compatible (e.g. portability demands smallness which does not go with ease of use), it is possible to use them in setting about improving memory aids or developing new ones.

I have already made some attempts along these lines and, for example, have come up with a micro-electronic memory aid (MEMA) for which I have drawn up general specifications, cabinet layout diagrams and modifications for special uses. At its most simple paired times (e.g. "12.45 p.m.") and reminder messages (e.g. "Telephone John Smith") are entered into the MEMA, the reminder being played baek at the time with which it was entered. The time is entered onto a display using a calculator type keyboard, and the reminder message is recorded via a microphone. A portable device of this type should prove effective as it can provide cues which meet the above mentioned criteria of being active, specific, and temporally proximate.

REFERENCES

Bower, G.H. and Clark, M.C. (1969). Narrative stories as mediators for serial learning. *Psychonomic Science*, 14, 181-182.

Flavell, J.H. and Wellman, H.M. (1977). Metamemory. In: *Perspectives on the Development of Memory and Cognition*. (R.V. Kail and J.W. Hagan eds.), Erlbaum, Hillsdale, N.J.

Morris, P.E. (1977). Practical strategies for human learning and remembering. In: *Human Learning*. (M.J.A. Howe ed.), pp.125-144. Wiley, London.

CULTURE AND MNEMONICS

Daniel A. Wagner
University of Pennsylvania
Philadelphia, Pa., USA

ABSTRACT

Theories of adult memory and memory development in children have made increasing reference to the importance of mnemonics, but only limited attention has been devoted to the varieties of cultural and societal experiences that induce or produce mnemonic use. A cross-cultural study was undertaken in Morocco which showed that mnemonic use varied importantly with such lifetime experiences as formal schooling and urbanization. This study, which contrasted a variety of populations including Koranic scholars and traditional rug sellers, provided evidence that mnemonic use may be culture-specific, or a function of specific life-time experiences. It was concluded that individual and group differences in memory may be largely a function of such differences in mnemonic use.

INTRODUCTION

The present paper is concerned with how culture may influence the use of "mnemonics," where the latter is defined as any strategy, skill or plan that is used to enhance memory performance. The topic is a difficult one primarily due to the problem of separating biological and cultural influences. However, many investigators appear to agree on a number of basic points. First, all normal human infants exhibit memory abilities as early as they can be tested. A variety of habituation and conditioning experiments attest to this fact, and to the fact that such abilities increase fairly rapidly over the first few years of life (see Stevenson, 1971, for a review). Second, there is evidence that such physiologically based changes asymptote by about four or five years of age, even though memory performance continues to improve until about adolescence. This latter phenomenon is generally explained as being a function of children's increasing linguistic and information processing skills (Hagen, Jongeward & Kail, 1975; Olson, 1973). More specifically, it is generally believed that the memory strategies or mnemonics -- sometimes referred to as "control processes" in adult models of memory (e.g. Atkinson & Shiffrin, 1968) -- are precisely what children acquire as they become adult-like memorizers (Brown, 1975; Flavell, 1970). The development of mnemonics or control processes has been found to begin as early as three years of age (Wellman, Ritter & Flavell, 1975), and increases up until about 13 years of age in school children tested on standard memory tasks. Mnemonic strategies that have been specifically investigated include: verbal rehearsal, clustering, categorization, semantic elaboration, and metamemorial skills (Brown, 1975; Flavell & Wellman, 1977; Hagen *et al.*, 1975). However, there are other, "structural" features of memory (Atkinson & Shiffrin, 1968) that, unlike mnemonics, are not under the subject's control. These include sensory, short-term, and long-term stores, and fixed decay rates. Structural features apparently develop rapidly in early development, and change little with age (see Wagner, 1978, for a review).

The central question of the present discussion is: What are the varieties of lifetime experiences that promote mnemonic use and memory development? It is suggested here that certain mnemonics are more likely to be demonstrated by individuals or groups of individuals who have had certain cultural and information processing experiences than those who have not. There are at least three general sources of evidence that are available to support this cultural (as opposed to biological) hypothesis. The first source of data come from individuals who have had experiences that are "supplementary" when compared to those of "normals." That is, they have learned (by chance or by effort) mnemonics that allow them to achieve greater than "normal" memory performance. (It is important to note here that "normality" is a relative term. When standard Western texts refer to (normal) adult memory and memory development in children, the reference is clearly to those that have been the subjects of study --that is, primarily Euro-American, middle-class college students or grade-school children. While such a definition is arbitrary, it provides a useful benchmark from which one may study superior or inferior to normal abilities.) There are, at present, a substantial number of case studies where individuals have been shown to have supranormal memory abilities. Some studies describe individuals who have consciously learned special mnemonic strategies, such as the Greek "method of loci," imagery techniques, and various recoding schemes (see Baddeley, 1976, for a review). Other studies describe individuals who seem to have acquired certain strategies without apparent training or intention, such as Luria's (1968) "S", and the British mathematician Aitken (described by Hunter in this Volume). These case studies provide rich detail into the mechanisms of human memory, and also tend to support the notion that memory ability may be highly malleable.

A second body of data is provided by the "training studies" of developmental psychologists. A distinguishing feature between younger and older children's memory performance has been found to be the latter's use of mnemonic strategies. Thus, a number of investigators have tried to teach such strategies to younger (or sometimes low I.Q.) children who typically showed little use of mnemonics. In general, it has been found that low performing children could be trained or taught to use such strategies as rehearsal and categorization, and subsequently showed improved memory performance (Brown, 1975; Campione & Brown, this Volume; Kingsley & Hagen, 1969; Wagner, 1975). While such training clearly demonstrates the acquisition of mnemonics through cultural intervention, children in such studies generally did not use the acquired strategies after the training was over.

A third source of data comes primarily from cross-cultural studies which attempt to compare and contrast populations which have differing cultural experiences. An early description of cultural differences in memory was provided by European ethnographers working primarily in Africa. Ethnographic accounts sometimes cited the supranormal memory abilities of "savages," while at other times seemed to support a point of view which attested to superior "rote" memory ability at the *expense* of critical thinking. Finally, some accounts provided evidence of culturally specific mnemonic aids, such as knot-tying among the Incas (for reviews, see Cole & Gay, 1972; Cole, Gay, Glick & Sharp, 1971). Recent cross-cultural research has attempted to: (1) investigate early ethnographic accounts; (2) test the generality of memory models; and (3) separate previously confounded environmental variables by careful selection of subject populations. For example, Cole *et al.* (1971) found that schooled Liberians used clustering strategies in free recall experiments, and thus attained higher memory performance than non-schooled Liberians. Another study in Liberia showed that degree of urbanization was significantly related to clustering strategies and subsequent recall (Scribner, 1974). While these studies seemed to show the influence of culture on memory, at least one other, highly-publicized study, conducted in Guatemala, suggested that memory is a "basic cognitive process," and that culturally and environmentally based differences *disappear* by adolescence (Kagan & Klein, 1973). Part of the difficulty in comparing such conflicting results and points of view resides in the fact that differing methodologies, tasks and populations were used.

The present study was designed to resolve some of the above difficulties by selecting well-defined, contrasting populations within a single general cultural group, and by using a variety of cognitive tasks. Thus, a study was undertaken in Morocco, where wide environmental variability provided an ideal setting for investigating the general influence of schooling and urbanization, as well as other, more specific experiences. Two main experiments will be briefly described below; further ethnographic, methodological, and statistical details of these and other experiments in Morocco have been published elsewhere (Wagner, 1977, 1978).

In both experiments, the subjects were 384 Moroccan males, and were selected so as to complete a three-way factorial design: age (7, 11, 14, and 19 mean years of age) X schooling (schooled *vs*. non-schooled) X environment (urban *vs*. rural). Thus, there were 16 groups and 24 subjects in each group. Additional groups of subjects were also tested in order to study the possible culture-specific influences on mnemonics: traditional Koranic scholars (Experiments I & II); Moroccan rug sellers and University of Michigan students (Experiment II). The memory tasks used in the experiments were chosen because they each tapped into aspects of structure and control processes.

EXPERIMENT I: SHORT-TERM RECALL

Method

The first experiment explored the development of short-term recall. A serial memory task, used extensively in the developmental literature, required the subject to locate the position of an animal drawing in a series of seven briefly presented drawings, where the to-be-remembered drawing varied in position from trial to trial over 14 trials. The subject was first shown each of the seven cards which were then placed face down after a brief presentation. Following the presentation of the seven cards, the subject was shown a single "probe" card with an animal drawing on it, and had to find the location of the same animal in the linear array of face down cards.

The task has been particularly useful because it provides a serial position curve, where the primacy effect has been shown to be a function of verbal rehearsal strategies (Hagen *et al*., 1975). Also, the recency effect provides a measure of short-term store, considered to be a structural feature of memory. Finally, the task provides an overall recall measure by calculating the percent correct over 14 trials. Analysis of the results is presented only briefly here since an earlier (though less extensive) study in Mexico (Wagner, 1974) produced similar results.

Results and discussion

Analyses of variance showed that recency recall was stable and relatively invariant across all population groups studied, regardless of age, schooling and environment. Primacy recall developed with age *only* for schooled subjects, and in a somewhat diminished form for non-schooled children who lived in an urban setting. Also, primacy recall was the most important factor in improved overall recall in the older schooled groups. The Koranic scholars' performance was similar to that of rural non-schooled subjects, who showed little primacy effect and no increase in recall with age.

Thus, Experiment I provides evidence that formal schooling and urbanization may contribute independently and positively to the development of control processes or mnemonics. It appears that the use of mnemonic strategies, such as rehearsal, may be linked to certain (as yet not well understood) cultural experiences, while short-term store -- a structural feature measured by the recency effect -- seems to be present in all individuals, regardless of age or special cultural experiences.

EXPERIMENT II: RECOGNITION MEMORY

Developmental studies of recognition memory -- in contrast to recall -- have been most often characterized by a lack of age-related trends in performance. Such invariance with age is considered to be evidence of the degree to which recognition memory does *not* require mnemonic strategies (Brown, 1975). Furthermore, a variety of studies has shown that forgetting rates (the continuous decay of information from memory as a function of time or intervening information to be remembered) are also invariant from childhood through adulthood (Nelson, 1971; Wickelgren, 1975).

Method

The subjects were the same as those in Experiment I, except for the addition of two groups: adult Moroccan rug sellers, and University of Michigan students. All subjects were tested on a modified version of the continuous recognition memory task of Shepard and Teghtsoonian (1961), which provides a measure of forgetting rate as well as overall recognition performance. The stimuli consisted of 207 black and white photographs of Oriental rugs. The experiment included a practice test of 30 trials, followed by the experimental task of 177 trials. The experimental task consisted of 88 different rug patterns and 88 exact duplicates, which were arranged in a sequential array so that duplicates formed "lags" of 1, 5, 10, and 25 intervening items. Both practice and experimental stimuli were arranged in large notebooks, so that when the next pattern was exposed, it covered the previous pattern. The subject was instructed to look at each rug carefully, and say whether the present pattern was appearing for the first or second time. The subject was allowed about five seconds to look and respond to each item before turning to the next item.

Results and discussion

Results were based on five derived measures of performance: total correct (sum of hits and correct rejections); and *d'* for each of the four lags. For each of these measures, three-way analyses of variance were performed. The most important features of these analyses were: (1) chronological age produced little or no reliable effects for any of the measures; (2) schooling produced a significant effect, but primarily at longer lags; (3) the effect of environment was highly significant, but contrary to the recall task, the *rural* subjects were superior on total correct recognition; and (4) Michigan students and Rug Sellers performed as well as the best rural subjects, while the Koranic scholars scored near the bottom. Statistical profile analyses of forgetting rates (the decline in *d'* over lag) showed that the curves were, in general, invariant or parallel to one another across both age and population groups, including the three additional groups.

In general, these data on recognition memory support previous research that indicated little age-related change in forgetting rates. Furthermore, forgetting rates were invariant with respect to schooling and environment. While it is unclear why rural subjects performed so much better than urban subjects on total correct, one potential hypothesis is that rural subjects were more familiar with rugs than urban subjects (but, for more discussion, see Wagner, 1978). Finally, the Rug Sellers (with little formal education) scored as well or better than all other Moroccan groups. While familiarity might again be invoked as a hypothesis, it seems likely that Rug Sellers are able to pick out distinctive features in rugs as a function of occupational experience. Furthermore, recent evidence suggests that some Rug Sellers also use categorization strategies to aid in recall of rugs as part of daily commerce.

CONCLUSIONS AND COMMENTS

The combined results of the two experiments support the hypothesis that experiential factors, such as formal schooling and living in an urban environment, may influence the development of control processes in memory. The results of the recall experiment showed that verbal rehearsal appeared to be used only by older schooled subjects, and to some extent by urban non-schooled subjects. These data, reflecting the stable use of rehearsal strategies by about age 13, are consistent with data collected among American school children. From the recognition experiment there is some further evidence that encoding strategies may be used by Rug Sellers to aid in recognition. The ontogeny of these strategies is less clear, because age-related changes were not observed among these subjects.

It is also important to note which features of memory were *not* evidently influenced by the experiential contrasts of this study. Specifically, it appears that structural features of memory were least affected: a relatively fixed-capacity short-term store was found in all groups; and forgetting rates were also found to be relatively invariant. Thus, it may be concluded that references to an "inherent program" of "basic cognitive processes" (mentioned earlier, Kagan & Klein, 1973) should be limited to estimates of memory performance that tap primarily structural features, rather than those that may involve the use of mnemonics.

We have seen a variety of evidence that suggests that control processes or mnemonics may be *culture-specific* -- that is, a function of the particular socialization of individuals or groups of individuals. Formal schooling and urban society have been found to be exemplars of such "cultures." Additional evidence is available form other sources. It is well-known that remembering the words to a song is greatly facilitated by singing the song -- the tune and rhythm serve as mnemonics. Among the Kpelle in Liberia, Lancy (1975) has reported that "my informants had great difficulty recalling the songs unless they were singing *and dancing* (p. 9; italics added)." Thus we see a motoric or kinesthetic mnemonic that aids recall. Similar evidence was recently gathered in a study of memory in deaf children (Liben & Drury, 1976). In this study, deaf children created their own, apparently culture-specific or deaf-specific mnemonics for remembering. The authors observed the use of finger spelling and the use of mime representations as mnemonics. Also, as mentioned earlier, there are numerous examples of mnemonic aids that have been used to carry forward oral traditions of differing cultures (e.g. Yates, 1966).

In the study of culture-specific mnemonics, there remain at least two serious problems. The first concerns the origin of mnemonics that are not overtly taught. A few studies have described the acquisition of mnemonics in young children (e.g. Wellman *et al*., 1975), yet, in most cases, we do *not* know the origins of the general use of rehearsal and clustering strategies by school children. What are the information processing tasks in school and in everyday life that produce these spontaneous processes? And what experiences may be lacking in children who do not use these strategies? We know very little about the answers to such questions. A second problem concerns the difficulty of measurement. It is often difficult to distinguish between those who have not acquired a mnemonic and those who "have" it, but do not apply it on the appropriate task. In Experiments I and II, Koranic scholars showed poor memory performance, and little use of mnemonics. Yet, a more recent study (with different subjects at the same Koranic school in Morocco) shows that beginning students learn quickly how to use chanting as a way of "keeping track" of Koranic verse. And, only later do more advanced students learn to "chunk" passages into units to aid in remembering. In Liberia, Scribner (personal communication) has also found that Koranic students use mnemonics, but only when the task makes use of serial ordering skills. Such evidence suggests that we should be careful in generalizations about the availability of cognitive skills in differing populations. These two problems will have to be addressed more fully in order to construct a comprehensive model of memory.

REFERENCES

Atkinson, R.C. and Shiffrin, R.M. (1968). Human memory: A proposed system and its control processes. In K.W. Spence & J. T. Spence (Eds.), *The Psychology of Learning and Motivation: Advances in Theory and Research*. Vol. 2, New York: Academic Press.

Baddeley, A.D. (1976). *The Psychology of Memory*. New York: Basic Books.

Brown, A.L. (1975). The development of memory: Knowing, knowing about knowing, and knowing how to know. In H.W. Reese (Ed.), *Advances in Child Development and Behavior*. Vol. 10. New York: Academic Press.

Cole, M., and Gay, J. (1972). Culture and memory. *American Anthropologist*, 74, 1066-1084.

Cole, M., Gay, J., Glick, J., and Sharp, D. (1971). *The Cultural Context of Learning and Thinking*. New York: Basic Books.

Flavell, J.H., and Wellman, H. (1977). Metamemory. In R.V. Kail & J.W. Hagen (Eds.), *Perspectives on the Development of Memory and Cognition*. Hillsdale, N.J.: L. Erlbaum.

Hagen, J.W., Jongeward, R.H., and Kail, R.V.,Jr. (1975). Cognitive perspectives on the development of memory. In H.W. Reese (Ed.), *Advances in Child Development and Behavior*. Vol. 10. New York: Academic Press.

Kagan, J., and Klein, R.E. (1973). Cross-cultural perspectives on early development. *American Psychologist*, 28, 947-961.

Kingsley, P.R., and Hagen, J.W. (1969). Induced versus spontaneous rehearsal in short-term memory in nursery school children. *Developmental Psychology*, 1, 40-46.

Lancy, D.F. (1975). *Studies in memory in culture*. Paper presented at the Conference on Issues in Cross-cultural research, New York Academy of Sciences.

Liben, L.S., and Drury, A.M. (1977). Short-term memory in deaf and hearing children in relation to stimulus characteristics. *Journal of Experimental Child Psychology*, 24, 60-73.

Luria, A.R. (1968). *The Mind of a Mnemonist*. New York: Basic Books.

Nelson, K.E. (1971). Memory development in children: Evidence from non-verbal tasks. *Psychonomic Science*, 25, 346-348.

Olson, G.M. (1973). Developmental changes in memory and the acquisition of language. In T.E. Moore (Ed.), *Cognitive Development and the Acquisition of Language*. New York: Academic Press.

Stevenson, H.W. (1971). *Children's Learning*. New York: Appleton-Century-Crofts.

Wagner, D.A. (1974). The development of short-term and incidental memory: A cross-cultural study. *Child Development*, 45, 389-396.

Wagner, D.A. (1975). The effects of verbal labeling on short-term and incidental memory: A cross-cultural and developmental study. *Memory and Cognition*, 3, 595-598.

Wagner, D. A. (1977). Ontogeny of the Ponzo illusion: Effects of age, schooling and environment. *International Journal of Psychology*, 12, 161-176.

Wagner, D.A. (1978). Memories of Morocco: The influence of age schooling and environment on memory. *Cognitive Psychology*, 10, 1-28.

Wellman, H., Ritter, A., and Flavell, J.H. (1975). Deliberate memory behavior in the delay reactions of very young children. *Developmental Psychology*, 11, 78¼-787.

Wickelgren, W.A. (1975). Age and storage dynamics in continuous recognition memory. *Developmental Psychology*, 11, 165-169

Yates, F.A. (1966). *The Art of Memory*. Chicago: University of Chicago Press.

KNOWLEDGE AND RETENTION: THE FEELING OF KNOWING AND REMINISCENCE

M.M. Gruneberg and R.N. Sykes

Department of Psychology,
University College of Swansea,
Swansea, Wales

The knowledge that we have about the capabilities of our own memory systems has been of growing interest to psychologists since the publication of two seminal articles in the 1960's, one by Brown & McNeil (1966), on the tip of the tongue phenomenon, and one by Hart (1965), on the feeling of knowing phenomenon. Brown & McNeil, using definitions of rare words, found that when subjects were in a tip of the tongue state (i.e. knew the answer, but could not get it back) they could produce many of the characteristics of the missing word, such as the number of syllables and the first letter of the missing word. Hart, in his studies, was concerned with the whole range of the feeling of knowing recall failure, from the tip of the tongue state at one extreme, to certainty that subjects felt they did not know the missing word at the other. He examined the accuracy of such feeling of knowing (FOK) judgements in relation to later evidence of retention as measured by recognition, and found that the greater the expressed feeling of knowing for items not recalled, the greater the probability of later recognition. He interpreted these and similar results to indicate a memory monitoring mechanism which tells the subject whether an item not retrieved is in store and therefore whether a further memory search is worthwhile.

Our own interest in the FOK phenomenon arose out of an interest in examining practical problems of memory. In an experiment by Gruneberg, Winfrow & Woods (1973) we were interested in memory blocks - largely equivalent to the T.O.T. phenomenon except that many people are able to express themselves certain they know an answer but are temporarily unable to recall it, without any obvious accompanying emotional reactions. We were interested in seeing what kind of memory blocks subjects themselves could be induced to report, and to examine the time course of recovery of such blocks. Subjects were asked to produce their own blocks in their own way, and despite some initial puzzlement, all but 4 of the 20 subjects did this by searching through categories such as old school friends, until they came upon a particular face they could not name, or a capital they could not name and so on. Categories were suggested for 4 subjects.

20 subjects reported a total of 206 blocks. 66% were recalled after a search during the experimental session,and 15 were recalled following a second retrieval attempt between 2-9 hours later. Whilst the majority of blocks were recalled within about 30 seconds of their being reported, 15 blocks took more than 90 seconds before successful recall, a period of time which is subjectively quite considerable. No block was recovered spontaneously between the first and second retrieval attempt without an active search being initiated, so that if memory blocks do recover spontaneously during other ongoing activity, there is no evidence for this in our study.

One of the strategies subjects used in the study was to go through the alphabet to see if they could hit the first letter of the missing item, and thus to trigger off the missing word. The use of first letter cueing had previously been examined by Earhard (1967), who showed the facilitative effects of such cueing in recall. First letter cueing is also the basis of mnemonic aids, such as Richard Of York Gave Battle In Vain, and we thought it would be useful to examine the relationship between the degree of feeling of knowing, and recall following first letter cueing. If there were a major effect, it suggests that first letter cueing might operate to aid recall in situations where S's were suffering a memory block. It would suggest that mnemonic aids which incorporate first letter cueing might be particularly useful in situations where memory blocks are likely to occur - in examinations say.

The first experiment we conducted on this (Gruneberg & Monks, 1974) involved presenting a list of 25 countries to Geography students individually and asking them to name the capitals. We chose capitals as this was a category frequently chosen spontaneously in the first experiment, for blocking, and we chose Geography students in the fond but mistaken hope that they would be familiar with capitals, but just block on a few. If S's could not name the capital they had to give an FOK rating from 1-3, or say they did not know the item ($\overline{FOK}$). There then followed a second uncued retrieval attempt following which all items still not recalled were cued with the first letter. On a final trial, items still not recalled were cued with the first and second letter.

As far as results are concerned we found, as did Hart and others, the greater the expressed FOK, the greater the evidence of subsequent retention. The results indicated that being presented with a first letter gives over 50% recall where S's are in a state of certainty or near certainty regarding their knowledge.

There are, unfortunately, at least two methodological problems with the experiment. In the first place the time taken for memory search for FOK items is significantly greater than for $\overline{FOK}$ items. In the second place, the relationship between FOK and subsequent cued recall varies with the nature of the material. These problems are dealt with in turn.

The fact that the time taken to search for items previously given an FOK rating is significantly greater than is the time taken to search following an $\overline{FOK}$ rating, leaves open the possibility that differences in the probability of recall following cueing for FOK and $\overline{FOK}$ items might be due to the greater motivation and greater time spent in searching for FOK items. We therefore carried out an experiment, (Gruneberg, Monks & Sykes, 1978) which tried to increase the time spent on memory search for $\overline{FOK}$ items by offering a reward of 5p for cued recall of items previously given an $\overline{FOK}$ rating, and not offering a reward for items previously given an FOK rating. Subjects were presented with the same experimental situation as in the feeling of knowing study, but were told at the beginning of the cueing trial that for certain items they would be rewarded with 5p if they could give the correct answer.

The experiment worked, at least in inducing subjects to spend as long searching for $\overline{FOK}$ as FOK items. However, FOK rated items were still significantly more likely to be recalled following first letter cueing than were $\overline{FOK}$ rated items ($p < .001$). The recall probabilities overall were .38 for FOK and .14 for $\overline{FOK}$. It can therefore be concluded that greater search time per se, is not likely to be the reason for the greater cued recall of FOK items.

The second problem is perhaps more difficult, namely that the relationship between FOK and subsequent recall varies with the nature of the material employed. In 1923 Brown conducted an experiment which involved subjects writing down as many states of the Union as they could on two successive occasions. It was found that the probability of recall following an initial retrieval failure was likely to be greater for items where the group as a whole had had a high initial recall. Given this finding, it was decided to re-examine Gruneberg & Monks' data for any possible interaction of group recall level with the relationship between expressed feeling of knowing following retrieval failure, and recall following first letter cueing. Countries were divided into those above the median in terms of the number of subjects giving the correct capital on the first trial, i.e. where more than 14 subjects gave the correct answer (the 'high' recall set) and those below the median, i.e. where less than 14 subjects gave the correct answer (the 'low' recall set). Recall probabilities following first letter cueing for items unrecalled on the first trial for the high and low sets for each subject were obtained.

The results clearly indicated the differential effect of initial group knowledge on the relationship between rated feeling of knowing and subsequent cued recall. Such a finding is perhaps not surprising in what where subjects give an FOK rating to such well known capitals as those of Belgium and Sweden, they are more likely to be in error regarding their lack of knowledge, than when they claim not to know less prominent capitals, of, say, Malaya or Zambia. In other words, for items given the same feeling of knowing rating, and presumably therefore, having the same subjective characteristics for the S in terms of feeling of knowing, subsequent probability of recall following cueing can nevertheless be shown to vary systematically with group knowledge.

Given this finding, we wondered whether in addition, for different kinds of material, the relationship between FOK and subsequent recall would vary. Hart (1967) in a little known study, showed a relationship between FOK and reminiscence. We therefore decided to examine further the relationship between FOK and reminiscence for different kinds of material i.e. uncued recall following a retrieval failure. We used three kinds of material, Capitals of Countries, Miscellaneous General Knowledge and Definitions of Words.

The experimental design involved presenting 25 items from each section individually and requiring Ss to give an FOK rating from 1-6 for items not recalled, 1 = certainly known, 6 = certainly not known. The sections were presented in random order for each subject, and following the presentation of all 75 questions, S's were again presented with unrecalled items and asked for a second retrieval attempt.

The probability of recall following a second retrieval attempt for each section is given in Table I.

Table I
OVERALL AVERAGE PROBABILITIES OF RECALL ON A SECOND RETRIEVAL ATTEMPT

	FOK					
	1	2	3	4	5	6
Definitions	.30	.28	.12	.10	.15	.13
Famous People	.19	.27	.10	.10	.08	.10
Capitals	.17	.10	.08	.04	.02	.02

Recall probability for FOK 1, 2 and 3 combined is significantly greater than for FOK 4, 5 and 6 combined (for all kinds of material, $P < .005$ one-tailed test).

Overall probability of recall of Definitions is significantly higher than Capitals P .01. Probability of recall of Famous People is significantly higher than Capitals $P < .02$. (two-tailed test)

For FOK ratings 1, 2 and 3 combined
Recall probability of Definitions and Capitals differ significantly at $P < .05$. (two-tailed test)

For FOK ratings 4, 5 and 6 combined
Recall probabilities of Definitions and Capitals differ significantly $P < .01$, and Famous People and Capitals differ significantly $P < .02$. (two-tailed test)

All were tested by Wilcoxon Matched Pairs Signed Ranks Test.

As can be seen, for all sections, FOK recall probability is significantly greater than is that for $\overline{FOK}$ items. However, there are significant differences between sections. For example, recall probabilities for FOK 1, 2 and 3 for Definitions and Capitals differ significantly ($P < .05$). Thus for different kinds of material, where FOK ratings are identical and therefore presumably have the same subjective feeling as far as the individual is concerned, there can nevertheless be a significant difference in the probability of recall dependent on the nature of the material involved.

Given the finding of within material differences for different levels of group knowledge, in the study of Gruneberg, Monks & Sykes (1978) it is possible that differences between materials in terms of the relationship between FOK and subsequent recall can be accounted for by the higher level of initial knowledge of particular materials. In the present experiment overall recall on the first trial is considerably greater for Definitions and Famous People than for Capitals and although Definitions and Famous People do differ significantly, the actual mean difference is small.

Where individual items from Capitals, however, are matched with those of Famous People and Definitions in terms of initial group recall, then differences in the probability of recall for both FOK and $\overline{FOK}$ items fail to reach significance (see Table II).

Table II
MATCHED ITEMS FROM CAPITALS, DEFINITIONS and PEOPLE

	FOK	$\overline{FOK}$
Capitals	.17	.08
People	.13	.07
N	37	12
	N.S.	N.S.
Capitals	.19	.04
Definitions	.16	.07
N	29	10
	N.S.	N.S.

N = numbers of paired comparisons used in Wilcoxon matched pairs signed ranks test.

Whilst little can be made of a failure to find significant differences for the FOK comparisons, because of the small number of comparisons involved, the number of comparisons for the FOK condition is sufficient to allow the conclusion that the difference in recall probabilities for different kinds of FOK rated material in the present experiment can be accounted for by differences in the level of initial group knowledge, rather than in terms of intrinsic differences in the nature of the material.

The question arises of course as to why initial group knowledge should be so important a variable. One possibility is that for well known items the individual is likely to have more close associates of the missing item to aid him with search and retrieval, compared to little known capitals, where the sought-for-item might be well known to the subject for idiosyncratic reasons.

What then is the significance of studies of feeling of knowing?

(1) Studies of feeling of knowing tell us something of the way our cognitive structure is organised. Studies such as Brown & McNeil are illustrations of aspects of organisation.

(2) A number of studies show that how an individual feels about his state of memory can affect mnemonic strategies. For example, in free recall tasks, the last items tend to be recalled first and subjects frequently report that the most recently presented items will disappear unless they are rapidly reported.

(3) The present study on FOK and reminiscence shows the importance of existing cognitive structure in relation to memory performance. Whilst the current emphasis on strategies employed by subjects is to be welcomed, such findings warn us not to ignore the importance of existing structural aspects of memory.

(4) An examination of factors involved in making judgements of confidence about memory have been shown by Deffenbacher (this volume) to have practical implications in, for example, eye-witness testimony. Their finding that confidence in judgements about their memory was not an accurate predictor of success for event material contrasts with laboratory findings. Little work, however, seems to have been done in this area despite its considerable practical significance and, apart from the question of why

laboratory and 'real life' findings differ, the whole question of individual differences in confidence judgements remains to be examined. Are certain individual more accurate in their judgements about the contents of their memories, and if so, can they be readily identified?

Whatever the merits or otherwise of our own contribution to the field, we do feel that this is an area which has been grossly neglected by memory researchers in the recent past, both from a theoretical and practical level.

REFERENCES

Brown, R. and McNeill, D. (1966) The 'tip of the tongue' phenomenon. *Journal of Verbal Learning and Verbal Behavior*, 5, 325-337.

Earhard, M. (1967) Cued recall and free recall as a function of the number of items for cue. *Journal of Verbal Learning and Verbal Behavior*, 6, 257-263.

Gruneberg, M.M., Winfrow, P. and Woods, R. (1973) An investigation into memory blocking. *Acta Psychologica*, 37, 187-196.

Gruneberg, M.M. and Monks, J. (1974) Feeling of knowing and cued recall. *Acta Psychologica*, 38, 257-265.

Gruneberg, M.M., Monks, J. and Sykes, R.N. (1977) Some methodological problems with feeling of knowing studies. *Acta Psychologica*, 41, 365-371.

Hart, J.T. (1965) Memory and the feeling of knowing experience. *Journal of Educational Psychology*, 56, 208-216.

Hart, J.T. (1967) Second try recall, recognition and the memory-monitoring process. *Journal of Educational Psychology*, 58, 193-197.

EYEWITNESSING

A CRITIQUE OF EYEWITNESS RESEARCH

Brian Clifford
Department of Psychology
North East London Polytechnic
Three Mills, Abbey Lane,
London E15 2RP.

While research into eyewitness behaviour has a long history its present status is a source of concern. This may reflect the current state of applied research in general, of which Littman (1961) wrote that when other professions come to psychology for advice "they are disappointed and, indeed, often aggrieved. What they begin to read with enthusiasm they put down with depression. What seems promising turns out to be sterile, palpably trivial, or false and, in any case, a waste of time." (p.232). The argument that this indictment does not apply to the particular case of eyewitness research is not substantiated by a reading of the Devlin Report (1976) on Evidence of Identification in Criminal Cases. This report, while stating explicitly that one of the Committee's first tasks was to enquire whether studies in forensic and general psychology threw any light on the problem which they were addressing, concluded that "... it has been represented to us that a gap exists between academic research into the powers of the human mind and the practical requirements of courts of law and the stage seems not yet to have been reached at which the conclusions of psychological research are sufficiently widely accepted or tailored to the needs of the judicial process to become the basis for procedural change." (p.73).

Given its long history, this condemnation of eyewitness research is worrying. What is the reason for this incapacity? At base it stems from the different orientations of pure and applied research. The former tends to have a theoretical orientation and is concerned with formal elegance and logical rigour, while the latter has a problem-centred orientation and is concerned with situationally valid, socially relevant and publicly usable knowledge. The implicit and explicit assumptions of these respective orientations have implications for testimony research because eyewitness memory straddles both pure and applied fields. While researchers of basic theory are able to maintain direction and focus by demonstrating how their operations apply to a theory (Wells, 1978) eyewitness researchers have no such focus. Thus, because eyewitness behaviour is at base a perceptual-memory phenomenon the assumption has been made that the paradigms of visual memory research can be employed wholesale. This has restricted independent variable manipulation, dependent variable measurement, and the ecological validity of experimentation. Further, by making recourse to standard memory paradigms eyewitness research has absorbed the simplifying heuristics which characterize pure research, such as perceiving man as passive, rather than active; and decoupling memory from both other cognitive processes and other more socially-based processes such as attitudes, beliefs and feelings (Clifford and Bull, 1978).

This lack of an appropriate focus, plus the seduction by simplifying assumptions and procedures has led eyewitness research into a situation where it lacks a unifying paradigm and as a result exhibits problems of agreement, generalizability and comprehensiveness.

The lack of a standard paradigm in eyewitness research

While the history of eyewitness research has exhibited four main strands (Clifford, 1979) two basic styles of experimentation are central - 'live' and 'representational' designs. In live experimentation subjects are witness to a live event and subsequent recognition is made of a live target (Live-Live, L-L). In the representational mode the subjects are presented with picture, film or videotape material and the ensuing recognition is made in the same medium (Representational-Representational, R-R). Of course hybrid designs are possible, i.e. L-R or R-L.

We can now go one stage further and superimpose this live-representational dichotomy on the experimental and mundane realism dichotomy proposed by Carlsmith, Ellsworth and Aronson (1976). These authors suggest an experiment has experimental realism if it is "realistic to the subjects... (and)...has an impact on them, and mundane realism if it produces a situation "likely to occur in the 'real world'". By juxtaposing the two dichotomies we now have: (a) Live-Live experimentation which is high in both experimental and mundane realism, (b)Live-Representational designs similarly high on both realisms, (c) Representational-Live procedures which (depending on the nature of the stimuli) lose out on both experimental and mundane realism, and (d) Representational-Representational paradigms which again have low experimental and mundane realism.

Now the problem for applicability is that as one moves from high to low dual realism (i.e. L-L, L-R, R-L, R-R) so the number of eyewitness experiments increase. Thus while the event or live methodology has the greatest ecological validity it is the least used method. This is unfortunate because lawyers and police just do not believe that psychologists can extrapolate from picture processing to crime witnessing without serious remainder. I have argued elsewhere (Clifford, 1979) that the utilization of the event methodology is a necessary (although not sufficient) precondition for an eyewitness research effort to not only be relevant but to be seen to be relevant.

The lack of agreement in eyewitness research

The problem with the four historical streams of research in eyewitness testimony (old and new research with photographs, and with event methodology) is that they are conflicting. Thus when interested parties ask such questions as: How good is visual memory? Does delay have an effect on witness memory? Are men and women potentially equal as witnesses? and so on, we have no clear answer - it all depends!

Because of space only one example will be elaborated to make the point. The answer to the first question would depend upon the source of research consulted. If we consulted picture memory data estimates of visual memory would be somewhere in the 90% accurate range (e.g. Nickerson, 1965; Shepard, 1967; Standing, 1973; Standing, Conezio and Haber, 1970). If we consulted face photograph research estimates would range from 90%+ (Hochberg and Galper, 1974; Yin, 1969) through 80%+ (Shepherd and Ellis, 1973) and 70%+ (Chance, Goldstein and McBride, 1975; Elliott, Wills and Goldstein, 1973; Goldstein and Chance, 1971; Malpass and Kravitz, 1969; Scapinello and Yarmey, 1970), to the comparatively low estimate of 50%+ (Cross, Cross and Daly, 1971). However if one consults event methodology (e.g. Buckhout, 1974; Dent, 1977; Dent and Gray, 1975) estimates are between 12 and 13%. Where relatively high accuracy has been shown for live targets this is usually accounted for by over long exposure durations (e.g. Laughery, 1972), biasing manipulations (e.g.

Buckhout, 1974, exp.1) or is qualified by high false positive rates (e.g. Adkins, Egan, Peterson, Pittner and Goldstein, 1974).

From the conflict existing in the area of face memory (and many others space does not allow to be indicated) it can be seen that findings are highly paradigm specific and little agreement exists, at least as far as relevant methodology is concerned. The need for a valid research methodology is thereby strengthened.

The lack of generalizability in eyewitness research

A problem of generalizability exists in eyewitness research which is more fundamental than simply lack of uniformity of estimates. Specifically, generalizability is inhibited by methodological artificiality, procedural biases, statistical treatment and lack of theoretical sophistication.

Methodologically, the dominant paradigm lacks isomorphism with real-life, and thus renders inflated estimates of eyewitness ability (Clifford, 1975, 1979). Pictures are static: criminal events are dynamic; pictures are information light: events are information dense; while pictures predispose focussed attention, events of a criminal nature predispose diffuse attention. While preparatory set characterizes picture methodology it is easy to create surprise with the event method. Allied to this, emotion can be insinuated into event paradigms, in picture paradigms only with the most crippling artificiality.

In addition to problems of isomorphism the use of photographs predispose methods of measuring witness accuracy which is incongruent with actual police practice. Picture research traditionally presents a large number of target stimuli and seeks recognition of these within a small ensemble of distractors. In real-life quite the opposite happens: the number of observed criminals is small and detection is made either with 8-10 distractors (a line-up) or a very large number of 'distractors' (mugshot album). While the former method is economical in terms of experimental man-hours it is less meaningful in terms of application or generalization. Not only the *number* but also the *nature* of these distractors cause concern. Distractor faces in the laboratory traditionally are selected randomly whereas in criminal line-ups the distractors are (or should be) selected to be similar to the suspect. Traditional memory research tells us that the more dissimilar the target and the distractor the better will recognition be thus once again, as Laughery, Fessler, Lenorovitz and Yoblick (1974) indicate, laboratory studies set the upper limit for recognition performance.

Generalization is also inhibited procedurally because, according to Wells (1978), "the literature is replete with biases." For example, while laboratory witnesses, unlike real witnesses, always know before they identify that an observed event was staged the knowledge that no important consequences will follow their actions may increase the tendency to try and identify in the former group. In a similar vein while police tend to use only witnesses who espouse ability to identify, in the laboratory every subject exposed to the study phase of an experiment must perform the test phase. Thirdly, because researchers tend to select criminal-confederates (stooges) on the basis of having 'no distinguishing characteristics' this non-random selection could artifically be dropping identification accuracy estimates. Lastly, Wells (1978) points out that low accuracy rates in eyewitness research may be preferred to high accuracy rates, the latter being an implicit null hypothesis to be rejected. There seems little evidence for this however.

Statistically the generalizability of eyewitness findings may be of doubtful validity. Analysis of data often fails to proceed beyond the statement of percentages or the drawing of graphs, and when inferential statistics are employed it often seems that a large number of subjects need to be consumed in order to obtain a significant effect at the 5% level. This criticism seems to apply particularly to leading questions research. Additionally, especially in eyewitness research, the degree of association may be as important as a significant difference between manipulated variables. Obviously trivial associations may show up as significant results when the sample sizes are very large.

Not only the conception, planning, conducting and analysing of eyewitness experiments create problems of extrapolation. As Schlenker and Bonoma (1976) pointed out generalizations are made on the basis of corroborated theory and not only data alone. However there is very little evidence of theoretical developments that would yield applicability (but see Clifford, 1976; Clifford and Richards, 1977; Loftus, 1975). From its inception eyewitness research has been focussed mainly on supporting the negative assertion that witnesses are fallible. Further, research has been hampered by a concern with main effects rather than with interactions (see Clifford and Scott, 1978).

The lack of comprehensiveness in eyewitness research

Many questions to which interested parties seek answers

have either not yet been addressed or are poorly consolidated. This may be due to eyewitness research being driven internally by memory theory rather than propelled externally by consideration of criminal episode parameters. In real-life criminal incidents testimony is frequently given of various aspects of different crimes by different types of people after varying exposure to one or more criminals who, while perhaps distinctive can alter their later appearance. Eight research areas reside within the above statement: only a few have been addressed or addressed comprehensively by researchers.

Police and Courts frequently wish to know if some crimes are more difficult to remember than others, at least generally. Photographic research cannot address the question for reasons of artificiality mentioned above. Using police records Kuehn (1974) found that the completeness of victims descriptions of assailants decreased as severity of crime increased. This has not been followed up. Clifford and Scott (1978) showed that recall of targets' actions and appearance was poorer for violent episodes than for non violent episodes, and Clifford and Hollin (in prep. a) showed the same relationship for identification. Both Johnson and Scott (1976) and Lieppe, Wells and Ostrom (1978) argue that moderately severe crimes may produce greater accuracy than either highly severe or trivially severe crimes. This curvilinear relationship awaits verification or falsification but will not be resolved by experiments which only use 2 point plots from which extrapolation and interpolation is impossible.

The explanation of the above 'nature of crime' effect is predicated upon the concept of arousal. Despite the troublesome nature of this concept, both theoretically and empirically (e.g. Eysenck, 1977) two research reports have attempted to manipulate arousal experimentally via white noise and to observe the effect on eyewitness accuracy. The two results conflict. While Majcher (1974) found white noise improved recognition performance, Clifford and Hollin (in prep. b) found that white noise decremented both recall and recognition of targets relative to a control group.

If we can accept that different crimes produce different degrees of arousal a legitimate (and practically important) question to raise is whether different individuals or groups react differently to this stress. While a general finding in photographic research has been a female superiority effect in terms of observer accuracy (e.g. Cross, et al.,1971; Ellis, et al.,1973; Goldstein and Chance, 1971; Witryol and Kaess, 1957) there is some evidence that in real-life (Kuehn, 1974) and in violent staged incidents (Clifford and Scott, 1978;

cf. Lipton, 1977) females make poorer witnesses than males. This clearly is an area in urgent need of clarification and consolidation.

The finding by Cross et al. (1971) and Goldstein (1977) that there are vast differences in both recognizability and erroneous recognizability of certain faces has never been followed up. It would seem that ready made research foci in this field exist in the areas of facial attributes (e.g. attractiveness - Cross et al, 1971; Shephard and Ellis, 1973; Fleishman, Buckley, Klosinsky, Smith and Tuck, 1976; Yarmey, 1977), facial gestalts (e.g. Homa, Haver and Schwart, 1976) and features-in-combination (e.g. Fisher and Cox, 1975), but these await applied development.

In real-life, criminals can alter their appearance. The effect this can have on recognition accuracy has barely been considered. Transformation studies (e.g. inversion studies and photographic negatives) were performed to address idiosyncratic theoretical questions. However studies by McKelvie (1976), using schematic faces, masking eyes and/or mouth, and Patterson and Baddeley (1977), using photographs, looking at the effect of addition or removal of wigs, glasses and/or beards clearly demonstrate that cover or disguise can have powerful effects. Altered appearance should now be examined with a live event methodology.

Can we identify two or three criminals as well as one? While Wall (1965) implied we could, and Tichner and Poulton (1975) found no significant difference in detection of one, two or three people in a film of a street scene, Clifford and Hollin, (in prep. a) indicated that both recall and recognition decreased progressively for one, three and five targets in a mugging incident. This, like most of the above, is a vitally important practical question which has barely been addressed.

These then are just a few of the areas of eyewitness behaviour to which other professions would like clear and consistent answers, but which at the moment are either poorly or inadequately researched. They must progressively be addressed by a variety of converging operations.

Conclusion

If Littman's (1961) indictment is to be denied and Devlin's (1976) criticism answered eyewitness researchers must face squarely the problems of paradigm, agreement, generalizability and comprehensiveness. While overall specific questions need to be addressed, developed and consolidated, nowhere in psychology does the viability of a research area depend more on a reorientation of its methodology than in eyewitness research. With this reorientation the area will flourish: without this reorientation it will die.

REFERENCES

Adkins, C., Egan, D., Peterson, L., Pittner, M. and Goldstein, A.G. (1974). *The effects of exposure, delay and method of presentation on eyewitness identification.* Unpublished manuscript.

Buckhout, R. (1974). Eyewitness testimony. *Scientific American.* 231, 23-31.

Carlsmith, J.M., Ellsworth, P.C. and Aronson, E. (1976). *Methods of Research in Social Psychology.* Addison-Wesley Publishing Comp.: California.

Chance, J., Goldstein, A.G. and McBride, L. (1975). Differential experience and recognition memory for faces. *Journal of Social Psychology.* 97, 243-253.

Clifford, B. (1975). The case of mistaken identities. *Psychology Today.* 1, 15-19; 58.

Clifford, B. (1976). Police as Eyewitnesses. *New Society.* 36, 176-177.

Clifford, B. (1979). Eyewitness Testimony: The bridging of a credibility gap. *Psychology Law and Legal Processes.* (D. Farrington and P. Hawkins eds). Macmillan, London. in press.

Clifford, B. and Richards, G. (1977). Comparison of recall by policemen and civilians under conditions of long and short durations of exposure. *Perceptual and Motor Skills.* 45, 39-45.

Clifford, B. and Bull, R. (1978). *The Psychology of Person Identification.* Routledge Kegan Paul, London.

Cliford, B. and Scott, J. (1978). Individual and situational factors in eyewitness testimony. *Journal of Applied Psychology.* 63, 352-359.

Clifford, B. and Hollin, C. The effect of number of targets on recall and recognition of live targets. in prep. a.

Clifford, B. and Hollin, C. Experimentally manipulated arousal and eyewitness testimony. in prep. b.

Clifford, B. and Hollin, C. Testimony accuracy as a function of questioner status. in prep. c.

Cross, J., Cross, J. and Daly, J. (1971). Sex, race, age and beauty as factors in recognition of faces. *Perception and Psychophysics.* 10, 393-396.

Dent, H. (1977). Stress as a factor influencing person recognition in identification parades. *Bulletin of the British Psychological Society*. 30, 339-340.

Dent, H. and Gray, F. (1975). Identification on parade. *New Behaviour*. 1, 366-369.

Devlin, Lord P. (1976). *Report to the Secretary of State for the Home Department of the Departmental Committee on Evidence of Identification in Criminal Cases*. H.M.S.O. London.

Elliott, E., Wills, E. and Goldstein, A.G. (1973). The effect of discrimination training on the recognition of white and oriental faces. *Bulletin of Psychonomic Society*. 2, 71-73.

Ellis, H.D., Shepherd, J. and Bruce, A. (1973). The effect of age and sex upon adolescent recognition of faces. *Journal of Genetic Psychology*. 123, 173-174.

Eysenck, M.W. (1977). *Human Memory: Theory, research and individual differences*. Pergamon Press, Oxford, England.

Fisher, G. and Cox, R. (1975). Recognizing human faces. *Applied Ergonomics*. 6, 104-109.

Fleishman, J., Buckley, M., Klosinsky, M., Smith, N. and Tuck B. (1976). Judged attractiveness in recognition memory of woman's faces. *Perceptual and Motor Skills*. 43, 709-710.

Goldstein, A.G. (1977). The Fallibility of the Eyewitness: Psychological Evidence. In: *Psychology in the Legal Process*. (B.D. Sales ed). Spectrum, New York.

Goldstein, A.G. and Chance, J. (1971). Visual recognition memory for complex configurations. *Perception and Psychophysics*. 9, 237-241.

Hochberg, J. and Galper, R. (1974). Attribution of intention as a function of physiognomy. *Memory and Cognition*. 2, 39-42.

Homa, D., Haver, B. and Schwartz, T. (1976). Perceptibility of schematic face stimuli: evidence for a perceptual Gestalt. *Memory and Cognition*. 4, 176-185.

Johnson, C. and Scott, B. (1976). *Eyewitness testimony and suspect identification as a function of arousal, sex of witness, and scheduling of interrogation*. Paper presented at American Psychological Association Meeting, Washington, D.C.

Kuehn, L. (1974). Looking down a gun barrel: person perception and violent crime. *Perceptual and Motor Skills*. 39, 1159-1164.

Laughery, K. (1972). Photograph type and cross-racial factors in facial identification. In: *Personal Appearance Identification*. (A. Zavola and J.J. Paley eds.) Charles C. Thomas, Springfield, Illinois.

Laughery, K., Fessler, P., Lenorovitz, D. and Yoblick, D. (1974). Time delay and similarity effects in facial recognition. *Journal of Applied Psychology*. 55, 477-483.

Leippe, M., Wells, G.L. and Ostrom, T. (1978). Crime seriousness as a determiner of accuracy in eyewitness identification. *Journal of Applied Psychology*. in press.

Lipton, J. (1977). On the psychology of eyewitness testimony. *Journal of Applied Psychology*. 62, 90-95.

Littman, R. (1961). Psychology. The Socially Indifferent Science. *American Psychologist*. 16, 232-236.

Loftus, E. (1975). Leading questions and the eyewitness report. *Cognitive Psychology*. 7, 560-572.

Majcher, L.L. (1974). *Facial recognition as a function of arousal level, exposure and duration and delay interval*. Unpublished Masters Thesis, University of Missouri.

Malpass, R. and Kravitz, J. (1969). Recognition for faces of own and other 'race'. *Journal of Personality and Social Psychology*. 13, 330-335.

McKelvie, S. (1976). The role of eyes and mouth in recognition memory for faces. *American Journal of Psychology*. 89, 311-323.

Nickerson, R. (1965). Short term memory for complex, meaningful visual configurations: a demonstration of capacity. *Canadian Journal of Psychology*. 19, 155-160.

Patterson, K.E. and Baddeley, A.D. (1977). When face recognition fails. *Journal of Experimental Psychology: Human Learning and Memory*. 3, 406-417.

Scapinello, K. and Yarmey, D. (1970). The role of familiarity and orientation in immediate and delayed recognition of pictorial stimuli. *Psychonomic Science*. 21, 329-330.

Schlenker, B.R. and Bonoma, T.V. (1976). *Fun and games: The validity of games for the study of conflict*. Unpublished University of Florida Manuscript.

Shepard, R. (1967). Recognition memory for words, sentences and pictures. *Journal of Verbal Learning and Verbal Behaviour*. 6, 156-163.

Shepherd, J. and Ellis, H.D. (1973). The effect of attractiveness on recognition memory for faces. *American Journal of Psychology*. 86, 627-633.

Shepherd, J., Deregowski, J. and Ellis, H.D. (1974). A cross-cultural study of recognition memory for faces. *International Journal of Psychology*. 9, 205-211.

Standing, L. (1973). Learning 10,000 pictures. *Quarterly Journal of Experimental Psychology*. 25, 207-222.

Standing, L., Conezio, J. and Haber, R. (1970). Perception and memory for pictures: single trial learning of 2,560 visual stimuli. *Psychonomic Science*. 19, 73-74.
Tichner, A. and Poulton, E. (1975). Watching for people and actions. *Ergonomics*. 18, 35-51.
Wall, P. (1965). *Eyewitness Identification in Criminal Cases*. Thomas, New York.
Warr, P. (1973). Towards a more human psychology. *Bulletin of the British Psychological Society*. 26, 1-8.
Wells, G.L. (1978). Applied Eyewitness-Testimony Research: System Variables and Estimator Variables. *Journal of Personality and Social Psychology*. in press.
Witryol, S. and Kaess, W. (1957). Sex differences in social memory tasks. *Journal of Abnormal and Social Psychology*. 54, 343-346.
Yarmey, D. (1977). *The effects of attractiveness, feature saliency and liking on memory for faces*. Paper presented at the International Conference on Love and Attraction. Swansea, Wales. September 1977.
Yin, R. (1969). Looking at upside-down faces. *Journal of Experimental Psychology*. 81, 141-145.

EYEWITNESSES ALSO HAVE EARS

Ray Bull
Department of Psychology
North East London Polytechnic
Three Mills, Abbey Lane
London E15 2RP

In 1976 the Devlin Committee, which reported to the Home Secretary its findings in respect of evidence of identification in criminal cases, stated that, "research should proceed as rapidly as possible into the practicability of voice identification parades with the use of tape recorders or any other appropriate method, which among other things, would have to take into account the dangers of disguising the voice and the extent of changes, produced by stress". Just two months ago Brian Clifford and myself commenced our programme of research on voice recognition which is being funded by the Home Office and this explains why, today, I shall not be presenting any data of my own but I trust that the review I shall now present of some previous research will be of interest to you.

The Devlin Committee also stated that in connection with person identification by voice, "as far as we can ascertain there has been no scientific research into this question". Brian and I have commented on this committee's report in our recently published book *The Psychology of Person Identification* and time does not permit me to do this today. However, it is true to say that the Devlin Committee did not avail itself of much of the psychological information which is available. There has in fact been quite a lot of research conducted on voice recognition though most of it has been concerned with the electro-mechanical, spectrographic analysis of speech and this I shall briefly mention once I have presented information concerning experiments using human listeners.

The study of voice recognition suffers from a lack of an appropriate descriptive vocabulary. Most identification situations involve the observer using visual cues but there are some instances when both visual and verbal information is available, and others when only verbal clues exist. In obscene telephone calls, for example, often the only possible method of identifying the speaker is by his voice. Similarly in kidnap cases information concerning the kidnapper's voice is sometimes made available by him over the telephone. In such situations, when a suspect is in the hands of the police a voice-matching exercise may be entered into. Here a witness may be asked whether the suspect's voice is the same, or resembles, the criminal's, or a machine may be employed in an attempt to answer these questions if a record (e.g. a tape) of the original criminal voice is available.

In as early as 1937 psychologists had begun to examine the reliability of voice identification. McGehee (1937) was concerned with attempting to answer the questions: (i) what is the influence of time-interval upon memory for voices?; (ii) what is the effect of increasing the number of voices heard in a series in which occurs a voice to be subsequently recognized?; (iii) to what extent is a voice recognized as having been heard previously when disguised by a change in pitch?; (iv) are there sex differences in the recognition of voices? The experimental procedure involved groups of students listening to an adult reading aloud a paragraph of fifty-six words from behind a screen. Each of the readers was unacquainted with any of the listeners and none had a noticeable dialect or speech defect. In all there were 31 male and 18 female readers, there being a total of 740 listeners. All the groups of listeners were tested for voice recognition after time intervals ranging from one day to five months. In the recognition situation each of five readers successively read aloud the initial passage and the listeners were required to note down which of the five readers they had heard previously. For listeners who initially heard only one reader McGehee observed 83, 83, 81 and 81 per cent accuracy for time intervals of one, two, three and seven days respectively. After an interval of two weeks performance dropped to 69 per cent and after a further week to 51 per cent. Intervals of three and five months led to accuracy scores of 35 and 13 per cent respectively. Thus, it was concluded that with the passage of time, "there is a general trend towards a decrease in percentage of listeners who were able to correctly recognize a voice the second time it is heard".

During the initial part of the experiment some listeners heard not one voice but several and it was found that the more voices heard initially the more difficult was it to recognize subsequently any one of them (83 per cent accuracy for the case in which only one voice was heard initially, down to 50 per cent when more than three voices were heard initially). As noted above, the case in which only one voice was heard initially resulted in 83 per cent recognition on the next day when on both occasions the voice demonstrated its normal pitch. If, however, on the second day the voice was disguised by a change in pitch then only 67 per cent of the listeners recognized it.

Concerning sex differences, McGehee found men to be better voice recognizers than women (84 per cent accuracy vs. 59 per cent), but that male voices were no better recognized than were female voices (72 per cent vs. 71 per cent). Significant interactions were noted in that men were very good at recognizing female voices (96 per cent) but were not so good with male voices (73 per cent), whereas women were better with male voices (72 per cent) than with female voices (47 per cent).

In 1973 Bartholomeus examined voice identification by nursery school children five months after the start of the school year. She played to two groups of children, aged four and five years, tape-recorded speech samples obtained from their classmates and teachers. Each child was provided with a series of recorded voices and was required to identify each speaker in turn having been told that they were classmates or teachers. In one condition the stimulus consisted of a two-sentence-long speech sample and the child was required to say out loud the name of the person who had provided the speech sample. In another condition the same stimuli were given but the identification response required the child to pick out from an array the photograph of the speaker. The third condition provided speech samples that were played backwards and each child was asked to name the speaker. In a fourth condition each child was required to name the classmates and teachers in the photographs shown to him. Four teachers also acted as subjects in this study. For each child (and teacher) the face-naming task produced the highest accuracy score (97 per cent for the children and 100 per cent for the teachers). In the voice-to-face-matching task the children's accuracy score dropped substantially to 58 per cent and that of the teachers to 81 per cent. Bartholomeus pointed out that errors in this task cannot be attributed to failures at picking out the right face having correctly identified the voice because the children were almost perfect at face naming. Scores in the voice-naming task were similar (56 per cent for the children and 68 per cent for the teachers) and again Bartholomeus argues that here the errors made cannot be attributed to the unavailability of appropriate verbal labels (i.e. not knowing the names of the children in the class). As one might expect the speech played backwards occasioned the lowest identification scores (41 per cent for the children and 63 per cent for the adults) but such a level of accuracy is still greater than could be expected by chance alone and this led Bartholomeus to claim that, "These results demonstrate substantial ability in the identification of voices from samples of unintelligible speech."

At first glance it might seem surprising that the teachers were not perfect at identifying the voices of children with whom they had interacted for several hours a day for five months. However, it is important to note that the children were all of a similar age and therefore their voices would be quite similar to one another, at least in pitch. Bartholomeus noted that one or two voices were consistently easily identified in any condition and some others were constantly mis-identified. She believes that the inaccuracies in the voice-naming and voice-to-face-matching tasks can be attributed to inefficient processing of available auditory cues, and that this may be because the auditory cues concerning an individual's identity are normally analysed during or after the processing of simultaneously presented linguistic information whereas purely non-verbal visual cues are processed immediately. That is, when a voice is heard the input is analysed for the meaning of the words being spoken and the act of doing this may to some extent prevent details of the actual voice being remembered.

Bartholomeus noted that some listeners were reliably much better at speaker identification than were others with the teachers tending to be most accurate of all. However, since the best teacher's score was equalled or exceeded by some of the children on each test, it can be concluded that at least some of these 4- and 5-year-olds were as accurate as were adults at voice identification. This being the case Bartholomeus believes that, "a lack of substantial improvement in speaker recognition after early childhood would be consistent with the adoption of a perceptual strategy which optimizes efficient decoding of linguistic information by relying on vision, rather than audition, for information concerning an individual's identity." The results in this experiment also provided evidence of correct recognition of the sex of the speaker in cases of incorrect identifications. Bartholomeus takes these findings to indicate that speaker identification involves a hierarchical sequence of judgments in which absolute identification is preceded by categorization of voices with respect to different variables such as age or sex. How this may be done was not commented on and Bartholomeus believes that, "the cues used by listeners when identifying voices remain largely unknown." Within the confines of this experiment there was no doubt that voice identification was more difficult than face identification. However, to what extent this difference was a function of the testing situation is not known.

There have been some attempts to examine the utility of possible identification cues in speech. Scherer (1974) tried not so much to determine which cues are used in identification but to see whether listeners could agree in their attribution of certain voice characteristics to various voices. In his study a large number of voice attributes was employed rather than the more restricted number relating to energy and frequency which are employed in electroacoustic equipment measures. In his experiment Scherer played to listeners twenty-second speech samples of various adult male speakers. Each sample was from only one speaker but it consisted of a number of randomly arranged mini-samples, each of less than one second duration so that the resultant sample conveyed minimal meaning in terms of containing intelligible words. Each listener was required to rate each voice for such things as pitch, height and range, loudness, breathiness, creak, glottal tension and nasality, on a thirty-five-item voice quality attribute rating form. The listeners consisted of the speaker himself, three of his acquaintances, six experienced phoeneticians who were deemed to be expert judges, and groups of adult females who were considered to be lay judges. Each listener was provided with two minutes worth of voice sample per speaker by continuous repetition of each twenty-second speech sample. Inter-agreement was fairly high for the ratings by the expert judges, especially for judgments of loudness, pitch height and pitch range, and several of the attributes being judged were found to be interrelated. However, when the ratings from the expert judges were compared with measures of the speech samples obtained by the use of a computerized filter-bank spectrum-analyser (i.e. average energy, energy variation, average pitch and pitch variation) very few significant correlations were found. The ratings by the expert judges were also compared with those of the lay judges and some measure of agreement was found, especially for pitch and loudness. This led Scherer to view pitch and loudness as the most powerful vocal dimensions affecting lay judgements. Neither the acquaintances nor the speakers themselves agreed with the expert and lay judges for ratings of the loudness, pitch or resonance of their friends' voices. Scherer points out that, "The lack of strong correspondence between self and acquaintance ratings of voice quality and expert ratings raises the interesting question of the validity of self and acquaintance ratings of voice." He believes that, "It is possible that if one has been acquainted with a person for a long period of time and has heard that person's voice in many situations, the resulting wealth of experience interferes with the accuracy of the description of the voice."

It may be worth while to bear Scherer's comments in mind when assessing the findings of studies such as that of Bartholomeus (1973). However, the voice stimuli provided in Scherer's study could seem so artificial as to make the study of little value to those interested in the identification of persons by the way they speak. Nevertheless, Scherer did find that there was a difference in voice quality between German and American speakers and this may have some bearing upon the possibility of regional dialects playing a role in person identification. There seems little doubt that the voices of various people do differ reliably from each other since we often appear able, for example, to recognize the voice of someone on the telephone even when they do not announce who they are. People from different walks of life and different parts of the country do speak in a variety of ways.

Bortz (1970) investigated how one's own voice may influence the judgments of the voices of others. Tapes were made of students each reading three texts and each reader judged his own voice and the voices of others. The voices were also rated by a number of psychologists. It was found that (i) raters with high-pitched voices judged others as having low-pitched voices, and vice versa; (ii) raters with strongly dynamic voices overestimated existing differences of expression in the voices of others whereas raters with less dynamic voices underestimated such differences. The rater-ratee interaction was concluded to be such that the closer a rater identifies with the voice of the ratee, the less suitable was his own voice as an objective standard of comparison.

In an early and rather limited study Pollack, Pickett and Sumby (1954) played to seven listeners, for varying durations the voices of men that they knew. It was found that the larger the speech sample the more accurate were the identifications, this effect being due to the greater speech repertoire evidenced in the longer samples since repetition of short samples did not increase the number of correct identifications. Whispered speech, which contains little pitch inflection, and which is of similar pitch for various speakers led to some correct identifications but far fewer than normal speech. Bricker and Pruzansky (1966) also examined the effect of stimulus duration and content upon talker identification. For the voices of people who worked together they found 98 per cent correct identification when spoken sentences were provided, 84 per cent for syllables and 56 per cent for vowel excerpts. When the accuracy scores were plotted either against the number of different phonemes contained in the speech sample or against its duration the former was found to provide a better picture of the relationships than was the latter. Bricker and Pruzansky concluded that the improvement in identification with sample duration is due to an increased sample of the talker's repertoire being provided.

Murray and Cort (1971) also investigated the ability to identify speakers on the basis of the duration and repertoire of the speech sample and they concluded that the repertoire available in a speech sample of a sentence in length is sufficient for identification performance to reach an asymptote and they conclude that for their subjects a fifteen-syllable sentence provided sufficient cues for voice identification. However, like the subjects in the study conducted by Bartholomeus, in this experiment the children had been together in the same class for at least several months. The conclusions which can be drawn from these experiments for the situations wherein recognition is required of a stranger who provided only one speech sample are tentative to say the least.

Though the police and judicial procedures for the recognition of persons by the way they speak are not as firmly laid down as they are for visual identification, the topic of identification by voice is one which has received quite a lot of attention from those wishing to develop electrical hardware to this end. Some success has been claimed for voice identification by spectrographic analysis but space does not permit a full discussion of these claims. (For this refer to Clifford and Bull, 1978).

Kersta was one of the first advocates of spectrographic voice analysis and he claimed that voiceprint identification is closely analogous to fingerprint identification. However, one of the questions that has only infrequently been asked of spectrographic voice identification is whether it is any better than simple human identification by ear. It would seem rather a waste of time and money if this were not the case. Stevens, William, Carbonell and Woods (1968) found error rates of over 20 per cent for speaker identification employing spectrograms, but the persons who matched the spectrograms in this study were not extensively trained in the art as Kersta claims they should be. (It was noted that as the study proceeded the examiners' efficiency increased.) These examiners were required both to identify speakers by visually comparing spectrograms and also to identify speakers by simply listening to the tape recordings on which the spectrograms were made. It was found that the identification performance accuracy from aural comparisons was far higher than that resulting from the visual comparison of spectrograms (94 vs. 79 per cent at the end of the study), and that the time taken to arrive at the identifications was less for the aural input. Overall not only did the aural tests lead to better performance at the beginning of the study they also were the ones which derived the greatest improvement with practice. Further, for the aural information the length of utterance required for identification was shorter than that required by the spectrographic comparisons. Stevens concluded that, "Authentication of voices is much poorer on a visual basis than on an aural basis". This suggests that spectrographic voice analysis may certainly be no better than comparing the same voices by ear, a conclusion also arrived at by Hecker (1971) who concluded his literature survey by pointing out that, "In speculating on possible reasons for the superiority of listeners over machines in recognizing speakers, it is well to remember that even the most naive listener has lived in a speech environment for a considerably longer period of time than any machine. The experience he has thus acquired cannot be readily defined and analogized."

Thus, to conclude, there is evidence that the performance of electro-mechanical, spectrographic voice identification systems is no more accurate than that of human listeners. This being the case it is worth while for psychologists to conduct research on the topic of voice identification by human listeners, and this we are now doing.

References

Bartholomeus, B. (1973). Voice identification by nursery school children. *Canadian Journal of Psychology*, 27, 464-472.

Bortz, J. (1970). On the reciprocal relationships between rating of speakers voices and the voice of the rater. *Archiv fur Psychologie*, 122, 231-48.

Bricker, P. and Pruzansky, S. (1966). Effects of stimulus content and duration on talker identification. *Journal of the Acoustical Society of America*, 40, 1441-9.

Clifford, B. and Bull, R. (1978). *The Psychology of Person Identification*. Routledge and Kegan Paul, London.

Hecker, M. (1971). Speaker recognition. *American Speech and Hearing Association*, monograph no.16.

McGehee, F. (1937). The reliability of the identification of the human voice. *Journal of General Psychology*, 17, 249-71.

Murray, T. and Cort, S. (1971). Aural identification of children's voices. *Journal of Auditory Research*, 11, 260-2.

Pollack, I., Pickett, J. and Sumby, W. (1954). On the identification of speakers by voice. *Journal of the Acoustical Society of America*, 26, 403-6.

Scherer, K. (1974). Voice quality analysis of American and German speakers. *Journal of Psycholinguistic Research*, 3, 281-98.

Stevens, K., Williams, C., Carbonell, J. and Woods, B. (1968). Speaker authentication and identification: A comparison of spectrographic and auditory presentation of speech material. *Journal of the Acoustical Society of America*, 44, 1596-1607.

SOME PREDICTORS OF EYEWITNESS MEMORY ACCURACY

K.A. Deffenbacher, E.L. Brown, and W. Sturgill
University of Nebraska at Omaha
Omaha, Nebraska

ABSTRACT

We have found accuracy to vary considerably as a function of several task parameters. 1) Witnesses recognize faces better than they recall circumstances of encounter, the advantage of recognition being more pronounced when they are aware of a crime's occurrence. 2) Witness confidence is not a reliable predictor of either recognition or recall accuracy across eyewitnesses and task variables. 3) Number and kind of previous encounters with a suspect strongly affect his/her chances of indictment. 4) Though we have not generally found accuracy to be predicted by individual difference variables, sex of witness has been an exception, showing both main effects and interactions with sex of suspect.

INTRODUCTION

In the past 10 years, research relevant to eyewitnessing has dealt primarily with the issue of just how good face recognition may be. Under optimal conditions produced in the laboratory, recognition can be quite good indeed, with accuracy rates of 90% or better not being uncommon (Brown, Deffenbacher and Sturgill, 1977; Hochberg and Galper, 1967; Patterson and Baddeley, 1977; Yin, 1969). This finding of 90% accuracy is a robust one in the sense that it obtains across a number of procedural variations: number of facial photos presented, quantity of cues in each photo, similarity among photos, manner of their presentation, time allowed for their inspection and method of recognition testing.

The subjects in the previously cited studies shared at least three things in common. They were all aware that they were to study the faces in order that they might later recognize them. Photos to be recognized were identical at presentation and test. Presumably subjects in these studies were also not in a state of high arousal that may be more typical of real life eyewitness situations. However, even though subjects may possess these three advantages, 90+% recognition accuracy is by no means assured. Goldstein (1977) reviewed a number of studies in the face recognition literature that showed accuracy rates averaging about 75%. A plausible reason for this discrepancy is that investigators have used samples of faces that have varied in intra-sample similarity from laboratory to laboratory. As Laughery, Fessler, Lenorovitz and Yoblick (1974) found, increases in intra-sample similarity led to poorer recognition performance. Hence the higher error rate in the studies reviewed by Goldstein may simply be due to greater facial similarity amongst photographs used.

When witnesses are tested under the three conditions mentioned in the preceding paragraph, then, face recognition accuracy typically varies from around 75% to over 90%. However, a significant further drop in accuracy occurs if any one of the three conditions is made less than optimal. Consider what happens when eyewitnesses are not warned they will be asked later whether they recognize the faces of people presently being encountered. In a master's thesis project completed in our laboratory, Sturgill (1976) showed that when this was the case the hit rate (the rate at which faces previously encountered were correctly recognized) dropped to 56%. Worse, the false alarm rate (the rate at which faces not seen before were falsely indicted) was 44%, yielding a d' statistic of just .30 where a d' of 0.0 would have indicated chance discrimination of old from new faces. Or consider what happens when the stimulus situation is not identical at presentation and test. Patterson and Baddeley (1977) showed that there was a significant drop in hit rate from 91% to 82% when the pose and expression of a face were changed from presentation to test. These same investigators found an even greater decline in accuracy when faces were disguised by adding or removing a beard or glasses or changing the hair style. The average hit rate dropped to 45%, while the average d' score declined from 1.67 to .58. Finally consider what occurs when eyewitness arousal is increased by increasing the level of violence of the critical incident. Clifford and Scott (1978) showed that there was a marked decrease in accuracy of recall of details concerning more violent incidents.

Regardless of how good eyewitnesses are at recognizing faces seen before, they must also be able to recall where the faces have been encountered. If an eyewitness were sufficiently confused as to whether a suspect's face might have been seen in police mugshots, newspaper or television presentations, or in fact at the scene of the crime, he or she might indict a suspect on the basis of face recognition alone.

In what follows, we first shall examine the results of two studies we have done that compare accuracy of face recognition and cued recall of circumstances of their encounter. We shall also describe results of other studies we have done documenting how accuracy of eyewitness report varies as a function of degree of awareness that a critical incident has occurred, degree of eyewitness confidence, nature of previous encounters with a suspect, and certain individual difference variables.

MEMORY FOR FACES AND CIRCUMSTANCES OF THEIR ENCOUNTER

Initially, we compared accuracy of memory for faces and circumstances of their encounter using a task that should have permitted optimal performance (Brown *et al.* 1977, Exp. 1). The three previously mentioned conditions obtained in this study, as did a 20-sec initial presentation rate and a self-paced test presentation rate. Tested individually, subjects were shown 25 facial photos in one room and 2 hours later, in another, radically different, room 25 more such photos. Two days later, in yet a third room, they were shown 100 photos presented as 50 old-new pairs. They indicated for each pair which picture they had seen before and the room in which they had seen it. The mean hit rate for face recognition was 96%, with all 14 subjects scoring reliably above chance; the group d' for this two-alternative, forced-choice situation was 2.48. Much less impressive was the recall of circumstances of encounter for correctly recognized faces. The average hit rate in this case was only 61%, yielding a group d' of .40. Though the group hit rate and d' score were above chance, this does not mean all individuals recalled at an above chance rate. As a matter of fact, only 5 of 14 subjects did so (rates of 66%-69%), with the others achieving recall scores ranging from 49% to 61%. Even the performance of the former subjects is hardly satisfactory for criminal justice systems that place great faith in the reliability of eyewitness testimony and that are biased in favor of the innocent. Nevertheless, it might be useful to know if there are individual difference variables that predict the recall performance of the more successful subjects. Police and others who must rely on eyewitness report in their investigative work could use such information for selection and training. We are proceeding with research designed to this end.

A test of significance between the d' scores indicated that subjects in this study discriminated among faces better than among circumstances of their encounter. This indeed raises the possibility that on some occasions witnesses might indict a suspect on face recognition alone. Insofar as we have investigated the matter, the pronounced advantage of recognition over recall holds only for the situation where witnesses are aware their memory will be tested later. In an experiment where they were not so aware (Sturgill, 1976), d' scores for recognition and recall were uniformly small and rather close in value, .30 and .20, respectively, with both values reflecting better than chance discrimination due to a large n. Apparently, then, when eyewitnesses are operating at the lower limits of memory, both face recognition and recall of circumstances of their encounter are relatively weak.

EYEWITNESS CONFIDENCE AND ACCURACY OF REPORT

Popular belief would have it that confidence and accuracy are positively related. Hence, jurors may well be more likely to believe eyewitnesses who are highly certain of their testimony rather than those who are less certain. Indeed, there is at least one report in the literature supporting this notion, Lipton's (1977) finding of a significant positive correlation between accuracy and confidence ($r = +.44$) in an experimental setting where subjects were not warned they would have to testify later about details of a filmed crime they were shown. Buckhout, Alper, Chern, Silverberg and Slomovits (1974) noted, however, that their most accurate group of witnesses were less confident than the next most accurate group. Intrigued by Buckhout *et al*'s finding, we have measured eyewitness confidence across some 400 individuals and a number of task variables (Brown *et al*. 1977, Exps. 2 and 3; Sturgill, 1976). Regardless of whether subjects know of a later memory test, regardless of whether recognition of faces or recall of circumstances of encounter is tested, despite a number of other procedural variations, we have found no evidence of a significant positive correlation between confidence of judgment and accuracy of judgment. Our Pearson coefficients have ranged from -.03 to +.12. Perhaps it is not surprising, then, that we have also consistently found a significant positive correlation between confidence when accurate and confidence when inaccurate; Pearson rs have ranged from +.51 to +.70. These two sets of findings, taken together with the very recent corroborating evidence of Leippe, Wells, and Ostrom (1978) and Clifford and Scott (1978), suggest that confident eyewitnesses are no more apt to be accurate than less confident ones, while a given witness will tend to exhibit a particular level of confidence whether right or wrong.

ACCURACY AND NATURE OF PREVIOUS ENCOUNTER

We must agree with Egan, Pittner, and Goldstein (1977) that "relatively little systematic research has been done to define the factors that affect accuracy of identification in lineups or other methods of personal identification used by criminal investigators." In 3 of 4 published papers on this topic (Buckhout *et al*.,1974; Buckhout, Figueroa, and Hoff, 1975; Egan *et al*.,1977), live presentation of 1 or 2 "criminals" was followed at an interval ranging from 2 up to as many as 56 days by either a lineup or a photospread. Buckhout *et al*. (1974) found that only 13.5% of their witnesses made no errors of identification, while Egan *et al*. (1977) found as many as 28% of theirs making no errors. The greater accuracy in the latter study was probably due to the witnesses having been warned of a later memory test. Egan *et al*.also found that a live lineup produced greater accuracy than a photospread, perhaps because the former procedure reproduced more of the cues present in the original presentation. Finally, Buckhout *et al*.(1975) showed that biased instructions and photospreads increased the indictment rate of the affected suspect, whether guilty or not.

In our own work, we have modelled not only the situation of following a live "criminal" presentation with a live lineup but also the common criminal identification procedure of having exposure to mugshots inserted between these two occurrences (Brown *et al*.,1977, Exps. 2 and 3; Sturgill, 1976). We have been particularly interested in documenting any confusions or biases introduced by the latter procedure. In this regard, Experiment 2 of the Brown *et al*.study indicates how type of previous encounter with a suspect strongly affects his chances of indictment, even when witnesses are aware of later memory tests. In a lineup, suspects previously seen at the "crime" and subsequently in mugshots were indicted more (65%) than suspects seen only at the crime (51%), innocents seen only in mugshots (20%), and innocents never seen before (8%). All pair-wise comparisons of these indictment rates were significant, as were d' scores computed for each possible pairing. The average d' score for comparisons of criminals with innocents was 1.32. Except for telling suspects to wear different upper clothing for each appearance and the insertion of a mugshot session between the crime and the lineup, the procedure of this experiment included all three conditions described earlier as promoting a high level of face recognition. However, even though there was significant discrimination of criminal from innocent, these results are not overly confidence inspiring if they generalize at all to real-life criminal identification. Certainly the evidence of eyewitness fallibility here is ample. The miss rates were rather high, .35 and .49 for the two criminal suspect conditions, and the false alarm rates for the two groups of innocents were higher than any criminal justice system biased in favor of the innocent would presumably tolerate. The use of mugshots hindered as well as aided the cause of justice. Their use decreased the miss rate when a person at the crime was also viewed in a mugshot but such use also increased the likelihood that an innocent would be falsely indicted. Hence this particular criminal identification procedure may produce a tendency to mistake having seen a mugshot for having seen a person.

When eyewitnesses have not been warned of subsequent memory tests and may not even have taken proper notice of faces encountered, mugshot-induced biases may be even greater Brown *et al.*,1977, Exp. 3). In this instance, suspects seen at the crime and in mugshots were again indicted more (45%) than suspects seen only at the crime (24%), innocents seen only in mugshots (29%), and innocents never before seen (18%). The indictment rate for suspects encountered only at the crime was not significantly different from those of the two groups of innocents! This finding is particularly important from a forensic standpoint. As Lipton (1977) points out, real-life eyewitness incidents often occur without warning. When this is the case, subsequent indictments of suspects by witnesses who have previously seen their mugshots should not be admissible as evidence.

INDIVIDUAL DIFFERENCE VARIABLES AND ACCURACY

Studies in the face recognition literature have reported no difference between the sexes in accuracy, a consistent advantage for females, or an interaction of sex of subject and sex of face, with females recognizing female faces better than do males (Ellis, 1975). Our own experience had been that of finding the interaction (Shroder, 1975). Against this background, Sturgill's (1976) findings regarding the sex variable came as a bit of a surprise. Live presentation of 2 male-female pairs, each pair in a different setting, was followed without warning a week later by a live lineup of 4 males and 4 females. Sturgill found female suspects (d'=.38) better recognized than male suspects (d'=.20), while female witnesses were less accurate (d'=.20) than males (d'=.46). The direction of both main effects is accounted for by the male witnesses' accuracy when indicting female suspects (d'= .69). The main effect for face of suspect was not unexpected, the other findings were.

Sex effects with regard to recall of circumstances of encounter were just the reverse! Sturgill (1976) found encounters with male suspects better recalled (d'=.40) than those with females (d'=.05). On the other hand, female witnesses recalled where they had encountered suspects (d'=.30) better than did male witnesses (d'=.05), though this difference was not significant. The direction of both these effects is explained by the accuracy of female witnesses at associating male suspects with the proper setting (d'=.56). Perhaps most relevant here is Clifford and Scott's (1978) finding that female witnesses showed a slight, but not significantly better recall than that of males for details of a nonviolent incident.

Our search for other individual differences predictors of eyewitness memory accuracy has with few exceptions yielded only nonsignificant correlations. Consider the results of Deffenbacher, Brown, and Sturgill (1975). Subjects were a stratified random sample of 45 students who had participated in Experiment 3 of the Brown *et al.* (1977) study. Six measures were obtained from them: accuracy on a face recognition task involving warning of a later test, and scores on the spatial relations subtest of the Differential Aptitude Tests (a measure of nonverbal intelligence), the Manifest Anxiety-Defensiveness Scale (a measure of the first factor of self-endorsement personality inventories), the Sensation Seeking Scale (a measure of the second factor, extroversion-introversion), the Vividness of Visual Imagery Questionnaire, and a timed test of proofreading accuracy. None of these measures correlated significantly with accuracy at the lineup staged in Experiment 3 of the Brown *et al.* study, though the correlation with the face recognition task approached significance (r=-.28, $p < .10$, 2-tailed). Apparently, then, accuracy at a lineup may not even be predicted by accuracy at the typical laboratory recognition of facial photos task, at least where the lineup occurs after an unannounced eyewitness incident. One other result may be worthy of mention. There was a significant multiple correlation between accuracy at the face recognition task and the most efficiently weighted linear combination of scores on the Sensation Seeking Scale and the test of proofreading accuracy (r=+.39). Extroverts who were good proofreaders tended to do better at this task.

REFERENCES

Brown, E.L., Deffenbacher, K.A. and Sturgill, W. (1977). Memory for Faces and the Circumstances of Encounter. *Journal of Applied Psychology*. 62, 311-318.

Buckhout, R., Alper, A., Chern, S., Silverberg, G. and Slomovits, M. (1974). Determinants of Eyewitness Performance on a Lineup. *Bulletin of the Psychonomic Society*. 4, 191-192.

Buckhout, R., Figueroa, D. and Hoff, E. (1975). Eyewitness Identification: Effects of Suggestion and Bias in Identification from Photographs. *Bulletin of the Psychonomic Society*. 6, 71-74.

Clifford, B.R. and Scott, J. (1978). Individual and Situational Factors in Eyewitness Testimony. *Journal of Applied Psychology*. 63, 352-359.

Deffenbacher, K.A., Brown, E.L. and Sturgill, W. (1975). Unpublished Data. *University of Nebraska at Omaha*.

Egan, D., Pittner, M. and Goldstein, A.G. (1977). Eyewitness Identification: Photographs vs. Live Models. *Law and Human Behavior*. 1, 199-206.

Ellis, H.D. (1975). Recognising Faces. *British Journal of Psychology*. 66, 409-426.

Goldstein, A.G. (1977). The Fallibility of the Eyewitness: Psychological Evidence. In: *Psychology in the Legal Process*. (B. Sales, ed.). Spectrum, Jamaica, New York.

Hochberg, J. and Galper, R. (1967). Recognition of Faces: I. An Exploratory Study. *Psychonomic Science*. 9, 619-620.

Laughery, K.R., Fessler, P.K., Lenorovitz, D.R. and Yoblick, D.A. (1974). Time Delay and Similarity Effects in Facial Recognition. *Journal of Applied Psychology*. 59, 490-496.

Leippe, M.R., Wells, G.L. and Ostrom, T.M. (1978). Crime Seriousness as a Determinant of Accuracy in Eyewitness Identification. *Journal of Applied Psychology*. 63, 345-351.

Lipton, J.P. (1977). On the Psychology of Eyewitness Testimony. *Journal of Applied Psychology*. 62, 90-95.

Patterson, K.E. and Baddeley, A.D. (1977). When Face Recognition Fails. *Journal of Experimental Psychology: Human Learning and Memory*. 3, 406-417.

Shroder, E.E. (1975). Recognition and Attractiveness as a Function of Sex and Race. *Unpublished Master's Thesis, University of Nebraska at Omaha*.

Sturgill, W. (1976). Memory for Persons, Encounters and Sex. *Unpublished Master's Thesis, University of Nebraska at Omaha*.

Yin, R.K. Looking at Upside-Down Faces. *Journal of Experimental Psychology*. 81, 141-145.

PERSON RECOGNITION: MORE THAN A PRETTY FACE

K.E. Patterson
MRC Applied Psychology Unit, 15 Chaucer Road, Cambridge, England

ABSTRACT

People are encountered in a variety of "formats", and sometimes initial and subsequent encounter of a person are characterised by different formats. In the present study, target people were presented as still photographs of the face or film clips of the whole moving person. The identification test occurred either in the same format as learning (*slide-slide* and *film-film* conditions) or in the alternative format (*slide-film* and *film-slide*). The latter two groups showed dramatically reduced performance, relative to the former two, in identifying the targets.

INTRODUCTION

While the typical study of person recognition is based on still photographs of faces, the current experiment utilised films of whole moving people in combination with still photographs. There were three justifications for suffering the difficulties incurred by film as an experimental medium.

(1) As perhaps witnessed by the existence of this book, psychological researchers are experiencing a drive towards ecological validity, which recommends not only meaningful as opposed to meaningless stimuli but also dynamic rather than static stimulus situations (Neisser, 1976). Photographs of faces are patently meaningful but they are not dynamic.

(2) Perception and recognition of facial photographs is a common enough phenomenon in real life; what is perhaps unrepresentative about most experiments is that *both* presentation and test are based on photographs. When photographs occur in the real world, they almost always do so as one stage: you become familiar with a whole, moving person and later see a photograph or (less frequently) the other way round. There are countless experiments on recognition of previously seen photographs of faces, but only a very few (e.g. Dent and Gray, 1975; Laughery, Fessler, Lenorovitz and

Yoblick, 1974) involving recognition of photographs when the initial exposure was to a whole, moving person.

(3) The study of person recognition has been somewhat disappointing in terms of cognitive theoretical content. It is easy to demonstrate major effects of physical variables such as duration of presentation, similarity among targets and distractors, changes in appearance of targets. But the kinds of manipulations which often interest cognitive psychologists, such as type of processing or subject strategy, seem to have rather minor consequences. Depth-of-processing effects, while significant, tend to be small (Bower and Karlin, 1974; Strnad and Mueller, 1977; Warrington and Ackroyd, 1975; Winograd, 1976), especially if the shallow processing task directs attention to the whole face (Patterson and Baddeley, 1977) rather than just a single feature. Context effects in face recognition tend to be minimal (Bower and Karlin, 1974) or even if significant (Watkins, Ho and Tulving, 1976; Winograd and Rivers-Bulkeley, 1977) of small magnitude relative to such effects with verbal materials. But attempts to evaluate processing and context issues at least bring person recognition into the sphere of our knowledge about recognition memory for other sorts of objects and events, and the present study of different formats of information (moving film versus facial photographs) was partially motivated by the same goal. Varying format of information is germane to the general issue of recognising something (a person, object, event, message) as "the same" when the stimulus configuration has changed between initial and subsequent encounter. Studies of recognition memory for verbal material have attempted to separate memory for underlying message and for its representational form by maintaining the message while changing the form. With sentences, for example, representational form can vary in syntax (Sachs, 1967), lexical selection (Levy, 1975), orthography (Kolers and Ostry, 1974); with single words, there have been variations in modality of input (Kirsner, 1974) and speaking voice (Craik and Kirsner, 1974). If a person's identity can be considered the "message" of a picture in the way that the meaning of a word or sentence represents the message of its presentation, then effects of representational form on memory for content can be assessed in person recognition as well as in verbal recognition memory.

In the present study, subjects learned to identify target people by name, studying either still photographs of their faces or short film sequences of them moving about. The recognition test which followed occurred either in the same format as learning (*slide-slide* and *film-film* conditions) or different format (*slide-film* and *film-slide*). The test also included manipulations of changes in appearance and angle of view of the targets, which had been shown to produce major effects on identification in a more traditional *slide-slide* experiment (Patterson and Baddeley, 1977).

METHOD

Design

Twelve clean-shaven men of varying age were both filmed and photographed (all black-and-white) in four different appearances: natural appearance, with a beard added, with a wig added, and with both beard and wig. Each of the four appearances was captured both in full-face and in profile view, yielding eight different versions. The still photographs, which were made into 35 mm slides, were ordinary portrait-style photographs of the head and shoulders. In the 16 mm film sequences, one for each version of each man, the man walked across an empty car park (in front of a building) over to a chair, picking up a brief-case on his way. During the walk across he was in profile view. At the chair first, with his back to the viewer, he put down the brief-case and removed a book from it; he then either paused facing away from the viewer for about 3 sec. or turned to face the viewer for 3 sec; finally he pivoted to profile view again and walked off the screen. The films with the pause facing away from the viewer will be called profile view, since the target's face was seen only in profile for these sequences. The films with the pause facing toward the viewer will be called full-face view, although of course these sequences also showed the target in profile when he was walking. The films were taken at a distance of about 8 metres, where the men filled most of the vertical frame.

Two target sets (A and B) of four men each were selected for the learning phase of the experiment, and one of the four versions of appearance (natural, beard, wig, beard and wig) was selected without replacement for each target within a set. For both slide and film conditions, subjects studied a target set of four, all targets in full-face view, each target in one appearance only. The test consisted of a series of 96 slides or 96 film sequences, including all eight versions of appearance and angle-of-view of all twelve men. Treatment at study and at test produced four experimental conditions (learn on slides, test on slides; learn on films, test on films; learn on slides, test on films; learn on films, test on slides) which combined with two target sets yielded eight experimental groups. Group size varied from ten to fifteen members of the Applied Psychology Unit subject panel, all female.

Procedure

In the learning phase, subjects were presented with the target set six times, each time in a different order, and they learned a name for each target (Roger Shaw, Peter Clark, Geoffrey Reed, Simon Mills). In the procedure for name learning, initially the experimenter called out the target names and subsequently the subjects did so (details can be found in Patterson and Baddeley, 1977, Experiment II). Regarding duration of presentation, the film sequences varied as a result of each man's natural walking speed, but were in the range of 12-15 seconds each. The slides were each shown for about 10 sec. at each exposure during learning, providing a slightly shorter total viewing time but a longer duration of full-face exposure than the film sequences. Between learning and test, full instructions were given on the nature and format of the recognition test, including the facts that the targets would appear multiple times each, that their appearances would be altered by addition and removal of beards and wigs, that they would sometimes appear only in profile view, and that the distractors were more numerous than the targets. For each slide or film sequence in the test series, subjects underlined one of the four target names or the word *none*. For groups tested on films, the film sequences were shown in their entirety but without a break between successive ones; thus subjects had to make a response during the latter part of each sequence. For groups tested on slides, the slides of faces alternated with blank slides (for response intervals) at an automatic 5 sec. rate.

RESULTS

Performance on target sets A and B was comparable, and therefore the data have been combined on this variable. The proportion of correct identification of targets is displayed in Fig. 1 as a function of the major manipulations: format at learning and test (the four columns of Fig.1), version of appearance (the four bars within each sub-graph), and angle of view (top vs. bottom half of Fig.1). By analysis of variance for min F', allowing generalisation across both subjects and targets, six effects were significant beyond the .05 level: (1) A change in the format of information from learning to test dramatically reduced the probability

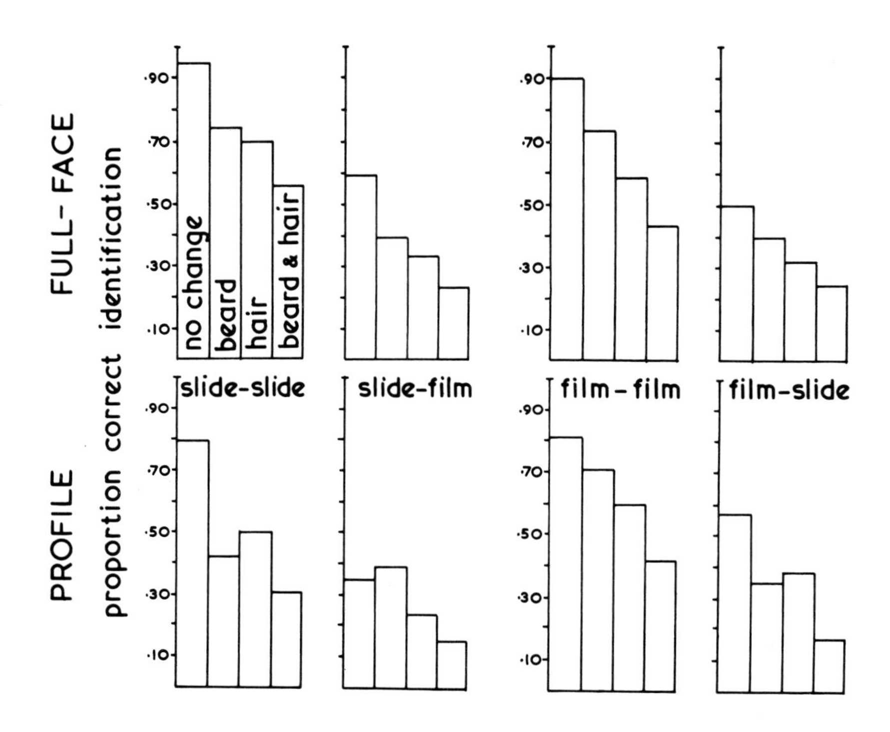

Fig. 1 Identification as a function of condition (slide-slide, slide-film, film-film, film-slide), version of appearance (no change, change in beard, change in hair style, change in both beard and hair), and angle of view (full-face, profile). Version of appearance is labelled on one sub-graph only, but follows the same order on all sub-graphs. Change in beard (hair) includes both addition and removal of beard (wig).

of correct identification; this effect is shown visually by pairs of contiguous sub-graphs in Fig.1 and statistically by a massive interaction between presentation format and test format. Neither learning nor test format yielded a significant main effect: slides and films provided equally good media for both learning and identifying, with performance dependent only on whether the medium was the same or different on the two occasions. (2) The addition or removal of a target's beard between learning and test significantly reduced correct identifications, as did (3) a change in hair style. (4) Identification was poorer when the test film or slide showed the target in profile rather than full-face view. This main effect must however be qualified by (5) the existence of a significant interaction between angle of view and learning format. It is not surprising that the angle-of-view effect was almost entirely attributable to the conditions where learning was on slides, since the learning films provided both full-face and profile views. Finally (6) a three-way interaction between test format, angle of view, and change in beard indicates that recognition of facial photographs in profile was more vulnerable to beard change than were the other types of test items.

For a brief summary of performance on distractor items, the false positive rate for the experiment as a whole was .21, and there are two relevant breakdowns of this figure. First, by condition, the false positive rate was roughly comparable for three of the four conditions (*slide-slide* .16, *film-film* .19, *film-slide* .19) but sharply increased for the remaining condition (*slide-film* .32). Thus the *direction* of change in format (slide to film or vice versa) made little difference to correct identifications but a major difference to false identifications of non-target people. Second, distractors as well as targets appeared in all four versions of appearance. Compared to the false positive rate for distractor items in their natural appearance (.16), the addition of a wig increased this rate very little (.18), the addition of a beard somewhat more (.22), and the addition of both rather notably (.28). Thus any man with both wig and beard was more likely to be identified as a target. This response bias does not improve identification performance: for the targets, the changes in beard and/or hair between learning and test were as frequently deletions as additions of beard/wig.

DISCUSSION

The results of the present experiment afford the basis for discussion of several different issues, but the joint goals of brevity and relevance to the symposium topic limit discussion to a single issue: the effects of change in format of information. Taking only cases where there was no alteration in the target's appearance and averaging, for the moment, over type of format and angle of view, subjects correctly identified their targets with probability .86 when learning and test format were the same, .50 when the formats were different. The magnitude of this effect is emphasised by two contrasts. First, a change in format reduced identification performance almost as much as an alteration in *both* beard and hair style, though intuitively one might have expected "disguise" (as the very term implies) to have a more devastating effect than changed format of representation. Secondly, in a subsequent experiment subjects learned to identify targets from the presentation films described here but were tested on films taken at a distance of 20 metres rather than 8. Although these "distance" films engender a substantial reduction in detailed information available, and did accordingly produce poorer identification performance than tests on the "close-up" films, this decrement was not nearly so large as the effect of changing from slide to film or film to slide.

The format effect has both theoretical and practical implications. Theoretically, the results argue against the notion that a person's identity is simply abstracted and recognised independently of the form in which it is represented. Although Kolers and Ostry's (1974) formulation of the recognition process takes its empirical support from studies of reading and sentence recognition, it seems applicable to the present results. "Recognition ... occurs as the reactivation of cognitive procedures, cognitive operations, and not necessarily by matching of semantic contents, propositions, or deep structures" (Kolers and Ostry, 1974, p.609). It is not of course easy to specify the cognitive operations involved in studying photographs of faces and films of people. But the data suggest that these operations differ for photographs and films, yielding superior recognition if the same operations can be reactivated on second encounter. A person's identity may be the "message" of a photograph or film; but the medium of that message cannot be considered a separate or irrelevant dimension. The fact that you easily recognise photographs of people you know well may merely attest the variety and complexity of the processing that occurs when you see a person repeatedly from different angles, with different expressions, etc.

Practically, the results argue for caution whenever recognition of a not-so-well-known person involves a change in the format of information. The *film-slide* condition seems a reasonable experimental analogue of the witness to a crime who (with less exposure to the target, often, than the experimental subjects) is asked to identify a suspect from a set of facial photographs. Such identification may be intended merely as the basis for subsequent identification in person. However, Loftus, Miller and Burns (1978) have shown that relevant information which arrives subsequent to viewing an event can be integrated into the memory for the original event. Loftus *et al* used verbal presentation of the intervening relevant information, but it is plausible that intervening visual information might be accorded the same integrative treatment. The caution, then, derives from the following scenario. A witness to a crime may be quite poor at recognising a facial photograph of the perpetrator (cf. the low identification rate in condition *film-slide*). Although the false positive rate was not inordinately high in this condition, given certain demand characteristics of the situation the witness might select a photograph of the wrong individual. The face of that unfortunate character might then get integrated into the witness' memory for the original event. And in a subsequent identification-in-person, the witness might provide honest but mistaken eyewitness testimony.

ACKNOWLEDGEMENTS

D.C.V. Simmonds, as camera man and photographer, was truly a *sine qua non* of this research. Further valuable assistance came from A.D. Baddeley, A.K. Copeman, J.M. Lawrence, C.A.S. Robinson, and M.M. Woodhead.

REFERENCES

Bower, G.H. and Karlin, M.B. (1974). Depth of Processing Pictures of Faces and Recognition Memory. *Journal of Experimental Psychology*, 103, 751-757.

Craik, F.I.M. and Kirsner, K. (1974). Voice Effects in Word Recognition. *Quarterly Journal of Experimental Psychology*, 26, 274-284.

Dent, H. and Gray, F. (1975). Identification on Parade. *New Behaviour*, 2, 366-369.

Kirsner, K. (1974). Modality Differences in Recognition Memory for Words and their Attributes. *Journal of Experimental Psychology*, 102, 579-584.

Kolers, P.A. and Ostry, D.J. (1974). Time Course of Loss of Information Regarding Pattern Analyzing Operations. *Journal of Verbal Learning and Verbal Behavior*, 13, 599-612.

Laughery, K.R., Fessler, P.K., Lenorovitz, D.R. and Yoblick, D.A. (1974). Time Delay and Similarity Effects in Facial Recognition. *Journal of Applied Psychology*, 59, 490-496.

Levy, B.A. (1975). Vocalization and Suppression Effects in Sentence Memory. *Journal of Verbal Learning and Verbal Behavior*, 14, 304-316.

Loftus, E.F., Miller, D.G. and Burns, H.J. (1978). Semantic Integration of Verbal Information into a Visual Memory. *Journal of Experimental Psychology: Human Learning and Memory*, 4, 19-31.

Neisser, U. (1976). *Cognition and Reality*. W.H. Freeman & Co., San Francisco.

Patterson, K.E. and Baddeley, A.D. (1977). When Face Recognition Fails. *Journal of Experimental Psychology: Human Learning and Memory*, 3, 406-417.

Sachs, J.S. (1967). Recognition Memory for Syntactic and Semantic Aspects of Connected Discourse. *Perception and Psychophysics*, 2, 437-442.

Strnad, B.N. and Mueller, J.H. (1977). Levels of Processing in Facial Recognition Memory. *Bulletin of the Psychonomic Society*, 9, 17-18.

Warrington, E.K. and Ackroyd, C. (1975). The Effect of Orienting Tasks on Recognition Memory. *Memory and Cognition*, 3, 140-142.

Watkins, M.J., Ho, E. and Tulving, E. (1976). Context Effects in Recognition Memory for Faces. *Journal of Verbal Learning and Verbal Behavior*, 15, 505-517.

Winograd, E. (1976). Recognition Memory for Faces following Nine Different Judgments. *Bulletin of the Psychonomic Society*, 8, 419-421.

Winograd, E. and Rivers-Bulkeley, N.T. (1977). Effects of Changing Context on Remembering Faces. *Journal of Experimental Psychology: Human Learning and Memory*, 3, 397-405.

INTERVIEWING CHILD WITNESSES

Helen R. Dent
*Department of Psychology,
University of Nottingham,
Nottingham, England.*

ABSTRACT

Research (Dent and Stephenson, in press) has shown that different questioning techniques significantly affect the accuracy of testimony elicited from juvenile witnesses. A preliminary analysis is presented in the following paper of an experiment designed to identify the questioning skills employed by effective interviewers. "Experienced" and "inexperienced" interviewers were required to elicit 10/11 year old children's recall of an incident staged in their schools the previous day. The interviewers were free to use whatever strategies they considered appropriate. Differences between the two groups of interviewers are identified and discussed relative to a number of performance criteria.

INTRODUCTION

Children are regularly called upon to give evidence both in juvenile and "adult" courts; whilst this fact alone provides adequate justification for studying the extent to which children's testimony can be relied upon to be accurate, a number of considerations accentuate the need for such research.

Perhaps the most important of these is the degree of complacency that exists amongst at least some of the professionals concerned. In particular I have become acquainted with the views of the police towards child witnesses. Although there is ample evidence from psychology alone to demonstrate the many ways in which children's recall can be inaccurate (Stern, 1939; Trankell, 1972), some police officers at all levels simply view young children as "innocents" who have no cause to lie, and will, therefore, give accurate evidence. There is a general tendency to play down the significance of the fact that existing research into testimony demonstrates that the use of present techniques can result in inaccurate testimony, even from the most honest child witness.

The task of eliciting verbal testimony from a witness can be considered to be one of helping the witness to create an accurate reconstruction of past events. In order to do so effectively, it is necessary to be aware of the ways in which recall is likely to be impaired, and how different methods of elicitation increase or decrease the likelihood of accurate recall.

There is a considerable amount of literature concerning the perceptual factors which tend to distort or otherwise impair recall (Buckhout, 1974; Neisser, 1976); but little detailed information concerning the effects of different techniques of elicitation upon the accuracy of children's recall. My previous experimental work was therefore designed to investigate the effects of elicitation upon the accuracy of children's recall.

The experiments in this research were all conducted with 10/11 year old school children, who witnessed a filmed crime or a live incident staged in their classrooms and were subsequently interviewed on successive occasions for a period of two months following the incident. The aims of the experiments were to compare the relative efficiency of free report, the use of general questions and the use of specific questions.

The overall results showed that any form of prompting impaired the accuracy of children's verbal recall. Free reports produced much more accurate, though less complete recall than answers to general or specific questions. More detailed analyses of the results revealed that whereas descriptions of people were particularly impaired by prompting, narrative information was more robust and was even enhanced by the minimal prompting involved in the general questions.

Whilst these experiments clearly demonstrated that overall free reports produce the most accurate information, there is no guarantee that a witness will unaided produce relevant information. In real life investigations such a constraint is unlikely to be tolerated even though this involves the risk of a reduction in accuracy. The demands of accuracy and the demands of completeness will often be in competition. A sensitive and flexible repertoire of questioning skills will be required to cope with such conflicts. The present investigation was designed to examine the likely make up of such a repertoire.

DESIGN AND PROCEDURE OF EXPERIMENT

The major difference between this study and my previous work was that the interviewers were left free to choose their own strategies in questioning the children. The performance of two groups of interviewers was compared. The first group was composed of three policemen and three teachers; the common characteristic of the members of this group was that they all had professional experience with children. The second group consisted of four parents and two voluntary youth workers. Though the members of this group did not deal in a professional capacity with children they were nevertheless involved with children in one way or another. I originally wished to compare a group of policemen and women with an alternative group of interviewers, but policemen proved hard to come by and policewomen impossible in school hours.

The experiment was carried out in the following manner: a live incident was staged in 4th year classrooms in a cross-section of Nottingham Junior Schools, with only the teacher's prior knowledge. The incident involved three men and one woman.

The following day ten children from each class were interviewed about the incident. Half were interviewed by a "professionally experienced" person and half by a "professionally inexperienced" person. The interviews took place in the Psychology Department and were recorded on video-tape. The interviewers were simply told "Yesterday, soon after the mid-morning playtime, the children's lesson was interrupted, and at some point a bag was taken from the classroom". They were asked to find out what the child could remember about the incident and to produce a written statement of the child's recall at the end of each interview.

Following the main interview, the interviewer and child were separately asked to go through the written statement created during the interview, in order to indicate those parts of the recall about which each felt the child was certain, doubtful, or purely guessing. The child was assisted in this task by another adult who did not know what had happened in the incident. Gauld and Stephenson (1967) found that adult subjects required to rate their own version of a story previously heard were able to identify correctly their errors. If children are similarly able to recognise the parts of their testimony which are erroneous, it clearly becomes part of the skill of the interviewer to identify those parts. This second stage of the experiment was designed to investigate both whether or not the children's levels of certainty would coincide with accuracy of information, and what degree of convergence there would be between the interviewer and the child's scoring of the statement.

Finally, after interviewing all five children, each interviewer was asked to write a report of what he or she thought happened in the incident and to answer a questionaire designed to probe the interviewer's perception of his or her interviewing technique.

RESULTS AND DISCUSSION

The analysis of the experiment is still ongoing; this paper is mainly concerned with the initial quantitative analysis. The transcripts of the interviews, the statements created during the interviews and the interviewers' final reports were all scored for accuracy, using a prepared checklist. The measures used were correct points and incorrect points, with the further subdivision of correct and incorrect descriptive points. Obviously, only information concerned with the incident and about which the accuracy was known was scored. The major objective of the analysis was to identify differences between the experienced and inexperienced interviewers on simple outcome measures, in order to provide a formal basis for later, more detailed analyses. These simple measures were used in a number of ways to establish criteria against which performance was evaluated.

Relative to the transcript scores, a good performance is indicated by a high correct point score, or by a low incorrect point score, or preferably by a combination of the two. The results included here were based on the simple uncombined scores.

For the statement scores, I have chosen to consider that a good statement faithfully records the relevant contents of the interview. Hence, in a good statement, the number of correct and incorrect points should equal the transcript scores.

No direct evaluation of the interviewers' skill in creating final reports will be presented in this paper. The final reports were, however, used to examine in more detail differences between the "experienced" and "inexperienced" groups suggested by the transcript scores.

Certainty/Doubt Scoring of Statements

Before discussing the between group comparisons, I shall deal briefly with the interviewers' and children's scoring of the statements in terms of certainty and doubt. The most consistent result that emerged was that the children expressed certainty about most of the information included in the statement. The only information they admitted to having guessed concerned the ages of people involved in the incident. The interviewers, on the other hand, produced a greater range of scoring, but their perceptions of the children's levels of certainty or doubt did not consistently coincide with the accuracy or inaccuracy of the information. This result does not, of course, rule out the possibility that skilled judgments about the status of the information were made by interviewers prior to or during the production of the statements.

Transcript Scores

The "experienced" interviewers elicited both more correct and more incorrect points from the children than did the "inexperienced" interviewers. The mean scores for the "experienced" group were 30.57 correct points and 5.33 incorrect points, and for the "inexperienced" group 17.27 correct points and 2.9 incorrect points. Analyses of variance failed to show reliable differences between the two groups, but when the interviewers were ranked according to who had the highest correct scores, five of the top six positions were occupied by "experienced" interviewers. The first two positions were in fact occupied by policemen; they also had the highest incorrect scores. The third policeman, however, occupied the tenth position in the list.

The differences between the two groups were maintained when descriptive information was extracted from these scores. The mean descriptive scores for the "experienced" group were 12.06 correct points and 3.59 incorrect points; and for the "inexperienced" group 4.93 correct points and 1.30 incorrect points. Analyses of variance failed to show a reliable difference between the incorrect scores, but showed a significant difference between the correct scores ($df=1,10$, $F = 6.10$, $P < 0.03$).

Little can be said of direct relevance to differences in questioning strategies on the basis of these scores. Previous research (Dent and Stephenson, in press) does, however, suggest the possibility that those questioners who obtained high numbers of correct and incorrect points were using strategies which involved closer structuring of the children's recall, than questioners who obtained low scores on each measure.

One final point worth mentioning concerning these scores

is that the difference between the two groups of interviewers was not consistent across all five children. The difference between the groups was greatest at the beginning of the interviewing sessions. The "inexperienced" interviewers increased their mean correct and incorrect scores across the five interviews so that the differences between the groups became less distinct. This result may indicate that the "inexperienced" interviewers increased the specificity of their questioning over the course of the five interviews. Such a change in strategy would certainly be consistent with the data.

Statement Scores

With respect to the statement scores, the situation was slightly different. Both groups had fewer correct and incorrect points in their statements than in the transcripts. In other words they did not make use of all the relevant information that was available to them. However, the "inexperienced" interviewers produced a more faithful reproduction of the transcript scores than did the "experienced" interviewers. The difference between the groups was rather small, however, and not statistically reliable. The reduction in incorrect points may indicate that both groups of interviewers attempted, with some success, to exclude points of dubious accuracy from the statements. The reduction in numbers of correct points may indicate incorrect judgments of the likely accuracy of the information. It may also be the case that the interviewers were unaware of all the information generated by the children, or that omitted information was considered to be irrelevant.

Final Report Analysis

The "experienced" interviewers' mean incorrect score was lower for the final reports than for the transcripts (final report = 2.5, transcript = 5.33). The corresponding difference was less for the "inexperienced" interviewers (final report = 2.5, transcript = 2.90). This result suggests that the "experienced" group are more skilled at recognising incorrect information than the "inexperienced" group. Whether this skill is exercised during individual interviews or whether it is based upon inconsistencies between the accounts of different children, is not yet known.

Within the limits of the interviewers' report-making skills, the final reports approximate to précis of the information obtained from each group of five children. A detailed analysis of these reports was therefore carried out to clarify those differences between the two groups of interviewers already suggested by the transcript scores. This analysis was based upon the number of information points specific to each group of interviewers. Information points common to both groups were not included in the analysis. The results of the analysis showed that there were equal numbers of incorrect points specific to each group (n=6), but the number of correct points specific to the "experienced" group (n=29) was greater than the number specific to the "inexperienced" group (n=1). Of the 29 correct points specific to the "experienced" group, 19 were concerned with the description of people, and 5 with the description of objects. These results provide support for the transcript scores which indicated the importance of descriptive information in differentiating the performance of the two groups.

FINAL COMMENTS

The major aim of this investigation is to identify sensitive and flexible interviewing techniques that will enable questioners to obtain recall from children that satisfies criteria of accuracy and completeness. Previous research showed that optimal accuracy was only possible at the expense of completeness and vice versa. Whether or not the interviews recorded for this investigation will provide a sufficient range of strategies to realise its objectives is not fully ascertainable from the analyses carried out so far. A number of points do, however, lend some justification for optimism. Some interviewers obtained very full accounts of the incident, whereas others elicited very little relevant information. Examples of strategies associated with completeness will therefore be available. With respect to the management of the accuracy/completeness dilemma, there are indications that at least some interviewers employ a wide range of evaluative skills to assess the accuracy of the information they obtained. An example demonstrating the use of this repertoire of skills concerns the elicitation of descriptive information. An impressive amount of detailed descriptive information was obtained in response to specific questioning, without the accompanying decrease in accuracy found in previous experiments. A clear implication of this result is that some use was made of "checking" strategies, when eliciting this type of information.

ACKNOWLEDGEMENTS

This research is funded by a grant from the S.S.R.C. (No H.R. 4522) held jointly by myself and Professor Geoffrey Stephenson. Thanks are also due to Paddy Donovan and Pauline Williams for invaluable assistance in the production of this paper.

REFERENCES

Buckhout, R. (1974). Eye witness testimony. *Scientific American*. Dec. Vol 231, No 6, 23-31.

Dent, H.R. and Stephenson, G.M. An experimental study of the effectiveness of different techniques of questioning child witnesses. *British Journal of Social and Clinical Psychology*. In press.

Gauld, A. and Stephenson, G.M. (1967). Some experiments relating to Bartlett's theory of remembering. *British Journal of Psychology*. 58, 1 & 2, 39-49.

Neisser, U. (1976). *Cognition and Reality*. W.H.Freeman & Co. San Francisco.

Stern, W. (1939). The psychology of testimony. *Journal of Abnormal and Social Psychology*. 34, 3-20.

Trankell, A. (1972). *Reliability of Evidence*. Beckmans.

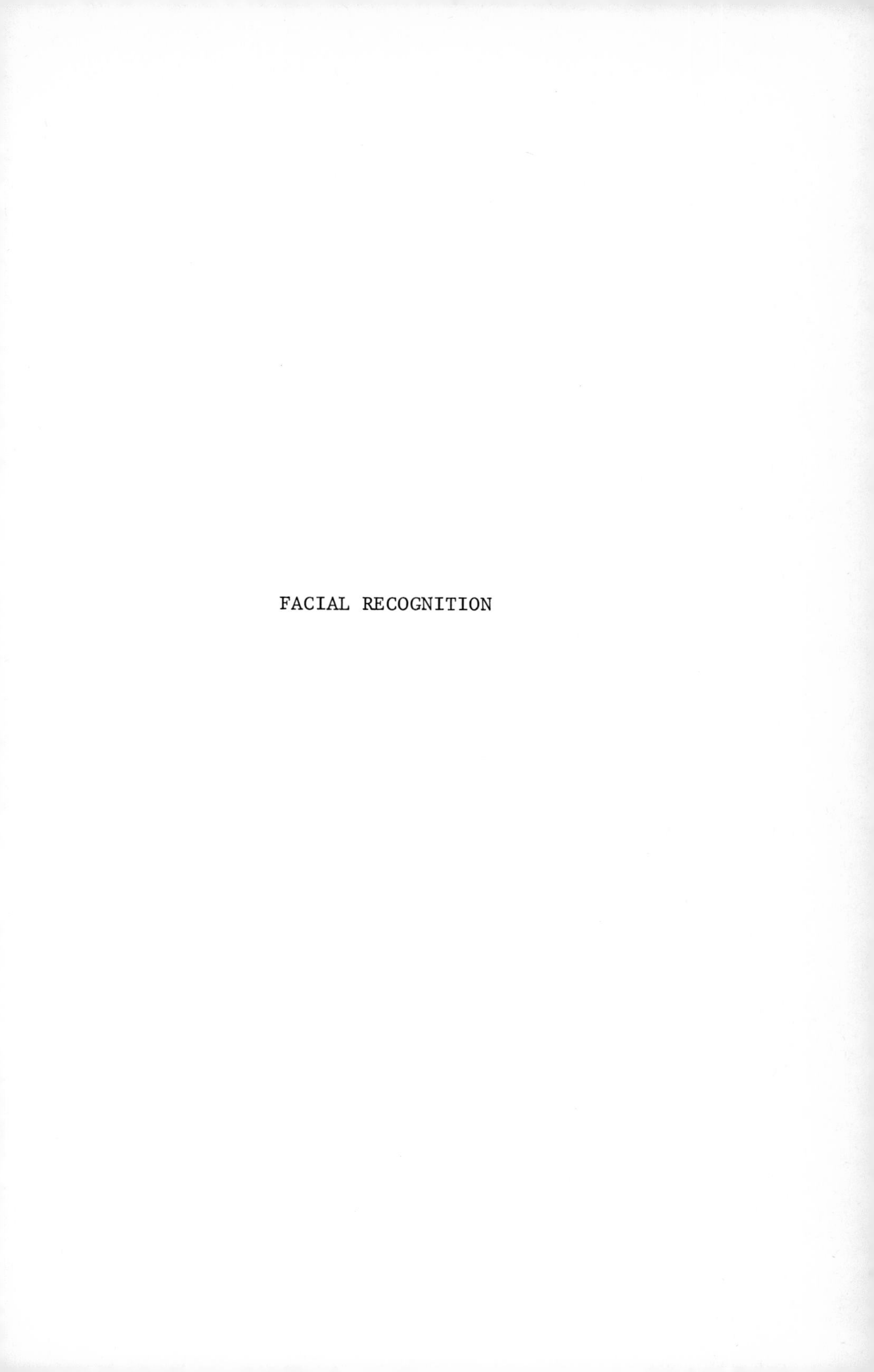

FACIAL RECOGNITION

FACE RECOGNITION: ISSUES AND THEORIES

G. M. Davies
Department of Psychology, The University, Old Aberdeen, Scotland.

A review is provided of the issues raised, and theories generated, by recent research on face recognition.

A review of this kind can only hope to introduce the reader to the growing research on face recognition. A more comprehensive account has been provided by Ellis (1975). Accordingly, this paper highlights issues and theories, drawing wherever possible on material published since the appearance of Ellis' review.

ISSUES

People appear to be very good at recognising photographs of strangers' faces under laboratory conditions. Subjects exposed to a set of 20 faces are able to select them from alternatives with an accuracy of up to 90% (see Goldstein, 1977 for a review). The effect is a fairly robust one, surviving changes of pose and expression between study and test (Patterson and Baddeley, 1977) and holds up well over time delays, a fact testified to by the ability of professors to recognise photographs of contemporaries from their undergraduate days (Bahrick, Bahrick and Wittlinger, 1975). However, the introduction of disguise disrupts performance: the addition of a wig or beard much more so than spectacles (Patterson and Baddeley, 1977).

Faces vary in their memorability. Individuals with particularly distinctive features are better recognised than those without (Going and Read, 1974), a point capitalised upon by cartoonists (Perkins, 1975). However, physical distinctiveness is not the only cue which distinguishes easily remembered faces: attributed properties like beauty or attractiveness also influence recognition accuracy (Fleishman, Buckley, Klosinsky, Smith and Tuck, 1976). The relationship between physical and attributional judgements is unclear: are beautiful faces also physically deviant or do the two factors enjoy a degree of independence?

Statements about memorability must be made with reference

to the context in which recognition takes place. A condition in which a face is placed among others which are physically similar produces a much higher false alarm rate than one in which the same face is placed among dissimilar faces (Laughery, Fessler, Lenorovitz and Yoblick, 1974; Patterson and Baddeley, 1977).

People also differ in their ability to remember faces, though the reasons for this are much less clear. One personality factor, that of field-dependence (Goodenough, 1976), has received perhaps disproportionate attention in the literature. According to theory, the individual who relies upon those around him for his frames of reference, should show a greater aptitude for face recognition than the field-independent person. Recent results have not supported this view and have even found significant trends in the reverse direction (Lavrakas, Buri and Mayzner, 1976; Hoffman and Kagan, 1977). The influence of other relevant personality factors such as introversion-extraversion has received little systematic investigation; it is clear that a great deal remains to be done in this area.

The influence of sex and race variables is more complex with the level of performance being a function of the nature of the sample and the type of stimulus material. The precise form of the interaction has shown some variation across studies.

As regards sex, women generally show higher accuracy scores on female than male faces whereas these trends are often reversed in male subjects (see McKelvie, this symposium). Earlier claims that this female advantage was present from the cradle have not been supported by later research (see Fagan, in press) and could well reflect a more general female preoccupation with social observation (McCall, Mazanec, Erickson and Smith, 1974).

As regards race, tests of caucasian subjects invariably show a higher rate of accuracy on white relative to black faces while a trend in the reverse direction has often been found for negro subjects (see Ellis, 1975). It is tempting to ascribe all such effects to differences in the cues essential to discriminate between members of different races and there is evidence that whites and blacks do differ in the way they describe faces (Ellis, Deregowski and Shepherd, 1975). However, an explanation purely in terms of differences in attentional strategy seems implausible given the fact that white subjects can learn to discriminate black faces under laboratory conditions (Malpass, 1975). Moreover, quantity of contact seems less important than quality: number of black friends, for instance, predicts performance but sheer amount of interracial contact does not (Lavrakas et al.,1976). While a purely social explanation (e.g. Luce, 1974) seems implausible, there is no doubt that attitudinal factors will play a part in any complete account of racial effects.

THEORIES

Face recognition studies have suffered from a dearth of theories to guide research. The one theory to arise from face research is that most closely associated with Yin (1970), that face identification requires a special mechanism additional to normal perceptual processing. Supporters of this hypothesis rely on three areas of research to support their position; in all of these areas there is reason to doubt whether the facts demand the interpretation placed upon them.

First, it is claimed that during early infancy, development of face perception proceeds independently of general perceptual learning. While there is no doubt that faces loom large in the child's perceptual world, the development of face discrimination appears to be no more rapid than for other non-social abstract patterns (Fagan, in press).

Second, Yin (1969) has claimed that the inversion of a face has a disrupting effect on recognition which is disproportionate relative to other mono-oriented objects. However, recent research, reviewed by Rock (1974) challenges Yin's conclusions: when stimuli equated for complexity and familiarity are inverted, the effects on recognition appear to be as great as for faces.

A final line of evidence concerns prosapagnosia, a rare clinical condition characterised by an inability to recognise faces. However, critical examination of the literature suggests such patients suffer from a more general impairment to complex visual discrimination, of which an inability to recognise faces is only one part; further the syndrome is associated with lesions scattered over a wide variety of neurological sites (Meadows, 1974).

Thus, there appears to be no compelling evidence which demands the assumption of a special mechanism. However, Yin's emphasis on the unique social significance of the face must be borne in mind in evaluating theories which treat face recognition in terms of more general information processing models. Such approaches will be referred to as feature and gestalt theories, paralleling the distinction drawn in pattern recognition between feature analysis and template matching.

Models which assume successive sampling of key features or dimensions can draw on three areas of research for support. First, there are the results of discrimination studies involving pairs of faces made from 'Identikit' parts where the faces differ in number of common features. Bradshaw and Wallace (1971) found comparisons involving multiple feature change to be much faster than those where the stimuli differed in only one respect. However, later studies which have manipulated a wider range of changes have produced results which are not consistent with a simple feature testing model (e.g. Matthews, 1978).

Second, there are the studies which have examined how recognition accuracy is affected by the omission or alteration of features within the face. In general, such studies suggest that upper features (hair, eyes) contribute more to recognition than lower (chin, mouth)(see Davies, Ellis and Shepherd, 1977).

Third, there are the studies of Harmon (1973) which demonstrate that feature information can be used as an effective tool in searching for and identifying target faces in a large population of alternatives. However, as Perkins (1975) has noted, the fact that subjects are able to use such information does not necessarily imply that this is the normal, or indeed the most effective, method of searching for a face.

Against this evidence may be set a number of findings which appear more compatible with the view that the face is stored as a total gestalt rather than a bundle of features.

First, photographed faces which are blurred to the point where most specific feature information is lost can still be recognised quite accurately (Harmon, 1973). Conversely, photographs converted into line drawings where most of the feature information is still present are identified surprisingly poorly (Davies, Ellis and Shepherd, 1977).

Second, observers are ineffective at remembering feature information: subjects can provide only vague and limited details on even well known faces (see Phillips, and Shepherd, Davies and Ellis, this symposium) and their performance with 'Photofit', a face reconstruction tool which uses photographed features, is unimpressive (Ellis, Davies and Shepherd, 1978).

On the basis of existing evidence it is too early to decide between feature and gestalt approaches. Serious consideration needs also to be given to the middle ground: models involving both types of processing (e.g. Matthews, 1978). However all such theories need to take account of the dual role of the face as physical stimulus and social object. As was observed in the review of the findings, attitudinal and contextual factors derived from the social role of faces seem to be important in influencing recognition accuracy.

The power of attributional judgements is further illustrated by a series of studies which have examined the influence of attitudinal judgements and contextual information on face recognition.

First, there are the results from studies which have extended the 'levels of processing' approach to memory into face research (Bower and Karlin, 1974). It has been discovered that asking subjects to rate faces on such global factors as 'intelligence' or 'attractiveness' leads to better subsequent recognition than if the faces are rated directly on physical features like nose-length or distance between the eyes (Winograd, 1976; Patterson and Baddeley, 1977, and see Winograd, this symposium).

Second, if a face is presented along with a descriptive statement such as 'enjoys skateboarding', that face is subsequently better recognised in the context of the original description than if it is presented with no statement or a different one (Watkins, Ho and Tulving, 1976; see also Winograd and Rivers-Bulkeley, 1977).

Finally, if subjects search for faces among alternatives which are drawn from the same social context as the targets (e.g. TV stars, politicians), rate of identification is significantly slowed relative to conditions in which the targets are embedded among contextually unrelated faces (Bruce,1977).

CONCLUSIONS

These findings, together with those discussed earlier on race and attractiveness, seem to indicate that attributional information has a role to play independent of feature information. It is, of course, possible to argue that these judgements are ultimately translations of statements about physical features. However, such reductionism appears to beg the question of why they are made in the first place.

The unique social dimension of the face can be accommodated in either a feature or a gestalt model. Whatever the ultimate resolution of that conflict, it is important that any general information processing theory that deals with faces does not lose sight of their wider significance. It is not necessary to go all the way with Yin to agree that 'faces *are* special'.

ACKNOWLEDGEMENTS

My thanks to Hadyn Ellis and John Shepherd for their criticisms and comments. The Aberdeen Bibliography of Face Research is supported by Home Office Grant POL/73 1675/24/1.

REFERENCES

Bahrick, G.P., Bahrick, P.O. and Wittlinger, R.P. (1975). Fifty Years of Memory for Names and Faces: A Cross-Sectional Approach. *Journal of Experimental Psychology: General:* 104, 54-75.

Bower, G.H. and Karlin, M.B. (1974). Depth of Processing Pictures and Recognition Memory. *Journal of Experimental Psychology*, 103, 751-757.

Bradshaw, J.L. and Wallace, G. (1971). Models for the Processing and Identification of Faces. *Perception and Psychophysics*, 9, 443-448.

Bruce, V. (1977). Searching for Politicians: An Information-Processing Approach to Face Recognition. Presented at a meeting of the Experimental Psychology Society, Sheffield.

Davies, G.M., Ellis, H.D. and Shepherd, J.W. (1977). Cue Saliency in Faces as Assessed by the Photofit Technique. *Perception*, 6, 262-269.

Davies, G.M., Ellis, H.D. and Shepherd, J.W. (1978). Face Recognition Accuracy as a Function of Mode of Representation. *Journal of Applied Psychology*, 63, 180-187.

Ellis, H.D. (1975). Recognising Faces. *British Journal of Psychology*, 66, 409-426.

Ellis, H.D., Davies, G.M. and Shepherd, J.W. (1978). A Critical Examination of the Photofit System for Recalling Faces. *Ergonomics*, 21, 297-307.

Ellis, H.D., Deregowski, J.B. and Shepherd, J.W. (1975). Descriptions of White and Black Faces by White and Black Subjects. *International Journal of Psychology*, 10, 119-123.

Fagan, J.F. (in press). The Origins of Facial Pattern Recognition. In: *Psychological Development from Infancy*. (M. Bornstein and W. Kessen, eds). Erlbaum, Hillsdale, New Jersey.

Fleishman, J.J., Buckley, M.L., Klosinsky, M.J., Smith, N. and Tuck, B. (1976). Judged Attractiveness in Recognition Memory of Women's Faces. *Perceptual and Motor Skills*, 43, 709-710.

Going, M. and Read, J.D. (1974). Effects of Uniqueness, Sex of Subjects, and Sex of Photograph on Facial Recognition. *Perceptual and Motor Skills*, 39, 109-110.

Goldstein, A.G. (1977). The Fallibility of the Eyewitness: Psychological Evidence. In: *Psychology in the Legal Process*. (B.D. Sales, ed.). Spectrum Publications, New York.

Goodenough, D.R. (1976). The Role of Individual Differences in Field Dependence as a Factor in Learning and Memory. *Psychological Bulletin*, 83, 675-694.

Harmon, L.D. (1973). The Recognition of Faces. *Scientific American*, 229, 71-82.

Hoffman, C. and Kagan, S. (1977). Field Dependence and Facial Recognition. *Perceptual and Motor Skills*, 44, 119-124.

Laughery, K.R., Fessler, P.K., Lenorovitz, D.R. and Yoblick, D.A. (1974). Time Delay and Similarity Effects in Facial Recognition. *Journal of Applied Psychology*, 59, 490-496.

Lavrakas, P.J., Buri, J.R. and Mayzner, M.S. (1976). A Perspective on the Recognition of Other-Race Faces. *Perception and Psychophysics*, 20, 475-481.

Luce, T.S. (1974). Blacks, Whites and Yellows: They All Look Alike to Me. *Psychology Today*, 8, 105-108.

McCall, G.J., Mazanec, N., Erickson, W.L. and Smith, H.W. (1974). Same Sex Recall Effects in Tests of Observational Accuracy. *Perceptual and Motor Skills*, 38, 830.

Malpass, R.S. (1975). Towards a Theoretical Basis for Understanding Differential Face Recognition. Presented at a meeting of the Mid-Western Psychological Association, Chicago.

Matthews, M.L. (1978). Discrimination of Identikit Constructions of Faces: Evidence for a Dual Processing Strategy. *Perception and Psychophysics*, 23, 153-161.

Meadows, J.C. (1974). The Anatomical Basis of Prosopagnosia. *Journal of Neurology, Neurosurgery, and Psychiatry*, 37, 489-501.

Patterson, K.E. and Baddeley, A.D. (1977). When Face Recognition Fails. *Journal of Experimental Psychology: Human Learning and Memory*, 3, 406-417.

Perkins, D. (1975). A Definition of Caricature and Caricature and Recognition. *Studies in the Antropology of Visual Communication*, 2, 1-24.

Rock, I. (1974). The Perception of Disoriented Figures. *Scientific American*, 230, 78-85.

Watkins, M.J., Ho, E. and Tulving, E. (1976). Context Effects in Recognition Memory for Faces. *Journal of Verbal Learning and Verbal Behavior*, 15, 505-517.

Winograd, E. (1976). Recognition Memory for Faces following Nine Different Judgements. *Bulletin of the Psychonomic Society*, 8, 419-421.

Winograd, E. and Rivers-Bulkeley, N.T. (1977). Effects of Changing Context on Remembering Faces. *Journal of Experimental Psychology: Human Learning and Memory*, 3,

397-405.
Yin, R.K. (1969). Looking at Upside-down Faces. *Journal of Experimental Psychology*, 81, 141-145.
Yin, R.K. (1970). Face Recognition: A Special Process? Rand Report, Number 4419, Rand Institute, New York, U.S.A.

ENCODING OPERATIONS WHICH FACILITATE MEMORY FOR FACES ACROSS THE LIFE SPAN

Eugene Winograd
Emory University
Atlanta, Georgia 30322

What is the best way to go about examining an unfamiliar face if your purpose is to remember it later? The major purpose of this chapter is to review recent research dealing with this question. At the outset, the reader should realize that we are dealing here only with the problem of recognizing a face as familiar and not with the problem of recalling the name associated with the face or the equally vexing problem in everyday life of recalling the context in which we encountered that person. Familiarity is the brute fact of memory and is so basic a cognitive operation that it is usually taken for granted. Note that it is only for a face which appears familiar that we bother to instigate a memory search for its name or original setting. Recognition of the face as familiar is thus the prior psychological operation; it precedes recall, and is the focus of the research discussed here.

Recognition of faces is an important social skill and is essential to many occupations such as police work. The embarrassment accompanying failure to recognize a person we have met before, when that person does remember us, is a universal reaction to a lapse of facial recognition. There exists a clinical condition called prosopagnosia in which unfortunate adults who have suffered brain lesions due to cerebral accident in the nondominant hemisphere are apparently unable to recognize any face as familiar although not showing symptoms of a more general amnesia.

Recent research on recognizing faces which have not been seen prior to the experiment has largely been concerned with amplifying the finding of Bower and Karlin (1974) that judgments about the honesty or likeableness of a picture of a person lead to better recognition of that person than judgments as to the gender of the person. (It should be said at the outset that all of the research reviewed in this chapter deals with the recognition of pictures of faces rather than actual people). Bower and Karlin approached the problem of memory for faces in the theoretical context of "levels of processing" as set forth by Craik and Lockhart (1972). Essentially, Craik and Lockhart argued that memory for an event is a function of how deeply that event was registered in memory at the time it was originally encountered. Specification of depth was made for verbal materials by assuming that judgments about the orthography of a word, or how it appears, are less deep than judgments about how it sounds and that semantic judgments in turn give rise to even deeper processing. Bower and Karlin, by analogy, assumed that deeper processing is involved in deciding whether a person appears to be honest than whether that person is male or female. At about the same time, Warrington and Ackroyd (1975) demonstrated, among an older group of subjects, that memory for faces was better following judgments of pleasantness than either judgments of height or no judgments at all. This latter group, which was simply told to try to remember the faces, will be termed a "standard" condition here. It is the usual intentional learning condition of most human memory experiments and we will be particularly interested here in studies containing this condition.

Since Bower and Karlin's (1974) paper, research concerned with memory for faces has mainly been concerned with comparisons between groups which have made judgments about personality characteristics or traits and groups which have been asked questions about specific physical features. For example, in one study Winograd (1976) included trait questions about anxiety, friendliness, and intelligence as well as feature questions about size of nose, straightness of hair and the more ambiguous category of heaviness. It is common in these studies to either ask the subjects a simple yes-no question such as "Does he look friendly?" or "Does he have straight hair?" about each face as it is presented or to ask the subjects to rate the queried trait or feature on a scale. Winograd found that 62% of the faces which were judged with respect to physical features were remembered compared to about 75% of the faces judged for traits, with heaviness judgments yielding recognition performance indistinguishable from the trait judgments. Winograd's study also included three judgments of occupations ("Does he look like a teacher?") and found memory performance comparable to the character trait judgments.

Essentially, the judgments of specific features led to poorer memory for faces than all of the other judgments, which differed little among themselves. Similar results have been reported by Mueller, Carlomusto, and Goldstein (1978). They found poorer memory for faces judged with respect to physical features (size of nose, thickness of lips, interocular distance, and height of forehead) than faces judged on traits (intelligence, friendliness, generosity, and confidence). Faces judged on more global aspects of physical appearance such as height, weight, muscularity, and posture were remembered as well as those judged for traits but better than faces rated on features. As Winograd (1976) had reported, Mueller et al found no differences associated with particular tasks of the same type. Patterson and Baddeley (1977) found the strongest evidence of all for poorer memory following encoding of features by demanding four successive judgments for each face. Their subjects were allowed 28 seconds to study each face, during which time they rated the face either on four physical features or on four traits. Even with such extended study time and the increase in number of judgments made, Patterson and Baddeley found better recognition for the faces rated on traits. Further evidence along these lines comes from developmental studies to be presented later. An additional point of some importance is that Winograd (1976) found that memory was not related to the outcome of the judgment made at encoding. That is, faces judged to be friendly were remembered as well as those thought to be unfriendly; the same pattern was found for all the dimensions. What seems to be important is the type of judgment required, not the outcome.

Before presenting the findings from research into some developmental aspects of memory for faces, there are some observations to be made. From a practical point of view, it can be said that research on memory for faces has identified a useful mnemonic aid. If you want to increase your power to remember the appearance of faces, simple mental effort or intent to remember is not as effective as implicitly asking yourself some form of the following question at the time you meet someone you wish to remember: Would I buy a used car from this person? The studies reviewed so far indicate that such a procedure is superior in general to choosing a physical feature at random and examining it closely. The research to be presented in the next section will confirm the finding of Warrington and Ackroyd (1975) that simple intent to remember is not as efficient as making a judgment about the personality of the person you are trying to remember. An interesting sidelight on the practical implications of this dictum comes from informal observations on metamemory

I have made while talking to classes about this research. When asked to predict the outcome of these studies, a clear majority is invariably found for the physical feature strategy. Most people are apparently of the opinion that time would be more profitably spent on doing a physical feature analysis than in asking what seem to be silly questions involving chancy inferences about character based on appearance.

It is interesting to note that books written with the explicit purpose of providing practical advice on improving memory functioning usually suggest a physical feature strategy for faces (see Cermak, 1975, Higbee, 1977, and Penry, 1971). However, there is a potentially important difference between the feature strategy most of these writers suggest and the feature strategy so extensively studied recently. The writers of mnemonics books urge the reader to survey the face he or she wishes to remember and select the most distinctive feature of that face for coding. Whereas the studies reviewed above all specify in advance for the subject which feature of each face should be carefully scrutinized, the memory books leave the choice of the feature up to the viewer with the admonishment to choose a highly distinctive or informative feature, that is, the feature which might set that face apart. We report here the outcome of an experiment which allows subjects to choose a distinctive feature for each face in line with the advice of the memory trainers.

DISTINCTIVE PHYSICAL FEATURES

Design and Procedure. One large class of college students enrolled in an introductory psychology class was tested at the same time. Booklets were prepared with the cover sheet providing one of three sets of encoding strategies and the booklets were distributed at random. In the Distinctive Features group (n=14), subjects were instructed to place a checkmark under the feature that was most distinctive for that particular face. The following column headings appeared at the top of the study page: eyes, nose, chin, ears, hair, head shape, brows, mouth, skin, other, none. In the Constrained Features group (n=14), one of three feature questions appeared for each face (does he have a big nose, straight hair, square jaw). In the Traits group (n=16), one of three personality characteristics was queried for each face (does he look honest, friendly, intelligent). These questions were counterbalanced across faces for the latter two groups by constructing different forms. The 72 faces were shown for 8 seconds each. The recognition test followed immediately afterwards with the 72 old faces randomly intermixed with 67 distractor faces. All of the faces were 35mm black and white slides of adult white males of various ages taken from a British casting directory and chosen to be unknown to American students. On the test, the faces were shown at a 5 second rate. All faces and subjects were male.

Results and Discussion. The proportions of hits and false alarms and d' scores are shown in Table 1. The outcome of the

Table 1. Hit and False Alarm Proportions and d'

	Distinctive Features	Constrained Features	Traits
Hits	.78	.64	.73
False Alarms	.19	.25	.16
d'	1.65	1.04	1.60

experiment is quite clear. The usual difference between trait and feature conditions appears in the two columns on the right and performance for the Distinctive Features condition equals the Trait condition. Analysis of variance is significant for all three measures. Allowing subjects to select which feature is most distinctive or prominent for each face has produced recognition performance markedly better than asking them about a feature chosen by the experimenter and raised performance to a level equivalent to that obtained following making judgments about personality characteristics. The Distinctive Features group and the Traits group are equivalent, in short. The advice of the memory trainer, then, is as useful as our advice to ask whether you would buy a used car from this person, but not more useful.

There is little space here for theoretical considerations, but we find little comfort for a depth of processing view in these data. Searching for a distinctive feature should lead to processing on a surface level whereas making a personality judgment should lead to deeper processing. Yet, the conditions produce equivalent performance. The findings are more compatible with a simple feature sampling model which assumes that recognition memory is a positive function of the number of features encoded. Trait judgments and searching for distinctive features lead to more features being encoded than answering a question about one feature. The finding of Patterson and Baddeley (1977) that trait judgments led to better memory for faces even when four features or traits were evaluated does not necessarily contradict the feature sampling hypothesis in that more physical features are likely to have been sampled in answering the trait questions even with multiple questions of each type.

DEVELOPMENTAL ASPECTS OF MEMORY FOR FACES

We present in this section the outcomes of two studies concerned with the effects of encoding strategies on memory for faces at ages spanning eight decades. Since both studies have been published, a general description will suffice. Smith and Winograd (1978) compared memory for faces between young and elderly (aged 50-80 years) adults. At each age there were three encoding conditions, a Standard group which was told to try to remember the faces, a Feature group which judged nose size for each face, and a Trait group which judged the friendliness of each face. Subjects in the Feature and Trait groups were told that their memory for the faces would be tested. The results are depicted in Figure 1. There are three aspects of the

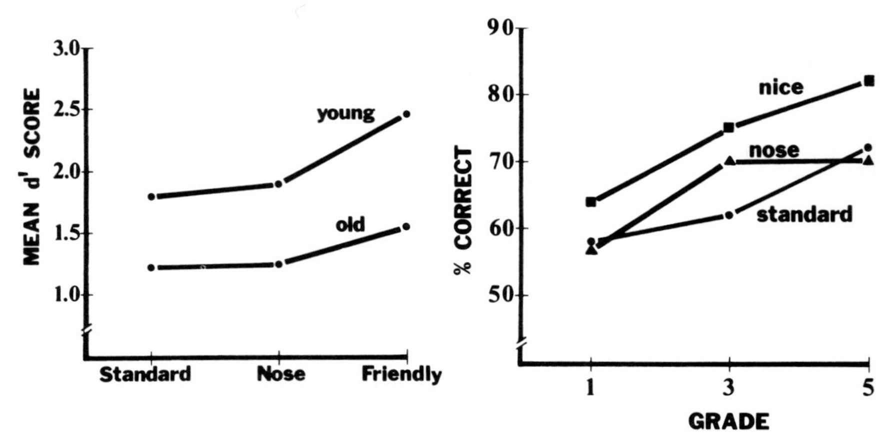

Fig. 1. Adult age differences in remembering faces. Adapted from Smith & Winograd (1978).

Fig. 2. Memory for faces in children of different ages. Adapted from Blaney & Winograd (1978).

results to be noted. First, at both ages judgments of friendliness facilitated recognition memory relative to the other two conditions which in turn did not differ from each other; secondly, memory for faces encountered for the first time declined markedly with age; thirdly, there was no interaction evident between age and encoding task. The last finding, that the mnemonic advantage of trait judgments benefited both age groups equally, is of theoretical interest in that the "processing-deficit" hypothesis of M. Eysenck (1974) is based on the finding that, in recall of verbal material, older subjects were found to derive less benefit from semantic or deeper processing than the young. Eysenck proposed that the memory problems associated with aging are largely due to difficulties with deep processing. The results of Smith and Winograd's study of recognition memory for faces do not support this hypothesis in that no interaction was seen.

A similar study was reported by Blaney and Winograd (1978) with children at three ages. Twenty faces were studied and tested with a 3-alternative forced-choice test. The results of this study are shown in Figure 2. It can be seen that older children remember more faces in each encoding condition, that judging whether the face was nice or not led to better memory, and that there was no interaction between encoding task and age. Aside from the expected finding that at these ages performance increases with age, the results parallel those of Smith and Winograd. The story, then, is much the same at all ages tested with respect to the variable of interest here, encoding strategy. More faces are remembered following a judgment of friendliness than judgments about physical features or, interestingly, instructions to try to remember the faces. It is clear that, when left to their own devices, people tend to encode faces less than optimally.

SUMMARY AND CONCLUSIONS

A review of the literature relating encoding strategies to memory for faces has found a high degree of consistency among studies and across the life span. Memory for faces is facilitated if an inference is made about some personality characteristic of the face at the time it is studied. Answering a question about a particular physical feature or just studying the face with intent to remember it both produce performance at a lower level. However, new data suggest that if subjects are induced to scan a face in search of its most distinctive feature they will remember the face as well as if they had made a personality judgment. A simple hypothesis is offered which states that memory for faces is an increasing function of the number of features encoded at study. Inferences about personality traits facilitate memory only because they lead to broader feature sampling. It would be of practical significance to know whether combining the two most effective encoding strategies, making a trait judgment and finding the most distinctive feature, would increase memory for faces.

REFERENCES

Blaney, R.L. and Winograd, E. (1978). Developmental differences in children's recognition memory for faces. *Developmental Psychology*. 14, 441-442.

Bower, G.H. and Karlin, M.B. (1974). Depth of processing pictures of faces and recognition memory. *Journal of Experimental Psychology*. 103, 751-757.

Cermak, L.S. (1975). *Improving Your Memory*. McGraw-Hill, N.Y.

Craik, F.I.M. and Lockhart, R.S. (1972). Levels of processing: A framework for memory research. *Journal of Verbal Learning and Verbal Behavior*. 1972, 11, 671-684.

Eysenck, M.W. (1974). Age differences in incidental learning. *Developmental Psychology*. 10, 936-941.

Higbee, K.L. (1977). *Your Memory*. Prentice-Hall, Englewood Cliffs, New Jersey.

Mueller, J.H., Carlomusto, M., and Goldstein, A.G. (1978). Orienting task and study time in facial recognition. *Bulletin of the Psychonomic Society*. 11, 313-316.

Patterson, K.E. and Baddeley, A.D. (1977). When face recognition fails. *Journal of Experimental Psychology: Human Learning and Memory*. 3, 406-417.

Penry, J. (1971). *Looking at Faces and Remembering Them: A Guide to Facial Identification*. Elek Books, London.

Smith, A.D. and Winograd, E. (1978). Adult age differences in remembering faces. *Developmental Psychology*. 14, 443-444.

Warrington, E.K. and Ackroyd, C. (1975). The effect of orienting tasks on recognition memory. *Memory and Cognition*. 3, 140-142.

Winograd, E. (1976). Recognition memory for faces following nine different judgments. *Bulletin of the Psychonomic Society*. 8, 419-421.

SEX DIFFERENCES IN FACIAL MEMORY

S.J. McKelvie
Bishop's University, Lennoxville,
Quebec J1M 1Z7, Canada

Four experiments studied recognition memory of male and female subjects (Canadian students and some adults) for male and female faces. In two of the experiments, which employed Canadian faces, there was an interaction between sex of subject and sex of stimulus, reflecting a relative superiority of females on female faces. In the other two, however, with British faces, this interaction was absent. It is suggested that the sex-linked interaction may only occur if viewers (particularly females) identify with the faces presented.

While the research literature on sex differences in recognition memory of faces is not entirely consistent, it suggests that females are superior to males, particularly on female faces. Most studies reporting a complete analysis of their sex data (Borges and Vaughn, 1977; Cross, Cross and Daly, 1971; Shepherd, Deregowski and Ellis, 1974; Feinman and Entwistle, 1976; Going and Read, 1974; Stefanatos, Brouwers and Mononen, 1978; Yarmey, 1975) have shown no overall significant difference between male and female recognition accuracy, although some (Ellis, Shepherd and Bruce, 1973; Yarmey, 1974; Yarmey and Paskaruk, 1975) favour females over males. However, six of these 10 studies yielded a significant interaction between sex of subject and sex of face. In four cases (Cross et al. 1971; Feinman and Entwistle, 1976; Going and Read, 1974; Yarmey and Paskaruk, 1975) females recognized more female than male faces, whereas males performed equally well on both types, and in the remaining two (Ellis et al., 1973; Stefanatos et al., 1978) males recognized fewer female than male faces, whereas females' performance was not significantly different.

Although other investigators (for example, Ellis, 1975) have also reached the conclusion that females, relative to males, recognize female better than male faces, the effect is by no means clearly established (four out of the 10 studies cited above found no significant sex interaction). The purpose of the present experiments is to explore the conditions under which the sex interaction emerges. Experiment I was designed to replicate the results of Ellis et al. (1973), using a modified version of the same stimuli.

EXPERIMENT I

Method

Subjects The subjects were 44 (22 males, 22 females) volunteers from the local community. The majority (18 males, 18 females) were university students, and the others were working adults. All subjects were recruited at a Science Fair held at Bishop's University; they offered their services in response to an offer to 'test your memory for faces'.

Materials The stimuli were 72 (36 male, 36 female) (5.0 x 5.0 cm) black and white slides of British undergraduates (aged 17-20). They were selected from a pool containing 148 male and 200 female slides (rephotographed in black and white and enlarged from the colour slides used by Ellis et al., 1973) so that they consisted of 36(18 male, 18 female) matched pairs. The basis of the matching was 'general similarity' - sex of subject, hairstyle, head and eye direction and facial expression. One member of each pair was arbitrarily assigned to the presentation set, and the 36 matched pairs constituted the recognition set.

Procedure The 36 presentation faces were randomly ordered and shown individually to subjects at a 5 sec rate with a Sawyer carousel projector. Subjects were instructed to view each picture carefully, in anticipation of a future recognition test. Before receiving the test, subjects spent 10-12 min filling out a visual imagery questionnaire. The recognition test (in which the order of the presentation stimuli was preserved) consisted of the 36 matched pairs of faces, shown at a rate of one pair every 15 sec. Subjects were asked to indicate, on a prepared answer sheet, which member of the pair (left or right) had been seen before and to rate their confidence on a four-point scale.

Results and Discussion

The present analysis is confined to the hit scores (number of correct recognition choices) which are displayed in Table I. The apparent similarity of the scores in each condition was confirmed by a 2x2 (sex of subject, sex of face) analysis

TABLE I

Mean Number of Hits (Standard Deviations in Brackets) in Each Condition

Subjects	Male Faces	Female Faces
Males	14.95(2.28)	15.09(1.87)
Females	15.18(1.65)	15.68(1.99)

Note Maximum score = 18

of variance (repeated measures on the second factor), which showed that the main effects and the interaction were not significant ($ps > .05$).

One factor which may have inhibited the emergence of a significant interaction is the nationality difference between subjects (Canadians) and stimuli (British). In view of the fact that all the studies reporting the sex effect appear to have utilized 'local' faces the next two experiments adopted this strategy. Experiment II replicated the method of Experiment I as closely as possible, and Experiment III introduced some procedural variations; they also employed two new sets of local (Canadian) faces.

EXPERIMENTS II AND III

Method

Subjects The subjects in Experiment II were 68 (31 males, 37 females) Introductory Psychology undergraduates; those in Experiment III were 50 (22 male, 28 female) students representing a variety of disciplines. All subjects were recruited from classes at Bishop's University, and were aged 18-20.

Materials The stimuli for Experiment II were 72 (36 male, 36 female) black and white slides of faces (cut out around chin and perimeter of hair) of students (aged 16-17) attending high schools in the Province of Quebec. They were chosen from a pool of 200 male and 200 female pictures (taken from school yearbooks) and matched in the same way as in Experiment I. In Experiment III, the faces were 60 (30 male, 30 female) black and white slides of adults (aged 15-60) obtained from a local photographer.

Procedure The procedure for Experiment II was similar to that of Experiment I. In Experiment III, however, a number of modifications were introduced: (a) the order of stimulus presentation was not preserved on recognition (it was random), (b) the delay interval was two days and (c) no imagery questionnaires were administered.

Results and Discussion

Both sets of data, which were again analyzed with 2x2 analysis of variance, are presented in Table II. In Experiment II, the interaction between sex of subject and sex of

TABLE II

Mean Number of Hits (Standard Deviations in Brackets)

	Experiment II		Experiment III	
Subjects	Male Faces	Female Faces	Male Faces	Female Faces
Males	14.81(2.07)	14.39(1.76)	14.09(1.38)	13.18(1.53)
Females	15.00(2.12)	15.68(1.72)	13.50(1.32)	13.75(1.40)

Note Maximum score = 18 *Note* Maximum score = 15

face was significant, $F(1,66) = 5.06$, $p < .05$. Post hoc tests showed that females recognized more female than male faces, $F(1,66) = 7.81$, $p < .01$, whereas males did not differ in the number of male and female faces recognized, and that, on female faces, females performed better than males, $F(1,66) = 8.06$, $p < .01$, whereas, on male faces, the subjects did not differ. In Experiment III, the interaction was again the only significant effect, $F(1,48) = 6.06$, $p < .02$. Of the four post hoc tests, only one (male vs. female faces for males) attained significance, $F(1,48) = 14.95$, $p < .01$, indicating that males recognized fewer female than male faces.

These two experiments, which respectively demonstrate strong female performance and weak male performance on female faces, support the earlier conclusion that, when an interaction between sex of subject and sex of face on facial recognition memory occurs, it reflects a relative female superiority on female faces. These results contrast with those obtained in Experiment I, which did not employ local faces.

Interesting as these findings may be, they do not show

why Canadian subjects respond differently to British and Canadian faces. Experiment IV was designed to test the possibility that subjects in Experiment I did not differentiate male and female faces or did not process them 'deeply' enough. To accomplish this, subjects in Experiment IV were shown a set of British faces and asked to categorize them for sex or liking. It was expected that faces judged for liking would be better remembered than those judged for sex (Bower and Karlin, 1974), but the major question was: would the interaction between sex of subject and sex of face emerge under one or both of these conditions?

EXPERIMENT IV

Method

Subjects Forty four (22 male, 22 female) 18-20 yr old psychology undergraduates at Bishop's University took part in this experiment.

Materials The stimuli were 192 (96 male, 96 female) black and white slides of British undergraduates (80 male, 96 female) and British footballers (16 male). The former were chosen from the same pool used in Experiment I (and included the stimuli used in Experiment I); the latter were selected from a set of 119 slides (rephotographed in black and white from pictures provided by Dr. Hadyn Ellis at the University of Aberdeen). Again, the stimuli constituted 96 matched pairs. The 96 presentation faces were formed into eight blocks of 12 faces, each block containing six female students, five male students and one male footballer.

Procedure Faces within each block were presented individually at a 7 sec rate, each block being separated by 7 sec. Subjects were instructed to view each picture carefully, in anticipation of a subsequent recognition test, and, for each block of faces, to categorize faces within the block according to sex (male, female) or liking (I would like/dislike this person) (judgements being recorded on prepared sheets). During the 7 sec period between blocks, subjects were instructed which judgement to make. Two orders were used - alternately sex and liking beginning with sex or liking. Following a 10 min unfilled delay interval, the 96 matched pairs (randomly mixed) were presented to subjects at a 15 sec rate.

Results

The hit scores (see Table III) were subjected to a 2x2x2 (sex of subject, judgement, sex of face) analysis of variance (with repeated measures on the last two factors). Two main effects were significant, judgement, $F(1,42) = 5.48$, $p < .05$,

TABLE III

Mean number of Hits (Standard Deviations in Brackets)

	Sex		Liking	
Subjects	Male Faces	Female Faces	Male Faces	Female Faces
Males	19.86(2.05)	19.18(3.03)	21.05(2.26)	19.82(2.48)
Females	20.14(2.42)	20.36(2.48)	21.18(1.62)	20.68(1.96)

Note Maximum score = 24

reflecting a greater number of hits on faces judged for liking than for sex, and sex of face, $F(1,42) = 4.15$, $p < .05$, reflecting better performance on male than on female faces. None of the interactions attained significance.

GENERAL DISCUSSION

Despite inducing subjects to differentiate some faces according to sex, and to process others more deeply, Experiment IV failed to yield the sex of subject by sex of stimulus interaction found in Experiments II and III. Taken together, however, the four experiments suggest that the relationship between subject and stimulus face is a factor in the appearance of the relative superiority of females on female faces.

Why does the sex interaction appear in the present experiments which employed local faces? One possibility is that subjects (particularly females) must identify with the faces (particularly females) in order for them to demonstrate their relative superiority on female faces.

In view of the fact that Feinman and Entwhistle (1976) report this result when children viewed pictures of children, this notion could be tested by asking adults and children to recognize adult and child faces, the expectation being that the sex interaction would only emerge when subjects observed faces of their peers.

REFERENCES

Borges, M.A. and Vaughn, L.S. (1977). Cognitive differences between the sexes in memory for names and faces. *Perceptual and Motor Skills*. 45, 317-318.

Bower, G.H. and Karlin, M.B. (1974). Depth of processing pictures of faces and recognition memory. *Journal of Experimental Psychology*. 103, 751-757.

Cross, J.F., Cross, J., and Daly, J. (1971). Sex, race, age, and beauty as factors in recognition of faces. *Perception and Psychophysics*. 10, 393-396.

Ellis, H.D. (1975). Recognizing faces. *British Journal of Psychology*. 66, 409-426.

Ellis, H.D., Shepherd, J., and Bruce, A. (1973). The effects of age and sex upon adolescents' recognition of faces. *Journal of Genetic Psychology*. 123, 173-174.

Feinman, S. and Entwhistle, D.R. (1976). Children's ability to recognize other children's faces. *Child Development*. 47, 506-510.

Going, M. and Read, J.D. (1974). Effects of uniqueness, sex of subject, and sex of photograph on facial recognition. *Perceptual and Motor Skills*. 39, 109-110.

Shepherd, J.W., Deregowski, J.B., and Ellis, H.D. (1974). A cross-cultural study of recognition memory for faces. *International Journal of Psychology*. 9. 205-212.

Stefanatos, G., Brouwers, E.Y.M., and Mononen, L.J. (1978). Visual field differences in the recognition of male and female faces. Paper presented at the Canadian Psychological Association.

Yarmey, D. (1974). Proactive interference in short-term retention of human faces. *Canadian Journal of Psychology*. 28, 333-338.

Yarmey, D. (1975). Social-emotional factors in recall and recognition of human faces. Paper presented at Midwestern Psychological Association.

Yarmey, D. and Paskaruk, S. (1975). The influence of affect, ego-involvement and sex differences in recognition of faces. Unpublished manuscript, University of Guelph.

RECOGNITION, RECALL AND IMAGERY OF FACES

Richard J. Phillips
Perception Laboratory, Royal College of Art, London SW7 2EU

Two exploratory studies are reported on the relationship between recognition, recall and imagery of faces. The first investigated undergraduates' memory of a single well known face. The second was a correlational study testing faces in general. Both studies suggest that subjects' reported imagery ratings for faces reflect performance on face recognition tasks more strongly than performance on recall tasks. It is argued that our difficulty in recalling faces arises principally from problems of recoding rather than retrieval.

INTRODUCTION

Without doubt, the most important and most difficult practical problem for research on faces is recall. An effective system for recalling faces would not only help the police catch criminals but also allow members of the public to communicate the appearances of faces among themselves. Furthermore it would prevent some of the injustices from misidentification which the publication of the Devlin report (1976) has done little to alleviate.

Recognizing faces is usually an easy task and from this we know that locked away in our heads we must carry substantial amounts of information about a whole gallery of faces. But all current research points to the conclusion that there is no easy way of getting this information out. Ellis, Davies and Shepherd (1976) in an apposite series of experiments on recall, using verbal descriptions and drawings as well as Photo-fit reconstructions found again and again that recall did not begin to approach the performance found with recognition.

This paper asks: why are faces difficult to recall? It is argued that the explanations offered for recall from verbal memory are inadequate for faces. Two exploratory studies are described and these are discussed with other evidence.

DATA FROM A SINGLE FACE

A study was conducted to compare performance on the recognition and recall of a single well known face--Cliff Michelmore. He has been appearing regularly on British television in a wide variety of programmes for the last 20 years, and is moderately well known to the British undergraduates who took part in this study. They were 45 men and 59 women who were tested in two groups: the first had 70 and the second, 34.

A printed page was prepared with a photograph of Michelmore among 11 other men of similar age and appearance. The first group was told that one of the faces was well known to people living in the United Kingdom and the second group was told that one of the faces was Michelmore. 87 per cent of the first group and 88 per cent of the second group identified the correct photograph, but only 57 per cent of the first group could name Michelmore or say who he was. It is likely that some of the undergraduates failed the recognition test because they had never seen Michelmore. However, the important point is that a large majority had no difficulty recognizing him.

20 minutes later the first group was told the identity of the target face and was asked to try to form a visual image of Michelmore's face. The procedure for this is given in the Appendix, but question 2 was excluded. 89 per cent reported they could form an image, 53 per cent rated their images as 'clear' or 'very clear' and 76 per cent could change the expression of the imaged face.

The first group then had 3 minutes to write a description of Michelmore which would help someone intending to meet him at a railway station. Descriptions were to be of his head and face only, and were to be as detailed as possible. The second group had the same instructions except they wrote their description while viewing the photograph of Michelmore. Five subjects in the first group did not attempt a written description and so there were only 99 descriptions in all. These were typed and 99 undergraduates at an American university acted as judges. Each was given a single description and attempted to pick out the face from the same 12 faces used in the recognition test. American undergraduates are most unlikely to have heard of Michelmore.

With the descriptions written from memory by the first group, 23 per cent were matched to the correct face. With the descriptions of the photograph written by the second group, 26 per cent were correctly matched. Both are significantly above the level expected by chance ($\chi^2 = 18.5$ and 14.7, both $p < .001$) but they do not differ significantly from each other ($\chi^2 = 0.016$, $p > .5$).

86 per cent of students could recognize Michelmore but only 23 per cent wrote a description which could identify him

among the same set of photographs. This demonstrates the disparity between recognition and recall. Especially interesting is the finding that performance on recall was similar for descriptions made from a photograph and made from memory.

Ellis *et al.*(1976) have reported a similar phenomenon with Photofit: a police method of reconstructing faces from photographs of facial features. There was no reliable difference between Photofit reconstructions made when a photograph of the target face was present and reconstructions made from memory. However, when university students were asked to sketch a face from memory their drawings were considerably worse than those made with a photograph present. These facts suggest that our difficulty in recalling faces is not simply a problem of retrieving information from memory.

VISUAL IMAGERY

The imagery ratings suggest that the majority could form clear visual images of the face. Of course, it is possible for people to exaggerate when rating the quality of their visual images but an experiment by Gordon and Hayward (1973) shows that images of faces do carry information. They found that subjects can make reliable similarity judgments between imaged pairs of well known faces. There was good agreement between judgments made in this way and judgments from pairs of photographs of the same faces.

If there is a blockage in the neural pipeline which joins recognition and recall, on which side of this blockage does imagery lie? Imagery could be regarded as a type of recall, but imaging a face appears to be much easier than drawing it, describing it in words, or making a Photofit reconstruction. One approach to this question is a correlation study. Howells (1938) presents some data to suggest that recognizing faces does not correlate with the recall of details. But would imagery ratings correlate positively with performance on either recognition or recall? Ellis *et al.*(1976) failed to find any relationship between people's ability at using Photofit and their imagery ratings, and Forbes (1975) also found no relationship between the recognition of faces and imagery. However, both studies were using general measures of visual imagery: it is possible that a test which specifically measures images of faces would give different results.

CORRELATION STUDY

95 volunteers from university admission candidates, divided into several small groups, participated on the same day that they were interviewed and given selection tests. There

were 30 men and 65 women. The questions are described in the order they were given, which was the same for all subjects.

The first three questions required subjects to rate the strength and quality of the visual images they could form with their eyes closed. The first was the Vividness of Visual Imagery Questionnaire (Marks, 1975). The second asked subjects to image the face of a close friend or relative and then answer the Imagery for a Face Questionnaire which is described in the Appendix. The third was Gordon's (1949) Control of Imagery Questionnaire slightly modified.

The face recognition test followed about 15 minutes later when subjects had completed some unrelated tests. The test employed 30 full face photographs of white male university students without glasses, beards or other obtrusive features. Subjects were asked to remember 20 faces projected at a 3s rate. After about 30s, subjects saw a further 20 faces consisting of 10 old and 10 new items projected at a 6s rate. They were asked to write 'old' or 'new' for each picture, guessing when uncertain. The score was d'.

This was followed immediately by an unexpected request to recall the last face which had been projected. 21 multiple choice questions similar to those used by Goldstein, Harmon and Lesk (1972) were used. The test was repeated without the element of surprise using a different face. Eight judges determined the correct answers, but on some of the multiple choice questions where judges showed little agreement it was necessary to allow more than one correct answer or to not count a question at all.

On the recognition test, mean d' was 2.16. For the first recall question the mean was 8.3 and for the second it was 11.2, both out of a maximum of 18. Pearson correlation coefficients between these and the imagery scores are shown in Table I.

TABLE I

The correlation matrix. FRN = face recognition test; FL1,FL2 = face recall, parts 1 and 2; FIM = imagery of a face; VVI = vividness of visual imagery; COI = control of imagery.
* = *p*<.05, ** = p<.01, *one tail.*

	FRN	FL1	FL2	FIM	VVI	COI	SEX♀+
FRN	---	-.02	.07	.24**	-.10	-.02	.14
FL1	-.02	---	.15	.00	.01	.07	.10
FL2	.07	.15	---	.11	.00	.08	.04
FIM	.24**	.00	.11	---	.31**	.30**	.22*
VVI	-.10	.01	.00	.31**	---	.26**	.11
COI	-.02	.07	.08	.30**	.26**	---	.11
SEX♀+	.14	.10	.04	.22*	.11	.11	---

The only statistically significant correlation between memory performance and imagery is the coefficient of 0.24 between face recognition and face imagery. In order to check this, the same two questions were given in the reverse order to a different group of 80 undergraduates. The Pearson correlation was 0.20 which is also statistically significant ($p<.05$, one tail). Although the correlation coefficients are small the replication suggests there is indeed a tendency for people who are better at face recognition to form stronger images of faces. The failure to find a similar result for recall suggests that the formation of an image of a face is more similar as a skill to recognition than to recall.

DISCUSSION

If we can *visualize* the position of furniture in a room we can also recall its position; for most types of information, imagery guarantees recall. But for faces this is not so. Everyday life experience, confirmed by the first study, tells us that it is much easier to visualise a face than to recall the details. The correlations found in the second study suggest imagery draws more strongly on the skills we use in recognition than those of recall.

One explanation for the difficulty in recalling a face in words is that our vocabulary for describing faces is very limited. The limitations of other methods of recalling faces can also be explained by production difficulties, for example, poor drawing skill when sketching a face, or interference problems with Photofit. However, the fact is that despite the motivation of a pressing practical problem no one has devised an adequate procedure for recalling faces, and this might suggest that the difficulty is not from a number of separate production difficulties, but from a more general cause arising from the way the brain codes faces.

Presumably when we look at a face we generate an internal code which can be stored in order to remember it. Phillips (1977, 1978) has suggested that the code loses nearly all of the spatial information about a face. A code rather like a car registration number would explain the disparity between recognition and recall. If the only thing we could remember about a car was its number, we would be unable to describe its shape, size or colour, but nevertheless if we saw it again we could be quite confident it was the same car; in other words, we could recognize it but not recall it. But this analogy breaks down when we introduce imagery. A registration number does not enable us to visualize a car, but the internal code we generate of faces does give us imagery.

This suggests that we code faces in a way which loses

spatial information but is still meaningful because it gives us facial expression. But this is still not quite right. When people describe images of faces they report that some spatial details can be seen in addition to the facial expression: it is not a case of 'a grin without a cat'. Perhaps the act of visualising a face involves two operations: loading into immediate memory a code which holds information about facial expression but little or no spatial information and simultaneously loading a stereotyped face which gives the spatial relationships between eyes, nose and mouth which are common to all faces. When these two are combined, we might have the paradoxical experience of a vivid mental image but nevertheless one from which it is difficult to extract specific details.

If this view is correct, our difficulty in recalling faces is principally a problem of recoding information. Retrieval factors may also play a part but it is the translation of a highly abstracted code which forms the biggest obstacle. If the same code is used for both memory and perception it is clear why under certain circumstances recall should be of similar difficulty with a face present or absent.

While the brain excels at recognizing faces it lets us down when we need to recall them. We need to recognize so much more frequently than we need to recall that the evolution of memory for faces must have been governed almost entirely by the demands of recognition. There is probably no simple solution to the practical problem of recalling faces. It is possible that an effective system of recall can only be achieved by a programme of training as part of school education. If this is so, it is a necessary price to pay for living in an urban society: in the country most faces are familiar, but in cities we are unequipped to cope with such enormous numbers of people.

ACKNOWLEDGEMENTS

I would like to thank everyone who has helped with this research, especially R.E. Rawles of University College London, Alan DeLucia of the University of Idaho, and Patricia Owtram of BBC television.

REFERENCES

Devlin, Lord (1976). *Report to the Secretary of State for the Home Department of the departmental committee on evidence of identification in criminal cases*. HMSO, London.

Ellis, H.D., Davies, G.M. and Shepherd, J.W. (1976). *An investigation of the Photo-fit system for recalling faces*.

Final report to SSRC project HR 3123/1.
Forbes, D.D.S. (1975). *An investigation into pictorial memory, with particular reference to facial recognition.* Ph.D. Thesis, Aberdeen University, Scotland.
Goldstein, A.J., Harmon, L.D. and Lesk, A.B. (1972). Man-machine interaction in human-face identification. *Bell System Technical Journal*. 51, 399-427.
Gordon, I.E. and Hayward, S. (1973). Second-order isomorphism of internal representations of familiar faces. *Perception and Psychophysics*. 14, 334-336.
Gordon, R. (1949). An investigation into some of the factors that favour the formation of stereotyped images. *British Journal of Psychology*. 39, 156-167.
Howells, T.H. (1938). A study of ability to recognize faces. *Journal of Abnormal and Social Psychology*. 33, 124-127.
Marks, D.F. (1973). Visual imagery differences in the recall of pictures. *British Journal of Psychology*. 64, 17-24.
Phillips, R.J. (1977). *A Comparison of Memory for Faces and other Visual Stimuli*. Ph.D. Thesis, London University.
Phillips, R.J. (1978). Some exploratory experiments on memory for photographs of faces. *Acta Psychologica*. 42. in press.

APPENDIX

'Imagery for a Face' Questionnaire

Subjects are asked to close their eyes and to try to form a clear image of the face. After 30s these instructions are read slowly, pausing between sentences.

"I expect most of you have been able to form some sort of image by now. Don't open your eyes yet. Can you see whether your image is coloured, or is it just grey, rather like a black and white photograph? For example, are you able to see the colour of the eyes? Now, still keeping your eyes shut, I want to know whether you can change the expression on the face. For example, if it is a smiling face, can you change the expression to 'thoughtful' or to 'angry'? Can you try this now? Please open your eyes now, turn over the page and answer the four questions as accurately as you can."

The questionnaire is reproduced below. It is scored simply by numbering the answers from left to right, and adding up the total. For example, someone who answered,"clear". "clearly coloured", "yes, easily" and "the image disappeared ...", would score 4 + 3 + 3 + 2 = 12. Anyone who answers "unable to form an image" to question 1 is given a score of 4, regardless of their other answers. Pearson correlation coefficients between the four questions are shown in Table II.

For each question, circle the best answer.

1. How vivid was your image of the face?

Unable to form an image	Very faint	Rather faint	Clear	Very clear

2. Was your image coloured?

Not coloured	Faintly coloured	Clearly coloured	Clearly coloured including colour of eyes

3. Were you able to change the expression on the face?

Unable to do this	Yes, with difficulty	Yes, easily

4. Were you able to maintain the image of the face, or did it frequently disappear?

The image frequently disappeared and was difficult to bring back	The image disappeared but could easily be brought back	The image was easy to maintain and rarely disappeared

TABLE II

Pearson correlation coefficients between the four questions (N = 280).

	(1)	(2)	(3)
(2)	.56		
(3)	.48	.27	
(4)	.43	.38	.41

HOW BEST SHALL A FACE BE DESCRIBED?

J. W. Shepherd, G. M. Davies and H. D. Ellis
University of Aberdeen

ABSTRACT

Three experiments are reported in which subjects were required to identify photographs of strangers, or named familiar men on the basis of different kinds of verbal description. In the first experiment, ratings, physical descriptions and descriptions including physical and character inferences of photographs of faces led to equally good recognition of the faces by judges. Character descriptions alone led to chance results. In the second and third experiments men were described by colleagues using free descriptions or ratings. Other colleagues could identify the targets equally well from the two modes of description, as could strangers who were asked to identify photographs. The practical advantages of rating scales are briefly discussed.

If we wish to convey to someone what another person looks like, we are most likely to do so by giving a verbal description of that person. Although techniques such as Photofit and Identikit are sometimes used by police forces for obtaining visual impressions in the absence of photographs, verbal descriptions are still the primary means of communicating information about appearance.

The efficiency with which the receiver will be able to identify the target person will depend in part upon the ability of the informant to imagine or visualise the target, his competence in translating details of the image into words, and the receiver's ability to convert the verbal information into some form of image to serve as the basis for recognition. Improvement at any of these stages may have some practical value, and may perhaps shed some light on the processes involved in face recognition and recall.

Verbal descriptions of faces typically consist of a list of details about the individual features of the face. Our vocabulary is short of terms to characterise the general physical conformation of the face, although, when trying to convey a general impression of a face, we frequently resort to character or mood attributions which appear to be associated with particular facial features.

One of the well replicated findings in face recognition research is that subjects who, during the inspection phase of the experiment, are asked to make some character or aesthetic attribution to the faces, show better recognition performance than subjects who are asked to make more superficial judgements, or to list the physical characteristics of those faces (e.g. Bower and Karlin, 1974). It is also the case that when we ourselves have asked subjects who have sorted large numbers of faces into groups of similar faces to label the groups, a number of them resort to attributional terms for their labels. In some way, then, drawing an inference from the physical features may facilitate subsequent recognition or immediate classification of faces in comparison with simply providing a physical description.

These considerations led us to consider whether encouraging subjects to use attributional or inferential terms would improve their ability to communicate the appearance of a face, over that of subjects providing a purely physical description.

One disadvantage of free descriptions is that their effectiveness will be susceptible to the personal idiosyncracies of the describer's selection of features and vocabulary. It may be possible to overcome this by providing a standard set of features to which the describer may refer. In an attempt to develop such a standard set of features, we have analysed numerous free descriptions and carried out factor analyses on ratings of the most frequently mentioned features (Shepherd, Ellis and Davies 1977). As a result of these studies we believe we have a set of scales which refer to the most salient facial features. Descriptions of faces using these scales may lack the richness and detail of free descriptions but should provide information about the generally most important parts of the face.

In our first experiment, then, we set out to compare the effectiveness of four different modes of describing faces to a stranger. These modes were: free description using physical features only, free description using attributional terms only, free descriptions using both physical and attributional terms, and rating scales.

METHOD

The experiment involved two stages. For the first stage, 16 full-face black and white photographs of men's faces were selected from a larger pool of photographs. Those selected varied in age, and length of hair, but had no moustache, beard or spectacles. This set of 16 was divided into two matched sets of 8.

A describer was asked to describe one of these sets of 8 faces, using one mode of the four modes of description.

The free descriptions were given orally and recorded, and were later transcribed. The rating scales were presented in the form of 5 point bipolar scales with each point verbally labelled. The features used were fatness of face, length of hair, thickness of hair, darkness of hair, thickness of eyebrows, size of eyes, length of nose, size of chin and size of mouth. In addition, an estimate of age within a decade was requested.

The describers were 64 undergraduates from Aberdeen University; 32 males - 32 females. Eight describers were allocated to each mode of description for each set of photographs.

In the second stage, a new group of subjects were given a description of a face, and were asked to select the person described from a group of four faces. For this stage of the experiment, each of the original target faces was presented together with three new faces. One of these faces was similar to the target face as determined by a cluster analysis of similarity judgements of 100 faces. The other two faces were dissimilar to the target as determined by the same analysis. Each subject was presented with 4 descriptions in each of the 4 modes, so that he received descriptions of all 16 targets. Each description was from a different describer, and the order of descriptive mode was counter balanced among subjects.

The subjects in the second stage were a further 32 male and female undergraduates from the University of Aberdeen.

RESULTS

The maximum number of faces each subject could identify within any particular descriptive mode was 4. The obtained means were, for physical descriptions 3.0, for character descriptions 1.5, for joint physical and character descriptions 2.9 and for ratings 2.9. Three of the descriptive modes were thus virtually identical, while the fourth mode, using only character descriptions, was significantly worse than the other three ($F(3.93) = 20.16$) and barely above the chance level of 1 correct.

An alternative way of examining the data is to consider performance on each target face. Eight subjects attempted to identify each target from each mode of description. On a chance basis, 2 of these should be correct. Using physical description or joint physical and character description, subjects identified 13 of the 16 targets at above chance level (with a mean of 5.9 for each target); using ratings, 12 targets were identified at above chance (mean 5.8/target), while for character judgements only 3 targets were identified at above chance (mean of 3.0).

When errors are considered, 77% of erroneous choices in the physical, joint and rating conditions were for the similar distractor in the group, compared with only 38% in the character descriptions.

In brief, three of the modes of descriptions were equally good and very successful for enabling a subject to select a face from among 3 others, while one, the character description alone, provided little information and resulted in a performance at chance level.

It is clear that whatever the value of making attributional judgements of a face may be to a subject who is later required to recognise that face, these judgements are of little value in communicating information about facial appearance to another person.

The success of the other modes of description have been demonstrated under what may be regarded as optimal conditions. The target was visible to the describers while they gave their descriptions, and the identical photograph was used at the recognition phase. A more stringent test would require the descriptions to be made from memory, and the subjects to identify the targets without visual aid. To do this it is necessary to have targets who are well-known both to describers and subjects.

The second experiment was therefore carried out among members of the psychology department at Aberdeen University.

METHOD

Targets, describers and subjects were all members of the department who were well-known to each other. Eight targets were selected using as criteria that they were male, had no moustache or beard, and did not normally wear spectacles. Two groups of 8 describers were then selected, the groups being matched for sex, age and function (academic, technical, secretarial). One group of describers were asked individually to give a free description of the physical facial appearance of each of the 8 targets; the other group were asked individually to provide ratings of the targets.

In the second stage a set of 8 descriptions, one of each of the targets provided by a different describer, was presented to a subject who was asked to match them to a list of names of the 8 targets. For half the subjects the free descriptions were given first, then a week later the same task was repeated using the ratings. The other half of the subjects received the conditions in the reverse order.

There were 32 subjects, 16 of whom were members of staff or postgraduates who had been in the department at least 3 years and had not been used as describers, and 16 who were final (i.e. 4th) year honours students in psychology.

RESULTS

Out of a possible 8 correct identifications subjects made an average of 3.8 correct choices from free descriptions and 3.8 from ratings, with a range of scores from 1 to 8 for each mode. The staff group had a mean recognition rate of 4.25 for free descriptions and 3.9 for ratings, while the student group had rates of 3.4 for free descriptions and 3.6 for ratings. None of these differences was significant.

When the data were compared by target the similarity of the results from free descriptions and ratings was also marked. The percentage of subjects identifying each target varied from 69% to 28% for the free descriptions, and from 81% to 31% for the ratings. The rank order correlation between the recognition rates for the targets from the two modes of description was +.57, which is not significant for an N of 8. Perhaps more interesting is a comparison of the errors for the two modes. This was done by compiling for each mode of description a matrix of the number of times confusion occurred between each possible pair of targets (i.e. the number of times the description of target A was assigned to target B was added to the number of times the description of target B was assigned to target A). The rank order correlation between the cells of the two matrices was rho = +.69, indicating a similar <u>pattern</u> of errors for the two modes of description.

The considerable correspondence between the two sets of results would suggest that not only were our rating scales as effective as free descriptions in leading to identification of a target, but were communicating essentially the same information about the targets, even though ratings and free descriptions were provided by different describers from their memory of the appearance of the targets, and the subjects were also required to identify the targets from their memory of them. If one or more of these sources of error were reduced, a greater degree of correspondence between the two sets of results might be found.

An opportunity to test this arose when the University held an Open Day for all the citizens in the region. Visitors were encouraged, by the offer of a monetary prize, to try to identify the targets described by ratings or free descriptions.

METHOD

Sets of descriptions of the targets, either as ratings or as free descriptions, were prepared from the materials of the previous experiment. In addition, full face and profile colour photographs were prepared of each of the targets, and these were mounted on cards, each with a code letter. Each subject was randomly assigned a set of ratings or of free descriptions, and was asked to match the numbered descriptions with the letters of the targets. A total of 100 subjects, none of whom was acquainted with any of the targets, were run, with 50 Ss being assigned to each descriptive mode.

RESULTS

The mean identification rate for subjects with the ratings mode was 3.2 (cf. 3.8 in the previous experiment), and for subjects with the free description mode it was 3.1 (cf. 3.8 in the previous experiment). There was no difference between the two conditions, nor was the difference in recognition rate in the present experiment significantly different from the rate in the previous experiment for either mode of information.

Examination of the data by target again illustrated the similarity between the results. Identification rates for targets in the free description mode ranged from 64% to 20% with a mean of 39%, and in the ratings mode from 60% to 24% with a mean of 41%. The rank order correlation between recognition of targets in the free descriptions mode and in the ratings mode was rho = +.89 ($p < .01$).

A comparison of errors for the two modes was carried out in the same way as in the previous experiment. The correlations between the cells in the two confusion matrices in this case was rho = +0.74, even though the two matrices were based upon independent groups of subjects.

The results of the third experiment confirm the previous conclusion that essentially the same information about the targets is provided by our rating scales as by the free descriptions we obtained.

The practical implications of these results concern the most effective ways of eliciting verbal descriptions of targets from witnesses. In the experiments reported here the conditions for obtaining all the descriptions were very favourable. Describers either had a photograph in front of them or were describing someone whom they knew well. The atmosphere in which the descriptions were given was relaxed and free from time restraint and emotional stress. Under these conditions, an uncued free description may be as informative as a set of ratings. However, under more stressful conditions some cueing of recall may be necessary, and an efficient set of rating scales may be the best way of achieving this, particularly if the witness is inarticulate.

In the experiments reported here, undergraduates and University staff were used. This usually fairly verbose group generated 7.5 items in describing photographs and only 5.7 items in describing familiar colleagues from memory. Describers, particularly when working from memory, do not recall much detail about the targets, but 7 items may be sufficient for most practical face recognition purposes. For example, Goldstein, Harmon and Lesk (1971) report that their subjects had considerable success in identifying a target from among 255 photographs on the basis of information provided in the form of ratings , using the 7 most extremely rated features.

In our own data, longer descriptions did not result in superior identification. Precision on a few critical features may be better than a less precise but more detailed account of a face.

However, it is important that these critical features be mentioned. Rating scales provide a method for eliciting judgements of these critical features from less articulate describers. In addition, ratings have the advantage that measures of agreement and a summary description derived from numerous accounts can be more readily obtained than with free descriptions. The rating scales could, further, be coordinated with a retrieval system for photographs.

A final, incidental, point concerns the similar pattern of results obtained in experiments 2 and 3. Conventionally, photographs are used in face recognition studies because of their convenience and availability. Their use raises the question of generalising from the results of such studies to those involving 'real life' faces. The results of the present experiments suggest that in recognising faces from verbal descriptions, real faces and photographs may be regarded as equivalent, indeed, photographs and memories of 'real' faces may be equivalent. The correlations between the error patterns for memories and photographs were above +.60 (similar to the value of the correlations between error patterns for ratings and free descriptions within each experiment). These occurred in spite of the variation among describers, which was not 'smoothed out' by an averaging procedure, and in the subjects' memory ability in the memory experiment, as well as in the judges' competence in the photograph conditions.

REFERENCES

Bower, G. H. and Karlin, M. B. (1974). Depth of processing pictures of faces and recognition memory. *Journal of Experimental Psychology*, 103, 751-757.

Goldstein, A. J., Harmon, L. D. and Lesk, A. B. (1971). Identification of human faces. *Proceedings of I.E.E.E.* 59, 748-760.

Shepherd, J. W., Ellis, H. D. and Davies, G. M. (1977). Perceiving and remembering faces. Technical report to Home Office under contract POL/73/1675/24/1.

EYE MOVEMENTS DURING RECOGNITION OF FACES

M. Cook

Department of Psychology
University College of Swansea,
Swansea, Wales

ABSTRACT

Eye movements of eight subjects were recorded while they looked at and later recognised unfamiliar faces and while recognising familiar ones. Data on number, target and order of points looked at are generally consistent with a feature testing model of recognition, with two important exceptions, that are more consistent with a pattern matching model.

Research on the way people recognise faces has both practical and theoretical interests. So too has research on the contribution of parts of the face to ease of recognition. Fisher and Cox (1975) showed that the eyes were the single most important feature, but also found that the eyes alone were not enough to identify the face. Only 12% of their faces could be recognised from the eyes alone. The combination of eyes and nose could be identified in 23% of cases, and the combination of mouth and nose in 16%. These findings lead one to expect that at least two parts of the face will be looked at before identification can be made.

METHOD

Subjects were eight students, five female and three male.

Faces To Be Recognised

Experiment 1. Ten faces were used, taken from a textbook of physical anthropology, to give the greatest diversity possible, within the limits that all were male, white and had neither facial hair, nor spectacles. The faces were photographed in black and white and turned into 2" x 2" slides.

Experiment 2. Nine pictures of well known public figures, e.g. Gerald Ford, H.M. Queen, Paul Newman, appearing in colour supplements, were photographed and turned into 2" x 2" colour slides. The tenth picture was of an unknown London solicitor.

Procedure

Experiment 1. Five faces were shown to the subjects, for 8-9 seconds each. The subject was told to look at each carefully because he/she would be required to remember it shortly. Immediately after the last had been shown the subject was told that the same five faces would be shown again, in a different order and mixed randomly with five new faces. His/her task was to decide as quickly as possible if he had seen the face before and to say 'New' or 'Old'.

Experiment 2. Subjects were told that ten faces of well known people would be shown, and that their task was to name the person or say how he knew the face, e.g. football player, TV actor, or say 'Don't know', as quickly as possible.

Apparatus

The subject's replies were tape recorded. His speech also operated a voice relay which lit a small light bulb.

The subject's eye movements were recorded by a NAC eye-mark camera. This apparatus employs a light which is reflected off the surface of the eyeball at differing angles as the eye moves. The image of the reflected light is added to an image of the subject's field of view and transmitted down a fibre optic cable to a TV camera and video-recorder. The equipment allows the subject's point of fixation to be determined to within 1 degree of visual field and to the nearest 1/50 second. The successive scans of the TV camera were numbered by a videotimer, and the image of the light operated by the voice relay mixed into the record, giving a rough measure of the subject's recognition time. The calibration of the equipment was checked at the beginning and end of each phase of the study.

RESULTS AND DISCUSSION

Eye Movements While Looking At The Five Faces To Be Remembered

The eight subjects recorded a total of 1,011 fixations.

Table I shows that the eyes were most frequently looked at, followed by the nose. Then the upper region of the face - forehead, hair and hairline, and ears - while the mouth and the lower part of the face were looked at relatively little. These results confirm those of earlier studies of eye movements while looking at faces, described by Argyle and Cook (1976), in finding that the eyes are the most frequently looked at part of the face. The fixations on the eyes were generally on the surround of the eye - brow, corners of eye, lines under the eye, and few were directed at the eyeball itself.

Table 1

REGIONS OF THE FACE FIXATED DURING PRELIMINARY EXPOSURE (EXPERIMENT 1) AND RECOGNITION (EXPERIMENTS 1 AND 2)

		Percent Directed At:-					
	Number of Fixations	Eyes	Nose	Mouth	Fore-head	Hair & Ears	Cheeks & Chin
Exposure of unfamiliar faces	1,011	41	18	8	14	13	5
Recognition of unfamiliar faces	401	36	27	17	5	3	10
Recognition of familiar faces	507	39	23	16	3	6	13

The eight subjects varied considerably in the parts of the faces they looked at, the range in proportion of gazes at the eye region being 22% to 59%. The five faces on the other hand differed very little in the way they were looked at.

The first two fixations within the face were almost always - on 72 of 80 possible occasions - directed at the eyes or nose, rarely at the mouth or forehead and never at the edge of the face.

Eye Movements During Recognition Of Faces Seen Once Before (Experiment 1)

Subjects made few or no errors in deciding whether they had seen the face before. The distributions of number of fixations made up to time of recognition, and the latencies of recognition were both markedly skewed. The modal number of fixations to recognition was 3 or 4, and the modal time .90 of a second.

Table 1 shows what part of the face the subjects looked at while recognising it, compared with when first looking at it. During recognition, the eyes are looked at most often, followed by the nose, then the mouth. However subjects looked at the nose more ($p = .035$, Sign test) during recognition, and looked less at the forehead ($p = .035$) hair and ears ($p = .004$).Six of the eight subjects also looked rarely or never at the lower face during recognition, but two subjects differed strikingly, one directing 24% of fixations during recognition at this region, the other 50%.

Table 2 plots the distribution of targets for the first five fixations. The first fixation was most frequently on the eyes or nose, as was the second. Those subjects who looked at other parts of the face did so on the second or subsequent fixations, and rarely or never on the first fixation, reflecting the order of fixations noted in the exposure part of the experiment.

Table 2

THE POINTS FIXATED DURING THE FIRST FIVE FIXATIONS OF RECOGNITION, IN EXPERIMENTS 1 AND 2

	Fixation No.				
	1	2	3	4	5
Experiment 1					
Eyes	30	23	28	29	16
Nose	39	25	14	5	2
Mouth	5	19	16	6	5
Forehead	1	2	3	5	6
Hair and Ears	0	0	2	2	3
Cheeks and Chin	2	8	11	6	2
Experiment 2					
Eyes	38	20	17	36	22
Nose	16	30	27	8	5
Mouth	8	20	20	7	4
Forehead	1	0	3	2	2
Hair and Ears	1	0	0	1	6
Cheeks and Chin	15	9	4	12	2

Figure 1 illustrates the data by showing the first five fixations by all subjects while recognising one face.

Experiment 2. Recognition Of Well Known Faces. Subjects found the task quite difficult, none getting all nine answers right; scores ranged from 2 to 8.

The distributions of number of fixations to recognition and of recognition times were both skewed; the modal number of fixations required was 4, and the modal recognition time 1.30 seconds.

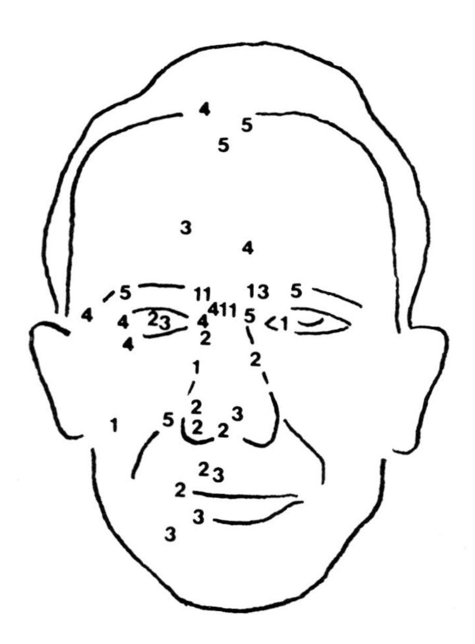

Fig. 1 Eight Subjects' Fixations During Recognising An Unfamiliar Face, In Order

Plotting the distribution of the regions of the face looked at yielded essentially the same results as in study 1 (Table 1) the region of the eyes being looked at most, followed by nose and mouth (but with wide variation between the subjects).

Table 2 plots the distribution of targets for the first five fixations.

The first and fourth fixations typically are on the eye region, while the second and third fixations are on the nose and mouth. The lower face attracts fifteen first fixation and twelve fourth fixations, reflecting the pattern for the eyes. It will be recalled that when looking at faces seen once or never before subjects never looked first at the cheeks or chin. The fifteen first fixations in this region were plotted to see if they fell near enough the eyes, nose or mouth possibly to count as fixating on one of these points; in fact they fell mostly on the centre of the cheeks.

Most of the subjects, most of the time, recognise the faces after looking at 3 or 4 points within the face. The 3 or 4 points include the eyes, the nose and the mouth, the outer areas of the face being looked at more rarely, and later in the sequence of fixations. In an unfamiliar face the nose and eyes are looked at first, but in the familiar face the eyes are looked at first, followed by the nose and mouth, then the eyes again. These data are consistent with the theory that faces are recognised by examining the significant features in turn and comparing them with stored memory.

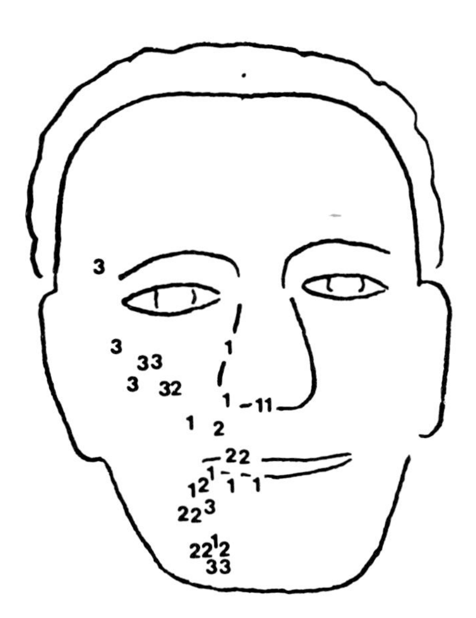

Fig. 2 Subject DH's Fixations While Recognising Unfamiliar Faces, In Order

However while the pattern described above is the typical pattern, there are two important exceptions. The first is that a substantial proportion of first fixations on familiar faces are on the featureless areas of the cheeks and chin. The second is that one subject when looking at faces seen once or never before directs 50% of her fixations at this region, and achieves recognition in 2 or 3 fixations, more quickly than the other Ss. Figure 2 shows that this subject rarely looks at the eyes, yet still knows whether she has seen the face before or not. This subject's eye movements during recognition fit the theory that the perceived form or shape of the face is compared with a stored image, instead of the component features being looked at one by one. The fact that several other subjects also look first in these relatively featureless regions, when looking at well known faces, suggests that they may sometimes identify faces by their form. A glance directed at the middle of the cheek of course takes in peripherally the rest of the face. The fact that faces can be still recognised when presented tachistoscopically, for too short a time to allow change of fixation, suggests that everyone *can* recognise faces without scanning their main features, if they have to, but the present data indicate that most subjects prefer, especially when looking at unfamiliar faces, to look at 3 or 4 areas before reaching a decision. There are not enough mistakes or 'Don't knows' in the present data to determine whether one or other pattern of fixation gives more success in recognising the face.

REFERENCES

Argyle, M. and Cook, M. (1976) *Gaze and Mutual Gaze.* Cambridge University Press.

Fisher, G.H. and Cox, R.L. (1975) Recognising Human Faces. *Applied Ergonomics*, 6, 104-109.

AROUSAL AND STRESS

AROUSAL AND STRESS IN HUMAN MEMORY: SOME METHODOLOGICAL AND THEORETICAL CONSIDERATIONS

Robert Hockey

Department of Psychology,
University of Durham,
England

INTRODUCTION

The aim of the present paper is to examine the evidence relating to effects of stress and arousal in human memory. In the space available it is not possible to review this field in any breadth. Instead, I will try to indicate some key theoretical and methodological issues which are critical for the interpretation of this body of data. In the main these points have been over-looked in current accounts, which give the impression that the relationship between arousal and memory is a simple one. The general view is that short-term memory (STM) is impaired by high arousal while long-term memory (LTM) is enhanced. In the following discussion I have not made any attempt to relate this STM/LTM distinction to any particular theory of memory organisation: work in this field has rarely paid much attention to theoretical developments. The operational distinction between the two is also somewhat inconsistent. LTM may refer to retention over a week, or over a few minutes. I have attempted to restrict my discussion to central issues which are relatively neutral with respect to these problems. First, let me state the evidence on which this generalisation is based.

THE INTERACTION OF AROUSAL WITH TIME OF TESTING

The original demonstration of this effect is found in an experiment by Kleinsmith and Kaplan (1963) on paired-associate (PA) learning. Arousal was defined in terms of the magnitude of GSR associated with the presentation of individual stimulus items, i.e. separately for each subject. After a single study trial retention tests were carried out immediately or at varying delays up to a week. The familiar data are shown in Figure 1. The results have been replicated

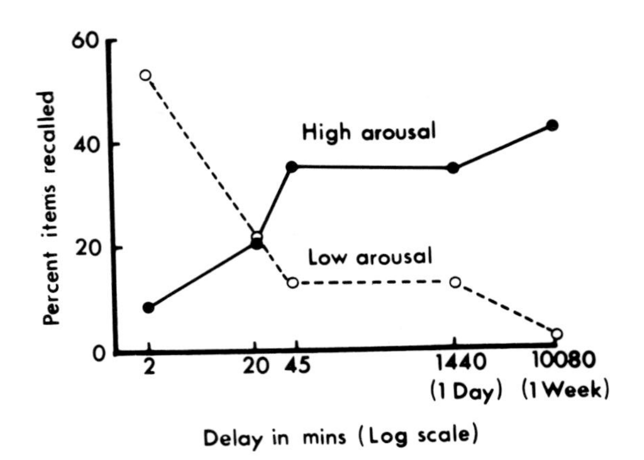

Fig.1 The interaction of arousal level with time of testing. Redrawn from Kleinsmith and Kaplan (1963)

in a number of other studies, and appear to have some generality (e.g. Kleinsmith and Kaplan, 1964; Walker and Tarte, 1963).

All the above studies used item-induced GSR as the index of arousal. The same general pattern of results has, however, been found for noise-induced arousal. Berlyne, Borsa, Craw, Gelman and Mandell (1965) found impaired immediate recall in a PA task with noise but improved performance in the noise condition after a 24-hr delay. A similar result was obtained by McClean (1969), also using PA learning. A number of other studies providing supporting evidence are reviewed by Craik and Blankenstein (1975). Among these are a separate group of experiments showing impaired STM for material presented at high points in the normal diurnal rhythm of the body: it has been suggested that this may be equivalent to high arousal of other kinds.

The simple generalisation that high arousal leads to worse STM but better LTM thus appears to be supported by a number of findings. In the next few pages I would like to examine this conclusion in more detail. Such a conclusion has important educational implications, over and above its intrinsic theoretical value, and it is therefore necessary to ensure that we have interpreted the findings correctly. As I will show, in fact, such a conclusion turns out to be somewhat misleading except in a rather superficial sense. Let us first consider the nature of arousal effects in STM.

EFFECTS OF AROUSAL ON STM

One of the principal limitations in the generality of the impaired STM conclusion concerns the use of the PA task itself. Let me illustrate the difficulty by referring to an experiment of our own (Hamilton, Hockey and Quinn, 1972). In this study we compared a conventional PA task (in which the order of the stimulus-response pairs is randomised from study to test trials) with one in which the order is kept constant. When the conventional task was used the effect of 85 dBC noise was to impair recall (in comparison to a control condition of 55 dBC), though the decrement was not significant. However, when the item pairs were kept in the same order from study to test trials, noise resulted in a clear improvement in recall. The pattern of these results suggests that the effect of noise is to change the way in which information is processed in the task, rather than simply alter the efficiency of learning, or whatever. Subjects appear to make more use of order information in the noise state. Such a strategy is clearly advantageous when the order of items is retained on successive trials, but is actually a hinderance when (as is usually the case in PA tasks) it is changed. No studies, to my knowledge, have been carried out using this kind of comparison with the Kleinsmith and Kaplan paradigm. A direct implication would be that high GSR items would give rise to better immediate recall in a fixed order PA task, though there may well be important differences between the two ways of manipulating arousal. (I shall say more about this later.) The impairment of immediate recall with high arousal may therefore be an artifact of the rather artificial PA task. Instead of stopping at the observation that performance is impaired (or improved) it is important to go a step further and ask what is the nature of the underlying change in the system producing the behaviour.

The suggestion that noise produces greater reliance on order information is supported by evidence from Dornic (1974) and Schwartz (1974). Dornic found that ordered recall was unimpaired by a number of stress conditions, while a free recall criterion (including as correct those items in the wrong order) did show an effect of stress. Schwartz has also found deleterious effects of noise only with material which was not strongly dependent on order. Daee and Wilding (1977) have shown the same kind of effect of noise, but on positional, rather than sequential aspects of order information, in a free recall task.

One other component of the nature of these changes should

be mentioned. Hockey and Hamilton (1970) presented a single list of words for immediate recall, then tested unexpectedly for recall of the location of words on the screen. Whereas word recall was marginally better in noise, location information was recalled better in quiet. This is a difficult result to include in the arousal/STM discussion since it shows opposing effects on two different aspects of the task. We have suggested on the basis of other evidence that this result fits in better with the interpretation that noise biases attention towards dominant sources of information. Because the primary task of the subject is to recall the list of words, this feature of the situation is attended to more strongly at the expense of the incidental location cue. The result has been replicated by Davies and Jones (1975), who also showed the same effect for monetary incentive, and by Anderson and Hockey (1975), for the effects of nicotine.

The suggestion that STM is worse in high arousal can therefore be seen to misrepresent the evidence. Although much more fundamental data needs to be obtained at the present time the idea of an attentional change seems basic to our interpretation of these effects. In sequentially presented material the order of items may be regarded as an important source of information, so is attended to more strongly. It is possible that location information would also be treated in this way if it was a critical feature of the situation (in memory for scenes, or spatially separated verbal material, for example). I do not know of any studies of this type. Whether immediate recall will be impaired or not will thus depend on how these changes in strategy relate to the task requirements. If a dominant cue (such as order, or position in a spatial array) is made incompatible with correct recall, we can expect performance to suffer. This is the case with the traditional PA paradigm, and may not be representative of real-life learning. An understanding of the underlying mechanics of arousal effects may prevent us from misusing this information. Let us now consider effects on LTM. Although these are difficult in some cases to distinguish from those of STM an examination of the data reveals similar problems of interpretation.

EFFECTS OF AROUSAL ON LTM

As we have seen in the previous section, not only is the interpretation of STM effects not as straightforward as first appears, but the actual evidence is rather ambiguous. A number of studies have found either no effect of arousal on STM or an improvement, depending on the conditions of the task. This is not the case with delayed recall. are generally consistent in showing improved rec learned under high arousal. It appears, howevel high degree of agreement may also be an artifac of test that have been used to measure LTM.

Almost every study in which this result is observed is of the kind which Tulving (1972) identifies as depending upon episodic memory. Subjects are required to recall unrelated items (as in free recall tests) or associations between items (in PA tests). There have been very few studies in which subjects are required to make use of semantic information in delayed recall, though such studies do indicate that LTM may be worse for material learned under high arousal.

Schwartz (1974) found an impairment in the retention of sentences with noise, but no effect on that of unconnected words. Other studies have found a reduction in the degree of semantic clustering with noise (Hörmann and Osterkamp, 1966; Daee and Wilding, 1977). An unpublished study of our own also indicates this kind of effect, and shows a reversal of the "normal" arousal/time of testing pattern. Immediate recall of a story (in verbatim form) was better after presentation in noise, while performance on a comprehension task after a 10-min delay was impaired by noise.

A generalisation which seems better to capture the pattern of these results is that high arousal leads to better episodic memory but worse semantic memory. This is almost certainly also an oversimplification, but highlights the apparent dissociation in the LTM data. If basically true, can this be incorporated into our attentional explanation of STM changes? One line of argument is to suggest that the rather restricted use of cues in the aroused state is less useful for forming semantic associations than for storing isolated events. Episodic memory is characteristically organised in terms of specific times and locations, which may be better coded in high arousal, so long as they are relevant in the situation. Our general picture of the pattern of learning produced by noise is one of stronger ordering and literal storage, though information is less readily accessed in other ways. As I have already said this is an area with very little useful data. Before we can begin to interpret the nature of stress effects in LTM in a more analytic way much more research is needed. Clearly, however, as with STM, the facts are not as clear-cut as is usually taken to be the case.

Before summarising what I believe to be the few useful practical implications to come from this area of memory research, I would like, briefly, to turn my attention to a consideration of the nature of arousal effects in these and other experiments.

THE NATURE OF AROUSAL

Arousal has usually been thought of as a kind of non-specific "volume control", increasing or decreasing performance uniformly. In the preceding pages we have seen, however, that there is a selectivity (or "tuning") component to the effect of noise (say); different components of performance are affected differently. This is even more true when effects across the whole range of performance measures are considered. In brief, to take noise, about which more is known than any other arousal agent, its effects on performance may be described as a pattern, of which these effects on memory are but a part. It is important to remember this, since memory tasks in real-life are rarely carried out for their own sake, but as part of a more complex sequence of information processing operations. Arousal may be best thought of not in terms of a level of activity, but as describing a "state" of the hardware associated with the whole of this cognitive system (Hamilton, Hockey and Rejman, 1977). This state will be more appropriate for some activities than for others, and may differ in detail for the various conditions assumed to be representative of "high arousal" in the usual sense. I have not had time to go into these differences here. It is clear that we cannot equate tonic arousal changes induced by continuous noise with the phasic arousal increments resulting from the occurrence of particular stimulus words. Similarly, the kinds of changes associated with natural variations in arousal such as those brought about by circadian rhythm may well be quite different to those which are imposed on the subject by manipulation of stimulus or environmental conditions. The non-specific volume control concept of arousal no longer seems useful as a means of integrating effects of stressors on human performance (Hamilton et al.,1977), and we should begin to take such differences more seriously than has been the case in the past. These differences between stressors and stress states are likely to be at least as important as the obvious similarities in their effects on performance. In the memory field, for example, phasic and tonic changes in state may well be associated with different features or stages of the cognitive processes involved in learning (orienting, encoding, storage, etc). If this is the case it becomes even more necessary to consider arousal in qualitative, rather than quantitative, terms. While "arousal level" may be useful to distinguish between states of sleep and waking, or even to identify phasic responses to sudden noises, it does not readily distinguish between the vast range of normal states, or sustained tonic changes brought about by continuous noise, sleep deprivation or the like. Effects of arousal on memory will only become meaningful, I believe, when we move away from this traditional concept, and think in terms of detailed performance patterns associated with particular stress-induced states. See Hamilton et al.(1977) for a fuller discussion of this argument.

A FEW PRACTICAL IMPLICATIONS

In view of the difficulties of interpretation which I have indicated I believe it is not possible to offer much useful advice on how best to "harness" arousal effects for efficient learning. There are, however, guidelines which should be considered when such a possibility arises (say, in educational planning). Firstly, it is worth noting that the size of the effects in these studies may be quite large, often between 10 and 20%, and therefore of some practical, as well as theoretical significance. Secondly, whether learning should take place under high arousal or not must depend on the nature of the task and how the information is going to be used. Since practical situations are primarily concerned with LTM we would expect that routine learning of ordered lists or highly structured material would be better under high arousal. The indications are, however, that the more flexible learning that we value as creative or original thinking may actually be acquired in a more suitable form under normal arousal conditions. The many gaps in the research literature make it impossible to be more precise than this.

REFERENCES

Andersson, K. and Hockey, G. R. J. (1975). Effects of cigarette smoking on incidental memory. *University of Stockholm reports No. 455.*

Berlyne, D. E., Borsa, D. M., Craw, M. A., Gelman, R. S. and Mandell, E. E. (1965). Effects of stimulus complexity and induced arousal on paired-associate learning. *Journal of Verbal Learning and Verbal Behaviour*, 4, 291-299.

Craik, F. I. and Blankenstein, K. R. (1975). Psychophysiology and human memory. In *Research in Psychophysiology* (P. H. Venables and M. J. Christie, (eds.). Wiley, London.

Daee, S. and Wilding, J. M. (1977). Effects of high intensity white noise in short-term memory for position in a list and sequence. *British Journal of Psychology*, 68, 335-349.

Davies, D. R. and Jones, D. M. (1975). The effects of noise and incentives upon attention in short-term memory. *British Journal of Psychology*, 66, 61-68.

Dornic, S. (1974). Order error in attended and non-attended tasks. In *Attention and Performance*, Vol. 4. (S. Kornblum, ed.). Academic Press, New York.

Hamilton, P., Hockey, G. R. J. and Quinn, J. G. (1972). Information selection, arousal and memory. *Journal of Psychology*, 63, 181-190.

Hamilton, P., Hockey, G. R. J. and Rejman, M. (1977). The place of the concept of activation in human information processing theory. In *Attention and Performance*, Vol. 6. (S. Dornic, ed.). Lawrence Erlbaum, Hillsdale, N. J.

Hockey, G. R. J. and Hamilton, P. (1970). Arousal and information selection in short-term memory. *Nature*, 226, 866-867.

Hörmann, H. and Osterkamp, U. (1966). Uber den einfluss von kontinuerlichem lärm auf die organisation von gedachtnisinhalten. *Zeitschrift fur Experimentell und Angewande Psychologie*, 13, 31-38.

Kleinsmith, L. J. and Kaplan, S. (1963). Paired associate learning as a function of arousal and interpolated interval. *Journal of Experimental Psychology*, 65, 190-193.

Kleinsmith, L. J. and Kaplan, S. (1964). Interaction of arousal and recall interval in nonsense syllable paired associate learning. *Journal of Experimental Psychology*, 67, 124-126.

McClean, P. D. (1969). Induced arousal and time of recall as determinants of paired-associate recall. *British Journal of Psychology*, 60, 57-62.

Schwartz, S. (1974). The effects of arousal on recall, recognition and the organisation of memory: *University of Northern Illinois, unpublished manuscripts.*

Tulving, E. (1972). Episodic and semantic memory. In *Organisation of Memory* (E. Tulving and W. Donaldson, eds.). Academic Press, New York.

Walker, E. L. and Tarte, R. D. (1963). Memory storage as a function of arousal and time with homogeneous and hetergeneous lists. *Journal of Verbal Learning and Verbal Behaviour*, 2, 113-119.

TIME OF DAY EFFECTS IN IMMEDIATE AND DELAYED MEMORY

Simon Folkard and Timothy H. Monk

M.R.C. Perceptual and Cognitive Performance Unit
Laboratory of Experimental Psychology
University of Sussex
Brighton, BN1 9QG

ABSTRACT

Three experiments are described that examined the effects of time of day on memory for information presented in naturalistic contexts. The time at which information was presented consistently influenced immediate and delayed retention in opposite directions; but there was no evidence that retrieval efficiency varied with time of day. In general, the results favour an interpretation assuming changes in arousal level, rather than one based on proactive and retroactive interference. These findings may have important practical implications in educational and other settings where people attempt to commit information to memory.

INTRODUCTION

Interest in the effects of time of day on memory originated from practical considerations as to the optimal scheduling of different subjects within the school day. The early studies in this area found various measures of 'immediate' memory, such as digit span, to be superior in the mid-morning, but performance on various perceptual-motor tasks to be better in the afternoon. As a result of these findings Gates (1916) concluded that "In general the forenoon is the best time for strictly mental work ... while the afternoon may best be taken up with school subjects in which the motor factors are predominant" (p 149).

More recent published studies in this area have confirmed these findings, and have interpreted them as reflecting variations in basal arousal level. Thus Colquhoun (1971) argues that, with the exception of a 'post-lunch' dip, arousal level parallels the circadian rhythm in body temperature (being at a minimum at 04:00, and reaching a maximum at about 20:00), while some studies have found immediate memory to be impaired under high arousal. However, Craik and Blankstein (1975) point out that the effects of heightened arousal on immediate memory are inconsistent, and similar inconsistencies have been found in unpublished studies of the effects of time of day (e.g. Jones 1974). The first study was thus designed to examine whether time of day affected immediate memory for the information presented in a factual article. In addition, it examined the potential effects of time of day on the efficiency of retrieval from long-term, or semantic, memory since it has recently been suggested that such retrieval may be affected by people's arousal level (Eysenck 1976).

EXPERIMENT 1

Method

14 female and 22 male undergraduates (mean age=21.3 years) were tested at three hourly intervals from 08:00 to 23:00 in a cyclic Latin square design. At each session the subjects read a different 1500 word article, from 'New Scientist' for three minutes, indicated how far they read, and were then given ten multiple-choice questions. The subjects were instructed to "read for comprehension" but to read as much as they reasonably could in the time allowed. The questions tapped memory for the factual information presented in the articles, and did not require any inference to be drawn.

After completing these questions, the subjects were given a category instance generation task. (See Eysenck 1976). They were given five minutes to write down as many instances as possible from two categories printed at the top of a page. The six pairs of categories used were matched in terms of the number of common instances. The subjects were allowed to switch between categories as often as they liked.

Results

The results from the articles read were scored in terms of the number of words read (speed), and the number of questions answered correctly, expressed as a percentage of the number of questions the subject could have answered given how far he had read (immediate memory). There was no effect of time of day on reading speed ($p>0.10$), although the mean number of words read increased from 716 to 764 (about 7%) between 08:00 and 11.00 and then remained within $\pm$ 3% of the 11:00 level over the rest of the day. In contrast the immediate memory scores showed a significant main effect of time of day ($p < 0.05$). These results are shown in Figure 1, in which the scores have been corrected for guessing and then expressed as a percentage of the overall mean for the day. This figure also shows the results of a similar study conducted by Laird (1925) in which subjects read a short passage and then made an immediate written 'free' recall of the 'ideas' contained in it.

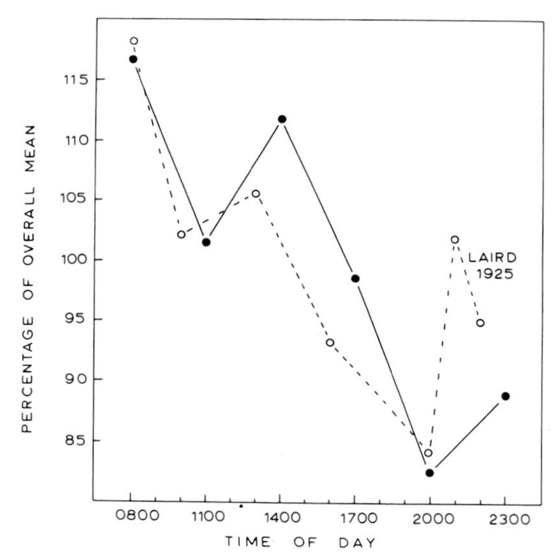

Fig. 1 Immediate memory for the information presented in prose as a function of time of day.

In both the present study, and that of Laird (1925), immediate memory varied substantially (± 15%) over the day, being highest at 08:00 and lowest at 20:00. In addition, both studies show a slight, short-lived, improvement in immediate memory after lunch (at 13:00 or 14:00), corresponding to the 'post-lunch dip' thought to occur in arousal level; and a later improvement after 20:00, when arousal level is thought to start decreasing again.

There was no evidence of an effect of time of day on the number of category instances retrieved ($p > 0.10$) although there was a slight improvement of about 7% from a minimum of 40.4 at 08:00 to a maximum of 43.2 at 14:00 and 20:00.

Discussion

Time of day had a fairly substantial effect on people's immediate memory for the information presented in prose, but apparently had no effect on their ability to retrieve information from long-term/semantic memory as measured by the category instance task. There are, however, two further ways in which variations in arousal level over the day might affect memory. First, Craik and Blankstein (1975) conclude that high arousal at presentation consistently results in superior long-term memory, suggesting that delayed retention may be superior following presentation later in the day. Secondly, there is some evidence that retrieval from long-term memory may be superior when the subject is in the same physiological 'state' as during the original presentation. Thus the delayed retrieval of information may be superior at the same time of day at which the presentation occurred, compared to other times of day. (Strictly speaking this prediction could be made independently of the arousal theory since virtually all physiological measures exhibit a circadian rhythm.)

EXPERIMENT 2

This study has been described elsewhere (Folkard, Monk, Bradbury & Rosenthall 1977). Briefly, six matched groups of school children were played a tape recording of a story at either 09:00 or 15:00, and were then given a multiple-choice questionnaire on its contents. For two groups this was given immediately (3-4 minutes) after the end of the story, while for the remaining four groups it was given seven days later, either at the 'same' or 'different' time of day to the original presentation. The questions ranged from those of factual detail to those demanding a more general understanding in that they required an inference to be drawn.

The raw scores were corrected for guessing and converted to 'percent-corrects'. In line with the results of experiment 1, immediate memory was superior following 09:00 presentation (78.7%) to that following 15:00 presentation (68.0%); but when recall was delayed by a week, 15:00 presentation (60.0%) resulted in *superior* retention to 09:00 presentation (52.7%). In contrast, there was no evidence that time of day affected the ability to retrieve information from long-term memory (09:00 recall = 57.3%, 15:00 recall = 56.0%), nor was delayed retention better at the 'same' time of day as the original presentation had occurred ('same' = 57.7%, 'different' = 55.7%). However, there is some evidence (Goodwin, Powell, Bremer, Haine & Stern 1969) that recognition measures are less sensitive than recall ones to 'state dependent' effects, suggesting that such an effect might be found if recall measures were used at more extreme times of day, i.e. 04:00 and 20:00.

More importantly, the effects of time of presentation were not entirely consistent with the arousal theory and may be open to alternative interpretations. The available evidence suggests that the "crossover" between inferior immediate memory and superior delayed memory, under high arousal occurs about 10-15 minutes after presentation (Craik & Blankstein (1975). In view of the length of the story approximately 10 minutes elapsed between the presentation, and the 'immediate' testing, of a piece of information in the present study; a delay at which effectively no difference would be predicted by the arousal and memory literature. An alternative explanation of the effect of time of day of presentation on both immediate and delayed retention invokes interference theory. Thus the decrease in immediate memory over the day might reflect increasing proactive interference, while the superior delayed retention following afternoon presentation might reflect the reduced potential for retroactive interference occurring between presentation and the subsequent sleep period.

An opportunity arose to test the state dependency predictions at more extreme times of day (04:00 and 20:30), and to distinguish between the arousal and interference interpretations of the time of presentation effects, as part of a large scale shiftwork study. In view of the inverted sleep/wake cycle of the night workers that took part in this study the arousal and interference theories make opposite predictions. If there is no adjustment to night work, the arousal theory predicts superior immediate memory, but inferior delayed retention, following 04:00 presentation when arousal level is normally at a low ebb. In contrast, the interference theory predicts inferior immediate memory, and superior delayed retention, at this time due to increased proactive interference but a reduction in the potential for retroactive interference between presentation and the start of the subsequent sleep period (c.11.00). A full report of this aspect of the study is in preparation, while a partial report has appeared elsewhere (Monk & Folkard 1978).

EXPERIMENT 3

Method

50 female nurses were shown a 10 minute film on the use of Radium therapy as part of their 'inservice' training programme. 26 nurses were shown it at 20:30, and 24 at 04:00 , on

either their first or second night of a span of successive night shifts. Within each of these four groups, approximately half the nurses were full-time night staff who showed partial adjustment of their circadian rhythms to night work, while the remainder were part-time night workers or students, who showed little such adjustment (Folkard, Monk & Lobban 1978). The nurses retention was tested both immediately, and after 28 days, by means of two parallel questionnaires used in a counterbalanced order. Each consisted of 15 open-ended questions requiring a single word or short phrase answer, and 5 multiple-choice questions. Both types of question tapped memory for the factual details presented. The 28 day delayed test was given to half the nurses at the 'same'time of day as they had originally seen the film, and half at the 'different' time.

Results

The analyses were based on the overall scores since there was no evidence that the results from the two types of question differed. The 28 day delayed scores yielded no evidence of a state dependent effect ('same' = 34.8%, 'different' = 40.7%), or of a straight time of retrieval effect (20:30 = 37.3%, 04:00 = 38.8%). This lack of any effect of the time of retrieval was fairly consistent over the various subgroups.

In contrast, the time of original presentation had a reliable and consistent effect on the 28 day delayed retention (20:30 = 43.0%, 04:00 = 32.7%; $p<0.01$), but no overall effect on the immediate recall level (20:30 = 56.3%, 04:00 = 55.4%) However, this failure to obtain an 04:00 superiority in immediate memory was not consistent across the various subgroups, and was influenced by the degree to which the nurses' circadian rhythms had adjusted to night work. In the least adjusted subgroup (the part-time and student nurses on the first night of a span) there was an 04:00 superiority in immediate memory (20:30 = 54.5%. 04:00 = 68.0%), but this pattern reversed to a 20:30 superiority (20:30 = 58.1%, 04:00 = 44.5%) in the most adjusted subgroup (full-timers on their second night shift). This interaction between level of adjustment and the time of presentation was significant ($p<0.05$).

Discussion

The inferior delayed retention following presentation at 04:00 obviously favours the arousal theory, rather than one based on retroactive interference. Nor can this finding be easily attributed to sleep deprivation since the part-time staff had considerably less sleep than the full-timers (Folkard, Monk & Lobban 1978), but showed slightly superior delayed retention following 04:00 presentation (part-timers = 35.6%, full-timers = 28.5%).

The effects of time of presentation on immediate memory, while rather more complex, again favour interpretation in terms of arousal level rather than proactive interference. Thus although there was no overall 04:00 superiority in immediate memory, a proactive interference explanation of the results cannot account for the interaction between time of presentation and adjustment of circadian rhythms. In contrast, the arousal theory can do so if it is assumed that adjustment of physiological circadian rhythms is accompanied by adjustment of the circadian rhythm in basal arousal level. The main problem with such an assumption is the failure to find a similar interaction between time of presentation and degree of adjustment in the delayed retention scores. Although there is some evidence that the circadian rhythms in different types of performance function adjust to night work at different rates (e.g. Hughes & Folkard 1976), it is logically impossible for a single mediating function (i.e. arousal) to do so. Thus these results necessitate the adoption of a multifactor model of arousal, such as that of Broadbent (1971), and the assumptions (i) that different subcomponents of such a model are responsible for immediate and delayed retention, and (ii) that these subcomponents differ in the rate at which they adjust to night work.

CONCLUSIONS

Two main conclusions emerge from these studies. First, it would seem that the time of day at which information is presented has a fairly substantial effect on people's immediate and delayed retention of it, but in opposite directions. Presentation during the morning results in better immediate retention, but worse delayed retention, than presentation in the afternoon or evening. In general, this pattern of results is consistent with the arousal theory (Colquhoun 1971), although the results of Experiment 3 suggest that a multifactor theory is required. Secondly, it would appear that even extreme times of day have little effect on people's ability to retrieve information from memory, in either a 'straight' or 'state dependent' manner.

It is unclear as to why arousal should differentially affect immediate and delayed retention, and why in the present studies 'immediate' memory showed a morning superiority given the effective delay of c.10 minutes that occurred in Experiments 2 and 3. Nor is it clear whether these effects hold for all types of information and/or presentation. Nevertheless, it would seem that the time at which information is presented may be an important factor in determining its retention, and that the early recommendation that the more 'academic' school subjects should be taught in the morning may have been ill-founded. To date, the evidence suggests that delayed retention will be best following afternoon or evening presentation, although further research is clearly needed. However, despite the obvious implications for people attempting to commit information to memory, psychologists have virtually ignored this area in recent years.

REFERENCES

Broadbent, D.E. (1971). *Decision and Stress*. Academic Press, London.

Colquhoun, W.P. (1971). *Biological Rhythms and Human Performance*. pp39-107. Academic Press, London.

Craik, F.I.M. and Blankstein, K.R. (1975). Psychophysiology and human memory. In:*Research in Psychophysiology* (P.H. Venables and M.J. Christie eds) pp 388-417. Wiley, London.

Eysenck, M.W. (1976). Arousal, learning and memory. *Psychological Bulletin*. 83, 389-404.

Folkard, S.,Monk, T.H.,Bradbury, R. and Rosenthall, J. (1977). Time of day effects in school children's immediate and delayed recall of meaningful material. *British Journal of Psychology*. 58, 45-50.

Folkard, S.,Monk, T.H.,and Lobban, M.C. (1978). Short and long-term adjustment of circadian rhythms in 'permanent' night nurses, *Ergonomics*. 21, In press.

Gates, A.I. (1916) Variations in efficiency during the day. *University of California Publication in Psychology* 2 1-156.

Goodwin, D.W.,Powell, B.,Bremer, D.,Haine, H. and Stern, J. (1969). Alcohol and recall: State-dependent effects in man. *Science*. 163, 1358-1360.

Hughes, D.and Folkard, S. (1976). Adaptation to an 8-h shift in living routine by members of a socially isolated community. *Nature*. 264, 432-434.

Jones, D.M. (1974). The allocation of attention in a multicomponent memory task at different times of day (Abstract). *Bulletin of the British Psychological Society*. 27, 77.

Laird, D.A. (1925). Relative performance of college students as conditioned by time of day and time of week. *Journal of Experimental Psychology*. 8, 50-63.

Monk, T.H. and Folkard, S. (1978) Concealed inefficiency of late night study. *Nature*. 273, 296-297.

SLEEP AND MEMORY IN HUMANS

C. Idzikowski,
University Dept. of Psychiatry,
(Royal Edinburgh Hospital),
Edinburgh EH10 5HF.

INTRODUCTION

In this paper, I shall bring up to date the last review on human sleep and memory (Van Ormer, 1933). There are two current reviews of the animal literature (Vogel, 1975; Fishbein and Gutwein, 1977).

Essentially, two techniques have been used in sleep and memory research: 1. Sleep-deprivation; 2. Selective sleep-deprivation. The latter technique normally involves comparisons between groups that have been REM-deprived (or Stage 4 deprived) and groups who have been woken out of other sleep stages. Both short-term memory (STM) and long-term memory have been investigated.

SHORT-TERM MEMORY

It is well known that as little as 24h sleep loss will cause lapses (very short periods of sleep) to occur (Williams, Lubin and Goodnow, 1959). It is important, therefore, to ensure adequate sensory registration of test material. Many studies show that sleep-deprivation impairs STM (Elkin and Murray, 1974; Lubin, Moses, Johnson and Naitoh, 1974; Polzella, 1975; Williams, Giesking and Lubin, 1966; Williams and Williams, 1966). Those studies that do not ensure sensory registration, should be approached with caution (Edwards, 1941; Kollar, Pasnau, Rubin, Naitoh, Slater and Kales, 1969; Williams et al., 1959, Vojtechovsky, Safratova, Votava and Feit, 1971).

There is little indication as to which sleep stage is important for STM (Feldman, 1969; Johnson, Naitoh, Moses and Lubin, 1974; Sampson, 1966).

LONG-TERM MEMORY

I take the view that LTM is based on some type of protein substrate. There is substantial evidence that links LTM with protein synthesis (Barraco and Stettner, 1976; Glassman, 1974, Rose, Hambley and Haywood, 1976) and there is growing evidence that suggests that the rate of protein synthesis during sleep is higher than during wakefulness (Adam and Oswald, 1977). Therefore, it would make sense to find that sleep benefits LTM.

The principal support for the notion that sleep benefits LTM arises from Jenkins and Dallenbach's (1924) experiment and those experiments of the same genre. Typically, an 8h retention interval is used, and a comparison is made between daytime wakefulness and night-time sleep (Benson and Feinberg, 1975, 1977; Ekstrand, 1967, Lovatt and Warr, 1968; Newman, 1939). There are two difficulties with this comparison: 1. Night and day are being compared, apart from sleep and wakefulness; 2. Circadian variations in either learning or recall may confound the results. Night and day differ for reasons other than sleep, e.g. plasma cortisol levels are low in the early hours of the night and high thereafter. This circadian variation is not sleep-dependent, i.e. sleep-deprived subjects will show the same variation (Weitzman, 1977). Cortisol enhances degradation, so degradation is increased during the day and reduced during the night. Put another way, this alone would mean that the rate of net protein synthesis would be higher during the night than during the day. This difference in the relative rates of synthesis and degradation could produce the differences in the Jenkins and Dallenbach type of experiment without sleep being directly related.

On the other hand growth hormone (GH), which enhances synthesis, displays a sleep-dependent circadian rhythm; GH secretion is greatly enhanced during sleep stages 3 and 4 (Sassin, 1977). Normally, this enhanced secretion of GH occurs at a time when cortisol levels are low, when therefore on hormonal grounds the rate of net protein synthesis would be expected to be high. This may be one of the ways in which sleep influences LTM. If sleep is not allowed to occur at the normal time, but is delayed for several hours, then the peak in GH secretion will coincide with high levels of cortisol; thus sleep's effect of increasing protein synthesis (through GH) will be diminished (as Rudman, Friedes, Patterson and Gibbas, 1973, found). This may explain why Hockey, Davis and Gray (1972) found 5h's sleep during the night more beneficial to memory than 5h's sleep during the morning.

Generally when the Jenkins and Dallenbach type of experiment is extended by using retention intervals longer than 8h, then the following picture emerges: 1. With retention intervals of 16-24h, if both groups have slept, then there will be no differences between the two groups (Benson et al., 1977; Ekstrand, Barrett, West and Maier, 1977; Gibb, 1937; Graves, 1937; Richardson and Gough, 1963); if one group has not slept then their memory will be impaired (Benson et al., 1977; Ekstrand et al., 1977). 2. With retention intervals of one week, the subjects who have been allowed to sleep first (e.g. evening-learners), will recall the most (Graves, 1937; Richardson et al, 1963). Unfortunately, the evidence is not completely consistent with this picture, (Benson et al., 1977; McGaugh and Hostetter, 1963).

Rather than comparing night and day, the best experiment to show that sleep has an effect on LTM would be one that does not allow a night's sleep in one group and allows a night's sleep in another. Sadly, the only published experiments that do this are difficult to interpret. Williams et al. (1959) found that sleep-deprivation was deleterious but their subjects were learning at a time when they were already suffering from the effects of prior sleep-deprivation. Vojtechovsky et al. (1971) reported impairment with a sleep-deprived group but it was unclear whether they were showing impairment of STM or LTM. I have conducted experiments using a 24h retention interval, which show without ambiguity that sleep-deprivation impairs LTM. Further, in one experiment I allowed two groups to have one night's sleep after learning; one group was subsequently sleep-deprived and the other was allowed to sleep. No differences emerged between these two groups, suggesting that sleep-deprivation will not affect LTM once consolidation has been allowed to take place (during the first night's sleep).

There is little indication as to which stage of sleep is important for LTM. At present, there are more experiments showing that REM-deprivation does not impair LTM (Castaldo, Krynicki and Goldstein, 1974; Chernik, 1972; Ekstrand, Sullivan, Parker and West, 1971; Feldman, 1969, Muzio, 1971) than those that do (Cartwright, Lloyd, Butters, Weiner, McCarthy and Hancock, 1975; Empson and Clarke, 1970; Grieser, Greenberg and Harrison, 1972). Lewin and Glaubman (1975) actually report that REM-deprivation may improve recall of nonsense syllables. Those studies which do not show impairment invariably use rote-learned material, whereas studies which show impairment use material that may be learnt incidentally. Although there are claims that REM improves consolidation, the successful studies have only shown that recall performance may be adversely affected by REM-deprivation.

In a series of experiments, Ekstrand's group compared the sleep found in the first half of the night (containing a low proportion of REM) with the sleep found in the second half of the night (containing a high proportion of REM). They found that sleep in the first half of the night was more beneficial to LTM than sleep in the second half of the night, which in turn was more beneficial than wakefulness (Barrett and Ekstrand, 1972; Ekstrand, 1972; Fowler, Sullivan and Ekstrand, 1973; Yaroush, Sullivan and Ekstrand, 1971). Unfortunately, as little as half an hour's sleep immediately prior to learning will impair subsequent recall (Ekstrand et al., 1977; Stones, 1973, 1977; Worchel and Marks, 1951). This "prior sleep" effect seems to dissipate after about 6h sleep. It is difficult to assess Ekstrand's experiments, as most of his subjects and especially his "second half of the night" subjects will undoubtedly have been suffering from the effects of "prior sleep".

CONCLUSIONS

There is little doubt that STM is impaired when a subject is sleep-deprived. This is consistent with those studies that show STM performance to be superior in the morning and to decline progressively throughout the day (Baddeley, Hatter, Scott and Snashall, 1970; Blake, 1967). LTM is also impaired by sleep-deprivation. Although sleep has a modulating effect in both STM and LTM, it is not clear what mechanisms are involved or what stages of sleep are important.

ACKNOWLEDGEMENT

The author was supported by an MRC scholarship.

REFERENCES

Adam, K. and Oswald, I. (1977). Sleep is for tissue restoration. *Journal of the Royal College of Physicians*, 11, 376-388.

Baddeley, A.D., Hatter, J.E., Scott, D. and Snashall, A. (1970). Memory and time of day. *Quarterly Journal of Experimental Psychology*, 22, 605-609.

Barraco, R.A. and Stettner, L.J. (1976). Antibiotics and memory. *Psychological Bulletin*, 83, 242-302.

Barrett, T.R. and Ekstrand, B.R. (1972). Effects of sleep on memory: III Controlling for time-of-day effects. *Journal of Experimental Psychology*, 96, 321-327.

Benson, K. and Feinberg, I. (1975). Sleep and memory: Retention 8 and 24 hours after initial learning. *Psychophysiology*, 12, 192-195.

Benson, K. and Feinberg, I. (1977). The beneficial effect of sleep in an extended Jenkins and Dallenbach paradigm. *Psychophysiology*, 14, 375-384.

Blake, M.J.F. (1967). Time of day effects on performance in a range of tasks. *Psychonomic Science*, 9, 349-350.

Cartwright, R.D., Lloyd, S., Butters, E., Weiner, L. McCarthy, L. and Hancock, J. (1975). Effects of REM time on what is recalled. *Psychophysiology*, 12, 561-568.

Castaldo, V., Krynicki, V. and Goldstein, J. (1974). Sleep stages and verbal memory. *Perceptual and Motor Skills*, 39, 1022-1030.

Chernik, D.A. (1972). Effect of REM sleep deprivation on learning and recall by humans. *Perceptual and Motor Skills*, 34, 283-294.

Edwards, A.S. (1941). Effects of the loss of 100 hours of sleep. *American Journal of Psychology*, 54, 80-91.

Ekstrand, B.R. (1967). Effect of sleep on memory. *Journal of Experimental Psychology*, 75, 64-72.

Ekstrand, B.R. (1972). To sleep perchance to dream (about why we forget). In: *Festschrift for Benton J. Underwood*. (C.P. Duncan, L. Sechrest and A. Melton, eds), pp59-82, Appleton-Century-Crofts, New York.

Ekstrand, B.R., Barrett, T.R., West, J.N. and Maier, W.G. (1977). The effect of sleep on humand long-term memory. In: *Neurobiology of sleep and memory*. (R. Drucker-Colin and J.L. McGaugh, eds), pp419-438, Academic Press, New York.

Ekstrand, B.R., Sullivan, M.J. Parker, D.F. and West, J.N. (1971). Spontaneous recovery and sleep. *Journal of Experimental Psychology*, 88, 142-144.

Elkin, A.J. and Murray, D.J. (1974). The effects of sleep loss on short-term recognition memory. *Canadian Journal of Psychology*, 28, 192-198.

Empson, J.A.C. and Clarke, P.R.F. (1970). Rapid eye movements and remembering. *Nature*, 227, 287-288.

Feldman, R.E. (1969). *The effect of deprivation of rapid eye movement sleep on learning*. (Doctoral dissertation, Stanford University), University Microfilms, No. 70-1, 525; Ann Arbor.

Fishbein, W. and Gutwein, B.M. (1977). Paradoxical sleep and memory storage processes. *Behavioural Biology*, 19, 425-464.

Fowler, M. Sullivan, M. and Ekstrand, B.R. Sleep and memory. *Science*, 179, 302-304.

Gibb, J.R. (1937). *The relative effects of sleep and waking* (M.A. thesis, Brigham Young University).

Glassman, B.E. (1974). Macromolecules and behaviour: A commentary. In: *The Neurosciences, Third Study Program.* (F.O. Schmitt and F.G. Worden, eds), pp667-677, MIT Press, Cambridge, Mass.

Graves, E.A. (1937). The effect of sleep on retention. *Journal of Experimental Psychology*, 19, 316-322.

Grieser, C., Greenberg, R. and Harrison, R.H. (1972). The adaptive function of sleep: The differential effects of sleep and dreaming on recall. *Journal of Abnormal Psychology*, 80, 280-286.

Hockey, G.R.J., Davies, S. and Gray, M.M. (1972). Forgetting as a function of sleep at different times of day. *Quarterly Journal of Experimental Psychology*, 24, 386-393.

Jenkins, J.G. and Dallenbach, K.M. (1924). Oblivescence during sleep and waking. *American Journal of Psychology*, 35, 605-612.

Johnson, L.C., Naitoh, P., Moses, J.M. and Lubin, A. (1974). Interaction of REM deprivation and stage 4 deprivation with total sleep loss: Experiment 2. *Psychophysiology*, 11, 147-159.

Kollar, E.J., Pasnau, R.O., Rubin, R.T., Naitoh, P., Slater, G.G. and Kales, A. (1969). Psychological, Psychophysiological and Biochemical Correlates of prolonged sleep deprivation. *American Journal of Psychiatry*, 126, 70-79.

Lewin, I. and Glaubman, H. (1975). The effect of REM-deprivation: Is it detrimental, beneficial or neutral? *Psychophysiology*, 12, 349-353.

Lovatt, D.J. and Warr, P.B. (1968). Recall after sleep. *American Journal of Psychology*, 81, 253-257.

Lubin, A., Moses, J.M., Johnson, L.C. and Naitoh, P. (1974). The recuperative effects of REM sleep and stage 4 sleep on human performance after complete sleep loss: Experiment 1. *Psychophysiology*, 11, 133-146.

McGaugh, J.L. and Hostetter, R.C. (1961). In: *Introduction to Psychology*, (E.R. Hilgard and R.C. Atkinson), pp 338-339, 4th edition, Harcourt, Brace and World Inc., New York.

Muzio, J.N. (1971). *Alterations in the normal human sleep EEG pattern and retention of meaningful verbal material.* (Doctoral dissertation, Columbia University), University Microfilms, No. 72-4177, Ann Arbor.

Newman, E.B. (1939). Forgetting of meaningful material during sleep and waking. *American Journal of Psychology*, 52, 65-71.

Polzella, D.J. (1975). Effect of sleep-deprivation on short-term recognition memory. *Journal of Experimental Psychology, Human Learning and Memory*, 104, -94-200.

Richardson, A. and Gough, J.E. (1963). The long range effect of sleep on retention. *Australian Journal of Psychology*, 15, 37-41.

Rose, S.P.R., Hambley, J. and Haywood, J. (1976). Neurochemical approaches to developmental plasticity and learning. In: *Neural Mechanisms of Learning and Memory*. (M.R. Rosenzweig and E.L. Bennett, eds), pp293-310 MIT press, Cambridge, Mass.

Rudman, D. Freides, D. Patterson, J.H. and Gibbas, D.L. (1973). Diurnal variation in responsiveness to human growth hormone. *Journal of Clinical Investigation*, 52, 912-918.

Sampson, H. (1966). Psychological effects of deprivation of dreaming sleep. *Journal of Nervous and Mental Disorders*. 143, 305-317.

Sassin, J.F. (1977). Sleep-related hormones. In: *Neurobiology of sleep and memory*. (R. Drucker-Colin and J.L. McGaugh, eds), pp361-373, Academic Press, New York.

Stones, M.J. (1973). The effect of prior sleep on rehearsal, recoding and memory. *British Journal of Psychology*, 64, 537-543.

Stones, M.J. (1977). Memory performance after arousal from different sleep stages. *British Journal of Psychology*, 68, 177-181-

Van Ormer, E.B. (1933). Sleep and retention. *Psychological Bulletin*, 30, 415-439.

Vogel, G.W. (1975). A review of REM-sleep deprivation. *Archives of General Psychiatry*, 32, 749-761.

Vojtechovsky, M., Safratova, V., Votava, Z. and Feit, V. (1971). The effect of sleep-deprivation on learning and memory in healthy volunteers. *Activas Nervosa Superior*, 13, 143-144.

Weitzman, E.D. (1977). Memory and sleep: Neuroendocrinological considerations. In: *Neurobiology of Sleep and Memory*, (R. Drucker-Colin and J.L. McGaugh, eds), pp401-417, Academic Press, New York.

Williams, H.L., Giesking, C.F. and Lubin, A. (1966). Some effects of sleep loss on memory. *Perceptual and Motor Skills*, 23, 1287-1293.

Williams, H.L., Lubin, A. and Goodnow, J.J. (1959). Impaired performance with acute sleep loss. *Psychological Monographs*, 73, No.14 (Whole No. 484).

Williams, H.L. and Williams, C.L. (1966). Nocturnal EEG profiles and performance. *Psychophysiology*, 2, 164-175.
Worchel, P. and Marks, M.H. (1951). The effect of prior sleep on learning. *Journal of Experimental Psychology*, 42, 313-316.
Yaroush, R., Sullivan, M.J. and Ekstrand, B.R. (1971). Effect of sleep on memory: Differential effect of the first and second half of the night. *Journal of Experimental Psychology*, 88, 361-366.

SHORT-TERM MEMORY DURING THE NORMAL WORKING DAY

D. M. Jones
Department of Applied Psychology, UWIST, Cardiff
D.R. Davies, K.M. Hogan, J. Patrick and W.G. Cumberbatch
Department of Applied Psychology
University of Aston in Birmingham

ABSTRACT

Seven studies of short-term memory are described in which comparisons are made between performance in the morning and in the afternoon. No reliable time of day effects were found with four auditory tasks. Afternoon performance was superior in two visual tasks. This superiority was due to a reduction in errors in the recency portion of the serial position curve and was abolished by a 30-second filled delay between presentation and recall. No significant time of day effect was found for a visual task with a very slow presentation rate. Possible reasons for these findings are discussed.

INTRODUCTION

It is well established that the time of day at which testing is conducted can reliably affect performance at a number of different tasks (Hockey and Colquhoun, 1972). However the phenomenon is not clearly understood and no adequate explanation exists for the inconsistencies that are apparent in the research literature on this topic. Performance of most tasks tends to improve from early to late in the day; examples include card sorting and mental arithmetic, where speed of performance increases (Blake, 1967; Kleitman, 1939), vigilance (Blake, 1967; Colquhoun, 1962), letter cancellation and five-choice serial reaction performance (Blake, 1967) and mirror drawing, hand steadiness, copying and coding (Kleitman, 1939).

The direction of time of day effects on performance seems to depend on whether a memory or a non-memory task is employed. Performance on tasks requiring short-term retention tends to deteriorate as the day progresses. Using an auditory presentation, this result has been obtained with 9-digit span (Blake, 1967) and the immediate free recall of common bisyllabic nouns (Hockey, Davies and Gray, 1972). However, there is at least one study where the opposite result has been obtained. Adams (1973) found afternoon performance to be superior in a task requiring the recall of digit sequences varying in length from 7 to 11 items. Only the experiments of Baddeley *et al*. and of Adams employed testing times entirely within the normal working day and in Blake's study it is unclear which differences were significant since only the result of an analysis of variance was reported. The largest difference, however, was between scores obtained at 1030 and at 2130 hours.

In the experiments to be reported here we are concerned with variations in short-term memory during the working day. We have explored differences in presentation modality, presentation rate, the type of material to be recalled and the duration of the task as they affect the 'inverse' rhythm of memory. All the experiments have certain features in common. First, we tested independent groups of subjects, who were either University or Technical College students aged between 18 and 30, between 0800 and 1700 hours. Second, short-term retention was assessed using correct serial position scores. Third, in most cases, subjects were given some practice at the task before testing began.

AUDITORY SHORT-TERM MEMORY DURING THE NORMAL WORKING DAY

The first four experiments to be described employed auditory tasks. The first was a replication of Baddeley *et al*. (1970), although that experiment used a repeated measures design. Two groups of 16 male subjects performed a task requiring the immediate recall of 24 9-digit sequences. The presentation rate was 1 digit per second, 11 seconds were allowed for recall following the presentation of each sequence and the task duration was 8 minutes. One group of subjects performed the task between 0900 and 1030 hours and the other between 1500 and 1700 hours.

The second experiment was essentially the same as the first except that high-frequency monosyllabic words rather than digits were used as experimental materials. The task consisted of 20 9-word sequences and 30 seconds were allowed for recall following the presentation of each sequence. The task duration was 13 minutes. Two groups of 10 subjects, 5 men and 5 women, performed the task either in the morning (1000 hours) or the afternoon (1600 hours).

The third experiment used the same presentation rate as the first two (1 item per second) but required subjects to recall the letters from a 12-item mixed letter digit sequence (for example, 7L6K3H2N9R4X). This procedure was considered to demand some active organization of the material to be remembered. Twenty sequences were presented to two groups of 20 male subjects either at 0930 hours or at 1630 hours. Ten seconds were allowed for recall following each sequence and the task duration was approximately 8 minutes.

In the final auditory experiment, Experiment 4, a slower presentation rate (1 item per 3 seconds) was used, thus allowing greater opportunity for the rehearsal and recoding of the presented information. The task consisted of 5 lists of 12 high-frequency monosyllabic words. 1 minute was allowed for recall following each list and the task duration was approximately 10 minutes. Two groups of 12 subjects (8 men and 4 women) performed the task either at 0800 or at 1600 hours.

Results

The results of Experiments 1-4 are presented in Table 1 and it can be seen that no reliable effect of time of day was found in any experiment.

TABLE 1 : Percent correctly recalled in Experiments 1,2,3 and 4 in the morning (AM) and in the afternoon (PM) NS = No Significant difference

	AM	PM	
Experiment 1	77.9%	74.7%	NS
Experiment 2	47.3%	47.6%	NS
Experiment 3	77.2%	78.7%	NS
Experiment 4	31.2%	39.7%	NS

In Experiment 1 a slight difference of 3.2% favouring the morning group was found. This finding is in the same direction as that of Baddeley et al. (1970) who obtained a significant difference of 5.6%. The differences in Experiments 2 and 3 are even smaller than that of Experiment 1, being 0.3% and 1.5% respectively. The largest difference between morning and afternoon performance, 8.5%, was obtained in Experiment 4, in which a slower presentation rate was used, and here afternoon performance was superior. In the experiment oral temperature measures were taken before and after the experimental session and, as expected, were found to be significantly higher ($P<.05$) in the afternoon. There was thus a tendency for short-term memory to be positively related to body temperature, a result in the opposite direction to that obtained by Hockey et al. (1972). The results of these experiments, then, suggest that differences in the performance of auditory short-term memory tasks are slight and provide little evidence of morning superiority.

VISUAL SHORT-TERM MEMORY DURING THE NORMAL WORKING DAY

The remaining three experiments are concerned with the effects of time of day on visual memory. Since differences in arousal level between different times of day are sometimes put forward as an explanation of time of day effects upon performance (Baddeley _et al_., 1970), the level of arousal being assumed to be higher later in the day, Experiment 5 employed a visual memory task previously used in studies of the effects of induced arousal (Davies and Jones, 1975; Hockey and Hamilton, 1970). This task consisted of a sequence of 8 common bisyllabic adjectives, each word being presented in a different corner of the viewing screen, with the constraint that successive words should not appear in the same corner. Following the presentation of the 8-word sequence, at a rate of one item per 2 seconds, subjects were allowed 1 minute to recall the words and were subsequently asked to indicate the location in which each of the words had appeared. The task duration was thus about 1½ minutes. Compared to a control condition both loud noise and monetary incentives improve the recall of words (in terms of correct serial position scores) but impair the recall of locations. It was hypothesized that afternoon testing, compared to morning testing, would have similar effects and 17 male subjects were therefore tested on the task at 1000 hours and 25 male subjects at 1600 hours. The results of Experiment 5 are shown in Table 2 and it can be seen that this hypothesis is confirmed. The recall of words is significantly better in the afternoon ($P<.01$), while the recall of locations is better in the morning, although this differences is not significant.

TABLE 2 : Percent words correctly recalled and percent locations correctly recalled in the morning (AM) and the afternoon (PM) sessions of Experiment 5 NS = No significant difference

	AM	PM	
Percent words correctly recalled	42.0%	57.4%	$P<.01$
Percent locations correctly recalled	46.2%	39.3%	NS

An examination of morning and afternoon serial position curves revealed that the largest differences in error scores were found for items 5-8, with fewer errors being made in the afternoon. The difference for item 6 was significant ($P<.05$). The afternoon superiority for word recall thus results from the reduction of errors in the recency portion of the serial position curve.

In Experiment 6 a more conventional task was used in an attempt to confirm the results of Experiment 5 and at the same time to abolish or attenuate any recency effect by interposing a 30-second filled delay between presentation and recall. The task was a visual version of that used in Experiment 4 and consisted of 10 sequences of 12 high-frequency monosyllabic words. The presentation rate was 1 word per 3 seconds, 1 minute was allowed for recall and the task duration was approximately 12½ minutes. For each subject 5 lists were followed by immediate and 5 by delayed recall, randomized within the 10-list sequence. Subjects thus did not know whether they would be asked to recall a particular list immediately or after a delay. Whether or not subjects _know_ that recall will be immediate or delayed does not seem to affect the serial position curves obtained (Cumberbatch, 1971). During the delay period subjects counted backwards in 3s from a 3-digit number given to them at the end of the word sequence. Two groups of 12 subjects were tested either at 0930 or 1630 hours. The results are shown in Table 3. For immediate recall it can be seen that performance is reliably superior in the afternoon, while no such effect is apparent for delayed recall, although the direction of the difference is the same in both conditions. Serial position curves for morning and afternoon sessions were compared for both immediate and delayed recall. For immediate recall, differences in error rates were significant for item 12, the final item, and item 3 ($P<0.5$ in each case), fewer errors being made in the afternoon. No recency effect was observed for delayed recall and when serial position curves for morning and afternoon sessions were compared no significant differences were found. Differences between error rates for immediate and delayed recall over the last 4 serial positions were marked, particularly in the afternoon. It therefore appears that for this task, the recency portion of the serial position curve makes an important contribution to the overall difference in recall scores. Delayed recall abolishes the recency effect and prevents the occurrence of the time of day effect.

TABLE 3 : Percent correctly recalled for immediate and delayed recall conditions of Experiment 6 in the morning (AM) and afternoon (PM)
NS = No Significant difference

	AM	PM	
Immediate recall	25.1%	39.4%	$P<.05$
Delayed recall	13.8%	21.1%	NS

Experiments 4 and 6 were comparable in all respects except presentation modality. For immediate recall afternoon superiority was found in both cases but was reliable only for the visual task. Both experiments used slow presentation rates (1 item per 3 seconds) and in Experiment 7 an even slower presentation rate (1 item per 5 seconds) and a shorter list (9 items rather than 12) were employed in the expectation that a larger difference favouring the afternoon would be found. Slowing down the presentation rate exerts little effect on recency (Glanzer, 1972) but performance at visual memory tasks invariably improves (Penney, 1975), possibly because the material to be remembered is more actively processed. In Experiment 7 two groups of 9 subjects (6 men and 3 women) performed a task consisting of 10 sequences of 9 high-frequency monosyllabic words either at 1000 or at 1600 hours. One minute was allowed for recall after each list and the task duration was approximately 17½ minutes. The results are presented in Table 4. For the task as a whole there was

TABLE 4 : Percent correctly recalled in the morning (AM) and and afternoon (PM) sessions of Experiment 7 NS = No Significant difference

	AM	PM	
Whole task	60.9%	50.0%	NS
Second half only	68.6%	49.6%	$P<.05$

no effect of time of day, although there was a tendency for morning performance to be superior. However for the morning session a reliable improvement in performance ($P<.05$) emerged. When second-half serial position curves were compared, the greatest differences were found in the recency portion of the curve, error rates being significantly lower ($P<.05$) for items 7 and 8. In Experiment 7 then, for the second half of the task, the direction of the time of day effect found in Experiments 5 and 6 is reversed.

DISCUSSION

It is clear that although the effects of time of day on auditory memory are small, and in our experiments not significant, fairly substantial differences can be found between morning and afternoon performance when visual tasks are used. First, the results of Experiment 5 seem to indicate that afternoon testing increases the allocation of attention to a high priority task and in this respect resembles loud noise and monetary incentives, both of which have been considered to increase the level of arousal. Some support for the view that arousal level increases later in the day also comes from Experiment 4, in which body temperature was significantly higher in the afternoon and in which there was a tendency for memory performance and body temperature to be positively related. Thus similar results may be obtained, with some memory tasks at least, to those found with non-memory tasks, and, as Hockey and Colquhoun (1972) point out, an improvement in memory performance is frequently associated with an increase in arousal.

Second, the memory tasks showing reliable time of day differences have slow presentation rates and it is likely that presentation modality and presentation rate influence the type of processing strategy subjects adopt. Possibly visual presentation at slow rates tends to favour an active processing strategy, which is facilitated by an increase in arousal. The slower the presentation rate, the greater the opportunity for encoding to-be-remembered items in a variety of different ways. However, increasing the variety of encoding operations may improve performance only up to a certain point and thereafter impair it, depending upon the task demands. Where the task is to link together in sequence a series of items, too great a breadth of encoding may cause performance to deteriorate. This possibility is tentatively put forward as an explanation of the results in Experiment 7.

Third, time of day effects, whatever their direction, seem to be largely attributable to a reduction in recency errors. This could result from attentional changes, an enhancement of primary memory capacity or a shift of processing strategy and, no doubt, there are other possible explanations. Further experiments using different kinds of memory task and varying different task parameters may help to illuminate these possibilities.

REFERENCES.

Adams, A.H. (1973) Time of day effects on short term memory. *Royal Aircraft Establishment Technical Memorandum HFG*, 122, 1-9.

Baddeley, A.D., Hatter, J.E., Scott, D. and Snashall, A. (1970) Memory and time of day. *British Journal of Psychology*, 22, 605-609.

Blake, M.J.F. (1967) Time of day effects on the performance in a range of tasks. *Psychonomic Science*, 13, 103-104.

Colquhoun, W.P. (1962) The effects of a small dose of alcohol and of certain other factors on performance in a vigilance task. *Bulletin du CERP*, 11, 27-44.

Cumberbatch, W.G. (1971) Rehearsal and recall in short-term memory. *Unpublished doctoral dissertation, University of Leicester*.

Davies, D.R. and Jones, D.M. (1975) The effects of noise and incentive upon attention in short-term memory. *British Journal of Psychology*, 66, 61-68.

Glanzer, M. (1972) Storage mechanisms in recall. In : *The Psychology of Learning and Motivation*. (G. Bower, ed.) 129-193. Academic Press, London.

Hockey, G.R.J. and Colquhoun, W.T. (1972) Diurnal variation in human performance : a review. In :*Aspects of Human Efficiency*. (W.P. Colquhoun, ed.) 1-24. English Universities Press, London.

Hockey, G.R.J. and Hamilton, P. (1970) Arousal and information selection in short-term memory. *Nature*, 226, 866-867

Hockey, G.R.J., Davies, S. and Gray, M.M. (1972) Forgetting as a function of sleep and phase of the circadian cycle. *Quarterly Journal of Experimental Psychology*, 24, 386-393.

Kleitman, N. (1939) *Sleep and Wakefulness*. Chicago University Press, Chicago.

Penney, C.G. (1975) Modality effects in short-term verbal memory. *Psychological Bulletin*, 82, 68-84.

NOISE AND MEMORY

J. Russell Thomas
Department of Applied Psychology,
UWIST, Cardiff, Wales.

ABSTRACT

This paper critically evaluates studies showing effects of noise on retention. Views which emphasize noise effects at input are contrasted with results which indicate beneficial effects of noise at output. The role of noise as an inducer of strategic changes in memory is considered and special emphasis is placed upon experimental evidence indicating changes in subjects' caution in noise. Such studies are contrasted with those which have considered noise to act by narrowing attentional focus and with experiments which consider that noise interacts with task difficulty. The evidence indicates that noise effects upon memory are beneficial for long term recall but in the case of immediate recall are dependent upon noise intensity. It is also apparent that noise effects are often mediated by changes in the subjects' level of caution.

INTRODUCTION

Studies investigating the effects of noise-induced arousal on memory have often considered the situation as being due to the cognitive value of noise as an aversive stimulus, rather than its function as an arouser. The present paper explores some of the effects of noise on memory which may be due to cognitive factors rather than changes in the level of physiological arousal. The role of cognitive factors in situations where physiological arousal exists has been well established (Schacter and Singer, 1962). It therefore is highly probable that the supposedly arousing source can have a strategic effect on the subject's performance, other than one conventionally associated with an increase in non-specific arousal level.

In a recent review of arousal and memory Jones (1979) has proposed that noise acts by altering the processing strategies that the subject adopts, rather than affecting the general level of arousal. He also states that the existing evidence indicates that noise brings about strategic changes rather than changes in processing capacity or changes in the contents of a particular store. In support of this view Jones cites two lines of evidence. The first is that there are indications that noise influences the organisation of material by changing the use of cues for recall. The second is that there is evidence of a consistent interaction between noise and task difficulty, which indicates that noise may bring about changes in caution.

EFFECTS AT INPUT AND OUTPUT

Attempts to find the locus of noise induced deficits have been equivocal in demonstrating effects at input or output. The influence of noise on memory tasks has been seen to occur at either the input or retrieval stages. Work by Berlyne and his colleagues at Toronto has emphasised the role of noise induced arousal (NIA) acting as a "reinforcer" of the learned material. This view has evolved out of a series of studies (Berlyne, Borsa, Craw, Gelman and Mandell 1965; Berlyne, Borsa, Hamacher and Koenig 1966; Berlyne and Carey 1968) in which moderate (72dB to 75dB) and high (85db to 90dB) levels of noise at encoding have been shown to result in improved recall 24 hours after the initial learning trial. When immediate recall is considered, the findings are less clear cut. Berlyne *et al.*(1965) and McLean (1969) both reported impaired immediate recall, whereas Berlyne *et al.*(1966) and Wickelgren (1975) all reported no effect on immediate recall. When impairment of immediate recall has been found, it has been attributed to action decrement (Walker 1958) which is seen as inhibiting short term recall in order to preserve the trace and to protect it against disruption, thereby providing a stronger long-term trace.

When slightly lower noise intensities are used (65dB) Berlyne *et al.*(1965) and Wesner (1972), improved immediate recall is the usual result. Berlyne *et al.*(1965) have postulated that there exists a non-monotonic relationship between the intensity of the arousal source and recall. The general form of this relationship is taken to be that of an inverted "U". Such a view is supported by Uehling and Spinkle (1968). They found that material learned in quiet showed improved recall 24 hours and one week later, if subjects were subjected to three minutes of intermittent white noise prior to testing. Subjects showed no improvement on an immediate recall task but this was considered to be due to a ceiling effect as both subjects in quiet and with NIA were operating at the maximum level of performance. These findings were interpreted as implying that there exists an optimal level of physiological arousal at which task performance is maximised.

From the above studies it would appear that noise is having an effect both at input and output stages. If an effect occurs at output, it implies that there cannot be any modification of the existing engram, and therefore any improvement in recall must be due to a change in retrieval strategy. One possible effect may be a change in decision criterion.

STRATEGIC CHANGES

Schwartz (1974) was interested in the hypothesis that noise acts by affecting the retrieval strategy of "pigeonholing" (Broadbent 1971) rather than by affecting the input strategy of filtering. Evidence for such a view comes from the work of Broadbent and Gregory (1965) who found that in a vigilance task, noise influenced the subjects' response criterion in their judgements of confidence. In quiet, subjects tended to use intermediate levels of confidence, whereas in noise they made judgements at more extreme confidence levels. Such a finding would seem to favour a pigeonholing interpretation of noise effects rather than one based upon filtering. Items processed using a filtering strategy are selected at input on the basis of their possessing a particular feature. Thus any noise effects at input would be reflected in changes in the decision theory measure of d', which has been associated with a filtering interpretation. Pigeonholing occurs at output and represents a bias towards responding with certain category states. Changes in this strategy are reflected in the decision theory parameter of β (Broadbent 1971, Schwartz 1974).

Schwartz (1974) found that noise influenced both the parameters of d' and β in a task where subjects were required to give confidence judgements to probe items in a recognition task. Subjects in quiet tended to employ significantly more cautious criteria for items of low taxonomic frequency (rare surnames) and riskier criteria for items of high taxonomic frequency (common surnames). In noise, subjects adopted similar criteria for both classes of surname. At the same time the d' measure of sensitivity indicated an increase in sensitivity for common surnames. The results of this study were interpreted by Schwartz (1974) as supporting the hypothesis that arousal affects the accessibility of information for retrieval and thereby supporting an interpretation based on pigeonholing.

There are a number of features of Schwartz's (1974) study which do not agree well with previous work. First is the finding that in terms of hit rate and d', common surnames were superior to rare surnames. These findings contrast with those of Ingleby (1969), Schulman (1974) and Rabinowitz, Mandeler and Patterson (1977) who found that recognition of items of low taxonomic frequency was superior, in terms of both hit rate and d', to items of high taxonomic frequency. The second aspect of Schwartz's (1974) study that is problematical is the interaction of changes in β with d'. It is possible that the d' change for common surnames represents a facilitatory effect of noise at input and therefore detracts to some extent from the pigeonholing interpretation in favour of one emphasizing filtering. Schwartz (1974) suggests that the d' changes he found could be due to auditory masking by the noise source of the auditorily presented material.

In an attempt to clarify Schwartz's (1974) findings an experiment was undertaken in which a prose passage was presented visually (see Jones and Thomas, in preparation, for a detailed description). There were two main reasons for this modification of Schwartz's (1974) procedure. First to see if auditory masking could account for the observed changes. If d' changes occurred with visual presentation this would lend support to a filtering interpretation possibly as a result of 'central masking'. This latter view is due to Poulton (1977) who proposes that noise, acts by masking sub-vocal articulation in a rehearsal loop. The second aim of this experiment was to test a later theoretical interpretation of his study by Schwartz (1975). In this interpretation he associates change in d' with changes in the encoding of episodic components of memory and changes in β with semantic memory. He therefore sees noise acting in such a way as to increase the time and effort needed to encode the memory trace at the cost of the semantic components. This reduced level of semantic processing arises out of the time pressure imposed by his auditory mode of presentation. Less time pressure should be evident with visual presentation and hence this mode of presentation would offer an opportunity for deeper semantic processing.

In this study, subjects were presented with a prose passage, via a TV monitor, in either noise (85dB) or quiet (60dB) conditions. All subjects were tested on recognition of three classes of material: rare surnames, common surnames, and individual words. The recognition task was presented in quiet and consisted of transcripts of the presented stories in which some of the items were underlined. Subjects had to indicate their judgements and level of certainty as to the presence of the underlined item in the original material. The mode of presentation was such that subjects had ample opportunity to recapitulate sections of the material.

The results of the study are in two main sections. First the findings of Schwartz (1974), with regard to the drop in β for rare surnames in noise was replicated and found to be significant at $p < 0.05$. At the same time there was no increase in β for common surnames as had occurred in Schwartz's (1974) study, in fact there was a modest decline in β for common surnames. This suggests that these differences between the two studies may be due to an effect based upon the initial values of β in quiet. This is similar to a view proposed by Broadbent (1971) who proposed that there exists a null point of β at which β will remain unchanged when arousal is increased and that all values above and below this point will converge to the null point when arousal is increased.

A second aspect of the findings are those associated with hit rate and d'. Hit rate data in this study indicated a significant main effect ($p < 0.01$) due to the class of stimulus, the rank order of which (rare surnames, common surnames and synonyms) agree with those found in previous studies (Ingleby 1969, Schulman 1974, Rabinowitz et al.1977). There was no main effect of noise nor an interaction between class of stimuli and noise level. The d' findings largely mirror those for hit rate with the difference between classes of stimuli being significant ($p < 0.01$) but in contrast there was no main effect of noise nor an interaction between class of stimuli and noise level.

One of the main aspects of the study that contrasts with that of Schwartz (1974) was the absence of an interaction between d' and β with noise. The lack of such an interaction when combined with the drop in β for rare surnames in noise substantially supports Broadbent's (1971) pigeonholing hypothesis. At the same time the lack of any significant increase in d' with noise also supports such a view. Schwartz's (1974) contention that his d' changes are due to auditory masking is brought into doubt by these findings. Auditory masking would lead to a change in d' rather than β.

The lack of a significant effect on d' in noise also casts doubts on the central masking hypothesis. It might be expected that interference by noise of items in a sub-vocal articulatory loop would be reflected in a decline in input sensitivity (d').

EFFECTS OF ATTENTIONAL FOCUSSING AND TASK DIFFICULTY

A view that places noise effects at input has been developed out of Easterbrook's (1959) proposal that increased arousal results in a narrowing of attention. A study by Hockey and Hamilton (1970) indicated that noise presented during a paired associates task resulted in the focussing of attention on the high priority task accompanied by a diminution in the encoding of secondary material. One aspect of Hockey *et al.'s* (1970) data which indicated an improvement of recall performance in noise was their finding that recall in correct order was superior (P = 0.055) in noise to that in quiet. This finding was further supported by Hamilton, Hockey and Quinn (1972), who found that noise facilitated the recall of order information without any corresponding loss of associative pairings. They emphasised that in conditions of high arousal subjects take in less information, but attend to it more, and that the extra capacity so allocated is used to preserve order information. In contrast Dornic (1975) sees noise acting like other methods of increasing task difficulty such that subjects adopt a more rudimentary method of processing material. This method of processing increases the probability that subjects will adopt a strategy of "parroting back" material which they have learned. It would appear that it is as a result of such a "parroting back" strategy that Hamilton *et al.* (1972) obtained their results indicating increased recall of order information. Other studies which have provided supportive evidence for Dornic's (1975) view are those which have shown a decrease in clustering during recall in noise. A recent study by Daee and Wilding (1977) also provides evidence to show that order cues are better recalled in noise than in quiet. One factor from their study which proves to be problematical to Dornic's (1975) view is that recall of sequence was optimal at 75dB and was impaired both in quiet and 85dB of noise. Such a finding cannot be accounted for by either Dornic's (1975) or Hamilton *et al.*'s (1972) views.

CONCLUSIONS

To summarise the main points, there appears to be unequivocal evidence that noise during encoding facilitates recall after a delay of 24 hours. It would appear that such facilitation can also be achieved by subjecting subjects to a short period of noise induced arousal prior to recall, particularly for material originally learned in quiet. From a theoretical point of view these two findings are in conflict with each other, with one emphasising noise effects at encoding and one at retrieval, but a degree of harmony can be achieved in the case of studies using paired associates by classifying findings on the basis of the noise intensity used in the study. A noise level of 65dB appears to be optimal for immediate recall, with studies using noise at this intensity demonstrating facilitation of recall. Studies using moderate noise intensities often show no effect of noise and those studies using high intensities showing a detrimental effect of noise. In studies which have looked at changes in recall strategy the results would seem to indicate that noise acts by altering the subject's degree of caution at recall. One other effect of noise is its tendency to cause subjects to adopt a lower and more rudimentary level of processing. This lower level of processing increases the probability that subjects will adopt a linear recall strategy and parrot back learned material.

In conclusion it would appear from these different lines of research of noise effects upon memory, that noise is having effects other than those resulting from increased activation of the nervous system. These effects can be combined under the rubric of strategy changes, which often include changes in the subject's level of caution. One ubiquitous factor in the present review is the tendency for noise effects to be non-monotonically related to performance. It would seem probable that as noise intensity increases, subjects adopt differing strategies in an attempt to maintain a high level of successful performance and that at very high noise intensities these strategies often break down.

REFERENCES

Berlyne, D.E., Borsa, D.M., Craw, M.A., Gelman, R.S. and Mandell, E.E. (1965). Effects of stimulus complexity and induced arousal on paired-associate learning. *Journal of Verbal Learning and Verbal Behaviour*. 4, 291-299

Berlyne, D.E., Borsa, D.M., Hamacher, J.H. and Koenig, I.D.V. (1966). Paired-associate learning and the timing of arousal. *Journal of Experimental Psychology*. 72, 1-6.

Berlyne, D.E. and Carey, S.T. (1968). Incidental learning and the timing of arousal. *Psychonomic Science*. 13, 103-104.

Broadbent, D.E. (1971). *Decision and stress*. Academic Press, London.

Broadbent, D.E. and Gregory, M. (1965). Effects of noise and signal rate upon vigilance analysed by means of decision theory. *Human Factors*. 7, 155-162.

Daee, S. and Wilding, J.M. (1977). Effects of high intensity white noise on short-term memory for position in a list sequence. *British Journal of Psychology*. 68, 335-349.

Dornic, S. (1975). Some studies on the retention of order information. In : *Attention and performance*. Vol. 5. (P.M.A. Rabbitt and S. Dornic eds), pp 203-239. Academic Press, London

Hamilton, P., Hockey, G.R.J. and Quinn, J.G. (1972). Information selection, arousal and memory. *British Journal of Psychology*. 63, 181-189.

Hockey, G.R.J. and Hamilton, P. (1970). Arousal and information selection in short-term memory. *Nature*, London. 226, 866-867.

Ingleby, J.D. (1969). *Decision-making processes in human perception and memory*. Ph.D. Thesis, University of Cambridge, Cambridge.

Jones, D.M. (1979). Stress, arousal and memory. In *Applied Problems in Memory*. (M. Gruneberg and P. Morris eds). Academic Press, London.

Jones, D.M. and Thomas, J.R. (1979). Memory for prose items in noise. In preparation.

McLean, P.D. (1969). Induced arousal and the time of recall as determinants of paired-associate recall. *British Journal of Psychology.* 60, 57-62.

Poulton, E.C. (1977). Continuous intense noise masks auditory feedback and inner speech. *Psychological Bulletin.* 5, 977-1001.

Rabinowitz, J.C., Mandler, G. and Patterson, K.E. (1977). Determinants of recognition and recall: accessibility and generation. *Journal of Experimental Psychology: General.* 106, 303-329.

Schacter, S. and Singer, J.E. (1962). Cognitive, social and physiological determinants of emotional state. *Psychological Review.* 69, 379-399.

Schulman, A.I. (1974). The declining course of recognition memory. *Memory and Cognition.* 2, 14-18.

Schwartz, S. (1974). Arousal and recall: effects of noise on two retrieval strategies. *Journal of Experimental Psychology.* 102, 896-898.

Schwartz, S. (1975). Decision processes in recognition memory. In : *Human judgement and decision processes.* (M.F. Kaplan and S, Schwartz eds), Academic Press, New York.

Sloboda, W. and Smith, E.S. (1968). Disruption effects in human short-term memory: some negative findings. *Perceptual and Motor Skills.* 27, 575-582.

Ushling, B.S. and Spinkle, R. (1968). Recall of a serial list as a function of arousal and retention interval. *Journal of Experimental Psychology.* 78, 103-106.

Walker, E.K. (1958). Action decrement and its relation to attention. *Psychological Review.* 65, 129-142.

Wesner, C.E. (1972). Induced arousal and word-recognition learning be mongoloids and normals. *Perceptual and Motor Skills.* 35, 586.

Wickelgren, W.A. (1975). Alcoholic intoxication and memory storage dynamics. *Memory and Cognition.* 3, 385-389.

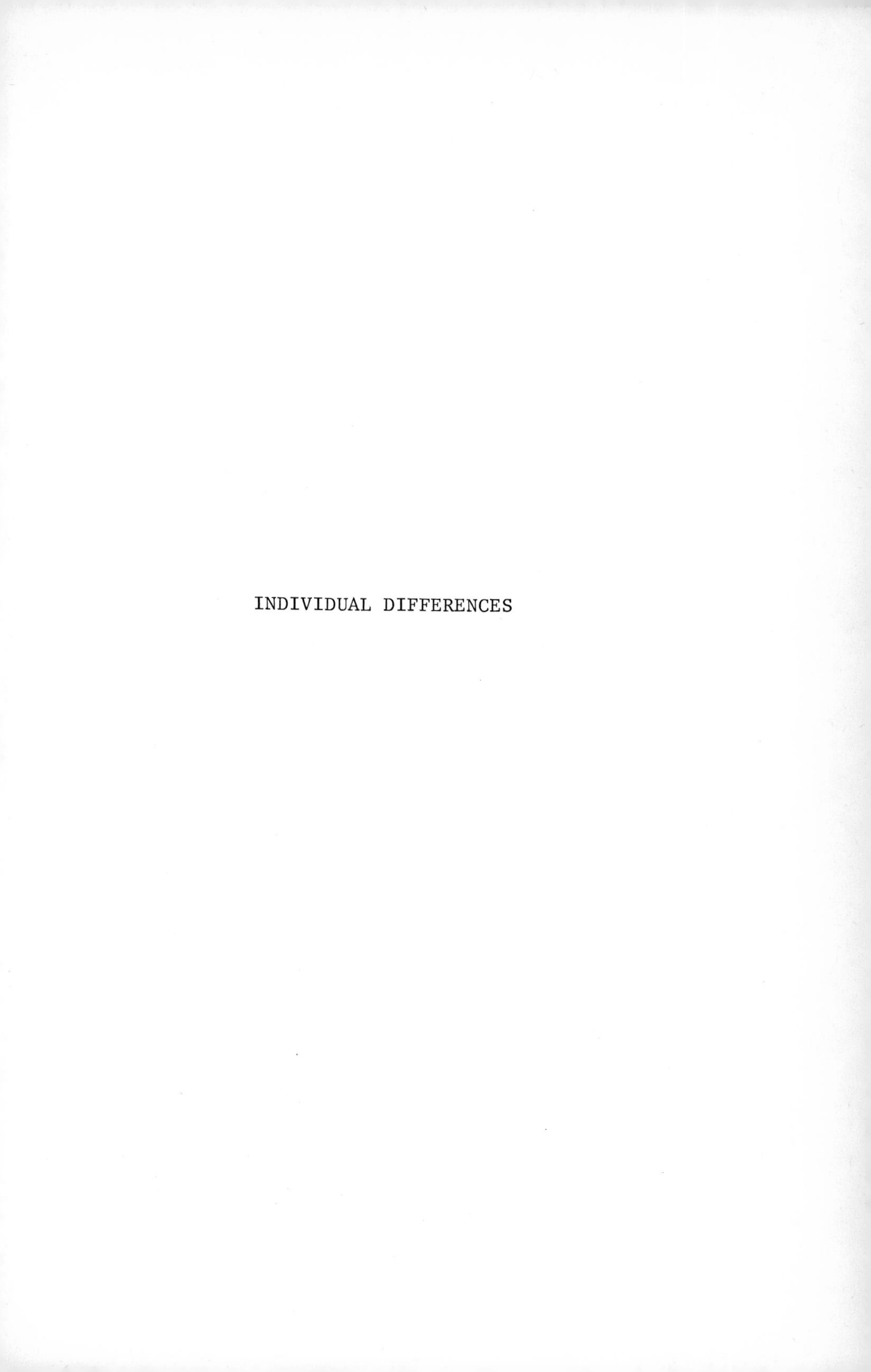

INDIVIDUAL DIFFERENCES

THE ROLE OF MEMORY IN EXPERT MENTAL CALCULATIONS

I. M. L. Hunter
Department of Psychology,
University of Keele,
Staffordshire, England.

In this paper I shall consider memory as a resource which serves the purposes of numerical calculation at large and of expert mental calculation in particular. So, to set the scene, let me ask: what does numerical calculation, mental or otherwise, require in the way of memory resources?

1. WHAT DOES CALCULATION DEMAND OF MEMORY?

Numerical calculation can be done in a very great variety of ways, e.g., by paper and pencil, by electronic computer, by abacus, by logarithms, entirely in the head. But however it is done, it always makes demands on memory. Furthermore, these demands are always of three distinguishable kinds. (i) Memory for calculative method. (ii) Memory for numerical equivalents. (iii) Memory for interrupted working. To illustrate, consider a sample calculation.

Suppose you are asked to multiply 123 by 456 and suppose you work the problem by using a paper-and-pencil procedure which is commonly taught in school. You write down the two numbers, as shown, and go through a sequence of steps.

```
  456
  123
 1368
 912
456
56088
```

3 times 6 is 18, write 8, carry 1; 3 times 5 is 15, add 1, write 6, carry 1; and so on until you reach the answer, the digits of which will appear in right-to-left sequence.

This calculation shows the three demands on memory. (i) Memory for calculative method, i.e., for a schematic procedure which decomposes your working into a pre-arranged sequence of steps. (ii) Memory for numerical equivalents, e.g., that 3 times 6 is equivalent to 18, that 3 times 5 is 15, that 6 plus 2 is 8. These equivalents are the basic constituent steps of your calculation. (iii) Memory for interrupted working. At several junctures you leave a loose end which you lay aside temporarily while you get on with something else, and to which you later return.

Notice that you meet the first two demands mainly by calling on your long-term memory. You run off the calculative method you learned at school and, in the process, you throw up a succession of specific numerical questions which you answer from your learnt repertoire of numerical equivalents. By contrast, you meet the third demand by using some form of temporary storage. Significantly, you do not keep every loose end in your head but write most of them on paper, each in a pre-arranged location where you can find it later. The writing serves as an external memory store without which you would have great difficulty in dealing with memory for interrupted working.

2. EXPERT MENTAL CALCULATORS

Expert mental calculators, like virtuosos in any sphere, differ greatly, one from another, in the details and in the style of their working. Also we must appreciate that the methods of calculation which are taught in school are not generally suitable for use without external memory aids; and for this reason, we are likely to be struck by the unconventionality of the methods used by expert mental calculators. These unconventional methods are highly intriguing but, in this paper, I wish to concentrate on general characteristics. So let us ask: how, in general terms, do expert mental calculators satisfy the three types of memory demand made by their calculations? The answer turns out to be clear, and it runs as follows.

Experts have, through years of experience, acquired a vastly large fund of numerical equivalents upon which they can draw with speed and accuracy. Experts have also acquired a large repertoire of calculative methods which enables them to calculate in ways that make maximally effective use of the fund of equivalents and which keep interrupted working to a minimum. In short, experts build up vast resources of long-term memory, and they shift the burden of calculation onto long-term memory while, at the same time, minimizing their reliance on temporary memory.

To illustrate what expert mental calculation can be like, listen to a tape-recorded excerpt from a session I held with A. C. Aitken, a virtuoso if ever there was one. (In the tape, I ask him to square the following three-digit numbers: 281, 572, 193, and 915. Then to express the following fractions as decimals: 3/408, 2/63, 3/78, and 1/752. I then give the following numbers and, for each, he has to say whether it is a prime or, if not, what its factors are: 113, 719, 533, 391, 871, 1211, 313, 417, 529.) This recording shows us calculation which is impressively rapid and yet is clearly being done by a human being and not a robot. Here is ingenuity and skill and intelligence in action.

The recording leaves us in no doubt that Aitken has, in long-term memory, a vast store of rapidly accessible numerical equivalents. Consider how this store serves his calculative performances. For example, when asked to multiply 123 by 456, he is silent for two seconds and then speaks the answer, 56088, giving the digits in their natural left-to-right order (as he always does, for he works with numbers and not digits). Then he comments as follows. "I do this in two moves: I see at once that 123 times 45 is 5535 and that 123 times 6 is 738; I hardly have to think. Then 55350 plus 738 gives 56088. Even at the moment of registering 56088, I have checked it by dividing by 8, so 7011, and this by 9, 779. I recognize 779 as 41 by 19; and 41 by 3 is 123, 19 by 24 is 456. A check you see; and it passes by in about one second." Notice how the working is decomposed into large, prefabricated segments which he handles by appeal to long-term memory; and how, as a consequence, he does relatively little actual calculation. His store of numerical equivalents saves a lot of calculative effort.

Here is another example which illustrates the same general point. After calculating the decimal equivalent of the fraction 1/851, Aitken comments as follows. "The instant observation was that 851 is 23 times 37. I use this fact as follows. 1/37 is 0.027027027 and so on repeated. This I divide mentally by 23. 23 into 0.027 is 0.001 with remainder 4. In a flash I can get that 23 into 4027 is 175 with remainder 2. And into 2027 is 88 with remainder 3. And into 3027 is 131 with remainder 14. And even into 14027 is 609 with remainder 20. And so on like that. Also, before I even start this, I know that there is a recurring period of sixty-six places."

In addition to his store of numerical equivalents, Aitken also has a store of unconventional calculative methods. The following quotation from Aitken illustrates the point. "It is not generally known that one can divide by a number like 59, or 79, or 109, or 599, and so on, by short division. Take for example 1/59, which is nearly 1/60. Set out the division thus:

```
6 / 1.016949152...
    0.0169491525...
```

Here we have the decimal for 1/59, obtained by dividing 1 by 60; as we obtain each digit we merely enter it in the dividend, one place later, and continue with the division. As another example consider 5/23. Write it as 15/69. Then proceed:

```
7 / 15.21739130...
     0.217391304...
```

One could equally well have written it as 65/299, then carrying out division by 3, two digits at a time, and entering in the dividend two places further along."

To return to general considerations, notice that all of the above examples involve interrupted working with which Aitken has no difficulty. Does this not contradict what I said earlier about experts keeping interrupted working to a minimum? It does not, and for the following reason. Given Aitken's resources of long-term memory, there are at least four aspects which help, up to a point, to make light work of temporary memory. Firstly, a number, such as 5535, is a distinctive entity which is easy to remember. Secondly, the speed of working reduces the time during which loose ends need to be held in temporary store. Thirdly, in the decimalizing examples, he is pursuing a familiar, repeated cycle of operations on which he has a well practised grip. Fourthly, when going through a repeated cycle of operations, he makes use of a strong, steady rhythm which helps him, as it were, to throw forward a loose end and then catch it at an appropriate later moment -- like a footballer dribbling a ball.

In the light of these considerations, then, we see that the above calculations place no great strain on Aitken's temporary memory. However, numerical problems do arise which threaten even Aitken with excessive demands on temporary memory. When this happens, he either hits on a method which minimizes the extent of interrupted working, or he reaches for external memory-aids such as paper-and-pencil or a calculating machine.

Let me now return to the central question: what role does memory play in expert mental calculations? And let me attempt a two-part answer which applies, not only to Aitken, but to all virtuoso mental calculators about whom we have a reasonable amount of information. Firstly, the expert brings to the calculation unusually large resources of long-term memory, that is, a store of numerical equivalents and calculative methods. These resources enable the expert to detect an efficient way of tackling the problem and to carry through the working in a rapid, orderly sequence of large steps. Secondly, in contrast to these resources of long-term memory, the expert has relatively slender resources by which to meet the demands of temporary memory. The expert goes quite a way to meet these demands, partly by the speed and quality of working, and partly by devising calculative methods which evade an excess of interrupted working. But there comes a point at which the demands of temporary memory can no longer be met. At this point, the expert must, like the rest of us, seek the assistance of external memory aids.

3. ACQUIRING THE STORE OF KNOWLEDGE

We have seen that expert mental calculators depend heavily on a large, readily accessible store of knowledge about numerical equivalences and calculative methods. Such a store is not acquired overnight but through years of experience and practice. Now, if we generalize from our own experiences at school, we might suppose that the acquisition of this store involves a great deal of deliberate memorization. Interestingly, the biographies of the experts show that this supposition is wrong. The store builds up, piece by piece, as a byproduct of its usefulness in pursuits which interest the individual. There is relatively little deliberate memorization bleakly undertaken for its own sake: if there were, the likely outcome would be boredom and discouragement.

Consider the three experts A. C. Aitken, G. P. Bidder, and S. Devi. They differ considerably in their social backgrounds and in their developmental paths. But in their formative years, each found in numbers and in calculations a field which was thrilling for its own sake. They enjoyed exploring this field, discovering new things about it, finding new ways of tackling problems, and developing their competence. In later years, to be sure, each of the three turned their calculative skill to other ends but, in the early stages, the skill was acquired as an end in itself.

To illustrate, listen to a comment made by Aitken. "It is a good exercise to ask oneself the question: what can be said about this number? Where does it occur in mathematics, and in what context? What properties has it? For instance, is it a prime of the form $4n+1$, and so expressible as the sum of two squares in one way only? Is it the numerator of a Bernoullian number, or one occurring in some continued fraction? And so on. Sometimes a number has almost no properties at all, like 811, and sometimes a number, like 41, is deeply involved in many theorems that you know." This is the comment of someone who already knows a lot about numbers and is using this knowledge to find out more. The comment reflects an exploratory process which will lead to an enlarged store of knowledge, but not through voluntary memorization as normally understood.

The main point is that the store of knowledge is acquired as a byproduct of its interest and use rather than through head-on memorization. This point seems to hold for experts in any field whatever -- music, language, horticulture, the law. In the acquisition of expertise over the years, what always seems to matter most is interest, use, and usefulness. This point is, in a way, obvious. But it is too easily lost sight of when we focus narrowly on memory processes which occupy only seconds, minutes, or even days.

4. THE TREND TOWARD EXTERNAL STORAGE

In everyday life most people calculate by using external memory-aiding devices of some sort -- written records, printed tables, calculating machines. Furthermore, the history of numerical calculation throughout the centuries is dominated by a trend toward a greater and greater use of external storage devices as a way of meeting the memory demands of calculation.

To illustrate, an early external memory-aid was the counting-board or counting-frame on which pebbles or beads were placed and physically moved around: the word 'calculate' comes from the Latin calculus, meaning 'a small stone'. A later external aid was a written notation for numbers (the arabic notation we use today) which made it possible to calculate by writing. These two devices help mainly with memory for interrupted working. Other external memory-aids help mainly by providing a ready made store of numerical equivalents, e.g., ready-reckoners and printed multiplication tables. Yet other external aids help mainly by providing shortcut methods, e.g., slide-rules and tables of logarithms. In the present day, the historical trend toward external storage is best exemplified by the electronic computer which enables people to relegate most of their calculative effort to a device which provides an external store of numerical equivalents and calculative methods, and an external means of storing interrupted working.

Now, mental calculators clearly fly in the face of this historical trend toward external storage. For this reason, high expertise in mental calculation may well become a thing of the past. In present-day literate culture, there is little incentive to develop such expertise. It is not, in practical terms, competitive with calculation as done by, say, an electronic computer. Nor is it granted the social value of an art or of an athletic sport. In the modern world, the development of high expertise in mental calculation is not so much laudible as freakish, and so it is probably doomed to extinction, except possibly in so-called underdeveloped parts of the world. If this is so, we are fortunate to have some information about expert mental calculations because, as I hope I have shown, it illumines our understanding of the functions and uses of memory.

REFERENCES

Aitken, A.C. (1954) The art of mental calculation: with demonstrations. *Transactions of the Society of Engineers, London*, 44, 295-309.

Bidder, G.P. (1956) On mental calculation. *Minutes of Proceedings, Institution of Civil Engineers*, 15, 251-280.

Binet, A. (1894) *Psychologie des Grand Calculateurs et Joueurs d'Echecs*. Hachette, Paris.

Devi, S. (1977) *Figuring*. Andre Deutsch, London.

Hunter, I.M.L. (1962) An exceptional talent for calculative thinking. *British Journal of Psychology*, 53, 243-258.

Hunter, I.M.L. (1977) An exceptional memory. *British Journal of Psychology*, 68, 155-164.

Hunter, I.M.L. (1977) Mental calculation. In: *Thinking*. (P.N. Johnson-Laird and P.C. Wasen, eds), pp. 35-45. Cambridge University Press.

Kojima, T. (1954) *The Japanese Abacus*. Tuttle, Tokyo.

Menninger, K. (1969) *Number Words and Number Symbols*. The M.I.T. Press, Cambridge, Massachusetts.

Mitchell, F.D. (1907) Mathematical prodigies. *American Journal of Psychology*, 18, 61-143.

Scripture, E.W. (1891) Arithmetical prodigies. *American Journal of Psychology*, 4, 1-59.

INDIVIDUAL DIFFERENCES IN THE RELATION OF RECOGNITION TO RECALL

J. Brown and A. Monk
University of Bristol, Department of Psychology, 8-10, Berkeley Square, Bristol, England.

The potential importance of individual differences in the relationship of recall to recognition is discussed and two studies are described. In the first, involving tests of both episodic and semantic memory, no individual differences of this type were found and recall recognition correlations were correspondingly high. In the second, where learning was to a recall criterion with study and test phases alternating, individual differences in the relationship emerged.

INTRODUCTION

We all know that there are individual differences in memory. We also know that memory can be assessed by either a recall or a recognition method. Consequently it is not surprising if there are individual differences in recall and there are individual differences in recognition. If recall and recognition make the same demands on memory, then these two sets of individual differences should be perfectly correlated. However, there is evidence that learning for recall and learning for recognition are not identical. If there are individual differences in these two learning abilities, individual differences in recognition and recall will *not* correlate perfectly. Put another way, there will be individual differences in the relation of recognition to recall. Such individual differences will be called RRIDs (Recognition-Recall-Individual-Differences).

RRIDs are of interest for both theoretical and practical reasons. The study of RRIDs should throw light on the processes underlying both recall and recognition. One interesting possibility is that the recall-recognition discrepancy for a subject may prove to depend on the learning strategies he employs. One practical reason RRIDs are of interest is that essay-type examinations rely heavily on recall whereas multiple-choice examinations are essentially tests of recognition memory. Accordingly, if there are RRIDs, the two types of examination will order individuals differently and are not equivalent.

RECOGNITION-RECALL CORRELATIONS

The heading of this section reflects the fact that, although the studies reported below were designed to investigate RRIDs, the main interest of the results lies in the recognition-recall correlations obtained. Eight tests were used. In these tests, memory was tested in immediate succession first by a recall method and then by a recognition method, except that for Test 3 recognition preceded recall. The advantage of this procedure is that it allows recall and recognition to be assessed on the same material following the same learning experience. The disadvantage is that the test taken first may affect the test taken second. However, carryover effects appear to be slight (Brown, 1976) and, even if they were appreciable, they would not necessarily affect the magnitude of RRIDs. Great care was taken to ensure, through pilot studies, that floor and ceiling effects were avoided. If recall for the group is close to zero because the task is too difficult, what appear to be RRIDs will reflect only differences in recognition. Similarly, if recognition is almost perfect because the task is too easy, differences in recall will produce apparent RRIDs for the same reason. To achieve this balance between recognition and recall performance levels in tests 1-4 (free recall), a filled delay of several minutes was interpolated between presentation and testing.

Method

TABLE I

Summary of tests and recall-recognition correlations

Test	Material	Presentation	Delay	r
1	20 CVC words	Read out once	10 min	0.69
2	40 common nouns	Read out twice	20 min	0.72
3	As test 2 but recognition before recall			0.62
4	40 common nouns	Read out 3 times recall after each presentation	1 week	0.61
4	40 adjective-noun pairs	Read out once	None	0.80
6	General knowledge questions			0.87
7	40 uncommon nouns, word-to-definition			0.69
8	40 uncommon nouns definition-to-word			0.80

Tests Table I summarises the tests used. The first four tests involved written free recall for two minutes and an unpaced recognition test. In each case, the recognition test consisted of an equal number of old and new words in random order, the old and new words having been drawn from a common pool. Each word was rated (see below). Test 5 was a paired associates task. For the recall test, the nouns were listed on a sheet and the task was to write down the correct adjective beside each noun. For recognition, 20 of the original pairs and 20 new pairs (obtained by rearranging the original pairs) were listed in random order. The rate of presentation of the list was 1.5 sec per word for tests 1 to 4 and 2.0 sec per pair for test 5. Test 6 consisted of general knowledge questions such as 'What is the fish whose roe is caviar?' Recognition was tested by presenting the same questions, half with the correct answer and half with a plausible incorrect answer. In test 7, the definition of an uncommon word such as 'sextant' was provided and the task was to recall or recognize the word. For recall, the initial letter of the target word was given. In test 8, the task was reversed : the word was given and the task was to recall or recognize the definition. Tests 1 to 5 concern episodic memory (memory for what was presented on a particular occasion) whereas tests 6 to 8 concern semantic memory. Not more than two tests (always involving non-confusable materials) were given during a single session and a week or more separated sessions.

Subjects The subjects were 24 psychology undergraduates at Bristol University. Only 18 were available for tests 1, 4 and 6.

Measures Recall was measured by the proportion of correct responses. Intrusion errors occurred but were infrequent. All the recognition tests consisted of correct and incorrect items in random order and each item was rated on a 4 point scale. From these ratings the area under the ROC curve (R) can be estimated with very small bias (Brown 1974). A criterion-free recognition measure is important because apparent RRIDs might reflect no more than differences in the recognition criterion used by different subjects. However, R itself has a chance value of 0.5. Accordingly, the difference between recognition and recall was taken to be the difference between 2R-1 and the recall probability, since 2R-1 has a value of 0 when recognition is at the chance level of 1 when recognition is perfect (cf. Brown 1976).

Analysis Each retention test, recall and recognition, was split at random into two halves. This allowed the results to be treated by analysis of variance in which both materials and subjects were treated as random variables. It also allowed split half correlations to be calculated from which the reliabilities of the tests could be assessed using the Spearman-Brown formula. Both within and between test correlations (product moment) were calculated between recognition and recall. The maximum possible between-test correlations were estimated as the square root of the product of the reliabilities of the retention tests involved.

Results

The analysis of variance failed to reveal statistically significant individual differences in the recognition recall discrepancies with any of the tests (no significant RRIDs). The within-test correlations are given in Table I. Both the reliabilities of the retention tests involved in these correlations and the correlations themselves are statistically significant. High between-test correlations were observed for tests using highly similar test materials. Tests 2 and 3 both involve free recall of words and tests 7 and 8 both involve knowledge of vocabulary. The correlations are shown in Table II. Here 23 is the correlation between recall in test 2 and recognition in test 3, 32 recall in 3 and recognition in 2 and so on. The second line of the table shows the maximum possible correlation estimated from the reliabilities of the tests involved: it is not possible to do this for the within-test correlations because they are concerned with recognition and recall of the same materials. Comparison with the estimated maxima indicates that these between-test correlations are high.

TABLE II

Between-test correlations of recognition and recall

Tests	23	32	78	87
r	0.65	0.66	0.65	0.59
max.r	0.78	0.83	0.84	0.77

Discussion

Both the between- and the within-test correlations were fairly high. We have to consider 1) why correlations reported in the literature are lower 2) the relation between recall recognition correlations and RRIDs and 3) the failure of the within-test correlations to exceed the between-test correlations.

Many correlations reported in the recent literature concern recall and recognition tasks which are not directly comparable. For example, a subject might be presented with a series of line drawings at acquisition, one of which is a cup: the recall task is to produce the word 'cup' whereas the recognition task is to recognize the original line drawing (Bahrick and Boucher, 1968; Tversky, 1973). Here the stored information immediately relevent to recall is verbal whereas the information immediately relevant to recognition is visual. A similar situation arises if cued recall is correlated with uncued recognition. Here provision of the cue in the recall test will facilitate retrieval of the stored code for the cue-target combination and this changes the recall task relative to the recognition task. In our study, the recall and recognition tasks were as nearly alike as possible : the major and inevitable difference was the provision of the target itself in recognition.

Conceptually, the relation between recall-recognition correlations and individual differences in the relation of recall to recognition (RRIDs) is straightforward. If recall and recognition correlate perfectly, then the recall score can be predicted from the recognition score (or vice versa) so that RRIDs are impossible. If the correlation is less than perfect, room emerges for RRIDs. In our study, the observed between-test correlations are high in relation to the maximum values permitted by the reliabilities. Accordingly, the absence of RRIDs in the analysis of variance is not unexpected given the magnitudes of these correlations. The relation between the within-test correlations and the possibility of RRIDs is more complicated because these correlations are not limited in the same way by the reliabilities. In order to clarify the situation, tests 2 and 5 were repeated with a fresh group of 24 comparable subjects except that the recall test was followed by a second recall test instead of by a recognition test. The resulting within-test recall-recall correlations were 0.92 and 0.97 respectively : these are substantially and significantly ($P < 0.05$ and $p < 0.01$ respectively) greater than the corresponding recall-recognition correlations. This suggests that the latter could have been substantially higher so that these within-test correlations do not in themselves preclude RRIDs.

The failure of the within-test correlations to exceed the between-test correlations, together with the higher recall-recall correlations just reported, can be explained as follows. The simple generate-recognize model of recall is now discredited. However, recalling an item does *sometimes* involve generation of the item followed by recognition

(Brown 1965, 1976). Associated with the generation process is generation variance. Generation variance reduces the correlation between recall and recognition. This applies to both within-test and between-test correlations and helps to make the two sorts of correlation comparable in magnitude. Generation variance does not prevent a high correlation between two recall tests given in immediate succession because, if an item is generated in the first test, it is then likely to be generated also in the second test.

PRESENCE OF RRIDs FOLLOWING LEARNING TO CRITERION

With the exception of test 4, the experiments on episodic memory so far described involved a single presentation of the stimulus material or two presentations without an intervening test phase. The next experiment involved multi-trial free recall until a criterion of 50% recall was reached. Accordingly study and test phases alternated, as in test 4. This may encourage the emergence of differential learning strategies and hence of RRIDs. With test 4, statistically significant RRIDs were found for a pilot group.

Method

17 subjects from the previous study were tested individually and learned a list of 30 common adjectives and abverbs by multi-trial free-recall to a 50% criterion. Presentation was oral at 1.5 sec per word and 30 sec was allowed for written free recall. Next 9 min were spent completing a questionnaire on the use of learning strategies. Finally a further free recall test, lasting 2 min, was given followed by an unpaced recognition test. The latter took the same form as the recognition tests in Tests 1 to 4 except that synonyms and antonyms of the list words were used as the distractors in order to prevent too high a level of recognition.

Results and Discussion

The number of trials to criterion varied from 2 to 11 with subjects fairly evenly distributed across this range. In the delayed tests, mean recall was 0.52 and recognition was 0.71. Recognition improved with trials to criterion ($r = 0.53$, $P < 0.05$) whereas recall performance deteriorated although not significantly ($r = -0.32$). This latter result, if reliable, may reflect greater criterion overshoot by fast learners. Little relationship was found between questionnaire answers and trials to criterion. For analysis of variance, the recall and recognition tests were split randomly into two halves so that both subjects and materials could be treated as random variables. There were significant RRIDs ($F(16,16) =$

3.96, P< 0.01). There were also significant IDs in recognition but not in recall (F(16,16) = 4.67. p < .01 and F(16,16) = 0.78 respectively). The absence of IDs in recall can be attributed to the fact that original learning was to a recall criterion.

The experiment demonstrates RRIDs but not following a constant opportunity to learn for all subjects since trials to criterion varied. Such RRIDs may have practical significance. For example, suppose candidates prepare for an examination concerned with factual knowledge and use self-testing (recall) to a common criterion. Then the relative performance of slow learners should be much better in a multiple-choice (recognition) examination because their ability to recognize the relevant information will have improved more quickly than their ability to recall it.

GENERAL DISCUSSION

Our subjects were British university students selected for university on the basis of essay-type examinations, which depend heavily on recall. This will have tended to screen out candidates poor at recall relative to recognition. This may explain our failure to find RRIDs with the first set of tests. It would be interesting to give similar tests to other populations of subjects, including children and old people and young adults with a poor educational background.

In the learning to criterion experiment, significant differences in the relation (RRIDs) were found even in our student population. We have suggested that the alternation of study and test trials during the learning phase of this experiment stimulated the adoption of differential learning strategies. Whether or not this suggestion is correct, the experiment clearly demonstrates that learning for recall and learning for recognition can be different, since subjects achieved a common level of recall but different levels of recognition, confirming previous studies of differential effects on learning. It should be noted that in our study, differences between subjects resulted in the non-equivalence of learning for recall and learning for recognition : they were not the result of an experimental manipulation.

The studies reported here show that RRIDs, with university students are somewhat elusive. However, the possibility that there are RRIDs for certain types of test and for certain populations of subjects warrants wide-ranging investigation. We need to know when and whether multiple-choice and essay type examinations of factual knowledge are equivalent. Finally, where RRIDs are found special training such as emphasizing the importance of organisation in learning, may help those with high recall-recognition discrepancies to improve their recall performance.

ACKNOWLEDGEMENT

This research was supported by the Social Sciences Research Council.

REFERENCES

Bahrick, H.P. and Boucher, B. (1968). Retention of visual and verbal codes of the same stimuli. *Journal of Experimental Psychology*, 78, 417-422.

Brown, J. (1965). A comparison of recognition and recall by a multiple-response method, *Journal of verbal learning and verbal behaviour*, 4, 401-408.

Brown, J. (1974). Recognition assessed by rating and ranking, *British Journal of Psychology*, 65, 13-22.

Brown, J. (1976). An analysis of recognition and recall and problems in their comparison. In: *Recall and Recognition*. (Brown, J. ed) pp 1-36, John Wiley and Sons, London.

Cooper, A.J.R. and Monk, A.F. Learning for recall and recognition. In: *Recall and Recognition*. (Brown, J. ed) pp 131-156, John Wiley and Sons, London.

Tversky, B. (1973). Encoding processes in recognition and recall, *Cognitive Psychology*, 5, 275-285.

ASSESSMENT OF INDIVIDUAL VARIATION IN MEMORY ABILITY

Maryanne Martin
University of Oxford
Department of Experimental Psychology
South Parks Road
Oxford OX 13UD
England

The assessment of individual variation in memory ability is discussed. An experiment is reported which investigated whether the immediate digit span measure traditionally used in the assessment of individual differences in cognition is a good predictor of performance on other memory tasks. It was concluded that an individual's digit span reflects his ability to retain information about the order of a sequence of events rather than the capacity of his short- or long-term memory.

One of the most frequent remarks of a person on being introduced to a psychologist, besides the question "Are you going to psychoanalyze me?", is "How can I improve my memory?" Many people, though normal healthy individuals, complain that they have poor memories. Sometimes the complaint is specific about what cannot be remembered (perhaps most commonly, people's names), but it may also be general in nature. Though there has been a great deal of research leading to the formulation of theoretical models of memory, comparatively little research effort has been directed towards discovering the extent of individual differences between people. Most research articles report only the mean level of recall and occasionally the variance. It is usually neglected whether a person is consistently good at the test or not (i.e., test-retest reliability) or whether a person who is good at remembering one type of material is similarly good at other types of material. The answers to these questions are important both practically and theoretically. If people's performance is relatively consistent and the same people are good at remembering a range of materials it might then be possible to devise a single memory test assessing mnemonic ability to be of use in personnel selection and clinical screening. Theoretically, this would be consistent with the existence of a single general processing limit as proposed originally by Broadbent (1958). In contrast, if some people are good at remembering a particular type of material then a battery of tests may be necessary in order to assess these various types of memory (Erickson & Scott, 1977).

The most commonly used measure of memory is that of digit span, that is, the magnitude of the longest string of unrelated digits which a person can reliably recall immediately after a single presentation. It was used as an indicator of mental capacity by Galton (1887) and by Jacobs (1887) nearly a hundred years ago, and is currently widely employed both in tests of intelligence, with a correlation of .37 existing between digit span and full scale WISC IQ (Wechsler, 1974), and in clinical diagnosis (see Burgemeister, 1962; Mayer-Gross, Slater & Roth, 1969; Payne, 1973; Rundel & Denckla, 1974; Warrington, 1970). Its appeal presumably lies in its simplicity and its intuitive validity as a measure of short-term memory. This idea has been supported by some recent papers in cognitive psychology which have renewed interest in the relationship between memory span (for other types of material as well as digits) and other measures of memory and cognitive processing (e.g., Baddeley, Thomson & Buchanan, 1975; Cavanagh, 1972; Watkins, 1977). Cavanagh (1972) reported a linear relationship between scanning time and the reciprocal of memory span: for different materials, the greater the memory span the less the scanning time per item as measured in the item-recognition paradigm of Sternberg (1966). Baddeley, Thomson & Buchanan (1975) showed that memory span and reading rate for words composed of varying numbers of syllables were highly correlated. Watkins (1977) showed that span was largest with high frequency words, smallest for low frequency words and intermediate for lists of mixed high and low frequency words. However, all these studies involved correlations over different types of material rather than over different people. Thus the important question arises whether individual differences in memory span among people correlate with other measures of memory ability.

In the last 20 years theorists have commonly distinguished two components of human memory: short-term memory and long-term memory. However, the term "short-term memory" has been used in connection with both a distinct mechanism or process and also any memory experiment involving short retention intervals. For clarity, the terminology of Waugh & Norman (1965) will be followed here. They reserved the above terms for the memory paradigms, and characterized two independent theoretical stores as primary and secondary memory, using terms introduced by James (1890). Both stores could be involved in retrieval of material after short delays, because an assumption was made of rapid transfer of information from primary to secondary memory. The distinction between the two stores is not universally recognised (e.g., Gruneberg, 1970, 1972), but reviews of this area can be found in Murdock (1974) and Baddeley (1976). The present paper investigates the relationship of memory span to both short- and long-term memory performance and to primary and secondary memory capabilities.

Probably the most widely used experimental task for investigating short- and long-term memory is free recall. A list of unrelated words is presented, and is followed by recall of the words either immediately or after an interval which has been filled by a distractor task. Immediate free recall may be taken as the prototypical short-term memory task, and delayed free recall as the prototypical long-term memory task.

The primary memory store is assumed to be of limited capacity, and several techniques have been proposed for estimating the magnitude of this. Probably the most widely used is the technique devised by Waugh & Norman (1965), who proposed that the capacity of primary memory may be estimated from the U shaped serial position curve reliably obtained for immediate free recall, as follows.

If the probabilities of recall from primary memory (PM_i) and secondary memory (SM_i) are assumed to be independent, then the overall recall probability (R_i) is given by

$$R_i = PM_i + SM_i - PM_i SM_i \qquad (1)$$

which can be rearranged to give

$$PM_i = \frac{R_i - SM_i}{1-SM_i} \quad . \qquad (2)$$

For this purpose i is usually taken to refer to presentation serial position over the final part of a list (Waugh & Norman originally identified i as the lag between presentation and recall of an item). Waugh and Norman (1965) assumed that, apart from the more rehearsed first few serial positions of a list, the value of $\overline{SM_i}$ is constant, and can be estimated for the terminal part of a list as the average value of $\overline{R_i}$ over the central part of the list (this was taken as serial positions 4 to 7 in the 13-item lists of the present study). Thus the value of $\overline{PM_i}$ can be calculated from Equation 2 for each of the terminal positions of the list (in the present case, 8 to 13), and summed to yield an estimate of the total capacity of primary memory. The amount stored in secondary memory in the present experiment was calculated as the sum of the above asymptotic values over the terminal positions together with the total recalled in the pre-terminal positions.

An alternative model of memory postulates separate representation of item and order information (e.g., Brown, 1958; Crossman, 1961; Healy, 1974; Murdock, 1976; Schwartz & Wiedel, 1978). One method of measuring memory for the latter is to require subjects to recall the order as well as the identity of items: an item is scored correct if and only if it is recalled in the correct serial position. Other more elaborate methods for calculating order information have also recently been proposed (Lee & Estes, 1977; Snodgrass, Burns & Pirone, 1978; Sperling & Melcher, 1976), but as yet no decisive advantage appears to have been established for a particular one, and thus here the simple method of estimating order information will be employed. The experiment was carried out to determine whether individual subjects' memory spans were related to their memory stores' capacities, or to their abilities to retain order information, or to both.

METHOD

Subjects. There were 38 subjects in this experiment. They were aged between 18 and 30 years and were members of the Oxford Subject Panel.

Materials. Three sets of stimuli were prepared as follows.

Immediate digit span lists were composed of the 10 numbers zero to nine. Sets of 10 lists were prepared, one of each length between three and twelve numbers. Three such sets were prepared.

Twelve free-recall lists of 13 words each were generated by sampling without replacement from the Kucera & Francis (1967) corpus of eight-letter words with frequencies in the categories 4 to 7.

Four order-recall twelve-items lists of decimal digits were prepared. No digit was repeated more than once in a list.

Procedure. All lists were auditorily recorded, and presented over speakers to the subjects. Digit span was tested first, followed by free recall and then ordered recall. Recall was written in each case.

For immediate digit span each list was preceded by the word "ready" 5 sec. before the onset of the list. This was spoken at a rate of one digit per second. The assessment of digit span was by the method recommended by Woodworth & Schlosberg (1954). Three sets of digit-span lists were given. Thus if, for example, a subject correctly recalled all the lists up to and including 6 digits, a basal value of 6 was alloted. If above that value he succeeded twice with a 7-digit list, not at all with 8, once with 9, and none further, his total score was 6 + 3/3 = 7, since equal credit was given for each correct recall above the basal level.

For free recall the word "ready" was spoken 5 secs. before the start of each list as a warning signal. It was followed by the words at a rate of one every 2 sec. After the presentation there was either a visual instruction to recall or else a three-figure number was first shown for 30 secs. In the latter case subjects had to count backwards in threes as fast as possible, and write down the number they reached. Two minutes was allowed for the recall of each list.

For ordered recall the word "ready" preceded each list by 5 secs. It was followed by the digits at a rate of one per second. At the end of the list, those digits which could be remembered were written in answer booklets in columns corresponding to the different serial positions of input.

RESULTS

The means and standard deviations of subjects' scores on the different measures are shown in Table I. The correlation between subjects' digit spans and immediate free recall scores was not significant, $r(36) = .12$. Similarly the correlation between digit spans and delayed free recall scores failed to reach significance, $r(36) = .12$. Thus digit span is not a good predictor of performance on either short-term or long-term memory tasks. However, the correlation between immediate and delayed free recall was significant, $r(36) = .57$, $p < .001$.

TABLE I

Group means and standard deviations.

Measure	Mean	Standard deviation
Digit span	7.4	1.3
Ordered Recall	48.8%	16.1%
Immediate free recall	48.6%	7.9%
Delayed free recall	28.4%	9.3%
Estimate of primary memory	3.2	0.7
Estimate of secondary memory	4.2	1.5

The correlation between digit span and the estimate of primary memory using the Waugh & Norman (1965) method also failed to reach significance, $r(36) = .11$. Similarly the correlation between digit span and the estimate of secondary memory failed to reach significant, $r(36) = .00$. Thus performance on digit span is not a good indicator of either the capacity of primary memory or the number of items which enter secondary memory in a given situation.

In contrast to the above, the correlation between digit span and ordered recall was highly significant, $r(36) = .66$, $p < .001$. Hence digit span appears to be a good indicator of memory for the order of items, but not for the retention of the items themselves.

The lack of correlation between digit span and scores on tasks involving memory for item information might, however, have resulted from the measures themselves being unreliable. The possibility was examined by calculating in each case a split-half reliability statistic, r, using the Spearman-Brown formula. The measures for each subject were recalculated for alternate lists (i.e., odd- and even-numbered lists) separately. Generally the agreement between the measures derived from the two was satisfactorily high. The values of the split-half reliability were as follows: for immediate free recall $r = .72$, for delayed free recall $r = .76$, for the primary memory estimate $r = .76$ and for the secondary memory esttimate $r = .72$.

DISCUSSION

The results of this experiment support the hypothesis that the digit-span score is a good predictor of the ability to remember temporal sequence, but not of the ability to remember item information. This outcome is consistent with those models of memory which postulate separate representation of item and order information (e.g., Brown, 1958; Crossman, 1961; Healy, 1974; Murdock, 1976). It has been proposed that retention of order information requires more learning than that of item information alone (Fuchs, 1969; Gruneberg & Melton, 1972). However, Dornic (1975) has proposed that it is easier to learn items with order information than without because this facilitates the concatenation of traces phonologically to form a "chunk", in the terminology of Miller (1956). Healy (1977) provided further evidence implicating such coding in temporal recall by demonstrating that recall of temporal order is disrupted by tasks involving vocalization, whereas that of spatial order is disrupted by tasks demanding processing of spatial information. In support of his view, Dornic (1975) demonstrated that the retention of item information alone was adversely affected more than that of combined order and item information by difficult conditions such as the division of attention, a high additional information load, or the consumption of alcohol.

Further evidence consistent with the present view comes from studies investigating the relationship between recall from supraspan lists and IQ. Cohen and Sandberg (1977) divided such lists into three parts and found a consistently high correlation between IQ and the recall of recency items but not of primacy or central items. In contrast no such relationship was found by Ellis, McCarver and Ashurst (1970) or Fagan (1972). However, the salient difference between the two conflicting groups of studies is that the former required items to be recalled in serial order, but the latter did not. This is complementary to the hypothesis proposed here that digit span is chiefly a measure of ordered information.

In conclusion it appears that digit-span score does not provide a general measure of performance on short- or long-term memory tasks nor of the theoretical concepts of primary and secondary memory, but rather it depends upon the ability to remember the order in which events occur. It is suggested therefore that, for the assessment of individual differences in cognition, the traditional digit-span procedure may usefully be supplemented by one based upon free recall.

REFERENCES

Baddeley, A. D. (1976). *The Psychology of Memory* Harper and Row, New York.

Baddeley, A. D., Thomson, N., and Buchanan, M. (1975). Word length and the structure of short-term memory. *Journal of Verbal Learning and Verbal Behavior*, 14, 575-589.

Broadbent, D. E. (1958). *Perception and Communication.* Pergamon, London.

Brown, J. (1958). Some tests of the decay theory of immediate memory. *Quarterly Journal of Experimental Psychology.* 10, 12-21.

Burgemeister, B. B. (1962). *Psychological Techniques in Neurological Diagnosis.* Harper and Row, New York.

Cavanagh, J. P. (1972). Relation between the immediate memory span and the memory search rate. *Psychological Review* 79, 525-530.

Cohen, R. L. and Sandberg, T. (1977). Relation between intelligence and short-term memory. *Cognitive Psychology*, 9, 534-554.

Crossman, E.R.F.W. (1961). Information and serial order in human immediate memory. In: *Information Theory.* (C. Cherry, ed.), pp. 147-161, Butterworths, London.

Dornic, S. (1975). Some studies on the retention of order information. In: *Attention and Performance V.* (P. Rabbitt and S. Dornic, eds.), pp. 230-240. Academic Press, London.

Ellis, N. R., McCarver, R. B., and Ashurst, H. M. (1970). Short-term memory in the retarded: ability level and stimulus meaningfulness. *American Journal of Mental Deficiency.* 75, 72-80.

Erickson, R. C. and Scott, M. L. (1977). Clinical memory testing: A review. *Psychological Bulletin.* 84, 1130-1149.

Fagan, J. F. (1972). Rehearsal and free recall in children of superior and average intelligence. *Psychonomic Science.* 28, 352-354.

Fuchs, A. H. (1969). Recall for order and content of serial word lists in short-term memory. *Journal of Experimental Psychology,* 82, 14-21.

Galton, F. (1887). Supplementary notes on 'prehension' in idiots. *Mind.* 12, 79-82.

Gruneberg, M. M. (1970). A dichotomous theory of memory - unproved and unprovable? *Acta Psychologica.* 34, 489-498.

Gruneberg, M. M. (1972). The serial position curve and the distinction between short- and long-term memory. *Acta Psychologica.* 36, 221-225.

Gruneberg, M. M. and Melton, K. C. (1972). Acoustic confusions and order forgetting. *Acta Psychologica.* 36, 48-53.

Healy, A. F. (1974). Separating item from order information in short-term memory. *Journal of Verbal Learning and Verbal Behavior.* 13, 644-655.

Healy, A. F. (1977). Pattern coding of spatial order information in short-term memory. *Journal of Verbal Learning and Verbal Behavior.* 16, 419-437.

Jacobs, J. (1887). Experiments on "prehension". *Mind.* 12, 75-79.

James, W. (1890). *Principles of Psychology.* Holt, New York.

Kucera, H. and Francis, W. H. (1967). *Computational Analysis of Present Day American English.* Brown University Press, Providence R.I.

Lee, C. L. and Estes, W. K. (1977). Order and position in primary memory for letter strings. *Journal of Verbal Learning and Verbal Behavior.* 16, 395-418.

Mayer-Gross, W., Slater, E., and Roth, M. (1969). *Clinical Psychiatry.*(3rd Edn. revised by E. Slater and M. Roth). Bouiliere, Tindall and Cassell, London.

Miller, G. A. (1956). The magical number seven, plus or minus two: Some limits on our capacity for processing information. *Psychological Review.* 63, 81-97.

Murdock, B. B. Jr. (1974). *Human Memory: Theory and Data.* Earlbaum, Potomac Md.

Murdock, B. B. Jr. (1976). Item and order information in short-term serial memory. *Journal of Experimental Psychology: General.* 105, 191-216.

Payne, R. W. (1973). Cognitive Abnormalities. In: *Handbook of Abnormal Psychology.* (H. J. Eysenck, ed.), pp. 420-483. Pitman Medical, Belfast.

Rudel, R. G. and Denckla, M. B. (1974). Relation of forward and backward digit repetition to neurological impairment in children with learning disabilities. *Neuropsychologia.* 12, 109-118.

Schwartz, S. and Wiedel, T. C. (1978). Individual differences in cognition: Relationship between verbal ability and memory for order. *Intelligence.* in press.

Snodgrass, J. C., Burns, P. M., and Pirone, G. V. (1978). Pictures and words and space and time: In search of the elusive interaction. *Journal of Experimental Psychology: General.* 107, 206-230.

Sperling, G. and Melchner, M. J. (1976). Estimating item and order information. *Journal of Mathematical Psychology.* 13, 192-213.

Sternberg, S. (1966). High-speed scanning in human memory. *Science.* 153, 652-654.

Warrington, E. K. (1970). Neurological deficits. In: *The Psychological Assessment of Mental and Physical Handicaps.* (P. Mittler, ed.), pp. 261-288. Tavistock Publications, London.

Watkins, M. J. (1977). The intricacy of memory span. *Memory and Cognition.* 5, 529-534.

Waugh, N. C. and Norman, D. A. (1965). Primary memory. *Psychological Review.* 72, 82-104.

Wechsler, D. (1974). *Wechsler Intelligence Scale for Children: Revised.* The Psychological Corporation, New York.

Wickelgren, W. A. (1969). Context-sensitive coding, associative memory, and serial order in (speech) behavior. *Psychological Review.* 67, 1-15.

Woodworth, R. A. and Schlosberg, H. (1954). *Experimental Psychology.* Methuen, London.

AGE, EXPERIENCE AND SHORT TERM MEMORY

H. Murrell and S. Humphries
Department of Applied Psychology
University of Wales Institute of Science and Technology
Llwyn-y-Grant
Cardiff

There are basically two approaches to the study of skill decrement with age. The earlier sought to examine those aspects of performance which were affected by normal age decrement, and thus map ongoing age related deterioration in a number of areas. The second, later approach which we have adopted, seeks to examine the role that experience plays in compensating for normal age decrement. The present experiment examines the role of experience in memory using a sample of experienced simultaneous translators in a shadowing. task.

As there is a time lag between input and output in ST some form of short term storage must occur. Various authors have proposed models for ST and these all involve storage. In much psychological work assumptions have to be made - we cannot hold a memory in our hand - we depend on evidence. We believed that the evidence of memory intervening in ST and shadowing is adequate: so we used simultaneous translators as our 'experienced' Ss in a speech shadowing task which closely resembles ST and is used in training translators.

PROCEDURE

The passages to be shadowed were recorded on tape and the Ss' talk-back was also recorded for subsequent examination. Ear-voice span was obtained by comparing a voice-trace of each S with that of the master tape and measuring time-lag on 20 pre-selected key words.

For familiarization, Ss shadowed a short passage at 130 words/min. Each then shaddowed a passage taken from G.K. Chesterton recorded at 187 words/min. Finally, naive Ss were given a 'training' schedule of six passages at increasing rates from 130-180 words/min.

The young experienced Ss were just completing a 7-month intensive course in ST; the old experienced were professional simultaneous interpretors with an average of 16 years experience. The naive Ss were drawn from the Department's subject pool. Their ages were:

Naive	Young; 25.2(N = 6)	Old; 56.3 (N = 13)
Experienced	Young; 25.2(N = 6)	Old; 58.0 (N = 6)

RESULTS

For ERRORS, four classifications were used; omission, addition, substitution and mis-pronunciation. The young and old naive Ss had mean total errors of 35% and 59% respectively with $p < .05$; but the corresponding performances of the experienced Ss were 22% and 23% which are obviously not significant. The correlation between errors and age for the naive Ss was significant at $\tau = +.52$, but that for the experienced group was non-significant at $\tau = +.21$; and this was largely due to one S who was almost 70 years old but still working! Without him the correlation was almost zero.

EAR VOICE spans showed little experience effect and averaged between 1 - 1.4 secs. It was, however, longer for both older groups. With the experienced Ss, but not with the naive, there was significant correlation between errors and ear-voice span at $\tau = +.86$ (young) and $\tau = +.87$ (old).

Finally, we discovered an apparent sex difference between the older naive Ss only. To explore this we tested an additional 7 Ss. It appeared that males of 50+ years were comitting many more errors than were females of similar ages. In fact, when over 60 some male Ss were incapable of shadowing. This further testing enabled us to make comparisons:

Males 50-60, 65% errors compared with females 50-60, 40% errors $p < .05$
Males 50-60, 65% errors compared with females 60+, 50% errors not significant
Males 50+ 73% errors compared with females 60+, 50% errors $p < .05$

It must be emphasized that similar results could <u>not</u> be found with experienced subjects. It would seem that older naive women are about a decade 'better' than men at shadowing. We can suggest no reason for this.

OUTCOME

Assuming that memory is involved in shadowing our results confirm decrements with age in naive Ss reported by others. They also support the findings of our other research (e.g. Murrell et al., 1962; Murrell and Edwards, 1963) that these age decrements are not found with experienced Ss. We can argue that experience is synonymous with extensive practice which itself is extended training; hence that the type of memory with which we experimented can be trained, probably other types of memory also. We must all know of instances from everyday life where people are successfully using memory in their jobs in ways which would baffle most of us (e.g. in the dyeing of wool) and it would be idiosyncratic not to accept that this is not due to extensive training (=experience).

This must lead us also to question the validity of some experiments with naive Ss. If our experiment had been done only with psychology students we would have reported an error rate of 35% which is a long way from practical performance at 22% and even further from older performance at 59%. If we had used a population cross-section the discrepancy would have been even greater since we would have reported a mean error rate for all ages of 51%. So if we are interested in memory in real life we should use as Ss people who regularly use memory in the manner which we are investigating if we are to produce a true measure of real life performance.

ACKNOWLEDGEMENT

The research was supported by the Social Science Research Council. Thanks are due to Professor D. Wallis for providing facilities at the Department of Applied Psychology, UWIST which enabled the research to continue after Professor Murrell retired.

REFERENCES

Murrell, H (1970) The effect of extensive practice on age differences in reaction time. *Journal of Gerontology*, 25, 268-274.

Murrell, H. and Edwards, E. (1963) Field studies of an indicator of machine tool travel with special reference to the ageing worker. *Occupational Psychology*, 37, 267-275.

Murrell, H., Powesland, P.F. and Forsaith, B. (1962) A study of pillar-drilling in relation to age. *Occupational Psychology*, 36, 45-52.

MEMORY IN CHILDREN

DEVELOPMENTAL ASPECTS OF MEMORY: A REVIEW

P. L. Harris
Developmental Psychology, Free University
Amsterdam, The Netherlands

Memory development in three areas is considered; potential age changes in the structural capacity of working memory; the increasing use with age of mnemonic strategies for remembering list materials and the possibility of training young children to use such strategies; finally, the schemata that children bring to bear on textual materials such as stories, and the emergence with age of the capacity to monitor and improve comprehension in a strategic fashion.

INTRODUCTION

Consider three tasks, ordered in terms of complexity: first,the traditional digit-span test; second, a task that exceeds the span of immediate memory in which the child is asked to remember a list of words or pictures for a few minutes; and third, a task which appears to approximate some of the complexity of everyday recollection - re-telling of a story. How does memory at these three levels of complexity develop and what practical steps can be taken to improve a child's performance.

WORKING MEMORY

Developmental psychologists have long considered the possibility that growth might bring about some basic change in the capacity or longevity of memory. For example, the visual icon might fade more rapidly, or visual recognition might be less robust in the young child as compared with the adult. One strong candidate for such a structural change has been the size of working memory. First, it has been known since the initiation of intelligence testing that digit-span increases with age. Second it has been assumed that digit-span might index the capacity of working memory particularly since Baddeley and Hitch (1974) showed that trying to remember several digits impairs performance on other cognitive tasks such as sentence comprehension. If younger children indeed possess a smaller working memory, this would have important practical implications. Many tasks in primary school such as learning to read or solving mental arithmetic problems depend upon working memory. Hence the evidence for such a fundamental development in information-processing capacity deserves careful analysis. Huttenlocher and Burke (1976),arguing against the hypothesis of structural change, point out that there are several findings in the literature showing that span is reduced when items are less easily identified on input. Thus the increase with age in the size of the digit -span may reflect age changes in perceptual encoding rather than memory capacity.

STRATEGIES AND LISTS

Turning to the second task mentioned above - memory for a list of items - there is a good deal of evidence which suggests that when the younger child remembers fewer items than the older child, this is because he is making less effective use of his memory rather than because he has an inferior memory capacity (Brown, 1975; Harris, 1978). In particular, the young child makes less use of various mnemonic strategies to improve his performance. A landmark experiment was performed by Flavell, Beach and Chinsky (1966). Children were shown a set of pictures and asked to remember their names for a few minutes (the pictures were not visible in this delay period). Not surprisingly, younger children remembered fewer pictures than older children. Flavell and his colleagues went on to find out why. A lip-reader observed that older children were more likely to mouth the names of the pictures in the delay period. The implication was that the older children were benefitting from the use of sub-vocal rehearsal. This conclusion was strengthened by training the younger child to rehearse. After training, they remembered as many pictures as the older children.

There are several noteworthy features of this experiment. First, it illustrates what has become a general finding in developmental work on memory: the younger child is likely to be less strategic in his memorizing. He adopts a planless and overly optimistic approach to the task. Second, by using the lip-reading technique, Flavell showed how age-changes in the use of strategies can be directly measured rather than inferred post-hoc from subsequent performance. Third, the training results showed not only that rehearsal is an effective mnemonic but also that the younger child's initial poor performance was not due to any basic incapacity since the younger child can produce and benefit from the rehearsal strategy.

Similar age-changes have been found for other mnemonic strategies. For example, younger children make less effective use than older children of grouping strategies and retrieval aids (Moely, 1977; Kobasigawa, 1977). As in the case of rehearsal these deficiencies can be reduced by training. Thus the general conclusion is that the younger child is less likely to anticipate and forestall memory problems by using a strategy. Exactly how such strategies are acquired in the course of development is not yet clear, but cross-cultural work strongly suggests that some aspect of Western urbanization, particularly schooling is responsible. Schooled adolescents in Morocco, for example, exhibit a primacy effect in short term memory tasks - presumably attributable to rehearsal - but their unschooled peers do not (Wagner, 1978).

From a practical point of view, the above results are encouraging. Young children can be trained to perform in a more mature fashion. However there are difficulties. In the first place young children frequently abandon a strategy if they are no longer instructed to use it (Keeney, Cannizzo & Flavell, 1967). In the second place, even if subjects maintain a strategy after training, they may fail to transfer it appropriately. For example, Brown, Campione and Murphy (1974) found that retarded adolescents could maintain rehearsal training over a six-month period but did not transfer that training to new materials (Campione & Brown, 1977)

Why might a child fail to produce a strategy spontaneously and even when trained, fail to transfer it appropriately? The answer to both queries may be that the child is simply unable to assess the adequacy of his memory for a given task. (Such insight into the strengths and weaknesses of memory has come to be called metamemory, Flavell & Wellman, 1977). If this hypothesis is correct, it suggests that a child trained to assess the fit or the gap between his own memory and a particular task will be more likely to exhibit transfer of a strategy than a child who is trained to use a strategy but does not realise why it is useful. However, transfer problems arise even when one attempts to improve a child's metamemorial insight. For example, Brown,

Campione and Murphy (1976) attempted to provide retarded children with a more realistic estimate of the size of their immediate memory span. Prior to training subjects were grossly over optimistic about how many pictures they could recall. After training in which subjects were shown how over-optimistic they had been, subjects made more realistic estimates, but when asked in a transfer task to assess how many digits they could remember, subjects reverted to their earlier optimism and made unrealistic estimates.

In summary, young children's memory can be improved for list-like materials, but so far at least, only local improvments have been produced. It remains possible that if we knew more about how the child comes to discover the weaknesses of his memory and the ways in which those weaknesses can be circumvented, the training programmes might be more effective. Until now however, developmental psychologists have had little success in achieving anything except brief or local accelerations in a pervasive process which Western schooling appears to bring about in an informal and indirect fashion.

REMEMBERING AND UNDERSTANDING TEXTS

There are two reasons why investigators have turned increasingly to meaningful materials such as stories. First, although the young child does not often recruit strategies in so-called intentional memory tasks, he clearly performs well in certain tasks where no deliberate mnemonic effort appears to be exercised. For example, the five-year old child, who rarely exhibits spontaneous rehearsal, nonetheless has a good grasp of the phonology, syntax and semantics of his mother tongue. Accordingly, investigators have begun to use meaningful materials where retention is typically an unintended by-product of comprehension. In this context, then, it becomes sensible to tell children stories and to see what they can remember. A second reason for focussing on stories has been the development of text grammars which offer a more detailed analysis of what parts of a story are remembered and what parts are forgotten.

As a result of Piaget's work (Piaget, 1926) it was assumed until quite recently that the child's recall of a story is poor. There is some indication that Piaget created difficulties for his subjects by telling them stories which contained bizarre causal sequences. For example:

"Once upon a time there was a lady who was called Niobe, and who had 12 sons and 12 daughters. She met a fairy who had only one son and no daughter. Then the lady laughed at the fairy because the fairy had only one boy. Then the fairy was angry and fastened the lady to a rock. The lady cried for ten years. In the end she turned into a rock and her tears made a stream which still runs today."

Since we know from Bartlett's work that even adults distort unfamiliar materials, it is not surprising that young children distort the story of Niobe and the fairy. Working with more prosaic materials, several investigators have reported greater accuracy among young children (Brown, 1976; Stein & Glenn, 1977a) Moreover, children seem to realise from an early age that a story is composed of structured episodes, the typical episode being composed of an initiating event that arouses some goal in the hero; an ensuing course of action and the eventual consequence of that action. That children appreciate what constitutes a well-formed episode is indicated by several pieces of evidence. First, if any part of an episode is omitted, for example the initiating event such as the appearance of the giant or the disappearance of the damsel, children tend to fill in the omission on subsequent recall (Stein & Glenn, 1977b). Second, if part of an episode is displaced in a story, for example the initiating event is mentioned toward the end rather than at the outset, children have greater difficulty in recalling the story accurately and tend to reorganise it on recall by shifting the initiating event to its conventional place in the story. Third, across many different stories it has been found that the critical components of an episode are well recalled, particularly the initiating event and the consequence. On the other hand, information which is more incidental to the main episodic structure of the story - the mental reactions of the hero to the eventual outcome of the episode - is less well recalled.

At present the status of the episode schema is unclear. There are at least three possibilities. First, it might reflect a schema that children use in understanding all social episodes, whether they occur in real life or in stories. Second,since most of the data collected so far has been based on the free recall of stories by children, the episode schema might reflect a very general encoding and retrieval strategy; the child might store a story as a temporally organized sequence of events and retrieve information from that representation by first scrutinising the end-anchors, that is to say the initiating event and the eventual consequence (Trabasso, 1975; Brown, 1976). Third, the episode schema may reflect not a general strategy for dealing with an ordered set of items, but rather a prototype of what constitutes a proper episode, a prototype that could be abstracted from the child's experience with stories.

What are the practical implications of this work? At present it is too early to point to any specific applications. However, it is worth stressing the way in which this research might be applied. Whereas the work on the development of strategies has been directed at changing the child research on text processing may eventually suggest how we can change what we expose the child to. An analogy with the acquisition of language can be made here. Deliberate efforts to remember are scarcely characteristic of the first language learner. Nor do we see mothers and older children making any effort to equip the language learner with memory strategies. What they do attempt to do, by various types of message simplification, contextual support and repetition is to make their message understood (Snow & Ferguson, 1978). In the same way, I anticipate that the next decade will put us in a much better position to monitor the suitability of the textual materials that the young child gets exposed to in the school and the nursery.

Having implied that practical efforts should sometimes be directed away from the child, I want to discuss in conclusion an area where attempts to change the child could have potentially far-reaching consequences. Although we are inclined to think of comprehension as a more or less involuntary, automatic process, it is clear that both in reading and in listening this is not entirely true. Not only can we pay more or less attention to a speaker or a text, we can monitor our comprehension processes and if necessary redirect them by asking for more information, by re-reading a text, by reading more slowly, by vocalising the words and so forth. These re-direction strategies presuppose that we can evaluate the progress of our comprehension processes. Recent evidence indicates that this is a skill which emerges quite late, at least at the level of text comprehension. Brown and Smiley (1977) asked children at various ages to decide which parts of a story were central and which were unimportant details. Until the age of ten years children's ratings were more or less random, but after ten years their ratings became increasingly sensitive. Nonetheless, all children, irrespective of age tended to remember the central parts of the story better than the details. This study suggests therefore that young children engage in some type of selective encoding at an unconscious level. In the course of development, access to these hitherto unconscious processes is achieved and can be used to guide the child's ratings. A similar conclusion emerges from some recent studies that I have been carrying out with Meerum Terwogt (Harris & Meerum Terwogt, 1978). We have given young children stories similar to those devised by Bransford and Johnson (1973) which remain ambiguous unless the title is provided. For example: "Peter and John go to stand in line. Peter can already reach the railing with one hand. John stands behind him. When they are at the top, Peter sits down. John gives him a push. There goes Peter. How fast he goes. It only lasts a moment and then he is there. Peter turns around. There comes John behind him".

If the title - "On the slide" - is provided before the story is heard, the story is more easily understood. Children heard two such stories, one with and the other without a disambiguating title, and were then asked to decide which they had found more difficult to understand. Again, until about ten years of age children were random in their selection, whereas older children appreciated that the story with a title was easier to understand. Despite this age-change in self-monitoring capacity all age groups found the story with a title easier to remember, indicating that all age-groups, irrespective of their introspections, found that the title facilitated comprehension. Similar results were obtained in a second study in which subjects read the stories rather than listened to them. Again ten year olds but not younger children selected the titled story as being easier.

Combining the results of these various experiments it appears that for Western schoolchildren at least, an ability to monitor text comprehension processes emerges at about ten years of age. The next question to ask is whether or not the child can use this self-monitoring in a planful way to direct their comprehension and ultimately their retention of a text. Brown and Campione provide more information on this issue in a subsequent chapter.

CONCLUSIONS

Research on the development of memory is not untypical of the rest of developmental psychology. While we have a solid description of the age-changes that occur for a variety of tasks, the key weakness of the work - and the most disappointing for the psychologist interested in practical application - is that we have much less understanding of how such changes are brought about. My own guess is that we need to look in two directions. We cannot hope to understand the development of memory if we continue to stress the inabilities of the pre-school child and ignore his outstanding abilities. Indeed we need to push the study of memory backwards chronologically, so that we learn more about its origins; although now know a good deal about the infant's perceptual capacities, we have not linked this to a systematic study of memory (Harris, 1979). Second, we need to be less afraid of regarding the child as a self-monitoring organism, whose psychological insight increases in the course of development. To understand how this self-knowledge emerges, we need to look closely at a variety of educational settings, since these settings appear to produce mental changes that are much more pervasive than anything we can produce in the laboratory at this time.

REFERENCES

Baddeley, A.D. and Hitch, G. (1974). Working memory. In: *Psychology of Learning and Motivation*. Vol 8.(G. Bower), Academic Press, New York.

Bransford, J.D. and Johnson, M.K. (1973). Consideration of some problems of comprehension. In: *Visual Information Processing*. (W.G. Chase). Academic Press, New York.

Brown, A.L. (1975). The development of memory. In: *Advances in Child Development and Behaviour*. Vol 10.(H.W. Reese). Academic Press, New York.

Brown, A.L. (1976). The construction of temporal succession by preoperational children. In: *Minnesota Symposium on Child Psychology*.Vol 10.(A.Pick).University of Minnesota Press, Minnesota.

Brown, A.L.,Campione,J.C.and Murphy,M.(1974).Keeping track of changing variables: Long-term retention of a trained rehearsal strategy by retarded adolescents. *American Journal of Mental Deficiency*. 78, 446-453.

Brown, A.L.,Campione,J.C. and Murphy,M.(1976).Maintenance and generalization of trained metamnemonic awareness by educable retarded children: Span estimation. Unpublished manuscript,University of Illinois.

Brown, A.L. and Smiley, S.(1977).Rating the importance of structural units of prose passages:A problem of metacognitive development. *Child Development*. 48, 1-8.

Brown, A.L. and Campione, J.C. (1978). Recall of prose and study strategies. This volume.

Campione, J.C. and Brown, A.L. (1977). Memory and metamemory development in educable retarded children. In: *Perspectives on the Development of Memory and Cognition*.(R.V. Kail and J.W. Hagen), Lawrence Erlbaum Associates, New Jersey.

Flavell, J.H., Beach, D.R. and Chinsky, J.M. (1966). Spontaneous verbal rehearsal in a memory task as a function of age. *Child Development*. 37, 283-289.

Flavell, J.H. and Wellman, H.M. (1977). Metamemory. In: *Perspectives on the Development of Memory and Cognition*. (R.V. Kail and J.W. Hagen). Lawrence Erlbaum Associates, New Jersey.

Harris, P.L. (1978). Developmental aspects of memory. In: *Aspects of Memory*. (M. Gruneberg and P.E. Morris). Methuen, London.

Harris, P.L. (1979). Origins of perception and cognition in infancy. In: *Psychology Survey*. No. 2. (K. Connolly), George, Allen and Unwin, London.

Harris, P.L. and Meerum Terwogt, M. (1978). Monitoring incomprehension. Unpublished manuscript, Free University.

Huttenlocher, J and Burke, D. (1976). Why does memory span increase with age ? *Cognitive Psychology*, 8

Keeney, T.J., Cannizzo, S.R. and Flavell, J.H. (1967). Spontaneous and induced verbal rehearsal in a recall task. *Child Development*. 38, 953-966.

Kobasigawa, A. (1977). Retrieval strategies in the development of memory. In: *Perspectives on the Development of Memory and Cognition*. (R.V. Kail and J.W. Hagen). Lawrence Erlbaum Associates, New Jersey.

Moely, B.E. (1977). Organizational factors in the development of Memory. In: *Perspectives on the Development of Memory and Cognition*. (R.V. Kail and J.W. Hagen). Lawrence Erlbaum Associates, New Jersey.

Piaget, J. (1926). *The Language and Thought of the Child*. Routledge, London.

Snow, C.E. and Ferguson, C.A. (1978). *Talking to Children*. Cambridge University Press, Cambridge.

Stein, N.L. and Glenn, C.G. (1977a). An analysis of story comprehension in elementary school children. In: *Multidisciplinary approaches to Discourse Comprehension*. (R. Freedle). Ablex, Inc., Hillsdale, New Jersey.

Stein, N.L. and Glenn, C.G. (1977b). The role of structural variation in children's recall of simple stories. Paper presented at meeting of Society for Research in Child Development, New Orleans.

Trabasso, T. (1975). Representation, memory and reasoning. How do we make transitive inferences? In: *Minnesota Symposium on Child Psychology*. Vol 9. (A.D. Pick). University of Minnesota Press, Minneapolis.

Wagner, D.A. (1978). Memories of Morocco: The influence of environment on memory. *Cognitive Psychology*, 10, 1-28.

THE EFFECTS OF KNOWLEDGE AND EXPERIENCE ON THE FORMATION OF RETRIEVAL PLANS FOR STUDYING FROM TEXTS

A.L. Brown and J.C. Campione
University of Illinois
Champaign, Illinois

Effective reading, including the ability to study prose passages, is an essential prerequisite for success in any academic milieu. Yet there is considerable evidence that mastery of such skills is quite late in developing, and it is by no means a safe assumption that all college students possess a serviceable, flexible, repertoire of effective study skills. Over the past few years we have been conducting a series of studies concerned with the general question of how children go about the complex task of studying texts. In these studies, we have examined a variety of reading tasks, especially reading for meaning, reading for doing (instruction following) and reading for remembering (studying). In this paper we will limit our attention to one simple skill involved in studying, the selection of retrieval cues to aid recall. As with our previous studies concerned with text learning we consider the problem in the context of what is already known about learning, memory, attention and "meta" knowledge in children and how such preexisting developmental data can be applied to understanding practical tasks of learning from texts. (Brown, 1978)

We have a good deal of evidence that children only gradually come to understand and appreciate the nature and use of retrieval cues (Flavell, 1977), however, the majority of prior studies, have concentrated on variations of list-learning tasks. But the ability to plan ahead for future recall is an essential prerequisite for effective study in a whole variety of situations, not the least of which are the typical learning activities that occur in schools. Students engaged in studying texts are equally dependent on a variety of retrieval cue activities that no doubt include sophisticated note-taking, underlining, summarizations and selective re-reading-activities that serve to focus attention on important elements. (Brown & Smiley, 1978)

What would a learner have to know in order to form an adequate retrieval plan for studying from tests: at least he must know something about a) his own ability to recall prose, b) strategies to enhance recall if it falls short of a desirable level of acuracy and c) the structure of the passage, particularly its important and unimportant aspects. In this series of studies we will consider the development of such knowledge.

First, what does the recall of prose passages look like in young children? Using folk tales as materials we have found that the pattern of recall is remarkably similar across ages. While older subjects recalled slightly more than younger ones the general pattern of results is consistent across the age range of 8 to 18 years, the least important units of a story are recalled less frequently than all other units and the most important units are most often recalled. (Brown & Smiley, 1977) Even young children reproduce the gist of stories favoring the main theme or important elements in their recall.

If there is an essential similarity across ages in how children construct a message from prose passages, are there any interesting developmental trends? As children mature they become better able to identify the essential organizing features and crucial elements of texts. This is an essential prerequirement for effective use of a limited processing capacity and limited time when studying. Without such knowledge it would be difficult for the child to select important units for strategic study.

We examined the child's increasing sensitivity to textual importance by asking students to rate the importance level of units of the Japanese stories. This procedure has interesting qualities for it provides us with a means of ascertaining whether the child has sufficient knowledge to determine what are the important elements. There was a clear developmental trend with a gradual improvement in the sensitivity to degree of importance emerging over the entire age range studied. Apparently sensitivity to the importance of constituent units develops gradually and is still being refined in college populations. Thus, although young children's recall may follow a similar pattern to that of adults, they do not possess the metacognitive information concerning what are important elements of complex texts. In a previous series of studies (Brown & Smiley, 1978) we have found that this lack of foresight seriously hinders their ability to benefit from extra study time. Children who are aware of the degrees of textual importance (and possess a suitable study strategy) improve their recall after studying by concentrating on the essential at the expense of trivia. Subsequently they recall more important material but their retention of less essential information is not influenced by extra time. Younger children, not so prescient, fail to improve their recall of important units substantially even after extra study time.

How would this difficulty with identifying important elements influence retrieval cue selection? Adequate retrieval cue selection must include at least two elements of knowledge a) that textual elements vary in importance and the recall of important units is essential for coherence; and b) that one should concentrate one's efforts on important material that one has previously failed to recall or that one suspects, via self-testing, that one will fail to recall. As we have seen young children are less than adequately informed of the varying degrees of textual importance, at least of the passages used in this series of studies. There is some evidence that the strategy of studying previously missed information may also cause problems. Masur, McIntyre & Flavell (1973), investigating this study strategy in a simple list-learning task concluded that "the strategy of deliberately concentrating one's study activities on the less well mastered segments of materials to be learned, like other elementary memory strategies cannot automatically be assumed to be part of a young child's repertoire of learning techniques". In the present series of studies we considered the ability in older children studying texts to display their study-time judiciously.

STUDY I: THE EFFECTS OF EXPERIENCE ON THE FORMATION OF A RETRIEVAL PLAN

Students from three age groups--fifth grade, seventh and eighth grade, and eleventh and twelth grade, together with college students, were given the idea units of two Japanese stories printed on index cards. They were asked to select twelve (out of approximately 50) units that they would like to have as retrieval cues when recalling the passage. Half of each group were asked to select units before experience with the passage while the remainder were first given practice studying and recalling the passage. The selection data are presented in Figure 1. The pattern of results appears to be quite similar for the naive student of all ages. But a developmental trend was found in the experienced subjects. Naive students at all ages show a marked preference for Level 4 units (the most important text elements). The school students do not change their pattern of choices following experience recalling the text. Now, their prime targets for retrieval cues are the two intermediate levels of importance (Level 2 and 3). After experience with the passages, college students still reject the least important units (Level 1) as potential retrieval cues but they now also reject the most important elements. The most commonly offered explanation for this change (on posttest interrogation) was that students realized they would remember the main theme without further

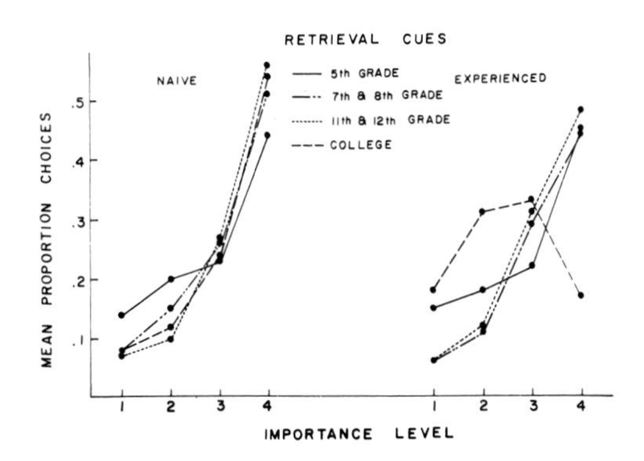

Fig. 1 The distribution of retrieval cue choices as a function of age and experience

effort, but in order to improve overall performance they would need to concentrate on the intermediate level material which caused them much more trouble on their previous recall attempt. Therefore they selected intermediate units as retrieval cucs. This shift in selection represents a sensitive awareness of the important elements of texts, and of the function of retrieval cues in recall, a sensitivity not displayed by even the eleventh and twelfth grade school sample.

The selection of suitable retrieval cues to aid in the recall of complex passages is by no means a simple task. It requires a fine sensitivity to the relative importance of various elements of texts, understanding of suitable study strategies, and an appreciation of the complex interweaving of these factors. Because of this complexity, we find a very late emergence of a suitable retrieval strategy. Only college students change their pattern of responses dramatically after one experience studying the passage, selecting units of intermediate importance to form the scaffolding for their subsequent recall attempt. This modification is an intelligent one, for approximately 80% of the most important units would have been recalled on their first try without the use of retrieval cues (Brown & Smiley, 1977, 1978). Thus, selection of relatively less central units as retrieval cues would be an optimal plan for a second recall attempt. We know that in a simpler paradigm, much younger children seem to be aware that items they have failed to recall should be given extra study. But it is not until college age that this knowledge is reflected in suitable retrieval plan modification for studying text materials.

STUDY II: REPEATED EXPERIENCE AND RETRIEVAL CUE SELECTION

In the previous study we found that only college students modified their selection of retrieval cues after experiencing a study-recall attempt with the target passage. School children continued to select mainly important units, thereby failing to show the fine metacognitive judgment displayed by the more experienced studiers, the college students. In the next experiment we examine whether increased experience alone would be sufficient to induce the same form of retrieval cue shift in younger children.

School students from fifth through twelth grade and college students were given the retrieval cue selection instructions from the previous study; however, in the second experiment they had multiple trials of the "study-select cue-recall" activity. On each trial the students were told to do anything they liked to help them remember. After termination of the study period they selected twelve retrieval cues which they kept with them during their free recall attempt. After recall and a rest period the entire prodedure was repeated, three times for college students and older school children, up to six times for the younger participants. We will consider only the first 3 trials. Note that on Trial 1 all students were naive in the sense of never having recalled the passage; on all subsequent trials they were, of course, experienced.

The data from the older participants are presented in Figure 2. Consider first the college students. The pattern of

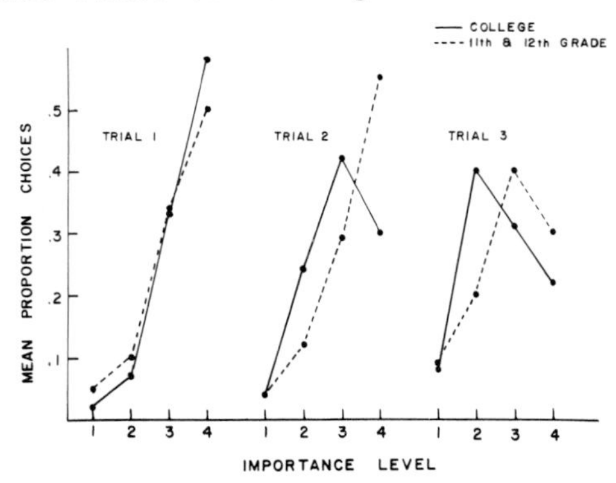

Fig. 2

Retrieval cue selection over trials for the older subjects.

the previous study was replicated. On the naive Trial 1 the students selected predominantly important (Level 4) units for retrieval aids. On the first experienced trial (Trial 2) they shifted to a preference for Level 3 units while on the second experienced trial (Trial 3) they preferred Level 2 units. On all three trials Level 1 units were treated appropriately as trivia. This is a nice replication of the shifting pattern of cue selection reflecting the gradual acquisition of the material.

Did any of our school children show this fine sensitivity? There is some encouraging data from the oldest group. Although, on the first experienced trial (Trial 2) they do not shift preference, by the second experienced trial their selections are beginning to change in a fashion comparable to college students. This age difference is illustrated in Figure 2. On trial 2 (first experience) only the college students shift their choices away from predominantly Level 4 units. But by Trial 3 eleventh and twelth graders also show the shift; they are precisely one trial behind. This lag could be due to slower learning -- i.e., both groups shift when they reach the same criterion of learning but the younger students take an extra trial to reach that criterion. It could also be due to a slower selection of the effective study strategy of switching to less important units -- i.e., both groups learn as much on each trial but it takes the school students longer to realize they need to shift cue selection. We are currently analyzing the relation between cue selection and recall levels to distinguish between these alternatives.

The data from the younger students suggest that the ability to rapidly modify one's retrieval plans as a function of the current state of learning is a late developing skill. There was some slight evidence of a decrease in Level 4 unit selection over trials for the ninth graders but it was not dramatic. Even less sensitivity was shown by the eighth graders who were remarkably consistent in their choices across trials. Indeed, they tended to choose the same cues on each trial even though their learning state changed. They tended to settle on a set of cues on Trial 1 and repeated the same selection on each succeeding trial--not exactly an effective study strategy.

SUMMARY: As we have found with prior work concerned with other study strategies such as underlining, note-taking, summarization, etc., (Brown, 1978; Brown & Smiley 1978) the ability to select suitable retrieval cues is a late-developing skill, because it requires a fine degree of sensitivity to the demands of gist recall tasks. The successful user of the flexible retrieval plan illustrated in these studies must have a) information concerning his current state of knowledge, i.e., what he knows of the text and what he does not yet know; b) knowledge of the fine gradation of importance of various elements of texts, i.e., what is important to know and what can be disregarded; and c) the strategic knowledge to select for retrieval cues information that he has missed previously. For it's not just the deployment of a strategy and the knowledge base upon which it must operate. The knowledge base must include at least some forms of self knowledge (i.e., myself as a memorizer), task knowledge (gist recall features) and text knowledge (importance vs. trivia, organization of text, etc.) The orchestration and coordination of these forms of knowledge demands a sophisticated learner and it is therefore, not surprising that efficient performance is so late in emerging.

ACKNOWLEDGMENTS: This research was supported by grants HD 06864, HD 05951 and a Research Career Development award HD 00111 to the first author.

REFERENCES

Brown, A.L, Metacognitive development and reading. In R.J. Spiro, B. Bruce & W.F. Brewer (Eds) *Theoretical Issues in Reading Comprehension*. Hillsdale, N.J.: Lawrence Erlbaum Associates, 1978. in press

Brown, A.L, & Smiley, S.S. Rating the importance of structural units of prose passages: A problem of metacognitive development. *Child Development*. 1977. 48 1-8.

Brown, A.L. & Smiley, S.S. The development of strategies for studying texts. *Child Development*. 1978, in press

Flavell, J.H, Metacognitive development, Paper presented at the NATO Advanced Study Institute on Structural/Process Theories of Complex Human Behavior, Banaff, Alberta. Canada, June 1977.

Masur, E.F., McIntyre, C.W. & Flavell, J.H. Developmental changes in apportionment of study time away items in a multi-trial free recall task. *Journal of Experimental Child Psychology*. 1973, 15 237-246.

HOW DOES MEMORY WRITE A SYNOPSIS ?

P. L. Harris and M. Meerum Terwogt
Developmental Psychology, Free University
Amsterdam, The Netherlands

Children of 5, 8 and 10 years were asked to recall a simple story after a delay of minutes or of several days. All age groups recalled the original story in a synoptic fashion, particularly after the longer delay. Analysis of the most complete protocols (i.e. those produced by the oldest children after the shorter delay) showed that a semi-hierarchical network guided recall; propositions placed low in the network were cued by propositions placed high in the network. The network analysis is used to explain how delay produces an increasingly synoptic version of the original story.

INTRODUCTION

Recent work on children's memory suggests that although the younger and the older child may have the same basic memory capacity, the older child uses that capacity more effectively. His encoding and retrieval of material is more planful and he is more sensitive to the deficiencies of his own memory, particularly with respect to non-meaningful material such as word-lists or digits (Harris, 1978). The younger, child, in contrast, tends toward a planless optimism. He treats his memory in the same way that Mr. Micawber treated his pocket: "something is sure to turn up".

No doubt, the young child's optimism is frequently justified. He can easily produce and understand his mother tongue, find his way to school, recognise his friends and learn to skate-board with no deliberate mnemonic strategy. Thus in order to get a representative picture of the development of memory, we must also study memory in situations where strategies might play a relatively minor role. Accordingly, the present study examined the development of story recall.

Following Bartlett (1932), long term memory for stories by adult subjects has received considerable experimental attention. The findings indicate that adults' recall of a story is increasingly synoptic as the delay between initial hearing and eventual recall is lengthened. The distortions in recall which Bartlett reported have not always been found in subsequent studies; distortions appear to be unlikely if the story contains prosaic materials which the subject can readily assimilate to his own schemata (Dooling & Christianssen, 1977).

Since virtually nothing is known about the young child's delayed recall of stories - although there is limited data on immediate recall - we asked whether the tendency toward increasing synopsis, so prevalent in adults, is also found in children. The data collected also served as a basis for constructing a model of the synoptic process. In order to minimize the likelihood of distortion, a story with a simple and common-place causal sequence was deliberately used.

METHOD

A total of 96 children were tested, divided into three age groups (5 years; 8 years; 10 years). Half the subjects in each age group recalled the story after a brief delay (20 minutes) and half after a long delay (approximately 9 days). All subjects were told the following story (translated from the original Dutch): "There was a little boy who liked biscuits very much. When his mother was not at home one morning, he secretly tried to get a biscuit, but he could not reach it because the dish with biscuits was much too high. So he put a chair beside the cupboard and climbed on it. When he wanted to take a biscuit, he knocked against a lemonade bottle with his arm. The bottle fell on the ground and broke. When his mother came home, she was very angry and gave him a telling-off. To make his mother happy again, he picked some flowers for her."

Subjects were then asked to recall the story in their own words after either a delay of 20 minutes or several days. Their narrative was tape-recorded.

RESULTS

To get an overall picture of accuracy of recall, the original story was divided into 22 propositions and protocols were scored in terms of whether or not they contained the gist of each proposition. Protocols were also scored for inaccuracies: a _distortion_ consisted of the replacement of an original proposition by a new one (e.g. the protocol stated that a bottle of milk was knocked over rather than a bottle of lemonade). Each such substitution was counted as one distortion. An elaboration was scored if subjects added to the original story without distorting it (e.g. the protocol stated that the boy's mother had gone out to do some shopping rather than that she had simply gone out). The results indicated that delay systematically reduced the number of accurately recalled propositions for all three age groups, but despite this sharp reduction in total accuracy, subjects did not supplement their recall by distortion or by elaboration. Both these tendencies were equally rare in immediate and delayed recall(See Table I).

TABLE I

Accurate recall of propositions, distortions and elaborations

Age		Accurate Recall	Distortions	Elaborations
5	Imm.	7.25	0.38	1.38
	Delay	2.38	0.25	0.31
8	Imm.	10.25	0.81	0.56
	Delay	5.56	0.62	1.31
10	Imm.	14.93	0.81	1.68
	Delay	7.25	0.56	1.31

Table 1 clearly indicates that children, like adults, produce an increasingly synoptic version of the original story over time. The drop in accurate recall reflects omission rather than distortion.

A true synopsis depends upon selective omission rather than random omission. To what extent were subjects selective in their omission? Examination of the set of protocols indicated that propositions were omitted asymmetrically with respect to one another. More specifically one of a pair of propositions could appear in a protocol without the other but not vice versa. For example although subjects who mentioned that the bottle fell, frequently omitted to say that the boy knocked it, the reverse was not true. Whenever they said that the boy knocked the bottle, they also said that it fell. Intuitively, this asymmetry is plausible because the falling of the bottle is more central to the gist of the story than the exact reason for its falling.

Such asymmetries were also recursive. For example, subjects would not say that the boy knocked the bottle without saying that it fell, but in addition, they would not say that the bottle fell without adding that the boy was trying to get a biscuit. A tree-structure was derived from these asymmetries, using the protocols of the oldest subjects engaged in immediate recall (i.e. the most complete protocols) as a data base. The protocols of each of the remaining five groups of subjects were subsequently checked for their fit with this tree-structure.

The tree-structure was derived as follows: each proposition was successively designated a target proposition; propositions adjacent to this target in the original story were examined one by one to find the nearest proposition which was present in all the protocols of subjects containing the target. Adjacency was defined in terms of the order of propositions in the original story and propositions were examined in the order: n - 1, n + 1, n - 2, n + 2, n - 3, etc. The total set of asymmetries obtained in this way is depicted in Figure 1.

Figure 1: The Propositional Network

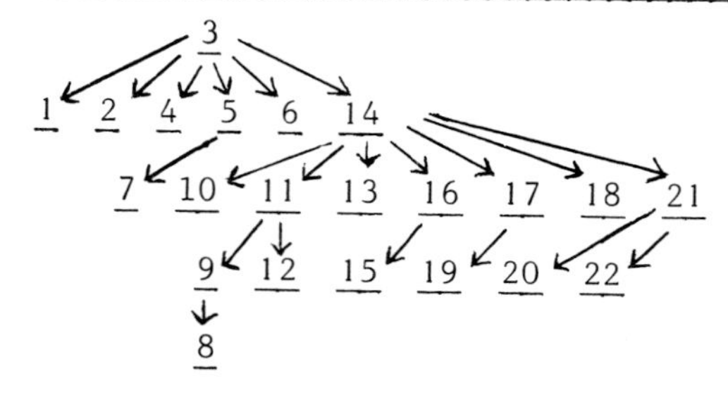

(Key to propositions: 1) Mother was not at home 2) one morning 3) he tried to get a cookie 4) secretly 5) but he could not reach it 6) the dish 7) was much too high 8) so he put 9) a chair by the cupboard 10) when he wanted to take a cookie 11) he knocked against 12) with his arm 13) the lemonade bottle 14) which fell 15) on the ground 16) and broke 17) when his mother came home 18) she was very angry 19) and gave him a telling-off 20) to make her happy again 21) flowers 22) he picked)

Any proposition in this structure is only found in a protocol if all the propositions which lie on a path up to and including the highest placed proposition (i.e. No. 3) are also found. For example, no subject mentioned proposition 20 unless he had also mentioned propositions 21, 14, and 3. We may now ask whether this structure fits the protocols of younger children and/or children engaged in delayed recall. A child recalling propositions at random would violate the structure because many propositions would be mentioned in the absence of propositions lying on a path from that proposition up to and including proposition 3. On the other hand, if propositions are chiefly dropped from the bottom of the tree-structure, few violations can occur.

To check whether propositions were mentioned at random, the number of violations actually produced by subjects within each combination of age and delay was compared to the number of violations that would be expected if production was indeed random. (The method for estimating the latter is explained in Appendix 1) For all five groups (i.e. ignoring the group which served as a data-base for the tree-structure) the observed number of violations was much smaller than would be expected given random production ($t \geq 3.78$, $p < .001$, in all 5 cases).

As a final step in data analysis, the tree structure was used to distinguish three levels in subjects' protocols: an upper level (proposition 3 plus all propositions immediately below it, i.e. 1,2,4,5,6,14) a middle level (propositions 7, 10,11,13,16,17,18,21) and a lower level (propositions 9,12, 15,19,20,22 and 8). The number of propositions recalled at each level is given in Table II.

TABLE II

Propositional Recall as a function of Level in the Tree

Age		Upper	Middle	Lower
5	Imm.	2.19	2.79	1.88
	Delay	1.00	0.66	0.63
8	Imm.	3.50	3.39	2.88
	Delay	2.69	1.97	0.63
10	Imm.	4.75	4.92	4.56
	Delay	3.13	2.24	1.56

A three way analysis of this data (Age X Time of Recall X Level) confirmed that recall increased with age and declined from immediate to delayed recall. More interesting, is the main effect of Level (F, 2,90,=8.945, $p < .01$) and the interaction of Level X Time of Recall (F, 2,90,=3.174, $p < .05$). Recall was better for the upper levels. The interaction indicated that this was especially true for delayed recall since memory loss was most severe for propositions located at lower levels in the network.

In summary, although younger children recall fewer propositions than older children, a semi-hierarchical network of propositions appears to underlie the recall of all age-groups. Delayed recall is characterised by selective omission with little tendency toward distortion or elaboration - at least for the simple materials used in the present study. Omission is selective in the sense that propositions located at lower levels in the network are more vulnerable to omission than higher level propositions.

DISCUSSION

The above results can be used to develop a more detailed model of the process of recall. Assume that the story is reconstructed from the top to the bottom of the network: a retrieval cue from the experimenter initially activates the highest placed proposition (i.e. 3 in this case) which serves as a cue in its turn for propositions which are directly linked to it (i.e. 1,2,4,5,6,14), which in their turn can cue still lower propositions.

Given this simple model of the retrieval process, how would memory for a story become more synoptic over time ? We may make the further assumption that the cue function of each proposition becomes weaker over time. Propositions which depend for their retrieval upon the completion of a long chain of cues from the top of the network to the bottom will be especially vulnerable to retrieval failure in delayed recall because of the occurrence of a break in the retrieval chain. Higher placed propositions depend upon a shorter chain and should therefore be less vulnerable to loss. This result was of course obtained: propositions at the lowest level in the network were especially likely to be omitted in delayed recall. However, the upper level propositions, which are presumably more central to the gist of the story remained accessible and could be formulated into an accurate albeit highly synoptic version of the original story

Alternative accounts of synoptic processes run into difficulties. For example, one might suppose that propositions decayed at different rates, propositions central to the story decaying more slowly than propositions concerned with minor details, but this would require the tagging of propositions during input with an index of centrality or importance. Yet young children (Brown & Smiley, 1977) are unable to engage in such a rating task, although their recall tends to emphasize the more important propositions. The advantage of the hypothesis proposed above is that differential memory loss is an incidental by-product of location in the network, and not something that the child must consciously specify. Nonetheless, we are left with a further question, namely how are propositions assigned their place in the network ? We note first of all, that several authors (Bransford & Johnson, 1973; Bransford & McCarrell, 1975) have argued that comprehension and later recall depend upon the ability to locate incoming propositions within a context. These authors have restricted their attention, however, to the role of a single initial context such as might be provided by the title of a story or an illustration. We propose that contexts are generated throughout the story by the subject in an iterative fashion. One proposition can serve as the context of storage for a second proposition which can serve as a context of storage for a third. Each such context can subsequently provide a recall cue for the retrieval of other contexts. To take a concrete example from the present study: proposition 3 (the boy wants a cookie) can serve as a context for his ensuing course of action and its eventual outcome (the eventual falling of the bottle, proposition 14); this latter proposition can serve as a context for his mother's anger, proposition 18.

How should age differences be explained in terms of the network analysis ? Two hypotheses may be considered. In the first place one might argue, particularly on the basis of the similarity between immediate recall in younger children and delayed recall in older children (see Table I) that younger children are more susceptible to a loss of the cue function provided by propositional contexts. If the cue function declines more quickly over time in young children, their immediate recall should approximate delayed recall in older children. The difficulty with this account is that it predicts that the difference between older and younger children should increase over time. No such interaction between Age and Time of Recall was observed however.

A second hypothesis is not vulnerable to the above difficulty. If we assume that younger children make a less exhaustive use of the cue function provided by each proposition, they should recover fewer propositions at each level than older children. Other evidence (Kobasigawa, 1977) confirms that young children are less systematic in their use of retrieval cues. The untested implication of this hypothesis is that the difference between spontaneous and prompted recall should be greater for younger children.

From a practical point of view the above results are encouraging. The young child, like the older child appears to adopt a hierarchical retrieval plan. This should not blind us, of course, to the important differences between younger and older children in the knowledge that they may bring to bear in their initial construction of a network during comprehension and in their spontaneous use of that network as a retrieval plan. It does indicate, however, that we can reasonably ask young children to talk or write about stories that they have heard or episodes that they may have witnessed.

REFERENCES

Bartlett, F.C. (1932). *Remembering*. Cambridge University Press, Cambridge.

Bransford, J.D. and Johnson, M.K. (1973). Consideration of some problems of comprehension. In: *Visual Information Processing*. (W.G.Chase). Academic, New York.

Bransford, J.D. and McCarrell, N.S.(1975). A sketch of a cognitive approach to comprehension. In: *Cognition and the Symbolic Processes*. (W.B. Weimer and D.S. Palermo). Lawrence Erlbaum Associates, New Jersey.

Brown, A.L. and Smiley, S.S.(1977). Rating the importance of structural units of prose passages:A problem of metacognitive development. *Child Development*. 48, 1-8.

Dooling, D.J. & Christianssen, R.E. (1977). Levels of encoding and the retention of prose. In: *The Psychology of Learning and Motivation*. Vol 11.(G.Bower). Academic, New York.

Harris, P.L.(1978). Developmental aspects of memory. In: *Aspects of Memory*. (M.M.Gruneberg and P.E.Morris). Methuen, London.

Kobasigawa, A. (1977). Retrieval strategies in the development of memory. In: *Perspectives on the Development of Memory and Cognition*. (R.V.Kail and J.W.Hagen). Lawrence Erlbaum Associates, New Jersey.

APPENDIX: The expected number of violations =

$$\frac{\text{number of propositions recalled}}{\text{Total possible(i.e. 22)}} \times \frac{22 - \text{number recalled}}{22 - 1}$$

X 44 (i.e. the total number of loci in the network where a violation could occur.)

WHY OLDER CHILDREN REMEMBER MORE: CONTRIBUTIONS OF STRATEGIES AND EXISTING KNOWLEDGE TO DEVELOPMENTAL CHANGES IN MEMORY

M.J.A. Howe
University of Exeter,
Exeter, England.
S.J. Ceci
University of North Dakota,
Grand Falls,
North Dakota 58201, U.S.A.

ABSTRACT

As children get older they acquire more effective strategies for coding, organizing, rehearsing and retrieving items in memory. Older children and adults were observed to exhibit more resourcefulness than younger children in searching the contents of memory. When subjects organized word lists in two alternative ways, older children could switch between the two organizations to retrieve items. Their greater retrieval flexibility led to improved recall. It was also found that when effective retrieval cues were available to all subjects, young children recalled as many items as older children. If recall cues elicited meanings that were incompatible with to-be-remembered words for older children, the younger subjects correctly recalled more items than their elders.

INTRODUCTION

Why do older children perform better on memory tasks than younger children? The view that developmental changes take place after early childhood in the basic capacity or "hardware" of the memory system receives little support from recent research. Memory development appears to be caused by age-related improvements in strategies and plans (including ones that are completely automatic and unaccompanied by awareness), by changes in executive memory processes, and by increases in the degree of knowledge about the particular materials that are to be remembered. Some researchers, for instance Chi (1976) and Huttenlocher and Burke (1976) have expressed the view that children's increasing knowledgeability about items is a more fundamental cause of age-related memory improvements than increases in their use of effective strategies. More often than not, however, the above factors work in combination to produce changes in the ability to remember. The lines of demarcation between the different causes are somewhat fuzzy. The present investigations concern the joint contributions to remembering of the knowledge children possess and the strategies by which they use their knowledge in order to remember.

A STUDY OF RETRIEVAL FLEXIBILITY

We were interested in the strategies that children use to aid in retrieving items that have been retained, and we conducted one experiment to examine an aspect of retrieval in which it appeared likely that age-related strategy differences would contribute to performance. We investigated what may be called 'retrieval flexibility'. The findings of previous research suggest that when recall of items retained in memory is required, older children and adults exhibit greater resourcefulness in searching the contents of their memories to retrieve correct items. The kind of flexibility that was examined in the present experiment is indicated by constructing a list of items that can be categorised in two alternative ways. Imagine a list like the following one:

Stagecoach Buffalo Sled Caribou

These items can be categorised into *taxonomic classes*, as follows:

Stagecoach Sled ('Transport') and *Buffalo Caribou* ('Animals'). Alternatively they can be grouped into *themes*, as follows:

Stagecoach Buffalo ('The Wild West') and *Sled Caribou* ('The Frozen North').

Let us assume that a person is trying to recall such a list. At the time of recall he uses category headings as cues to facilitate recall of the individual items. There comes a time when he can remember no more of the items in a given category. At this point an individual who has a flexible retrieval strategy will be able to switch from retrieving items on the basis of one kind of categorization (say, taxonomic classes) to another (say, themes). Another person may rely exclusively on either one of the alternative forms of classification in order to provide retrieval cues. The former, more flexible, strategy yields higher levels of recall, since it provides the learner with additional retrieval cues when no more words can be generated by one system of classification.

The experimental subjects in the present study (Ceci and Howe, 1978a) were children aged four years, seven years, and ten years, there being 24 subjects at each age. The materials to be recalled were 25 black-and-white drawings of familiar objects that could be classified in each of two ways, first thematically, into five themes (The Wild West, The Orient, The Desert, The Alps, The North Pole) with five items in each, and, second, taxonomically, on the basis of word class, into five semantic categories (Travel, Animals, People, Clothing, Homes), again with five items in each. For instance, a picture of a camel could be taxonomically classified as belonging to the group of Animals and it could also be thematically classified as belonging to the group of Desert items.

In a training session the children were shown the pictures one at a time, and they were asked to name them. Afterwards the children were shown the items in the five taxonomic or thematic groups. Half the subjects practiced grouping the items thematically until they could replicate the correct groupings and then they repeated the process with taxonomic grouping. The other children trained with taxonomic grouping first. Immediately after the training in grouping, each child received a cued-recall test. The cues corresponded to the five taxonomic labels and the five thematic labels used in grouping the items. There was very little difference in performance at this test between the eldest and the youngest children. It appears that there were no substantial age differences in *retention* of the items. However, when a free recall test was administered 24 hours later, the obtained pattern of results was very different, the oldest children recalling fifty percent more items than the youngest. The average number of items recalled (out of 25) was 12.25 for the four-year-olds, 16.75 for the seven-year-olds and 18.50 for the ten-year-olds. Clearly, when explicit recall cues were *not* available, the older children performed much better. In trying to explain why, we examined the recall protocols of individual subjects. Investigation revealed that during retrieval the ten-year-olds switched between modes, that is, from the thematic to taxonomic or *vice versa*, more than twice as often as seven-year olds and four times as often as the four-year-olds. In every 60 instances in which the words recalled by ten-year-olds went from one group of items to another group, 38 of these instances involved a switch between the two modes. However, in the four-year-olds, in every 60 instances in which recall of an item in one group was followed by an item from a different group there was a switch between thematic and taxonomic modes on only nine occasions.

It is conceivable that the observed age-related differences in switching between modes during retrieval were not due to variations in switching *per se*, but to differences in the number of items that were actually encoded in the different modes. However, using a technique devised by Tulving and Watkins (1975) on the cued-recall test data to measure memory trace composition, we found that there were very similar proportions of traces containing both modes of information in children at different ages.

The findings showed that younger children infrequently switched between the thematic and taxonomic modes of classifying the items on occasions when such a strategy would have facilitated retrieval and hence increased the level of recall. When the older children had exhausted the items they could recall from one group, they were much more likely to make a switch, enabling them to recall more items. As a consequence, the gap between what was initially retained in memory and what was successfully retrieved 24 hours later was much less in the older than in the younger subjects.

Would it be possible to improve young children's performance by training them to switch more? At present we don't know. The very limited amount of switching observed in four-year-olds may indicate a specific deficit in the strategy of making switches, or it may be indicative of a more general limitation in the ability to keep more than one dimension in mind at the same time. If the limited switching in the present study is due to a broadly based limitation in young children, specific training in switching between modes of organization at the time of recall would be ineffective. However, if the limitation is a more specific one, training may improve memory test performance considerably.

THE INFLUENCE OF KNOWLEDGE ON RETRIEVAL

We were also interested in the contribution to memory of the greater amount of knowledge possessed by older children, compared with younger children. In a pilot study Stephen Ceci (Howe, 1976) showed pictures of animals to children aged three and four years. He explained to them that the birth of each animal occurred in one of three different ways, placental, monotreme and marsupial.

Some other children of similar age, who formed a control group, spent an equal amount of time looking at pictures of the same animals but the experimenter did not describe to them the semantic attribute of means of birth. On a later session the children were shown nine of the original pictures again, and after a ten-minute period they were asked to recall the animals they had recently seen. At this stage it was found that those children to whom the semantic attribute of natal class had been explained were able to remember significantly more items than the other subjects. Furthermore, when the order of the words recalled by each child was examined, it was found that the former children showed almost total clustering into groups defined by the different natal classes. No equivalent semantic grouping was observed in the other children. In short, children who had acquired appropriate knowledge about semantic features of words spontaneously categorised the items on the basis of this knowledge, without being given any instructions to do so. Categorising items in this way increased the accuracy of recall.

Research by Tulving and others has shown that if a word is presented to a subject together with an associated word, and a new word that is also an associate of the original word is presented at the time of recall, the new word will not always facilitate recall of the original item, even though the new word might appear to provide a cue for retrieving the original item. Instead, there is a degree of what Tulving terms 'Encoding Specificity'. The specific encoding operations that take place when the item to be remembered is first presented determine whether a particular cue that is provided at the time of recall will be effective or not. Only if the information or meaning that is coded when the original word and the accompanying item are presented is the same as a meaning of the new word used as a retrieval cue will the latter help a subject to recall the correct item. Thus, if the original word to be remembered, *BALL* was accompanied by *dance*, subsequent presentation of the *bat* as a retrieval cue would be ineffective. Although *bat* is semantically related to *BALL* it does not elicit the particular meaning inherent in the original *dance*-*BALL* pair.

The encoding specificity effect can be used as the basis of a technique for providing information about relationships between a person's knowledge and his ability to remember things. Two experiments by Ceci and Howe (1976) were undertaken to discover whether differences in the knowledge possessed by children of different ages contributes to developmental improvements in memory test performance. If young children semantically encode word items they perceive, one would expect that they would be as susceptible as adults to the compatibility of the meanings evoked by, first, the input pair comprising a word to be remembered and a related word item and, second, the output pair consisting of the word provided as a recall cue and the to-be-remembered word.

In one experiment, we compared recall by children aged seven, ten and thirteen years in a situation in which previous preparation of appropriate materials, using a large sample of other children, had established the likelihood of children at the various ages knowing the different meanings of the words used to produce compatible and incompatible pairings. As expected, children at all ages performed better when the output cue words prompted similar (that is, compatible) meanings to the input cues. In fact, in those circumstances in which the meanings of input and output cues were known to the children, and they were compatible, there were *no* differences in performance between older and younger children. Among the four conditions, in which the compatibility of input and output word pairs was manipulated, as was the presence or absence of their meanings by the children, the only condition in which the older children *did* perform significantly better than the younger ones was the one in which the children all knew the meanings of the different word pairs, but the meanings of input and output pairs were different, or incompatible, so that the output word would *not* serve as an effective retrieval cue for the word to be remembered. In this condition the thirteen-year-olds did much better than the seven-year-olds, recalling about twice as many correct items. To hark back for a moment to the retrieval flexibility experiment, this latter condition provides precisely the kind of situation in which a flexible retrieval strategy would have the greatest effect. The results of the earlier experiment might encourage us to predict the present finding that older children (who make the switches associated with a flexible retrieval plan) would perform much better than the younger children.

In another experiment we followed up a specific prediction that arises from the encoding specificity research. Imagine a situation that involves incompatible output and input cue pairs. The words are chosen so that older children know all the meanings of the words that are necessary for the incompatibility to be discerned, but the younger children lack knowledge of the word pair meanings that are incompatible. For the younger children, although the output cue would not evoke the correct word, neither would it evoke a meaning that was different from one that had been acquired from the input pair. Hence it would not 'lead the subject astray' along an erroneous retrieval path or route, in the way that would happen in the case of a subject who did know all the pair meanings. Under such circumstances we would predict that the younger children would actually recall *more* items than older children. This is precisely what we found. When older children possessed sufficient knowledge about a to-be-remembered word so that its input and output cue pairings elicited incompatible encodings, their performance was substantially inferior to that of younger children who lacked this knowledge. Comparing recall of the same word materials by children at different ages, performance on materials involving incompatible cues always dropped dramatically at the precise age at which the children's semantic knowledge became sufficient for them to discern the incompatibility.

The findings of another study (Ceci, Lea and Howe, 1978) indicate that the common view that young children encode items only on the basis of physical and perceptual attributes, and cannot encode semantically may be quite wrong. We have established that the relative proportions of semantic location and colour information in children's memory traces remain substantially constant from age four upwards. In conclusion, it appears that increases in knowledge, in metamemory, and in the ability to use strategies account for many if not all of the observed developmental changes in memory after infancy.

REFERENCES

Ceci, S.J. and Howe, M.J.A. (1978a). Age-related differences in free recall as a function of retrieval flexibility. *Journal of Experimental Child Psychology*. In Press.

Ceci, S.J. and Howe, M.J.A. (1978b). Semantic knowledge as a determinant of developmental differences in recall. *Journal of Experimental Child Psychology*. In Press.

Ceci, S.J., Lea, S.E.G. and Howe, M.J.A. (1978). Structural analysis of memory traces in children from age four to age ten. *Journal of Experimental Child Psychology*. In Press.

Chi, M.T.H. (1976). Short-term memory limitations in children: Capacity or processing deficits? *Memory and Cognition*. 4, 559-572.

Howe, M.J.A. (1976). Good learners and poor learners. *Bulletin of the British Psychological Society*. 29, 16-19.

Huttenlocher, J. and Burke, D. (1976). Why does memory span increase with age? *Cognitive Psychology*. 8, 1-31.

Tulving, E. and Watkins, M.J. (1975). The structure of a memory trace. *Psychological Review*. 82, 438-543.

MEMORY, VOLITION, AND THE STRUCTURE OF ACTIVITY IN CHILDREN

Donald H Sykes
Queen's University, Belfast
Northern Ireland

My interest is not so much in memory for its own sake, but rather in the development of control of voluntary behaviour in children. A brief reflection on such a topic quickly leads to an appreciation that memory must play some part in that development. The fine discriminative judgements which are a notable feature of voluntary behaviour, require the extraction of relevant information from the environment and the interpretation of that information within the context of knowledge. Clearly, parts of this process involve elements of what is referred to as memory. The question then is, what are the characteristics of memory and its development that have implications for our understanding of volition and its development?

We tend to view the higher psychological processes such as "sensation and perception, attention and memory, association and logical relation, judgement and reasoning" (Luria, 1971) as the cognitive precursors and major determinants of the form and structure of the particular behaviours that we observe. If at times we seem to place relatively little emphasis on the nature and content of the problem in determining the structure of the observed behaviour of the individual, we give even less attention to the influence of these factors in determining the structure of the psychological processes which we infer are involved in the behaviour.

The case that I will argue is that the form and content of the problem on which the subject acts determine not only the type of activity in which the subject will engage, but are also major determinants of the structure of the psychological processes brought to bear upon the task. Within the context of the development of the child, I will argue that there is no reason to believe that there are qualitative changes with age in the structure of processes such as memory. Rather, what changes with age is the child's knowledge of the world, the type and range of activities in which he engages, and his relative familiarity with tasks. It is these factors that have a major influence in shaping some of the observed differences in memory with age.

DETERMINANTS OF MEMORY

The Task

The experimental paradigm that I have used has been to give different children different tasks to perform on the same stimulus material, namely words, and to examine the consequences of the different activities for memory. For example, in one study (Sykes, 1976) each child was assigned to one of six experimental conditions. Three of the conditions required a structural analysis of the stimuli, that is the children had to state in the case of each word whether or not it contained the letter A. The other three conditions required a semantic analysis, since each word had to be categorized according to whether it was the name of an animal or a country. Following these tasks, the children's recognition memory for the stimuli was tested.

Not surprisingly, memory strength, as measured by 'd', was less following a structural analysis as compared to a semantic analysis ($F(1,96) = 30.63, p < .001$: $\overline{X}$ semantic = 2.32; $\overline{X}$ structural = 1.58). This is perfectly understandable in the context of the writings of such individuals as Craik & Lockhart (1972), Jenkins (1974), and Schulman (1971). What was more interesting from our present point of view was the significant interaction between age and the experimental condition. Recognition memory following a semantic analysis was similar for all three age groups ($F(2,48) = 0.54$, ns; $\overline{X}$ 8 yr = 2.19; $\overline{X}$ 10 yr = 2.44; $\overline{X}$ 12 yr = 2.34), whereas, following a structural analysis the younger children's memory was significantly inferior to that of the older children ($F(2,48) = 11.37, p < .001$; $\overline{X}$ 8 yr = 0.97; $\overline{X}$ 10 yr = 1.78; $\overline{X}$ 12 yr = 1.98). The conclusion that I draw from this finding is that the age differences found in this study cannot be ascribed to qualitatively different memory states in the different aged children. If this were so, then you would expect these qualitative differences in memory structure to manifest themselves in the semantic condition also. They did not.

Levels of Skill

The second point that I wish to make concerns the level of skill brought to the task by the child, and the consequences of this for memory. In the structural condition the younger children, while achieving the same degree of accuracy in categorizing the stimuli, took noticeably longer than the older children. ($F(2,36) = 23.60$, $p < .001$; $\bar{X}$ 8 yr = 2.23; $\bar{X}$ 10 yr = 1.76; $\bar{X}$ 12 yr = 1.38). I think that it is reasonable to interpret the longer latencies of the younger children as indicating a lower level of automatization of the component skills brought to the task. This had a significant effect on memory. For, it was the case that while the younger children's memory following a structural analysis of the stimuli was significantly worse than that following a semantic analysis, as the children get older the difference in memory performance following the two conditions became less. If you accept that an analysis of words in terms of the presence or absence of the letter A is not a sound basis for the later recognition of those words, then one must conclude that with the older children, in addition to their structural analysis of the stimuli, they were also carrying out additional analyses of the stimuli in terms of their meaning. This suggests that in the case of the younger children, the low level of automatization of the component skills brought to the task precludes them from carrying out additional analyses on the semantic content of the stimuli. In effect, a difference in memory performance between younger and older children would appear to reflect, in this case, not a quantitative or qualitative difference between the different aged children in memory structure, but rather a difference in the level of organization of the component cognitive skills brought to the task.

The findings from the second study (Sykes, 1978) that I wish to mention relate to two issues. Firstly, the relative importance in determining memory of task versus person characteristics, and secondly, the nature of the influence on memory of the content or material of the task. As regards the first issue, if there is an inherent structure to memory, then you would expect that there would be individual variation in that structure, which should express itself in performance. In effect, then, this is an additional test concerning the source of the structure observed in memory.

Task Versus Person Characteristics

The individual difference dimension that I have chosen for this test is that of reflection-impulsivity. I have chosen it because it has been claimed by Messer (1976) that what distinguishes the reflective from the impulsive child is that "... the reflective (child) not only spends more time evaluating his hypothesis but also gathers more information on which to base his decisions, and he gathers it more systematically than the impulsive" (Messer, 1976, p.1028). The relevance of that claim to memory is, of course, obvious.

In this second study there were sixty boys of about eight years of age. There were three experimental conditions. There was a structural condition, as in the first study, where the subjects had simply to indicate whether or not the word contained a letter A. There was a semantic condition, where the subjects had to provide a verbal definition for each word. In the third condition the subjects were told that they were to learn each word, and that their memory for the words was to be tested later. This condition I refer to as the intentional condition,for here the focus of the activity was the intention to remember. The other two tasks are incidental tasks, in that memorization was not the primary focus of the activity carried out on the stimuli. In addition to the experimental condition to which each subject had been assigned, I had for each subject a measure of his latency of responding and number of errors on the Matching Familiar Figures Test (Kagan, Rosman, Day, Albert & Phillips, 1964), which measures are commonly used to distinguish the reflective from the impulsive child. Latency, errors, and the experimental condition were the predictors in a multiple regression analysis (Kerlinger & Pedhazur, 1973), with the criteria being predicted being the subject's memory and response bias, as measured by the non-parametric signal-detection measures, A' (Grier, 1971; Berch,1975) and RI (Berch, 1975). There were two recognition tests, one immediately after the initial presentation of the items and the second a week later.

On the first recognition test, a substantial 49% of the variation in A' was determined by the predictors (Multiple R= 0.70, $F(3,56)= 18.18$, $p<.001$), which explained variation was solely attributable to the experimental conditions. A week later, the influence of the experimental conditions has declined, now accounting for some 29% of the variation in A', and the cognitive style dimension has emerged, accounting for 11% of the variation (Multiple R= 0.63, $F(4,55)= 9.20, p<.001$). A similar picture holds for RI, the measure of the response bias that the subject brings to the task, with the difference that far less of the variation in RI is determined by the predictors. Of the 21% of the variance determined by the independent variables on the first recognition test (Multiple R= 0.45, $F(4,55)= 3.55$, $p<.025$), 17% was attributable to the experimental conditions, with a non-significant 4% contributed by the cognitive style dimension. A week later, the experimental conditions account for some 15% of the variation, with cognitive style contributing a further 8% (Multiple R= 0.48, $F(3,56)= 5.63$, $p< .005$).

My interpretation of these results is, again, that the task is a major determining factor for memory, and further, that the task is a constraining factor for memory, in that it can swamp or suppress potentially relevant personal characteristics. Only as the constraints placed on memory by the task are weakened, in this case by the passage of time, do personal characteristics emerge as determining factors.

The Content of the Task

The second point that I want to make concerns the role of the material in determining memory. In the studies that I have described, the stimuli have always been words. The central characteristic of words is that they have meaning. The other characteristics of words, such as the fact that they are composed of letters, different letters, and different serial positions of letters, for example, are trivial in comparison to the semantic aspect of words. It is not surprising therefore that memory for words is greater following a semantic analysis of the words than following a structural analysis in terms of the presence or absence of the letter A. The latter type of analysis does not allow a distinction to be made between old and new words. It could only do that if, for example, all the old words contained a letter A, and none of the new words did. In which case of course, the observation of that fact by the subject would lead to a perfectly accurate distinction between the items in the two categories.

It is not therefore simply a question of the semantic analysis being a deeper level of analysis than the structural analysis (Craik & Lockhart, 1972). Rather it is the question of the relevance of the analysis to the material being analysed. The better memory for the stimuli following a semantic analysis reflects the fact that in a situation where you are required to distinguish between words, the best means of achieving this is in terms of their meaning, since that is the characteristic on which all words differ. If you were ignorant of the language it would still be possible to achieve a high recognition if the subject carried out a deep analysis of the constituent letters of each of the words, coding them perhaps in some numerical fashion. But this would be very costly in terms of time and cognitive effort.

Memory, to an extent that is not always recognized, is locked into the material. Observed memory appears to reflect the influence not so much of some hypothetical memory structure, but rather the characteristics of the material, and the nature of the activity carried out on the material. The activity performed on the material can itself be determined, in part, by the material. There was evidence for this from both studies. In the first study it was evident that in the structural condition, where a semantic analysis of the stimuli was not required, nonetheless the older subjects, who came to the task with a relatively high level of information processing skills, engaged, I would suggest involuntarily, in a simultaneous analysis of meaning. In the second study, memory following the intentional condition was very similar to that following the semantic condition. Essentially, this indicates that when you are told to memorize words, insofar as you can do so you study their meaning, for that is the commanding feature of words.

MEMORY AND VOLITION

At the beginning of this paper I said that I was really interested in volition and its development. What does memory contribute to that? In the second study you will recall that I had two measures, A' and RI. The latter was the measure of response bias. This measure varies between a bias to respond 'not seen before' to all items, which we could label a cautious attitude, to a bias to respond 'seen before' to all items. Let me suggest that the measure of response bias, RI, has some elements in common with the concept of volition, since volition is essentially concerned with the question of when to respond and which response to make. What then is the relation between our measure of memory, A' and RI? I analyzed the three experimental conditions separately. (A note of caution has to be introduced, since the correlations that I will mention are now based on only 20 subjects in each instance, which makes for some unreliability).

In the structural condition, where memory strength was the weakest, the values of RI were also the lowest, indicating that if you have very little memory for the stimuli then you tend to a cautious response mode. Following the intentional condition, where memory is stronger, so the subject becomes less cautious. With the semantic condition, where memory was the strongest, the subjects are the least cautious. That is the general finding as regards the absolute values for A' and RI. If now you correlate individual A' and RI scores in the three conditions separately, what you find is that in the structural condition there is no correlation between the two measures (1st recognition: $r= -0.14$, df 18, ns; 2nd recognition: $r= 0.13$, df 18, ns), nor is there a correlation between the two measures in the semantic condition

(1st recognition: r= 0.04, df 18, ns; 2nd recognition: r=0.08, df 18, ns), but in the intentional condition there is a significant correlation between the two measures, with an r= 0.40(df 18, $p < .05$) on the first test, and an r= 0.48(df 18, $p < .025$) on the second test. In other words, in the two incidental conditions, where intentional memorization was not the focus of the activity, even though the absolute RI values reflect the absolute A' values, at the individual level memory does not determine response bias. Only in the intentional condition does this occur.

CONCLUDING COMMENTS

You will no doubt appreciate that the interpretations that I have given to the experimental findings go, to use a well-known expression, beyond the information given. However, in support of the interpretations I would point out that they are quite compatible and convergent with certain other developments in psychology. Very briefly, in an area of psychological functioning closely related to memory, namely attention, Kahneman (1973) has argued that the allocation of effort is determined primarily by task characteristics. Still in the area of attention,but dealing with an aspect of attention that we usually think of as having a greater degree of structure, namely the orienting response, Barham & Boersma (1975) have found that there is no uniform orienting reaction across different task conditions. Rather, the structure of the orienting response at any one time appears to be a function of such variables as the task, the subject's age, and the response mode. The authors conclude that the orienting response is multidimensional in character, with its structure changing in response to changes in task structure.

Luria (1971; 1976), in a social and historical context,has argued that the characteristics and structure of the higher psychological processes cannot be understood simply as reflecting the characteristics of nervous tissue. Rather he says, they are social in origin and they are mediated in their structure. Cofer (Cofer, Chmielewski & Brockway, 1976), on the basis of his experimental work with prose recall, states his conclusions concerning the nature of memory when he says that, "Fundamentally, the problem anyone faces in a task situation is to figure out what must be done to satisfy the demands of that situation. Our subjects in experiments calling for recall, generated statements, and sorting... showed substantial adaptibility to task demands. That is, they did what we asked and what they did varied as a function of what we asked"(Cofer et al.,1976,p.200). And later he says, "The point of all this discussion is to warn against an irreversible decision opting for a conception of human memory that contains fixed structural arrangements. Knowledge may be arranged somewhere in our heads...but the operations we perform on knowledge, in the light of the tasks that we are asked to perform, suggest to us those arrangements can be highly flexible"(Cofer et al., 1976, p.202).

Flexibility, adaptibility, modifiability, these are key words when conceptualizing the higher psychological processes. In the last ten thousand years or so, the major thrust of evolution has not been in the direction of new anatomical structures. Rather, the major development has been in terms of activities and functions. What differentiates 20th Century man from, let us say, pre-historic man, is less a difference in structure and more a difference in function and the range of activities that 20th Century man can and does engage in. The evolution of function and action has occurred in close conjunction with the evolution of, to use Popper's terminology (Popper, 1972), objective knowledge. The majority of man's activities are a function of that knowledge, and are structured by that knowledge. The complexity of present day knowledge, and the complexity and range of man's activities, could not have happened if they had had to develop on the basis of fixed and structured psychological processes.

As psychologists, to understand the nature of psychological processes, such as memory, we must understand more deeply than we do at present, the nature of human or objective knowledge, and then study the manner in which individual minds interact with that knowledge. When we do that we will emerge with a far more complex, and sophisticated picture of the remarkable flexibility of the human mind. Let me now end with a quotation from Karl Popper, who said, in the context of memory, "Such things cannot be explained, I think, by a mere repetitive mechanism, but only, I feel inclined to conjecture, by the action which a discerning mind exerts upon memory contents - contents which are related to the World of theories and of action programmes"(Popper & Eccles, 1977, p.143).

REFERENCES

Barham,R.M. & Boersma,F.J.(1975). *Orienting Responses in a Selection of Cognitive Tasks.* Rotterdam University Press, Rotterdam.

Berch,D.B.(1975). Measures of sensitivity and response bias for the probe-type serial memory task. *Journal of Experimental Child Psychology.* 20, 149-158.

Cofer,C.N., Chmielewski,D.L. & Brockway,J.P.(1976).

Constructive processes and the structure of human memory. In: *The Structure of Human Memory.* (C.N.Cofer,ed), pp. 190-203. Freeman & Co., San Francisco.

Craik, F.I.M. & Lockhart, R.S.(1972). Levels of processing: a framework for memory research. *Journal of Verbal Learning and Verbal Behavior.* 11, 671-684.

Grier, J.B.(1971). Nonparametric indexes for sensitivity and bias: computing formulas. *Psychological Bulletin.* 75, 424-429.

Jenkins,J.J.(1974). Remember that old theory of memory? Well, forget it. *American Psychologist.* 29, 785-795.

Kagan,J., Rosman,B.L., Day,D., Albert,J. & Phillips,W.(1964). Information processing in the child: significance of analytic and reflective attitudes. *Psychological Monographs.* 78, (1, Whole No. 578).

Kahneman, D. (1973). *Attention and Effort.* Prentice-Hall, New Jersey.

Kerlinger, F.N. & Pedhazur,E.J. (1973). *Multiple Regression in Behavioral Research.* Holt, Rinehart & Winston,New York.

Luria,A.R.(1971). Towards the problem of the historical nature of psychological processes. *International Journal of Psychology.* 6, 259-272.

Luria,A.R.(1976). *Cognitive Development. Its Cultural and Social Foundations.* Harvard University Press,Cambridge, Mass.

Messer,S.B.(1976). Reflection-impulsivity: a review. *Psychological Bulletin.* 83, 1026-1052.

Popper,K.R.(1972). *Objective Knowledge. An Evolutionary Approach.* Clarendon Press, Oxford.

Popper,K.R. & Eccles,J.C.(1977). *The Self and Its Brain. An Argument for Interactionism.* Springer, Berlin.

Schulman,A.I. (1971). Recognition memory for targets from a scanned word list. *British Journal of Psychology.* 62, 335-346.

Sykes,D.H.(1976). Stimulus processing and recognition memory in children. *British Journal of Psychology.* 76, 429-438.

Sykes,D.H.(1978). Determinants of memory and judgement in reflective and impulsive children. *Unpublished manuscript.*

TRAINING GENERAL METACOGNITIVE SKILLS IN RETARDED CHILDREN

J.C. Campione and A.L. Brown
University of Illinois
Champaign, Illinois

INTRODUCTION

While research concerned with the memory performance of retarded children has a long history, more recent work is noteworthy for its reliance on what has been called the instructional approach to this problem. While there are important theoretical reasons for this emphasis, there are also obvious practical ones, and it is these which will concern us here. The impetus for this work stems directly from experimentation addressed at the role and use of various strategies in determining memory performance. It has become clear that mature memorizers use an impressive array of strategic devices when faced with the problem of trying to commit material to memory, and that these strategies vary considerably with subtle changes in the task demands and requirements. It is by now also apparent that immature memorizers in general, and retarded individuals in particular, do not generate such strategies when faced with tasks in which they would be appropriate.

The educational implications of this state of affairs are straightforward. Given that poor performance reflects, at least in part, a failure on the part of retarded individuals to employ task-appropriate strategies, it becomes an obvious next step to see if teaching them such strategies would result in enhanced performance. The answer to this question is a clear and emphatic "yes." In a large number of experiments, the results have been consistent in showing that even brief training is effective, and that with more intensive and carefully designed training, dramatic improvements in performance could be effected (Belmont & Butterfield, 1977; Brown, 1974; Campione & Brown, 1977). Thus, this line of research has both identified an area where retarded individuals experience problems and shown that instruction can lead to worthwhile improvement <u>on the training vehicle</u>.

These results were extremely encouraging, and follow-up

research was then designed to evaluate the potential educational benefits in more detail. Specifically, the training programs were evaluated against three basic criteria of effectiveness: (1) performance should improve as the result of instruction, both in terms of accuracy and in terms of the strategies used to effect this improvement; (2) the effects of this training must be durable; it is obviously desirable to show that what has been trained can be detected after a reasonable time period has elapsed; and (3) training must result in generalization to a class of similar situations where the trained activity would be appropriate, for without evidence of such generalization, the practical utility of the instruction would be minimal.

While there was no problem satisfying the first criterion, criteria 2 and 3 caused more difficulty. Although relatively brief instruction would lead to temporarily improved performance, the less experienced memorizer showed a marked tendency to abandon a trained strategy when not explicitly instructed to continue in its use. However, additional progress has been made with regard to the second criterion, and a number of recent studies have shown that more extended training can result in durability of a trained behavior for at least a year, although the tendency of subjects to show such maintenance does appear to be related to developmental level. Very young or retarded individuals are more likely to abandon the strategy than are slightly more sophisticated trainees (cf. Brown, 1978).

The criterion which has presented the most serious problem is generalization, or transfer to appropriate new situations. There is general agreement that evidence for flexible generalization to new situations is sadly lacking. This inflexibility in the use of trained skills in new situations is particularly problematic when the trainee is a retarded child. Both American and Soviet psychologists, not to mention parents and teachers, have repeatedly observed the difficulty mildly retarded children experience with generalization. Indeed it has been suggested that one of the major problems with slow-learning children is that they tend to use new information only in the specific situation in which it was acquired. Successfully training the child to use a simple skill in one specified situation seems to be well within our competence as instructors; getting the child to use the information appropriately in other settings appears to be the major hurdle.

To summarize, inefficient and slow-learning children tend not to use a variety of simple memory strategies spontaneously. However, they can be instructed to execute those strategies quite easily. This improvement can be relatively durable on the specific task on which the training took place, but flexible use of the skill in new situations is rarely found. Adopting the view that our task as instructors is to induce generalization, we need to consider how this might be accomplished, i.e., what changes in research strategy would seem desirable? We have elsewhere (Brown & Campione, 1978) summarized a number of possible approaches based on the design of training routines *per se* or on the processes which we target for training. It is the latter with which the present research was concerned. Rather than training routines specifically tailored to the needs of a specific task, we attempted to inculcate more general knowledge concerning strategies and their use--a class of metacognitive skills. These skills, including such processes as checking, planning, self-testing, etc. are characteristically lacking in retarded children's laboratory learning performance; further, they are the very processes implicated in breakdowns of effective generalization (Campione & Brown, 1978).

INSTRUCTIONAL PHASE

The data to be reported here were collected as part of a larger project investigating the effects of teaching retarded students drawn from special education classes a simple "stop-check-and-study" routine. The larger project consisted of an initial training program, followed by a number of tests for maintenance of the instructed routines and finally, one year after the initial instruction, a probe for generalization. The original sample was divided into two groups based on functioning level. Both groups had a mean IQ of approximately 70, but the mean mental ages were around 8 years for the Old group and 6 for the Young group. The training phase, described in detail in Brown and Barclay (1976), made use of a simple ordered recall task. Briefly, the students were required to study a set of pictures for as long as they wished, with the task being to indicate when they were sure they could recall the items perfectly and in order. Thus, they were asked to study the items, monitor the correct state of their learning, and terminate study only when they had mastered the items sufficiently well that they were prepared for the recall requirement.

Prior to any intervention, performance on this task was exceedingly poor, and students regularly terminated study well before they were able to recall all the items. Both the Young and Old students were then divided into three groups for purposes of training. Two of the groups were trained in the use of strategies, anticipation or rehearsal, which involve self-testing elements, and the third a strategy, labeling, which does not. This latter condition served primarily as a control treatment. In each group, the students were required to go through the list once, naming each picture. This labeling trial was followed by a series of three more trials on which the procedures varied with group membership. Those in the Anticipation group were trained to anticipate the next picture in the sequence by saying its name before looking at it. The Rehearsal subjects were trained to rehearse the items in sets of three. Finally, the Label group was told to go through the list three more times, labeling each item. All groups were further encouraged to continue with the instructed activity until they were sure they could recall all the items.

All students were given a series of post-tests following the training. As expected, the Label subjects continued to perform poorly, but those in the Rehearsal and Anticipation groups improved their accuracy significantly. For the Old subjects, the effects of training were maintained over a one-year period; however, the Young children reverted to pre-training levels of performance as soon as the experimenter stopped reminding them to continue with the instructed routine.

GENERALIZATION

The generalization phase of the study took place about 15 months after the end of the training sessions. As the Young students had failed to show evidence of maintaining the strategies on the training task itself, it was decided not to test them for generalization. We were able to locate and test 33 of the 39 students comprising the original Old sample, 12, 11, and 10 from the Anticipation, Rehearsal and Label groups, respectively. In addition, a New group of 17 subjects was included in the design. These children shared the same classes as the trained subjects and were of comparable IQ and mental age as those students; however, they had no previous experience in our training program.

The generalization task selected was one which we believed to be more representative of the type of study activity required in the classroom. Most studying requires the student to extract the main ideas of prose passages and regurgitate the gist of the ideas in his own words. Our question was, would training recall-readiness on the simple rote-list learning task help children on the more typical school study activity of preparing for gist recall of prose passages? Although strategies of anticipation and rehearsal are useful on a prose learning task they would have to be modified considerably from the straight forward procedures suitable for learning lists of words. Rehearsal or anticipation of individual words would be inefficient and the subject would have to attempt anticipation or rehearsal of longer chunks of material. In addition, the criteria for judging readiness are much more subtle. In the rote recall task readiness is reached when the learner can recall all items verbatim and it is relatively easy for the learner to check this prior to recall attempts. But in the gist recall tasks, the learner must gauge when he has grasped the main ideas of the material, for verbatim recall is not required. Thus, the training and transfer tasks were quite different in their strategy-use and strategy-monitoring requirements even though they demanded the same general "stop-check-study-recheck" routine.

The stimulus materials consisted of a set of 12 simple stories written to be of second grade difficulty. The stories were divided into idea units by independent groups of college students, with the stories ranging in length from 10 to 19 idea units. The stories were then retyped with one idea unit per line and given to other independent groups of college students who were asked to rate the idea units in terms of the importance to the story following a procedure introduced by Johnson (1970). This resulted in the identification of the least important third of the units (Level 1 units), the middle third (Level 2 units), and the most important third (Level 3 units).

Each subject was seen individually on a total of six days. No mention of the prior testing was made to the subjects. Each day consisted of having them study and recall a randomly selected pair of the 12 stories. The experimenter read each story to the subjects, and then the subjects read it back twice with the experimenter sounding out and explaining any words the subjects could not read or understand. The subjects were then told to read the story over, as many times as necessary in order to try to remember everything that happened. When they were sure they could tell all that happened _in their own words_, they were to ring a desk bell (indicating that they were ready) and then try to tell the story.

Performance was averaged across the 12 stories for each subject. The data of interest are shown in Figure 1, where recall accuracy is plotted as a function of Groups (Anticipation, Rehearsal, Label, and New) and Importance of the constituent idea units. An analysis of variance revealed significant ($p < .001$ in all cases) effects due to Group, Importance, and the Groups x Importance interaction. The Groups effect indicated that the Anticipation (mean recall = 50%) and Rehearsal (49%) groups outperformed the Label (35%) and New

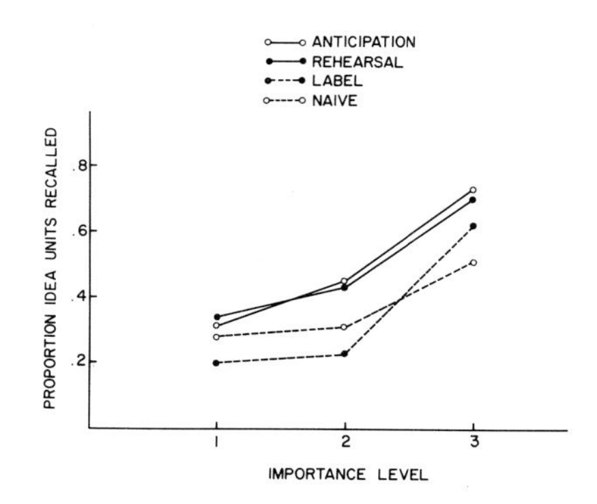

Fig. 1 Recall of idea units as a function of Groups and Importance.

(37%) subjects. Thus, students trained in the use of task-appropriate self-testing strategies did recall more than the two control groups.

The Importance Level main effect indicated that recall improved as thematic importance increased. While the latter trend was reliable for all groups ($\underline{p} < .001$), as indicated by simple effects analyses, the pattern differed across groups. Scheffé follow-ups to the simple effects analyses indicated that for the Anticipation and Rehearsal groups, there were significant ($\underline{p} < .05$) differences between Level 1 and Level 2 units, as well as between Level 2 and Level 3 units. For the Label and New groups, however, the Level 1 and Level 2 units produced comparable recall levels. For these groups, Level 3 units were recalled more frequently than Level 2 units. This pattern fits in nicely with results from prior studies of prose recall in children. Students of third grade or above differentiate all levels of importance in their recall of stories; however, less mature children, while they do favor the most important elements somewhat, fail to differentiate the lower levels of importance in recall. The less mature pattern has been found in poor readers of normal intelligence, mildly retarded children, and normal children younger than third grade. Thus, the appropriately trained subjects in this study both recalled more and demonstrated a more mature pattern of recall than did the less appropriately trained or naive controls.

SUMMARY

This study represents our first successful attempt at inculcating a generalized cognitive skill in EMR children. Students trained to use common mnemonics that embody self-testing routines were found to perform much better on the list-learning, recall-readiness task that was the vehicle of the original training. The durable effects of training were still present even a year later. Those students who successfully maintained adequate recall-readiness for a list-learning task also revealed the benefits of this training on a quite dissimilar recall-readiness task involving prose learning. Students trained in the task-appropriate strategies of anticipation and rehearsal both recalled more idea units than control subjects and showed more mature patterns of recall. We attribute the success of this training program to the redirection in our thinking concerning what skills to train. Having failed to effect generalization when attempting to inculcate specific mnemonics we turned to a more general problem solving routine involving self-testing of the effects of these mnemonics. The monitoring routine necessary for adequate recall-readiness estimation does appear to be (a) susceptible to training and (b) generalizable across quite distinct tasks.

As a result of both our success and failure in attempting to train EMR children to perform more effectively on a common memorization task we suggest that the types of cognitive activities which are most suitable for intensive intervention should have certain properties, (a) they should have wide transsituational applicability, (b) they should readily be seen _by the child_ to be reasonable activities _that work_, (c) they should have some counterpart in real-life experiences, and (d) their component processes should be well understood so that effective training techniques can be devised. This bias directs us to a concentration on a subset of general metacognitive activities (Brown, 1978) which we feel admirably fit this prescription. These include checking, monitoring, and reality testing. The initial results are certainly encouraging, and we are hopeful that future work will succeed in identifying the essential components of instructional routines which can inculcate generalizable cognitive skills.

REFERENCES

Belmont, J.M. and Butterfield, E.C. The instruction approach to developmental cognitive research. In R.V. Kail, Jr. and J.W. Hagen (Eds.), *Perspectives on the development of memory and cognition*. Hillsdale, N.J.: Erlbaum, 1977.

Brown, A.L. The role of strategic behavior in retardate memory. In N.R. Ellis (Ed.), *International review of research in mental retardation*, Vol. 7. New York: Academic Press, 1974.

Brown, A.L. Knowing when, where, and how to remember: A problem of metacognition. In R. Glaser (Ed.), *Advances in instructional psychology*, Vol. 1. Hillsdale, N.J.: Erlbaum, 1978.

Brown, A.L., and Barclay, C.R. The effects of training specific mnemonics on the metamnemonic efficiency of retarded children. *Child Development*, 1976, 47, 70-80.

Brown, A.L., and Campione, J.C. Permissible inferences from the outcome of training studies in cognitive development research. In W.S. Hall and M. Cole (Eds.), *Quarterly newsletter of the Institute for Comparative Human Development*, 1978, 2, 46-53.

Campione, J.C., and Brown, A.L. Memory and metamemory development in educable retarded children. In R.V. Kail, Jr., and J.W. Hagen (Eds.), *Perspectives on the development of memory and cognition*. Hillsdale, N.J.: Erlbaum, 1977.

Campione, J.C., and Brown, A.L. Toward a theory of intelligence: Contributions from research with retarded children. *Intelligence*, 1978, 2, 279-304.

Johnson, R.E. Recall of prose as a function of the structural importance of the linguistic unit. *Journal of Verbal Learning and Verbal Behavior*, 1970, 9, 12-20.

TRAINING RETARDED PEOPLE TO GENERALIZE MEMORIZATION METHODS ACROSS MEMORY TASKS

J.M. Belmont and E.C. Butterfield
University of Kansas Medical Center
Kansas City, Kansas
J.G. Borkowski
Notre Dame University
Notre Dame, Indiana

ABSTRACT

Eighteen retarded adolescents memorized 50 lists of letters over 2 sessions. Session 1 had 2 slightly different recall tasks. All subjects were trained to use an appropriate memorization method for the first task; on the second task, 9 were given generalization training. Two weeks later all subjects faced 4 tasks: The 2 previous ones; 1 slightly different (delayed near generalization); 1 very different (delayed far generalization). Both groups managed immediate generalization, but only the twice-trained group showed delayed generalization.

INTRODUCTION

If you know how to perform some particular cognitive task very well, you can fashion instructions to induce a child to do what is necessary. The dependable result is that the child shows a large increase in performance on the training task, but he may quickly lose this learning, and he will rarely generalize it to another task. Why, the field is asking, does the noninstructed child not instruct himself? Why does he not solve the problem of developing a good method for that task? And why is our training so immediately effective, yet so transient and non-generalized? In asking such questions, developmentalists have shifted their attention away from specific mechanisms needed to perform specific tasks. They are now considering instead the child's executive management of his own thinking (Belmont, 1978; Belmont & Butterfield, 1977; Butterfield & Belmont, 1977; Brown, 1975; Flavell & Wellman, 1977), and a good deal of the current work is concerned with training generalization skills. This emphasis on training and generalization has arisen, no doubt, because training of specific skills for specific tasks has proven so immediately successful, and the ability to foster executive management of one's own thinking--especially in retarded children--has such obvious human value.

Ann Brown and Joe Campione (in press) have a beautiful analysis of permissible inferences from outcomes of cognitive training studies, and they have summarized the prevailing hypotheses. Borkowski and Cavanaugh (in press) have also captured the main idea, which boils down to this simple formula: Teach what you want to be learned. If you want the child to learn a specific method for a specific task, teach the method around the task. But do not "teach and hope" (Stokes & Baer, 1977). If you hope for generalization, then treat generalization as the task to be mastered, analyze it, and teach a method derived from that analysis.

Viewing generalization as problem-solving, Brown and Campione suggested at least this list of trainable problem-solving skills: Planning, checking, asking questions, self-testing, monitoring one's efforts. In the present training study we focused on such activities. Moreover, to give the child a model for generalization, we trained him in two separate episodes, using one form of the mnemonic method in the first, a distinctly different form of the same method in the second, and calling his attention to the similarities and differences between the two. Thus we tried to conform to two of Brown and Campione's additional suggestions for generalization training: Train in multiple settings; give direct instruction concerning generalization.

METHOD

Subjects

The 18 children in this study were mentally retarded students in a suburban Kansas Jr. High School special class system. Their age ranged from 12 to 15 years. Their word-reading level ranged from nil to 3rd grade, with an average around 2nd grade. We assigned 9 children to each of two treatment groups, one of which we trained on one form of a memorization method, the other on two forms of that method.

The General Task

On each of 50 trials the child paced himself through a list of 7 different random letters, seeing each for 0.6 seconds in a separate window, the windows being laid out in a row. No letter was repeated in a list. No list was repeated in the series. The child was free to pause however long he wished before exposing each letter in turn. Immediately after seeing the last letter in a list he attempted to execute whatever recall requirement was currently in force.

Recall Requirements

We used 4 different recall requirements. The 3/4 circular recall task required the child to recall the last 3 letters in their order of presentation followed by the first 4 in their proper order. The 4/3 circular task required him to recall the last 4 letters and then the first 3. The 2/5 task had him recall the last 2 and then the first 5. In the Position Probe task, immediately following the disappearance of the 7th letter, the child saw in the 8th window a test letter that remained until he responded. Instead of vocally recalling all of the letters, he simply pushed the window where he recalled the last letter to have appeared in the list just seen.

Study Design

There were 26 lists in Session 1. Two weeks later came Session 2 with 24 lists. The first session had 8 lists of 3/4 circular recall; then 8 more of the same, but with intensive training on a memorization method designed to meet the 3/4 requirement; then there were 5 lists of 4/3 circular recall without training; and finally 5 more lists of 4/3 circular recall. In this last block, Group 2 only were trained intensively on a variant of the previously trained memorization method.

For Session 2 the children were tested by a person they had never seen before, who did not know whether any particular child had previously received only one or both training episodes. The new tester gave no training, nor did he mention or discuss possible approaches to handling the 4 recall requirements he dealt out: 7 lists of Probe Recall (Block 5); 6 of 2/5 circular recall (Block 6); 5 of 3/4 circular (Block 7); and finally 5 lists of 4/3 circular (Block 8).

Training Routines for Session 1

Block 1. Each child tried to recall each list under the 3/4 circular recall requirement. There was no mention of memorization methods.

Block 2. We trained each child to prepare for 3/4 recall by dividing each list into two parts. He was shown that by dashing through the last 3 letters, he could easily recall them immediately in the right order without thinking much about them. This fast-finish method met the first part of 3/4 recall. To meet the second part, the child was trained to memorize the first 4 letters by moving slowly through them, building them up into a rhythmically rehearsable chunk, and then rehearsing them enough to guarantee their retrievability following the fast-finish. On every trial we tried to show the child what it means to evaluate what he was doing in the combined cumulative-rehearsal-fast-finish method, and how well it ultimately influenced recall.

Block 3. Each child tried to recall each list under the 4/3 circular recall requirement, which represents a close variant on the previous 3/4 task. There was no mention of memorization methods during these 5 trials.

Block 4. The 9 Group 1 (control) children continued under the 4/3 requirement without instruction. The 9 Group 2 (twice-trained) children, in contrast, were treated to a thorough discussion of how, first of all, a fast-finish is much more difficult with 4 letters than with 3, so a little repetition of those 4 terminal letters is appropriate; but on the other hand the rehearsal of the early 3 letters is easier than the previous 4-letter rehearsal. By such comparisons we tried to have the child understand the harmony of input and output processes, and the similarities and differences between the cumulative-rehearsal-fast-finish method for the 3/4 circular recall task and that for the 4/3 task.

Outcome Measures

Every inter-letter pause was automatically recorded to within .04 sec. There were 6 inter-letter pauses recorded for each 7-letter list. As well as being hand recorded, all spoken recall was tape recorded for later scoring. In the analyses to be reported here, we used a strict scoring of the circular recall protocols, in which every letter had to be spoken in exactly the correct position. Anything recalled after an omission not replaced by an intrusion, was scored as totally incorrect. We will here be concerned with recall accuracy for the delayed-recall portion of the lists, i.e., the items that should have been rehearsed in an appropriate cumulative-rehearsal-fast-finish method. For the Position Probe test, we will look at recall in the first 3 positions. The results are similar if we look at the first 4 positions.

RESULTS

Even though all children were treated alike over Session 1's first 3 trial blocks, the random assignment to treatment groups did not result in the two groups having precisely equal recall accuracies prior to Group 2's receiving its crucial second training episode. Group 2 was slightly but consistently more accurate than Group 1 over Blocks 1 through 3. To be sure that this inexplicable advantage would not confound the interpretation of post-treatment groups differences, we paired children across treatments according to their recall accuracies on the first 3 blocks. The members of each pair had to be closely similar to one another on *each* of these 3 blocks. Five very good pairings were found. The results over Blocks 4 through 8 for these matched groups of 5 children were closely similar to those obtained for the total groups of 9 children each. We here present the matched groups' results for all 8 blocks.

To obtain group-average pause patterns, we computed each child's average pattern for the last 3 trials of each block. We then averaged these average patterns across children within groups. Figure 1 shows these group average pause patterns for each of the 8 blocks. The onced-trained group's pause patterns are signified by 1---1; the twice-trained group's by 2——2. For each block, the two groups' overall average recall for the entire block is shown by a pair of numbered bars to the left of the pair of pause patterns. The black bars are for training trials, including Block 2 for both groups and Block 4 for Group 2 only. Above each pair of bars is Group 1's recall expressed as a percentage of Group 2's. Thus, for Block 1, the two groups each recalled about 13% of the early items, and Group 1 was 104% as accurate as Group 2. Over Blocks 1, 2 and 3, Group 1's recall averaged 108% of Group 2's, but starting with Block 4 (Group 2's 2nd training episode),

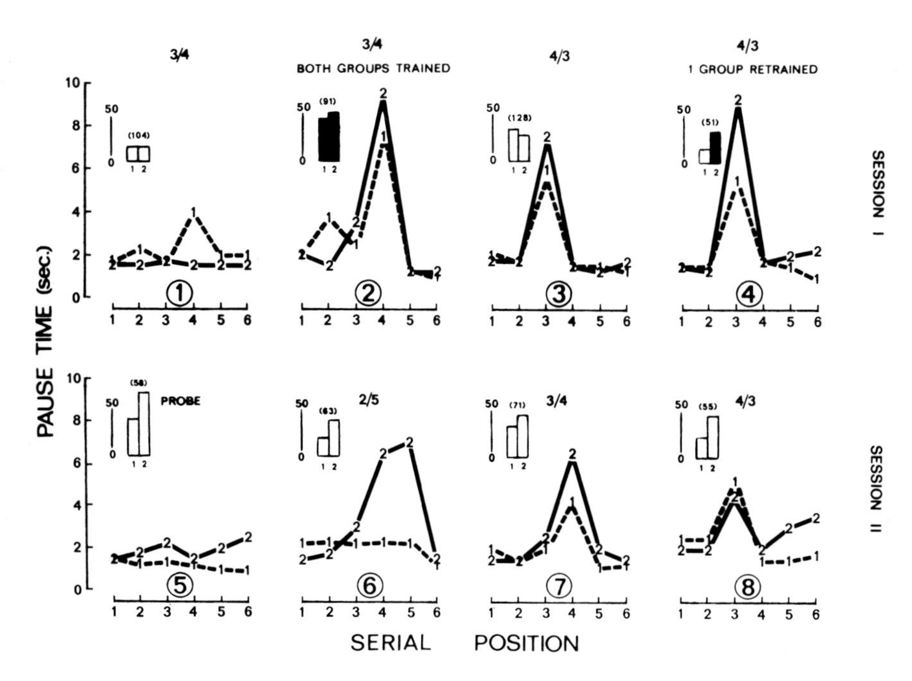

Fig. 1. Input pause patterns and recall accuracies for two groups of differently trained retarded children on each of 8 test and training blocks.

Group 1 dropped to 51% of Group 2, and averaged 60% relative accuracy over the last 5 blocks. Clearly, the second training (Block 4) gave Group 2 the edge, not only immediately, but throughout the various task changes experienced in the 2nd Session 2 weeks later.

Now, what of the pause patterns? Neither group was notably active in Block 1. Untrained retarded people rarely ever become active information processors. The pattern in Block 2 naturally conforms to the trained cumulative-rehearsal-fast-finish method that all subjects were constrained to use to meet the 3/4 circular recall requirement. The huge leap in recall accuracy attests to the method's usefulness. Going from Block 2 to Block 3, there is a shift in major pause position, from Position 4 to Position 3. This shows that both groups nicely generalized the cumulative-rehearsal-fast-finish strategy to conform to the new 4/3 circular recall requirement.

Moving to Block 4, the resumption of training clearly influenced Group 2 to become substantially more active on the early items, and to slightly polish the last 4 items (as seen in the slight divergence of the two pause patterns over Positions 4 - 6). The recall accuracy comparison in Block 4 shows that Group 1 was apparently losing interest (note their accuracy drop from Block 3), whereas Group 2, being heavily constrained to perform a pure method, held up beautifully in recall accuracy.

They never lost their advantage. Two weeks later, on the toughest generalization (Block 5's Probe Recall test), Group 2 showed an increasing pause pattern similar in shape and elevation to that obtained from university students on a 7-item probe test. Meanwhile, Group 1 reverted precisely to the typical retarded group's slightly descending pause curve for position probe (see the relevant comparisons in Belmont & Butterfield, 1971, Figure 1 b).

In Block 6, Group 2 again distinguished itself, this time on the novel 2/5 near-generalization task, by showing a lovely active 5/2 method. Group 1, in contrast, failed the test miserably. They did, however, show long-term retention on Block 7's 3/4 test and Block 8's 4/3 test. Group 2 also retained what they had learned, even including the upswing of pausing on terminal items to meet Block 8's 4/3 requirement.

We conclude that the combination of careful attention to the particulars of a method, coupled with ample feedback on how the trainee's efforts are serving him, can lead to immediate generalization of the method to a closely similar situation, and can lead to retention of the trained method over a 2-week interval. We learn from the twice-trained group, moreover, that deliberately comparing and contrasting methods for coping with similar tasks yields a bonus in far-generalization and long-term near-generalization above and beyond the benefits realized by a single training episode.

These results, derived as they are from considering both the processes and the products of memory, certainly support Brown and Campione's (in press) and Borkowski and Cavanaugh's (in press) suggestions for training generalization. We look forward to seeing the scheme much expanded, in expectation of discovering ways to bolster children's problem-solving skills across a wide range of cognitive and perhaps even social situations.

ACKNOWLEDGMENTS

This work was supported by USPHS Grants HD-00870 and HD-00026.

REFERENCES

Belmont, J.M. (1978). Individual differences in memory: The cases of normal and retarded development. In: *Aspects of Memory*. (M. Gruneberg and P. Morris eds.), pp 153-185 Methuen, London.

Belmont, J.M. and Butterfield, E.C. (1977). The instructional approach to developmental cognitive research. In: *Perspectives on the Development of Memory and Cognition*. (R. Kail and J. Hagen eds.), pp. 437-481. Erlbaum, Hillsdale, New Jersey.

Borkowski, J.G. and Cavanaugh, J.C. (in press). Maintenance and generalization of skills and strategies by the retarded. In: *Handbook of Mental Deficiency: Psychological Theory and Research*. 2nd Ed. (N. Ellis ed.) Erlbaum, Hillsdale, New Jersey.

Brown, A.L. (1975). The development of memory: Knowing, knowing about knowing, and knowing how to know. In: *Advances in Child Development and Behavior*. Vol. 10. (H. Reese ed.), pp. 103-152. Academic Press, New York.

Brown, A.L. and Campione, J.C. (in press). Permissible inferences from the outcome of training studies in cognitive development research. *Quarterly Newletter of the Institute for Comparative Human Development*.

Butterfield, E.C. and Belmont, J.M. (1977). Assessing and improving the cognitive functions of mentally retarded people. In: *The Psychology of Mental Retardation: Issues and Approaches*. (I. Bialer and M. Sternlicht eds.), pp. 277-318. Psychological Dimensions, New York.

Butterfield, E.C., Wambold, C. and Belmont, J.M. (1973). On the theory and practice of improving short-term memory. *American Journal of Mental Deficiency*. 77, 654-669.

Flavell, J.H. and Wellman, H.M. (1977). Metamemory. In: *Perspectives on the Development of Memory and Cognition*. (R. Kail and J. Hagen eds.), pp. 3-33. Erlbaum, Hillsdale, New Jersey.

Stokes, T.F. and Baer, D.M. (1977). An implicit technology of generalization. *Journal of Applied Behavior Analysis*. 10, 349-367.

MEMORY FOR SOCIAL RELATIONSHIPS IN YOUNG CHILDREN

Peter K. Smith and Patricia Delfosse
Department of Psychology, University of Sheffield, Sheffield, England

ABSTRACT

The memory of young children for social relationships has implications for both social development and memory research; relevant work is reviewed. An empirical study is described which illustrates a technique for assessing memory for companions in preschool children.

INTRODUCTION AND REVIEW

Generally, studies of memory and retention have been on aspects of the physical world - objects, words, motor skills. Memory for people, or for skills in social relationships, has not attracted much interest outside a few studies in social and child development. These studies are not often reviewed in textbooks on memory.

Nevertheless, on theoretical and practical grounds the importance of social knowledge and social relationships in the development of memory deserves more consideration. From a phylogenetic perspective, it has been argued by Humphrey (1976) that intelligence in the higher primates and humans is primarily social in origin - that it evolved largely under a selection pressure to understand and manipulate increasingly complex social relationships. While plausible, this is difficult to substantiate; but if we consider the ontogenesis of intelligence and memory in the young child the case for social origins can be more strongly put. Babies are pre-adapted to be interested in social beings and to enjoy and be able in a simple way to participate in contingent social interactions (Goldberg, 1977). Further, some would argue that knowledge and symbolic functioning develop from the start as an interactive process between the child and adults in which cultural meanings begin to be transmitted (Trevarthen, 1975; Newson and Newson, 1975). A number of empirical studies on infant-adult and peer-peer relations in children certainly attest to the important cognitive impact of the child's social world, even if questions of primacy must at present remain debatable.

Considering infant-adult relationships, many studies have found that stages of person permanence (recognising and reacting to a person as a particular, permanent entity rather than just a transient stimulus configuration) are typically well ahead of stages of object permanence. This is what Piaget refers to as horizontal decalage. While much of this decalage as reported may be due to differing task demands, even when these are controlled for, some evidence for decalage remains (Jackson, Campos and Fischer, 1978).

The development of attachment relationships between children and adults depends on the development of person permanence concepts. However it is more than just the recognition of someone as mother, father, or other particular person. Attachment is linked to the motivational aspect of relationships, and cognitive theorists such as Kagan (1974) argue that motivation, related to attempts to assimilate information, depends mainly on static stimulus discrepancy/familiarity only for the first 8 months or so of life. Beyond this age, the babies' expectations of cause-effect relations in the environment, its hypotheses as to consequences, become increasingly important. The research literature on wariness or fear of strangers in young children generally bears out the supposition that much depends on how well the baby feels it can interact with the stranger - in a sense, how much it has learnt and remembered about interactions with that person, as well as how much it can transfer from other interaction relationships (Smith, in press).

This would suggest a crucial role for memory in limiting the number of adults a child can effectively learn to develop secure relationships with; that is, the effective number of caretakers. We know from studies in social development that a child under three years can successfully be reared by up to five or ten caretakers (Weisner and Gallimore, 1977; Marvin, VanDevender, Iwanaga, LeVine and LeVine, 1977) but that having more than 20 or 30 caretakers, as often occurs in institutional care, may mean that no deep attachment relationships develop (Stephens, 1971; Tizard and Rees, 1975). This in turn may have adverse consequences later (Tizard and Hodges, 1978). Thus the question of how many caretakers a young child can cope with is of crucial practical importance. It is presumably in some inverse relationship to the time needed for the child to learn and retain the interaction skills developed with one particular person. Yet little research is available on how quickly children can learn such skills, though some beginnings have been made (e.g. Bretherton, 1978).

It is no doubt easier for young children to learn about relationships in which the partner behaves reasonably predictably; hence the importance of how the adult behaves, in the formation of attachment and affiliative relations and the waning of stranger wariness. Conversely, it seems more difficult for children under two years to learn and remember effective interaction sequences with same-age peers. As Bronson (1974) puts it, "the feedback given by peers is too variable and often too delayed to allow the baby to develop firm predictive expectancies of links between his behaviour and the actions of a peer". While this suggests a limitation which memory may put on the early development of peer interaction, we also know that children at this age are very interested in peers. Lewis, Young, Brooks and Michalson (1975) found that 12 to 18 month old children spent more time looking at an unfamiliar peer than either a familiar or unfamiliar adult. Given interest in peers, it is likely that early attempts at social interaction may play an important if not leading role in providing a context for the development of memory in real-life situations.

Some support for this comes from a study by Sluckin and Smith (1977) of peer relationships at 3 and 4 years. The study focussed on aggression and dominance relations in two preschool playgroups. It was found that the 4 year olds could report, and generally agree on, the ordering of dominance relations in their group. This implies some ability to carry out a seriation task, at an age as early as has been found by Bryant (1974) using non-social tasks, and for which he suggests memory is a crucial factor. The reported dominance orderings actually correlated well with the observed frequencies of aggression initiation by the children. These findings are compatible with the idea that preschool children pay considerable social attention to others, remember the initiation of aggressive acts by others, and use this information in at least as cognitively sophisticated a way as they would non-social information, when asked to rank the children in their group.

The studies reviewed above are suggestive, but the precise way in which memory capacities may place limitations on social relationships, and conversely how the motive to develop social relationships may provide real life practice for memorial abilities, is an under-researched area. One practical difficulty is that of finding suitable metrics for social memory, while retaining the naturalistic kind of setting which does not grossly distort actual social encounters. The study to be described here develops a suitable quantitative metric, in the context of preschool children's memory for friendly relations with others.

METHOD

The study was carried out in a part-time nursery class containing 10 girls and 8 boys aged 3 years 1 month to 4 years 7 months at the start of the term. Observations were made of children's play companions, and they were also interviewed individually. Three younger boys refused to be interviewed, but otherwise all the children cooperated well.

Observations were made every morning during two 2-week periods, one at the beginning of term and one at the end, after an eight-week interval. The class was scanned for a period of 50 minutes at the beginning of each morning, once all the children had arrived; free play was allowed during this period, after which more structured activities were typically organised. A scan was made every 2 minutes, and the names of all children in group play (Smith and Connolly, 1972) were recorded; inter-observer concordance was 83%.

Interviews about friendships were conducted using the picture sociometric technique developed by McCandless and Marshall (1957). After identifying head-and-shoulders photographs of his or her classmates, each child was asked "who did you play with a lot today?". By naming a child or pointing to a photograph, one or more nominations were obtained. The child was then asked "who did you play with a lot yesterday?". These interviews were carried out on all the observation days, except Mondays, in the latter period of the morning. All 15 children could be interviewed over two mornings, so that two 'today' and two 'yesterday' questions were asked of each child, each week. In addition, during the second week of both the initial and final two-week periods, each child was asked (twice) "who did you play with a lot last week?", and at the end of the study (final two days) each child was asked (once) "who did you play with a lot at the beginning of nursery?". Since attendance averaged 93%, and never fell below 15 during the study period, a fairly complete record was obtained.

Nominations from the picture sociometric technique were compared with who a child actually played with in the period referred to, from the observational data; to the same morning for 'today' questions, the previous morning for 'yesterday' questions, the previous week for 'last week' questions, and the whole of the initial two weeks for 'beginning of nursery' questions. Any set of observational data provided a ranking from 1 to 17 for the frequency with which a particular child was actually seen in group play with a child interviewed; thus the accuracy of a nomination could be scored from 1 to 17, with 9 representing a 'chance' baseline level if children were guessing randomly.

RESULTS

All children gave one nomination to each question, sometimes two or three. For successive nominations for each question, the mean accuracy score averaged over children is shown in Figure 1. (Means are plotted for all entries where one or more replies were received from at least half the children interviewed.) First nominations are significantly more accurate than chance levels for 'today' questions, $t(14)=11.22$, $p<.001$; 'yesterday' questions, $t(14)=9.34$, $p<.001$; 'last week' questions, $t(14)=5.22$, $p<.001$, and 'beginning of nursery' questions, $t(11)=3.00$, $p<.05$. Second nominations are significantly above chance for 'today' questions, $t(14)=6.20$, $p<.01$, and 'yesterday' questions, $t(13)=3.62$, $p<.01$, while third nominations are significantly better than chance for 'today' questions only, $t(11)=2.67$, $p<.05$.

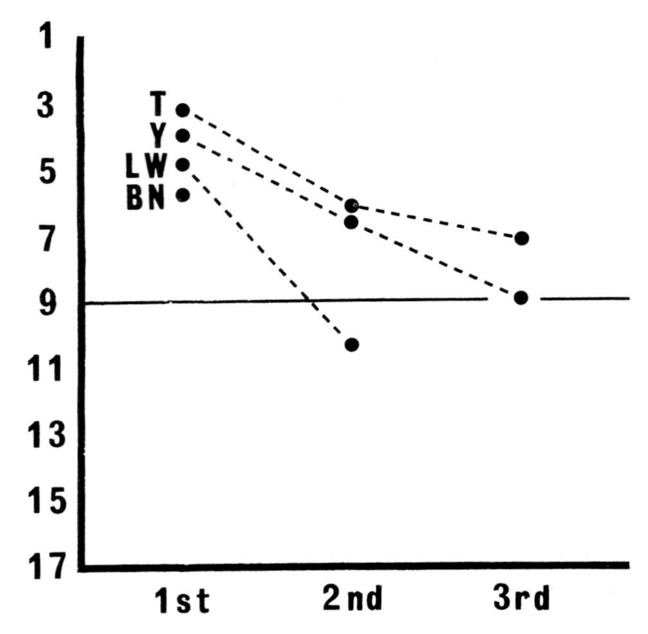

Fig. 1. Mean accuracies of successive nominations for today (T), yesterday (Y), last week (LW) and beginning of nursery (BN) questions.

The mean accuracy scores clearly decrease not only with further nominations, but also with more delayed recall. Nevertheless, the results suggest some ability to remember friendships even as early as 8 to 10 weeks previously. However before ascribing the above-chance results to long term recall, it must be borne in mind that play companionships do show some moderate but declining stability over increasing time periods. Thus, it could be that the children were unable to really recall earlier companions, but relied instead on nominating present companions in reply to all questions. This could give a pattern of results similar to those actually found.

To check whether this was indeed happening, the accuracy of 'yesterday', 'last week' and 'beginning of nursery' nominations were scored against the observations of companions on the morning of the particular interview. This should either increase accuracy (if the child was always nominating present companions) or decrease accuracy (if the child was really recalling earlier companions). Results are shown in Figure 2, which clearly favours the latter hypothesis. Acc-

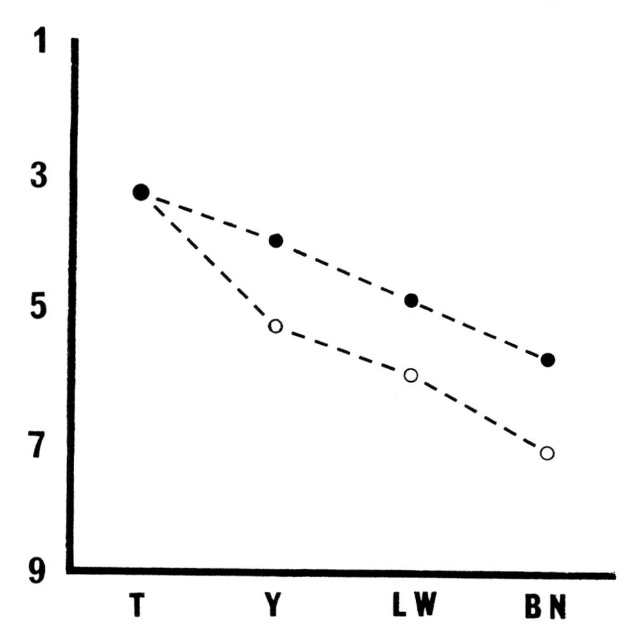

Fig. 2. Mean accuracies of first nominations (●----●) as compared with accuracies when scored against present companions (o----o).

uracies when referred to present companions are significantly worse for 'yesterday' questions, $t(14)=3.16$, $p<.01$, 'last week' questions, $t(14)=2.87$, $p<.05$, and 'beginning of nursery' questions, $t(11)=1.89$, $p<.10$. This strongly indicates that the children were using true recall strategies in the original interview situation.

CONCLUSIONS

The ability of the children to recall earlier friendships is perhaps surprising. Not only are mean responses above chance, but 52% of the 'yesterday' responses, 40% of the 'last week' responses, and 25% of 'beginning of nursery' responses nominate the child actually recorded as most played with then (accuracy score of 1). These findings support the notion that the child's social world is highly salient, for memory in particular as well as cognitive processes in general. The study provides a quantitative approach to memory research in a naturalistic social domain; further work could usefully attempt to compare memory capacities in social and non-social domains at this age range.

ACKNOWLEDGEMENTS

The authors wish to thank the children and staff of the Mushroom Lane Nursery, Sheffield, for their cooperation.

REFERENCES

Bretherton, I. (1978). Making friends with one-year-olds: an experimental study of infant-stranger interaction. *Merrill-Palmer Quarterly* 24, 29-51.

Bronson, W.C. (1974). Competence and the growth of personality. In: *The Growth of Competence* (K Connolly and J Bruner eds), pp241-264. Academic Press, London.

Bryant, P. (1974). *Perception and Understanding in Young Children*. Methuen, London.

Goldberg, S. (1977). Social competence in infancy: a model of parent-infant interaction. *Merrill-Palmer Quarterly* 23, 163-177.

Humphrey, N.K. (1976). The social function of intellect. In: *Growing Points in Ethology* (P P G Bateson and R A Hinde eds), pp303-317. Cambridge University Press, Cambridge.

Jackson, E., Campos, J.J., and Fischer, K.W. (1978). The question of decalage between object permanence and person permanence. *Developmental Psychology* 14, 1-10.

Kagan, J. (1974). Discrepancy, temperament, and infant distress. In: *The Origins of Fear* (M Lewis and L A Rosenblum eds), pp229-248. John Wiley & Sons, New York.
Lewis, M., Young, G., Brooks, J., and Michalson, L. (1975). The beginning of friendship. In: *Friendship and Peer Relations* (M Lewis and L A Rosenblum eds), pp27-65, John Wiley & Sons, New York.
Marvin, R.S., VanDevender, T.L., Iwanaga, M.I., LeVine, S., and LeVine, R.A. (1977). Infant-caregiver attachment among the Hausa of Nigeria. In: *Ecological Factors in Human Development* (H McGurk ed), pp247-260. North Holland Publishing Company, Amsterdam.
Marshall, H.R. and McCandless, B.R. (1957). A study in prediction of social behavior of preschool children. *Child Development* 28, 149-159.
Newson, J. and Newson, E. (1975). Intersubjectivity and the transmission of culture: on the social origins of symbolic functioning. *Bulletin of the British Psychological Society* 28, 437-446.
Sluckin, A.M. and Smith, P.K. (1977). Two approaches to the concept of dominance in preschool children. *Child Development* 48, 917-923.
Smith, P.K. (in press). The ontogency of fear in children. In: *The Development of Fear in Animals and Man* (W Sluckin ed). Van Nostrand, New Jersey.
Smith, P.K. and Connolly, K. (1972). Patterns of play and social interaction in pre-school children. In: *Ethological Studies of Child Behaviour* (N Blurton Jones ed), pp65-95. Cambridge University Press, Cambridge.
Stevens, A.G. (1971). Attachment behaviour, separation anxiety, and stranger anxiety in polymatrically reared infants. In: *The Origins of Human Social Relations* (H R Schaffer ed), pp137-144. Academic Press, London.
Tizard, B. and Hodges, J. (1978). The effect of early institutional rearing on the development of eight year old children. *Journal of Child Psychology and Psychiatry* 19, 99-118.
Tizard, B. and Rees, J. (1975). The effect of early institutional rearing on the behaviour problems and affectional relationships of four-year-old children. *Journal of Child Psychology and Psychiatry* 16, 61-73.
Trevarthen, C. (1975). Early attempts at speech. In: *Child Alive* (R Lewin ed), pp62-80. Temple Smith, London.
Weisner, T.S. and Gallimore, R. (1977). My brother's keeper: child and sibling caretaking. *Current Anthropology* 18, 169-180.

EFFECTS OF HUMOUR UPON CHILDREN'S MEMORY

H.C.Foot, C.A.Sweeney and A.J.Chapman
U.W.I.S.T.,
Cardiff, Wales.

According to Zajonc's theory of social facilitation, learning is characteristically impaired by the presence of a group. In a classroom situation variables which offset the distractive, arousing effects of the group need to be explored. This study examined the influence of humour that is related to the material to be learned by children in solitary and group settings. Neither humour nor the social condition directly affected memory for the information, but boys' recognition performance was superior to that of girls, a difference that is attributed to visual attentiveness.

INTRODUCTION

Studies of group learning and performance in an educational setting have been prompted by the inescapable fact of life that children are almost invariably taught in groups and rarely on a one-to-one basis. Social and educational psychologists have long been interested in the effects of group situations for learning both in terms of their beneficial effects and in terms of their detrimental effects, and this interest has directly or indirectly helped to shape educational policy vis-a -vis size of class, streaming, peer group assignments, and so on. Zajonc's (1965) well-known theory of social facilitation concerning the relative merits of the presence of others for learning and performance has received such widespread acceptance that it has to some extent blunted further research in social facilitation processes. According to this theory, the presence of others increases drive strength which enhances the emission of dominant already learned responses at the expense of non-dominant new responses in the process of being acquired. There is no doubt that many studies have supported the generality of this conclusion in a wide range of learning and performance situations. Geen (1971, 1973), for example, has shown that an audience tends to impair short-term recall in paired-associate learning but to facilitate long-term recall, a finding which points to differential effects of high arousal during the assimilation and consolidation processes.

Even if educationalists have to accept that the group setting is not ideal for the learning of new information, they might be well advised to explore other variables or educational aids which to some extent offset the over-arousing and distractive effects of the class, and maintain the child's attention in what s/he is learning. Humour is one such educational aid which, although very often assumed to be an effective means of communication enhancement in advertising, has received very little systematic empirical study in relation to learning by adults or by children.

It is not our intention to review the limited research upon the effectiveness of humour as an educational aid to learning and memory. This will be undertaken in another article in this book (by Chapman and Crompton). Suffice it to say here that despite the somewhat confusing findings, there is some evidence, particularly from Kaplan and Pascoe (1977), that humour which is related to or built into the information to be learned is more likely to enhance memory for that information than no humour or humour which is incidental or unrelated to the information. Tangential evidence for this view also comes from behavioural studies which have shown that humour responsiveness is enhanced by the presence of others and that humour stimuli serve to hold an audience's attention (cf. Chapman, 1973; Foot, Chapman and Smith, 1977).

The purpose of the empirical study to be described was to investigate among a group of seven-to-eight year-old children whether humour that is related to the information to be learned can help to counteract the impairment to learning which is expected as a consequence of the group situation. In addition to humour and social situation, sex was also selected as an independent variable on the basis of differences previously established between boys and girls with respect to their social responsiveness in humorous situations and with respect to their humour appreciation. Girls have been found to be more expressively responsive than boys in their nonverbal behaviours such as smiling and eye-contact (Chapman, 1973, 1975; Foot *et al.* 1977) and are more concerned with the social situation per se (Chapman, 1975; Foot, Chapman and Smith, 1979). Girls are also more sensitive than boys to their own and others' overt reactions to humour when judging the funniness of humour stimuli (Leventhal and Mace, 1970).

METHOD

Subjects and Materials

Forty-eight children were selected for the study, twenty-four boys and twenty-four girls aged between seven and eight years.

The study was conducted in a mobile laboratory designed for working on location in local junior and infant schools, and comprising a specially equipped children's playroom with hidden video-cameras and microphones. The material to be learned was presented through a series of nine slides (eight experimental and one practice), each depicting a different animal and each conveying a piece of information about that animal (see Table I). This information was selected on the basis that it would be of equal interest to boys and girls.

TABLE I

Information about Animals to be Learned

1. A full-grown elephant weighs 6 tons (Practice)
2. A camel's hump holds 50 gallons of water
3. A cheetah runs at 50 miles an hour
4. A chicken lays 200 eggs a year
5. A dolphin stays under water for 15 minutes
6. A flamingo's legs are 3 feet long
7. A kangaroo keeps its baby in its pouch for 8 months
8. A giraffe's neck is 8 feet long
9. A walrus' tusks are 3 feet long

In the 'humour' condition the feature of the animal about which a fact has to be learned was visually distorted or accentuated in an incongruously comical way. Also the essential element of information to be learned was displayed in a corner of the slide. In the 'nonhumour' condition exactly the same information was to be learned about the same animals. The drawings,however, were normal, non-humorous representations of the animals with no visual distortion of the feature of the animal relating to the information to be learned.

Procedure and Design

Each slide was presented for ten seconds by a caramate projector synchronised with a tape-recorder. The tape-recording consisted of the experimenter's voice verbalizing the information to be learned, as in Table I. In addition to the humour or nonhumour conditions, subjects were either allocated to a solitary or group condition. The group condition consisted of same-sex triads with the children suitably spaced to prevent copying during the recognition series that followed. Sex, humour and social conditions were therefore the three factors in this 2 x 2 x 2 independent groups design. Subjects were randomly allocated to humour and social conditions, and the presentation order of stimulus material was systematically varied.

The learning series was followed by a recognition series. The children were shown the same set of humorous or nonhumorous slides with which they had been presented during the learning series, in identical order and in the same social condition, solitary or group. In a corner of each slide, however, a set of four alternative responses was provided from which the child had to select what s/he deemed the correct response. Again, by means of a synchronised tape-recording, questions pertaining to the learned information were posed by the experimenter, for example : 'how many gallons of water does a camel's hump hold ? 20, 30, 40 or 50 gallons'. Correct responses were embedded systematically in each response position. For purposes of responding booklets were prepared requiring the child merely to tick off the response s/he judged as correct for each slide. The objective measure of memory taken was the child's correct recognitions. The experimenter sat with the children during both the learning and recognition phases of the study, adopting a low-key role and ensuring that no overt copying occurred in the group condition. The entire testing session was video-tape-recorded.

Finally in relation to the procedure, a validation of the picture stimuli was undertaken in terms of whether the children perceived as funnier those stimuli designated as humorous than those designated as nonhumorous. Twenty of the children selected randomly from those who had undergone the solitary social conditions were shown both the humorous and nonhumorous sets of stimuli in random order and asked to rate each picture for its funniness. For this purpose a modification of the simple rating procedure adopted by Davies (1977) was used, whereby the children were given a set of four line-drawn faces each depicting a stage of increased amusement (curve of the mouth). The child's task was to select the face which appeared to be expressing the same amount of amusement as s/he was experiencing in relation to each of the animal pictures.

RESULTS

Taking first the results of this follow-up validation study, there was little doubt that the animal stimuli designated as humorous were perceived by the children as substantially more amusing than those designated as non-humorous. The humour ratings for the animal stimuli are presented in Table II, from which substantial mean differences (averaging 1.4 on a four-point scale) are evident between the humour and nonhumour series. Boys and girls showed very similar ratings for both sets of stimuli.

TABLE II

Mean Ratings (Scale : 1-4) of Humorous and Nonhumorous Animal Pictures

Animal	Humorous	Nonhumorous
Camel	3.75	1.80
Cheetah	3.45	1.55
Chicken	3.60	1.90
Dolphin	3.30	1.80
Flamingo	3.35	2.25
Kangaroo	3.45	2.10
Giraffe	3.20	2.25
Walrus	3.40	2.70

The main analyses were conducted firstly on the correct recognitions by the children in the different conditions and, secondly , on certain aspects of their nonverbal behaviours extracted from the video-tape-recordings during learning. Table III sets out the mean correct recognitions from which the effects of humour and social condition can be inspected. In fact neither of these factors produced significant differences upon recognition performance. Sex was the only factor which had a significant effect, the boys recognising on average 1.2 items more than the girls ($F = 5.36$; $df = 1,40$; $p < .05$). Surprisingly this sex difference did not interact with social condition: although there was a slight overall tendency for solitary performance ($\bar{X} = 4.4$) to be superior to group performance ($\bar{X} = 3.9$), girls were not more susceptible to the distractive effects of the group by virtue of their increased social responsiveness, as had been expected.

TABLE III
Facts about Animals : Mean Correct Recognitions

	Humour		Nonhumour	
	Solitary	Group	Solitary	Group
Boys	5.3	3.8	4.7	5.2
Girls	3.3	3.2	4.2	3.5

Before returning to the sex difference it should be mentioned that further analyses were conducted on order effects and on differences in relation to the individual stimuli, from which no significant differences emerged.

Since neither the humour stimuli nor the social situation appeared to account for the sex difference in recognition performance, the video-recordings were analysed with a view to searching for other situational factors which might be responsible. Two main measures were examined during the learning phase of the test sessions: visual attention during stimulus presentation, as measured by the duration of time spent gazing at the slides, and emotional responsiveness as measured by the occurrence of smiling and laughter during stimulus presentation. These data were obtained for the eight best boy performers and the eight worst girl performers.

In relation to visual attention, two significant differences emerged: (i) boys were more attentive to the stimuli than were girls ($F = 5.84$; $df = 1,20$; $p < .02$). The latter result is partially reflected by the slight superiority in recognition performance in the solitary condition, which applies to both boys and girls. The sex difference in visual attentiveness appears to provide a relatively straightforward explanation for the recognition superiority of boys: they simply were more attentive to the stimuli and paid less attention to the experimenter or towards other environmental cues.

Analyses of emotional expression did not yield significant differences, largely due to the wide inter-subject variance. In terms of average scores, boys and especially girls, were more responsive in the group than in the solitary condition.

Reviewing the results of the study briefly, it can be concluded :

(i) Humour that is directly associated with the information to be learned did not facilitate memory for that information.

(ii) The social situation did not significantly affect recognition performance but solitary learning did facilitate visual attentiveness relative to group learning.

(iii) Boys produced a superior recognition performance to girls, a finding which appears to be in part, if not wholly, explicable in terms of their increased visual attentiveness. As we claimed earlier, the stimulus material was selected on the basis of its being of equal interest to boys and girls, and this is borne out by the very similar ratings of the material by both sexes.

As a final cautionary comment it would be hasty, in our view, to conclude from this study that humour related to the information to be learned is not beneficial to memory. We used stimuli which had high interest value for children as evidenced by their high visual attentiveness to the non-humorous as well as to the humorous stimuli. If stimulus material was used which was of much lower intrinsic interest to children (for example, facts about geometric shapes or historical events), then it may well be that related humour will have greater impact upon learning and memory.

REFERENCES

Chapman, A.J. (1973). Social facilitation of laughter in children. *Journal of Experimental Social Psychology*, 9, 528-541.

Chapman, A.J. (1975). Humorous laughter in children. *Journal of Personality and Social Psychology*, 31, 42-49.

Davies, A.P. (1977). The importance of humour in childhood learning. Unpublished doctoral thesis, University of Wales.

Foot, H.C., Chapman, A.J., and Smith, J.R. (1977). Friendship and social responsiveness in boys and girls. *Journal of Personality and Social Psychology*, 35, 401-411.

Foot, H.C., Chapman, A.J., and Smith, J.R. (1978). Patterns of interaction in children's friendships. In : *Friendship and Social Relations in Children*. (H.C. Foot, A.J. Chapman and J.R. Smith - eds.), Wiley, Chichester.

Geen, R. (1973). Effects of being observed on short and long term recall. *Journal of Educational Psychology*, 69, 61-65.

Kaplan, R.M., and Pascoe, G.C. (1977). Humorous lectures and humorous examples : some effects upon comprehension and retention. *Journal of Educational Psychology*, 69, 61-65.

Leventhal, H., and Mace, W. (1970). The effect of laughter on evaluation of a slapstick movie. *Journal of Personality*, 38, 16-30.

Zajonc, R.B. (1965). Social facilitation. *Science*, 149, 269-274.

WHAT FORM OF MEMORY DO SCHOOLCHILDREN USE WHILST PERFORMING MENTAL ARITHMETIC?

John M. Findlay,

Department of Psychology,
University of Durham,
South Road,
Durham DH1 3LE

ABSTRACT.

Nine, ten and eleven year old children were presented with slides of single digit addition or subtraction sums and asked for each one to make a correct/incorrect judgement. The latencies of these judgements were used to investigate the processes involved. The latencies, particularly of addition sums, were systematically related to the numbers involved in a way which appears to implicate a counting process. However, other aspects of the results suggest the availability of associative links between numbers as well as a form of number representation which allows rapid magnitude comparison. It is concluded that children possess several forms of memory representation for number.

INTRODUCTION.

Manipulation of single digits (addition, multiplication etc.) forms the basis of arithmetic. It is frequently assumed particularly by those involved in mathematics education, that the form of memory involved in these single digit problems is 'simple association'. Empirical investigation suggests a different conclusion, at least in the case of addition problems. Groen and Parkman (1972), by examination of the response latencies to a variety of single digit addition sums, showed that the majority of 7 year old children use a specific strategy, designated the 'minimum addend' strategy. The time required for the children to produce an answer to problems of the type m + n = ? was found to show a linear dependency on a variable set equal to the smaller of the addends m or n. The interpretation of this result is that children solve the problem by first, using a comparison process to find which of the two digits is the smaller; then a counting process is initiated which starts from the larger digit and increments on from this by an amount equal to the size of the smaller digit. If it is further assumed that the variable part of the latency depends only on the counting and that this process requires a constant amount of time for each increment, the minimum addend strategy accounts well for the observations.

Groen and Parkman (1972) describe this as a reconstructive strategy, that is one which generates a response on the basis of a stored algorithmic rule, as opposed to a reproductive strategy, in which the response would be generated by a direct associational process. The form of memory required to solve single digit addition problems with the reconstructive strategy would consist of the appropriate (minimum addend) rule, together with a representation of number which consists of an ordered sequence to allow the necessary manipulations. Brainerd (1973) has used the term ordinal to denote this form of number representation, and has demonstrated that it is a form of number representation which develops early in childhood.

What occurs as the child grows older? One evident possibility is that the child might switch from using a reconstructive to using a reproductive strategy. The present study is an attempt to find out if this 'common sense' notion is valid. Some earlier work had suggested that the 9 - 11 year old age range might show this transition. Specifically, amongst a group of nine year olds presented with addition sums to answer, a different pattern of errors had been observed in the more proficient and the less proficient children. The more proficient showed a tendency to make errors such as responding '2' to the sum 7 + 5 =. If presentation of two numbers (in the case quoted 7 and 5) gives rise by some form of associational linkage to both the sum (12) and the difference (2), then these errors become understandable. The less proficient children, on the other hand, showed a significantly stronger tendency to make errors which were different by one from the correct answer (e.g. 7 + 5 = 11), which could obviously be interpreted as counting errors. This suggested that the less proficient children might be using a reconstructive counting strategy whereas the more proficient might be using a reproductive strategy. If this were the case and if proficiency developed with age, a change in the relative proportions of the two types of errors with age would be expected.

Since errors in single digit arithmetic problems are infrequent, it was decided also to look for an effect on solution latencies. The subjects were accordingly asked to make a two choice correct/incorrect decision when a complete single digit sum was presented (e.g. 5 + 6 = 11) which could be either correct or incorrect. The main hypothesis was that certain items ('wrong sign' incorrect sums and 'wrong by one' incorrect sums as discussed above) would result in longer latencies and increased errors and further that the relative effects of these two types of item would change with age. Finally the study was designed to investigate further the relationship found by Groen and Parkman (1972) discussed earlier, that the solution time for single digit addition sums was linearly related to the minimum addend in the sum. The relationship holds for 7 year old children and also for adults (Parkman and Groen, 1971). This study investigates an intermediate age range.

METHOD

Subjects

The subjects were children at a local junior school. From each of three classes, 20 children (10 boys and 10 girls) were selected at random. The age range in each group was twelve months and the mean ages for the three groups were 9 yr 6 months; 10 yr 3 months; 11 yr 8 months.

Apparatus and Material.

The sums were prepared on slides and were presented to the subject by means of back projection. The appearance of a slide on the projector initiated timing on a centisecond timer, which was terminated by the subject's response. The subjects held a button in each hand and were instructed to press one of these if the sum presented was, in fact, correct and the other if the sum was incorrect.

The stimulus material for each subject consisted of 60 single digit sums of which one half were additions and one half subtractions. In half of these (the 'correct items') the answer was correct (e.g. 7 - 2= 5) and in the other half (the 'incorrect items') the answer was incorrect (e.g. 7 - 2 = 9).

Design.

10 children (5M, 5F) from each class were presented with a set of 60 slides made up as follows; 30 correct items, 15 incorrect items in which the answer was one removed from the correct answer (e.g. 6 - 3 = 4), and 15 control incorrect items with no specific relation between the sum and the answer (e.g. 8 - 6 = 5). The other 10 children in each class received a set of 60 items in which the correct items and the control incorrect items were identical to those in the

first set. In place of the 'wrong by one' incorrect items, 15 'wrong sign' items appeared in which the answer represented the result of performing the opposite operation (addition or subtraction) to that actually shown on the left hand side digits (e.g. 8 + 6 = 2). The 60 slides were divided into two blocks of 30 and each child saw one block in one session and the other in a second session on the following day. The order of presentation of the blocks was balanced.

Procedure.

On the first day the child was shown the operation of the buttons and given a practice session which continued until he or she was responding appropriately. The test slides were then presented consecutively with only a brief pause between items. On the second day the child was reminded of the operation of the buttons and the test sequence shown. The duration of the test sequence was about five minutes.

RESULTS.

1. Errors on test and control incorrect items

Table 1 shows the distribution of errors on the various types of incorrect items.

	Errors on 'wrong by one' items	Errors on 'wrong sign' items	Errors on control items
9 yr olds	3.8% (60%)	14.4% (70%)	4.0% (40%)
10 yr olds	5.2% (40%)	12.8% (70%)	2.4% (25%)
11 yr olds	8.0% (60%)	13.4% (80%)	3.0% (35%)

Table 1. Proportion of errors made (and proportion of children making at least one error) on each type of incorrect item.

It is evident that 'wrong sign' items are particularly prone to error. Although there is a suggestion that 'wrong by one' items may occasion more errors than control items, this trend is not statistically significant.

2. Latencies on test and control incorrect items.

Table 2 shows the class median latency for each type of item.

	Correct items	Incorrect items		
		'wrong by one'	'wrong sign'	'control'
9 yr olds	3.25 s.	3.66 s.	3.12 s.	3.18 s.
10 yr olds	3.40 s.	4.12 s.	3.51 s.	3.42 s.
11 yr olds	2.28 s.	2.94 s.	2.14 s.	2.22 s.

Table 2. Class median latencies on each type of incorrect item.

Analysis of variance showed that the 'wrong by one' items were significantly slower. There was also a significant main effect of age but no interaction involving age. The finding that the ten year old group were slower than the nine year old group is almost certainly not a general characteristic. The class teachers had already noted the slowness of that particular group.

3. Strategies used on correct addition items.

If some algorithmic processing is being used to obtain the answer to a sum, then the latency for solution should depend in a lawful way on the components involved. Groen and Parkman (1972) consider various models for the process of simple addition of the single digit sum m+n=? Each different model produces a particular relationship between the latency for a sum m and n. For example if the subject commences at the value of m, and increments by a number n times, then the latency will be a linear function of n, assuming each increment takes the same time. Thus, according to this model, the data should show a linear regression of the latency for a sum against the value of n for that sum. A variety of possible models can be postulated

i) latency depends on the second addend, n.
ii) latency depends on the first addend, m.
iii) latency depends on the minimum of m and n.
iv) latency depends on the total, m+n.

It is possible to test each of these models against the data by performing a regression analysis of the addition latencies against the amount of counting predicted by a particular model. It is necessary to consider the data from each individual child separately because of the possibility that different children are using different strategies.

Accordingly for each child's latencies on the correct addition items, a linear regression was performed against the values for the amount of incrementing predicted by each model. The items used in this analysis were 12 correct addition items which were not 'doubles' (e.g. 6+6=12). It was evident from our work and also from earlier studies that doubles can be processed much more rapidly than other items. The regressions were performed against four parameters; the first addend, the second addend, the minimum addend, and the total sum. A significant regression against the total sum would be found if the subjects counted up through both addends. However such a process seems implausible and other explanations could be offered for this result.

A problem with the analysis is that the models are not mutually independent. High values of one addend on average are associated with high values of the total sum and the minimum addend. Correspondingly for many children, more than one model shows a good fit to the data. Table 3 gives the results of the regression analysis. The number of subjects are shown (out of 20 in every case), whose data show a significant correlation at two levels against the count values predicted by four models.

	9 year olds	10 year olds	11 year olds
First addend	13(6)	10(2)	7(1)
Second addend	7(3)	6(1)	9(3)
Minimum addend	15(13)	12(5)	6(4)
Total sum	16(13)	17(10)	14(8)

Table 3. Numbers of children in each age group whose data can be fitted with the different algorithmic counting models. The first figure in the table shows the number of children who show a regression significant at the 0.05 level and the second figure (in parentheses) shows the number of children who show a regression significant at the 0.01 level.

DISCUSSIONS

The data on errors show clearly that 'wrong sign' incorrect items are more likely to lead to errors than the other types. However, a different pattern is evident in the latency data. Here it is the 'wrong by one' items which produce the longer latencies. The dissociation is at first sight puzzling but a tentative explanation can be offered by invoking a further, totally different, strategy. It is possible to reject the sum 8 + 6 = 2 as incorrect without any specific knowledge concerning the correct answer by noting that the sum (2) is smaller than either addend. It seems plausible to suppose that this strategy could proceed rapidly and in cases where this strategy can be used, then fast responses might be found. A similar process could be used with subtraction items in which the total was greater than each initial item. This possibility had not been envisaged when the experiment was designed and in fact some 60% of the control incorrect items could be solved in this way. Detailed analysis of the responses (Findlay, Bates and Hutchinson, in preparation) revealed that these items did lead to faster responses, and so the apparent long responses of the wrong by one items may at least in part be ascribed to inadequacies in the control items. The wrong sign items were all potentially soluble using the approach under discussion. The fact that these items nonetheless gave so many errors shows that additional factors must be involved.

What form of memory representation is involved if the above considerations hold? It is one which must allow the rapid comparison of the magnitudes of two numbers and neither of the two processes discussed in the Introduction (reconstructive and reproductive) operates in this way. Investigators following a somewhat different line of investigation have had occasion to suggest an appropriate underlying representation. Moyer and Landauer (1967) followed by Restle (1970) showed that if subjects are presented with a pair of numbers and asked explicitly to judge which one is the larger, then the latency for this judgement is inversely related to the difference between the numbers. The similarity of the results in this situation to that obtained when subjects are asked to judge the relative lengths of two lines has led to the suggestion that number is represented in an analogue fashion.

The results from the analysis of strategies used for the correct addition items allow a direct comparison with the data obtained by Groen and Parkman (1972). The abbreviation G+P will be used in the subsequent section to describe this study. G+P report that 54% of their 7 year old children show a significant regression against the count values predicted by the 'minimum addend' model when a strict criterion (0.01) is used. With the same criterion, 65% of the nine year olds in this study show a significant regression against the minimum addend count values. There seems at first a close correspondence. However as shown in Figure 1, there is a major difference between our data and that of G+P. Whereas for their children the minimum addend model gave the best fit to the data in nearly all cases, in the present study the 'total sum' regressions assume much more importance. Indeed using a partial correlation analysis it emerged that in all but four cases overall, the apparent correlation with minimum addend count values was accounted for by the effect of the total sum (the partial correlation with the total sum held constant was not significant at the 0.5 level).

Both age differences and procedural differences might be involved. Regarding the latter, G+P used a production task as opposed to the verification task used in the present study. Also the children in our study were presented with both addition and subtraction problems whereas those of G+P had only additions. Further studies are needed to examine the effects of these differences but the data shown in Table 3 show that the minimum addend model predictions become less adequate as a function of age. Consequently it is tempting to suppose that a genuine age change could be occurring. This has some support from data on adults analysed by G+P where both minimum addend and total sum models do equally well. Analysis of individual latencies suggests that the possibility of averaging artefacts can be rejected (Findlay, Bates and Hutchinson, in preparation). One possible mechanism for this developmental progression is that reproductive type associations do not develop separately from the reconstructive strategy, but develop effectively as some form of automatization of this strategy. This could then explain why the pattern of latencies found mimics so closely the pattern found at an earlier age. This suggestion has some affinities with the suggestion of LaBerge and Samuels (1974) that a similar process occurs in reading development.

The experiment was originally based on the idea that a developmental transition might be observed across the nine to eleven year old age range. Any qualititative developmental trend seems conspicuously absent in the primary results on errors and latencies. Also the nine year olds in the present study show very similar patterns, at least when analyzed in terms of the minimum addend model, to the seven year olds of Groen and Parkman (1972). The prevalence of 'wrong sign' errors was held to argue for associative confusions, yet the fit of the data on solution latencies to models involving counting algorithms seem to demand reconstructive strategies. The necessary conclusion seems to be, as argued in the last paragraph, that the reproductive and reconstructive processess are not as separate as they appear to be and that the latter develops into the former.

How then can we describe the form of memory used by 9 - 11 year old children when performing mental arithmetic? Firstly, there is the counting algorithm that the child will have used in the early stages of learning. Secondly, a whole set of relations are in the process of development, initially making heavy use of the counting algorithm, but gradually developing to become effectively autonomous associations. Thirdly, there is the process of analogue comparison, which may be always operating as a check procedure. It is possible that even this list is not exhaustive.

ACKNOWLEDGEMENTS.

The assistance of Tony Bates and Clive Hutchinson in carrying out the experiments is gratefully acknowledged.

REFERENCES.

Brainerd, C.J. (1973) The origins of number concepts. *Scientific American*, 228, (December), 101-109.

Groen, G.J. and Parkman, J.M. (1972) A chronometric analysis of simple addition. *Psychological Review*, 79, 329-343.

LaBerge, D. and Samuels, S.J. (1974) Towards a theory of automatic information processing in reading. *Journal of Cognitive Psychology*, 6, 293-323.

Moyer, R.S. and Landauer, T.K. (1967) Time required for judgements in numerical inequality. *Nature*, 215, 1519-1520.

Parkman, J.M. and Groen, G.J. (1971) Temporal aspects of simple addition and comparison. *Journal of Experimental Psychology*, 102, 335-342.

Restle, F. (1970) Speed of adding and comparing numbers. *Journal of Experimental Psychology*, 83, 274-278.

HEMISPHERE DIFFERENCES IN MEMORY

J.P. Scully
Coleg Harlech
Gwynedd, Wales.

INTRODUCTION

Investigators of both memory and cerebral dominance have for some years been interested in verbal and non-verbal aspects of coding and retrieval (Brooks, 1968; Paivio and Csapo, 1969; Seamon, 1974; Kail and Siegel, 1977). But there have been few, if any, systematic attempts to integrate research in these two areas. Our practical knowledge, I believe, has suffered as a result. In this paper I will use an experiment connecting cerebral dominance and memory research to illustrate such integration, and explore some of the practical consequences of the theory that emerges as a result.

EXPERIMENT

The experiment compares the retention of verbal and spatial information presented to each of the visual half fields. Research to date very strongly suggests that verbal material is best handled by the left hemisphere in right handed people and that spatial information is dealt with more efficiently by the right hemisphere (McKeever & Huling, 1971; White, 1969; Kimura & Durnford, 1974). The experiment was designed to compare the retention of verbal and spatial characteristics for the same stimuli and possibly to demonstrate independent processing as postulated by Kail and Siegel (1977) and indicated by others (e.g. Byrne, 1974). Kail and Siegel also found sex differences in the absolute level of retention, boys being better at the spatial task and girls at the verbal task. Such sex differences are very interesting as, though there is "good evidence of a clear adult male superiority for a small nucleus of definitive spatial skills", "there are rarely significant findings in childhood" (Fairweather, 1976). There are even fewer findings of female verbal superiority. Therefore such sex differences should be demonstrable in adults if they are robust. So a secondary aim is to see if these sex differences will extend to adults on a tachistoscopic task.

Tachistoscopic techniques ensure exact registration of the stimulus within either the left or right visual field, if the subject is fixating on the centre of the target display. Therefore a 5 x 4 matrix ($1\frac{1}{4}$" horizontal x 1" vertical) was presented in the centre of the field of a Cambridge Instruments 2-field tachistoscope. Within the matrix there were 6 letters distributed pseudo-randomly among the cells (There was always one letter in the central column of the matrix. The others were distributed so that equal numbers of letters appeared in each column over the course of the experiment).

m				
		b		P
	1		t	
s				

Subjects were asked to recall the identity of the letters in one condition and the position of the letters in the other (half the subjects performed the identity recall condition first and the position recall task second and the other subjects vice-versa). To ensure that subjects were fixated on the centre of the display only those who were able to recall the position or identity of the central letter correctly in over 90% of the trials were included in the analysis. 20 consonants were used in the display so that the probability of answering correctly by chance was the same in both conditions.

Subjects were provided with answer sheets which had either the twenty consonants printed 24 times or the matrix printed 24 times. For each trial the subject either circled the letters they had seen in the display or put a cross in the squares of the matrix they thought the letters appeared in. A forced recognition paradigm was therefore used. There were 50 female subjects and 20 male subjects. All were experimentally naive university students.

ANALYSIS

Two 3 way analyses of variance (Anovar) were used to analyse the data, and t-tests for comparing sex differences and across sexes (ANOVAR - condition first x condition type x visual field).

SUMMARY OF RESULTS

There was no effect due to the condition that was performed first either as a main effect or in interaction for either sex. A single design was not used because of the large difference between the numbers of male and female subjects.

TABLE OF ANOVARS

SEX	SOURCE OF VARIANCE	F RATIO	PROBABILITY
FEMALE	CONDITION	8.13	$p < .01$
	VISUAL HALF FIELD	.30	N.S.
	CONDITION x V.H.F.	24.66	$p < .001$
MALE	CONDITION	1.046	$p > .25$
	VISUAL HALF FIELD	14.776	$p < .005$
	CONDITION x V.H.F.	1.931	$p < .25$

There are several interesting features about these results

1. They are not consistent over the two sexes.
2. Girls have a significantly better performance on the position task than on the identity task.
3. Girls have a L.V.F.A. (Left Visual Field Advantage) for the position task and a significantly different Right Visual Field Advantage for the identity task.
4. Boys have a significant L.V.F.A. for both tasks.

This is expressed graphically below:-

Bearing in mind these results certain tests across and between the sexes were made.

5. Irrespective of sex, the position task is performed better than the identity task. ($p <.025$, t test, over both visual fields). But this is due to a LVF difference ($p <.001$). There is no difference in performance between the tasks if only RVF scores are used. (This finding effectively eliminates any explanations of the difficulties of the recognition procedure being responsible for the difference in accuracy between conditions).

6a) There is no significant difference in RVF scores between the boys and the girls on the identity task. ($t = 1.14$).

6b) Boys have significantly higher LVF scores than girls for the identity task ($t = 2.73$ $p <.01$).

7a) There is no significant difference in RVF scores between the boys and the girls ($t = 1.61$).

7b) There is no significant difference in LVF scores between boys and the girls ($t <1$).

8. There is a significant ($t = 2.8$ $p <.01$) LVFA for both sexes on the position task.

These results do not support Kail and Siegel's findings so far as the task difficulty is concerned: both sexes perform better on the position task.

For the girls the postulate of independent processing is supported by the significant visual field interaction. This effect is also supported by the cerebral dominance literature.

For boys the postulate of independent processing is neither confirmed nor contradicted - the LVFA for the position task is in accord with the cerebral dominance literature but the LVFA for identity recall (not significant if taken alone) is anomalous. It could be explained by the left to right iconic scanning hypothesis (Fudin and Masterton, 1976) as such scanning would interact with any hemisphere dominance to the detriment of performance; the data would (post hoc) support this conclusion. But the fact that this only applies to the boys invites more questions than explanations.

1. In a 150ms presentation (the duration roughly of 1 fixation - a quick glance) information of the position of a verbal display is better processed than its identity.
2. There is a LEFT VISUAL FIELD advantage for recognition of position information.
3. For women there is a RIGHT VISUAL FIELD advantage for

the identity of the display. This is attributable to a significantly lower performance in the LVF, for this type of information, when compared to the boys.

DISCUSSION

These results and others in cerebral dominance research are especially interesting when considered in the perspective of memory theory and practice over the last 2,000 years.

The recall of large amounts of verbal material has often relied upon systems of memory which involve the use of a major spatial component. The place or "loci" system of memory whose origin is credited to Simonides of Ceos (Yates, 1966) is possibly the most famous such system. The system uses the idea of placing an object, word or concept in a particular well known location. When a previously learned set of locations is used, a chain of ideas can be consigned to memory and recalled subsequently by simply "walking through" the locations ("in ones mind"). Relying on such systems, rhetors could speak for hours entirely from memory and reproduce a given speech almost verbatim on a subsequent occasion. Thus a verbal skill, oratory, and more precisely verbal memory, depended on an artificial system based on spatial location. Having shown that even unfamiliar locations are better remembered than the information in them (in a quite circumscribed task), we return to modern problems to see more current research.

Normal text, such as on this page, has, of course, spatial attributes. Research on these properties of printed text (Rothkopf, 1971; Zechmeister, McKillip, Pasko and Bespalec, 1975) has indicated that awareness of location and knowledge of content are related and Zechmeister's (1975) conclusion that visually mediated spatial memory "may be of mnemonic worth" when retention of textual information is required, is reassuring in the light of previous discussion.

Somehow it would appear that different aspects of the same stimuli are processed separately before being integrated in memory. Following previous argument the better this integration, the better the memory. This is borne out by several studies (G.H. Bower, 1970; Briggs, Hawkins and Crovitz, 1970) where interaction between images in memory proved to be a more effective way to recall than bizarre associations. Also Moreau has shown better recall for place names when they are associated (in a typically French fashion) as a "Tour de France" (Moreau, 1973).

If integration of just two attributes by stimuli produces better recall whether imposed artificially (as in Loci) or naturally (as in "place on the page") it is an open question as to what effect the linking of other attributes would have.

There would seem to be a lot of value in an approach such as that of Underwood (1969) which could be used to link up temporal, spatial, frequency, modality and orthographic attributes of stimuli.

Underwood's thesis indicates a way of developing memory systems; the finding that spatial information is processed better in a short duration presentation gives a more precise direction to this contention. We now know of one attribute that is processed more easily. Information should be integrated by using such attributes with the specific aim of producing practical memory devices.

The use of spatial mnemonics by normal people is a convenience; but for brain damaged patients it could make a more normal life a real possibility. This has already been indicated by Marilyn Jones (1974), who demonstrated that visual imagery can be used to alleviate material specific memory disorders. The method of Loci itself has been used to help patients with dominant hemisphere lesions remember verbal material, (Patten, 1972). Both these examples indicate the power of verbal and spatial integration. The use of different types of imagery suitable for different circumstances, bearing in mind attributes of stimuli other than the spatial, could be applicable to many different varieties of memory disorder.

In a different field, the development of complex technology requires much information to be assimilated efficiently and often very quickly; complex visual displays such as those in aircraft are a perfect example. If a pilot is constantly using a central display with subsidiary but often vital information to either side the encoding of that information, especially if it is a rapidly changing display, should be as efficient as possible. If our data and current theory about spatial information are taken seriously then such information should be "fed" to the Left Visual Field. The correct placing of such instruments as artificial horizons could have a small but appreciable effect. The finding of the experiment that position information is more accurately recalled than identity after one fixation could also be utilized, by using more displays of the type where position is the factor which gives information rather than figures or letters.

REFERENCES

Bower, G.H. (1970) Imagery as a Relational Organizer in Associative Learning. *Journal of Verbal Learning and Verbal Behavior*, 9, 529-533.

Briggs, G.G., Hawkins, S. Crovitz, H.F. (1970) Bizarre Images in Artificial Memory. *Psychonomic Science*, 19. 353-354.

Brooks, L.R. (1968) Spatial and verbal components of the act of recall. *Canadian Journal of Psychology*, 22, 349-368.

Byrne, B. (1974) Item concreteness vs spatial organization as predictors of visual imagery. *Memory and Cognition*, 2, 53-59.

Dimond, S. and Beaumont, J.G. (Eds.) (1974) *Hemesphere Function in the Human Brain*. Elec. London

Fairweather, H. (1976) Sex differences in cognition. *Cognition*, 4, 231-280.

Fudin, R. and Masterton, C.C. (1976) Integration of post-exposural directional scanning and cerebral dominance: Explanations of lateral differences in tachistoscopic recognition. *Perceptual and Motor Skills*, 42, 355-359.

Higbee, K.L. (1977) *Your Memory*. Prentice Hall, New Jersey.

Jones, M.K. (1974) Imagery as a mnemonic aid after left temporal lobectomy. *Neuropsychologia*, 12, 21-30.

Kail, R.V. and Siegel, A.W. (1977) Sex differences in relation to verbal and spatial characteristics of stimuli. *Journal of Experimental Child Psychology*, 23, 341-347.

Kimura, D. and Durnford, M. (1974) Normal studies of the function of the right hemisphere in vision. In: Dimond, S. and Beaumont, J.G. (Eds.) Op.cit.

Moreau, A. (1973) Le role du shema dans l'apprentissage et l'evocation d'une tache verbale. *Anee Psychol.*, 73 521-533.

Paivio, A. and Czapo, K. (1969) Concrete image and verbal memory codes. *Psychological Review*, 76, 279-285.

Patten, B.M. (1972) The ancient art of memory. *Arch. Neurol.* 26, 25-31.

Rothkopf, E.Z. (1971) Incidental memory for location of information in text. *Journal of Verbal Learning and Verbal Behavior*, 10, 608-613.

Seamon, J.G. (1974) Coding and retrieval processes and the hemispheres of the brain. In: Dimond, S. and Beaumont, J.G. (Eds.) Op.cit.

Senter, R.J. and Hoffman, R.R. (1976) Bizarreness as a non-essential variable in mnemonic imagery: a confirmation. *Bulletin of the Psychonomic Society*, 7, 163-164.

Underwood, B.J. (1969) Attributes of memory. *Psychological Review*, 76, 559-573.

White, M.J. (1969) Laterality differences in perception. *Psychological Bulletin*, 72, 387-485.

Wollen, K.A., Weber, A. and Lowry, D.H. (1972) Bizarreness versus interaction of mental images as determinants of learning. *Cognitive Psychology*, 3, 518-523.

Yates, F.A. (1969) *The Art of Memory*. Penguin, Harmondsworth.

Zechmeister, E.B., McKillip, J., Pasko, S. and Bespalec, D. (1975) Visual memory for place on the page. *Journal of Genetic Psychology*, 92, 43-52.

MEMORY AND READING

ANALYZING THE READING PROCESS

G. Underwood and P. O'B. Holt
*Department of Psychology, University of Nottingham
Nottingham, England*

INTRODUCTION

There appear to be two distinct experimental approaches to the psychological analysis of the reading process, and although the differences are clear it is questionable whether the two are mutually exclusive or whether they should be interactive and dependent upon each other. These two supposedly opponent methods involve on the one hand what we might call the *analysis of component processes*, and on the other what we might call *reading dynamics*. One method relies upon the analysis of skills and processes which by themselves have little "ecological validity" but which are integral to the performance of the skilled reading task. Such processes as lexical access, pattern decoding, eye movement control, the integration of word meanings, and text comprehension may each be investigated in isolation where the factors which influence their performance can be observed clearly and without involvement of the other processes. The alternative method requires observation in the free-reading situation, and relies upon the manipulation of text materials to produce differences of reading time, comprehension, and interpretation errors. These are the two extremes, of course, and our description in terms of "supposedly opponent methods" gives away our conclusion that these two methods are both necessary for an understanding of what happens when the reader extracts meaning from the printed page. The Cardiff symposium was particularly reinforcing from this point of view, for although frequent comments were made regarding the ecological validity of some experiments, and the experimental unreliability of others, a number of papers were presented which had the effect of demonstrating that the two methods depend upon each other.

THE ANALYSIS OF COMPONENT PROCESSES

There has been, to use Chall's (1967) expression, something of a "Great Debate" amongst teachers of reading concerning the use of teaching methods, and a principal dichotomy in this debate is the use of phonics against the whole-word method. It is a debate which has been conducted by those concerned with the teaching of reading for several decades now, but without any signs of resolution in the classroom. This is one debate which can be settled not in the classroom but in the psychology laboratory, however, by an analysis of what the skilled reader needs to do to obtain lexical access and what is done with the accessed material. If he recognizes a word by phonological mediation and the decoding of print by the analysis of the constituent graphemes and then phonemes, then it would appear that a phonic method of teaching is necessary. Alternatively, if we can demonstrate that phonological encoding is unnecessary, and that the skilled reader can obtain the meanings of words visually, then it would appear that a whole-word approach to the teaching of reading would be most appropriate.

From the laboratory we have a number of demonstrations of the use of phonological encoding during reading tasks. Corcoran (1966) had readers cross out all instances of the letter "e" from a passage of text, and found that even though they read silently, they missed more "e's" which would not have been pronounced in speech (e.g., the second "e" in "breathe") than those which would have been pronounced had the subject been reading out aloud (e.g., the first "e" in "breathe"). Even in a silent reading task when a phonological encoding strategy leads to omission errors it appears that subjects prefer to translate the print into a sound-based code.

A second line of evidence for the phonological mediation hypothesis, and one followed up by Barron (this volume), concerns the pseudohomophone effect in the lexical decision task. When subjects are required to decide whether a letter-string forms a word or not, some interesting differences emerge between letter-strings which are not words, and therefore gain a "no" response (Rubinstein, Lewis and Rubinstein, 1971). Letter-strings which are orthographically illegal and unpronouncable (e.g. FKTE) are rejected easiest, those which are pronouncable gain the next fastest "no" (e.g. FIME), and those non-words which *sound* as if they are real words (e.g. FITE) are rejected slowest. This is the pseudohomophone effect, and has been taken to indicate that even in the ecologically invalid lexical decision task subjects employ a phonological encoding strategy when attempting to decode print. Moreover, Barron now reports that good and poor readers aged 11-12 years can be distinguished by their performance on the lexical decision task. Only the good readers show a reliable pseudohomophone effect, and Barron found a positive correlation between the size of the pseudohomophone effect (an indication of phonological encoding) and the speed of reading for these children. Evidently they could not avoid using a phonological encoding strategy even when it slowed them down on the lexical decision task. This is good evidence that readers prefer to use this strategy, but says nothing of course on the matter of whether lexical access could occur without recourse to phonological encoding. Coltheart (1978) has proposed a model of the lexical decision task in which two routes are used simultaneously in an attempt to locate the letter-string in the lexicon: a visual route and a phonological route. The availability of the visual access route was a feature of the experiments of Holt and Underwood (this volume), and the equipotentiality of the cerebral hemispheres in visual access might be taken to suggest that the lexicon is represented bilaterally. Coltheart argues that the two access processes are started together in the lexical decision task, and whereas visual access is a fast process, phonological encoding is slow. However, in the case of a non-word, with no visual access possible, phonological encoding may be completed before the decision is taken that no such word exists. When phonological encoding is completed then the pseudohomophone effect can emerge. In the case of Barron's experiment it may have been the case that the decision was always taken late by the good readers, who had by then successfully produced a phonological code of the non-word, but that the poor readers were so slow at producing this code that they generally made the decision before completion of the encoding process.

The hypothesis that phonological encoding is *essential* for the reading process has been questioned on theoretical grounds by Coltheart (1978) who suggests parallel visual and phonological access to the lexicon, and on experimental grounds in tasks which demonstrate that meaning can be extracted from print without using a phonological code (Baron, 1973; Kleiman, 1975; Underwood, 1977).

When asked to judge whether sentences are meaningful, subjects are no worse with homophonical nonsense (e.g., HE SEAS POORLY) than they are with non-homophonical nonsense (e.g., COME OVER ARE), indicating that they were not relying upon the phonological form of the homophonical nonsense in order to reject it, otherwise they would have produced incorrect "yes" responses and longer decision times (Baron, 1973). The suppression of vocalization by having subjects speaking something else whilst reading does not interfere with their judgements of the meaning of what is read (Kleiman, 1975), indicating that they do not need to produce a phonological code in order to extract meaning. Finally, it is possible to demonstrate the influence of the meanings of words when those words are unattended, and when the reader is unaware of them (Underwood, 1977). The experiment reported by Underwood, Parry and Bull (this volume) extended this conclusion by a demonstration that the context available during an eye-fixation is integrated with context available prior to that fixation. The reading response is dependent upon both prior and simultaneous context, and when both are available the facilitation effect is greater than when either of them is presented alone.

A query about the generality of these conclusions concerning the availability of parafoveal words has been raised by Rayner's (this volume) inability to raise an effect of the influence of the meanings of these words. Rayner presented a word in the parafovea (between 1° and 5° from fixation) and replaced it with another word during the saccade resulting in fixation upon the word. Changing the word from CHAIR to TABLE did not affect naming time but changing from TALKS to TABLE facilitated the response. The absence of an effect of the semantic relationship of the two words is surprising, and remains to be explained. Kennedy (1978), in a study of eye-movements using strings of sentences did find that the presence of two associates influenced comprehension time (slower if associates are present), reading time up to the second associate (faster if associates are present), and the number of fixations upon the second associate (more if associates are present).

READING DYNAMICS

The artificial nature of our dichotomy of methods is already apparent, for it is impossible to place the experiments by Kennedy in either group with any confidence - he is investigating microprocesses of reading (as are Barron, etc.) but using real text. That his results are in accord with those using single-fixation methods is encouraging.

In further observations of patterns of eye-movements, Kennedy (this volume) has investigated the comprehension of sentences in which a word in the second sentence has high or low conjoint frequency with a referant in the first sentence (e.g., "A *bus* came roaring round the corner. The *vehicle* nearly flattened a pedestrian." The two associates are in italics here, but not in the experiment). As reported by Garrod and Sanford (1977), sentences with high conjoint frequency (e.g. bus/vehicle) were read faster than those with low conjoint frequency (e.g. tank/vehicle). Kennedy's recordings indicated that readers spent longer looking at low conjoint frequency reference points. The control of eye-movements during reading appears to depend upon the relationships between word meanings in the text. The semantic processing of the text dictates the pattern of future fixations, both their period of fixation and location as well as their direction. An ingenious experiment by Wanat (1971) found that sentences containing deleted agents (e.g., "The ball was hit by the park") resulted in more regressive saccades than did those containing active agents (e.g., "The ball was hit by the boy"). If all information is not readily available (*who* hit the ball) the reader will search for it. The common usage of some words ("by" as an indicator of an agent rather than as an indicator of location) will bias interpretation, and the reinterpretation can be observed by eye-movement recordings.

The experiment reported by Sanford, Garrod and Bell (this volume) developed their earlier result to suggest that word relations are manipulated during reading through a mediating scenario. What Sanford *et al*.refer to as a scenario seems to be related to what Bartlett (1932) referred to as a schema, and are thematic structures organized in semantic memory.

Whereas skilled language users (adult subjects) demonstrate an intimate relationship between their appreciation of language and their extraction of information from print (*viz*, the data reported by Kennedy, Wanat, and Sanford *et al* mentioned above), such a relationship cannot be said to apply with young readers. Lunzer (this volume) found only a small positive correlation between language tests and reading tests in beginning readers (5 and 6 years old). A more striking correlation emerged between a visual sequencing test and reading. Lunzer interprets the correlation to indicate that a fundamental determinant of reading success is the ability to match a sequence of visual characters to sequence of phonological codes. In this respect the result confirms that of Barron (this volume) even though Lunzer used an approach which might be described as being ecologically valid, and Barron preferred to use a technique which certainly involves lexical access, and which involves little else.

There are valid reasons for employing the lexical access task when confounding processes need to be avoided. The fact that similar conclusions may be drawn using this variety of methods should only serve to encourage us to look not only *beyond* the laboratory, as Neisser (this volume) suggests, but to check what we observe outside with the appropriate analytical tools *within* the laboratory.

CONCLUSIONS

This brief review started with a compromise on methods of investigation, and will conclude with a compromise on the theoretical debate which emerged. It appears from a number of sources that phonological encoding serves some purpose during reading, but that reading *can* proceed in the absence of a phonological code being generated. What then is the purpose of mediating the reading response by transforming the text into a code which is not essential for the derivation of meaning? Lunzer's result gives us a clue, in that semantic analysis is not the only task for the beginning reader. He must sequence the visual display letters within a word, but he must also sequence the words across the page if he is ever to develop beyond a word-by-word level of skill. To put this another way, he needs to attend to sequences of words before he can bring his linguistic knowledge to bear upon the text. One possibility then is that phonological encoding is used as a method of attention control. By converting print into sound the importance of sequencing is emphasized to the beginner, and for this reason it may be that the faster learners are those who are adept with the generation of the phonological code.

REFERENCES

Baron, J. (1973). Phonemic stage not necessary for reading. *Quarterly Journal of Experimental Psychology*, 25, 241-246.

Bartlett, F.C. (1932). *Remembering*. London: Cambridge University Press.

Chall, J.S. (1967). *Learning to Read: The Great Debate*. New York: McGraw-Hill.

Coltheart, M. (1978). Lexical access in simple reading tasks. In *Strategies of Information Processing*. (G. Underwood, ed.), London: Academic Press.

Corcoran, D.W.J. (1966). An acoustic factor in letter cancellation. *Nature*, 210, 658.

Garrod, S. and Sanford, A.J. (1977). Interpreting anaphoric relations: The integration of semantic information while reading. *Journal of Verbal Learning and Verbal Behaviour*,

16, 77-90.

Kennedy, A. (1978). Reading sentences: Some observations on the control of eye movements. In *Strategies of Information Processing*. (G. Underwood, ed.), London: Academic Press.

Kleiman, G.M. (1975). Speech recoding in reading. *Journal of Verbal Learning and Verbal Behaviour*, 14, 323-339.

Rubinstein, H., Lewis, S.S. and Rubinstein, M.A. (1971). Evidence for phonemic recoding in visual word recognition. *Journal of Verbal Learning and Verbal Behaviour*, 10, 645-657.

Underwood, G. (1977). Attention, awareness and hemispheric differences in word recognition. *Neuropsychologia*, 15, 61-67.

Wanat, S.F. (1971). *Linguistic Structure and Visual Attention in Reading*. Newark, Delaware: International Reading Association Research Reports.

READING SKILL AND PHONOLOGICAL CODING IN LEXICAL ACCESS

R.W. Barron
Department of Psychology
University of Guelph
Guelph, Ontario, Canada N16 2W1

ABSTRACT

Use of graphemic and phonological codes in lexical access by good and poor readers was investigated with a word/nonword decision task. Good, but not poor readers, were slower on nonwords which sounded but did not look like homophones (e.g., RANE) than on control nonwords (e.g., RAME). Neither group responded more slowly to homophones than to nonhomophones. These and other results suggest that good are better able than poor readers to use a phonological code in lexical access, possibly because they can generate it more quickly. Differences in lexical access strategies and functions of access codes in reading are discussed.

INTRODUCTION

There is now a body of evidence indicating that it is not necessary to recode printed words into their phonological representations in order to obtain access to information stored in the internal lexicon (e.g., Baron, 1973), even for beginning readers (Barron and Baron, 1977). Rather, investigators have argued that both graphemic and phonological coding are carried out simultaneously and that either code can be used in lexical access. Coltheart, Davelaar, Jonasson and Besner (1977), however, have suggested that although both codes are processed in parallel, phonological coding may be slower than graphemic coding; hence, phonological coding may be less likely to be used in lexical access in some situations. Evidence consistent with this possibility was reported by Coltheart *et al.*(1977) in a lexical decision experiment in which subjects were required to decide whether or not a visually displayed string of letters was a word. Their subjects were presented with two types of items: 1) homophones which were the less frequent member of a homophone pair (e.g., HAUL instead of HALL) and 2) double pseudohomophones which are nonwords that are pronounced, but not spelled like homophones (e.g., WUN). They argued that if phonological codes were used in making lexical decisions about either homophones or pseudohomophones, then it would be necessary to check the spelling of the items (twice with double pseudohomophones) in order to avoid making errors. Presumably, the spelling check process would slow response times to the homophones and double pseudohomophones relative to their appropriate control items. They found that subjects were not any slower in responding yes to the homophones than to the nonhomophone control items. Subjects were, however, slower in responding no to the double pseudohomophones than to nonword control items which were not pseudohomophones, but were visually similar to them (i.e., they differed by only one letter from the pseudohomophones; e.g., VUN was the control item for WUN). These results suggest that subjects may have relied primarily upon graphemic codes in making their yes decisions and phonological codes in making their no decisions. The possibility that speed of code generation was responsible for the difference in the results obtained with the two response modes is suggested by the difference in the visual familiarity of the yes (words) and the no (nonwords) items. Subjects may have been able to use the greater visual familiarity of the words to generate more rapidly a graphemic code than a phonological code for the yes items. In the case of the no items, however, the graphemic codes may have been generated so slowly, due to the low visual familiarity of the nonwords, that there was sufficient time for the phonological codes to determine lexical access.

Stanovich and Bauer (1978) have also reported evidence suggesting that phonological codes are generated more slowly than graphemic codes. They used a lexical decision task, but investigated the use of phonological codes in lexical access by using words which were regular (e.g. GLOBE) or irregular (e.g., YACHT) in their conformity to spelling-to-sound correspondence rules. It was reasoned that the application of spelling rules would be more likely to result in accurate lexical access in the case of regular words, which obey the rules, than irregular words, which do not. They predicted that subjects would be faster on regular than irregular words if they were using a phonological code in lexical access and their results confirmed that prediction. They also found, however, that this spelling regularity effect disappeared when their subjects were instructed to decrease their response times at the expense of increasing their errors. These latter results suggest that a phonological code could not be generated fast enough to determine lexical access under conditions of high speed and low accuracy demands.

The results presented thus far suggest that task variables such as visual familiarity and speed/accuracy demands can influence the effectiveness of graphemic and phonological codes It is possible, however, that individual differences in reading skill, as well as task factors, might also influence the effectiveness of these two codes in determining lexical access. Perfetti and Hogaboam (1975), for example, have shown that good readers are faster and more accurate than poor readers in pronouncing low frequency words and nonwords. These results suggest that the readers may differ in the speed and accuracy with which they can apply spelling-to-sound correspondence rules to generate a phonological code. If good readers can generate a phonological code more quickly than poor readers, then they might be more likely than the poor readers to use a phonological code in lexical access. Furthermore, the use of this code should be related to the speed with which nonwords can be pronounced.

Langer (1977) obtained results in a lexical decision task which are consistent with the above predictions. She used grade six (11-12 years of age) good and poor readers who differed in reading comprehension skill, but not in nonverbal I.Q.. Like Stanovich and Bauer (1978), she varied the spelling regularity of the words. In addition, she also varied orthographic structure as measured by the summed single letter and bigram positional frequency values (Mayzner and Tresselt, 1965) of the letters making up the words. Thus one-half of the regular and irregular words had high summed single letter positional frequency values while the other one-half had low values. Langer (1977) found that the good readers were faster on regular than irregular words, but did not differ on the orthographic variable suggesting that they used a phonological code in lexical access. The poor readers, on the other hand, were faster on the high than the low single letter and bigram positional frequency words, but did not differ on the spelling regularity variable. These results suggest that they used a graphemic rather than a phonological code in lexical access. A subsequent experiment with Langer's (1977) subjects showed that the good readers were faster than the poor readers in pronouncing nonwords. Furthermore, fast pronunciation was related to the use of a phonological code whereas slow pronunciation was related to the use of a graphemic code in lexical access.

Although Langer's (1977) results suggest that good readers are more likely than poor readers to use a phonological code in lexical access, it seems important to provide some additional support for this conclusion, particularly as the spelling regularity effect was rather small in both Langer (1977) and Stanovich and Bauer's (1978) experiments. The lexical decision task used by Coltheart *et al* (1977) appears to be particularly useful for this purpose as it would be predicted that the good readers would show a larger pseudohomophone effect than the poor readers. Furthermore, it would be expected that the magnitude of the pseudohomophone effect would be negatively correlated with the speed with which subjects could pronounce nonwords. In fact, Patterson and Marcel (1977) have shown that the ability to pronounce nonwords is related to the likelihood of obtaining a pseudohomophone effect. They carried out a modified version of the task used by Coltheart *et al*.(1977) on two individuals with acquired dyslexia. These individuals appeared to have lost their ability to apply spelling-to-sound correspondence rules as they could not pronounce nonwords. Although these dyslexics could distinguish words from nonwords, they did not show any evidence of a pseudohomophone effect in the lexical decision task. Normal control subjects, however, were slower on the pseudohomophones than the control items. Accordingly, good and poor readers were required to carry out a lexical decision task very similar to that used by Coltheart *et al* (1977). In addition, the subjects' speed and accuracy of pronunciation was assessed by requiring them to pronounce lists of nonwords.

METHOD

The 32 good and 32 poor readers were made up of equal numbers of five and sixth grade children (10-12 years old). They were chosen from a larger group of children so that they did not differ in their scores on the nonverbal section of the Lorge-Thorndike Intelligence test (both groups had an average I.Q. score of 106), but did differ by over one standard deviation (SD=10) on the comprehension subsection of the Gates-MacGinitie Reading Test (60 and 43 for the good and poor readers, respectively; $t(62)=14.31$, $p<.001$). None of the children had been identified by their schools as having severe reading or learning disabilities.

A total of 160 stimulus items were presented to the subjects; 80 were words and required a yes response and 80 were nonwords and required a no response. Forty of the words were less frequent members of homophone pairs (e.g. SOAR rather than SORE). The remaining 40 words were control items that were not homophones, but nevertheless were identical to the homophones in length and very similar to them in word frequency (Carroll, Davis and Richman, 1971; average of grade 5 and 6 norms) and in summed single letter and bigram positional frequency values. The average values for the homophones and their controls, respectively, were 15.94 and 15.06 for word frequency, 1983 and 1988 for summed single letter positional frequency and 211 and 173 for summed bigram positional frequency. Forty of the nonwords were double pseudohomophones as they could all be pronounced like a homophone (e.g., WROLE). The remaining 40 nonwords were control items. They were not pseudohomophones, but they were pronounceable and, following Coltheart *et al*.(1977), they differed from the double pseudohomophones by only one letter (e.g., WROKE). In addition, the control nonwords were identical in length to the double pseudohomophones and very similar to them in summed single letter (2028 and 2014) and bigram (151 and 152) positional frequency.

The subjects were tested individually in a trailer located at their school. The items were back projected onto a screen by a slide projector and the maximum visual angle in the horizontal plane was less than three degrees. The subject initiated a trial by pressing a button which started a timer and opened a shutter displaying an item. Subjects responded yes or no by moving a small lever to the left or right. They were given feedback about their accuracy, but not their speed. Finally, following the lexical decision experiment, subjects were required to pronounce six lists of eight pronounceable nonwords as fast and as accurately as they could. These nonwords did not appear in the lexical decision experiment.

RESULTS

Median correct response times (milliseconds) and percent errors were taken for subjects (Ss) summed over words and for words (Ws) summed over subjects. Separate t-tests were computed for subjects and for words. Considering the no responses first, the good readers were slower on the double pseudohomophones (1087 Ss, 1048 Ws) than on the controls (1019 Ss, 988 Ws) by 68 milliseconds for subjects and 60 milliseconds for words. These differences were significant for both subjects, $t(31)=5.42$, $p<.001$, and for words, t(78)=2.38, p<.025. The poor readers were also slower on the double pseudohomophones (1129 Ss, 1082 Ws) than on the controls (1099 Ss, 1041 Ws), but the differences were 30 milliseconds for subjects and 41 milliseconds for words and were not significant for either subjects, t(31)=1.19, p>.10, or for words, t(78)=1.31, p>.10. The good readers made significantly more errors on the double pseudohomophones (16.81 Ss, 16.63 Ws) than on the controls (6.56 Ss, 6.15 Ws) for both subjects, t(31)=7.64, p<.001, and for words, t(78)=3.84, p<.001. The poor readers also made significantly more errors on the double pseudohomophones (22.38 Ss, 22.15 Ws) than on the controls (12.00 Ss, 11.73 Ws) and these differences were also significant for subjects, t(31)=5.62, p<.001, and for words, t(78)=3.05, p<.01. Analyses of the yes responses showed that the good readers were seven milliseconds slower for subjects and 14 milliseconds faster for words on the homophones (939 Ss, 905 Ws) than on the controls (932 Ss, 919 Ws). Similarily, the poor readers were 13 milliseconds slower for subjects and one millisecond slower for words on the homophones (986 Ss, 935 Ws) than on the control items (973 Ss, 934 Ws). These differences were not significant for subjects or for words in either group of readers (p>.50). The good readers made more errors on the homophones (11.00 Ss, 10.70 Ws) than on the controls (9.09 Ss, 8.80 Ws) and the poor readers also made more errors on the homophones (14.38 Ss, 14.03 Ws) than on the controls (12.13 Ss, 11.93 Ws). These differences were not, however, significant for subjects or for words in either group of readers, (p>.05). Finally, an analysis of the pronunciation data showed that the good readers were faster, t(62)=3.27, p<.01 and more accurate, t(62)=3.73, p<.001 than the poor readers in pronouncing nonwords. Furthermore, the pronunciation times were correlated negatively and significantly (r=-.30, t(62)=2.48, p<.02) with the size of the pseudohomophone effect across readers indicating that subjects with fast pronunciation times tended to have large pseudohomophone effects.

DISCUSSION

The results of this experiment indicate that the good readers were significantly slower on the pseudohomophones than on the control items suggesting that they used a phonological code in deciding that an item was not a word. Poor readers, however, did not show a reliable pseudohomophone effect suggesting that they did not use a phonological code in making their decisions about nonwords. Consistent with Coltheart *et al.*(1977), neither group of readers produced a reliable homophone effect suggesting that phonological coding was not used in word decisions. Finally, the significant negative correlation between the pronunciation times and the size of the pseudohomophone effect suggests that the subjects who were able to apply quickly spelling-to-sound correspondence rules also had a tendency to use a phonological code in lexical access. These results can be regarded as being consistent with Langer's (1977) results in two ways. First, they suggest that good readers are more likely than poor readers to use a phonological code in lexical access. Second, they suggest that use of a phonological code in lexical access is related to the speed with which that code can be generated. Finally, the results are also consistent with Patterson and Marcel (1977) as they suggest that phonological coding, as indicated by a pseudohomophone effect, is less likely to be obtained by subjects who are relatively deficient in their knowledge and use of spelling-to-sound correspondence rules.

The results of this experiment suggest that individuals may not be able to exercise much strategic control over the codes they use to obtain access to the internal lexicon, at least in this task. It is inefficient to use a phonological strategy in the Coltheart *et al.*(1977) task as the response times to both the homophones and pseudohomophones can be slowed by the resulting spelling check. Nevertheless, the good readers produced a substantial pseudohomophone effect suggesting that phonological coding proceeds automatically in this task and that readers do not have much strategic control over it. The fact that there was not much evidence for the use of phonological strategies in lexical access with the Coltheart *et al.*(1977) task does not, however, necessarily rule them out all together. In fact, Davelaar, Coltheart, Besner and Jonasson (1978) have shown recently that subjects will shift away from using a phonological code in lexical access (indicated by a homophone effect) when all of the nonwords are pseudohomophones which can be mistakenly identified as words.

Finally, the results of this and other experiments have shown that even though a phonological code is not necessary in lexical access, it is used nevertheless. Furthermore, it is more likely to be used by individuals who are relatively proficient in reading. If this is the case, then what is the role of phonological coding in reading? It may simply be a by-product of learning to pronounce words and has no utility except as a device for learning new words. Another possibility is that it plays a critical role in reading extended text by providing a means of retaining the wording of a sentence during comprehension. A third possibility is that it is not speed of phonological coding per se which distinguishes levels of reading skill, but rather the speed of accessing verbal information in memory. Additional research is needed to evaluate these and other possible roles of phonological coding in reading.

REFERENCES

Baron, J. (1973) Phonemic stage not necessary for reading. *Quarterly Journal of Experimental Psychology*, 25, 241-246.

Barron, R.W. and Baron, J. (1977). How children get meaning from printed words. *Child Development*, 48, 587-594.

Carroll, J.B., Davis, P. and Richman, B. (1971). *The Word Frequency Book*. Houghton, Mifflin Co., American Heritage Printing Co.: New York.

Coltheart, M., Davelaar, E., Jonasson, J.T. and Besner, D. (1977). Access to the internal lexicon. In: *Attention and Performance VI*. (S. Dornic, ed), Lawrence Erlbaum Associates: Hillsdale, N.J.

Davelaar, E., Coltheart, M., Besner, D. and Jonasson, J.T. (1978). Phonological recoding and lexical access. *Memory and Cognition*, 6, 391-402.

Langer, J.L. (1977). Effects of spatial frequency and pronunciation regularity on good and poor readers' performance on a lexical decision task. Unpublished masters thesis, University of Guelph.

Mayzner, M.S. and Tresselt, M.E. (1965). Tables of single-letter and digram frequency counts for various word length and letter position combinations. *Psychonomic Science Monograph Supplements*, 1, 13-32.

Patterson, K.E. and Marcel, A.J. (1977). Aphasia, dyslexia and the phonological coding of written words. *Quarterly Journal of Experimental Psychology*, 29, 307-318.

Perfetti, C.A. and Hogaboam, T. (1975). Relationships between single word decoding and reading comprehension skill. *Journal of Educational Psychology*, 67, 461-469.

Stanovich, K.E. and Bauer, D.N. (1978). Experiments on the spelling-to-sound regularity effect in word recognition. *Memory and Cognition*, 6, 410-415.

ASPECTS OF MEMORY DYNAMICS IN TEXT COMPREHENSION

A. J. Sanford, S. Garrod and E. Bell
Department of Psychology, University of Glasgow
Glasgow, Scotland

ABSTRACT

Inferences have been made about the processes of text comprehension from experiments on memory for text. An alternative approach is to try to study text processing operations directly by measuring the time taken to read each sentence of a text. In general, these approaches lead to a convergence of ideas. However, it is argued that memory studies may be confounded with retrieval or recognition operations. A specific example is given.

INTRODUCTION

In recent years memory experiments have been used widely to draw inferences about how text comprehension occurs. This approach is based on the argument that the memory trace for a text in large part consists of the products of comprehension (e.g. Thorndyke, 1975). An alternative approach has been to measure the time taken to read each sentence of a text, and draw conclusion about real time processing from that (e.g. Garrod & Sanford, 1977). For some ideas about comprehension, these two approaches are in broad agreement. For example, memory experiments indicate that inferences are made during text comprehension (Kintsch, 1974; Thorndyke 1975), and inference making of some types has been shown to be a time-consuming process during comprehension (Haviland & Clark, 1974; Garrod & Sanford, 1977). Furthermore, memory experiments show that more is retained of a text if it can be set into some broad orienting theme (Dooling & Mullett, 1973) or into some well-defined framework such as a story grammar (Thorndyke, 1975). Sanford & Garrod (1978; Garrod

& Sanford, in preparation) have shown that during on-line text comprehension, substantial thematic structures seem to be retrieved from memory, and are used as blocks of information to enable text to be integrated. These structures we term *scenarios,* and are broadly similar to the notion of *frames* discussed by Minsky (1975).

While memory experiments can take us so far in unravelling the mechanisms of text comprehension, the approach suffers the general criticism that it may reflect the processes of retrieval or recognition rather than what actually happens at the time of comprehension. For example, a high false recognition rate for plausible inferences not presented in text (Thorndyke, 1975) could be the result of plausible ideas not actually present in the memory trace itself, and maybe not even elicited by the text. Indeed, the increase in such intrusion with time since presentation (Dooling and Christiansen, 1977) is difficult to explain in terms of text processing, although it undoubtedly relates at some level. It is difficult to pinpoint the relationships accurately with memory experiments alone.

One point of agreement between the two approaches is the idea that the working representations of text used in comprehension contain more than just the propositions explicit in the text. In general the representations entertained are thought to be frame-like programs, containing slots which are waiting to be filled with appropriate data (or instantiations). For instance, if I saw 'I went to a birthday party' the representation would contain slots for guests, presents, activities etc. - all we would normally expect at a party. This idea works quite well, but has not yet been very well specified. Elsewhere we have discussed the problem more fully (Garrod & Sanford, in preparation). In the present paper, we shall examine a reported instance of the instantiation idea, carried out using a memory technique. By requiring subjects to read each sentence in a self-paced reading (SPR) situation, we feel we have evidence to disprove the contentions made on the basis of the memory study.

Instantiation and scenarios

The idea of frames as structures awaiting instantiation has been examined by Anderson, Pickert, Goetz, Schallert, Stevens and Trollip (1976) in a study which they termed 'The instantiation of general terms'. Consider a sentence like *'The woman was outstanding in the theatre'*. Anderson et al. suggest that the context in which we find *the woman* works in such a way that the woman becomes instantiated as an *actress*.

To check the validity of this intuition, they carried out a cued recall experiment in which subjects saw many sentences in which contextual restrictions suggested certain individuals. They then presented subjects with a recall cue, and asked them to remember the sentence suggested by that cue. They found that the cue *actress* resulted in superior performance to the cue *woman* in the example given above, even though woman was the actual word used. For a control sentence like *'The woman lived near the theatre' woman* was a better cue than *actress*. By invoking the principle of encoding in terms of specific exemplars wherever possible, they were able to give an explanation for this result. However, it should be noted that the general term itself is encoded within the memory package retrieved, since particular terms were *substituted* in the sentence recall produced in only about 11% of the cases. Anderson et al. suggest that a trace is retained of the surface form of the message.

This idea obviously has implications for comprehension at the time of reading. The tenor of Anderson et al.'s paper is such that they suppose instantiation to be the result of events occurring at the time of reading from the interplay of schemata addressed by the text. But if instantiation does occur at the time of comprehension, it seems reasonable to suppose it could be detected using the SPR paradigm. For example, if an instantiation has taken place, then we may well expect that subsequent references back to the instantiated individual would be as easy (or easier) if the instantiated form was used as it would be if the original (general) term was used.

Let us consider this in the light of a specific example, shown in Table 1.

Table 1

A passage with a cueing restriction in sentences 1 and 2

(1) A weapon was protruding from the corpse.
(2) There was blood all over the floor.
(3) *The assassin would easily be traced.
(4) *The police already had a suspect.
(5) The weapon/knife was covered with finger prints (TARGET).
(Question) Had the weapon killed the victim?
*Denotes noncueing sentences simply lengthening the passage (see text).

It should not take any longer to read (5) when it contains knife, strongly suggested by context, than when it contains weapon if the instantiation hypothesis is correct. Indeed, it may even take less time. In contrast, if knife is not suggested by the context, we would expect it to take longer to read a reference in which it was introduced. For example, consider the materials in Table 2.

Table 2

A passage with no cueing restriction (uncued).

---

(1) A weapon was bought from a shop in town.
(2) It was the only one of its kind.
(3) *The assasin would be easily traced.
(4) *The police already had a suspect.
(5) The weapon/knife was covered in fingerprints.
(Question) Was the weapon unique?

An experiment was carried out to examine this hypothesis.

A READING TIME STUDY OF CUEING

Method

A total of 20 materials like the example given above was made up, each consisting of a critical general noun-phrase embedded in a cueing or non-cueing context. The 20 pairs were further modified to give 40 pairs, 20 consisting of a three sentence version, and 20 a five sentence version by the inclusion of two additional sentences (marked with asterisks in the example). A check on the success of cueing was made by asking 20 students to indicate what specific instance of each general noun/phrase was suggested by the context. Fisher exact probabilities showed that 18 of the materials gave a reliable ($p < .01$) instantiation of the anticipated noun-phrase, and the others were near misses.

The SPR paradigm was used. Subjects sat at an IMLAC visual display unit, coupled to a NOVA 2 computer. By pressing a space-bar on the console they saw the materials one sentence at a time. Each paragraph was preceded by the sentence NEXT TRIAL. When the question came up, subjects answered by pressing N if the answer was 'no' (right hand) and Y if the answer was 'yes' (left hand). 20 subjects saw the three sentence paragraphs, and 20 the five sentence versions. All subjects received practice at SPR prior to the experiment proper. Instructions were to read as quickly as possible, without rushing, in order to be able to answer the questions. 16 sets of 3-sentence materials from another (different) study were mixed randomly with those from this study. Reading times and question-answering times were measured to the nearest msec by the computer.

Results

(a) *Target sentence data.* Mean reading times for the target sentences are shown in Table 3. An analysis of variance revealed that the targets were read more rapidly

Table 3

Target reading times (msecs)

Target:		Specific	General
Antecedent	(cued	1388	1330
	(uncued	1463	1390

when preceded by the cued antecedent than by the uncued $F(1, 38) = 9.925$, $p < .004$. The target sentences containing a specific term were read more slowly than those containing a repeat of the general term $F(1, 38) = 5.905$, $p < .02$. Contrary to the instantiation hypothesis, the interaction of these two effects was numerically small and quite unreliable, with $F(1, 38) < 1$. There was no reliable difference in reading time for targets appearing in the 3 or 5 sentence conditions $F(1, 38) = 0.28$, and no other interactions were significant, all F's $(1, 38) < 1$.

There are two striking features here. The first is that cueing does seem to influence target reading times - by speeding them up. The second is the almost total lack of interaction between target type and cueing.

(b) *Question answering times.* An analysis of mean question-answering times revealed that questions relating to cued materials were answered faster (2060 msecs) than those relating to uncued materials (2208 msecs), a reliable difference with $F(1, 38) = 14.3$, $p < .0008$. This parallels the target sentence data suggesting that the memory trace for cued materials is more accessible.

(c) *Sentence 4 of the 5-sentence condition.* It is possible that uncued materials produce a generally higher memory load which may influence any incoming materials. A comparison of reading times for sentence 4 in the 5 sentence condition shows cueing to have no effect (cued: 1482 msec, uncued: 1468 msec, $F (1, 19) = 0.48$). Consequently the cueing effect is specific to coreferential materials only.

Discussion of results

Our results indicate the instantiation hypothesis is wrong. Cueing an individual by context does not serve to privilege the specific form in terms of anaphoric reference, hence the specific form is not substituted for the general or made more readily available by the context.

The structure of cued and uncued materials did have an effect on subsequent ease of handling anaphoric materials. We suggest that this is because of the ease with which anaphoric statements as a whole may be integrated into the extant representation. We suggest that by their nature, cueing contexts portray situations which are more stereotyped for a subject, and that new information is more easily integrated into a stereotyped scenario. This makes sense in that it implies that passages requiring the integration of familiar, well portrayed events are easier to read - a point supported by the observation that such passages are read more rapidly even when proportional content is held constant (Kintsch, Kozminsky, Stretby, McKoon and Keenan, 1975). In order to test this point of view, 20 subjects were asked to produce short phrases or titles for each of the materials used in the experiment. They also had to indicate how easily they could do this on a 5-point scale. Similarly, they rated on a 5-point scale how readily they could produce a visual image of this situation, regardless of whether they could describe it. The results, shown below, indicate that both visual imagery and verbal descriptions come to mind more readily in the case of the cued materials:

Table 4

Mean ratings

Imagery:	Cued	Uncued	Verbal Description:	Cued	Uncued
	3.03	2.13		3.11	2.99
$p < .01$	(Sign test)		$p < .01$	(Sign test)	

Rather than instantiation, we suggest that the results are due to the ease of retrieving and maintaining a scenario. The results of Anderson et al.(1976) can be understood in these terms. Suppose the sentence 'The woman was outstanding in the theatre' produces an 'acting' scenario. Subsequent use of the retrieval cue 'actress' may serve to similarly elicit an 'acting'scenario, and hence lead to easy retrieval of the original material. On the other hand 'The woman lived near the theatre' may produce poorer, less well defined scenarios, since it is not obviously about anything and therefore cannot be expected to elicit scenario modules from memory. The 'actress' cue will produce a scenario which is largely irrelevant in this case. Finally, 'woman' will be a poor retrieval cue because it is not sufficiently well specified either to elicit a scenario or to produce one which will be likely to overlap with the representations of the previous materials.

In summary, we suggest that instantiation does not occur during reading, and that memory experiments suggesting it does are reflecting properties of retrieval mechanics. Furthermore, language input may perhaps be looked at as eliciting scenario or frame-like structures, which consist of modular information stored in long term memory. Fuller discussions of this may be found in Sanford and Garrod (1978) and Garrod and Sanford (in preparation).

REFERENCES

Anderson, R. C., Pickert, J. W., Goetz, E. T., Schallert, D.L., Stevens, K. V. and Trollip, S. R. (1976). Instantiation of general terms. *Journal of Verbal Learning and Verbal Behavior, 15,* 667-679.

Dooling, D. J. and Christiansen, R. E. (1977). Levels of encoding and retention of prose. In: *The Psychology of learning and motivation.* Vol. II, Academic Press, New York.

Dooling D. and Mullett, R. (1973). Locus of thematic effects in retention of prose. *Journal of Experimental Psychology, 97,* 404-406.

Garrod, S. and Sanford, A. J. (1977). Interpreting anaphoric relations: the integration of semantic information while reading. *Journal of Verbal Learning and Verbal Behavior, 16,* 77-90.

Garrod S. C. and Sanford, A. J. (in preparation).

Haviland, S. and Clark, H. H. (1974). What's new? Acquiring new information as a process in comprehension. *Journal of Verbal Learning and Verbal Behavior, 13,* 512-521.

Kintsch, W. (1974). *The representation of meaning in memory.* Erlbaum, Potomac, Md.
Kintsch, W., Kozminsky, E., Stretby, W. J., McKoon, G., and Keenan, J. M. (1975). Comprehension and recall of text as a function of content variable. *Journal of Verbal Learning and Verbal Behavior, 14*, 196-214.
Minsky, M. (1975). A framework for representing knowledge. In: *The psychology of computer vision.* (P. Winston, Ed). McGraw-Hill, New York.
Sanford, A. J. and Garrod, S. C. (1978). Memory and attention in text comprehension: the problem of reference. *Paper presented at the VIIth International Symposium on Attention and Performance, Princeton, New Jersey.*
Thorndyke, P. W. (1975). *Cognitive structures in human story comprehension and memory.* Ph.D. thesis: University of Stanford, California.

This research was supported by a grant No. 4814/1 from Social Science Research Council, awarded to Drs. Sanford & Garrod.

EYE MOVEMENTS AND THE INTEGRATION OF SEMANTIC INFORMATION DURING READING

Alan Kennedy
Department of Psychology,
The University, Dundee, Scotland.

INTRODUCTION

This paper is concerned with some of the mental operations which go on when people read and interpret short sequences of sentences. It is customary to speak in this context of the integration of information, implying that the reader is engaged in building in working memory some kind of stable mental representation of what is before him as he reads. The function of such a representation would be to free the reader from any long-term constraints imposed by the more superficial aspects of what is read - for example, its punctuation, syntax and exact word-order. Once these have served to provide an entry into working memory they are lost. From this point of view "comprehension" involves building a series of relatively short-term relationships between concepts which are part of our stable knowledge of the world: an activity which may also, of course, lead to permanent changes in long-term memory itself, reflecting the acquisition of new information.

The impetus for the experiment I wish to discuss was provided by a study carried out in Glasgow by Simon Garrod and Tony Sanford, (1977). They looked at the consequences of reading pairs of sentences such as

A bus came trundling round the corner

The vehicle nearly flattened a pedestrian ...

Clearly, to understand this narrative sequence it is necessary to grasp that the words *bus* and *vehicle* both refer to the same entity. The rules of English allow for a range of anaphoric relations of this kind, the most usual involving pronominalisation as in

When Henry fell over he was drunk

Read with normal stress it is accepted that *he* and *Henry* in this sentence refer to the same person. But when does the process of cross-reference - the forging of this link - take place? Garrod *et al.* argue that it is during reading itself, and is not an operation occurring later, and then only if further interpretation is necessary, as, for example, might be needed to answer the question: *Did the vehicle nearly flatten the pedestrian?* In other words they argue that when the sentence containing the word *vehicle* is first read it is related directly to the specific examplar named earlier; the subject does not simply enter information into memory about vehicles in general. The support they offer for this view is provided by the fact that the time taken to read sentences (silently) of the kind illustrated is influenced by the semantic distance (or conjoint frequency) between the category and the examplar. It takes longer to read the sentence *the vehicle nearly flattened a pedestrian* when it follows a reference to *tank* (low conjoint frequency) than to *bus* (high conjoint frequency).

Their study was of interest to me because I was at the same time trying to relate some aspects of text-processing to concurrent eye movements. One of the few reliable effects in this area is that fixation duration lengthens and saccade length shortens when material gets harder. It would clearly be of interest to examine the precise way in which subjects looked at contrasting sentences which were known, from other evidence, to produce reliable differences in reading time.

This is not the place to review models of eye movement control. However, if we consider simply general classes of model the most significant contrast is provided between some variant of a "gain control" system and some system of direct control via semantic and perceptual feedback. Looked at from the first point of view it could be argued that eye movement control is more or less decoupled from analysis of the content of what is being read. There is a simple gain control which moves the eye along the line in appropriately sized chunks. When the going gets difficult the feedback is such as to reduce the size of each saccade (Kolers, 1976). The effect shown by Garrod *et al.* may be related to the momentary influence of discovering a difficulty in interpretation which results in a general slowing down of reading rate.

The second class of model assumes, firstly that subjects can pick up in peripheral vision low grade information and extract enough from it to guide in part the size and direction of successive fixations. In addition, the process of understanding what one has read may itself lead, on a moment-to-moment basis, to organised plans for looking. It is as if, in this view, one rapidly normalises the eye-movement control system to particular type-faces, spacing, line lengths and separations and then uses this parametric information, in conjunction with knowledge of the content and structure of what is read, to guide the eyes from one informative region to another. This is not altogether as implausible as it may sound if what is meant, for example, is no more than to say that when reading *The hunters shot the rhinoceros*, if the eye falls on the centre of the word *hunters* it may be possible to plan to skip the short word identified in peripheral vision ("*the*") and hit the long word which is almost certainly the object of the verb which is already being processed (see O'Regan, 1975).

This paper is an attempt to distinguish between these models and to examine eye movements directly in a replication of part of the Garrod *et al.* study.

METHOD

Materials and Design

The materials were identical to those used by Garrod *et al.* (1977). These consisted of sixteen categories, each having a high and a low conjoint frequency examplar associated with it. The particular words were incorporated into sequences of sentences such as:

A (bus / tank) came trundling round the corner

The vehicle nearly flattened a pedestrian

Did the vehicle nearly flatten a pedestrian?

The critical measure was the time to read (silently) the second sentence following either a high or low conjoint frequency examplar. After each pair of sentences a question was added, with half of the questions arranged so that the required answer was true. The experiment was run with 12 subjects. After a series of practice trials each subject was given two blocks of sixteen experimental trials each block consisting of 8 high and 8 low conjoint frequency examplars. If the high conjoint frequency examplar occurred in the first block the second block would contain the low frequency examplar. Order of presentation of the two blocks was counterbalanced across subjects.

Procedure

The sentences were displayed on a VR-14 Display interfaced to a PDP-12A computer. Subjects were seated comfortably looking slightly upwards towards the display with the head held rigidly by means of a dental composition bite-bar fixed to a heavy metal frame. After calibration of the equipment subjects were told to read, in as natural a fashion as possible, the sentences which appeared on the screen. Sentences were displayed for up to 4048 msec with an inter-sentence interval of one second. There was a variable interval, averaging 3 sec, between each set of three sentences. The subject had a button under the right-hand index finger and was asked to press it lightly as soon as a particular sentence was read; when pressed, this button terminated the display. Subjects were also provided with a pair of buttons to indicate yes or no responses respectively to the questions appearing at the end of each sequence of three sentences. Subjects were not told, and appeared to be unaware, that the purpose of the experiment was to measure reading speed as distinct from the accuracy of answers to the questions.

Eye movements were measured using an infra-red reflection technique which recorded horizontal movements of the left eye. The camera provided an analogue input to the computer which stored sampled data on magnetic tape, - (for further details of the procedure see Kennedy, 1978). Eye movement data were sampled at a one msec rate with the mean of each 16 samples being stored in the form of an estimated horizontal screen position.

Analysis of the stored data was carried out using a pattern analyzing computer program. This generated for each sentence a table giving the total time during reading that the eye spent within the boundary of each word, together with the viewing time for the sentence as a whole, this latter measure being the "reading time" employed by Garrod *et al.*

RESULTS

The mean reading times for the second sentences of the

triples presented were 2045 msec for high and 2206 for low conjoint frequency examplars, with *min F'* $(1,24) = 6.6$, $p<.05$. This result compares with times of 1320 and 1401 msec by Garrod and Sanford. Clearly their primary finding is replicated, although the absolute times were much longer, probably as a result of the very different experimental situation.

The results of the eye-movement analysis showed that the total time spent looking at the critical word in sentence 2 was 70 msec per letter for high and 86 msec per letter for low conjoint frequency examplars, with *min F'* $(1,24) = 4.6$, $p<.05$. This result would appear to be specific to the critical words since a similar analysis performed on the (critical word + 2) showed no significant differences. This result suggests that subjects do indeed spend longer looking at points of cross-reference when these are of low conjoint frequency, and that this is an effect which occurs in the course of assimilating information.

To assess whether subjects simply made longer fixations or made regressive eye movements to particular words, further analyses were carried out using a measure of the number of inspections made of the category word in sentence 2 under the two conditions. These produced results of 1.30 inspections per word and 1.52 inspections per word for the high and low conjoint frequency examplars respectively, (*min F'* $(1,25) = 7.99$, $p<.05$). Although this difference is significant it is clearly not the case that critical words were subjected to more than one inspection in all cases and somewhat doubtful whether all the obtained difference in total inspection time can be accounted for in this way.

DISCUSSION

The most obvious reference point for these results is a recent study by Carpenter *et al.* (1978). They showed that in the reading of fairly long sequences of sentences the point of disambiguation of particular pronouns was associated with regressive eye movements to the appropriate antecedent in a previously read sentence. Subjects read sequences such as:

> *The guard mocked one of the prisoners in the machine shop*
>
> *The one who the guard mocked was the arsonist*
>
> *He had been at the prison for only one week*

It was the warden who never visited the machine shop

In the third sentence the word *he* could refer to either *the guard* or *the arsonist*, although the construction of the passage makes the latter interpretation more likely. Carpenter *et al.* showed that regressive eye movements occurred back to a particular referent in the second sentence after reading the pronoun in the third. It is not, of course, logically necessary to look back in this way if the relevant item has already been entered into a memory structure; it may however be that the simplest way to "re-enter" an item is to look at it afresh. The temporal sequence of eye fixations need bear no relationship to the logical sequence of what is read any more than the order of sentences need reflect the underlying chronology of a particular narrative sequence (Kintsch & Monk, 1972).

I would suggest that similar effects may be identified as operating in the present study. Subjects are very sensitive to reference within text. Even at the simplest level it can be shown that reading one word will alter the evidence needed to recognise or utter another related word. These processes of semantic "priming" may operate in a diffuse undifferentiated way but can also be influenced by both syntactic and semantic constraints. Further, they function as one of the inputs to the eye movement control system such that primed words are located more rapidly and may be fixated for a longer duration, (Kennedy, 1978). In the present case, as we have seen, the data are equivocal since fixation duration and number of fixations are confounded and we must therefore wait for additional experimental data to examine the proposal that subjects may look longer *and* more often at critical points in sentences of the present kind.

People often claim not only to know an item of information, but also to know where it is in terms of its location on a particular page. This incidental learning, which appears at first sight to have little functional significance, first found experimental support in a paper by Rothkopf (1971). Subjects were asked to remember the contents of a 12-page prose passage and could frequently also recall which page contained a particular fact and what part of a particular page contained it. Locative information of this kind could be remembered over long periods of time. In a more detailed study Christie and Just (1976) showed that subjects can, in fact, accurately remember the location of a particular sentence in a passage which contains critical information. I would suggest that both these studies are tapping the residue of very accurate fine-grain locative information which is available over the period of time needed to integrate information from the reading of successive sentences, and is used to control eye movements. People not only read the words but also appear to know quite exactly *where* what they have read is located on the page. This information may be essential if fluent reading - which involves mapping a particular temporal sequence of fixations on to a quite distinct sequence of concepts - is to take place at all.

The experimental data suggest that a simple gain control model of eye movement control, may be inadequate. The variations in fixation duration produced by changes in anaphoric reference take place over too short a time-scale for such a model to be plausible. It seems much more likely that the control system is sensitive to the results of the processes of interpretation going on during reading. What is read at a particular moment may play a part in determining where the eye falls next.

REFERENCES

Carpenter, P.A. and Just, M.A. (1978). Reading Comprehension as the eyes see it. In: *Cognitive Processes in Comprehension*. (M.A. Just and P.A. Carpenter,eds), Lawrence Erlbaum, New Jersey.

Christie, J. and Just, M.A. (1976). Remembering the location and content of sentences in a prose passage. *Journal of Educational Psychology*. *68*, 702-710.

Garrod, S. and Sanford, A. (1977). Interpreting anaphoric relations: the integration of semantic information while reading. *Journal of Verbal Learning and Verbal Behavior*. *16*, 77-90.

Kennedy, A. (1978). Reading sentences: some observations on the control of eye movements. In: *Strategies of Information Processing*. (G. Underwood, ed), Academic Press, London.

Kintsch, W. and Monk, D. (1972). Storage of complex information in memory: some implications of the speed with which inferences can be made. *Journal of Experimental Psychology*, *94*, 25-32.

Kolers, P.A. (1976). Buswell's discoveries. In: *Eye Movements and Psychological Processes*. (R.A. Monty and J.W. Senders, eds), Wiley: New York.

O'Regan, J.K. (1975). *Structural and Contextual Constraints on Eye Movements in Reading*. Unpublished doctoral thesis, University of Cambridge.

Rothkopf, E.Z. (1971). Incidental memory for location of information in text. *Journal of Verbal Learning and Verbal Behavior*, *10*, 608-613.

SEMANTIC PROCESSING OF WORDS: FOVEAL AND PARAFOVEAL DIFFERENCES IN READING

Keith Rayner
University of Massachusetts
Amherst, Massachusetts, U.S.A.

Experiments dealing with subjects' ability to obtain meaning from parafoveally presented words are described. In the experiments, eye movements were monitored and a stimulus (a word or letter string) appeared in parafoveal vision. Subjects made an eye movement toward the stimulus and during the saccade the initially presented stimulus was replaced by a word which the subject named. Results indicated that semantic information was not obtained from the parafoveal stimulus. The implications for reading are discussed.

INTRODUCTION

One of the most interesting findings that has emerged from recent research on word recognition is that subjects apparently know the meaning of a word before they know what the word is. In these experiments (Allport, 1977; Marcel and Patterson, 1978), words are presented for very short durations in foveal vision and a masking pattern that immediately follows the word makes it impossible for subjects to reliably indicate whether or not a word was presented prior to the mask. Yet these "unseen" words seem to affect subjects responses to a stimulus which follows after the mask. One implication of the results, Marcel (1978) has suggested, is that meaning is simultaneously available from a number of places on a page. For example, Marcel notes that if you turn the page of a book and are reading the top line, something at the bottom of the page may "catch your eye". Marcel argues that this is only possible if its meaning has been analyzed independently of where attention is directed.

While the results obtained by Marcel and by Allport are compelling, the generalization to an entire page of text is questionable. In reading normal text there is the obvious problem that acuity factors and lateral masking considerations make it difficult to identify words at increasing distances from the fixation point. Some information about the shape and length of words in parafoveal vision may be available, but it is unlikely that semantic access can occur from global shape or length attributes of words.

In this paper, I will focus on the distinction between foveal and parafoveal vision and the capability of obtaining meaning from these two areas. I will report some experiments that deal with subjects ability to obtain meaning from parafoveal vision. In the experiments, eye movements were monitored as subjects looked at the face of a Cathode-Ray Tube (CRT). A stimulus (a word or letter string) appeared in parafoveal vision and subjects were instructed to make an eye movement to the location of the stimulus. During the saccade, a computer monitoring the eye position rapidly replaced the initially presented stimulus with a word which the subjects were asked to name. Reaction times for naming the word present on the CRT after the eye movement were significantly affected by the characteristics of the initially presented stimulus. Like the experiments by Marcel and Allport, these experiments can be characterized as dealing with unconscious processes as the subjects were unable to report what the first stimulus was and were seldom able to tell that a display change had occurred on the CRT.

EXPERIMENTAL PROCEDURES

When subjects arrived for an experimental session, they were seated facing a CRT which was interfaced with a PDP-1140 computer. The CRT had a P-31 phosphor, which had the characteristic that removing a character resulted in a drop to 1% of maximum brightness in .25 msec. Eye position was determined by an infrared sensing device placed in front of the subject's right eye. The signal from the eye movement sensors was sampled every msec by the computer. The characteristics of the display were such that when the subject's eye was 48 cm from the face of the CRT three character spaces equalled 1° of visual angle. A forehead rest was used to stabilize the head.

After the eye movement sensors had been calibrated, subjects fixated on a dot in the center of the CRT and pushed a button held in the right hand. If the computer judged the eye to be fixated, a stimulus string (*initially displayed alternative*) appeared beginning either 1°, 3° or 5° to the right of fixation or ending 1°, 3° or 5° to the left. When the subject made a saccade toward the stimulus, the initially displayed alternative was removed by the computer and replaced by a word which the subject was asked to name (*base word*). The display change occurred within the time period of the saccade and a number of software constraints resulted in the repitition of a particular trial later in the sequence if the change did not occur during the eye movement. Since the latency of the eye movement was in the range of 150-200 msec, the amount of time that the initially displayed alternative was visible on the CRT approximated many fixation durations in reading.

The dependent variable in the experiments was the amount of time required for the subject to name the base word. Since the experiments are somewhat difficult for subjects, we have typically used a small group of well-practiced subjects (about 10 altogether) who were very familiar with the apparatus and with the set of base words. Although there are individual differences (particularly in overall naming time), the pattern of results for these subjects was quite consistent.

RESULTS

The basic pattern of results has been described in greater detail elsewhere (Rayner, 1978; Rayner, McConkie, and Ehrlich, 1978). Here, I will briefly describe the results of some of the earliest experiments prior to discussing the most recent research. More detail can be found in the original sources.

Figure 1 shows the typical pattern of results from the earliest experiments. The naming time is from the end of the eye movement until the subject began uttering the base word.

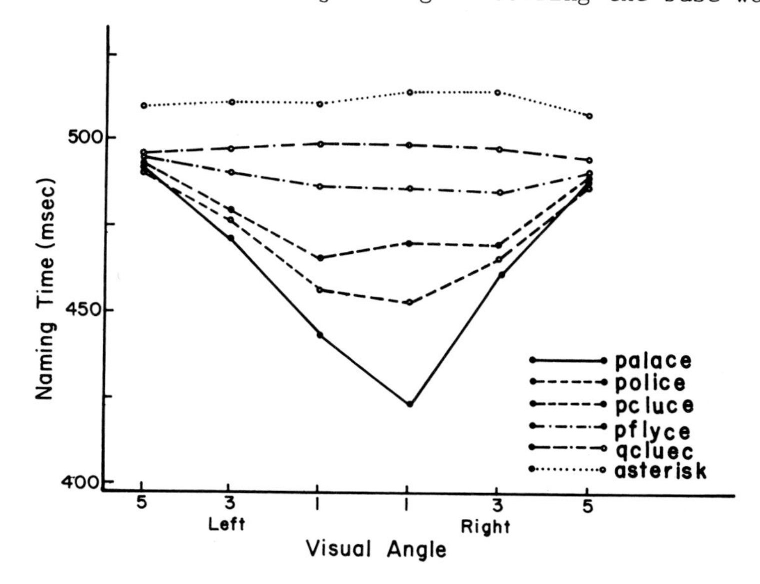

Fig. 1 Naming time as a function of visual angle. In the example shown, palace was the base word.

As seen in Figure 1, there were definite differences as a function of the distance that the initially displayed alternative was presented from the fixation point. More importantly, there were differences among the experimental conditions particularly when the initially displayed alternative was presented 1° or 3° from fixation. The legend in Figure 1 indicates different types of initially displayed alternatives when the base word was *palace*. Thus, a word (*police*) or nonword (*pcluce*) that was visually similar to the base word resulted in considerable facilitation in naming time compared to nonwords which had either the same beginning and end letters (but different word shape) as the base word or which had the same overall word shape (but different beginning and end letters).

One aspect of Figure 1 is particularly relevant to a discussion of obtaining semantic information from parafoveal vision. It could be argued that subjects identify the word from the parafoveal presentation and then simply check it against a few visual features following the eye movement prior to uttering it. Such a suggestion is very similar to the hypothesis testing view of reading but without contextual information to aid in generating the hypothesis. One way to test this suggestion is to examine what happens in the case when a word (such as *police*) is initially presented in parafoveal vision and then replaced by another word (*palace*) during the saccade. The data we have obtained indicate that the suggestion that subjects are identifying the parafoveal word is unlikely for a couple of reasons. First, if subjects do identify the parafoveal word prior to the eye movement and then check it against the visual features after the eye movement, on a number of trials the subject should verbalize the parafoveal word. In fact, subjects did not verbalize the parafoveal word and they did not make errors in naming the foveal word. Second, given that such intrusions do not occur, at least there should be a great deal of interference generated which would lead to longer naming times when *police* is initially presented and replaced by *palace*. If the parafoveal word were truly identified, then this "hypothesis" would be disconfirmed on the next fixation and considerable difficulty should result. In fact, there were no such inhibitory patterns in the data; as seen in Figure 1 there was substantial facilitation in this condition (when compared to the initial presentation of an asterisk). It is also interesting that there were not great differences between the initial presentation of nonwords like *pcluce* and words like *police* which are visually similar to the base word. If lexical information were the critical factor one would expect all conditions in which a nonword was initially presented should result in longer naming times. But, this was clearly not the case. Thus, any simple explanation for the effects we have observed involving the acquisition of either lexical or semantic information from the parafoveal stimulus does not seem to be supported by the data.

In subsequent experiments we have attempted to determine what type of information is obtained from the parafoveal word that facilitates the processing of the foveal word. One attractive alternative is that there is an Integrative Visual Buffer (see Rayner, 1978 for a discussion). According to this position, visual information is integrated across fixations; gross visual information obtained from the parafovea on the first fixation is stored in some type of temporary visual buffer and overlapped with information in the fovea on the second fixation. However, a series of experiments (Rayner, 1979) in which case changes occurred during the saccade have indicated that this alternative cannot be correct. In these experiments, for example, *chest* may initially appear in the parafovea and be replaced by *chest*, *CHEST*, *chart*, or *CHART*. Although word changes affected naming time, case changes did not. If strictly visual information were being overlapped across fixations, then surely there should be some disruption when case changes occurred; but this did not happen. It should also be noted that although the experiments described here have utilized a naming task, similar effects have been obtained when subjects were not required to verbalize the base word.

Figure 2 shows the results of a more recent experiment. In this experiment, the initially displayed alternatives were either semantic associates of the base word, words that looked very much like the semantic associate, words that had the same first two letters as the base word, or words that had the same last two letters as the base word. As seen in Figure 2, the semantic associate resulted in no facilitation of naming the base word. On the other hand, if the first two letters of the initially displayed alternative were the same as the first two letters of the base word, there was considerable facilitation. Thus, it appears that the type of information that subjects obtain from the parafoveal word that facilitates the naming of the foveal word is specific letter information that is independent of case considerations. Some type of preliminary letter identification of beginning letters of words seems to be responsible for the facilitation we have observed.

DISCUSSION

The major thrust of the experiments reported here is that

we have obtained no evidence that semantic information is obtained from the parafoveal presentation of a word. It is clear that if subjects are given sufficient time they can identify a word presented parafoveally. However, in the experiments described here where a word appeared parafoveally for 150-200 msec and was replaced by another word during the eye movement, the semantic content of the first word did not affect the naming time of the second word. The general conclusion that semantic information is not obtained from these parafoveal presentations is also consistent with the results of an experiment (Rayner, 1975) reported a few years ago. In that experiment, subjects read passages of text as their eye movements were monitored and certain critical words were changed on the display during the saccade. The results of that experiment suggested that readers do not obtain the meaning of words beginning six or more character positions to the right of the fixation point. However, in that experiment there was some indication that the combination of word shape and beginning letter information was obtained from parafoveal words. Stimuli used in that experiment were identical to those used in the experiment shown in Figure 1. The results of the experiments we have done with changing case and an experiment by McConkie (1979) now indicate that strictly visual information is not being integrated across fixations in read-

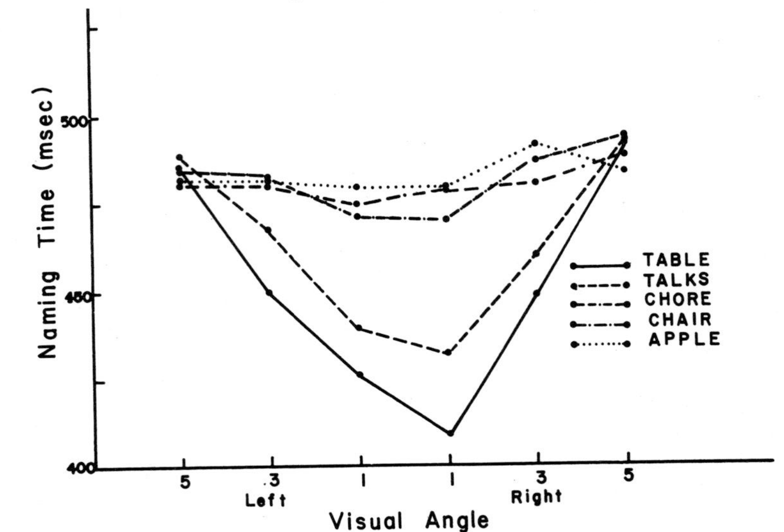

Fig. 2 Naming time as a function of visual angle. In the example shown, TABLE was the base word.

ing and that information about the beginning letters of the parafoveal word is the critical information obtained from words in parafoveal vision. Thus, some type of preliminary letter identification of the initial letters of words occurs for words in the parafovea so that the reader can devote more attention after the eye movement to letters other than those at the beginning of the word. The notion that preliminary letter identification occurs can also explain the finding that visually similar initially displayed alternatives resulted in a great deal of facilitation in the word naming task while an initially displayed alternative which was not visually similar to the base word resulted in no facilitation. Consider the cases in which *pcluce* and *pflyce* are presented parafoveally and replaced by *palace* during the saccade. Because the initial stimulus is presented parafoveally and followed temporally very rapidly by another word, preliminary letter identification begins on the parafoveal word. But due to acuity factors and lateral masking considerations the subject is able to identify the first letter and make some preliminary identification of the next two letters. However, since the c is confusable with *a* and shares many features in common with it, the probability is higher that the second letter will be identified as an *a* when *pcluce* is initially presented than when *pflyce* is presented initially. Thus, preliminary letter identification is influenced by the visual similarity of other letters. Such an explanation can also account for the finding reported previously (Rayner, 1975) that changes in the display in which word shape was changed while beginning letters remained constant provided more disruption during reading (in terms of fixation duration) than when word shape and beginning letters remained constant.

Returning now to Marcel's suggestion that during reading meaning is analyzed independently of where attention is directed, the present results provide no support for such a notion. One possibility why something at the bottom of the page may "catch your eye" when you turn the page and begin reading the top line is that as you moved your eye to bring it to the top of the page there was a short fixation near the bottom of the page. While the normal fixation duration is 200-250 msec, fixations as short as 35-50 msec do occur in reading. In particular, they occur quite frequently following the return sweep of the eye. These undershoots of the eye are then followed by a right-to-left saccade. While it is often suggested that the purpose of the brief fixation is to program a corrective saccade and not to abstract textual information, it is also true that readers generally do not refixate the area of the brief fixation. Thus, it may be that information gets into the system during these brief fixations, but is not fully processed until the eye has moved on. Whereas in normal eye fixations in reading, attention and the location of the fixation may be correlated, in these brief fixations they may not be. Thus, as the reader is reading the top line, the semantic content of the information obtained during the brief fixation near the bottom of the page may reach consciousness leading the reader to move the eye to the bottom of the page to see if that information was really there.

ACKNOWLEDGMENTS

This research was supported by NSF grant BNS76-05017 and by NICHHD grant HD12727. The author would like to thank A. Well and A. Pollatsek for their comments on an earlier draft.

REFERENCES

Allport, D.A. (1977). On knowing the meaning of words we are unable to report: The effects of masking. In *Attention and Performance V1*. (S. Dornic, ed.), Erlbaum, Hillsdale, New Jersey.

Marcel, T. (1978). Unconscious reading: Experiments on people who do not know they are reading. *Visible Language*, in press.

Marcel, T. and Patterson, K. (1978). Word recognition and production: Reciprocity in clinical and normal studies. In *Attention and Performance V11*. (J. Requin, ed.), Erlbaum, Hillsdale, New Jersey.

McConkie, G.W. (1979). On the role and control of eye movements in reading. In *Processing of Visible Language 1*, (P.A. Kolers, M. Wrolstad, and H. Bouma, eds.), Plenum, New York.

Rayner, K. (1975). The perceptual span and peripheral cues in reading. *Cognitive Psychology*, 7, 65-81.

Rayner, K. (1978). Foveal and parafoveal cues in reading. In *Attention and Performance V11*. (J. Requin, ed.), Erlbaum, Hillsdale, New Jersey.

Rayner, K. (1979). Eye movements in reading: Eye guidance and integration. In *Processing of Visible Language 1*, (P.A. Kolers, M. Wrolstad, and H. Bouma, eds.), Plenum, New York.

Rayner, K., McConkie, G.W., and Ehrlich, S. (1978). Eye movements and integrating information across fixations. *Journal of Experimental Psychology: Human Perception and Performance*, 4, in press.

SHORT TERM MEMORY AND READING, STAGE 1

E. A. Lunzer
University of Nottingham,
Nottingham, England.

ABSTRACT

In the course of study of children's cognitive abilities, it was found that reproducing a visual sequence at age 6 is highly correlated with progress in initial reading. The prediction is independent of language and intelligence. It is argued that this finding points to the importance of building up correspondences between letter and sound sequences in the early stages of reading.

INTRODUCTION

There are three possible positions one can take with regard to the mechanisms involved in reading, corresponding to the degree of emphasis one accords to data driven processes on the one hand and central control processes on the other. At the one extreme, we have the view of Gough (1972) who describes a continuous processing from the extraction of letter features to the assignment of meaning. Laberge and Samuels (1974) take a somewhat similar position although stressing the automaticity of the process in the skilled reader. At the other extreme Goodman (1967) insists on the primacy of the central information-seeking process. The third position is intermediate: the reader scans the visual input sequentially, but the amount of information he needs to extract tends to diminish for later letters within words and also for later words within phrases, in the measure that he is able to build up syntactic and semantic expectations. However, these latter do not in general enable him to identify words or phrases. What they do is to reduce recognition thresholds.

The findings to be reported were incidental in an inquiry the main purpose of which was quite another, viz. to establish whether Piaget's concept of operativity could be operationally defined and reliably measured. A second purpose was to explore the relation between operativity, language and S.T.M. Will operativity prove factorally distinct from language competence when each is represented by a number of separate measures in a battery? Is the correlation between S.T.M. and operativity sufficiently marked to sustain the hypothesis advanced by McLaughlin (1963) that the level of the child's reasoning is primarily a function of the number of judgements which he can hold in mind and compare at any one time, and this in turn is simply a matter of S.T.M.

It was found that (1) provided that sufficient tests are used, the measurement of operativity can be as reliable as a traditional intelligence test; (2) measures of operativity and language do group in such a way as to appear as distinct factors, but the factors themselves are highly correlated; (3) correlations between S.T.M. and operativity measures are positive but low.

This last finding should not be interpreted as in contradiction to the neo-Piagetian theory of Pascual-Leone (1970), since the latter is careful to insist that repetition of digits is an inadequate test of "M-power", which is concerned with the demand of information-processing strategies whose function is to operate on input and transform it, and not merely to reproduce it (cf. White, 1965). These results have been discussed elsewhere (Lunzer, Wilkinson and Dolan, 1976).

The main inquiry took place in 1972 when the subjects were just under six. A year later we were able to carry out a follow-up investigation, and this time we included a number of tests of reading. We were therefore in a position to establish how effective were the various measures included in the original battery in predicting achievement in reading one year later. Briefly, it was discovered that whereas the Piagetian tests gave the best prediction and the language measures were not much poorer, the correlations between these two were so high that language did not add significantly to the power of the prediction. On the other hand, tests of S.T.M., and especially of visual sequencing, did enhance the predictions. It is these aspects of the study that concern us here.

I would like first of all to give a few details regarding the measures, the procedures and results, and to briefly discuss their significance and limitations.

METHOD

There were 210 children in the original sample but these numbers were reduced to 183 who completed the reading tests in the second year. The sample was random within schools (21 in all), these being chosen to represent advantaged, average, or disadvantaged catchment areas.

The original battery included nine Piagetian measures, these including conservation, seriation, classification, and the reproduction of sequences. It also contained five measures of language, including the Crichton vocabulary and the E.P.V.T. There were also several measures of learning, including three of operative learning.

There were four measures of S.T.M. Two of these were the repetition of digits and of unassociated words. The remaining two are of special concern to this paper, being measures of memory for visual sequences. Both used a box of nine plaques in a three by three arrangement, each featuring a different symbol. The tester showed the child a series of cards featuring sequences of these symbols, increasing from an initial length of two, to three, four, etc. and left these exposed for four, six or eight seconds, etc., i.e. two seconds per item. After each such presentation, the child was required to select the correct plaques from the box and place them in the right order, the plaques being returned to the box in the same position after each trial. One of the two sets of symbols was geometric (half moon, lightning flash, plus sign, ring, etc.), the other was representational, showing sequences of outline animal drawings. The two tests differ in that the shapes are less easy to name.

To complete this section of the battery there were a number of measures of L.T.M., chiefly memory for stories but also including some memory for structured arrangements of drawings. All testing was individual.

Three tests of reading were given in 1973 including the Standard Reading Test, which uses sentences, and the Neale Analysis of Reading which uses whole passages. However, the correlations between these were so high that subsequent analyses were based on the most familiar test, the Schonell Word Recognition Test.

RESULTS

These are shown in Table 1. It will be seen that the two measures of audial STM are more strongly correlated with one another than the two measures of memory for visual sequencing. Nevertheless, the latter correlate (and factor) together.

TABLE 1

Intercorrelations among measures of STM (N=210)

	Digits	Words	Shapes
Words	.65		
Shapes	.30	.27	
Animals	.29	.35	.46

Correlations with reading (forward prediction)

Table 2 shows the zero order correlations of three sets of measures with reading one year later.

TABLE 2

Correlations with reading (decimals omitted)

Operativity		Language		STM	
Length conservation	25				
Number conservation	31	Comprehension I	35	Digits	26
Seriation	45	Comprehension II	41	Words	33
Multiple seriation	39	Watts	31	Shapes	29
Class inclusion	31	EPVT	38	Animals	51
All and Some	43	Crichton	45		
Reproduction of order	46				
Intersection	53				
Haptic recognition	28				

The best single predictor is one of the operativity measures: intersection (placement of multiple category objects in intersecting hoops corresponding to a Venn-diagram) Reproduction of order and seriation of rods are close. The Crichton Vocabulary test is the best predictor among the five measures of language. However, the second best predictor is the animal sequencing test of visual STM.

Multiple Regression

The relative contributions to the prediction of reading can be seen by combining the tests in Table 2 into sets. Most of the predictor sets in Table 3 are averages of several highly correlated tests as shown by the figures in brackets, raw scores having been standardised before averaging. Thus the two conservation tests are combined, as are the remaining seven operativity measures. The two modalities for STM appear separately as does the single best measure of language: Crichton vocabulary. Also included in the equation of Table 3 are the measures of learning and LTM, although these will not be discussed. The beta weights for the 183 subjects appear in the first column. Also shown are the corresponding beta weights calculated separately for each of the three groups of schools (n = 67,57 and 59 respectively, for socio-economic (SE) groups I, II and III).

TABLE 3

Comparison of β weights for the prediction of reading achievement by 10 sets of predictors (N=183)

	All Ss	SEI	SEII	SEIII
Conservation (2)	.02	.05	-.01	.13
Operativity (7)	.23	.16	.15	.32
Learning (complex) (4)	.21	.29	.03	.27
Learning (simple) (2)	.03	.09	-.01	-.03
Language (4)	.06	.09	.07	.53
Crichton (1)	.07	.11	.25	-.41
STM Audial (2)	.03	.05	.16	-.04
STM Visual (2)	.26	.26	.34	.02
LTM Content (5)	-.11	-.15	-.10	.07
LTM Structure (3)	.10	-.01	.25	-.10
R	.66	.65	.71	.77

It will be seen that the two measures of visual sequencing make a substantial contribution to the prediction for the whole sample and for each of the three sub-samples. Although the contribution is least for SE group 3, it is always substantially higher than that of audial S.T.M. One notes in passing the overwhelming importance of language for this group, with anomalous results from the Crichton test.

Beta weights for the remaining predictors are somewhat varying - due to the high intercorrelations between measures of operativity, language and learning.

The programme chosen to compute the data allows one to establish which of the predictors make a significant contribution, using an F test to weigh the covariance of the full predictor set with the criterion against that of each reduced set, after omitting one or more predictors (Veldman, 1967). The relevant F values are shown in Table 4, with significant values asterisked, together with the reduced values of R.

TABLE 4

Comparative Significance of Predictors

Omitted predictor set	All		SE-1		SE-2		SE-3	
	R	F	R	F	R	F	R	F
Unreduced set	.66	-	.65	-	71	-	77	-
All Piaget	.64	3.0*	.64	0.1	71	0.3	73	3.8*
All Learning	.64	2.9*	.61	2.4**	71	0.0	75	1.6
All Language	.65	1.1	.64	0.8	69	1.5	71	5.3**
All Memory	.61	4.1**	.59	1.8	59	3.6**	76	0.3

By comparing the statistics in Table 4 with those in Table 2, it should be clear that the contributions of the three first predictor sets are based on what is for the most part common variance. Comparison with Table 3 shows that the significance in the last row is mainly due to the two visual STM tests, these being moderately correlated with one another, as shown in Table 1.

Comparison of forward and concurrent prediction

Certain of the measures taken in 1972 were repeated in 1973, but in six schools only, these being different for the language and STM measures. Table 5 shows the means of the original testing together with those obtained one year later. Also shown are correlations with the reading scores (1973) and long-term reliability. All of these figures relate to the relevant sub samples only.

TABLE 5

Comparison of forward with concurrent predictions of reading

	Mean		Correlation with reading (1973)		long term reliability	N
	1972	1973	1972	1973		
Watts	31.9	54.9	.16	.42	.51	47
Crichton	23.2	28.8	.41	.41	.70	47
EPVT	17.0	23.3	.23	.22	.79	47
Digits	16.1	16.6	.31	.28	.74	58
Shapes	1.9	3.7	.45	.14	.31	58
Animals	2.9	3.8	.60	.51	.54	58

In five cases, the long term reliabilities are quite high. The exception is sequencing of shapes, where the weaker children obtained very poor results in 1972 (so enhancing the correlation with reading progress, probably by virtue of non specific variance, i.e. general intelligence).

While the three language measures correlate as well with reading in 1973 as they do in 1972 or better (Watts), prediction of reading from STM is better using the earlier set of measures.

DISCUSSION

The principal finding is the independent contribution of visual sequencing to the prediction of reading. Children who show themselves better at reproducing a sequence of pictures or diagrams are better at learning to read. The fact that the contribution is independent means that this is not a matter of general ability or of language.

It was once almost universally held that learning to read in English entails, in the first instance, learning to match a spatial sequence of visual characters with a temporal sequence of phonemes (Chall, 1967). It is precisely this that is denied by Goodman (Goodman, 1972; Cambourne, 1977; and cf. Smith, 1978). The present data suggest that at least for some children the orthodox view is correct and the guessing-game theory is at best exaggerated.

We concede at once that the present evidence is correlational and not experimental. More importantly, the finding is post hoc, which means the result should be regarded as provisional. But it should also be pointed out that independent prediction in a regression equation is rare, especially when all predictors are of the same sort (in this case measures of cognitive performance).

Finally, it should be said that the present evidence is confined to the beginning of reading. On general grounds it is useful to distinguish three stages in the acquisition of reading. In the first, the child learns to interpret a graphemic code. He is not involved in any effortful interpretation of meaning, because what he reads is well within his language competence. The second stage will extend the skill to cover a range of semantic and syntactic options which exceeds his spoken language. A third stage involves the ongoing evaluation of content and a consequent variation in reading style to suit its purpose.

It is possible that the letter read out from the visual eikon is relevant only at stage 1. In our own view, however, this phase in reading is crucial throughout, although this does not mean letters continue to be labelled or that all the letter information is used. The mature reader can operate on partial information, and regularly does so (Rawlinson, 1976).

However, the fact that the reader builds up a series of expectations which partially determines the identification of printed words and phrases, does not mean that reading is an almost free-wheeling centrally driven process. Those that argue that is have yet to give a coherent account of how the visual cues are sampled, when they are sampled. They will also need to account for the critical part played by the beginnings and endings of words in word recognition (Bruner and O'Dowd, 1958; and cf. Rawlinson).

REFERENCES

Bruner, J. and O'Dowd, D. (1958). A note on the informativeness of parts of words. *Language and Speech*, 1, 98-101.

Cambourne, B. (1977). Getting to Goodman: an analysis of the Goodman Model of Reading with some suggestions for evaluation. *Reading Research Quarterly*, 12, 605-636.

Chall, J.S. (1967). *Learning to Read: The Great Debate.* McGraw Hill, New York.

Goodman, K.S. (1967). Reading: a psycholinguistic guessing game. *Journal of the Reading Specialist*, 6, 126-135.

Goodman, K.S. (1972). Reading process - theory and practice. In: *Language and Learning to Read* (R.E. Hodges and E.H. Rudorf eds.). Houghton Mifflin, Boston.

Gough, P.B. (1972). One second of reading. In: *Language by Ear and Eye* (Kavanagh, J.F. and Mattingly, I.G. eds.). M.I.T. Press, Cambridge, Mass.

Laberge, D. and Samuels, S.J. (1974). Toward a theory of automatic information processing in reading. *Cognitive Psychology*, 6, 293-323.

Lunzer, E.A.,Wilkinson, J.E. and Dolan, T. (1976). The distinctiveness of operativity as a measure of cognitive functioning in five year old children. *British Journal of Educational Psychology*, 46, 280, 294.

McLaughlin, G.H. (1963). Psycho-logic: a possible alternative to Piaget's formulation. *British Journal of Educational Psychology*, 33, 61-67.

Pascual-Leone, J. (1970). A mathematical model for the transition rule in Piaget's developmental stages. *Acta Psychologica*, 32, 301-345.

Rawlinson, G. (1976). *The significance of letter position in word reorganisation.* Ph.D. thesis, University of Nottingham.

Smith, F. (1978). *Reading.* Cambridge University Press, London.

Veldman, D.J. (1967). *Fortran Programming for the Behavioural Sciences.* Holt, Rinehart and Winston, N.Y.

White, S.H. (1965). Evidence for a hierarchical arrangement of learning processes. In: *Advances in Child Behaviour and Development*, *Vol. 2.* (Lipsitt, L.P. and Spiker, C.C. eds.). Academic Press, New York.

LATERALITY, LEXICON AND DISCRIMINATION.

P. O'B. Holt and G. Underwood.
Department of Psychology, University of Nottingham, Nottingham, England.

ABSTRACT.

Is visual discrimination a unified process? Two experiments comparing nonverbal and verbal discrimination suggest bilateral representation in visual discrimination overall, and a RH superiority for nonverbal processing. It is concluded that the dichotomy visual/verbal is redundant and that visual discrimination comprises distinct subsystems, the control of which may provide a therapeutic tool.

INTRODUCTION.

There is evidence to indicate that left hemisphere (LH) damaged right handed global aphasics have remaining language functions and these can be approached visually. An artificial language training programme has been tried, using visual concrete symbols emphasising discrimination and some success has been reported (Glass, Gazzaniga and Premack 1973). It can be argued that the right, intact, hemisphere (RH) played a leading role here, and there is evidence that the RH is active in the recognition of written language on a visual basis (Gazzaniga 1974). A review of reading suggests that visual or graphemic representations can be accessed without a phonological stage (Bradshaw 1975) and a recent discussion of aphasia suggests that there are two direct access routes, one graphemic and the other phonemic (Marcel and Patterson in press) and recent expts. have provided further evidence for this (Spoehr 1978). The artificial language training would therefore seem to have involved a visual code for access and the question arises as to whether this code is comparable to other visual codes or whether there are many differing aspects of visual coding. First it is necessary to establish a description of nonverbal discrimination for comparison. The problems of attaining laterality differences using nonverbal stimulihave been reviewed (White 1972). However, expts. using same-different discrimination of faces (nonverbal task) have shown a RH superiority, which is depen -dent upon manual responses, and also a LH superiority for digit naming (verbal task), not dependent upon response mode (Geffen, Bradshaw and Wallace 1971). However, using digits in a discrimination task showed no hemisphere difference, but splitting the task between hemispheres was superior to presentations to one hemisphere (Davis and Schmit 1971) and when the task was to discriminate between letters on a verbal or visual basis, splitting the task was superior in both cases. It was concluded that the RH can only analyse on a visual basis, but the LH can analyse on both visual and verbal basis (Davis and Schmit 1973). Other expts. have shown similar results using letter matching on physical or name basis: a RH superiority was observed in the former and a LH superiority in the latter (Geffen, Bradshaw and Nettleton 1972). Expts. on coding in memory have given comparable results, eg. LH superiority was observed in verbal coding and a RH superiority in visual coding (Seamon and Gazzaniga 1973, Seamon 1974).

In expt. 1 colours are used as stimuli to establish a nonverbal baseline. This has the advantage for further research that colours can be coded verbally and nonverbally. The RH has been implicated in colour processing (Davidoff 1976, Pennal 1977) but not all expts. have shown a clear effect (Dimond and Beaumont 1972). It is hypothesised that a RH superiority, dependent upon response mode will be observed, also that performance will be superior when the task is split, implying bilateral representation in visual discrimination.

METHOD

Materials

Stimuli were red and blue coloured squares (3 x 2 cm) pasted on white cards.

Procedure

On each card two coloured squares were situated 4-7 cm from centre, both being on the left or right or one on the left and one on the right. The squares subtended a visual angle of 3°3'- 6°5' from centre. Colour categories were combined exhaustively. The two squares were placed vertically to each other when in one visual field, the distance between them being 0.5 cm, but when divided between fields they were placed horizontally to each other. The squares were presented in the LVF, the RVF and BVFs. A total of 12 cards, 4 in each hemifield condition, two requiring the response SAME and two the response DIFFERENT, were projected using a Campden Instruments Two-field Tachistoscope Model 610. Ss were presented with the stimuli consecutively using 3 exposure durations (ED) (100 ms, 50 ms, and 15 ms), ie. with the 12 stimuli within each ED, the order of which was independently randomised for each S. The stimuli were also independently randomised for each S. Illumination was kept constant throughout. Ss were instructed as to the nature of the task and emphasis was placed on fixation, speed and accuracy. Ss were required to judge whether the two squares presented were SAME or DIFFERENT in colour. Half the Ss responded vocally into a microphone connected to an Electronics Developments Voice Key which stopped a millisec timer (Campden Instruments Counter Timer Model 565); half the Ss responded bimanually by pushing the two nearer buttons to register one judgement and the two farther buttons on a keyboard to register the other. This stopped the millisec timer. The timer started when the stimuli were presented. Prior to each presentation Ss were told to fixate on a spot presented in field 1, which was illuminated before and after each trial. When errors were made, the stimulus was reintroduced later. Interstimulus interval was approx. 10 secs and the interval between ED conditions was approx. 3 mins.

Subjects

Twenty subjects were used. All had normal or corrected to normal vision and were right handed as determined by Annett's (1970) Handedness Questionaire. All were members of staff or students at Nottingham University and were naive as to the purpose and procedure of the expt.

RESULTS

The data were subjected to an analysis of variance by Response Mode, Exposure Duration, Hemifields and Type of Response. The last 3 factors having repeated measures. The Main Effect, Exposure Duration, was significant (F: 6.16 df:

2,36 $P < 0.005$), there being an increase in RT with decreasing ED (100 ms: 627.63 ms 50 ms:687.40 ms and 15 ms:695.85ms). The means were compared using Scheffe's test and this revealed a significant difference between 100 ms and 50 ms ED (t: 3.99 df: 2,958 $P < 0.01$) and between 100 ms and 15 ms ED (t: 4.55 df: 2,958 $P < 0.01$) but the difference between 50 ms and 15 ms ED was not significant (t: 0.56 df:2,958). Hemifields were also significant (F: 4.29 df: 2,36 $P < 0.05$) (LVF: 659.18 ms, RVF: 695.99 ms and BVFs: 655.70 ms). A comparison using Scheffe's test revealed a significant difference between RVF and BVFs (t: 2.64 df: 2,717 $P < 0.05$). The difference between LVF and BVFs was not significant (t: 0.23 df: 2,717) and the same applies to the difference between LVF and RVF (t:2.41 df 2,717), here the t value needs 0.041 to reach significance, this is worth bearing in mind considering the conservativeness of the Scheffe test. The interaction Response Mode X Hemifields was significant (F:5.64 df:2,36 $P < 0.01$), see Table 1. Two kinds of comparisons were made using the Scheffe test. 1. Within Response Mode but between Hemifields and 2. Within Hemifields but between Response Modes. 1. This revealed a significant difference between RVF(man) and LVF(man) (t:3.56 df:5,714 $P < 0.05$), and a significant difference between RVF(man) and BVFs(man) (t:4.08 df:5,714 $P < 0.01$) Type 2. comparisons revealed a significant difference between RVF(man) and RVF(voc) (t:3.42 df:5,714 $P < 0.05$). No other main effects or interactions reached significance.

Table 1

Means for the interaction, Response Mode x Hemifields

	RVF	LVF	BVFs
Vocal	657.59 ms	660.73 ms	664.99 ms
Manual	734.39 ms	657.63 ms	646.40 ms

DISCUSSION

The results verify those of Geffen *et al*.(1971), Davidoff (1976) and Pennal (1977) by showing a RH superiority, and the results of Davis and Schmit (1971, 1973) receive some substantiation, BVFs being superior to the LH in the Main Effect. The fact that no difference was observed between RH and BVFs is most likely due to the RH superiority for colour discrimination. The results imply that the absence of an effect using vocal responses is due to LH vocal output making up for any disadvantages in processing.

In expt. 2, two words are substituted for the two colours. If the words are verbally coded then some word combinations, where meaning conflicts with response, might cause a delay in RT, implying lexical access. The words used here are graphically dissimilar and this probably invites visual coding. If the words are discriminated on a verbal basis then a LH superiority might be observed, especially as it can be argued that the words are abstract (see eg. Day 1977). If a RH superiority is observed it would imply that nonverbal processing has taken place as described for faces and colours. A BVF superiority would imply bilateral representation. Only one ED was used as EDs did not interact in expt. 1.

METHOD

Materials

Stimuli were two words (SAME and DIFFERENT) made up of capital black letters 5 mm high, on white cards.

Procedure

Essentially the procedure was identical to expt. 1, the words being substituted for the coloured squares. The ED was 100 ms. Two millisec timers were used, an OMB Electronics Counter Timer Model 745 for the vocal responses and a Campden Instruments Counter Timer Model 565 for the manual responses.

Subjects

Ten Ss were used. All had normal or corrected to normal vision and were right handed as determined by Annett's (1970) Handedness Questionnaire. All were members of staff or students at Nottingham University and were naive as to the purpose and procedure of the experiment.

RESULTS

The data were subjected to an analysis of variance by Response Mode, Hemifields and Context. The last two factors having repeated measures. Hemifield emerged as a significant Main Effect (F: 5.33 df: 2,16 $P < 0.01$) (LVF = 1223.90ms, RVF = 1093.53 ms and BVFs = 1002.10 ms). A comparison of the means using the Scheffe test revealed a significant difference between LVF and BVFs (t: 3.25 df: 2,117 $P < 0.01$), but no difference was observed between RVF and LVF, or between RVF and BVFs (t: 1.91 and t: 1.34 df: 2,117 respectively). No other Main Effects and no interaction reached significance.

DISCUSSION

Bilateral processing is implied, at least in comparison with the RH. The noninvolvement of the LH might be explained on the basis of some degree of language involvement: this argument is comparable to the one made in expt. 1 concerning the absence of any difference between RH and BVFs, which was confirmed by the RH involvement in colour discrimination. Expt. 2 fails to imply lexical access, but a simultaneous matching task gives evidence for lexical access at least in SAME responses, DIFFERENT responses being less clear (Chambers and Forster 1975). The failure of expt. 2 to show this could be due to the very limited word sample. The above expt. used variations within a larger word sample to produce the effect. A RH superiority in word matching has been demonstrated (Gibson, Dimond and Gazzaniga 1972), but this expt. was procedurally different.

GENERAL DISCUSSION

Both expts. imply bilateral representation in simultaneous visual discrimination. Expt. 2 would imply that the discrimination of words is not identical to the discrimination of nonverbal items like colours, and there is no implication of the lexical-semantic system. Nonverbal discrimination is response dependent, but word discrimination is not, and this is similar to results obtained with digit naming (a verbal task) (Geffen *et al.* 1971). In both expts. comparison of BVFs with individual hemifields does indirectly imply laterality direction, RH for nonverbal, which is observed independently, and LH for verbal, although this is indirectly arguable. It is reasonable to assume that the visual aspects of language processing are at least to some extent bilaterally represented, especially in view of recent expts. implying that words of high imagery are bilaterally represented, but that the LH might be more proficient in handling low imageability or abstract words (see eg. Day 1977). In conclusion, it can be stated that the dichotomy visual/verbal seems redundant as the expts. reported here seem to imply a bilateral visual discrimination system, characterised by subsystems which are dependent on the nature of the stimuli, eg. visual-nonverbal codes as opposed to visual-verbal codes. These could be viewed as separate forms of discrimination. The bilateral implications of visual-verbal discrimination seem relevant to ideas concerning the rehabilitation of LH damaged aphasics and for patients with phonemic disabilities. If the visual-verbal aspects of graphemic access can be described and controlled, an important therapeutic tool will become available.

REFERENCES

Annett, A. (1970). A Classification of Hand Preference by Association Analysis. *British Journal of Psychology.* 61, pp303-321.

Bradshaw, S.L. (1975). Three Interrelated Problems in Reading: A Review. *Memory and Cognition.* Vol 3(2), pp123-134

Chambers, S.M. and Forster, K.I. (1975). Evidence for Lexical Access in a Simultaneous Matching Task. *Memory and Cognition.* Vol 3(5), pp549-559.

Davidoff, J. (1976). Hemispheric Sensitivity Differences in the Perception of Colour. *Quarterly Journal of Experimental Psychology.* 28, pp387-394.

Davis, R. and Schmit, V. (1971). Timing and Transfer of information between Hemispheres in Man. *Acta Psychologica.* 35, pp335-346.

Davis, R. and Schmit, V. (1973). Visual and Verbal Coding in the Interhemispheric Transfer of Information. *Acta Psychologica.* 37, pp229-240.

Dimond, S. and Beaumont, G. (1972). Hemisphere Function and Colour Naming. *Journal of Experimental Psychology.* Vol 96, No 1, pp87-91.

Day, J. (1977). Right-Hemisphere Language Processing in Normal Right-Handers. *Journal of Experimental Psychology: Human Perception and Performance.* Vol 3, No 3, pp518-528.

Gazzaniga, M.S. (1974). Cerebral Dominance Viewed as a Decision System. In: *Hemisphere Function in the Human Brain.* (S.Dimond and G.Beaumont, eds), pp367-382. Elek Science, London.

Geffen, G., Bradshaw, J.L. and Wallace, G. (1971). Interhemispheric Effects on Reaction Times to Verbal and Nonverbal Stimuli. *Journal of Experimental Psychology.* Vol 87, No 3, pp415-422.

Geffen, G., Bradshaw, J.L. and Nettleton, N.C. (1972). Hemispheric Asymmetry: Verbal and Spatial Encoding of Visual Stimuli. *Journal of Experimental Psychology.* Vol 95, No 1, pp25-31.

Gibson, A.R., Dimond, S.J. and Gazzaniga, M.S. (1972). Left Field Superiority for Word Matching. *Neuropsychologia.* Vol 10, pp463-466.

Glass, A., Gazzaniga, M.S. and Premack, D. (1973). Artificial Language Training in Global Aphasics. *Neuropsychologia.* Vol 11, pp95-103.

Marcel, T. and Patterson, K. (in press). Word Recognition

and Production: Reciprocity in Clinical and Normal Studies. In: *Attention and Performance VII*. (J.Requin, ed) pp?, Laurence Erlbaum Associates Inc., Hillsdale.

Pennal, B. (1977). Human Cerebral Asymmetry in Colour Discrimination. *Neuropsychologia*. Vol 15, pp563-568.

Seamon, J.G. (1974). Coding and Retrieval Processes and the Hemispheres of the Brain. In: *Hemisphere Function in the Human Brain*. (S. Dimond and G. Beaumont, eds) pp184-203, Elek Science. London.

Seamon, J.G. and Gazzaniga, M.S. (1973). Coding Strategies and Cerebral Laterality Effects. *Cognitive Psychology*. 5, pp249-256.

Spoehr, K.T. (1978). Phonological Encoding in Visual Word Recognition. *Journal of Verbal Learning and Verbal Behaviour*. 17, pp127-141.

White, M.J. (1972). Hemispheric Asymmetries in Tachistoscopic Information Processing. *British Journal of Psychology*. 63, 4, pp497-508.

SIMPLE READING TASKS ARE AFFECTED BY UNATTENDED CONTEXT

G. Underwood, R.S. Parry and L.A. Bull
Department of Psychology, University of Nottingham
Nottingham, England

ABSTRACT

Two experiments are reported in which adult skilled readers were asked to process single words which were briefly presented. In the first experiment a context-giving sentence, when semantically related to the word, aided the response to the word, which was to read it out aloud. When a further word was printed in the visual field and exposed at the same time then it too aided the reading response if it was associated to the word. When both the prior context and the simultaneous context were related to the word then recognition was further facilitated. The second experiment confirmed the effect of simultaneous context in a lexical decision task, and suggested that the effect was located at the stages of lexical access and processing rather than during response organisation.

INTRODUCTION

The influence of semantic and syntactic context upon reading performance has been demonstrated in a number of single-fixation and free-reading situations. The eye-voice span, for example, increases as each part of the text provides more information about succeeding parts (Morton, 1964). Context increases the statistical redundancy of the text and so facilitates the speed of reading. In a study using good and poor readers Willows (1974) found that unattended words which provided irrelevant information about a passage, but which were related to the passage, caused more disruption with the comprehension by the good readers. The poor readers behaved as if they had not seen the unattended words, possibly as a result of adopting a word-by-word reading strategy. Unfortunately with these free-reading tasks we cannot be certain as to the strategy used by the subject to get around the problems set by the experimenter, and in the case of the Willows experiment it is quite possible that the good readers actually looked at the so-called unattended words. The validation of her experiment must come from tests using a single fixation.

Experiments using tachistoscopic presentations have also indicated the influence of previous context upon the reading of single words. The study by Tulving and Gold (1963) varied the amount of context (0-8 words) spoken immediately prior to the exposure of a single word. The amount of context influenced the duration of exposure necessary for recognition of the word. An auditory analogue of this effect of context was demonstrated by Underwood (1977) who had listeners repeat sentences as they heard them (this is known as shadowing). The latency between presentation of the final word in the sentence, and the shadowing response to that word was then recorded as a function of the amount of contextual information given prior to the word, and as a function of the source of the context. By increasing the amount of attended context it was possible to reduce the shadowing latency to the final word. With unattended context a slightly different story emerges, in that a small amount of context was helpful, but increasing the amount of context further did nothing more to reduce the shadowing latency. A full sentence of unattended context was no more helpful than a few words.

The experiments to be described here were designed to provide information about the effects of unattended context in simple reading tasks. To avoid the problems of fixation in free-reading the present experiments used tachistoscopic exposures in which subjects were asked to recognise single words. In the first experiment skilled readers were presented with either an incomplete sentence prior to exposure or a single word (full or reduced context). The sentence or word was either semantically related or unrelated to a word which was presented to be read out (the TBR word, as we shall describe it). An unattended word was presented as the same time as the TBR word and was sometimes related to the prior context (and therefore sometimes related to the TBR word), and was sometimes unrelated. The effects of simultaneous context under these conditions speak to the questions of the structural nature of the facilitating effect of context during word recognition, and the effects of combinations of context from different sources.

EXPERIMENT 1

Method

Design and materials. On each trial of the experiment the subjects were required to read out aloud a single word (the TBR word). Five trials were used in each of sixteen conditions in a factorial design with four factors. These four factors were: amount of prior context (a word/a sentence); association between prior context and the TBR word (semantically related/unrelated); association between prior context and the simultaneous context word (related/unrelated); easy/difficult reading conditions.

The simultaneous context word was printed in lower case, below and to the right of the TBR word. The two words on the tachistoscope card each subtended an angle of between $2\frac{1}{2}^{\circ}$ and $5\frac{1}{2}^{\circ}$. The centres of the words were separated by 8° of visual angle. Both words were printed in black ink upon white card. Both words were selected from the Thorndike and Lorge (1944) list to have a frequency of between 50 and 100 times per million. The TBR words were all three syllables in length.

Half the trials were presented under "difficult" reading conditions in that the TBR word was printed in alternating lower and upper case. This condition was added to allow the simultaneous context more time to become activated.

The cards were viewed through a Campden Instruments two-field tachistoscope (model 610), and a vocal response triggered an Electronic Developments voice key. Operation of the tachistoscope started a Campden Instruments timer (model 565) which was stopped when the voice key was switched.

Subjects. Ten students with normal or corrected vision took part in the experiment. They were between 18-22 years.

Procedure. All subjects were presented with all stimuli, with a different random ordering of trial for each subject. The 80 test trials were preceded by 16 practice trials. A fixation dot appeared in the centre of the pre-exposure field of the tachistoscope, and subjects were asked to read out the word presented to fixation. The test field was exposed for 200 msec. The pre- and post-exposure fields were both illuminated and blank. Subjects were instructed to ignore any other words in the test field. The test field was exposed immediately after the incomplete sentence had been spoken, or after the single word of prior context.

Results

The reading latencies from the sixteen conditions are presented in Table 1, and were submitted to an analysis of variance.

TBR word:	Prior Context (Sentence) context related	Prior Context (Sentence) context unrelated	Prior Context (Word) context related	Prior Context (Word) context unrelated
Simultaneous Context Related to Prior Context				
Easy Reading	535(105)	603(136)	529(108)	543(96)
Diff. Reading	488(97)	582(139)	532(110)	553(102)
Simultaneous Context Unrelated to Prior Context				
Easy Reading	520(94)	557(121)	526(111)	579(121)
Diff. Reading	552(109)	569(125)	555(101)	552(121)

Table 1. Response latencies from Experiment 1. Standard deviations are given in brackets.

The analysis of variance indicated one main effect and a number of interactions. Providing appropriate context prior to the presentation of a word which is to be recognised aids that recognition (530 msec: 567 msec) in comparison with trials where the prior "context" is unrelated to the TBR word (F = 25.9, df = 1,9, p <.001). Although this effect exists for those trials in which a single word provided the prior context (536 msec: 557 msec) it was emphasized (523 msec: 587 msec) when a sentence was spoken before recognition (F = 10.6, df= 1,9,p <.01). An interesting interaction emerged between the aid provided by the two forms of context (F= 6.4, df= 1,9, p <.04). When the simultaneous context was unrelated to the prior context, the prior context gave a certain amount of facilitation (539 msec: 565 msec) but when these two forms of context were associated then the facilitation effect was doubled (521 msec: 570 msec). This effect held only for those cases where the prior context was a sentence: if a single word provided the context then no advantage was given by the simultaneous context (F= 11.1, df= 1,9, p<.01). A curious three-way interaction involved the easy/difficult reading conditions, the type of prior context, and the semantic relationship between the prior context and the simultaneous context ($F= 8.2$, $df= 1,9$, $p<.02$). In most cases the change from easy to difficult reading conditions resulted in a slower reading response, but in the case of a sentence providing the prior context, with related simultaneous context, the change of reading difficulty *speeded up* the response. A further three-way interaction also involved the easy/difficult reading treatment, the relationship between the TBR word and the prior context, and the relationship between the simultaneous context and the prior context ($F= 8.9$, $df= 1,9$, $p<.02$). When the TBR word was unrelated to the prior context, then changing the TBR word from lower case to alternating case made little difference to the speed of response, but when the prior context was associated with the TBR word two effects were present. An unrelated word acting as simultaneous context led to a slower response when the TBR word had alternating case, but if the simultaneous context was associated with the prior context (and also to the TBR word) then changing the case *facilitated* the response again.

Discussion

The main conclusions from this experiment were as follows. The results of Tulving and Gold (1963) and Underwood (1977) were confirmed for the case of appropriate prior context easing the recognition of words. This effect was increased by the presence of appropriate simultaneous context. Influencing the difficulty of reading produced no clear-cut results. The implications of the main results will be pursued after Experiment 2 has been described.

EXPERIMENT 2

To determine further the effects of simultaneous context a task was sought which provided context in a single fixation reading task and also in which the context itself could serve as an erroneous response. Whereas there is some evidence of the processing of simultaneous context from Experiment 1, the effects upon lexical access and response organisation are unclear. In this experiment a lexical decision task was used.

Method

Design and materials. Subjects were required to decide whether each presentation consisted of a word, or not, and to respond by pressing either a YES key or a NO key. A factorial design was used, with repeated measures on four factors: the letter string was a word/nonword; the letter string was presented to the right of fixation or to the left; the simultaneous context was a word or a nonword; and the simultaneous context was in the same visual field as the TBR word or in the opposite field. Whenever the two letter strings were both words then they were semantically related. A total of 160 trials was used, with ten trials in each of the conditions.

All words and nonwords were four letters in length, and the distance from the central fixation point to the centre of each letter string subtended an angle of 3°.

The apparatus was the same as that used for Experiment 1, except that a manual response keyboard was used.

Subjects. Eight students were used for this experiment. All had normal or corrected vision, and all claimed to be right-handed. They were aged between 18 and 22 years.

Procedure. Each pair of letter strings, printed on white card, with the TBR word (or nonword) printed in a red box, was exposed for 150 msec. The 160 trials were preceded by 16 practice trials. The pre-text field had a fixation point in the centre of the field and subjects were instructed to focus upon this point when given a warning shortly before exposure. The pre- and post-exposure fields were blank and illuminated. Subjects were instructed to ignore the distractor, and to decide as quickly as possible whether or not the letter string in the red box was a word, and to indicate their decision by pressing one of the two manual response keys.

Results

The result times from the sixteen conditions were submitted to an analysis of variance, and their means are in Table 2.

	TBR Word		TBR Nonword	
Simultaneous Context:	Word	Nonword	Word	Nonword
TBR item to Left Hemisphere (LH)				
Context to LH	675(65)	741(56)	757(56)	733(69)
Context to RH	621(49)	702(74)	683(54)	719(45)
TBR item to Right Hemisphere (RH)				
Context to LH	688(55)	771(48)	764(69)	724(68)
Context to RH	695(54)	756(82)	737(52)	720(52)

Table 2. Response latencies from the lexical decision task in Experiment 2. Standard deviations in brackets.

Errors were recorded on less than 6% of the trials, and were evenly distributed over conditions.

Faster responses were produced ($F = 10.9$, $df = 1,6$, $p < .02$) when the TBR item was a word (707 msec) than when it was a nonword (729 msec). When the simultaneous context was a word (702 msec) rather than a nonword (734 msec) a faster response was also produced ($F = 7.2$, $df = 1,6$, $p < .04$), although a two-way interaction indicated that the effect of context held only when the TBR item was itself a word, and therefore related to the context ($F = 34.3$, $df = 1,6$, $p < .002$). TBR items presented to the left rather than to the right hemisphere were processed marginally faster, but the effect shows only in the form of a two-way interaction with the factor of whether the TBR item is a word or not ($F = 7.0$, $df = 1,6$, $p < .04$). The left hemisphere advantage for words is more apparent than any advantage for non-words. Simultaneous context in the same hemifield as the TBR word produced slower responses (732 msec: 705 msec) than that in the same hemifield ($F = 6.6$, $df = 1,6$, $p < .05$), although no interactions involved this factor.

Discussion

As with the previous experiment, simultaneous context aided the response when a semantic relationship existed between two words. When the TBR item was a nonword then the context had no effect, facilitating or interfering. It was easier for subjects to decide that letter strings were words when they were presented to the left hemisphere, although there was little difference between the hemispheres when the letter string was a nonword. Letter strings in the same visual field interfere most with the processing of the TBR item, regardless of whether they are words, of whether the TBR items are words, and whether the TBR item is presented to the left or to the right hemisphere.

One finding specific to this experiment concerns the relationship between a proposed explanation of the facilitation effects and the separation here of the TBR item and the context which supplies the facilitation. By the absence of a three-way interaction involving the TBR item (word/nonword), context (word/nonword), and field of the two letter strings (same/opposite), it appears that spreading activation may operate *between* the two cerebral hemispheres, and therefore across the corpus collosum.

GENERAL DISCUSSION

Both experiments here demonstrate that simultaneous context has a facilitating effect upon reading during a single fixation. When awareness of the simultaneous material might have produced an inappropriate response in the lexical decision task of Experiment 2 it had no qualitative or quantitative effect upon the response, and so the effect of this context might be taken to be one of lexical access and processing prior to awareness. The first experiment suggests that the effect of simultaneous context is enhanced when preceded by associated words.

The absence of a convincing interference effect in Experiment 1, in those trials where the word was unrelated to both sources of context which were related to each other, suggests that any facilitation or interference effects can only be obtained when a semantic association exists between the word being attended and another source. In turn this suggests that these effects stem from the word which is processed intentionally, possibly through the phenomenon of spreading excitation.

These experiments indicate the importance of using semantically contextual information from two sources whilst reading. Previously presented words aid the reading task, and so do words available during the fixation but which are not attended. When these two sources of context are available together the combined effect is greater than the contribution from each.

REFERENCES

Meyer, D.E. and Schvaneveldt, R.W. (1971). Facilitation in recognizing paird of words: Evidence of a dependence between retrieval operations. *Journal of Experimental Psychology*, 90, 227-234.

Morton, J. (1964). The effects of context upon speed of reading, eye movements, and the eye-voice span. *Quarterly Journal of Experimental Psychology*, 16, 340-354.

Thorndike, E.L. and Lorge, I. (1944). *The Teacher's Word Book of 30,000 Words*. New York: Columbia Univ. Press.

Tulving, E. and Gold, C. (1963). Stimulus information and contextual information as determinants of tachistoscopic recognition of words. *Journal of Experimental Psychology*, 66, 319-327.

Underwood, G. (1977). Contextual facilitation from attended and unattended messages. *Journal of Verbal Learning and Verbal Behavior*, 16, 99-106.

Willows, D.M. (1974). Reading between the lines: Selective attention in good and poor readers. *Child Development*, 45, 408-415.

THE PRACTICAL USE OF SHORT-TERM MEMORY IN SPEAKING

Andrew W. Ellis
Department of Psychology,
University of Lancaster,
Bailrigg, Lancaster,
England

There is no shortage of evidence to demonstrate that when subjects are asked to repeat a list of disconnected words, letters, or syllables, they are apt to employ a phonemically-based code resulting in errors involving the substitution or exchange of phonemically-similar items. (Smith,1895; Conrad, 1964). There is also evidence that this form of coding may only be relied on in the absence of higher-order (syntactic, semantic, or associative) information as to the nature of the items or the order in which they occur (Crowder,1978; Morris, 1978). It has been a persistent problem for theories of memory to suggest an everyday use for such a phonemic (acoustic or articulatory) storage capacity (after a while the old example of retaining a telephone number in the interval between looking it up in a directory on one side of the room and dialling the number at the other side seems a trifle hackneyed - besides, who keeps their telephone and directory at opposite sides of the room?).

Morton (1964, 1970) has proposed a model in which phonemic short-term memory (STM) storage is mediated by a Response Buffer whose normal function is to allow the efficient programming of speech production. Within the model (see Figure 1), the Response Buffer holds preplanned stretches of impending speech in a serially-organized phonemic form and may be held responsible for phonemic speech errors, such as the sequential misordering of phonemes which occurs in Spoonerisms like keep a tape ⟶ "teep a kape", or feed the pooch ⟶ "food the peech" (Fromkin, 1973). Spoonerisms of this sort provide independent evidence of pre-articulatory phonemic storage in speech, and the maximum separation of phonemes in Spoonerisms (which may be taken as a measure of the limits of phonemic preplanning and, hence, of the required capacity of the Response Buffer) is of the order of 7 or 8 syllables (Nooteboom and Cohen, 1975), corresponding with the capacity

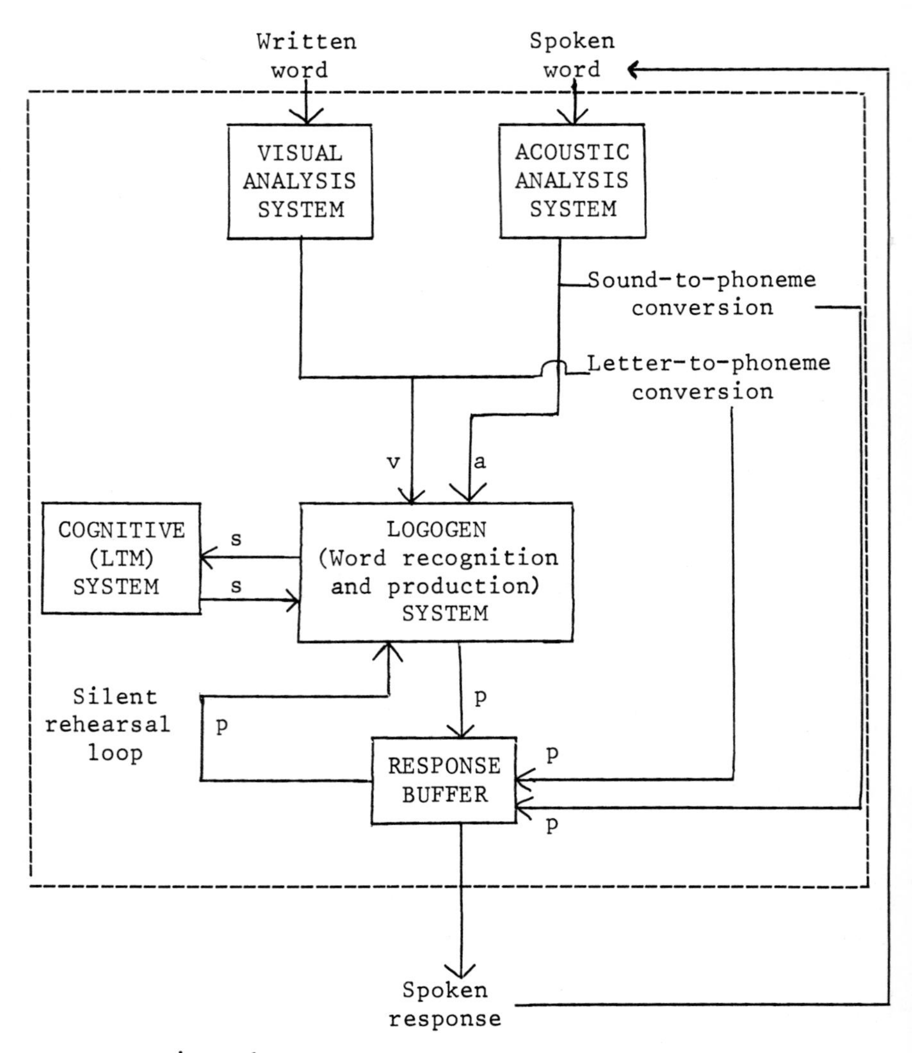

a = acoustic code
p = phonemic code
s = semantic code
v = visual code

Fig. 1 The Logogen Model (based on Morton, 1964; 1970; in press, and Ellis, in press)

required to explain STM performance.

Ellis (in press) has developed the implications of Morton's Logogen Model for accounts of STM and speech production in greater detail, and proposed a principle for testing the theory, in the form of an 'error equivalence hypothesis' which states: If one phonemic Response Buffer mediates both spontaneous speech production and phonemic short-term memory, and if that Response Buffer is prone to make certain particular types of error, then the same forms of phonemic error should be detectable in both speech and STM, and they should be influenced by the same variables in the same way. The error equivalence hypothesis has been tested in a series of experiments (Ellis, forthcoming) which investigate the effects of phonemic similarity and syllable position on transposition (order) errors and substitution (item) errors in immediate recall of lists of auditiorily- or visually-presented syllables. The results of these experiments may be summarized as follows:

1. The probability of transposition (exchange) between two consonant phonemes in a syllable sequence increases as the degree of similarity between them (defined in terms of the number of shared distinctive feature values) increases. This 'feature similarity effect' parallels the known effect of similarity on naturally-occurring Spoonerisms (Nooteboom, 1967; MacKay, 1970).
2. Pairs of consonants presented in syllables having identical vowels are more likely to transpose than pairs of consonants from syllables with dissimilar vowels. This 'contextual similarity effect' is also true of Spoonerisms in speech (Nooteboom, 1967; MacKay, 1970).
3. Occasionally, speech errors involve replacement of a phoneme by a different phoneme not present in the speech context (e.g. a trans<u>f</u>ormational rule → a trans<u>p</u>ormational rule). In such errors the replacing phoneme usually differs from the intended phoneme by only one or two distinctive features (Introduction to Fromkin, 1973). A comparable influence of feature similarity was demonstrated for substitution errors in STM. (One may note in passing that previous studies of so-called "accoustic confusion errors" in STM have either failed to separate transposition from substitution errors, or failed to distinguish between feature similarity and contextual similarity, or both).
4. Consonants transpose more frequently in STM than vowels which, in turn, transpose more frequently than whole syllable units. The same rank ordering applies to Spoonerisms (Nooteboom, 1967; MacKay, 1970).

5. In lists of mixed consonant-vowel (CV) and vowel-consonant (VC) syllables, both consonants and vowels tend to transpose with other consonants or vowels which originate in the same syllable positions (syllable-initial or syllable-final) rather than with consonants or vowels originating in different syllable positions. Thus, consonants in CV syllables transpose with other consonants from CV syllables in preference to consonants from VC syllables, and so forth. This mimics the effect of syllable position on Spoonerisms in natural speech (Nooteboom, 1967; Boomer and Laver, 1968; MacKay, 1970).

These results, together with other evidence for error equivalence which can be gleaned from surveying the literatures on speech and STM errors (Ellis, in press), provide strong corroborative support for the Response Buffer account of phonemic storage in STM. That account is also compatible with other lines of evidence which are embarrassing to theories which posit STM as a phonemic store intervening between sensory analysis systems and long-term/semantic memory (an example of such problematic evidence is Conrad's (1973) demonstration of phonemic confusions in articulate, but profoundly deaf, subjects).

Several authors (e.g. Meringer and Mayer, 1895; Marshall, 1977; Talo, 1977) have drawn attention to the similarity between the occasional tongue slips of normal speakers and the habitual errors of certain classes of aphasia, arguing the truth of Lenneberg's (1960) claim that some forms of aphasia are an abnormally augmented and sustained state which, in transient form, is not uncommon in persons without demonstrable pathology. Thus, there is scope for describing a variety of aphasic disorders which have as a common factor difficulties with the phonological aspects of speech production (e.g. Blumstein, 1973; Green and Howes, 1977) in terms of impairments of the Response Buffer and associated processes (Ellis, in press).

The model proposed must also, if it is to be accepted, be compatible with the clinical literature on memory disorders (N.B. there is, in any case, no clear distinction to be drawn between disorders of language and disorders of memory). The separation of the Response Buffer from the Cognitive (LTM) System permits explanation of normal memory spans in amnesic patients (Warrington and Weiskrantz, 1973). The fact that the Response Buffer is not the only (or indeed the normal) route of access of verbal input to the Cognitive System allows long-term memory to function at normal levels in patients who show drastically reduced short-term memory performance (Warrington and Shallice, 1969; Warrington, Logue and Pratt, 1971). From the model one would expect that patients showing impaired STM would also normally manifest speech production difficulties, and this does, indeed, seem to be the normal pattern (Green and Howes, 1977; Shallice and Warrington, 1975).

There exists, however, at least one patient in the literature who, whilst displaying severely-impaired STM, nevertheless appears to speak normally (the patient J.B., described by Warrington *et al.* 1971; Shallice and Butterworth, in press). Assuming J.B.'s speech is not abnormal in some way not revealed by Shallice and Butterworth's (in press) analysis, there is only one locus in the model where functional impairment could result in the observed constellation of symptoms, and that locus is the silent rehearsal loop. If information in the Response Buffer is subject to decay, as the results of Baddeley, Thomson and Buchanan (1975) suggest, then a patient with impairment of the silent rehearsal loop would, when attempting memory span or similar tasks, be unable to maintain the trace strength of early list items whilst registering later items in the Response Buffer. Such a patient's situation may be comparable with that of the subjects in experiments by Baddeley *et al.* (1975), Smith (1895) and Murray (1967) whose STM was impaired considerably through being required to articulate simple words or syllables constantly during presentation of the to-be-repeated items.

This tentative hypothesis as to the nature of J.B.'s disorder generates an interesting prediction as regards her ability to interpret orthographically-regular nonwords which are homophonous with real words (e.g. frute, bair). *Ex hypothesi*, J.B. should be able to read such nonwords aloud and, by hearing the word spoken, arrive at a semantic interpretation. However, since (within the model) the rehearsal loop also mediates silent 'phonic' recoding of words for which there is no visual representation in the Logogen System (Morton, in press), the patient should be unable to semantically decode (e.g. point to an appropriate picture of) homophonous nonwords. This prediction is a fairly strong one in the sense that it is readily testable whilst not being self-evident. If the prediction proves false, then the model is incorrect and stands in need of modification or abandonment. That prospect, however, should not alarm us unduly since all good theories are, ultimately, wrong.

ACKNOWLEDGEMENTS

This work was carried out while the author was a post-graduate student at the University of Edinburgh, Department of Psychology. I should like to thank Dr. Terry F. Myers and Dr. John D. Laver for advice and supervision, and the Medical Research Council for financial support.

REFERENCES

Baddeley, A.D., Thomson, N. and Buchanan, M. (1975). Word length and the structure of short-term memory. *Journal of Verbal Learning and Verbal Behaviour*. 14, 575-589.

Blumstein, S.E. (1973). *A Phonological Investigation of Aphasic Speech*. Mouton, The Hague.

Boomer, D.S. and Laver, J.D.M. (1968). Slips of the tongue. *British Journal of Disorders of Communication*. 3, 2-12. Reprinted in V.A. Fromkin (1973) *op.cit*.

Conrad, R. (1964). Acoustic confusions in immediate memory. *British Journal of Psychology*. 55, 75-84.

Conrad, R. (1973). Some correlates of speech coding in the short-term memory of the deaf. *Journal of Speech and Hearing Research*. 16, 375-384.

Crowder, R.G. (1978). Memory for phonologically uniform lists. *Journal of Verbal Learning and Verbal Behaviour*. 17, 73-89.

Ellis, A.W. (in press). Speech production and short-term memory. In: *Psycholinguistics Series* Vol 2. (J. Morton and J.C. Marshall eds). Elek Science, London/ MIT Press, Cambridge Mass.

Ellis, A.W. (forthcoming). Errors in speech and short-term memory : the effects of phonemic similarity and syllable position. Manuscript in preparation.

Fromkin, V.A. (1973). *Speech Errors as Linguistic Evidence*. Mouton, The Hague.

Green, E. and Howes, D.H. (1977). The nature of conduction aphasia: a study of anatomic and clinical features and of underlying mechanisms. In: *Studies in Neurolinguistics*. Vol 3 (H. Whitaker and H.A. Whitaker eds), pp. 123-156. Academic Press, New York.

Lenneberg, E.H. (1960). A review of Speech and Brain Mechanisms by W. Penfield and L.Roberts. *Language*. 36, 97-112. Reprinted in R.C. Oldfield and J.C. Marshall (1968). *op cit*.

MacKay, D.G. (1970). Spoonerisms: the structure of errors in the serial order of speech. *Neuropsychologia*. 8. 323-350. Reprinted in V.A. Fromkin (1973). *op.cit.*

Marshall, J.C. (1977). Disorders in the expression of language. In: *Psycholinguistics Series*. Vol 1 (J. Morton and J.C. Marshall eds), pp.125-160. Elek Science, London/ Cornell University Press, Ithaca.

Meringer, R. and Mayer, K. (1895). *Versprechen und Verlesen: eine psychologisch - linguistische Studie*. Goschen, Stuttgart. (Re-issue: John Benjamins, Amsterdam, 1978).

Morris, P.E. (1978). Encoding in short-term memory: a reply to Baddeley. *Bulletin of the British Psychological Society*. 31, 122.

Morton, J. (1964). A preliminary functional model for language behaviour. *International Audiology*. 3, 216-225. Reprinted in R.C. Oldfield and J.C. Marshall (1968) *op.cit.*

Morton, J. (1970). A functional model for memory. In: *Models of Human Memory*. (D.A. Norman ed.), pp. 203-254. Academic Press, New York.

Morton, J. (in press). Word recognition. In: *Psycholinguistics Series*. Vol 2. (J. Morton and J.C. Marshall eds). Elek Science, London/MIT Press, Cambridge, Mass.

Murray, D.J. (1967). The role of speech responses in short-term memory. *Canadian Journal of Psychology*. 21, 263-267.

Nooteboom, S.G. (1967). Some regularities in phonemic speech errors. *Instituut voor Perceptie Onderzoek (Eindhoven) Annual Progress Report*. 2, 65-70.

Nooteboom, S.G. and Cohen, A. (1975). Anticipation in speech production and its implications for perception. In: *Structure and Process in Speech Perception*. (A. Cohen and S.G. Nooteboom eds), pp.124-145. Springer-Verlag, Berlin.

Oldfield, R.C. and Marshall, J.C. (1968). *Language: Selected Readings*. Penguin Books, Harmondsworth England.

Shallice, T. and Butterworth, B. (in press). Short-term memory impairment and spontaneous speech. *Neuropsychologia*.

Shallice, T. and Warrington, E.K. (1975). Word recognition in a phonemic dyslexic patient. *Quarterly Journal of Experimental Psychology*. 27, 187-199.

Smith, W.G. (1895). The relation of attention to memory. *Mind*. 4. 47-73.

Talo, E.S. (1977). Slips of the tongue in normal and pathological speech. Paper presented at 12th International Congress of Linguists. Vienna, August-September, 1977.

Warrington, E.K., Logue, V. and Pratt, R.T.C. (1971). The anatomical localisation of selective impairment of auditory verbal short-term memory. *Neuropsychologia*. 9, 377-387.

Warrington, E.K. and Shallice, T. (1969). Selective impairment of auditory verbal short-term memory. *Brain*. 92, 885-896.

Warrington, E.K. and Weiskrantz, L. (1973). An analysis of short-term and long-term memory deficits in man. In: *The Physiological Basis of Memory*. (J.A. Deutsch ed), pp. 365-396. Academic Press, New York.

PREREQUISITES FOR A MORE APPLICABLE PSYCHOLOGY OF READING

Tony Marcel
Medical Research Council, Applied Psychology Unit, 15 Chaucer Road, Cambridge

ABSTRACT

The currently predominant approach to reading attempts to describe skilled reading and its deficits in terms of a structural, modular information-processing system. This is useful for diagnosis and remediation by substitution. However it is suggested that it is inadequate to deal with the fundamental problem:- teaching. Most difficulties in initial learning can be seen as problems primarily of understanding concepts expressed in particular ways, and secondarily of turning them into behaviour. Further, present models cannot capture the nature of the process of acquiring knowledge and how knowledge becomes action: they merely describe the operation of a system in a particular state, with or without specific components. In addition nothing follows about teaching from such approaches because they in no way include models of intervention, the relevant level being that of human communication, which is at the conscious level. A more pedagogical, cognitive and "phenomenological" approach is suggested.

In this paper I wish to express some qualms about the applicability of certain psychological approaches to reading and in doing so to grope towards some notions of what might be a helpful additional direction to take.

Necessarily, scientific enterprises are expressed in the forms of particular paradigms. Each paradigm has its own type of descriptive language and set of conceptual tools. These probably derive from the metascientific concerns which engender and drive the paradigm, and they generate a particular kind of research. More importantly, and the fundamental point of this paper, each paradigm and its descriptive language has certain "entailments" and lacks others.

To be blunt, each approach (to the extent of its individuality and integrity) is useful for some things and useless for others. In the present context the issue to which this is germane and which is to be faced is 'To what do we wish a psychology of reading to be applied?'

In the main, approaches to reading over the last century has been (a) Educational-Pedagogic, where the main concern has been on formal curriculum development; (b) Neurological, where the main concern has been with constraints imposed by the structure of the central and peripheral nervous system, but more generally with placing reading problems within a medical framework; (c) Psychometric, where the main concern has been to develop sensitive tests for assessment and diagnosis; (d) Social-Personality, where the main concern has been to explore how specific educational difficulties may arise from personality and social factors; and (e) Experimental Psychological. I shall direct most of my remarks to the last of these approaches but shall touch on other approaches either by implication or explicitly insofar as they are relevant.

Most psychologists who have been studying reading recently have been doing so in some version of what I will call the Information-Processing framework. The nature of that enterprise is to describe human behaviour in general and cognition in particular in terms of the structure of modular components. That is, what are the systems of epistemic representation and what are the processes which lead to and utilize those structures in various activities of the skilled performer? The aim is also to describe what changes as those skills and underlying representations are developed and break down. How this is applied to reading is exemplified in the many recent symposia that have been published. Whether the frequency of such publications reflects the presupposed usefulness of such approaches or their intrinsic interest, I am unsure. However I would not deny Huey's (1908) proposal that if we understood how people read we would understand a lot about cognition in general.

Achieving a full account of how a skilled reader performs various reading tasks is a wholly admirable aim for certain purposes. For example no systems analyst (electrical engineer, computer programmer, automobile mechanic or medical practitioner) can find out what is wrong with a suboptimal system unless he has a full specification of the working of that system, how it ought to be and exactly how it can be lacking or go wrong.

Thus when people who were competent readers suffer a partial or total reading impairment through brain damage, we can hardly expect therapists to begin helping the patient at a psychological level unless they know the specific nature of the dysfunction at that level. This applies equally to identifiable impairments in people who have not yet learnt to read in the first place. Thus a prime role for functional models of the information-processing kind is to guide diagnosis. But let us examine what such diagnosis may offer to the prospective helper. The most obvious example is what I wish to call Substitution or Surrogate therapy. Suppose a person loses both legs. They can be taught to use a wheelchair which substitutes a functionally different kind of locomotion for walking.

How might this apply to reading? Recently a "dual route" model of lexical access has been developing from both clinical and normal research (Marcel and Patterson, 1978). It is convenient to suppose that a store of information about words, a lexicon, intervenes between meaning or semantics and both linguistic input, spoken or written, and linguistic output, spoken or written. It is beginning to become clear that there are two ways that a reader can address the lexicon from printed words, one via a visual or graphic description, the other by converting a graphemic description to a soundlike or phonemic description. This latter route depends on equivalence rules and therefore will not work for words in English whose spelling maps onto sound in an irregular or ambiguous way (*sword, rough*). Just suppose that within this framework a particular patient's problem could be best accounted for as a loss of the ability to convert graphemes to phonemes by non-lexical equivalence rules without any other loss (as indeed Beauvois and Desrouesne (1978) have described one patient). In this case a therapist might be well advised to avoid phonic approaches in any attempt at remediating reading, and to supply a sight vocabulary of visuo-graphic addresses or to use visual heuristics. That is, the patient might be able to learn with appropriate mnemonics to associate whole-word or syllabic orthographies with semantic addresses or with entries in a preserved speech lexicon.

As a second more obvious example consider the congenitally profoundly deaf. While English orthography basically represents the sound of the language, however irregularly, it would be tortuous, if not pointless, to attempt to base any teaching of reading on that fact when dealing with such a population. Possibly any attempt to teach reading ought to be based on sign-language once acquired. But if so, it would be extremely useful to know just how the deaf process and represent sign-language, if we are to devise a reading curriculum for them. And this is just what information-processing approaches might contribute.

But can such approaches do anything more than aid diagnosis and suggest substitutes? In elucidating what I mean by "more", I will put forward a point of view. I would argue that the fundamental problems of literacy are of achieving it in the first place. There are those who read slowly and those who have problems in comprehension. I do not wish to diminish the problems in helping such people improve. But the major problem is in helping people to read *at all*, i.e. helping them to become independent readers who can manage more than a few sight words, who know what reading is about and can extend their own competence. Reid's (1972) review illustrates what I am referring to. She points out that in Clark's (1970) survey children who were backward by her criterion at the age of 7 were recognizing less than 10 words on Schonell's Graded Word List, including the items: tree, little, milk, egg, book, sit, frog, bun, road, clock, train. The backward 9 year-olds in Rutter, Tizard and Whitmore's (1970) survey were making around 14 errors on the first two passages of the Neale Analysis, i.e. on sentences like 'A black cat came to my house'. In the 1966 D.E.S. Survey and the N.F.E.R. follow up (Start and Wells, 1972) large groups of children of 11 years old were identified with virtually no ability to read at all nor understanding of what they were trying to learn. It is curious in this context that experimental psychologists spend so much time investigating the characteristics of poor readers whose problems are nowhere near as severe as those identified in the surveys reviewed by Reid. It also seems unhelpful if not misleading to characterize those they study by calling them 'dyslexic'. (See e.g. Ellis and Miles, 1978.)

Before attempting to specify the problems and assessing the ability of current approaches to deal with them, two points can be made. Firstly Merritt (1972) has reviewed the many psychometric, social-emotional, neurological and cognitive information-processing factors which have been identified with poor reading and reading failure. He has claimed that in the case of every factor it is possible to find children who perform or behave in the same way on those tasks as the poor readers and who therefore should be at risk, *but who can read perfectly well*. If this is indeed the case then we have to look to some other type of factor as crucial.

But of course there is an additional difficulty in interpreting psychological studies of the kind to which Merritt is referring. Many deficits found in poor readers, when compared to a normatively satisfactory population, may be the result of poor reading or lack of reading rather than its cause. Any memory deficit identified after poor reading has been identified may either be the result of an inability or impairment in coding input in the way that proficient literacy allows or may be due to the lack of proficiency in a kind of processing or transformation which results from practice at reading activities. An example of this kind of misleading correlation has been provided by Alegria (personal communication). Liberman, Shankweiler, Liberman, Fowler and Fischer (1977) found that poor readers had greater difficulty in phonetic segmentation than good readers. They suggested that this is a factor which constrains the achievement of reading. However they did not specify how the children they tested had been taught. Alegria has shown this to be rather important. He tried to teach Belgian children their equivalent of English secret languages (e.g. Black-Slang, Pig Latin) which require phonetic segmentation. He chose his children after the first year of formal reading instruction from schools which had started with a sight vocabulary and a look-say approach and from those which had started with a phonics approach. The children from the latter schools were clearly superior at learning the games. After the second year, when the two approaches were far less distinct, the difference diminished. In other words, proficiency in phonetic segmentation is at least as much a result of type of instruction as a determinant of reading proficiency.

As a way into examining psychological approaches, let me take the clearer case of neurological models of reading failure. Neurological approaches are inappropriate because they entail nothing about intervention. However true or valid neurological accounts of impairments are, one will never be able by neurological or physical means to either restore or donate the ability to read. (I exclude here the remediation of peripheral linguistic processing.) The reason is that reading is essentially an epistemological matter. It involves firstly the acquisition of concepts and secondly the translation of those concepts into skilled procedures or competences (e.g. that the graphic array represents a linguistic message in particular ways). Although reading relies on the central nervous system, it was invented not discovered. This of course is not to deny that particular forms of graphic languages (e.g. our own alphabetic system) have evolved to suit our capacities. Given this, it is hardly likely to be a successful enterprise to couch difficulties specific to reading in biological terms. But the main point is that even were such accounts valid they are useless practically since any remediation or initial teaching has to be at a psychological and a cognitive level.

In contrast, information-processing accounts are at a functional, psychological level. Indeed they do very well in capturing the functional nature of the problems of carrying out the various processes in reading. To take one example, mere vocalization may impose a considerable load on a child's capacity (Conrad, 1972), such that decoding operations together with retrieval of the output phonology of already lexicalized visual word-forms may overload the system. A common observation in MacKinnon's (1959) study of beginning readers, was that in successfully sounding out new words, children tended as a consequence to block on already familiar words in the same phrase. Hitch and Baddeley's (1976) concept of Working Memory, which has both executive and capacity aspects looks as if it can give an extremely good account of this problem. Yet my argument is that, in the fundamental teaching of reading such models fare no better than neurological descriptions.

Firstly, they do not specify courses of action: they do not tell you how to teach. In this they are as fatalist as any neurological or Piagetian model. That is, they may say that a person lacks x or has an impaired y. But they do not tell you what to do about it other than substitution. However well we specify such concepts as the lexicon or visual word-form, grapheme-phoneme conversion, visual memory or working memory, there is little in the models that tells us how to create these structures or processes in people or even how to improve them. Such models tell us nothing about *teaching*. The most obvious reason is that at present information processing models only deal with the operation of a system in a particular state, with or without particular components. They do not at present deal with how a system changes, acquires new knowledge or new structures, nor with the process of change. But more basic than this are two other reasons: (a) such models do not deal with the *relevant* aspects of learning to read, and (b) their descriptions of behaviour are at an inappropriate level.

I would like to argue that most difficulties in learning to read (as in initially learning other things) are difficulties of understanding. Learning to read entails the acquisition of a large number of knowledges or concepts and these knowledges must be turned into behaviour. Just four basic concepts emphasised by Rozin and Gleitman (1977) are that meaning is represented by visual symbols, that this is accomplished by mapping the symbols onto speech, that new elements can be generated by combining smaller elements for their sound values, and that the elements in alphabetic writing are approximately the phonemes. There are a large number of far more detailed concepts that have to be acquired relating to the graphical aspects of writing, linguistic aspects of speech and semantics, and their relationships. In addition procedural knowledge has to be acquired related to how to see and move over writing, how to use grapheme-phoneme rules and synthesise their results, and how to use the constraints of language and text. This is not the place to specify these necessary knowledges and examine their associated difficulties. However, unless a person acquires these concepts, not necessarily explicitly, but such that his behaviour is based on them, he will not be able to read. What needs to be considered is that individual differences may lie in the ease of *understanding* of what a teacher is attempting to convey in the cases of each of these different pieces of information. Understanding requires an internal representation onto which a communication can be mapped or from which a new one can be constructed. Thus what is vitally important is the concepts which a child coming to reading already has, and how they are internally represented. The point of this is that different people may require the same concepts to be expressed in radically different ways in order to comprehend them. Children's failure on conceptual tasks of a Piagetian kind is often taken to reflect a lack of the conceptual structure and apparatus necessary for such tasks. Yet the evidence reviewed by Donaldson (1978) suggests that if the question or the task is expressed in an appropriate way, then the child is often able to mobilise and apply his or her ability successfully. Donaldson's point is that apparent failures may not reflect lack of the prerequisite structures or abilities but either a failure on the adult's part to appreciate the child's communicative presuppositions or a difficulty on the child's part to use his abilities in a situationally detached and self-reflective way.

But the problem is not just one of fitting communicative representations to the constructs and presuppositions of the learner. It often involves doing so at a conscious, self-reflective level, because that is the level of comprehension and of the intentional aspects of learning and of turning knowledge into skill. A child who comes to school and can produce and understand speech obviously has the ability to parse and synthesise speech segments and categorize them into lexical formatives (e.g. root and bound morphemes). Yet a major problem for many such children is to understand this *explicitly*, as revealed by their apparent inability to intentionally segment and combine phonetically in tasks which require it, even in intrinsically motivating activities such as speaking secret languages like Pig Latin (Liberman et al.,1977; Rozin and Gleitman, 1977; Savin, 1972). A representation which is phonetically segmentable and combinable is exactly what graphemes have to be mapped onto. The problem here, as in other instances, may be one of creating insight, that is of aiding the child to gain conscious access to what he or she already knows tacitly. And one thing we know from the literature on problem solving is that gaining insight is crucially dependent on an appropriate representation. Thus one step is to try to find appropriate ways of expressing particular concepts according to the conceptual representations of individual children. The other step is indicated by Mattingly's (1972) suggestion that a powerful source of individual differences is in linguistic *awareness* as opposed to linguistic *ability*. It is to find ways of creating awareness.

The other reason why information-processing models have little bearing on teaching is the level of behaviour they seek to describe. The analogy of the electrical engineer will serve to illustrate this. He is successful not only because he has a model of the system with or without different components, but because he has an adequate model of what happens when he intervenes. He knows precisely what it is to join two terminals. Not only do we not know how to join two psychological "terminals", we do not have models of intervention at all. The reason for this is that the psychological level of intervention, of teaching, is that of communication. This is carried on at the level of consciousness. The problem for someone who learns a new concept about his own behaviour is that he needs to reflect upon his own processing in order that what is being communicated means anything to him. The problem for the teacher is not only to understand this and be sensitive to its individual variations, but to be able to modulate his or her own behaviour in accordance. This may sound rather vague. But it is so precisely because we have as yet no language for talking about such a process. The differences between the electrical engineer and the teacher is that the latter has to work through an intervening level. That level is the phenomenological one.

To summarize so far, I am suggesting that an applicable psychology of reading will be to a large extent a pedagogy of reading, and since pedagogy operates largely at the experiential level, our theoretical language will have to be capable of being mapped onto such processes at that level.

One of the ways in which the information-processing approach may actually have been misleading from the educational point of view is in its very emphasis on processes. Relative to modelling what is supposed to go on in a reader's head, it ignores the nature of the external representations upon which such processes operate. This means two things. Firstly we might pay more attention theoretically to specifying the nature of the graphic representation which confronts us and its relation to verbal language. Secondly, in the pedagogic context, several authors (Donaldson, 1978; Merritt, 1972; Rozin and Gleitman, 1977) have suggested that as opposed to teaching particular mappings and skills we might be far better off to attempt to convey from the start what reading is and the true nature of the graphic representation. There are two kinds of reasons for this. One is that in teaching particular skills we may involve the learner in apparent conflicts. Examples of this can be seen in (a) the relevance of sequential order for some things (letters for word identity, words for sentence meaning) and its irrelevance for others (letters for letter identity, words for word identity), and (b) what a child is told at different times about the relation between individual letters and sounds. The second reason is that unless the learner understands the nature of what he is attempting to learn he will have no way of avoiding the conflicts which are almost inevitable in English between individual relationships (e.g. the information conveyed by morphology and orthographic-sound relationships:- *sign-signature* versus *maintain-maintenance*). Indeed skills can sometimes develop "of themselves" once the underlying concept is understood (see, for example, the increases in reading speed achieved merely by pointing out the sequential redundancies in text, reported by Morton, 1959). This does not imply that the teacher should attempt to lecture verbally on the history of writing systems and the nature of articulatory constraints in the realization of phonetic segments in the speech wave. The curriculum devised by Rozin and Gleitman attempts to teach these very things by giving an operational understanding of (i.e., the ability to use) first a semasiography, then a logography, then phoneticization, then a syllabary and finally alphabeticization. While it is extremely doubtful that Rozin and Gleitman's pupils would have been able to verbalize about what they had learnt, nonetheless their successful acquisition of syllabic segmentation can be seen as evidence of their having explicit (intentionally available) access to what had been before only a tacit skill. Interestingly the greatest problem in the curriculum was in teaching alphabeticization (segmentation and synthesis of phone-phoneme sequences). But it is important to note that this is probably not a problem of gaining awareness of an already tacit ability, since it is by no means evident that speech is naturally categorized by a phonetic code in all or even some individuals. That is, due to phonetic coarticulation, the number of acoustic segments is usually less than the number of phonetic segments. It might even be possible to argue that the phonemic segmentation necessary to reading and spelling is a special invention of the alphabetic principle itself.

In this paper I have suggested that the most pressing practical issue in reading is teaching. I have tried to point to several aspects of this which we need to consider and about which the currently dominant theoretical language of information-processing has little to say. This implies several directions for research. Because of the level at which teaching and comprehension occur, we need to explore how teacher and learner experience each concept as it is conveyed. This must take account of the particular individual variations in conceptual structure, modes of explanation and modes of comprehension with regard to each of the concepts to be acquired. Naturally this also presupposes an appropriate description of each of the concepts which we wish to convey. Given this we should find ways of representing each concept that are compatible with the different forms of conceptual structure which learners bring with them. Since comprehension as well as communicative problems are often problems of achieving awareness, methods of creating self-reflective awareness for specific levels and types of knowledge would also seem to be an area of research which has been virtually ignored so far. This last is not only of interest for pedagogy but is exciting for both clinical reasons (Weiskrantz, 1977) and theoretical ones (Marcel, in press).

REFERENCES

Beauvois, M-F. and Desrouesne, J. (1978). Phonological Alexia: Study of a Case of Alexia without Aphasia or Agraphia. Paper delivered to Meeting of European Brain and Behaviour Society, London, July.

Clark, M.M. (1970). *Reading Difficulties in Schools.* Penguin, Harmondsworth.

Conrad, R. (1972). The developmental role of vocalizing in short-term memory. *Journal of Verbal Learning and Verbal Behavior.* 11, 521-533.

Department of Education and Science (1966). *Progress in Reading 1948-1964.* H.M.S.O. London.

Donaldson, M. (1978). *Children's Minds.* Fontana, Glasgow.

Ellis, N.C. and Miles, T.R. (1978). Visual Information Processing in Dyslexic Children. In: *Proceedings of the International Conference on Practical Aspects of Memory.* (M M Gruneberg, P E Morris and R N Sykes, eds). *Academic Press, London.*

Hitch, G.J. and Baddeley, A.D. (1976). Verbal Reasoning and Working Memory. *Quarterly Journal of Experimental Psychology,* 28, 603-621.

Huey, E.B. (1908). *The Psychology and Pedagogy of Reading.* M.I.T. Press (New Editition 1968), Cambridge.

Liberman, I.Y., Shankweiler, D., Liberman, A.M., Fowler, C. and Fischer, F.W. (1977). Phonetic Segmentation and Recoding in the Beginning Reader. In: *Toward a Psychology of Reading.* (A S Reber and D L Scarborough, eds). Erlbaum, Hillsdale, N.J.

MacKinnon, A.R. (1959). *How do children learn to read?* Copp Clark, Vancouver.

Marcel, A.J. (in press) Conscious and Unconscious Reading: the effects of Visual Masking on Word Perception. To appear in *Cognitive Psychology.*

Marcel, A.J. and Patterson, K.E. (1978). Word Recognition and Production: Reciprocity in Clinical and Normal Studies. In: *Attention and Performance.* Vol. 7. (J Requin ed). Erlbaum, Hillsdale, N.J.

Mattingly, I.G. (1972). Reading, the Linguistic Process, and Linguistic Awareness. In: *Language by Ear and by Eye.* M.I.T. Press, Cambridge.

Merritt, J.E. (1972). Reading Failure: a Reexamination. In: *Literacy at All Levels.* (V Southgate ed). Ward Lock Educational, London.

Morton, J. (1959). An investigation into the effects of a reading efficiency course. *Occupational Psychology,* 33, 222-238.

Reid, J.F. (1972). The Scope of the Reading Problem. In: *Reading: Problems and Practices.* (J F Reid ed). Ward Lock Educational, London.

Rozin, P. and Gleitman, L.R. (1977). The Structure and Acquisition of Reading II: The Reading Process and the Acquisition of the Alphabetic Principle. In: *Toward a Psychology of Reading.* (A S Reber and D L Scarborough eds). Erlbaum, Hillsdale, N.J.

Rutter, M., Tizard, J. and Whitmore, K. (1970). *Education Health and Behaviour.* Longman, London.

Savin, H.B. (1972). What the Child Knows about Speech When He Starts to Learn to Read. In: *Language by Ear and by Eye.* (J F Kavanagh and I G Mattingly eds). M.I.T. Press, Cambridge.

Start, K.B. and Wells, B.K. (1972). *The Trend of Reading Standards.* National Foundation for Educational Research, Slough.

Weiskrantz, L. (1977). Trying to bridge some neuropsychological gaps between monkey and man. *British Journal of Psychology,* 68, 431-445.

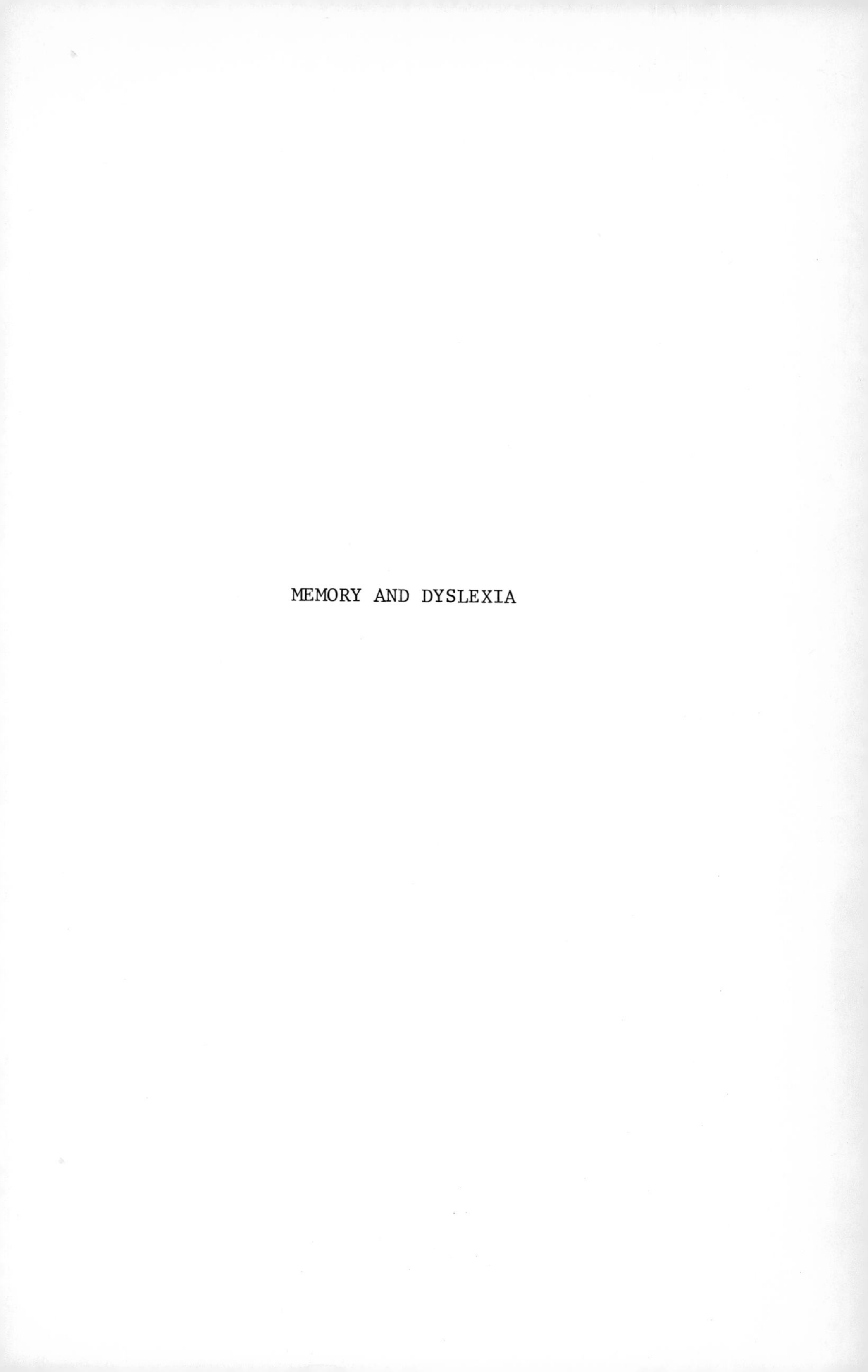

MEMORY AND DYSLEXIA

SOME ASPECTS OF MEMORY IN DYSLEXICS AND CONTROLS

M. E. Thomson and C. Wilsher
University of Aston, Birmingham B4 7ET

Aspects of memory have important implications for reading and spelling, in terms of retention of sound/symbol correspondences, retention and recognition of phoneme and grapheme sequences and so on. One category of written language difficulties is dyslexia, which one might describe as an individual difference in cognitive development, not favouring the easy acquisition of written language skills. See for example Newton, Thomson & Richards (1978) for descriptions as to the nature of 'dyslexia'.

Although many writers make clinical observations on memory deficits in dyslexia, there has been relatively little controlled research in this area.

Goldberg and Schiffman (1972) found a significant positive correlation between both visual sequential memory and visual memory and reading ability in dyslexics. Comparisons of memory differences using auditory and visual sequencing tests (eg ITPA) have found inferior performance in dyslexics (Stanley, 1973; Newton & Thomson, 1978).

Stanley and Hall (1973) review the passage of information through 'visual memory store' (iconic memory), short-term memory and long-term memory, examining the recall of arrays of letters using dyslexic and non-dyslexic subjects.

They found that an increase in duration produced an increase in the amount recalled. However the dyslexics' performance was inferior to the control group. This was interpreted as a 'maturational lag' in memory.

Scallon (1975) found dyslexics' performance was inferior to the controls' in both the processing of letters and symbols. He concluded that dyslexics have specific limitations at the early stages of information processing (eg. in the VIS) and transfer from VIS to short-term memory store takes longer in dyslexics, accounting for lower scores by dyslexics on memory tasks.

Miles and his co-workers suggested that the main feature in dyslexia was "an inability to retain complex information over time" (Miles and Wheeler, 1974). In various experiments Ellis and Miles (1977) varied amount of stimulus presented, duration of presentation and the interval between presentation and the time at which the subject is required to respond. They concluded that dyslexia is due to a limitation in processing capability, which accounts for the memory deficits.

Thomson (1977) found that dyslexics' showed an overall deficit in short-term recall of objects, although when examining the proportion of correct recall, the dyslexics errors were not significantly greater until 5 objects were to be recalled, suggesting a 'threshold level.

The aim of this paper is to explore the nature of these short term memory deficits and information processing models, as well as the concept of 'maturational lag' in terms of perceptual/memory skills by using both children and adult subjects.

METHOD

Subjects: Two main studies were undertaken (A and B), with children and adults. Both studies used a matched group design, subjects matched on age, sex (all male), socio-economic background and intelligence. The experimental groups were individuals who had been diagnosed as dyslexic, see Thomson (1978a) for details of the diagnostic criteria. The control groups were average or good readers. For Study A forty children were tested, twenty controls and twenty dyslexic, age range 9-11 years. In Study B 14 controls and 16 dyslexics formed the groups, age range 17-24 years.

Procedures: All subjects in both studies were given an auditory sequential memory test (WISC or WAIS) and a visual sequential memory test (ITPA).

Study A: (i) Free recall. A single string of 7 random digits were tachistoscopically presented to the subject, who was then asked to write down as many as he could remember, in any order, after presentation. 5 trials each at 0.2, 0.4, 0.7, 1 and 2 seconds were given. Scoring was number of digits correctly recalled. (ii) Recognition. The procedure was similar to (i) except that the subject was asked to pick out the correct string of digits from 6 alternatives shown after presentation. Scoring was number of correct strings recognised. (iii) Partial recall. The stimulus cards consisted of an array of digits. These consisted of 3x3, 3x4 and 3x5 rows of digits matrices, and presentation times as (i) and (ii). After presentation Ss were cued verbally as to which row they were required to recall.

Study B: (a) Serial learning task on a memory drum. This consisted of ten three letter nonsense syllables (cvc) of high association value. These syllables were presented

in conjunction with a number cue. The list of ten nonsense syllables took 70 secs to be presented and was followed by a 20 sec rest before the next trial. The experiment continued until the subject reached the criterion of two successive correct trials.
(b) 'Information absorption'. A projector with shutter speed control unit enabling slides to be shown at tachistoscopic speeds varying from 5ms upwards projected photographs of a horizontal random 6-digit number string. Subjects were asked to recall the numbers as soon as the display had ended. The speed of presentation was altered by successive approximations according to the subject's previous response down to a 50% threshold point at which ten exposures were recorded. An Information Absorption rate was arrived at by using the Miles and Wheeler (1977) method.

RESULTS

The dyslexic groups scored significantly less well on both auditory and visual sequential memory tests.

Study A: The results for the three tasks are presented in Table 1. Using analysis of variance dyslexics scored significantly less well on all measures than the control group ($p<.001$). For task (i) both groups performed significantly better with increase in exposure time ($p<.05$) whereas for task (ii) only the dyslexic group improved significantly with increased exposure time ($p<.05$). For task (iii) the control group performance increased significantly with longer presentation time up to 700 msecs, for all arrays ($p<.05$). However, the dyslexic groups' performance increased significantly only for the 3x3 array ($p<.01$).

			Presentation time (m.secs)				
			200	400	700	1000	2000
(i)	Dys		2.24	2.82	3.08	2.98	4.14
(i)	Cont.		3.52	3.76	4.32	4.58	5.36
(ii)	Dys		2.0	3.1	3.4	4.0	4.5
(ii)	Cont.		4.0	4.3	4.7	4.5	5.0
(iii)	Dys %	3x3	35.2	77.8	52.1	58.2	57.9
	cued	3x4	28.3	34.1	37.8	40.2	44.9
	row	3x5	24.9	24.7	22.3	28.7	35.8
(iii)	Cont.	3x3	58.1	60.9	67.3	79.1	78.8
	% cued	3x4	49.8	54.7	61.6	62.1	66.2
	row	3x5	40.1	50.8	56.2	55.3	55.8

Table 1 : Mean correct for Study A.

Study B: Table 2 presents the results for this study, (a) refers to serial learning and (b) to Information Absorption. Dyslexics were significantly poorer on both tasks ($p<.001$).

		Dys	Control
(a)	No trials	11.1	6.5
	Immediate Forgetting	6.0	1.9
(b)	Bits/sec	40.59	302.59
	Threshold m/s	737.5	138.52

Table 2 : Mean scores for Study B

DISCUSSION OF RESULTS

The poorer performance of dyslexics on the sequential memory tests suggests difficulties in the retention of symbolic information presented serially, a key feature in reading and spelling. These features have been described by many writers and of interest here is the finding that adult dyslexics have similar difficulties, suggesting a finite difference in "cognition" rather than a maturational lag in perceptual skills, delaying written language acquisition in children.

In Study A task (i) there is an increase in performance in both groups that corresponds to an increase in presentation time of the stimuli. The performance level of the dyslexic group is however inferior to that of the control group. This would suggest that it is deficit of memory recall and not just sequential memory in the dyslexic. Dyslexics at 2000 msec. have only just passed the level of performance of the Controls at 400 msec. presentation time, and it would appear, are slower at processing the information available. Ellis and Miles (1977) suggest that this may be due to deficits in the Visual Information Store (VIS).

In task (ii) the control group performance does not increase significantly with an increase in length of presentation time suggesting that the subjects have reached a 'threshold', or maximum performance. The dyslexics, however, show a significant increase and do not appear to reach a 'threshold', but only reach the level of performance of the controls' first trials (ie 200 msec) at 1000 msec.

The control group may be making greater and more profitable use of the Visual Information Store (Iconic Storage), at these lower presentation times. In a recognition task the subject is required to retain information about the items and then match it against another item; if the information he has processed from the previous item matches that of the new item then he recognises it. Obviously the more information he gathers from the first item the less mistakes he will make in correct recognition. It seems that the dyslexics appear less able to process information, having a limited capacity for information, and these results cannot be fully explained by the 'maturational lag' hypothesis.

In task (iii) dyslexics perform significantly less well in general on such a task than do controls. This is the same for each of the various arrays. In both groups the percentage of the cued row recalled in the 3x3 array is greater than that for the 3x4 and 3x5 arrays respectively. This would suggest that each group is only able to process a limited amount of information (ie a limited capacity). As the information available increases so the percentage recalled decreases.

There seems a 'threshold' of amount of information processed in both groups. As we have seen the dyslexic group performance is lower, this would indicate that dyslexics have a lower 'threshold' for the amount of information processed. This supports the work by Ellis and Miles (1977) and work by Thomson (1977) who have found that the dyslexics have a lower 'threshold' or a limited capacity for information.

The control groups' performance increases with an increase in presentation time for those times up to 700 msec (1000 msec in the case of 3x3 array) and then levels off. The overall increases are for all arrays. Possibly after 700 msec they are unable to 'take in' any more information. The dyslexics' percentage recall increase with increase in presentation time is only significant for the 3x3 array. This suggests that for the larger arrays the greater information available and the longer time for which it is available causes an 'information overload' and thus a decrease in performance.

An interesting point of the graph for the 3x3 array for dyslexics is the peak (better than controls) at 400 msec. Stanley (1973) has found that dyslexics have a greater persistence of Visual Information Storage. He estimates this to be 30-50% longer than non-dyslexics, which would increase the dyslexics VIS from 250 to about 400 msecs. This longer duration of VIS might cause the peak observed, as subjects would have a longer time in which to read off the information after 'cueing'. In the 3x4 and 3x5 arrays the information threshold has been reached and the extra information may cause interference.

Taking the three tasks together, it appears that dyslexics have poorer performance on the recall task, whereas in the recognition task the main feature was poor VIS, and increased presentation time improved their performance, whereas the control group seemed at maximum performance. Further increase in presentation time would investigate the possibility that the dyslexics would catch up. In partial recall the dyslexics were again poorer, and in this case although poorer at VIS generally, if they showed greater 'persistence' would have improved performance when the stimulus array is below their 'capacity'.

'Maturational lag' is not sufficient to account for the results obtained and they could be explained by a "limitation of information capacity". While both groups appeared to have a limitation of information capacity (this was especially evident in the Partial Recall experiments) dyslexics had a smaller capacity hence their poorer performance on memory tasks. This would also explain their poor memory for sequence. The sequence of an array of items contains information. If dyslexics have a smaller information capacity they may not use the information of the sequence, or they may not use it fully hence poor sequential memory.

In Study B the dyslexic group took almost twice as long to learn the ten nonsense syllables as the control group. Their performance was also erratic as measured by "Immediate Forgetting". This was recorded each instance when a nonsense syllable was learned and then forgotten on the very next trial. The dyslexics' frequency of this measure was over three times that of the student group. This measure typified the learning pattern of the dyslexic who did not build upon the items learned but forgot them. The pattern of learning showed irregularities with many instances of learning ceasing at some points.

In the Information Absorption study not only were means significantly different but the two distributions had different characteristics and were almost separate. To achieve mutually exclusive groups the ten "best" and "worst" readers and spellers were selected. The results revealed very large and significant differences. What is more the Information Absorption rate could be used as a predictor of reading and spelling. When the ten best and worst Information Absorbers were selected the groups differed by 6.4 year in Reading age and 4.4 years in Spelling age. For all groups together Information Absorption showed significant correlations of .79 and .82 with reading and spelling respectively. This suggests that not only were the two groups significantly different but that there was an even relationship with reading and spelling skills.

Practical implications for written language acquisition

Some of the processes involved in reading and spelling acquisition are reflected by the experimental tasks. Written language includes word patterns (sequence of phoneme contrasts) and spelling patterns (sequence of grapheme contrasts), and uses arbitrary symbols which must be combined in the correct order. (See Thómson, 1978 for a detailed review.) The retention of visual and auditory symbols in order, in short term memory is paralleled by the sequential memory taks. Spelling involves elements of recall, in that arbitrary symbols with a learnt sound attached to them must be recalled from a possible array (viz.Study A Task (i)). Reading involves elements of recognition, in that a 'template' of written symbols must be matched to a previously learnt sound/symbol pattern (viz.Study A task (ii)). The learning of the alphabetic sound/symbol system involves the arbitrary attachment of a sound to a visual symbol, (viz.Study B, serial learning task). The complex integration of visual, auditory and kinaesthetic skills in terms of sound/symbol relationships, spelling and word patterns, sequence of letters, combination of letters etc., requires that information be retained in time, and in 'short term memory' if learning is to take place (Study A, partial recall, Study B information absorption). The difficulties shown by dyslexics in recall and recognition of visual symbol information processing and in learning name/syllable relationships would obviously make reading and spelling a problem.

In general the results suggest an individual difference in memory processes, and in written language learning one would want to take account of these differences. In simple terms the dyslexic would need a much longer exposure to written language learning, with considerable 'overlearning' and 'overteaching'. There are however some more specific implications. In the recall task, and the sequential memory tests, increased 'exposure' time is of limited value. Here one would suggest presenting the written language to meet the learner. For example instead of learning s-t-r-i-n-g as string, six things to recall, spelling patterns can be taught as units, viz. str +ing (two elements to recall). Sound/symbol correspondence would need considerable 'overlearning' and use of mnemonics, and the recognition results would suggest that word patterns and letter recognition will require special teaching - possibly as whole (as opposed to serial combination) units, or using multisensory techniques. The relatively poor information processing capacity would suggest that teaching be highly structured, with small amounts of work being undertaken at any one time - eg one spelling rule, or sound. The 'overloading' of capacity by remedial programmes aimed at "enrichment" would be avoided, as would teaching a number of written language skills at the same time. Finally the recognition of the specific difficulties dyslexic individuals have is of primary importance, both in terms of understanding the problems, as well as planning appropriate teaching.

REFERENCES

Ellis N. C. and Miles T. R. (1977) Dyslexia as a limitation in the ability to process information. *Bull. of Orton. Soc.* 27, 73-81.

Goldberg H.K. and Schiffman G.B. (1972) *Dyslexia*. Grune & Stratton: New York.

Miles T.R. and Wheeler T. (1974) Towards a new theory of dyslexia. *Dyslexia Review 11*.

Miles T.R. and Wheeler T. (19-7) Responses of Dyslexic and non-dyslexics to tachistoscopically presented digits. *IRCS Medical Science 5:149*.

Newton M.J., Thomson M.E. and Richards I.L. (1978) *Readings in Dyslexia* Learning Development Aids.

Newton M.J. and Thomson M.E. (1978) A concurrent validity of the Aston Index. In *Readings in Dyslexia* (op. cit.).

Scallon P. (1975) Short term visual memory and information processing abilities of dyslexics. *MSc dissertation, University of Aston in Birmingham.*

Stanley G. and Hall R. (1973) A comparison of dyslexics and normals in recalling letter arrays and symbols after brief presentations. *Brit. J. Ed. Psych.* 43, 301-304.

Stanley G. (1973) Visual memory process. In *Short-term memory*. (Deutsch D & Deutsch S, eds) Academic Press London.

Thomson M.E. (1977) Individual differences in the acquisition of written language: implications for Dyslexia. *PhD thesis, University of Aston in Birmingham.*

Thomson M.E. (1978a) Identifying the dyslexic child. In *Readings in Dyslexia* (op. cit.).

Thomson M.E. (1978b) The nature of written language. In *Readings in Dyslexia* (op. cit.).

LEARNING, MEMORY, AND DYSLEXIA

D.J. Done and T.R. Miles
*University College of North Wales,
Bangor, Wales*

ABSTRACT

3 experiments are reported, each of which was designed to test the claim that dyslexic subjects are inferior to non-dyslexic subjects at remembering a sequence of items only when those items need to be verbally encoded.

INTRODUCTION

It is widely agreed that those poor readers and spellers designated as 'dyslexic' show a distinctive pattern of difficulties (Miles, 1978). What is not clear, however, is whether it is possible to specify in a general way the types of task at which they perform relatively less efficiently. Now Blank and Bridger (1966) have argued that translation of temporal sequences into spatial patterns involves a language element. It therefore seemed to us worth while to examine whether dyslexic subjects were distinctively weaker than controls at tasks which involved verbal labelling.

This hypothesis carries the following predictions. 1) Dyslexic subjects will perform less efficiently than controls in correctly recalling sequences of digits after brief visual presentation but will show no extra (differential) inferiority if nonsense shapes are substituted for digits. (This is because, in the absence of practice, the nonsense shapes, being nonsense, will have been as little verbalised by the control subjects as by the dyslexic subjects). 2) Since digits allow readily of verbal encoding, pictures are partly encodable, and nonsense shapes least encodable, the differentiation between the two groups will be greatest in the case of digits and least in the case of nonsense shapes. 3) If tasks which involve verbal retention are subjected to interference the differentiation will be reduced and may even disappear. 4) If labels are learned for what would otherwise be nonsense shapes the differentiation will again be found. Three experiments are reported which test these predictions.

Exp.1 relates to the first two predictions, exp.2 to the third, and exp.3 to the fourth.

METHOD AND RESULTS

In all cases a subject was classified as dyslexic if a sufficient number of the criteria set out by Miles (1978) were satisfied.

Exp. 1

Method. 18 dyslexic subjects(mean C.A. 13.2, mean spelling age 8.6) were matched with 18 control subjects (mean C.A. 13.2, mean spelling age 12.6), all being of at least average ability as judged by traditional intelligence tests. Sequences of digits, sequences of pictures, and sequences of nonsense shapes were presented in an Electronic Developments 2-field tachistoscope for periods of 2000 ms. There were 3 exposures of 5 items, 3 of 6 items, and 3 of 7 items; this made 9 exposures per item set. The subjects were required to respond immediately after stimulus offset by placing a ring round each item on a 'response board', comprising 10 items of the appropriate category, and a record was kept of the order in which the ringing was done.

Results. Each item placedin its correct serial position in the sequence was scored as one point. Since there were 3 exposures of 5 items, 3 of 6 items, and 3 of 7 items, this gives a maximum possible total for each subject of 54 (15 + 18 + 21). An ANOVA of individual responses indicated significant groups difference overall ($p < .001$), the scores for the controls being the higher. Differences between item sets were highly significant ($p < .001$) but neither order of presentation nor sequence length contributed significantly to the variability ($p > .05$). Of the interactions, there was a significant group x item set interaction ($p < .01$) due to group differences in respect of digits ($p < .05$), with differences in respect of pictures and nonsense shapes being in the predicted direction but not reaching an acceptable level of significance (compare table 1). There was also an item set x order of presentation interaction due to an apparent 'warm-up effect' with digits but not with pictures or nonsense shapes.

Table 1 gives the mean scores for the two groups of subjects in each item set (scores for all 9 exposures being pooled).

These results show the familiar pattern (Mackworth, 1963) of improved performance as items become more easily encodable. This advantage can be seen to be differentially greater in the non-dyslexic group, predictions 1 and 2 being therefore fulfilled.

TABLE 1

Comparison of mean scores (the sum of 9 exposures) of dyslexic and control subjects

	Digits	Pictures	Nonsense Shapes
Control subjects	43.2	25.02	15.75
Dyslexic subjects	32.4	18.9	13.41
Difference	10.8	6.12	2.34

Exp. 2.

Method. 15 dyslexic subjects (mean C.A. 15.3, mean spelling age 11.0) were matched with 15 control subjects (mean C.A. 15.2, mean spelling age 14.0), all being of at least average ability as judged by traditional intelligence tests. The verbal retention task was that of recalling tachistoscopically presented sequences of digits, and the type of interference chosen was that of articulatory suppression (AS). Sequences of 7 digits were presented in an Electronic Developments 2-field tachistoscope for exposure times of 2000 ms. The subject was instructed to respond at specified times after stimulus offset by placing 7 numbered tables (on which were inscribed the digits used in the experiment) in the order in which they had appeared in the tachistoscope. 6 conditions were used (see table 2) of which nos. 2, 3, 4, and 5 involved articulatory suppression. In these conditions the

TABLE 2

The 6 Recall Conditions of Digit Sequences in Exp.2

Condition No.	Description
1	Subject responds immediately after stimulus offset
2	Subject responds 5 secs(+AS) after stimulus offset
3	Subject responds 10 secs(+AS)after stimulus offset
4	Subject responds 15 secs (+AS)after stimulus offset
5	Subject responds 20 secs (+AS)after stimulus offset
6	Subject responds 20secs(No AS)after stimulus offset

subject repeated the word 'the' during the time interval after stimulus offset. During the delayed recall conditions (2 to 6) all subjects stacked plain cards on to a pile in front of them; this task was given as a means of maintaining a constant rate of articulatory suppression.

Results. Two different scoring systems were used to analyse S's responses, viz. (1) 'absolute position' (ABS), by which a point was awarded for each item in its correct serial position, and (2) 'adjacent pairs' (ADJ), by which a point was awarded for any correct sequence of two digits regardless of serial position. Fig.1 illustrates the results based on the two methods of scoring, both of which indicate a group convergence in the articulatory suppression conditions and a group divergence in the other two conditions. An ANOVA of condition totals for each S indicated a significant overall difference between groups ($p < .001$ ABS and $p < .01$ ADJ),

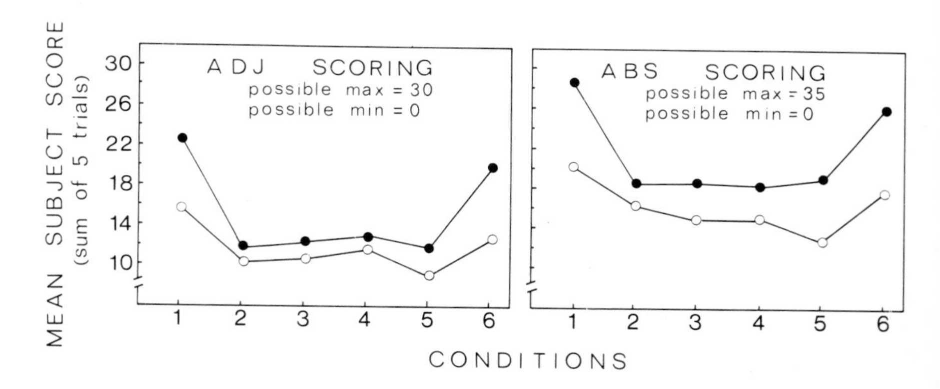

Fig. 1 The Effect of Retroactive Articulatory Suppression on Memory for Digit Sequences - Dyslexic (-○-) vs. Non-dyslexic (-●-) S's under 6 Conditions (see Table 2)

the performance of the controls being superior. Differences between conditions were also significant ($p < .001$ ABS and $p < .001$ ADJ), performance being reduced by articulatory suppression (see Fig.1). However, there was a highly significant group x conditions interaction ($p < .025$ ABS and $p < .01$ ADJ), which indicates that the controls suffered to a greater extent than the dyslexic subjects under the suppression conditions, which in themselves did not generate differing results.

It follows from this experiment that the third prediction

was also fulfilled: in other words, interference by means of a task which involves verbal retention affects the controls more than it affects the dyslexic subjects.

Exp.3.

Method. 10 dyslexic subjects (mean C.A.14.3, mean spelling age 9.6) were matched with 10 control subjects (mean age 14.4, mean spelling age 13.7), all being of at least average ability as judged by traditional intelligence tests. Subjects were selected as controls who, in a preliminary test, had a higher score on a digit sequencing task than their 'pair' but a similar score when the stimuli were nonsense shapes.

Sequences of 5 nonsense-shape stimuli were presented in an Electronic Developments 2-field tachistoscope for exposures of 2000 ms and 400 ms. As in condition 1 of exp.2 the subjects were required immediately after stimulus offset to recall the sequence by arranging tablets (test 1). Next they were given a paired-associate learning task (PAL) in which each shape was displayed in a memory drum at the rate of 1 presentation every 4 sec. and its paired-associate, a meaningless CVC trigram, was presented auditorily from a tape-recorder. After an initial introduction (i.e. a run of all 5 shape-CVC pairs) the subject was required to say the sound of the CVC trigram aloud while the stimulus was being exposed, after which the correct CVC trigram was auditorily presented as corrective information. This procedure continued until each subject had satisfied the criterion of 2 consecutive errorless trials. Next they were given a card with the shapes printed on it. There were eight rows, with nine shapes per row (i.e. 56 shapes altogether) and the subjects were instructed to begin with the first shape at the left side of the top row and name the shapes aloud as though reading through a page in a book. Finally, the nonsense shapes were once again tachistoscopically presented (test 2), with the subjects responding, as before, by arranging tablets.

A week later they were given the same paired-associate learning task and the same printed page, again with instructions to name the shapes line by line. Next the nonsense shapes were again tachistoscopically presented, with the subjects initially responding by arranging tablets (test 3), and finally the subjects were asked to respond orally by giving the 'names' of the shapes (test 4). Each test involved 7 trials with the same 5 nonsense shapes at each of the two exposure times.

The following represents a summary of the procedure:
(1) Test 1: pre-test on memory for sequence of nonsense shapes
(2) Paired-associate learning task (PAL 1)
(3) Test 2: test on memory for sequence of nonsense shapes
One week later:
(4) Re-learning of paired associates (PAL 2)
(5) Test 3: test on memory for sequence of nonsense shapes
(6) Test 4: test on memory for sequence of nonsense shapes (subjects being required to respond orally)

Results. Responses in Tests 1-4 were scored in the same way as in exp.1. Table 3 shows the mean scores for the two groups in the 4 different test conditions. Since the scores

TABLE 3

Comparison of mean scores (the sum of 14 exposures) of dyslexic and control subjects over the 4 tests of exp.3

	Test 1	Test 2	Test 3	Test 4
Control subjects	33.39	36.696	40.13	46.84
Dyslexic subjects	32.44	33.46	37.596	35.9
Difference:	0.95	3.236	2.534	10.94

at the two exposure times have been pooled the results relate to 2x7 (=14) trials of 5 shape sequences, the maximum possible score therefore being 70. An ANOVA of responses indicated significant overall group differences on the 4 tests combined ($p < .05$), the controls scoring higher than their dyslexic 'pairs'. Differences between tests were also significant ($p < .01$), the recall of sequences in tests 3 and 4 being superior as a result of prior learning. There was also an overall difference in score at the two different exposure times ($p < .025$), all subjects performing better at the longer exposure time (2000 ms). Of the interactions, the group x tests interaction was significant ($p < .025$); this result is due to a significant group difference ($p < .01$) on test 4, there being no significant differences on tests 1, 2 or 3(see Table 3). Table 4 gives the number of trials to criterion in PAL 1; with the exception of pair 2 the dyslexic member of each pair consistently needed a far larger number of trials (Wilcoxon, $T = 2$, $N = 10$, $p < .01$).

TABLE 4

Comparison of Dyslexic and Control Subjects in PAL 1 in Terms of Number of Trials Needed to Reach the Criterion

Pair No.	1	2	3	4	5	6	7	8	9	10
Control Subjects	11	17	12	6	10	13	11	13	16	11
Dyslexic Subjects	31	8	29	30	17	41	46	24	48	28

Finally, a table of correlations between some of the variables has been set out in Table 5. The most important inferences to be drawn from these correlations are:

TABLE 5

Spearman Rank Order Correlation Coefficients between No. of Trials in PAL 1, Mean Score on the Digit-sequencing Task (MDS), Spelling Age (SA), and Mean Scores on Tests 3 and 4 of exp.3. (N = 20)

	PAL 1	MDS	SA	Test 3	Test 4
PAL	-				
MDS	- 0.64*	-			
SA	- 0.59*	0.72*	-		
Test 3	- 0.12	0.58*	0.25	-	
Test 4	- 0.57*	0.79*	0.47	0.66*	-

* $p < .005$; df 18

1) Rapid paired associate learning is positively correlated with memory span for digit sequences and score on test 4 (verbal recall of shape sequences); 2) Memory for digit sequences is positively correlated with both tests 3 and 4. These results therefore support the prediction that when labels are acquired for nonsense shapes the differentiation between dyslexic and non-dyslexic subjects in memory for sequence tests will reappear.

CONCLUDING REMARKS

The results of all three experiments are compatible with the hypothesis that dyslexic subjects are inferior to control subjects at remembering a sequence of items only when those items need to verbally encoded.

That this is a correct account of the matter is given

further support by the fact that one of the most successful predictors of reading failure is said to be letter naming (Calfee, 1977). Moreover, the results of exp.1 make it likely that when the dyslexic child has to deal with letters, digits or other verbally encodable material he is less able than a non-dyslexic child, in the time available, to record the order in which the items were presented. Experience suggests that he can best be helped not by being told to 'try harder at remembering' but by being encouraged to pay attention to the 'job' which each letter does in representing a particular sound. If one considers some of the spelling mistakes made by dyslexic children, they are often in fact strikingly similar to those made by non-dyslexic subjects in short term memory (STM) experiments. Thus, the dyslexic mistake 'reamin' for *remain* exemplifies not only incorrect ordering but primacy and recency effects (since it is the middle-order items which are misplaced, cf. Bjork and Healy, 1974), while 'asisd' for *assist* is an example of confusion between similar sounding letters (cf. Conrad, 1964). There are grounds, therefore, for claiming that an important characteristic of dyslexia is some kind of limitation in the mechanisms of STM and that any programme of language training, if it is to be used successfully with dyslexic children or adults must take this limitation into account.

ACKNOWLEDGEMENT

The authors are grateful to the S.S.R.C. for the studentship awarded to Mr Done during the period of the research.

REFERENCES

Bjork, E.L. and Healy, A.F. (1974). 'Short-term order and item retention'. *Journal of Verbal Learning and Verbal Behaviour*. 13, 80-97.

Blank, M. and Bridger, W.H. (1966). 'Deficiencies in verbal labelling in retarded readers'. *American Journal of Orthopsychiatry*. 36, 840-847.

Calfee, R.C. (1977). Assessment of Independent Reading Skills: Basic Research and Practical Applications. In: *Toward a Psychology of Reading* (A.S. Reber and D.L. Scarborough eds), pp.317-320. Lawrence Erlbaum Associates, Hillsdale, New Jersey.

Conrad, R. (1964). 'Acoustic confusions in immediate memory'. *British Journal of Psychology*. 55, 75-84.

Mackworth, J.F. (1963). 'The relation between the visual image and post-perceptual immediate memory'. *Journal of Verbal Learning and Verbal Behaviour*. 2, 75-85.

Miles, T.R. (1978). *Understanding Dyslexia*. Hodder and Stoughton, London.

VISUAL INFORMATION PROCESSING IN DYSLEXIC CHILDREN

N.C. Ellis and T.R. Miles
Department of Psychology, University College of North Wales, Bangor, Wales

ABSTRACT

Four experiments are briefly reported. These were designed to test for differences between dyslexic and control children at successive stages from iconic memory to working memory.

The results are compatible with the theory that a relative slowness or inefficiency is found in dyslexic children at a stage of processing which involves name-encoding; and it is suggested that it is this deficit which limits their ability at reading. If these children are generally poor at dealing with articulatory information in working memory this could underlie and thus explain many of the apparently diverse dyslexic symptoms. The practical implications are briefly discussed.

INTRODUCTION

In all the experiments reported here the subjects were boys aged 10-15 years chronological age (CA). The dyslexic and control groups were matched for both CA and level of intelligence, with the criteria for dyslexia including a reading and spelling retardation of at least 2 years and the demonstration of other typical dyslexic symptoms.

EXPERIMENT 1

In order to reduce complications due to 'processing for meaning' it was decided to use digits as stimulus material in preference to words or phrases.

41 dyslexic and 41 control children were asked to report as many items as possible from 7 digit arrays presented at exposure times from 50-400 ms under backwards pattern masking in a tachistoscope. The results (fig. 1) demonstrate that dyslexic children are able to report significantly fewer

items at all the exposure times used ($p < .001$).

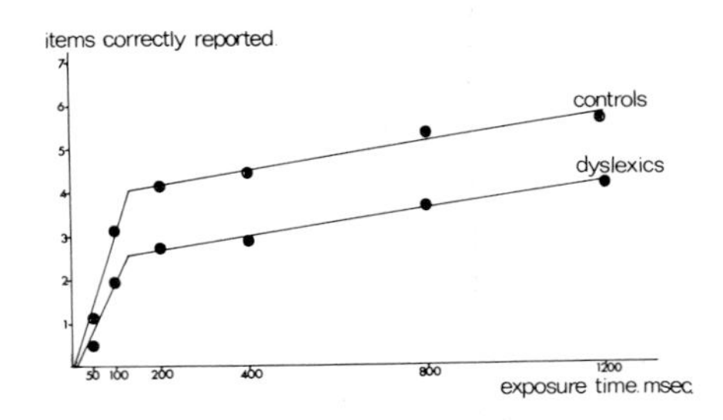

Fig.I. The number of digits correctly reported by the dyslexic and control children in the backwards masking procedure of Expt.I.

Since at shorter exposure times saccadic movements are impossible, it must be concluded that dyslexic children are relatively poor at 'reading digits' from a single fixation. From this it follows that the abnormal eye movements commonly associated with dyslexia (see for example Lesèvre, 1964) may be regarded as the result rather than the cause of any dyslexic deficit. Also, as this task involves negligible semantic processing demands, it must be concluded that while there may be problems associated with semantic analysis in dyslexic children, this is not the root cause of their reading difficulty.

Various component analyses have been suggested for this type of task. For example Sperling (1967) has proposed that item information is first represented in the visual information (iconic) store (VIS). The information in the VIS is scanned and converted into a 'program of motor instructions', an abstract name code, in the recognition buffer. The execution of these motor instructions, the conversion of the abstract name code into an articulatory code, is said to constitute rehearsal. Following this model, the points in Fig.1 at which the first steep limbs peak, the dogleg points, can be said to reflect the capacity limitations of the recognition buffers of the two types of subjects, the slope of the first limb reflecting the rate of the scan process. It would thus be concluded from the data of Fig.1 that dyslexic children differ from their normal reading peers in that they are both slow at the 'scan' process and have a recognition buffer of a reduced capacity.

Since there is evidence, however, of a visual code store which differs from the VIS in that the information contained in it is both more durable and less susceptible to masking (c.f. Phillips, 1974; Posner, 1969), Coltheart (1972)has suggested that the visual code may act as the buffer store between the icon and the articulatory code. According to this interpretation the dogleg point might reflect either the capacity of the visual code or the efficiency with which this trace is interpreted and converted into the articulatory code. From Fig.1 it would therefore be concluded either that the dyslexic children possess a visual code of a relatively smaller capacity, or that they are less efficient at articulatory encoding from this trace.

It might also be suggested that a deficit at the VIS level could explain the dyslexic childrens' low performance in visual information processing. If the VIS trace decayed relatively rapidly in dyslexic children then this would limit the amount of information processed, as in both models the VIS is the data base upon which further processing functions operate. This, however, cannot be the case for the following reasons: i) Differences between dyslexic and control subjects were obtained in Expt.1 where backwards masking was used. This technique is thought to eliminate the further processing of information residual in the VIS after stimulus offset, and therefore processing from the VIS after stimulus offset is not incurred in Expt.1. ii) Direct measures of VIS duration undertaken by Stanley and Hall (1973)and Ellis and Miles (1978a, b) demonstrate that in fact this store has a marginally longer duration in dyslexic subjects.

A priori, however, it is not possible to exclude any of the following areas as being the loci of the dyslexic's visual information processing deficit: the scan process, the capacity of the recognition buffer, the capacity of the visual code, or the articulatory encoding from the visual code. A visual code problem, for example, might be implied from the reversals (e.g. b/d) commonly seen in dyslexic script; scan or articulatory encoding problems might be expected from the findings of slow naming reaction times to simple picture stimuli (both Denckla and Rudel, 1976 and the present authors have observed this with dyslexic children using the Oldfield and Wingfield, 1965 picture stimuli). The following experiments are designed to test some of these alternatives.

EXPERIMENT 2

To test the speed of visual code production and matching, and the speed of matching name-identical letters the Posner, 1969 paradigm was used. The stimuli shown in Fig.2 were presented singly and in a randomised order to 21 dyslexic and 21 control children. These children were asked to say 'yes' if the 2 letters were the same, and 'no' if they were different, and to give their answer as soon as they knew it. The physical pairs (PS, PD, and PCD) could be judged same or different on the basis of their visual characteristics, whilst the name pairs had to be represented in some name code before this judgement could be made. In addition there were the confusing different pairs (PCD and NCD) where the pair members, although different, were either visually or acoustically similar.

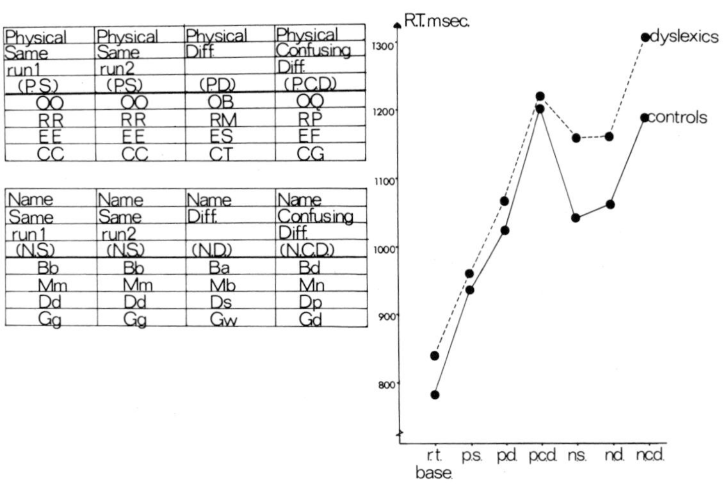

Physical Same run1 (P.S.)	Physical Same run2 (P.S.)	Physical Diff. (P.D.)	Physical Confusing Diff. (P.C.D.)
OO	OO	OB	OQ
RR	RR	RM	RP
EE	EE	ES	EF
CC	CC	CT	CG

Name Same run1 (N.S.)	Name Same run2 (N.S.)	Name Diff. (N.D.)	Name Confusing Diff. (N.C.D.)
Bb	Bb	Ba	Bd
Mm	Mm	Mb	Mn
Dd	Dd	Ds	Dp
Gg	Gg	Gw	Gd

Fig. 2. The letter pairs used in Expt. 2 and the resultant mean judgement reaction times (RT) in msec for the dyslexic and control children on each condition.

The RT base means, which do not differ significantly between the two groups, represent the mean reaction times obtained when the children were asked to respond 'yes' when a large solid circle was presented and 'no' if a small empty circle appeared. For the other conditions, a 3 factor ANOVA demonstrates that whilst there is no overall significant difference between the groups (F=1.59; df=1,40), there is a highly significant group x type interaction (F=9.01; df 1,280; $p < .001$): the dyslexics do not respond slower than the controls on the type of letter pairs which may be adjudged same or different on the basis of their visual characteristics, but they are much slower at adjudging the type of pair where the comparison is one of name codes. Supramanian and Audley (1976) have found a similar pattern of results with poor reading subjects. It is concluded that the speed of production and matching of visual codes is as fast and efficient in dyslexics as in controls. The production of name codes, however, takes on average 113ms longer for the dyslexics than for the controls. Whether this name code matching is based on abstract name codes, occurring for example as a result of the scan process, or on articulatory codes is a matter of debate. The fact, however, that Articulatory Suppression, a technique which interferes with articulatory encoding whilst having no effect on that information in the recognition buffer, appears neither to affect 'visual code' matching or 'name code' matching in undergraduates, suggests that the name code in operation in this task is abstract in form (Ellis, 1978). The slower name code matching in dyslexics is therefore evidence of a deficit in the speed of name code production, and this seems more likely to be that abstract name code of the recognition buffer, rather than an articulatory code. The parallel second limb slopes obtained in Fig.1 might further support this notion: in the Coltheart,(1972)model this shallow function is suggested to reflect articulatory encoding since its rate approximates to that of implicit speech. As the slope of this function is the same in dyslexic and controls, if the Coltheart (1972) model is correct, it follows that the dyslexic and control children are equally proficient at articulatory encoding.

EXPERIMENT 3

Dyslexics are prone to making reversal errors and it has often been assumed that they do have a visual orientation problem (for reviews see e.g. Critchley, 1970 and Vernon, 1971). The fact that the dyslexic children in this study are not slower on the P.C.D. pairs (which are not acoustically confusable c.f. b/d/p) suggests that the typical reversals seen (b/d) might be a result of confusion in the production of name codes for these stimuli rather than their visual confusability alone.

However, the stimuli used in Expt.2 were simple letter pairs, and it is possible that in the case of older dyslexic children, who had all received considerable remedial tuition, that learning overlay may have masked any visual code problem that they might have. Therefore a similar study to Expt.2 was run on the same children. This used the highly confusable stimuli shown in Fig.3. These stimuli are both unfamiliar, and difficult to name, and the child was asked to judge whether the two stimuli presented on any one trial were identical or otherwise. This task is again performed on the basis of comparison of information held in the visual code. Verbal reaction times were again recorded.

basic stimulus ↓	SAME				DIFFERENT			
	Run1.	Run2.	Run3.	Run4.	90°rot.	UDrev.	LRrev.	Mut'n.
1.								
2.								
3.								
4.								

Fig. 3. The stimuli used in Expt. 3.

A three factor ANOVA demonstrates no distinction between the dyslexic and control groups for judgement times on any of the conditions. The dyslexics, however, do make more errors on this task, but this should be regarded in the light of low overall error rates (5% for the controls and 10% for the dyslexics).

The visual code production and matching are as fast in dyslexics as in controls. Whilst the dyslexics are slightly less accurate on this task where novel and confusing stimuli are used, this difference is slight, and there is no difference in accuracy between the two groups when familiar letter stimuli are to be visually matched (Expt.2). It is therefore suggested that the typical dyslexic problems in reading and spelling cannot be ascribed to a visual code problem, but are attributable to a deficit in the translation of the visual stimulus representation into its name-code equivalents.

EXPERIMENT 4

To exclude the visual code entirely as an area of deficit in dyslexia there remains to be tested the capacity and decay rate of this store (for example it may be the case that the visual code decays more rapidly in dyslexic children, so impeding adequate name-coding).

To test this possibility a procedure devised by Phillips and Baddeley (1971) and Phillips (1974) was used. This involves showing the S a matrix similar to a 'randomized chessboard'. The simplest used here was a 4x4 (16 cell) matrix with half the cells filled in a random arrangement. First one such matrix is shown, and then, after a variable interstimulus interval (ISI), a second which is either identical to the first or, if different, differs in one cell only. The subject has to report if the two matrices are the same or different.

If the ISI is short (500 ms or less) and the 2 matrices are presented in the same physical location, any differences between the groups could be attributed to differences in capacity or decay rate of the VIS. If the ISIs are long, however, or filled with a masking stimulus, then such differences must involve the visual code store. The procedure can therefore be used to study the capacity of this store (by the inclusion of a larger number of cells in the matrix) and the decay rate from it (by the use of a wide range of ISIs).

61 male dyslexic children were tested on this task, mean CA 12.3 years, along with 22 male control children, mean CA 12.8 years, and 26 first year undergraduates. The matrices were shown on film, with each trial consisting of 24 frames matrix 1, variable ISI of either 1, 2, 5, 10, 48, or 143 frames, and 24 frames matrix 2. The film was projected at 24 f.p.s. giving a matrix exposure time of about 1 sec., and an ISI range from 40 ms to 9 sec. The ISI period was either mask-filled or blank. After the subjects had participated in this expt. they were shown a second film which used 25 cell matrices, with exposure times of roughly 2 sec. and with the ISI always unfilled.

The results were converted to give the proportion of each group giving correct responses on each trial. ANOVAs run on these data show no significant differences between the 3 groups on either the 4x4 or the 5x5 matrices. Whilst this is a rather crude procedure it does demonstrate that, within the range of this experiment at least, visual code 'capacity' and decay are similar in both dyslexic and control children and undergraduate adults, and therefore the dyslexic problems in visual information processing cannot be ascribed to problems in these areas.

CONCLUSIONS

From the results of Expts.1-4 it is concluded that the visual information processing deficit in dyslexic children lies neither in the speed of production, capacity, or speed of decay of the visual code. Rather the dyslexic children demonstrate problems at a name coding level. It is likely from the results of Expts.1 and 2 that this is a handicap at the stage of abstract name code production (the 'scan' and 'recognition buffer' stages of the Sperling (1967) model) rather than articulatory encoding per se.

This hypothesis makes sense of many of the other familiar manifestations of dyslexia, as described, for instance, by

Miles (1978). These include difficulty in recall of auditorily presented digits and of items in sequence such as mathematical tables and months of the year, as well as spelling difficulty in the sense of difficulty in remembering what letters go to make up a word. If verbal labelling of items in a sequence is slow but the decay rate remains the same, then the memory easily becomes overloaded, with resultant loss of detail.

On the practical side it seems important that teachers should be alerted to the fact that some children have a constitutionally caused limitation which affects their ability to deal with any kind of situation where naming the stimulus material is required; and an adjustment of standards is called for together with a willingness to appreciate the amount of compensatory effort which a dyslexic child needs to make. In addition it seems to follow from the results of exps.2 and 3 that training in shape discrimination will not necessarily lead to an improvement in reading and that games such as pelmanism will not necessarily 'train the memory' in a way that will lead to improved spelling. Nor is there reason to think that the reading of a dyslexic person will be improved by appropriate training of eye movements. What is in fact needed is the learning in a systematic way of grapheme-phoneme correspondences, with plenty of time being allowed for naming and for scrutiny of detail. It is interesting that programmes of this kind have in fact been devised by teachers of dyslexic children in several different parts of the world.

ACKNOWLEDGEMENTS

The authors are grateful to Alan Allport, Alan Baddeley, Max Coltheart and Don Mitchell for helpful comments on this work, and to the headmasters, Gerald Trump, John Walters and Kenneth Underwood, who allowed us into their schools.

REFERENCES

Coltheart, M. (1972). Visual information processing. In: *New Horizons in Psychology: 2.* (P. Dodwell ed), pp62-85. Penguin, Harmondsworth.

Critchley, M. (1970). *The Dyslexic Child.* Heinemann, London.

Denckla, M.B. and Rudel, R. (1976). Naming of object-drawings by dyslexic and other learning disabled children. *Brain and Language.* 3, 1-15.

Ellis, N.C. (1978). Visual information processing and working memory. In preparation.

Ellis, N.C. and Miles, T.R. (1978). Visual information processing speed as a determinant of reading speed. *Journal of Research in Reading*. 1, 108-120, in press.
Ellis, N.D. and Miles, T.R. (1978). The role of the visual information store in reading. In preparation.
Lesèvre, N. (1964). Les movements oculaires d'exploration. *Thèse de Paris*. Cited in Critchley, M. (1970). op.cit.
Miles, T.R. (1978). *Understanding Dyslexia*. Hodder and Stoughton, London.
Oldfield, R.C. and Wingfield, A. (1965). Response latencies in naming objects. *Quarterly Journal of Experimental Psychology*. 17, 273-281.
Phillips, W.A. (1974). On the distinction between sensory storage and short-term visual memory. *Perception and Psychophysics*. 16, 283-290.
Phillips, W.A. and Baddeley, A.D. (1971). Reaction time and short-term visual memory. *Psychonomic Science*. 22, 73-74.
Posner, M.I. (1969). Abstraction and the process of recognition. In: *The Psychology of Learning and Motivation*. Vol. 3. (J.T. Spence and G. Bower eds). Academic Press.
Sperling, G. (1967). Successive approximations to a model for short term memory. *Acta Psychologica*. 27, 285-292.
Stanley, G. and Hall, R. (1973). Short term visual information processing in dyslexics. *Child Development*. 44, 841-844.
Supramanian, S. and Audley, R.J. (1976). The role of naming difficulties in reading backwardness. Paper presented to the *British Association Annual Conference*.
Vernon, M.D. (1971). *Reading and Its Difficulties*. Cambridge University Press, Cambridge.

CODING OF SPELLING BY NORMAL AND DYSLEXIC READERS

P.H.K. Seymour and C.D. Porpodas
Department of Psychology,
The University, Dundee, Scotland.

1. INTRODUCTION

The difficulties encountered by dyslexic children in learning to spell are generally more severe than their difficulties in learning to read (Critchley, 1970). A possible implication is that the spelling and reading functions share a common component which is critical for the acquisition of reading skill and for the longer-term exercise of spelling skill. It is reasonable to propose that this common element is a permanent memory system in which physical properties of written words are stored. If this store was impoverished in dyslexia this could delay the development of lexical recognition systems (see Seymour & Porpodas (in press)) and deprive the spelling function of essential information about the letters contained in individual words or morphemes.

Unfortunately our knowledge of the manner in which spelling is coded in the permanent memories of competent writers of English is very limited. The code might specify all of the letters in a word, or only those which could not be reliably derived by application of phoneme-grapheme correspondence rules. It might be visual in character or speech-based. The ordering of the letters might be represented by a quasi-spatial code which specified properties of location, adjacency and direction or in some other more abstract form.

2. EXPERIMENT 1: VISUAL AND NAME CODING

The first experiment was conducted with the aim of determining whether letter-specific information is represented by a graphemic code or by a phonemic code. On each trial the subject was instructed to judge the shape or sound of the letter whose position in a 5-letter target word was indicated by a probe digit. The probe was visual in one experiment and auditory in the other. Under shape instructions subjects responded positively to letters possessing an ascender or descender and negatively to others. Under sound instructions they responded positively to letters whose names rhymed with "ee". Ten words were used (table, child, point, begin, plant, bread, blind, death, build, great) the last five being considered somewhat irregular in sound-to-spelling relation. Reaction times were recorded from onset of the visual or auditory probe to closure of a "Yes" or "No" switch, and a total of 100 trials was run under each condition.

The subjects for this and the other experiments to be described were: (1) a group of 7 competent readers aged 10-11 years; (2) two 10-year old dyslexic boys, AR and JM (see Seymour & Porpodas (in press) for details); and (3) five secondary school dyslexic boys with well-established histories of reading and writing impairment whose ages were 12 years (PA), 14 years (MH), 15 years (JH and GM), and 17 years (RE). The word sets and the shape and sound properties of the letters of the alphabet were communicated to all subjects in advance of the experiment and it was established that the dyslexic boys could spell the words.

The reaction times (RTs) of the competent readers were examined with the aim of determining whether there was a difference in the time needed to make shape or sound decisions, and whether such an effect was related to the regularity of the sound-to-spelling relation or to the modality of the probe digit. The average RT was 1700 ms and errors occurred on about 5 per cent of trials. Responses to auditory probes were about 400 ms faster than responses to visual probes but this effect did not interact with the decision required. Shape decisions were faster than sound decisions, and this effect was chiefly attributable to the words of irregular spelling. There was a large serial position effect, with RTs increasing at a rate of 288 ms per position over the digits 1-4 and then declining at the fifth and final position. Overall, these results support the conclusion that a graphemic code is favoured for letter-specific spelling information, at least for words of irregular spelling.

The mean RTs and error rates of the dyslexic subjects have been summarised in Table 1. It can be seen that one subject (GM) appears very similar to the control group, but that the others react much less rapidly, the delays being extreme for the younger subjects, AR and JM. The error rates of the dyslexics are also higher, particularly MH. A more detailed analysis of the data of the five secondary school subjects showed that their serial position curve was similar in shape to that of the controls but that the rate of increase over positions 1-4 was about 700 ms per

Subject		VISUAL PROBE		AUDITORY PROBE	
		Shape	Sound	Shape	Sound
Control	$\overline{X}$	1885 (3)	1985 (6)	1437 (6)	1596 (8)
	sd	182	120	303	347
Dyslexic					
GM		1501 (2)	1796 (0)	1422 (10)	1616 (6)
PA		3508 (6)	3863 (14)	2840 (6)	2843 (16)
MH		3232 (20)	3582 (48)	3302 (20)	3695 (30)
JH		3138 (10)	2793 (14)	2677 (4)	2895 (2)
RE		3147 (10)	3665 (26)	2733 (2)	3535 (18)
AR		9844 (12)	10391 (16)	13939 (12)	12085 (14)
JM		7235 (18)	8492 (36)	6411 (24)	5641 (26)

Table 1. Mean RTs (ms) and error rates (in brackets) for control and dyslexic subjects in the probe task.

letter. The effects of probe modality and decision type corresponded in direction to the control data but were not significant, and there was no evidence of an influence of spelling regularity. In general, therefore, the experiment demonstrates that our dyslexic subjects were slow to access numerically specified locations in words they knew, although we did not obtain clear evidence that their coding of spelling was atypical.

3. EXPERIMENT 2: MONTHS OF THE YEAR

In the second experiment the digit probe task was applied to the months of the year. On each trial a number from the series 1-12 was visually presented and the subject reacted by naming the month occupying that location (e.g. 8 —> "August"). The RT was recorded from onset of the probe to production of the vocal response.

The aim was to determine whether the impairment shown by the dyslexics in Experiment 1 was specific to spelling tasks or whether it extended to other sequentially organised categories. When adults retrieve month names the RT averages about 1 s and the RT profile takes the form of an inverted W. This pattern was approximated by the control group, although the level of the RT was slightly higher, at 1500 ms. The dyslexic subjects showed a clear delay of reaction, RTs being 3-4 s for AR and JM, and about 2300 ms for the five secondary school boys. Error frequencies were again elevated (usually responses of the month adjacent to the target month) and this was particularly evident in the data of MH.

This study confirms reports that dyslexia is often associated with difficulty in learning conventional sequences and concepts of clock and calendar time (Critchley, 1970). The interesting possibility emerges that the weekdays, months and other analogous semantic structures are dependent on a form of abstract (or quasi-spatial) coding which is also important in the representation of spelling and which is likely to be defective in cases of developmental dyslexia.

4. EXPERIMENT 3: RELATIVE JUDGEMENTS OF LOCATION

Characteristics of the code underlying ordered series and variations of magnitude have recently been studied by means of a relative judgement task. The subject is presented with pairs of items from a series and is instructed to indicate which has the greater (or lesser) value. It has been shown that the reaction time is sensitive to the degree of separation of the items, tending to decrease as the distance between them becomes larger. There is also a 'semantic congruity effect', that is a tendency for the choice of the larger of two items to be faster with large than with small items, and vice versa for the choice of the smaller of two items.

A test for the occurrence of these effects in our subjects was made using the weekdays and names of objects of varying size (bee, cup, cat, dog, cow, bus). The two sets were examined in separate blocks of 60 trials. On each trial the subject was instructed to choose the larger or smaller object or the earlier or later day. A display of two words side by side was then presented, and the subject indicated his choice by pressing a left or right switch.

An analysis of the results of the competent readers indicated that the general level of the RT was about 900 ms and that errors were infrequent (less than 3 per cent of trials). Both series produced a standard distance effect with the RT decreasing as the ordinal separation of the items increased. The RTs for choices between adjacent items were examined to determine whether there was a semantic congruity effect. The expected interaction occurred, and has been illustrated in Figure 1.

The dyslexic subjects were quite accurate on this task (errors occurred on only 3.4 per cent of trials) but, as is shown in Table 2, their RTs were in every case greater than those of the control subjects. Figure 1 shows that the secondary school boys demonstrated a semantic congruity effect. However, the distance effects were somewhat variable and were not significant statistically.

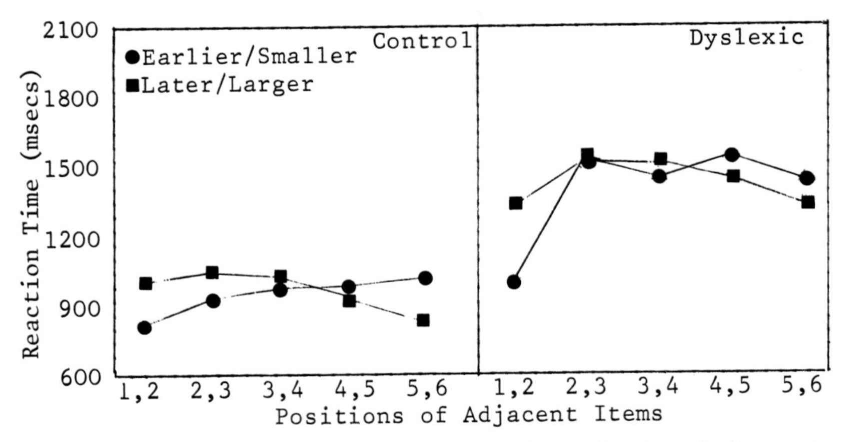

Fig. 1. Semantic congruity effects in relative judgements of weekdays and sizes.

The relative judgement task was then applied to choices of the earlier or later of pairs of letters from target words of regular spelling (bright, advice, winter, hungry) or irregular spelling (tongue, beauty, answer, weight) which were known by the dyslexic subjects. The judgement required (earlier or later) and the identity of the target word varied from trial to trial.

The mean RT of the control subjects was 1393 ms with an error rate of about 6 per cent. There was no effect of spelling regularity. The distance effect was significant but the interaction of earlier/later instructions and letter positions (required for the semantic congruity effect) was not. As is shown in Table 2 all dyslexic subjects other than GM had elevated RTs and error rates on this task, with MH being particularly error prone and AR and JM particularly slow. Like the controls, the older dyslexics produced a substantial distance effect but no semantic congruity effect. In general, the choice of the earlier of the two letters was faster than the choice of the later irrespective of serial position, and this effect was shown by both control and dyslexic subjects.

Subject	Regular Words	Irregular Words	Weekdays	Sizes
Control $\bar{X}$	1384 (4)	1401 (8)	899 (2)	933 (3)
sd	301	299	72	84
Dyslexic				
GM	1490 (7)	1530 (11)	1376 (6)	1274 (4)
PA	2105 (16)	1852 (18)	1058 (2)	1147 (3)
MH	1953 (25)	1905 (39)	1668 (6)	1774 (15)
JH	1700 (19)	1949 (19)	1405 (6)	1161 (8)
RE	2691 (14)	2911 (13)	1184 (0)	1405 (1)
AR	7446 (22)	6198 (26)	3090 (0)	2512 (0)
JM	5161 (17)	5917 (14)	2540 (0)	2639 (1)

Table 2. Mean RTs (ms) and error rates for relative judgements of positions of letters in words and items in series.

5. EXPERIMENT 4: FORWARD AND REVERSE SHIFTS

A further experiment was conducted with the aim of investigating the directional properties of spelling. On each trial the subject was given the instruction 'Forward' or 'Backward' followed by a target word. Five of the words used were regular in spelling (begin, black, drink, about, point) and five were somewhat irregular (ocean, blind, sugar, watch, laugh). A letter from the target word was then displayed in the tachistoscope, and the subject named the adjacent letter which followed or preceded it. The response "nothing" was given for backward shifts from the first letter and forward shifts from the last letter. There was a total of 100 trials.

The RT of the competent readers averaged about 1390 ms and errors occurred on fewer than 4 per cent of trials. Reactions were in general faster for words of regular spelling than for words of irregular spelling. Forward shifts were faster than backward shifts, but, as has been shown in Figure 2, this directional effect interacted with the serial position of the probe letter, being most evident for serial positions 3, 4 and 5. The data of the individual dyslexic subjects have been summarised in Table 3. All subjects other than GM exhibit an impairment, affecting both error frequency and RT. As in the previous experiments, MH made many errors and AR and JM were very slow. Figure 2 shows that the secondary school boys produce a serial position effect but no forward/backward effect. Thus, the property of 'directional polarisation' appears to be absent from their representation of spelling.

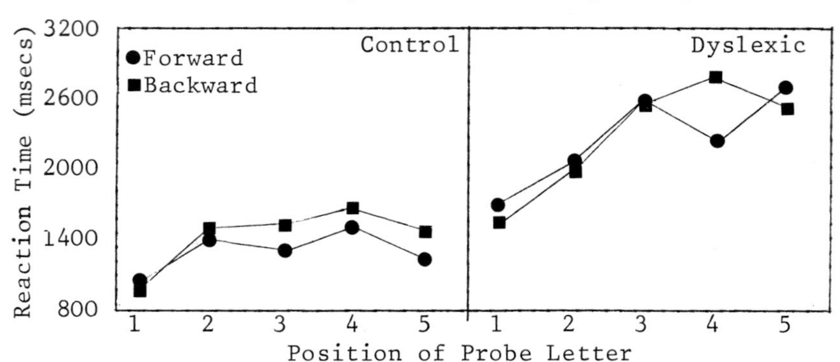

Fig. 2. Mean RTs (ms) for forward/reverse shifts in words.

The forward/reverse shift task was also undertaken with two sequentially organised categories - the weekdays and the spectral colours. The results, summarised in Table 3, indicate that the dyslexic subjects all show delayed RTs with colours, but that three of them (GM, JH and RE) fall within or very close to the confidence limits for the control mean with the days. There was a weak forward/backward effect for the controls, but this was absent in the data of the dyslexics.

Subject	Regular Words	Irregular Words	Days	Colours
Control $\overline{X}$	1359 (2)	1422 (5)	1057 (0)	1408 (2)
sd	178	186	140	123
Dyslexic				
GM	1412 (2)	1543 (6)	1157 (2)	1658 (2)
PA	2935 (6)	2603 (16)	1387 (2)	1970 (8)
MH	2862 (32)	3197 (38)	1750 (8)	2548 (8)
JH	1828 (16)	1733 (22)	1197 (8)	1884 (8)
RE	2962 (12)	3081 (12)	1060 (0)	3323 (24)
AR	8853 (26)	7286 (34)	4285 (2)	4476 (0)
JM	8630 (10)	8229 (36)	3211 (0)	5525 (0)

Table 3. Mean RTs (ms) and error rates (in brackets) for control and dyslexic subjects in the shift tasks.

6. CONCLUSIONS

These experiments demonstrate that dyslexic subjects are

impaired on tasks which require analytic operations on spelling knowledge. They are slow to make decisions about the physical characteristics, locations and orders of letters in words with which they are familiar, and make frequent errors. The reaction time deficit appears to be age-related, since RTs were always considerably greater for AR and JM than for the older subjects. The problem seems to be in part a matter of the speed at which locations in spelling structures are accessed (see Experiment 1) and this may well be linked to the defect in directional coding suggested by Experiment 4. We have also presented evidence that dyslexics may be impaired in their capacity to operate on other sequences, such as months, weekdays, sizes and spectral colours. This may imply a particular semantic defect concerned with the coding of direction and location which is disruptive of sequential processes necessary for reading and writing. Further research designed to isolate this defect and to determine its wider cognitive consequences would clearly be beneficial.

7. ACKNOWLEDGEMENTS

This research was supported by a grant to C.D. Porpodas from the Scottish Council for Research in Education. We are most grateful to our subjects, to Miss Catriona Collins of George Watson's College, Edinburgh, to the officers of the Tayside Dyslexia Association, and to the Headmistress and staff of the Park Place Primary School, Dundee, for their help and cooperation, and to Margaret Grubb for typing the manuscript.

REFERENCES

Critchley, M. (1970). *The Dyslexic Child.* Heinemann: London.

Seymour, P.H.K. and Porpodas, C.D. Graphemic and lexical processing in dyslexia. In: *Cognitive Processes in Spelling.* (U. Frith, ed), Academic Press: London. (In preparation).

MEMORY IN THE DEAF

DEAF PEOPLE'S MEMORY: THERE ARE PROBLEMS TESTING SPECIAL POPULATIONS

J.M. Belmont
Ralph Smith Mental Retardation Research Center
University of Kansas Medical Center
Kansas City, Kansas
M.A. Karchmer
Office of Demographic Studies
Gallaudet College
Washington, D.C.

ABSTRACT

Fourteen deaf and 14 normal-hearing high-school students intensively practiced a memory method involving active rehearsal and passive attention. They used these 2 processes to memorize pictured objects or the objects' printed names. The 2 groups were comparable on recall, except in rehearsal memory for words, on which the deaf were deficient. It was concluded that this peculiar memory deficiency simply reflects a mismatch between materials and linguistic competence.

INTRODUCTION

Are deaf people memory deficient? The question is simple enough, but to try to answer it is to become tangled up in a mess of ancillary problems: What do you mean by deaf? By memory? By deficient? Endlessly qualified, the simple question about deaf memory is never answered. The present study illustrates one problem that contributes to the question's unanswerability. This kind of problem is common to a wide range of cognitive studies with special populations.

The cardinal sign of difficulty in special-populations research is the pre-eminence of the design question, *what is the appropriate contrast group?* The contrast group is of course meant to provide the norms against which to view possible deficiencies. Yet special populations can differ in many ways from the norm, and they often do differ on noncognitive variables that can influence performance on basic cognitive tasks. Thus, cognitive psychologists who study a population to learn about that population, must control for a number of social, cultural and linguistic factors which do not ordinarily concern the researcher. In deaf studies one must ask, does the subject understand the task? Is he well motivated? Is he comfortable with the people who test him? Does something about the task proper detrimentally interact with his special linguistic apparatus? The present experiment with deaf people was designed to guarantee understanding, motivation and comfort, so that we could clearly explore the last possibility. We wanted to show that deaf people's particular linguistic requirements can lead us to underestimate their memory ability.

Imagine for a moment that your memory for verbal materials is tested using words from your second language. Unless you are perfectly fluent in that language, you will need to translate or at least muddle your way through some idiosyncratic articulation. In either case you will probably fail to recall some items because of shallow encoding or a badly oiled retrieval mechanism. We suppose that deaf people can be similarly handicapped: Performances inferior to normal-hearing contrast groups have often been reported for experimental tasks that involve English language materials (e.g., Craig, 1973; Wallace & Corballis, 1973; Conrad, 1973), whereas with nonverbal materials deaf and normal-hearing people often perform similarly (e.g., Blair, 1957; Doehring, 1960; Ross, 1969).

If the hypothesis of the imperfectly known second language can account for deaf-hearing recall differences, then we should be able to induce deaf and normal-hearing people to use exactly the same method to memorize English words or their non-English equivalents, and the groups' recall difference favoring hearing people should appear only with English words. Before running off to test the hypothesis, however, there is another point to think about.

We see the problem for deaf people arising not out of unfamiliarity with the English vocabulary itself, but rather the uses to which the words must be put. If the recall task requires very little preprocessing of materials into usable forms, then we should expect no deaf deficiency, regardless of the nature of the materials. If, however, memorization methods appropriate to the task's recall demands all involve semantic or articulatory coding, then we expect the use of imperfectly known materials to make a very large difference indeed. We therefore chose a task that has two parts. One part requires minimal processing.

The other definitely requires at least repetitive articulation. We had deaf and normal-hearing people do the task with pictures of common objects, or the objects' printed English noun equivalents. Under the hypothesis of imperfectly known language, we anticipated that deaf people would perform subnormally only with English words, and then only on the verbally demanding part of the task.

METHOD

Subjects

The subjects were 14 deaf and 14 normal-hearing high-school sophomores and juniors. The deaf students were in the academic track of the Kansas School for the Deaf. Their median age was 18 years. At the time of the study their median hearing loss was 100 dB (ISO) average in the better ear across the speech range. The minimum loss was 85 dB. Every student's onset of hearing loss occurred before age 2½.

The normal-hearing students' median age was 16 years. All were enrolled in summer school English classes. Although we have no other academic information, these students probably attended summer school because they were academically less capable than their normal-hearing age mates. Thus, any differences found in this study favoring the normal-hearing group should be regarded as conservative reflections of the deaf students' deficiencies. Likewise, any differences favoring the deaf would be liberal estimates of their relative strength.

Memory Task and Materials

We studied two verbally dissimilar memory systems simultaneously in a single experimental task. The task is best appreciated by taking the memorizer's viewpoint: You see a box with a row of 7 windows running along the bottom and one window centered above that row. Suppose that the items to be memorized are pictures of common objects. Your task is to study 7 different pictures that you expose one at a time, left to right, one per window. Then, in the upper window, you expose one of the 7 pictures you have just seen. Your recall requirement is to touch the lower window where you saw that picture.

Item presentation is actually done by pressing a foot switch. The first time you press it, the first picture appears briefly (0.7 sec.) in the first window. The second time you press the switch, the second picture appears briefly in the second window, and so forth. You may take as much time as you want between pictures. The last time you press the switch, the test picture appears in the upper window and stays there until, by touching one of the lower windows, you indicate where you recall having seen it. This item-exposure/item-test sequence is repeated many times in a single session, so that you will have tried to memorize many different lists and will have been tested several times for recall of pictures in each of the 7 windows.

By analyzing normal-hearing adults' approaches to this Position Probe task, we have found that the most efficient memorizers treat each 7-item list as though it has two distinct parts (Belmont & Butterfield, 1971; Butterfield & Belmont, 1971). The first part contains the first 4 items; the second contains the last 3. The efficient method calls for actively rehearsing the first 4 items as a group, but then spending very little time on the last 3 items, each of which is simply glanced at, or at the most labeled once. Since the test item can be exposed immediately, if it turns out to be one of the last 3 (which were just seen), its position among them can be recalled immediately and easily by echo alone. If, however, the test item was one of the first 4 in the list, its position among them can be recaptured by repeating the originally rehearsed items and associating them with the appropriate windows. The function of the "maintenance rehearsal" (Craik & Lockhart, 1972) applied to these early 4 items is, afterall, precisely to permit recall following some intervening activity, such as the echo memory processing that follows it. This method of rehearsing the 4 early items of a 7-item list but merely attending to the last 3 may be called a 4-3 "cumulative-rehearsal-fast-finish" method (Pinkus & Laughery, 1970). It is easily teachable to deaf or normal-hearing people (Belmont, Karchmer & Pilkonis, 1976). In combination with the materials variable (pictures vs. words), the memory demands variable (rehearsal vs. echo) provides the test we seek for the hypothesis of imperfectly known language: Only when tested for recall of rehearsed English words should the deaf students show a deficiency.

The materials were lists of 7 items. The items for each list were drawn without replacement from one or the other of two pools. One pool contained 12 line drawings, the other the 12 corresponding nouns, as shown in Fig. 1. Native signers had selected the pictures as having clear sign equivalents, and as being easily identifiable.

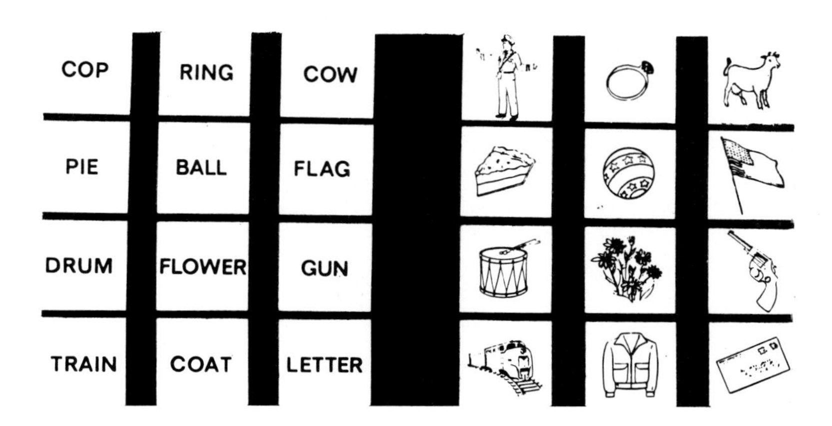

Fig. 1. The Stimulus Materials

Design

Each person was seen individually for 4 sessions. Each session involved 35 different lists, through each of which the person paced himself and then tried to recall the position where the test item had appeared in that list. The correct position varied unsystematically from list to list so as to be unpredictable, but to result in each position's being tested once every 7 lists. During the first session, nobody was given instruction about how to memorize the lists. For the remaining 3 sessions, everybody followed instructions to use the efficient 4-3 cumulative-rehearsal-fast-finish method in which the lists' first 4 items were to be rehearsed as a group (either signing or naming), followed by a rapid labeling of the last 3 items (signing or naming without rehearsal). Instructions were signed and spoken to the deaf; spoken to the hearing. In all sessions, the first 21 lists were pictures or words; the remaining 14 lists were done with the material not used in the first 21. Each session began with the type of material used at the end of the preceding session, an alternation that yielded an ABABABAB design. Seven people in each hearing-status group started Session I with words; the other seven started with pictures. All were introduced to Session I by being shown all of the words and pictures side-by-side, on the single display shown in Fig. 1, with the paired equivalents being explicitly drawn to their attention.

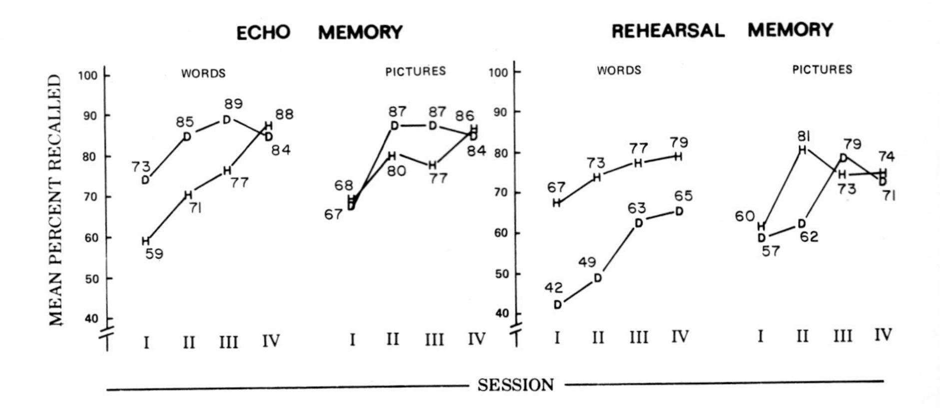

Fig. 2. Deaf (D) vs. Hearing (H) subjects' recall of pictures and words from rehearsal and nonrehearsal (echo) memory.

RESULTS AND DISCUSSION

Fig. 2 shows the two groups' recall accuracies as they changed across the 4 sessions. The left panel shows the changes for the last 3 (echo memory) items, which were not rehearsed under the 4-3 method used in Sessions II-IV. The right panel shows the session-by-session changes for the first 4 items, which were systematically rehearsed under the instructed method. For each memory system, the results for words and pictures are shown separately.

We note that for both systems and both materials, hearing and deaf groups alike improved their recall accuracy over sessions as they gained practice with the instructed method. This result confirms our previous study's finding (Belmont *et al*.1976) that the instructed method is effective for hearing and deaf people. That it was the instruction, and not simply practice that caused the gains over sessions, is confirmed by our earlier finding that uninstructed normal-hearing adolescents do not improve, even with extended practice on this task (Belmont & Butterfield, 1971).

Now consider the results for echo memory alone (Fig. 2, left panel). For each group the curve for pictures is similar to that for words, meaning that echo memory for words and pictures was not different. This leaves us with the already noted improvement over sessions, and an overall difference between the groups on echo memory: The deaf group was better than the hearing for both materials, except on the last session, where the hearing equalled the deaf.

Figure 2's right panel shows three things about rehearsal memory. First, both groups recalled both materials better under instruction (Sessions II-IV) than when free to memorize as they wished (Session I). Second, there is practically no overall group difference in rehearsal memory for pictures. Third, the deaf group showed a large and consistent recall deficit when tested with words. This specific recall deficiency, appearing as it does only with words (not pictures), and only for the rehearsed parts of the lists, suggests to us that the deaf subjects in this study had no fundamental memory deficiencies, nor did they have any trouble with the experimental situation itself. When they had received the same amount of practice with equivalent memory techniques, their rehearsal memory for pictures equalled that of a group of normal-hearing subjects (matched by school grade), and their echo memory somewhat exceeded the contrast group's for both materials. The deaf subjects did fall short, however, when they were required to actively memorize printed English words. Even the rehearsal technique that served them so well for pictures was insufficient alone to deal with the verbal materials. Bearing in mind that these deaf people were given 4 separate sessions of intensive practice at memorizing various subsets of a single pool of 12 simple English nouns, and these words were the names of the corresponding pictures, it appears that the deaf people's particular recall deficiency for words is not a trivial finding.

A simple thought experiment erases all doubt. Suppose that instead of words, we were to use pictures of finger-spelled letters, and instead of normal-hearing high-school students, we use normal-hearing college students who had been studying sign language. The apparent memory deficiency in such a study would be seen in normal-hearing people's rehearsal memory for finger-spelled letters, whereas for those materials the deaf people's rehearsal memory would be particularly strong: Thus, the results would be exactly opposite to those we have just reported. Did we observe a memory deficit in deaf people? The question seems to be meaningless, as it must also be when applied to any other special population whose noncognitive peculiarities influence cognitive test performance.

ACKNOWLEDGMENTS

This research was supported by USPHS research grants HD-00870 and HD-08911; RCDA HD-00026; and post-doctoral research training grant HD-00183. The Office of Demographic Studies (Raymand Trybus, Director) also provided support.

REFERENCES

Belmont, J.M. and Butterfield, E.C. (1971). Learning strategies as determinants of memory deficiencies. *Cognitive Psychology*. 2, 411-420.

Belmont, J.M., Karchmer, M.A., and Pilkonis, P.A. (1976). Instructed rehearsal strategies' influence on deaf memory processing. *Journal of Speech and Hearing Research*. 19, 36-47.

Blair, F.X. (1957). A study of the visual memory of deaf and hearing children. *American Annals of the Deaf*. 102, 254-263.

Butterfield, E.C. and Belmont, J.M. (1971). Relations of storage and retrieval strategies as short-term memory processes. *Journal of Experimental Psychology*. 89, 319-328.

Conrad, R. (1973). Some correlates of speech coding in the short-term memory of the deaf. *Journal of Speech and Hearing Research*. 16, 375-384.

Craig, E.M. (1973). Role of mental imagery in free recall of deaf, blind and normal subjects. *Journal of Experimental Psychology*. 97, 249-253.

Craik, F.I.M. and Lockhart, R.S. (1972). Levels of processing: A framework for memory research. *Journal of Verbal Learning and Verbal Behavior*. 11, 671-684.

Doehring, D.G. (1960). Visual spatial memory in aphasic children. *Journal of Speech and Hearing Research*. 3, 138-149.

Pinkus, A.L. and Laughery, K.R. (1970). Recoding and grouping processes in short-term memory: Effects of subject-paced presentation. *Journal of Experimental Psychology*. 85, 335-341.

Ross, B.M. (1969). Sequential visual memory and the limited magic of the number seven. *Journal of Experimental Psychology*. 80, 339-347.

Wallace, G. and Corballis, M.C. (1973). Short-term memory and coding strategies in the deaf. *Journal of Experimental Psychology*. 99, 334-348.

KINAESTHETIC MEMORY IN DEAF CHILDREN

E. Gulian, P. Hinds, F. Fallside, S. Brooks
Cambridge University Engineering Department, Cambridge, England.

ABSTRACT

Speech acquisition in profoundly deaf children is investigated in experimental (E) and control groups. The E group uses a computer-based aid which displays the visual information in the form of the shape of the vocal tract for single sounds as well as providing feedback about the success of the children's articulatory attempts. The results to date suggest a particular relationship between short and long term memory in kinaesthetic articulatory learning. This may be attributable to a priming mechanism necessary in order to ensure the encoding of the kinaesthetic information.

INTRODUCTION

Memory processes in the deaf have been studied for a long time. The overwhelming majority of these studies are of a laboratory-experimental type concerned with verbal memory, i.e. with the ability of deaf people to encode, store and retrieve linguistic information. Recent experiments on short-term memory (STM) in the deaf have shown that they use a different speech code type from normal-hearing people, (Conrad 1972). It was also found that they present deficiencies in the free recall of words (Craig 1973) and in the recognition of semantically related words (Frumkin and Anisfield 1977). Ling (1975) found that hearing-impaired people were least different from normal-hearing ones in the recall of nonverbal sequences, recalling syllable sequences with different vowels more accurately than nonverbal sequences, with consonant sequences poorly remembered.

The data presented here are derived from a project concerned with practical problems: 1) whether using a computer-based aid proves more beneficial in articulation acquisition than ordinary speech training methods; 2) whether training with the computer-aid allows generalization in the form of transfer of the learned sounds into spontaneous speech. Answering these practical questions raises a number of theoretical issues like the mechanisms enabling a child to use a visual input to master kinaesthetic response previously lacking; and the characteristic features of kinaesthetic memory which make possible the storage and retrieval of these patterns. Clinical and experimental evidence indicates that the control and perception of movements are very poor when the sensory channel mediating them is not functioning. Little is known about the specific characteristics of proprioceptive stimulation that allow the individual to control changes in position, rate or acceleration of his limbs. This is even more true for such fine movements as those of the articulators. In the case of deaf children we deal not only with subjects who lack practically any experience with their vocal apparatus, but who also are deprived of the normal feedback channel, the auditory one.

METHOD

Subjects

The investigation is carried out with 7 experimental (E) subjects, 4 juniors and 3 infants and 7 control (C) subjects in the same age range. All subjects are congenitally profoundly deaf (mean hearing loss 90 dB) and they have very poor speech, if any. The subjects' intelligence and emotionality scores cover the normal distribution range.

Apparatus

The E subjects are trained on a computer-based aid (CBA) which uses a linear prediction areas analysis to provide a display of approximate vocal tract shape for sustained sounds. There are two area traces in the display: 1) a stationary target trace which represents a correct sound and 2) the attempt trace appearing every time a subject utters a sound, and which represents the current segment of speech being analysed by the computer. In each, the horizontal axis is the linear distance along the vocal tract from glottis to the lips and the vertical axis is smoothed log area. When the subject's attempt is correct it overlaps the stationary display and 'freezes', so that the subject gets an immediate feedback. The display provides the means for gradual learning, from a rough approximation of the phoneme when the student's production freezes at level 1, to a normal utterance, when it freezes at level 5. Details about the CBA are given in

Fallside and Brooks (1976).

The training programme

The training programme common to E and C consists of teaching vowel (V) articulation, when Vs are embedded into meaningful monosyllabic words. The sequence of trained V follows the development of speech in normal-hearing children and emphasizes the contrasts between Vs. So far, the Ss have been trained on 10 phonemes. Each phoneme is practised for several consecutive sessions which form a training cycle. Some phonemes were practised for several training cycles (between 2 and 4), the time intervals between them varying between 2 months and 1 year. The training procedure differs between E and C Ss. The E Ss use the CBA for 5 to 10 min./per session according to age, following an instrumental type of learning: the Ss are presented with a visual input and their response to it is immediately reinforced, positively or negatively (the trace on the display freezes or disappears). The C Ss are trained by their teachers who use conventional techniques. All Ss are individually trained. However, the E infants were trained together during the first 3 months of the assessment.

Data processing

The raw results yielded by the Ss CBA-interface reflect performance proficiency at each of the five levels of difficulty. It was therefore necessary to calculate a composite index which reflects the overall performance in any one session. The index takes into account the correct responses against the total number of attempts at each level of difficulty, using a weighting which obeys a linear law, normalised to a total weighting of unity. This provides a learning score which shows the rate of learning at each stage weighted in favour of the most difficult level of performance. The data thus obtained were then plotted for repetition rate across subjects and phonemes, separately for infants and juniors. Other data derived from the identification test. In this task, panels of adult naive people were asked to listen to tape recordings of the children's speech. These samples of speech were elicited by pictures in the absence of the CBA, before training and after training at different intervals of time. When presented to the panels, the recordings were randomized over Ss and phonemes/words. The panel members were asked to write down what they heard or to leave a blank when they could not understand anything. Scoring as presented here takes into account correctly identified words and vowels trained. Results in this task yield intelligibility scores

(% correct). These results were plotted against time from the last day of training to the day of the recording, for every phoneme/per child and then averaged separately for E and C groups.

RESULTS

There are two angles from which we can evaluate whether and to what extent the speech skills acquired during training are subjected to decay over time. First, we consider what happens between the periods (cycles) of training. In this case, there is either a total lack of practice on the CBA (during holidays) or practice on different phonemes (during terms). It seemed a reasonable assumption that in either case, a rather long interval of time between clusters of sessions devoted to the training of the same sound would result in an initial decrement in performance when learning would be resumed, which would subsequently be superseded and performance would improve due to the renewed practice on the computer.

In Fig. 1 you can see the infants' performance level (successful attempts on the computer) during successive training cycles. It is notable that every new cycle of training begins and in general remains at a higher level than the previous one. It is as though no forgetting takes place between

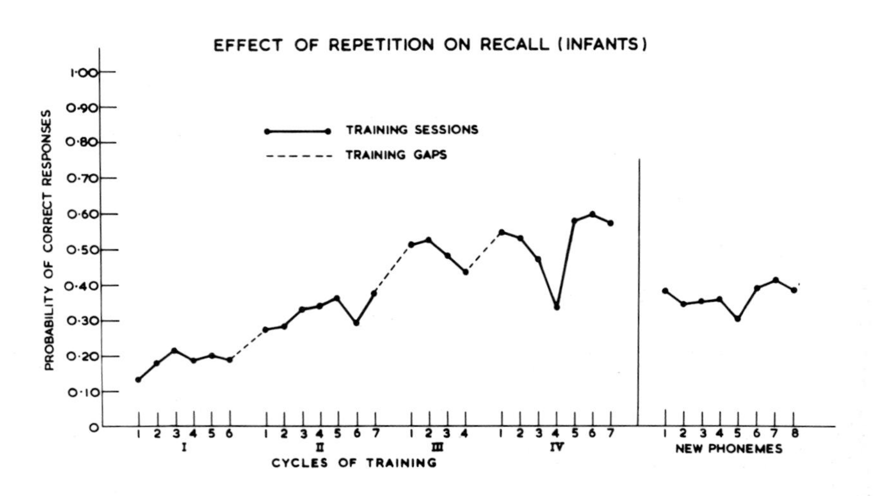

Fig. 1 Effect of repetition on recall (infants)

clusters of sessions. On the contrary, there is a definite improvement in their ability of matching the target with repetition on the CBA, but only after an interval of time. Within the same cycle of training there is little progress, if any. Thus, in the infants' case the hypothesis was disproved. What happens when new phonemes are introduced for training? In this case, the infants reach a lower performance level, but still higher than that achieved during the first training cycle. It seems that the infants have acquired to a certain extent the necessary ability to control their speech output: new but related tasks enable them to generalize this skill. A somewhat different picture emerges from the juniors' performance (Fig. 2). In their case, after the first two

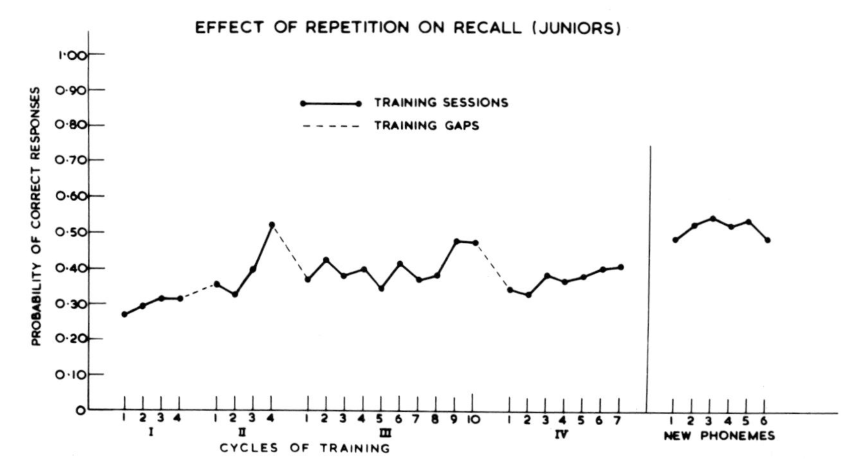

Fig. 2 Effect of repetition on recall (juniors)

training cycles performance reaches a kind of plateau. On the other hand, learning of new sounds produces definite progress. This suggests that recall in older children is less dependent on a great number of repetitions. Forgetting between training cycles, in their case too, seems not to occur. The control over the speech apparatus seems to be achieved quicker and to generalize to a greater extent than in infants. There are, thus, developmental differences in the articulatory proficiency and memory for particular articulatory movements and the transfer to other articulatory movements. The second way of looking at the deaf children's memory is to consider whether and to what extent their articulation of different phonemes/words deteriorates over time independently of their achievements on the CBA, i.e. when they have no visual input or feedback, and when the judgement of their articulatory proficiency is made by the human ear. In Figs 3 and 4 we present the intelligibility scores for juniors and infants (E and C groups) recorded at different intervals after

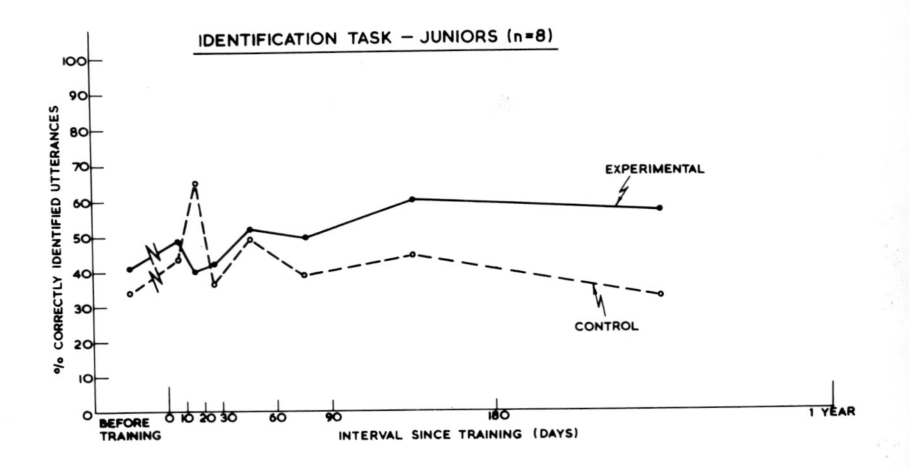

Fig. 3 Intelligibility scores in an identification test

training, as identified by naive listeners. It was hypothesized that the general trend would show a plateau in recall a short time after training, followed by a steady decay in memory over time. It can be seen that this hypothesis was confirmed only in the control group's case. The E children's speech production seems to be better recognized when the phonemes/words are recorded 3, 6, 9 or even more months after they were learned than within a month after training. Differences between E and C junior groups are close to statistical significance at the 60-90 days interval ($p = 0.0681$), but very clearly achieve it at the 90-180 and 180 days-1 year intervals (Mann Whitney U Test, $p = 0.0314$ and $p = 0.0256$, respectively). The same trend is found in infants, too; the E children's utterances are better understood when they are recorded a long time after training.

These results suggested that once a particular phoneme/word is learned, subsequent lack of training even for rather

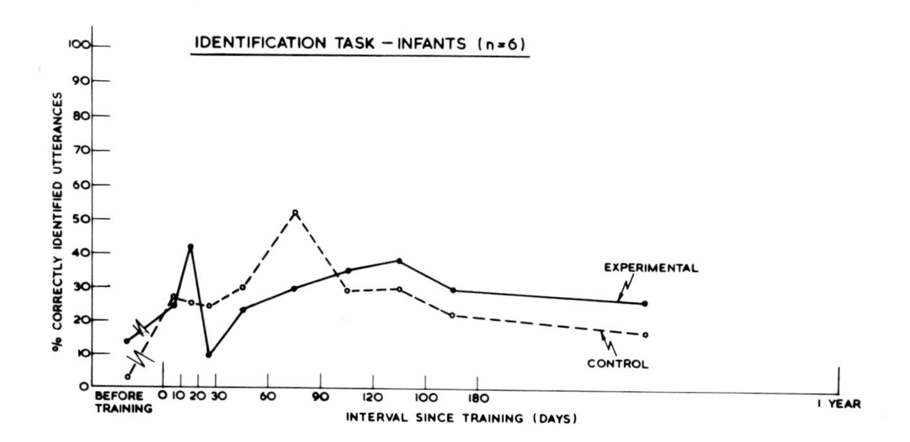

Fig. 4 Intelligibility scores in an identification test

long periods of time does not lead to a considerable impairment in articulatory proficiency, to forgetting. This is true for the E group who have benefited from the instrumental learning and the permanent feedback provided by the CBA, and it is not true for the C who missed this type of systematic training. To summarize: deaf juniors recall learned phonemes/words over a long period of time and they are able to use the acquired skills for producing new phonemes at higher levels of performance, Deaf infants benefit from many repetitions spaced in time. During these interruptions in the learning of particular phonemes/words not only no forgetting takes place but when resuming training an improvement is clearly noticeable. The slope of decay in memory is gradual: at some points in time they remember better a long rather than a short time after learning.

DISCUSSION

Our results point clearly towards a long term memory for articulatory skills in deaf children. In other words, what has been encoded and can be retrieved is not a particular phoneme or word as such, but the general ability of controlling the articulators. The evidence of this ongoing study points to the very strong role kinaesthetic input and feedback play in learning to articulate. In the absence of auditory cues, retention of this skill depends almost exclusively upon the intrinsic, proprioceptive cues. However, the differences in acquisition and retrieval observed between E and C Ss indicate that different learning strategies result in different achievements. Thus for E Ss during learning the visual feedback provided by the CBA has an important function in that it offers an immediate reinforcement, provides a standard criterion and ensures a consistent strategy in learning and rehearsal. But if the Ss relied entirely on this information, once this was removed their performance would steadily deteriorate to or near the pre-training level. The fact that little or no forgetting appears to take place for long periods of time shows that the kinaesthetic information plays the major role in learning and retention. On the other hand, this is what happens in the case of the C group. It is therefore likely that the instrumental reinforcement provided by the CBA facilitates the transfer from short to long term memory in a much more consistent way than the different and mixed procedures used with the C group. These findings are supported by the work of Belmont, Karchmer and Pilkonis (1976) who point to the dependence of primary memory processes (STM) on articulatory feedback and to the importance of instructed strategies in improving recall accuracy and speed.

The relationship between STM and LTM is further shown by the very slow decay found in articulatory ability over time. In normal-hearing children suffering from articulatory disorders it was found that recall of motor movements is relatively high over moderately long periods of time (5 days) and that retrieval of sounds from storage is presumably constrained by factors of facilitation and interference (Winitz and Bellerose 1975). Here, however, we presented evidence of retrieval from the memory store over much longer periods of time. It was shown that training sessions following closely together produce no marked improvement in performance and that clear-cut progress shows-up only after a training gap. This finding is akin to the phenomenon of reminiscence, which is described in a wide range of learning studies. In the present case, however, the chunks of time are of a totally different order than those found in reminiscence (months instead of minutes), but the bonus - the improvement in performance without practice is present. It is as if a facilitatory or priming mechanism is operating and ensures the encoding of the kinaesthetic information and its subsequent retrieval. Such improved proficiency in articulatory skills without any direct training fits the hypothesis of linguistic distinctive feature theory, too. A complementary explanation is that a process of generalization takes place. So far, no stimulus generalization gradient has been found in children suffering from articulatory disorders and generalization cannot be taken for granted (Costello and Bosler 1976). Nevertheless, it has been shown that sound training within the syllabic structure of words may accelerate generalization to unpracticed words, whereas training with isolated sequences may inhibit generalization to words (McReynolds 1972). Since the Ss in this study were trained on phonemes within monosyllabic words it is possible that generalization occurs consistently.

In conclusion: the stage we have reached in our research points to the ability of deaf children to master and remember articulatory skills. Hearing, while essential to clear articulation does not seem to be indispensable.

REFERENCES

Belmont, J.M., Karchmer, M.A., Pilkonis, P.A. (1976) Instructed rehearsal strategies influence on deaf memory processing, *Journal of Speech and Hearing Research*, 19, 36-47.

Costello, J., Bosler, S. (1976) Generalization and articulation instruction, *Journal of Speech and Hearing Disorders*, 41, 359-373.

Conrad, R. (1972) Short-term memory in the deaf: a test for speech coding, *British Journal of Psychology*, 63, 173-180.

Craig, E.M. (1973)Role of mental imagery in free recall of deaf, blind, and normal subjects, *Journal of Experimental Psychology*, 97, 249-253.

Fallside, F., Brooks, S. (1976) Real-time areagraph of continuous speech for analysis and speech training, *Electronics Letters*, 12, 515-516.

Frumkin, B., Anisfeld, M. (1977), Semantic and surface codes in the memory of deaf children, *Cognitive Psychology*, 9, 475-493.

Ling, A.H. (1975) Memory for verbal and nonverbal auditory sequences in hearing-impaired and normal-hearing children, *Journal of the American Audiology Society*, 1, 37-45.

McReynolds, L. (1972) Articulation generalization during articulation training, *Language and Speech*, 15, 149-155.

Winitz, H., Bellerose, B. (1975) Self-retrieval and articulatory retention, *Journal of Speech and Hearing Research*, 18, 166-177.

Acknowledgements. We thank the Medical Research Council for supporting this project. We also wish to acknowledge the valuable assistance given by Mr G. Bristow.

THE SHORT TERM MEMORY OF DEAF AND HEARING CHILDREN FOR SOME LETTERS OF THE ALPHABET

W.H. Edmondson
Department of Psychology
Bedford College (University of London),
Regent's Park, London NW1.

ABSTRACT

Performance of 36 deaf and 54 hearing children on a short-term memory test is reported, (see Conrad 1972). The test was designed to identify those deaf children consistently using a phonological memory code; the children concerned were participating in a study of deaf children's classroom communication. The results (consistent phonological coders - 0% of the deaf; 35% of the hearing) are not as straightforward as figures previously reported. Procedural improvements devised for the test facilitated the discovery of details of the children's coding schemes and similarities between deaf and hearing children. The role of handwriting as a memory code is discussed.

INTRODUCTION

An observational study of deaf children in classrooms is being done with a view to discovering more about the communication skills of the children and how these skills are suited to the classroom endeavour and communication with the teacher. It is of pedagogical importance to know more about the real behaviour of deaf children in what, for them, constitutes a difficult environment. This is because most of the teaching in classrooms in schools for the deaf depends on speech and the blackboard.

To support the analysis of the video-tapes made in the classrooms some information about the individual children has been gathered. One important measure is that of the use of phonological coding in memory. Conrad (1972) has shown that deaf and hearing children differ in respect of the use of such coding in short-term memory. This paper is concerned with the testing of the children for phonological coding in short-term memory.

METHOD

Conrad reports several methods for testing for phonological coding in short-term memory, all of which depend on analysis of recall/report errors when letters of the alphabet are used as stimuli, (1970,1972,1973). The scheme employed in this study is described below and the differences between the procedure used, and the approach of Conrad, are indicated.

Two groups of letters were used; B C D P T - the phonologically confusing set, and K N W X Y - the visually confusing set, (see Conrad 1973). The letter V was excluded from Conrad's groups (he used B C D P T V and K N V W X Y) because its membership of both groups might a) cause additional confusion, b) complicate analysis of the responses.

Use of two groups of five letters makes possible a second refinement. With ten 'words' composed of the same five letters each letter can appear equally often in each position and can be followed equally often by the other letters. Obvious letter sequences such as BCD, WXY can be excluded. Thus twenty 'words' are required for the two groups of letters. For presentation the B group and K group 'words' were intermingled in a pseudo-random way to avoid the possibility of a child predicting which group of letters would be displayed next. Conrad reports (1972, 1973) the presentation of the two types of 'word' in alternate succession. It was decided that the letters should be presented in groups of five, as opposed to five individual letters presented sequentially, so that each child was not obliged to use a sequential code if he did not wish to. Conrad has used sequential presentation (1973) and simultaneous presentation (1972).

The 'words' were produced by a Varityper Headliner Model 820. Two sizes of print were used: 1.8 cms high (V72/52U font at letter spacing of five machine units) and 0.7 cms high (V30/197 font, upper case, at five machine units letter spacing). The two fonts are sans serif.

KNWXY

BCDPT

Fig. 1 Examples of the two fonts used

The strip of photographic paper output from the machine was trimmed, cut up, and glued on to cards. The cards were covered with clear adhesive film to allow them to be kept clean. Conrad used letters 4 cms high (1972).

Conrad arranged for the display to be visible for a period of time equivalent to 1 second/letter, (1972), or for the letters to be presented at the rate of 1 letter/second, (1973). However, it is important to arrange for the task to be equally difficult for all the children, as far as possible. It is desired that the children make some errors and the nature of the errors is of interest. For comparison between the children to be possible they should be making equivalent numbers of errors. The method chosen to do this was as follows. The children were tested individually. Each child was given a few practice trials (with extra cards made for the purpose) where the display of the cards (held up one at a time, at 'reading' distance, by the experimenter) was monitored with a stopwatch to find a display time likely to yield about 50% errors - the experimenter assessing this informally. This time was then adhered to for the full set of 40 trials. Occasionally it proved necessary to adjust the presentation time after a few trials, when it was apparent that learning of the task was still taking place.

To recapitulate. The children were tested one at a time. The upper case letters were printed in groups of five, in carefully arranged order, and attached to display cards. These cards were shown, in pseudo-random order, one at a time, each for a period of time determined during practice trials. The display time was recorded.

The child wrote down her response immediately after the card was removed from view, but delays caused by rehearsal or forgetfulness were not discouraged. The child was obliged to guess rather than omit any item through lapse of memory. After twenty trials with one print size a new response sheet was produced and the child continued with twenty trials of the other print size. Thus for each size of print the child's responses were always available to her. Each size of print was equally often used first. As part of the explanation of the test routine each child was shown the packs of cards - both type sizes - and the nature of the 'words' printed.

The test was applied to 36 deaf children (17 girls, 19 boys. Mean age 11.7 years, s.d. 1.26) and 54 hearing children (27 girls, 27 boys. Mean age 11.5 years, s.d. 1.37). Seven schools were involved.

RESULTS

A child's responses can be one of four types:

1 KB Greater accuracy of report for the K group of letters and greater number of transposition errors for report of the B group.

2 BK Converse of type 1.

3 BB As type 1 but with greater accuracy of report for the B group.

4 KK As type 1 but with greater number of transposition errors for the K group.

(A transposition error is defined as an incorrect response from the appropriate stimulus group.)

The transposition errors are of interest because, it can be argued, it is the predominance of transposition errors for the B group, error type 1, which indicates the presence of phonological coding, (see Conrad 1973). Thus the great majority of hearing children, and those deaf children using a 'hearing-child-like' phonological code, will be expected to have responses of type 1.

TABLE 1

Error type	1 KB	2 BK	3 BB	4 KK	
Print size					Population
large	30	16	3	5	Hearing
(both)	(19)	(7)	(2)	(1)	
small	26	15	10	3	
large	3	17	11	5	Deaf
(both)	(0)	(13)	(5)	(4)	
small	2	20	10	4	

Table 1 shows the children's responses according to error type, stimulus print size, and population. The figures in brackets are the numbers of children making the same type of error regardless of stimulus print size, i.e. those children behaving consistently.

Two things are clear from the figures. Print size is important. Only 19 (35%) of the hearing children are consistent phonological coders, with none of the deaf children behaving consistently in the same error group.

Other relevant figures are presentation times - Deaf: mean 7.1 secs. s.d. 2.3; Hearing: mean 1.8secs. s.d. 0.47 - and correct response percentages - Deaf: mean 47.32% s.d.12.8; Hearing: mean 59.69% s.d.14.27. t tests on the correct response percentages show that the two groups are significantly different, but for responses of type 2 and 3 the populations are only different for the case of type 2 errors with large print stimuli.

Detailed statistical analysis indicates that type 2 and type 3 errors are especially interesting. These show that to a considerable extent the deaf and hearing children are behaving alike. Also, more detail is provided on the effect of print size.

Correlation of the 'response by position' and 'response by stimulus' confusion matrices reveals, for type 2 errors, that print size has only a slight effect on the deaf children, but a more pronounced effect on the hearing children. With large print stimuli the deaf and hearing children's responses (overall) correlate at about 0.5 ($P < 0.01$), but the responses to the K group stimuli fail to correlate significantly. With small print stimuli the overall responses correlate at about 0.35 ($P < 0.05$) but in this case both the B group and the K group responses fail to correlate and the two sets of K group responses appear very different.

For type 3 errors the analysis reveals that the deaf children are strongly affected by print size, the hearing children much less so. The correlation between deaf and hearing children's responses is about 0.5 ($P < 0.01$) for the small print case, and very low for the large print case. It also appears that the deaf children's responses to large print B group stimuli are unusual. Thus, with large print B group stimuli the deaf children making type 3 errors are making transpositions which are completely different from those made by deaf children shown small print, or hearing children shown either size of print.

DISCUSSION

The test has accomplished that for which it was devised - not one of the deaf children is a consistent phonological coder in the sense that hearing children can be. Deaf children could of course be using an entirely different phonological code, (see Dodd 1976, and Dodd and Hermelin 1977). However, it seems probable that for a phonological code based on lip-reading the B group will still constitute a phonologically confusing set of stimuli. Certainly the status of phonological memory codes in deaf children is a complex issue unlikely to be resolved by the results of simple tests such as that reported here.

The errors of type 2 and type 3 are particularly interesting. It is here that the similarity between the deaf and hearing children is revealed. Type 4 errors are made by a small section of the population studied (12 children in all) and are inexplicable. Both deaf and hearing children are strongly affected by print size and correlations between the two populations are poor (large print K group stimuli 0.36, small print B group stimuli -0.38).

The codings responsible for errors of type 2 or 3 are not obvious. Visual confusions amongst the K group of letters might give rise to type 2 errors - and also to errors of recognition. Wallace and Corballis (1973) showed the latter not to be a problem - with serial presentation and with different letters of the alphabet. It is not clear that their finding applies in this case. Other factors, many apparently common to both deaf and hearing children, cause further confusion, both for the subjects and the experimenter. These are, briefly; 1 - orthographic influence: responses are made to look word-like by the intrusion of vowels and consonants not present in the stimuli; 2 - semantic influence: TCP: a common disinfectant, PT: physical training; 3 - unfamiliarity with the alphabet: BCDPT are easy because 'they are at the beginning', KNWXY are difficult letters, 'don't use them much' - some of these explanations were quite convoluted; 4 - print size: big print 'easy to read', small print easy to 'see in a glance'; 5 - grouped nature of the stimuli not obvious; 6 - group similarities considered helpful: BCDPT are easy because they rhyme, KNWXY easy because they look alike - as with 3 and 4 above there is a problem with introspection here, and the children's responses do not always agree with their estimates; 7 - handwriting as a code:'air-writing' was sometimes done during rehearsal (Conrad also noted this - personal communication); 8 - stimulus or task specific codes: a'visual'code for 'acoustic' material, an 'acoustic' code for 'visual' material, or one code for the first three letters and a different code for the last two; 9 - idiosyncratic codes: Pelman systems, finger spelling (apparently not widely used as a code amongst the deaf), reverse ordered reporting;(factor 7 seemed too frequent for inclusion here).

A further problem is that the deaf children did not like being only 50% correct. They were very inclined to change their strategies in an attempt to improve performance (c.f. hearing children).

Despite all this the fact remains that four groups of

children can be distinguished on the basis of the types of errors made (the categorisations being clear) and two of these groups contain sufficient numbers of children for the causes of the errors to be worth considering.

It seems that the major difference between type 2 and type 3 responders is that errors of type 3 - the BB group - arise through unfamiliarity with the alphabet and with the K group in particular. This is manifest as a tendency for the B group letters to be favoured for response, yet when they were appropriate they were less accurate (c.f. type 2 response). In addition, fewer of these children know the alphabet. There is no significant age difference between the two groups of children.

The type 2 errors probably reflect no more than that the K group are visually confusing at the recognition level. The variety of codes used overtly by children in this group would seem to preclude any simple explanation based on memory code confusion.

GENERAL DISCUSSION

The possible role of handwriting as a memory code is worthy of comment. Apart from the observed behaviour of many of the children (mainly deaf), large numbers reported some of the letters in lower case (no instructions were given on this). Moreover, the use of upper case was strongly correlated with correctness of response (about 0.9 - $P < 0.05$) except for the deaf children making type 1 errors where the correlation is much lower. Lower case forms of the letters might be expected to be preferred for such a code because they are simpler to execute and more frequently encountered and used in classrooms Recall errors would lack any information about the upper case form of the letter and thus the response would be in lower case. The situation is not clear however, because 'upper-caseness' could be remembered as part of the task, and lapses in memory of this fact could cause errors to be reported in lower case.

Nonetheless the use of such a memory code makes a lot of sense from the child's point of view - the classroom is the location of many copying tasks and some of these may, for the child, involve nonesense material. Imagery based on handwriting, with or without a visual component, is well suited to the copying task.

Possible support for the suggestion of handwriting as a memory code comes from the Wallace and Corballis (1973) study, where recall was much improved in the non-oral deaf children by arranging for handwritten confirmation of the letters perceived, prior to recall of the sequences.

It is not suggested that handwriting in memory is a predominant code, merely that it is available. There is no reason to expect any one form of imagery to be predominant. The child who selects a memory code to suit the task is demonstrating that she has a repertoire of such codes available. This sort of behaviour reflects good experimental design (lack of constraint on the child to use a specific code) but at the same time makes the results of any simple test very confusing. The point raised by Morris (1977) - that effective codes do not show up in such tests - is pertinent, but nevertheless the results can be thought-provoking.

Important questions are raised but not answered by this sort of test. If a child seems unfamiliar with the alphabet, in memory, how has this arisen, what is its significance, and what should a teacher do about it? Why is print size important? If a child is using many different codes in task specific ways are these efficiently managed, or does the management cause problems? Development of task specific code usage has been explored (Samuels, Hiscock and Kinsbourne 1978), but the deaf population may be 'at risk' here. They may develop more idiosyncratic codes which cause problems as the child grows older and the codes become inadequate. For some children the problem seems severe - remembering how to remember. How do teachers identify these children and what do they do with them?

Is an answer to many of these questions to be found by studying semantic coding? Frumkin and Anisfeld (1977) note the 'weighty role of semantic coding in the memory of deaf children'. Does this arise, as seems possible, because of the stress placed on interpretation in communication with deaf chilren? Interpretation requires appreciation of context, and thus context dependent or semantically influenced codes might be expected. Some of the hearing children could be labouring under the same burden.

The test has revealed the need for a more effective assessment of imagery in memory, so that teachers, parents, psychologists, and others involved with children can better understand the problems encountered by children - deaf or hearing - who are trying to understand the world around them.

ACKNOWLEDGEMENTS

The author is grateful to the Leverhulme Trust Fund for financial support and to the staff and pupils in the schools participating in the study.

REFERENCES

Conrad, R. (1970). 'Short-term memory processes in the deaf.' *Br.J.Psychol.* 61(2), 179-195.

Conrad, R. (1972). 'Short-term memory in the deaf: a test for speech coding.' *Br.J.Psychol.* 63(2), 173-180.

Conrad, R. (1973). 'Some correlates of speech coding in the short-term memory of the deaf.' *Journal of Speech and Hearing Research.* 16, 375-384.

Dodd, B. (1976). 'The phonological systems of deaf chidren.' *Journal of Speech and Hearing Disorders.* 41(2), 185-198.

Dodd, B. and Hermelin, B. (1977). 'Phonolgical coding by the prelinguistically deaf.' *Perception and Psychophysics.* 21(5), 413-417.

Frumkin, B. and Anisfeld, M. (1977). 'Semantic and surface codes in the memory of deaf children.' *Cognitive Psychology.* 9, 475-493.

Morris, P.E. (1977). 'On the importance of acoustic encoding in short-term memory: the error of studying errors.' *Bulletin of The British Psychological Society.* 30, 380.

Samuels, M., Hiscock, M., and Kinsbourne, M. (1978). 'Development of Strategies for Recalling Letter Sequences.' *Journal of Experimental Child Psychology.* 25(2), 298-314.

Wallace, G. and Corballis, M.C. (1973). 'Short-term memory and coding strategies in the deaf.' *Journal of Experimental Psychology.* 99(3), 334-348.

STRATEGIES IN MEMORY

TEST EXPECTATIONS IN TEXT LEARNING

G. d'Ydewalle and H. Rosselle
Department of Psychology,
University of Leuven,
B-3000 Leuven (Belgium)

ABSTRACT

In the experiment, half of the subjects expected to be tested by a series of open questions, while the other half expected a multiple-choice test. Subjects were given 4 min. to learn a first text, and were immediately administered the first and expected test. After learning a second text, one group received its second and expected test, while another group received its second but unexpected test. A superior performance was found when the received test was expected. Further analyses indicated that the subjects used learning strategies which were appropriate for the expected test.

INTRODUCTION

In recent years, there has been a growing interest in the influence of test expectations. The first studies with lists of unrelated words produced either conflicting or undefined results (Freund, Brelsford, and Atkinson, 1969; Loftus, 1971; Postman and Jenkins, 1948). However, a clear pattern of findings has emerged in a number of recent studies: Expecting a recall test apparently enhances various subsequent test performances compared with the expectation of a recognition test, and this finding is particularly reliable when the test requires a recall performance (Bruce and Cofer, 1967; d'Ydewalle, 1977; Hall, Grossman, and Elwood, 1976; Hall, Miskiewicz, and Murray, 1977; Maisto, DeWaard, and Miller, 1977; Naus, Ornstein, and Kreshtool, 1976). Studies with texts and prose materials have produced a diffuse picture of results (Hakstian, 1971; Kulhavy, Dyer, and Silver, 1975; Kumar,

Rabinsky, and Pandey, 1977; Meyer, 1934 and 1936; Peeck and Knippenberg, 1977; Sax and Collet, 1968; Vallance, 1947). This absence of clear findings is interesting since several studies (Douglass and Tallmadge, 1934; Meyer, 1936; Silvey, 1951; Terry, 1933) reported that students believe that their learning strategies are affected by the type of test anticipated.

The present study was designed to gather further data on text learning, taking special care of the subjects' thorough understanding of the kind of test to be expected. This was done by giving a first learning session followed by the expected test. Only after learning a second text was the test manipulated so that half of the subjects received the expected test, while the other half received the other (unexpected) test. The subjects were provided with history texts containing a large amount of factual information (e.g., numerous names and dates). In contrast to lists of unrelated words, this factual information was integrated in a structure provided by the chronological sequence of major historical events. A restricted study time was used, making a perfect knowledge of the text impossible. It is assumed that this would enhance the use of different learning strategies most appropriate to the test expected. Two kinds of tests were used: A multiple-choice test and open questions. The open-questions test was a modified multiple-choice test without the response alternatives.

If the learning material can be acquired by different learning strategies, we assume that the subjects will use the learning strategies most appropriate to the expected test: Subjects with the expected test should show a superior performance compared to subjects given an unexpected test. However, studies using unrelated words indicated that a recall set enhances test performance, independently of the test form received. Therefore, one can formulate one alternative hypothesis that expecting open questions produces a better test performance, no matter whether the test consists of open questions or multiple-choice presentation.

METHOD

Material

To construct texts for this experiment, a book (Ploetz, 1969) containing a list of historical dates and events was used. Each text, one about the East-Roman Empire from 527 to 751 (Text I) and the other more specifically about the history of Constantinople from the 12th century till 1453 (Text II), contained 10 names of important persons, 10 historical dates, and 10 major events. With a few exceptions (e.g., 1453), no names, dates, and events could be expected to be known by most of the ubjects. For each text, the number of words was kept equal within narrow limits: The lengths of Text I and Text II were 479 and 441 words, respectively. Every effort was made to produce natural, readable texts. A single page presentation without paragraphs was used for each text. Thirty questions about the 10 names, 10 dates, and 10 major historical events were formulated. The incorrect responses from a preliminary experiment provided the material for choosing three distractors to each question. Accordingly, the questions in the multiple-choice test were followed by four response alternatives, one correct and three incorrect. A set of written instructions on a single page preceded each text. The texts were followed by the thirty questions on 8 pages. The presentation of the questions were organized in 10 triplets: Each triplet contained one question about a name, one question about a date, and one question about a major historical event. The triplets were printed in the order of information provided in the text. The written instructions, the text, and the questions were printed on paper of different colors.

Postexperimental questions were constructed to assess how the subjects experienced the whole experiment. Each question was followed by a 7 point scale, with a verbal description of the two extremes: (a) Was the provided study time sufficient ? (largely enough-not sufficient); (b) Was the information in the text difficult to learn ? (very difficult-very easy); (c) How interesting were the texts ? (very interesting-not interesting); (d) Was the second text easier or more difficult than the first text ? (more difficult-easier); (e) Did you concentrate highly, while learning the text ? (high-low); (f) Was the text well organized ? (clear-confusing); (g) Were there too many details ? (too many-not too many); (h) Did you learn the second text in a similar way as the first text ? (similarly-differently); (i) Was the provided time to answer the questions sufficient ? (largely enough-not sufficient).

Design and Procedure

The design consisted of a factorial combination of 2x2x2 conditions, resulting in eight different kinds of booklets. For the one half, Text I preceded Text II, while Text I followed Text II for the other half. The first presented text was followed either by open questions or the multiple-choice test. The test after the second text was either open questions or a multiple-choice test.

The experiment took place in a large classroom during a regular lecture on English language for first-year students at the University of Leuven (Belgium). Only very few students did not want to participate and were allowed to leave the classroom. The data of two students were discarded as clear indications were available that they did not work seriously on the two texts. The remaining group consisted of 70 male and 87 female students, 18 to 20 years old. The experimental session lasted up to 45 min.

The eight different booklets were randomly mixed, and quickly distributed to the whole classroom by four research assistants. One restriction to the randomization was made to minimize opportunities for cheating: The subjects received alternatively Text I and Text II as first presented text, so that students seated next to each other never had the same text at the same time. The experimenter emphasized not to turn the pages before a signal was given. The four research assistants checked carefully whether the instructions were continuously respected. The checking procedure was easy as the pages of the booklet were of different colors and quickly recognizable from a moderate distance.

On the first page, the subjects were instructed that they would have 4 min. available to learn a history text which would be followed either by open questions or multiple-choice test. To make instructions clear, subjects received an example of the anticipated question form. The 4 min. were clearly indicated by the experimenter: A signal was given every time one min. elapsed. Time to respond to the 30 questions was unrestricted and the experimenter waited till everyone finished responding. The same procedure was followed for the second text and its test. Time to respond to the postexperimental questionnaire was also subject-paced.

RESULTS

The responses from the open questions were corrected by two independent judges. To avoid any bias favoring one or another hypothesis, the correction was made without knowledge of the condition to which the responses belonged. As the responses to the open questions could be more or less correct, a stringent criterion for correctness was used. The correlation coefficient between the scores of the two judges was found to be 0.97 indicating a high interscorer reliability. When the two judges occasionally disagreed, the subject's response was considered to be incorrect. All F values reported in this paper are significant beyond the 5% level.

First/Second Performance

Six factors were involved in the analysis of variance (ANOVA): Two texts (Text I and II), two types of tests following the texts, sex of subjects, answers on the first and second test half, the kind of question (names, dates, and events), and the performance on the first and second presented text. The analysis was carried out only on the data of the subjects receiving twice the expected test.

As guessing is easier when response alternatives are presented, more correct answers occurred when a multiple-choice test was given than when open questions had to be answered, $F\ (1,73) = 194.859$. Moreover, answers on the first test half were better than on the second test half, $F\ (1,73) = 160.143$. This effect is due to a primacy effect confounded with a test priority effect, as the information first provided in the text is also first tested. No negative transfer occurred between learning the two texts. Actually, the performance after the second text was reliably better than the performance on the first presented text, $F\ (1,73) = 46.768$. Text II (441 words) was better memorized than Text I (479 words), $F\ (1,73) = 8.951$. This is only clear on the performance of the second test half, with a slightly opposite tendency on the first test half. Accordingly, the interaction with test halves was highly significant, $F\ (1,73) = 65.760$. The kind of questions (names, dates, and events) produced a significant effect, $F\ (2,146) = 36.050$. However, this main effect is difficult to describe as it was involved in a few interactions. Those interactions were produced by a few exceptions to the following pattern of findings: The highest and lowest performance are found on the questions about names and dates, respectively.

Test Expectations on the Second Performance

In the ANOVA on the data from the second presented text, the factor First/Second Performance was dropped and replaced by the factor Test Expectations. Obviously, a number of significant findings were replicated which will not be reported here again. The key variable was the effect of test expectations which was not significant as main effect ($F < 1$). However, its interaction with the test received was quite reliable, $F\ (1,141) = 10.099$. The subjects performed better when they were given the expected test. On the multiple-choice test, subjects expecting a multiple-choice test chose more often correct responses than subjects expecting open questions. A separate ANOVA on the data from the multiple-choice test produced a significant F value: $F\ (1,73) = 7.875$. The opposite emerged from the data of the open-questions test: The expectation of an open-questions test enhanced the performance beyond the performance level of subjects expecting a multiple-choice test, $F(1,70) = 4.776$. Except with the test received, the effect of test expectation did not produce any other first-order interactions. Only one fourth-order interaction was significant beyond the 5% level. Its description would burden the discussion unduly.

Postexperimental Questionnaire

A multivariate analysis of variance (MANOVA) preceded ANOVAs on the data from the nine questions to determine the effects of four variables: Text I/II, test received and expected, and sex of subjects. Two MANOVA effects were significant: Test expectation, $F(9,135) = 2.788$, and the test received, $F(9,135) = 4.011$. The MANOVA effect of test expectation was mainly due to its significant ANOVA effect on Question (a), $F(1,143) = 8.112$. Study time was especially too short for subjects expecting open questions. However, the subjects expecting a multiple-choice test but receiving open questions had also the impression that the given study time was too short, producing a significant interaction between test expectation and test received, $F(1,143) = 4.831$. The significant MANOVA effect of the test received has to be explained by 4 significant ANOVA effects. Two of them were involved with a significant interaction with test expectation: The data from Question (a) (its interaction was explained in the preceding paragraph) and from Question (d). The interaction on Question (d) is to be described by the responses from the subjects expecting a multiple-choice test, but receiving open questions. They considered the second text as much more difficult to learn than the subjects from the other conditions. The two remaining significant main effects of the test received are found in the responses to the Questions (h) and (i): Subjects with a multiple-choice test reported that they used more different learning strategies on the two texts, and they had more time to respond than the subjects with open questions.

Generally speaking, the data from the postexperimental questionnaire may be interpreted in the following way: Expecting and receiving open questions more or less independently contribute in producing a general impression of participating in a difficult experiment. Subjects who were less frustrated by the short study time were from conditions with a multiple-choice test expected and received. Receiving open questions while expecting a multiple-choice test produced an impression of a greater difficulty of the text. Answering open questions also gave the impression of insufficient time to respond.

DISCUSSION

The data confirm one of the two hypotheses from the introduction. As subjects performed better when they received the expected test, one may assume that they learned and encoded the texts as a function of the test they anticipated. This finding is obtained after learning a second text. The performance on the second text for subjects receiving the expected test was higher than the performance on the first text: Proactive interference was not found. The same explanation in terms of encoding strategies can be given for this fact. After a first test performance, subjects had a better insight into which learning strategy is most appropriate to the test. Accordingly, they improved their performance on the second text.

What is the most appropriate learning strategy for responding either to open questions or to a multiple-choice test ? Some studies (see Marton and Säljö, 1976) indicated that students experience that expecting a multiple-choice test leads to a more superficial level of processing, often expressed by subjects as "attending to details", while expecting an essay or open-questions test is reported as leading to focusing on general principles and main points. To examine this possibility, we tabulated in three classes the kind of answers with a zero-score on the open-questions test: Either no answers, a too general answer, or a detailed but wrong answer. We expected more general answers with the expectation of open questions, while more detailed answers should occur with subjects expecting a multiple-choice test. The tabulation provided some confirmation of the prediction. From the incorrect answers with subjects expecting open questions, 16% came from too general answers, while in conditions with a multiple-choice test expected, only 7% were too general. From conditions with the expectation of open questions and a multiple-choice test respectively, 57% and 58% of the questions produced no answers at all. The same percent of "no answers" in both conditions provides evidence for rejecting the hypothesis that the surprise of the unexpected test may explain the lower performance level: Surprise should have enhanced the number of questions without responses.

REFERENCES

Bruce, D. and Cofer, C.N. (1967). An explanation of recognition and free recall as measures of acquisition and long-term retention. *Journal of Experimental Psychology*. 75, 283-289.

Douglass, H.R. and Tallmadge, M. (1934). How university students prepare for the new types of examination.

School and Society. 39, 318-320.
d'Ydewalle, G. (1977). *Test Expectancies in Free Recall and Recognition*. Unpublished manuscript, University of Leuven.
Freund, R.D., Brelsford, J.W., and Atkinson, R.C. (1969). Recognition vs. recall: Storage or retrieval differences ? *Quarterly Journal of Experimental Psychology*. 21, 214-224.
Hakstian, A.R. (1971). The effects of type of examination anticipated on test preparation and performance. *Journal of Educational Research*. 64, 319-324.
Hall, J.W., Grossman, L.R., and Elwood, K.D. (1976). Differences in encoding for free recall vs. recognition. *Memory and Cognition*. 4, 507-513.
Hall, J.W., Miskiewicz, R., and Murray, C.G. (1977). Effects of test expectancy (recall vs. recognition) on children's recall and recognition. *Bulletin of the Psychonomic Society*. 10, 425-428.
Jacoby, L.L. (1973). Test appropriate strategies in retention of categorized lists. *Journal of Verbal Learning and Verbal Behavior*. 12, 675-682.
Kulhavy, R.W., Dyer, J.W., and Silver, L. (1975). The effects of notetaking and test expectancy on the learning of text material. *Journal of Educational Research*. 68, 363-365.
Kumar, V.K., Rabinsky, L., and Pandey, T.N. (1977). *Test Mode, Test Instructions and Retention*. Unpublished manuscript, Case Western Reserve University.
Loftus, G.R. (1971). Comparison of recognition and recall in a continuous memory task. *Journal of Experimental Psychology*. 91, 220-226.
Maisto, S.A., DeWaard, R.J., and Miller, M.E. (1977). Encoding processes for recall and recognition: The effect of instructions and auxiliary task performance. *Bulletin of the Psychonomic Society*. 9, 127-130.
Marton, F., and Säljö, R. (1976). On qualitative differences in learning: II-Outcome as a function of the learner's conception of the task. *British Journal of Educational Psychology*. 46, 115-127.
Meyer, G. (1934). An experimental study of the old and new types of examination: I. The effect of the examination set on memory. *Journal of Educational Psychology*. 25, 641-661.
Meyer, G. (1936). An experimental study of the old and new types of examination: II. Methods of study. *Journal of Educational Psychology*. 27, 30-40.
Naus, M.J., Ornstein, P.A., and Kreshtool, K. (1977). Developmental differences in recall and recognition: The relationship between rehearsal and memory as test expectation change *Journal of Experimental Child Psychology*. 23, 252-265.
Peeck, J., and Knippenberg, W.J.M. (1977). Test expectancy and

test performance. *Tijdschrift voor Onderwijsresearch*. 2, 270-274.
Ploetz, K. (1969). *Hauptdaten der Weltgeschichte*. Ploetz, Würzburg.
Postman, L., and Jenkins, W.O. (1948). An experimental analysis of set in rote learning: The interaction of learning instruction and retention performance. *Journal of Experimental Psychology*. 38, 683-689.
Sax, G., and Collet, L.S. (1968). An empirical comparison of the effects of recall and multiple-choice tests on student achievement. *Journal of Educational Measurement*. 5, 169-173.
Silvey, H.M. (1951). Student reaction to the objective and essay test. *School and Society*. 73, 377-378.
Terry, P.W. (1933). How students review for objective and essay tests. *Elementary School*. 33, 592-603.
Vallance, T.R. (1947). A comparison of essay and objective examinations as learning experiences. *Journal of Educational Research*. 41, 279-288.

THE EFFECT OF DEMARCATING THE TARGET SET ON IQ-RELATED INDIVIDUAL DIFFERENCES, IN THE PROBED SERIAL RECALL OF VERY RECENT ITEMS

Ronald L. Cohen and Kathy Lavin
Glendon College, York University, Toronto

ABSTRACT

Three experiments are reported, in which high and low IQ children were tested on the recall of the final 3 digits in a list, under conditions where the 3 target digits were distinguished from the remainder of the list solely by virtue of their serial position, and under conditions where the 3 target digits were demarcated in some way. Although demarcating the target set generally improved performance, the low IQ children did not attain the performance level of the high IQ children. The data are discussed in the context of an access explanation for IQ-related individual differences in probed tests of STM.

Using probed serial recall, Cohen and Sandberg (1977) demonstrated a reliable correlation between IQ and STM for the final 3 items in a 9-digit list, and a complete lack of a correlation when the first 3 digits in the list were probed. Possible explanations for this correlation, which have so far failed to receive empirical support, include IQ-related individual differences in chunking, in encoding individual items, in rehearsal, and in the retention of order information (Cohen and Sandberg, 1977; Cohen and Gowen, in press).

The present study tested a further possible explanation for these IQ/STM correlations. Probed serial recall does not simply involve echoing out what is available of the target set of items, but requires the subject to isolate the specified set from the other material in store. Two boundaries are important for demarcating a target set of items, these corresponding to the beginning and the end of the set. In the primacy set the start boundary is clearly marked, since the first item in the set is also the first item in the list; in the recency set the end boundary is well marked, whereas the start boundary is not. Since an IQ/STM correlation is found for recency items but not for primacy items, it can be concluded that if the isolation of the target set is the mechanism underlying these correlations, then it is the location of the start boundary, or point of entry, which is important.

In the following 3 experiments, high and low IQ children were tested on the probed serial recall of very recent items in digit lists. Performance under conditions in which the point of entry was not marked was compared with that under conditions in which the point of entry was clearly marked. If proficiency in locating the target set is responsible for IQ-related individual differences in this task, it could be expected that marking the point of entry would greatly decrease the difference between the high and low IQ groups.

EXPERIMENT 1

Method

Experiment 1 used auditory 9-digit serial lists, each of which was probed, following presentation, with the auditory letter A, B, or C, which asked for the recall of the first 3, middle 3 or final 3 digits respectively. In one condition the lists consisted only of the digits, presented at a rate of 2 digits/second. In a second condition the points of entry for the three sets of digits were marked by including the auditory letters A, B, and C at appropriate places during presentation. The two conditions can be represented by 123456789 and A123B456C789. Twelve lists were presented under each condition, and each serial position was probed 4 times. In all 3 experiments, presentation of the various conditions was blocked.

Subjects were children in the age range 9.5-11.5 years. One group (N = 16) had IQs in the range 65-95, with a mean of 80; the other group (N = 16) had IQs in the range 115-135, with a mean of 122. These subjects were used in all 3 experiments.

Results

Table 1 gives the results of Experiment 1.

The main result in Table 1 is that the difference in performance between the high and low subjects on the final 3 digits in fact increased when the markers were introduced, in spite of an obvious ceiling in the case of the high IQ subjects.

TABLE 1

Proportion correctly recalled in serial order

serial position of target set		A	B	C
without A,B,C markers	high IQ	.53	.47	.81
	low IQ	.44	.19	.32
	difference	.09	.28	.49
with A,B,C markers	high IQ	.44	.46	.94
	low IQ	.15	.10	.39
	difference	.29	.36	.55

A groups x conditions Anova performed on the recency scores yielded significant F-values for both variables, $F(1,30)\ 58.24$, $p <.05$, for groups, and $F(1,30)\ 5.47$, $p <.05$, for conditions. The interaction was not significant, $F(1,30)\ 1$. A post-test (Scheffé with a .10 significance level) showed that the marker produced a significant increase in performance in the high IQ group, but not in the low IQ group. However, the introduction of the letter markers appears to have had a deleterious effect on the performance of the low IQ subjects, at least in the case of the A and B digit sets. This conclusion is based not only on their scores but also on their manner of responding. Often, the low IQ subjects included the marker as part of their response, giving A123 or C789; in no case did a high IQ subject include the marker in his response. Consequently, any increase in ease of access due to marking the entry point to the final set, may have been offset by a decrease in the availability of these items.

EXPERIMENT 2

Method

In this experiment the target set of recency items was clearly differentiated from earlier list items, by virtue of their class. The basic control condition used 9-item lists of the form 123456789, while the easy access condition used 9-item lists consisting of 6 letters and 3 digits of the form ABCDEF123. Rate of presentation was again 2 items/second.

The subjects were post-cued to recall the first 6, or the final 3 items in the lists using the auditory cues first six and last three, respectively. Prior to testing, they were carefully instructed on the makeup of the lists. Thus all subjects knew that a last 3 cue following a letter-digit list asked for the recall of only digits, whereas a first 6 cue asked for the recall of only letters. Eight lists were given under each condition, the first and last positions of the list being probed 4 times each.

Results

Table 2 gives the results of Experiment 2.

TABLE 2

Proportion correctly recalled in serial order

		first 6	last 3
all-digits	high IQ	.42	.84
	low IQ	.24	.27
	difference	.18	.54
letters-digits	high IQ	.39	.93
	low IQ	.22	.53
	difference	.17	.40

In Table 2, it can be seen that the high IQ subjects were clearly superior to the low IQ subjects for both recency and prerecency items, the greatest difference occurring on the recency items. An analysis of variance performed on the recency data showed that the type of sequence had a significant effect on performance, $F(1,30)$ 22.65, $p < .05$. There was also a significant groups x sequence type interaction, $F(1,30)$ 5.66, $p < .05$, which reflects the fact that the type of sequence had a greater effect on the low IQ children than on the high IQ children. In view of the ceiling effects shown by the high IQ children, however, this interaction should probably be treated as artifactual, rather than evidence in support of the access hypothesis.

EXPERIMENT 3

Experiment 3 also avoided the negative effects ascribed to the letter markers in Experiment 1, by using empty pauses as entry point markers in a modified running memory task.

Method

Digit sequences of varying length (9-15 digits) were presented auditorily at rate of 3 digits/second. The subject's task was to recall the final 3 digits in each list, in serial order.

In the difficult access condition, the entry point of the target set was not distinguished in any way. In the easy access conditions the entry point to the target digits was marked by a one second pause which separated them from the rest of the list.

A pilot study using the easy access condition, showed that all subjects could perform this task perfectly, regardless of their IQ, probably because they ignored all items presented before the pause. In the experiment proper, therefore, the easy access sequences were presented with a probe, after or before, which indicated whether the subject was to recall the 3 digits following the pause, or the 3 digits preceding the pause. Two versions of this condition were used. In easy access condition 1, a probe test followed every marked set of 3 digits. In easy access condition 2, blind marked entry points were introduced so that a pause in the digit sequence did not necessarily signal a test. The terminal set of digits was tested on 6 trials in the difficult access condition and 4 times in each of the easy access conditions.

Results

Table 3 gives the results of Experiment 3.

TABLE 3

Proportion of items correctly recalled, in serial order, from the target sets comprising the final 3 digits in each sequence

	difficult access	easy access 1	easy access 2
high IQ	.91	.97	.98
low IQ	.50	.64	.71
difference	.41	.33	.27

Both groups of subjects showed improved performance as access was facilitated, the low IQ subjects showing a greater increase than the high IQ subjects. The obvious ceiling performances of the high IQ subjects make this observation difficult to interpret as support for our original prediction, however. An analysis of variance on the data for the low IQ group showed that the conditions had an effect, $F(2,30)$ 7.95, $p < .05$. A Scheffé test located a difference between the difficult access conditions and the two easy access conditions, but not between the two latter conditions.

DISCUSSION

All 3 experiments have demonstrated that demarcating the point of entry improves performance on the recency items, to some extent. For the high IQ subjects, this improvement was severely limited by ceiling performances, but the fact that increases occurred in these subjects in all 3 experiments suggests that the effect of isolating the target set is a reliable one. More substantial gains were made in the case of the low IQ subjects, except in Experiment 1, where the markers appeared to interfere with the task.

In Experiments 2 and 3, demarcating the point of entry to the recency target set did reduce the difference between the high and low IQ subjects. However, the ceiling performances produced by the high IQ subjects clearly weakens the case for regarding these data as support for the access hypothesis. Further, the relatively low levels of performance shown by the low IQ subjects when the target sets were well demarcated, suggest that the access operation plays at most a minor role in determining the IQ-related individual differences found in the probed recall of terminal serial items. Even under conditions where the terminal sets were clearly marked, the performance of the low IQ subjects was still well below the ceiling established by the high IQ subjects. In view of the failure of this study to produce convincing evidence for an access explanation, the original suggestion made by Cohen and Sandberg (1977), namely that IQ-related individual differences found in the probed recall of recency items are due to individual differences in the availability of the target set, regains much of its original attraction.

REFERENCES

Cohen, R.L. & Sandberg, T. (1977) Relation between intelligence and short-term memory. *Cognitive Psychology*, 9, 534-554.

Cohen, R.L. & Gowen, A. (in press) Recall and recognition of order and item information in probed running memory, as a function of IQ. *Intelligence*.

OPTIMUM REHEARSAL PATTERNS AND NAME LEARNING

T. K. Landauer
Bell Laboratories
Murray Hill, N. J., USA
R. A. Bjork
University of California, Los Angeles
Los Angeles, California, USA

ABSTRACT

Two kinds of practice are distinguished. In one, new information is presented repeatedly for study. In the other, often exemplified in name learning, a fact is presented just once, and subsequent rehearsal takes the form of "tests". Previous results and theory suggest that different schedules of rehearsal may be optimal in the two cases. We report experiments on name learning that compared various rehearsal patterns. Given a fixed number of rehearsals in a fixed period, a pattern of increasing intervals between successive rehearsals was best for test-type practice, while uniform spacing was slightly better if the information was repeated.

INTRODUCTION

Memorization usually occurs under circumstances in which an outside source provides the information anew on each practice trial, as when a student recites vocabulary words in preparation for a test. The proper scheduling of practice in this kind of situation has been much studied. Often, however, one wants to remember a fact that is presented just once, under circumstances in which it is difficult to record the information externally for later consultation. Name learning exemplifies the problem nicely. Writing down the names of people one meets at conferences is awkward; snapping pictures to pair with the names is downright gauche. The rehearsal mode that _is_ available in such situations can be characterized as a series of self-administered tests. The optimal scheduling of tests as learning trials has also been studied experimentally (e.g., Landauer and Eldridge, 1967; Izawa,

1966, 1967; Whitten and Bjork, 1977), but less extensively.

For good experimental reasons, investigations of scheduling effects in either mode have seldom involved more than variation in the spacing between two trials on the same item. There has been virtually no work on non-uniformly spaced sequences of 3 or more trials. (But see Foos and Smith, 1974.) However, real practice commonly utilizes many trials, and in test-type practice where new information may be totally lost without rehearsal, multiple trials and non-uniform patterns take on special interest.

One account of test-spacing effects (Landauer, 1969, 1975; Whitten and Bjork, 1977) assumes that tests with successful outcomes are like repetitions. The longer the interval from initial presentation to test, the lower the probability of success but the greater its benefit for long term retention. Expanded, this idea suggests that the optimal schedule for test-type rehearsal would be a pattern of increasing intervals between successive tests. A first test-trial at a short interval would be likely to succeed and strengthen an item sufficiently to survive a slightly longer interval that would yield a more effective second practice trial, etc. In contrast, when the information is repeated, very long intervals are not as much better than moderate intervals and very short intervals are worse (see e.g., Landauer, 1969) so uniform spacing should be better for repetition-type practice.

EXPERIMENT I: LAST NAMES FOR FIRST NAMES

Method

Subjects were the 468 students attending an introductory psychology lecture at the State University of New York at Stony Brook. (We thank them and Professor Z. Coulter.) Each student was given a prearranged deck of cards bearing - for initial presentation trials - first and last names of fictitious people or - for test trials - first names only. Subjects turned through the cards at a 9 sec. rate in time to a signal, studying and writing last-name answers as appropriate. Next there was a 30 min. retention interval filled with a distracting lecture, followed by a final retention test.

The subjects were told to imagine they were at a cocktail party, meeting people they wanted to remember. The 50 study phase cards "introduced" a total of 16 fictitious people, of which 4 were recency and primacy buffers. The remaining 12 names were presented and tested on cards whose order in the deck produced various rehearsal patterns. Two were presented once, i.e., both first and last name appeared on a card and neither name appeared again until final test. The rest of the names occurred four times each during the study phase. Initial presentation gave both names, the next three presentations only the first name and a space for attempted recall of the last name. There were, thus, three intervals, filled with other presentations and tests, separating the four study phase cards for each name. The number of intervening items in the three intervals were arranged in five classes of patterns, as follows. Uniform, short: (0,0,0 and 1,1,1. Uniform, moderate: 4,4,4 and 5,5,5. Uniform, long: $9 \leq (x,y,z) \leq 11$, mean = 9.3-10.3. Expanding: 0,3,10 and 1,4,10. Contracting: 10,3,0 and 10,4,1. Each subject's deck contained two examplars of each class. The mean interval of the uniform moderate patterns matches those of the expanding and contracting. The hypothesized superiority of the expanding patterns can thus be evaluated against both uniform patterns and patterns with the same distribution of intervals in the opposite order, where each contains the same practice events in the same total period. Uniform short mimics what naive people usually do (Landauer and Ross, 1976) and uniform long represents what one might prescribe on the basis of previous research on repetition-type spacing.

In addition to the information described above, for half of the critical names in each deck, study-phase test cards presented fictitious occupations for the named people. This manipulation had no discernable effect on rehearsal pattern differences. In producing card decks two entirely different sets of names were used. Rotation insured that particular names were used equally often in each pattern condition. Four different list orders were used; overall the list positions occupied by the first and last event in each pattern type were closely matched. Final tests were given in random order, and decks were distributed to subjects in random order.

Results

Fig. 1 shows proportions correct during the study phase of the experiment. The list position of each test relative to initial presentation of both names together is given on the abscissa. Variants of pattern classes that did not produce noticeable differences have been combined; (10,10.10 summarizes all variants of uniform-long spacing).

Fig. 2. Gives results on the final test. Here again variants of pattern classes yielding indistinguishable results have been combined. The abscissa is average spacing, e.g., 4,4,4 and 5,5,5 combined are plotted at 4.5.

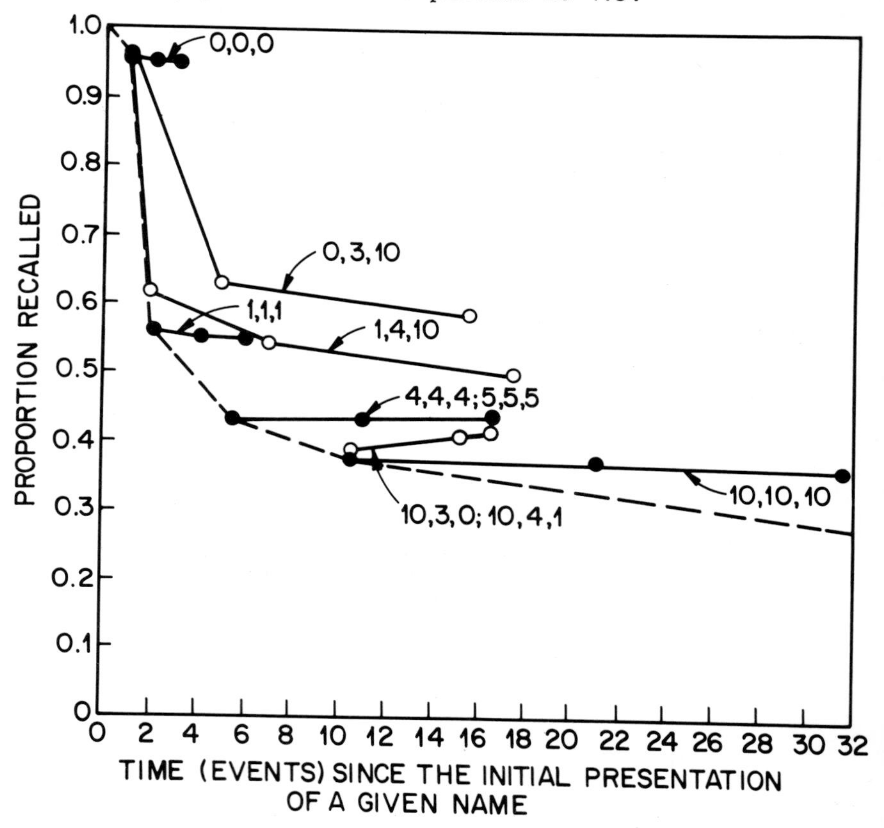

Fig. 1. *Exp. I. Performance on intralist tests.*

The expanding pattern produced almost twice as many correct final recalls as a presentation alone, the situation in which subjects determined their own rehearsal strategies. The expanding pattern was substantially better than the comparable uniform conditions, $z = 2.6$, $p < .01$, which were in turn somewhat but not significantly better than the contracting pattern. The forgetting curves in Fig. 1 are consistent with the idea, postulated above, that the expanding pattern is superior because it keeps the probability of a successful test relatively high. Note the short-term forgetting difference between the 0,3,10 and 1,4,10 patterns, which led to .49 and .45 correct on final tests respectively.

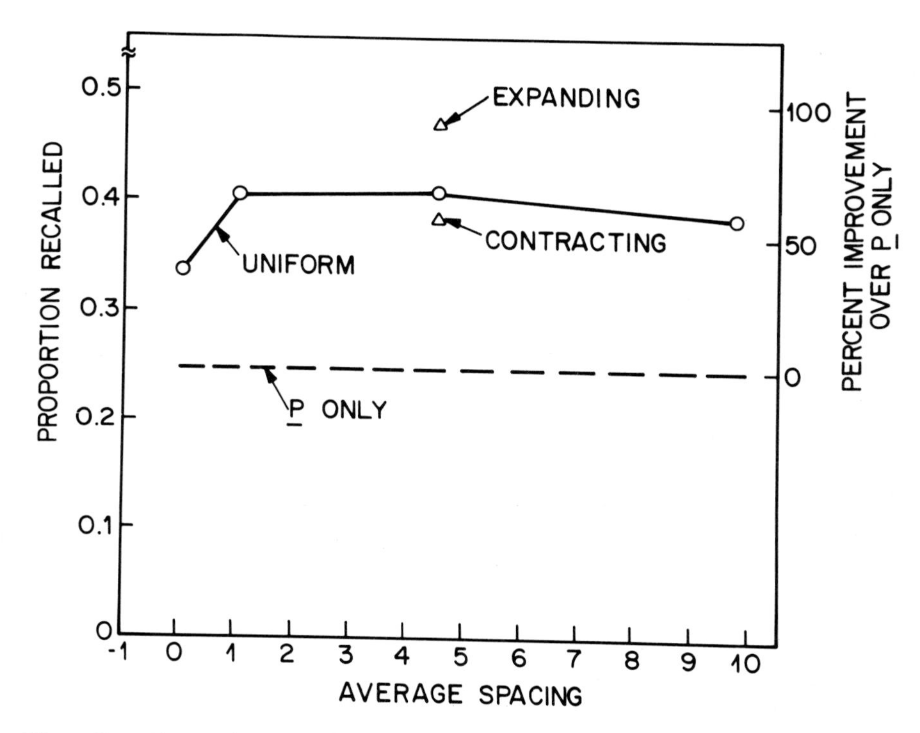

Fig. 2. *Exp. I. Performance on final tests. (P - names given only initial presentation).*

EXPERIMENT II: FIRST AND LAST NAMES FOR FACES

Method

Subjects were 218 students attending an Introductory Psychology lecture at the University of Illinois at Chicago Circle (we thank them and Professor E. Kent). The procedure (including control balancing) was similar to that of Exp. I with the following differences. The stimuli were standard, frontal photographs of heterogeneous faces. A 3x5 matrix of faces was projected in front of the class. The matrix disappeared and reappeared with the faces randomly permuted every 15 seconds. At each slide change, the subjects turned to a new card which bore a coordinate reference, e.g., A-5, to a particular face in the correspondingly labeled row and column of the display. The first time a face was referenced, both the first and last name were given on the card. During the study phase, succeeding cards referring to that face gave either only the first name or only the last name, the other to be written by the subject. Thus for a given fictitious person one name was subject to repetition practice, the other to test-type practice. Two rehearsal patterns were used; one of 3,3,3,3 intervening events, judged the best uniform spacing on the basis of results shown in Fig. 2, and an expanding pattern of the same mean interval, 0,1,3,8 ,which, also on evidence from Exp. I, was expected to be optimal. There were two exemplars of each pattern, one with the first name repeated and the second tested, and the other vice-versa, plus three "people" given only initial presentation, at equated list positions, plus 11 buffer cards involving 8 "people". On test trials face references only were given and subjects attempted to supply both names. Three sets of names were used. Face-name, and face-condition pairings were permuted across subjects.

Results

Proportions correct on both intralist and final tests for test-type practice are shown in Fig. 3. Because there were no differences dependent on whether first or last name was the one tested or repeated, this distinction is ignored, yielding 436 observations per point.

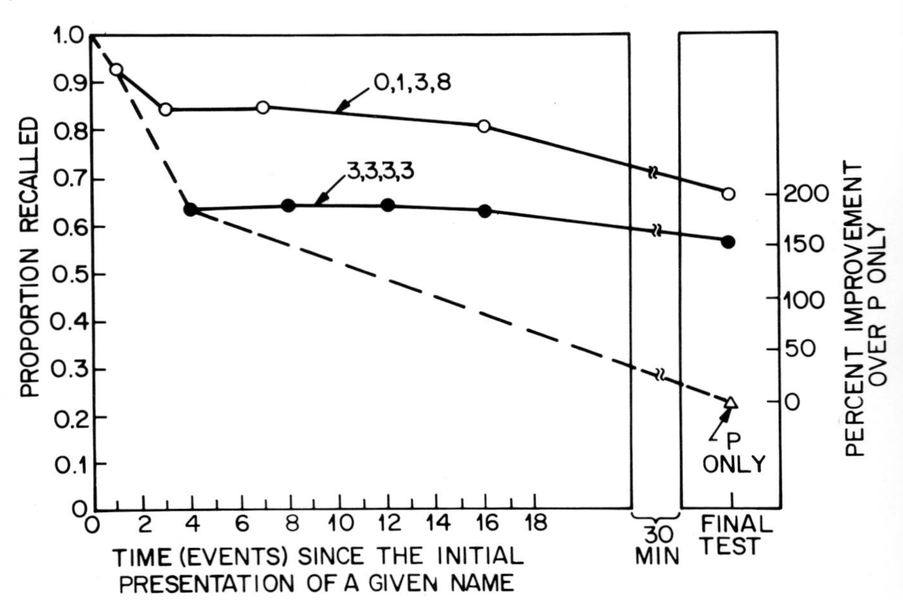

Fig. 3. *Results for test-type practice in Exp. II.*

As in Exp. I, the expanding pattern produced better final recall than the uniform pattern with the same average spacing; .66 and .56 correct respectively, $t = 3.16$, $d_f = 217$, $p < .01$. The absolute level of recall is impressively high for information presented just once as part of a long, highly similar list and tested over 30 minutes later. The proportions for which repeated information was recalled correctly were .58 and .62 for expanding and uniform patterns respectively. While this difference is not significant, the interaction between test-type and pattern is, $F = 18.72$, $d_f = 217$, $p < .001$. Thus, the expanding pattern is better than the uniform for test-type practice, but the uniform pattern is at least relatively better for repetitions.

It bears note that the best condition of all was the expanding test-type rehearsal, and it was significantly better than the corresponding expanding repetition pattern, $t = 3.56$, $d_f = 217$, $p < .01$.

Discussion

Expanding pattern test-type rehearsal offers an attractive mnemonic principle for retention of information that cannot be conveniently recorded. Indeed, popular mnemonic systems (see, e.g., Lorayne and Lucus, 1974) appear to induce just such a pattern of rehearsals, but attribute their claimed success to the demanding elaborative rituals in which the rehearsals are imbedded. The straight-forward rehearsal strategy suggested by the present results may be easier to apply in practical settings. To learn the name of a new acquaintance at a conference, one may be unwilling to shift cognitive power from technical discussion to rich associative imaginings, but may be willing to try the name as an implicit or explicit response to the face four or five times at increasing intervals.

Theoretically, the superiority of test-type practice over repetition in the expanding case can be explained if it is assumed that successful tests are more effective than repetitions. This could either be because tests induce greater encoding effort, or because they are more similar to the performance required at eventual recall. The expanding pattern may thus be seen as an effective shaping procedure for successively approximating the desired behavior of unaided recall at long delays.

ACKNOWLEDGEMENTS

We thank Karl Gutschera and Ann Boscardin for their help.

REFERENCES

Foos, P. W. and Smith, K. H. (1974). Effects of spacing and spacing patterns in free recall. *Journal of Experimental Psychology*, 103, 112-116.

Izawa, C. (1966). Reinforcement-test sequences in paired-associate learning. *Psychological Reports*, 18, 879-919.

Izawa, C. (1967). Function of tests in paired-associate learning. *Journal of Experimental Psychology*, 75, 194-209.

Landauer, T. K. (1969). Reinforcement as consolidation. *Psychological Review*, 76, 82-96.

Landauer, T. K. (1975). Memory without organization: Properties of a model with random storage and undirected retrieval. *Cognitive Psychology*, 7, 495-531.

Landauer, T. K. and Eldridge, L. (1967). Effects of tests without feedback and presentation-test interval in paired-associate learning. *Journal of Experimental Psychology*, 75, 290-298.

Landauer, T. K. and Ross, B. H. (1977). Can simple instruction to space practice improve ability to remember a fact? An experimental test using telephone numbers. *Bulletin of the Psychonomic Society*, 10, 215-218.

Lorayne, H. and Lucas, J. (1974). *Memory Book*, Stein and Day.

Whitten, W. B. and Bjork, R. A. (1977). Learning from tests: Effects of spacing. *Journal of Verbal Learning and Verbal Behavior*, 16, 465-478.

QUALITATIVE DIFFERENCES IN THE UNDERSTANDING AND RETENTION OF THE MAIN POINT IN SOME TEXTS BASED ON THE PRINCIPLE-EXAMPLE STRUCTURE

F. Marton and C-G. Wenestam
Institute of Education, University of Göteborg
Fack, S-431 20 Mölndal, Sweden

ABSTRACT

We carried out a study on the way people perceive and remember the intentional content of a certain kind of argumentative prose. Qualitative differences between individuals in understanding and qualitative differences within individuals in remembering were found to be of the same kind. One month after the texts used in the study had been read a number of individuals "moved" from one conception of the main point to another. All the conceptions which an individual "moved" to had, however, previously been exhibited by other individuals in their original understanding of the passage read.

In terms of changes in the conception of the main point, forgetting was found to be dramatically less than in studies in which verbatim recall of factual details is measured.

INTRODUCTION

In studies of verbal learning and remembering, the learning material used in the experiment frequently provides the standard against which the amount of learning or forgetting is measured. By comparing the subject's recall of a text or his answers to questions on it with what is actually said in the text, we arrive at a judgement concerning the extent to which the subject managed to learn or to remember the text.

The application of this method means, however, that something important is missed. A text is always perceived and remembered in one way or another. Formulating questions in terms of <u>how</u> the text is perceived and <u>how</u> it is remembered is often better than asking <u>to what extent</u> it is learned and remembered.

From such a starting point, we have, during the last few years, carried out a series of studies of the way people understand and remember texts. Repeatedly, we found qualitatively different ways of apprehending the content of the text read as well as qualitatively different ways of remembering it. Furthermore, the two sources of variation in the conception of content - between individuals on the same occasion and within individuals on different occasions - were found to be commensurable. This means that it was possible to use the same set of qualitatively different conceptions to describe the variation between as well as within individuals. The categories were the same in the case of immediate retention as in the case of delayed retention even if a certain number of individuals "moved" between the categories from one occasion to another (Marton, 1975 and Marton & Säljö, 1976).

From this perspective, both learning and remembering must be described in terms of the apprehended content. Since content differs from one study to another, the description of learning and remembering also varies. We have, however, found it extremely worthwhile to study and describe the qualitative differences concerning the different ways in which basic concepts and principles can be understood and retained.

Naturally, we can group texts, which are different from the content point of view, on the basis of structural similarities. In the study in question, we use four different texts based on the same structure, namely that of principle-example. This is a fairly common kind of argumentative prose; a principle is explained and this is done partly by making the principle explicit and partly by using a rather extensive example illustrating the principle.

Our intention with this study was to further illuminate our previous findings as to qualitative differences in the understanding and retention of the content of a text read as well as to the degree of commensurability between the inter- and intra-individual differences. Our aim was also to study these phenomena in relation to varying retention intervals.

On the structural level, we were interested in describing the variation in the way in which the principle-example structure is understood and remembered. On the content level we wanted to find out the different ways of perceiving and remembering the specific principles and concepts present in the texts used in the experiments.

In our study, four texts, all based on the principle-example structure, but differing as to specific content were used. Because of limitations of space and time, only one of these experiments will be discussed here.

METHOD

Procedure

The procedure was exactly the same in each of the four experiments. The subjects participating in the experiments were randomly divided into four subgroups corresponding to four different conditions. The independent variable was the length of the retention interval, varying between 0, 1, 7 and 30 days. Thus, all the groups except the first one participated in two sessions.

At the first session the subjects were asked to read a text in order to understand it as well as possible. They were also told that after having read the text they would be given some questions on the content. There was no time limit for reading which varied between approximately 5 to 20 minutes.

The subjects were asked to give written answers to some questions after they had read the text as well as on the second occasion. Two of the questions appeared on both occasions:

1. Write down what you remember of the text. Also include what you believe is obvious, i.e. do not leave anything implied. Write in full detail.

2. Try to summarize the text in a few sentences. In other words, what did the author want to say?

Six additional questions were given on the second occasion. The first group (with no retention interval) was included in order to be able to compare the answers to these six questions after varying delays following the reading of the texts. The results presented in this paper are, however, based entirely on answers to the two questions above.

Subjects

In all, 231 paid volunteers participated in the four experiments, 58 of them in the experiment reported in this paper. They were all students at local secondary schools (24 male, 34 female) and their average age was 19.9 years (s=1.3).

Texts

As mentioned above, all the four texts were based on the same structure though varying as to content. In each, a certain principle was made explicit and further illuminated by means of a fairly extensive example.

The text in the experiment from which the results are described below, consisted of 1 333 words and concerned the testing of hypotheses. It is an excerpt from Hempel (1966) and its main point is that hypotheses concerning causal factors are tested by comparing two otherwise identical conditions, one in which the presumptive causal factor is present and one in which it is absent. If the expected effect occurs, then the hypothesis is confirmed, otherwise not. This is illustrated by the Austro-Hungarian physician Ignaz Semmelweis' search for the cause of childbed fever in 1844-48. He tested one hypothesis after the other comparing the frequency of childbed fever between two hospital wards which were always identical except for one factor:

> "Various psychological explanations were attempted. One of them noted that the First Division was so arranged that a priest bearing the last sacrament to a dying woman had to pass through five wards before reaching the sickroom beyond: the appearance of the priest, preceded by an attendant ringing a bell, was held to have a terrifying and debilitating effect upon the patients in the wards and thus to make them more likely victims of childbed fever. In the Second Division, this adverse factor was absent, since the priest had direct access to the sickroom. Semmelweis decided to test this conjecture. He persuaded the priest to come by a roundabout route and without ringing of the bell, in order to reach the sick chamber silently and unobserved. But the mortality in the First Division did not decrease.
>
> A new idea was suggested to Semmelweis by the observation that in the First Division the women were delivered lying on their backs; in the Second Division, on their sides. Though he thought it unlikely, he decided 'like a drowning man clutching at a straw', to test whether this difference in procedure was significant. He introduced the use of the lateral position in the First Division, but again, the mortality remained unaffected." (Hempel, 1966, p.4)

etc. He was not able to discover any reliable differences until he tested the correct hypothesis, namely that of infection. He compared frequencies of childbed fever when the doctors examined women in labor directly after having carried out an autopsy and without having washed their hands (the common procedure) with when they carefully disinfected their hands between the autopsy and the examination of the women. As we know his hypothesis was confirmed.

RESULTS

After the collection of all the data, a very time-consuming, qualitative analysis of the written answers to the two questions above was initiated in order to find out how the subjects had understood what the text was about. The answers to the two questions from each person were treated together and, finally, a holistic judgement in each case was arrived at.

Again, it was established that on the one hand the main point of the text was understood in qualitatively different ways and on the other, the subjects' conceptions of the main point were changed qualitatively in many cases by the elapsing of the time after reading the text. Furthermore, it was possible to characterize the qualitative changes in remembering within individuals in terms of the initial differences in understanding between individuals. The most difficult moment in the research strategy adopted here is to discover the categories by means of which we can grasp and describe the qualitative variation. There is simply no algorithmic procedure for finding the distinct ways in which people's understanding of what they read about differ. The categories can not be "produced", they have to be found.

In this study four different ways of understanding and remembering the main point of the text appeared after a long period of intuitive, interpretative and holistic analysis. Once the categories were found they were made explicit by means of judgement instructions. Two judges working independently of each other arrived at identical judgements in 70 per cent of cases. Agreement in the remaining cases was reached after discussion between the two judges.

The main point of the text was thus understood and remembered in the following four qualitative different ways.

Category A

According to the answers in this category the text concerns the testing of hypotheses. The subjects who gave these answers realized that it was necessary to compare two conditions where the causal agent which the hypothesis concerns is present in one but not in the other. Furthermore, the way in which this procedure is exemplified by the case of Semmelweis is made explicit in the answer.

Excerpts from answers given by two subjects can exemplify this category.

Subject 45

"The text begins with how one sets about testing a hypothesis. One investigates two different groups, one of which will give a positive result and the other a negative result in relation to the hypothesis. If the hypothesis is faulty, then this difference won't be obtained and one will have to start again with a new hypothesis. This was illustrated by an example about Semmelweis. S. wondered why the mortality rate from childbed fever was so different (about 9% and about 2%) in wards 1 and 2 at the hospital in Vienna (1840's) ..."

Subject 66

"In scientific research, when one wants to investigate what caused an event one makes assumptions (hypotheses). These are tested by means of experiments in which one sets up two similar situations of which only one contains the assumed cause. If the expected event is obtained in the situation containing the assumed cause, the cause of the event is considered to have been found. If the experiment doesn't turn out as expected, that is, if the assumed cause doesn't respond in a certain situation, then the hypothesis is faulty and a new assumption has to be made. Semmelweis' investigations in 1844-48 concerning the alarmingly high death-rate from childbed fever was chosen as an example of this sort of research ..."

Category B

The answers in this category reveal an understanding of the fact that the text concerns the testing of hypotheses as well as that it is exemplified by the case of Semmelweis. There is, however, no indication of the subject's understanding of how the testing of hypotheses is exemplified by the case of Semmelweis (i.e. the comparison of two conditions alike in all respects except one). This conception of the main point thus represents a more superficial level of understanding than category A.

Subject 12

"The text is about how one investigates if one's hypotheses are correct and as an example of this the success in stopping childbed fever has been chosen. There was a doctor in the middle of the 19th century who was worried about the fact that so many women died of childbed fever. He decided to investigate why this happened and based his work on different hypotheses (his own and others). One of them was that there was an influenza epidemic which made the women ..."

Subject 86

"The text is about how one investigates a hypothesis (assumption). As an example they have taken Ignaz Semmelweis' investigation into why there were so many who died of childbed fever in ward 1 at a clinic in Vienna. Thus, he put forward a number of hypotheses and investigated whether they were correct. First, he assumed that it was caused by influenza, but since the other ward in the same clinic didn't have the same infant mortality rate he was forced ..."

Category C

In this case, the main point of the text is in fact replaced by another main point constructed by the subjects in order to render meaning and coherence to what they remember of the text. The testing of hypotheses as the main point is substituted by the more common sense notion of finding the cause or the explanation.

Subject 35

"In order to find the cause of a certain result one has to proceed by trial and error and perhaps repeat the tests many times in order to obtain the desired result. The Austrian doctor Semmelweis wanted to find out why so many women died of childbed fever in one ward but not so many in another. One theory was that the priest had to walk through so many wards in order to give a woman with childbed fever the extreme unction. On the way to ..."

Subject 56

"The account was about how one arrives at a "law" or theory. The man in the account had a lot of theories which he thought could be correct, but which proved not to be tenable. But even if the tests were wrong, they helped him along the right way because he was able to disregard certain areas. Even if, in this case it was an accident that helped him find the correct solution."

Category D

In this case, the principle-example structure of the text is entirely missing as the subjects believe that the text concerns what is said in the example. The example is thus not understood as an example but as the "main story".

Subject 54

"The text is about a professor who is going to find out the reason for childbed fever being so much higher in the first ward than in the others. It was about 9% while the others had only 2-3%. He tested a lot of different reasons, one of which was that he thought that it could be a priest who caused it all when he went through the ward with ..."

Subject 70

"The Hungarian doctor Semmelweis was going to investigate why childbed fever started at a hospital in Vienna. It was all very peculiar because the mortality rate in ward 1 was extremely high (about 8%) and in the adjoining ward the mortality rate was much lower. Different investigations were carried out in the different wards and then compared with each other. All this happened in the 1840's. He tested mental factors concerning whether the position during childbirth had any significance, the medicines, methods of investigation etc ..."

As was pointed out above, it was possible to characterize the initial variation in the understanding of the main point of the text in terms of these four categories. During the retention interval, qualitative changes occurred in a certain number of cases as to the way the main point was remembered. Also these changes could be described in terms of the four categories since all the subjects who changed their initial conception changed it to a conception which had been exhibited by some other subjects immediately after having read the text. The extent to which such changes occurred in the three different groups (group 1 with no retention interval is not included for obvious reasons) is shown in Table 1.

As can be seen, there are very few changes up to one week; and even after one month, half of the group exhibit the same conception of the main point as they did immediately after having read the text.

Table 1. *Qualitative changes in the conception of the main point after varying retention intervals. (Capital letters refer to the categories described above.)*

Immediate recall	After one day (Group 2)					After one week (Group 3)					After one month (Group 4)				
	A	B	C	D	Σ	A	B	C	D	Σ	A	B	C	D	Σ
A	2				2	3				3	1	3	2		6
B		4			4		3	1		4		1	1		2
C			4		4			6	1	7			3	1	4
D			1	4	5					0				2	2
Σ	2	4	5	4	15	3	3	7	1	14	1	4	6	3	. 14

The reason for carrying out four experiments with four texts differing in content but similar in structure was to study the way texts based on principle-example structure are understood and remembered. The sets of qualitatively different conceptions of the main point of the four different texts naturally differed in their content but, at the same time, there were some structural similarities. In actual fact, on a more general level than in the case of the four categories accounted for above, the differences in conceptions of the main point can be described in a way which applies to all the replications.

We found that the content of the four texts based on the principle-example was understood and remembered in the following different ways:

A. The principle and the example as well as the relationship between them is understood.

B. The principle and the example are understood (separately) but not sufficiently to understand the relationship between them.

C. The principle is not understood but constructed on the basis of the fragments retained.

D. The example in itself is seen as the main point of the text.

To recapitulate: it was possible to describe qualitative differences between individuals on the same occasion as well as within individuals on different occasions in terms of these categories. Thus, in this sense, qualitative changes in remembering means a transition from a higher to a lower level of understanding (in one case above, the change went in the "wrong" direction).

DISCUSSION

Thus, on a general level in the present study we have found further support for our earlier findings on qualitative differences in understanding as well as in remembering. Furthermore, the commensurability between these two sources of variation was again established. When describing qualitative changes in memory in terms of transition to lower levels of understanding, the degree of forgetting that took place was much lower than is normal in studies of verbal learning and memory.

On the level of the specific content, we have discovered four qualitatively different ways of understanding and remembering the exemplified principle of testing of hypotheses in scientific research.

To conclude, we should like to comment briefly on our results concerning the intermediate, structural level.

The categories at the specific content level refer to different conceptions of this specific content and the categories on the structural level refer mainly to different conceptions of the structure of the text.

As is the case with all argumentative prose texts based on the principle-example structure, these texts also have a dimension of depth, a hierarchical structure. Most obviously the principle is superordinate to the example. In previous studies by Wenestam (1978) and Marton and Säljö (1978) it has been shown that a common way of misunderstanding the principle-example structure is the abolishing of the depth dimension. By means of what has been called horizontalization, the hierarchical structure in the subjects' understanding becomes sequentially structured. In many cases, texts based on the principle-example are understood in terms of "first there was something about this (the principle) and then was something about that (the example)" instead of the realization that the example exemplifies the principle. Principle and example are thus not understood as principle and example but rather as two parts of the text, of equal importance and without any obvious connection. In Wenestam's and in Marton and Säljö's study, the interview method was used which makes it possible to ascertain in greater detail a phenomenon such as horizontalization. If asked further, the subjects in the present study, whose answers were classified into category D (conceptualizing the text as being about the example), would probably have been able to remember that something else was mentioned in the text as well (the principle). In all likelihood, category D is simply another example of horizontalization. Categories B and C are intermediate-between the complete understanding of the depth dimension (category A) and the absence of it (category D). Since we have described qualitative changes in remembering in terms of a transition to lower levels of understanding (i.e. from A to B, from B to C and from C to D), forgetting appears in this perspective in the form of a loss of depth in understanding.

ACKNOWLEDGEMENTS

The research reported here has been financially supported by the Swedish Council for Research in the Humanities and Social Sciences and from the University of Göteborg.

REFERENCES

Hempel, C.G. (1966). *Philosophy of Natural Science*. Prentice-Hall, Inc., Englewood Cliffs, N.J.

Marton, F. (1975). On non-verbatim learning. I. Level of processing and level of outcome. *Scandinavian Journal of Psychology*. 16, 273-279.

Marton, F. and Säljö, R. (1976). On qualitative differences in learning. I. Outcome and Process. *British Journal of Educational Psychology*. 46, 4-11.

Marton, F. and Säljö, R. (1978). Level of difficulty viewed as a relationship between the reader and the text. Paper presented at the XIXth International Congress of Applied Psychology, July 30 - August 5, 1978, Munich, West Germany.

Wenestam, C-G. (1978). Horisontalisering. Ett sätt att missuppfatta en text. (Horizontalization. A way of misunderstanding a text.) *Rapporter från Pedagogiska institutionen, Göteborgs universitet*. Nr 157.

STRATEGIES AND MEMORY

N. E. Wetherick
University of Aberdeen,
Aberdeen, Scotland.

Feigenbaum and Simon (1962) propose a theory of serial rote learning in which "anchor-points" are learned in one trial and other items in the list linked to these anchor-points over subsequent trials. Evidence will be presented that this theory may account equally well for the immediate recall of lists heard only once. Recall is either direct from residual, one-trial memory (which however registers only anchor-points) or else depends on the use of strategies of recall, often involving registration in forward or backward associative order beginning or ending at an anchor-point. Use of these strategies is age-dependent but the efficiency of residual memory is not.

The studies reported in this paper seek to elucidate some fundamental properties of memory that have already been the subject of many hundreds of experimental investigations. I am not sure whether an apology is due, I can only plead that it seemed to me that important questions regarding these properties had not as yet been asked. The first (Wetherick, 1975) was of the effect of semantic category membership of the words in a list on the number of words recalled. It seemed to me odd that although long-term memory was widely supposed to be organised on a semantic basis, semantics was nevertheless allowed no role in short-term recall. I shall describe the method in some detail since a similar method was employed in all the subsequent studies.

Lists of one-syllable words were presented verbally at the rate of one per second and immediate verbal recall was required. The words were drawn from one or more semantic categories - an 8-1 list consisted of eight words from one semantic category, a 1-8 list of one word from each of eight different semantic categories and so on ... Typical semantic categories were "colours", "birds", "trees", "parts of the body" etc. Where words from more than one category were presented no word ever followed another from the same category. Subjects might be instructed to recall these lists in any order (FR instructions) or in the order presented (SR instructions). However instructed, the subjects' responses might be scored either correct in correct order or correct irrespective of order. The difference between the total correct (S2) score and the correct in order (S1) score was called the residual score (words recalled but not in forward associative order).

The results obtained (using adult subjects) are shown in Fig.1. The decline left to right of S2 (total) scores is

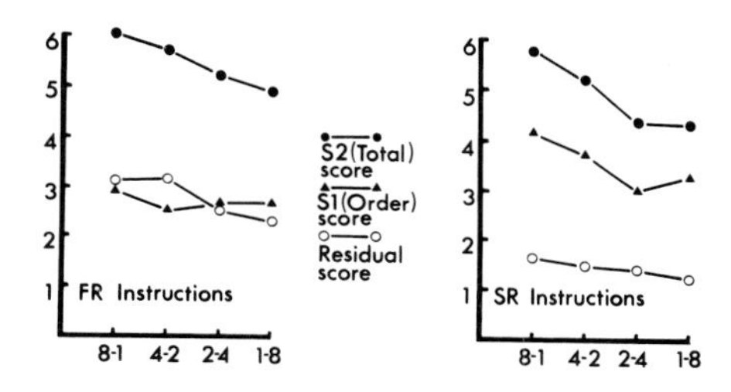

Fig.1 S1, S2 and residual scores in two instruction conditions (from Wetherick, 1975).

highly significant ($p < .001$) with FR and SR instructions. The more different categories the words are drawn from the fewer words are recalled. S2 scores are just significantly lower ($p = .05$) with SR instructions than FR instructions but, as was to be expected, S1 (order) scores are significantly higher ($p < .01$). The residual score was therefore necessarily lower with SR instructions. If instructed to recall in the order presented subjects try to do so but at the cost of recalling slightly fewer words overall. These results could be explained by hypothesizing a recall selector that takes longer to shift between semantic categories than between words within a category, operating on memory traces which remain detectable only for a limited time. If several traces have been initiated in one semantic category more will be detected in the time available than if the same number of traces had been initiated in two or more categories.

Fig. 2 shows serial position curves for S2 scores on the 8-1 and 1-8 lists. FR instructions give a conventional bowed curve but with SR instructions better recall of words in the first four serial positions is obtained at the cost of worse recall in the last four positions. The strong recency effect cannot be attributed to any tendency to recall the last words first; the last words were almost invariably recalled last if at all. It seemed to me noteworthy that in the FR instruction condition the serial position curve is of the

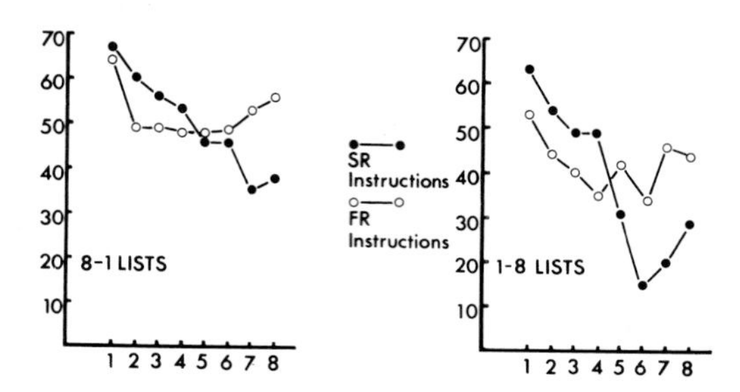

Fig.2 Serial position curves for S2 scores on two types of list (from Wetherick, 1975).

traditional form - ubiquitous in the recall of learning of strings of unrelated items, irrespective of the length of the string or the nature of the items. The curve appears to reflect the fact that the adult human subject is concerned above all to identify the beginning and end of any string to which he is exposed. The capacity to deal with strings of items cannot, however, be supposed to have evolved for the benefit of experimental psychologists, its primary function must clearly be to deal with strings of items in meaningful relation with each other i.e. regulated by syntactic rules. Nevertheless the capacity to identify the beginning and end of a string, even in the absence of meaning relations between items is fundamental. Without it order relationships between the items could not be preserved and language would have had to rely wholly on word inflexion. Feigenbaum and Simon (1962) advanced a theory of the serial position effect in rote learning which suggests that subjects consciously adopt a strategy of selecting "anchor points" in any list which is too long to be learned in one trial. These anchor points normally include the first and last items but can include any item which has "features of uniqueness" making it stand out from the rest. Anchor points may be learned in one trial but the remaining items can only be linked in forward associative order to one or other of the anchor points, over subsequent trials.

It seems possible that a similar procedure may be followed in immediate recall; if it is, then the strategy proposed by Feigenbaum and Simon may not be "consciously adopted" as they suggest but may simply reflect a fundamental non-conscious mode of coping with sequential material. Investigation of this possibility will involve plotting serial position curves for S1 and residual scores as well as for S2 (total) scores.

Wetherick and Alexander (1977) studied children aged from 5 to 9 years using the same method. Six as well as eight-word lists were presented and perhaps the most important finding was that the performance of the older children (aged 7 to 9) on six-word lists closely resembled that of adults on eight-word lists. Their performance on eight-word lists was not, however, very different from that of younger children (aged 5 to 6). The common observation that young childrens' recall depends on recency with primacy almost absent was repeated and the same negative relation between recall and number of semantic categories represented in the list was observed as in adults.

Wetherick and Morrice (unpub.) carried out an analysis of the serial position effect in a further study, using children as subjects. The results obtained are shown in Fig. 3.

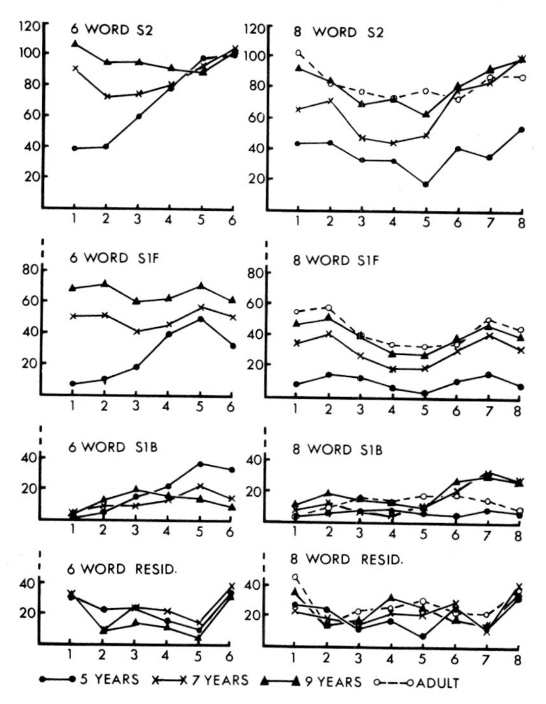

Fig.3 Serial position curves for S1F, S1B, S2 and residual scores on six and eight-word lists (Wetherick and Morrice, unpub.).

The top two graphs show serial position effects for S2 scores on six and eight-word lists. Five, seven and nine-year-old children were employed and, on the graph for eight-word lists, scores for adult subjects have been superimposed (taken from Wetherick, 1975). Immediately below are curves for S1F scores (words recalled in forward associative order). These have so far been referred to as S1 scores but analysis of the present data made it clear that the younger children in particular used backward associative order to a considerable extent. Separate curves are therefore plotted for S1B scores (words recalled in backward associative order). The residual score is, as before, the difference between the S2 (total) score and the S1 (F + B) score; i.e. the lower three graphs sum to the top one.

Looking first at the graph for S2 scores it may be seen that five-year-olds show absence of primacy on six-word lists and poor overall performance on eight-word lists as in the previous study. Five, seven and nine-year-olds (six-word lists) and seven,nine-year-olds and adults (eight-word lists) show similar recency effects. The increase in recall with age is significant ($p < .001$) in children but adults are not significantly better than nine-year-olds. Note that adult recall is poorer than that of seven and nine-year-olds in the last three serial positions.

The curve for S1F is typically of an elongated M shape though in five-year-olds the first peak of the M is missing. The characteristic shape of the curve appears to arise from the fact that the first and last words cannot figure in as many associative sequences as the second and last but one (which can either be first or second in a sequence whereas the former can only be first, or only last). S1F scores also increase significantly with age ($p < .001$) though again adults are not significantly better than nine-year-olds.

S1B scores appear to decline with age. Five-year-olds use backward association almost as extensively as forward association but backward scores (expressed as a proportion of forward scores) decline from 0.74 in five-year-olds to 0.25 in seven-year-olds and 0.19 in nine-year-olds. The fact that adult S2 scores are lower than those of seven and nine-year-old children in the last three serial positions seems to be directly due to the failure of adults to employ backward association.

Residual scores do not vary with age but are significantly higher on eight-word lists than on six-word lists ($p < .02$). The curve is typically of an elongated W shape.(Scores plotted here do not include any obtained by the recall of one word only. Children do occasionally recall one word only usually the first or last but counting these would invalidate comparison with S1F and S1B scores which can only be obtained from recall of a minimum of two words). The fact that S2 scores are almost invariably highest for the first and last words in a list appears to depend wholly on recall from residual memory.

The graphs suggest that immediate recall of a list of unrelated items may involve the registration in residual memory of "anchor points" at the beginning and end of the list. The efficiency of this function is independent of age. Any item in the list may be registered in residual memory if it catches the attention of the subject and, consequently, the more items the list contains the more will be recalled. However the first and last items are much the most likely to catch the attention. Note that while the first item may do so because it is an item where previously there was no item the last does so to the same extent and attention must here be caught by the fact that there is no item where the presence of an item was to be anticipated in the light of immediate previous experience.

Items that have been registered in the residual memory may be recalled independently or may form the beginning or end points of forward or backward associative sequences. The ability to form such sequences develops with age. On the face of it there is no reason to prefer forward to backward association and the five-year-old makes nearly equal use of both but only on the last items of the list (in the five-year-old earlier items appear to be erased by later). By the age of seven the child can retain two samples from the list instead of one, giving a primacy effect as well as a recency effect. The seven-year-old uses forward association more than the five-year-old and backward association less. In the nine-year-old and the adult forward association is dominant, perhaps as a result of increasing experience of language.

Clearly an analogy may be drawn between the processes employed in immediate recall and those hypothesized by Feigenbaum and Simon to account for the phenomena of serial rote learning, though it hardly seems possible to speak of a "strategy consciously adopted" in respect of childrens' immediate recall. However, Feigenbaum and Simon's theory also accounts for the Von Restorff effect. In serial rote learning this effect occurs when an item in the middle of a list has "features of uniqueness" which make it stand out. It may for example be presented in a different colour or type face or be a meaningful word in a list of nonsense syllables. Typically the odd item is learned in an early trial and shows up as a peak in the middle of the serial position curve. If a similar phenomenon could be shown to occur in immediate recall the proposed analogy would be greatly strengthened. Wetherick and Reynolds (unpub.) investigated this possibility. They presented nine-word lists to adult subjects in which eight words came from one semantic category and one (either the first, fifth or ninth) from a different category.

The "feature of uniqueness" was simply membership of a different semantic category. If the proposed analogy holds we might expect the odd word to be recalled more frequently from residual memory and less frequently in forward or backward association with adjacent items. Whether the odd word would be more frequently recalled overall and whether, if it were, it would be at the expense of less frequent recall of other items is difficult to say. Analysis of the results obtained shows that the three types of list (first, fifth or ninth word odd) did not differ in overall difficulty (F = 0.12, N.S.). Further analysis compared the forward,backward and residual scores for each serial position in each of the three types of list. Where, say, the fifth word is odd the residual score on the fifth word should according to our hypothesis be relatively high and the forward associative score relatively low, by comparison with the two types of list in which the fifth word is not odd. Significant differences in the predicted direction were observed in the fourth, fifth, eighth and ninth serial positions. Fig. 4

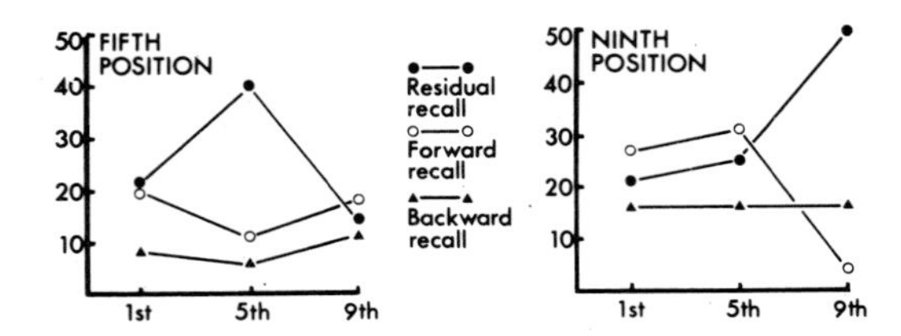

Fig.4 Incidence of forward (S1F), backward (S1B) and residual recall in lists where the fifth or ninth word is from a different semantic category (Wetherick and Reynolds, unpub.).

shows the results for the fifth and ninth positions. In each case residual recall is relatively high and forward recall low. The results for the fifth position suggest that total recall was higher than it would otherwise have been but since there was no difference overall between types of list this effect must have been compensated by lower recall of words in other serial positions. It is not perhaps surprising that no effect was observable in the first position since words in this position are recalled so well that a ceiling effect must have been in operation. The significant effects on the fourth position (where the fifth word was odd) and the eighth position (where the ninth word was odd) suggest that forward sequential recall operates more effectively within a semantic category than across category boundaries. Preliminary analysis of data from four, five and six-year-old children (Wetherick and Sutherland, unpub.) shows no evidence of an effect similar to the one obtained here with adults which suggests that at that age semantic category boundaries may not be firmly enough established.

Conclusions

The suggestion put forward is that memory may be rooted in a relatively primitive non-conscious "residual" system that registers only what catches its attention by some "feature of uniqueness" usually involving a change of perceptual state (a parallel may be drawn with retinal neurons that fire either at the onset or at the offset of stimulation in a particular area). Superimposed on this system are a variety of (possibly conscious) strategies that permit more information to be extracted from the input and retained. Broadly these strategies fall into two classes. In Chomsky's (1976) terms they involve either "grammar" or "common sense". In either case rules about what follows what (in "language" or in "reality") are employed to reduce the uncertainty of input sequences and increase the probability of registration of items which do not otherwise catch the attention. In the studies reported here the rules employed specify that *faute de mieux* order, particularly forward order, may be significant probably because in language order is significant.

REFERENCES

Chomsky, N. (1976). *Reflections on Language*. Fontana/Collins, Glasgow.

Feigenbaum, E.A. and Simon, H.A. (1962). A theory of the serial position effect. *British Journal of Psychology*. 53, 307-320.

Wetherick, N.E. (1975). The role of semantic information in short-term memory. *Journal of Verbal Learning and Verbal Behaviour*. 14, 471-480.

Wetherick, N.E. and Alexander, Jane. (1977). The role of semantic information in short-term memory in children aged 5 to 9 years. *British Journal of Psychology*. 68, 71-75.

EFFECTS OF INITIAL TESTING ON LATER RETENTION AS A FUNCTION OF THE INITIAL RETENTION INTERVAL

Vito Modigliani
Simon Fraser University
Burnaby, B.C., Canada

ABSTRACT

Two experiments confirmed past research to the effect that an initial recall increased later retention. They also extended previous results by showing that how an initial recall affects a later recall is dependent on the initial retention interval, that is, the time interval intervening between presentation of information (*words* in Experiment 1, *ideas* in Experiment 2) and its initial recall.

INTRODUCTION

It is not difficult to agree that the initial recall of some information affects the later retention of it. Surprisingly little, however, is known about the specific aspects of the process or processes involved. Yet, to understand how an initial recall may effect later retention is of practical importance since such an understanding could be used to determine the structure of review and practice sessions which would optimize retention of subject matter such as is learned in the schools. The topic of interest here did not go unnoticed by those interested in education. One of the first studies in this respect was by Spitzer (1939) who showed, among other things, that a group of children who had been tested immediately after reading a 577-word passage remembered, a week later, much more of it than another group of children who had not been given the initial test. A considerable body of research, recently summarized by Anderson and Biddle (1975), has also shown that questions asked after reading a passage increase the later retention of it.

These and other findings raise a number of interesting and largely unanswered questions. For example, how do coding activity at presentation and initial recall interact to determine later retention? What are the conditional probabilities of later retention given or not given a successful initial recall? Is the facilitatory effect of the initial recall a purely retrieval phenomenon, or does it entail a storage mechanism, or both? Before answering these questions, however, one must first deal with yet another question, whose importance has recently become apparent. Recent research has shown that the retention interval between the presentation of information and its initial recall is a crucial factor in determining how beneficial that recall is for later retention (Modigliani, 1976; Thios and D'Agostino, 1976; Whitten and Bjork, 1977). In previous research this factor was left completely uncontrolled, since its importance had not been suspected.

The present paper explored further the relationship between the retention interval of an initial test and later retention. In Experiment 1 results obtained by Modigliani (1976), who used a Brown-Peterson task, were extended to a free recall situation. Experiment 2 was designed to explore the effects of the initial retention interval on later retention in a more realist situation.

EXPERIMENT 1

The aim of this experiment was to study the effect of an initial recall on later retention under conditions in which the to-be-recalled information was presented serially and the possibility of rehearsal between items was either minimized (distraction condition) or maximized (overt rehearsal condition). In this task the initial retention interval was determined by input position. The retention test was either another recall or a recognition test. Because of space limitations, only the recall data are reported. The recognition data, however, completely mirrored the recall data.

Method

Nine 12-word lists were randomly drawn from a pool of common, concrete, nouns. Each list was divided into four word triads. All words in one triad were presented rapidly together and assigned the same input position. The time intervals between the first and second, the second and third, and the third and fourth triads were 13.5, 9.5, and 6.5 seconds, respectively. Lists were divided into 3 blocks of 3 lists each and the blocks were counterbalanced across subjects.

There were two main conditions. In the distraction condition each of 9 college students counted backwards by threes in the intervals between triads. In the overt rehearsal condition they repeated aloud the last triad heard until the next was presented. In both groups each list was initially recalled immediately after presentation of the fourth triad. One minute was allowed for this recall and then the next list was presented. These two groups will be referred to as the Initial Recall, or IR groups. Two more groups served as controls for item selection effects (see Modigliani, 1976, for the underlying rationale). Control groups were not engaged in the initial recall. Instead, they counted backwards by threes between list presentations. A final free recall test on the words from all lists was given to all subjects.

Results and Discussion

Figure 1 (A) shows the probability of initial recall as a function of input position (and initial retention interval) and of activity between triads (distraction or overt rehearsal) for the IR groups. Also shown in Figure 1 (A) is the number of rehearsals received by each triad in the overt rehearsal IR group. Initial recall decreased exponentially as the retention interval increased, that is, from position 4 to position 1. Contrary to previous findings (e.g., Rundus, 1971 number of overt rehearsals had no differential effects on recall even though it raised the whole curve with respect to the distraction condition.

Conditionalized final recall from the IR groups is shown in Figure 1 (B). The probability of final recall given a successful initial recall (FR/IR) *increased* in a negatively accelerated fashion with the initial retention interval. Most significantly, the overt rehearsal (OR) and distraction (D) curves for FR/IR were indistinguishable, except for random variations This is important because it means that if a word was initially recalled, then the probability of a later recall was independent of that word's previous history. The probability of final recall given an unsuccessful initial recall (FR/$\overline{\text{IR}}$) is shown by the broken line in Figure 1 (B). Because of the floor effect both groups were combined. Also, no point was plotted for FR/$\overline{\text{IR}}$ at position 4 because there were practically no words of the $\overline{\text{IR}}$ type at this position.

Unconditional probabilities of recall for all four groups are shown in Figure 1 (C). First, the IR groups outperformed the control groups, except for position 4. This indicates that an initial recall facilitates a later recall only when the initial retention interval is longer than a few seconds. Second, recall was better for the overt rehearsal groups than

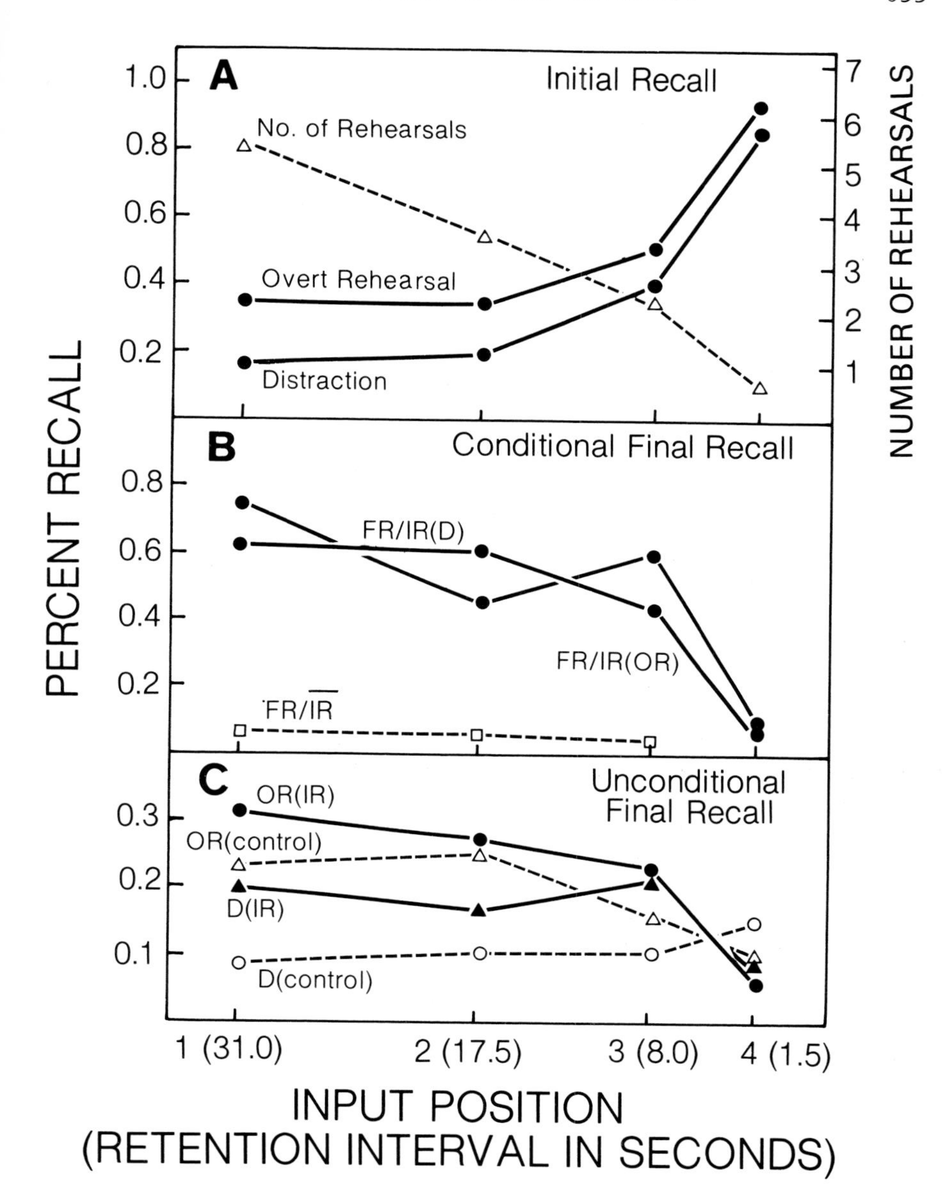

Fig. 1 (A) Percent initial recall and number of rehearsal (for the overt rehearsal condition) as a function of input position. (B) Conditional final recall. (C) Unconditional final recall.

the distraction groups. If it is remembered that the final recall was actually the first recall for the control subjects, then the recall data can be completely summarized as follows: (1) Rehearsal increased *initial* recall. (2) After initial recall, the probability of a later recall was entirely dependent on whether the initial recall had been successful or not. (3) The probability of final recall given a successful initial recall increased monotonically in a negatively accelerated way with the initial retention interval. (4) There was no benefit of an initial recall on a later recall when the initial retention interval was near zero.

EXPERIMENT 2

Experiment 2 represents the first step in an effort to study the processes evidenced in Experiment 1 in a more realistic situation. The aim of this experiment was to combine the rigorous control over time intervals which was possible in Experiment 1 with a task which would be more representative of real life settings.

Method

In the experimental group each of 16 college students listened to each of six tape recorded passages. Each passage was a complete story and the topics ranged in content from a description of caribou in Northern Canada and Alaska, to that of a train race between two American cities. Each passage consisted of 12 sentences (numbered 1 - 12) and each sentence contained two unique pieces of information (the "basic ideas") not duplicated elsewhere in the passage. In the tape recording of passages, each sentence began exactly every five seconds, all sentences being of such length as to blend into each other smoothly when spoken at a normal speed. After listening to a passage once a subject was asked four sentence-completion questions. The subject was given the stem of a sentence which had occurred during presentation and required to complete it. Such questions were asked at 0, 10, 20, and 30 seconds from the end of the passage. The sentences about which questions were asked were always those in positions 2, 6, 10, and 12 within the passage. However, the *order* of the passages as well as that of the questions at the end of each passage was counterbalanced across subjects. At the end of the experiment, that is, after the questions about the sixth passage had been answered, the subjects were given a final recall test on all stories. This test had the same form as the immediate test.

Two more groups of 8 subjects each acted as control. One group was not engaged in any initial recall. While subjects in the experimental group answered questions immediately after a passage, those in this control group were engaged in a distracting task (counting backwards by threes). This control group was given, at the end of the experiment, the same test as the experimental group. The other control group was given a free recall task both initially (after each passage) and finally (at the end of the experiment). In either case subjects were instructed to repeat the story they had heard in their own words. Subjects' responses were scored for meaning. Two judges independently determined whether a response contained basic ideas expressed in the original sentence or not. They agree on practically 100% of the cases.

Results and Discussion

The results are shown in Figure 2. The ordinate is the percent of basic ideas recalled out of the possible maximum number. The abscissa represents the initial retention interval, in units of 5 seconds, measured from the end of the time unit during which a sentence was spoken in the message to the time when the question about it, in the initial recall, was asked. In the Free control group the initial retention interval was not under experimental control and so only the average performance for both initial and final recall is reported. Similarly, there is no relationship to initial retention interval, since there was no initial recall test, in the distraction group and only the average final recall is reported for this group.

Figure 2 (A) shows initial recall for the experimental (IR) and free control group. The experimental group initial recall decreased in the usual way as a function of retention interval. Overall the performance of the IR and free control group was similar in the initial recall.

Figure 2 (B) shows the Final recall. Three measures for the IR group are reported: The conditional probability of recall given a successful initial recall, FR/IR, the conditional probability of recall given an unsuccessful initial recall, FR/$\overline{\text{IR}}$, and the unconditional probability of recall, FR(IR). Also shown in Figure 2 (B) are the unconditional probabilities of recall for the free and distraction control groups. The FR/IR curve replicates that obtained in Experiment 1, increasing rapidly with retention interval to reach asymptote at 10 seconds. Again FR/$\overline{\text{IR}}$ was very small. The FR(IR) curve was significantly above the FR(distraction) curve ($p < .05$), indicating that the initial recall strengthened the recalled sentences (see Modigliani, 1976), with the FR(Free) curve falling between the two. Overall, these results were very similar to those obtained in Experiment 1, indicating that the relationship between initial test and later retention as a function of initial retention interval has validity in a fairly realistic situation.

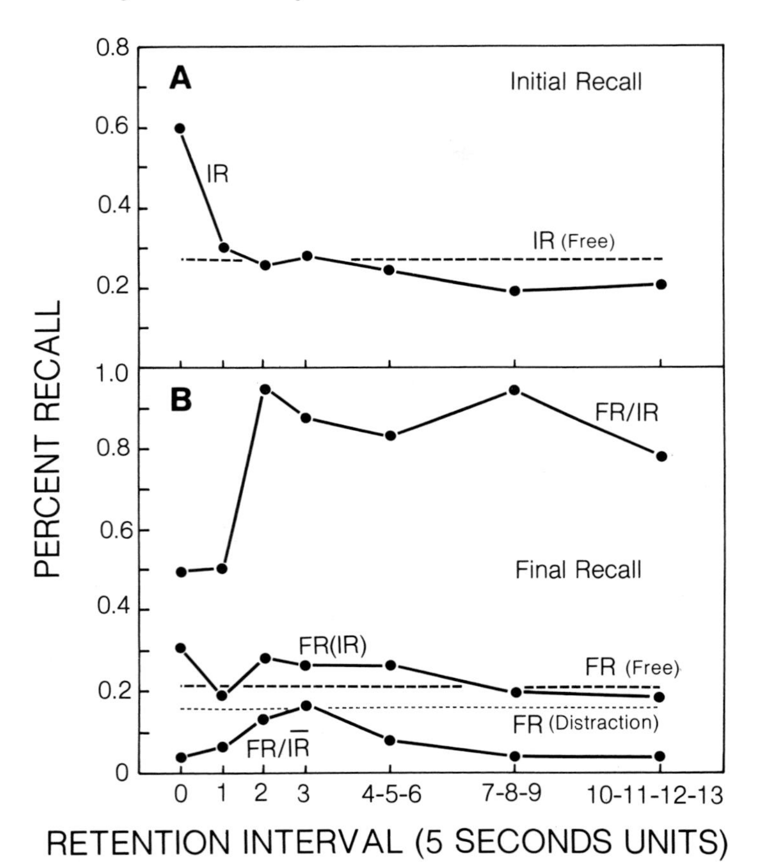

Fig. 2 (A) Initial recall for the IR and free group. (B) Final recall for the IR, free and distraction groups.

CONCLUSIONS

The results of the two experiments reported here confirm and extend those obtained in past research on the effect of asking questions after a passage (Anderson and Biddle, 1975).

They confirm the fact that unconditional final recall is better when preceded by an earlier initial recall than in its absence. They also confirm rather dramatically that it is information (*words* in Experiment 1 and *ideas* in Experiment 2) already recalled initially that is recalled in the later test. The Results extend previous findings by showing that an initial recall benefits a later recall only when the initial retention interval is greater than approximately few seconds.

The practical implications of this research with regard to how to structure practice in certain school subjects, for example, the multiplication tables, is clear. It would be much more efficacious *not* to repeat a particular multiplication, say 8 X 6, over and over again, but to repeat it once, do a different one which will take a few seconds, and then practice 8 X 6 again. Regarding the learning of written material, questions about important ideas would be most effective if asked only a few seconds, but not immediately, after they have been presented. This way the initial recall would still have a high probability of being successful and the few seconds delay would insure that the probability of a later recall would be increased.

ACKNOWLEDGEMENTS

This research was supported by National Research Council of Canada Grant A 0698. The author gratefully acknowledges the invaluable assistance of Don Hedges.

REFERENCES

Anderson, R.C., and Biddle, W.B. (1975). On asking people questions about what they are reading. In G.H. Bower (Ed.) *The Psychology of Learning and Motivation*. Vol. 9, New York: Academic Press, 1975.

Modigliani, V. (1976). Effects on a later recall by delaying initial recall. *Journal of Experimental Psychology: Human Learning and Memory*, 2, 609-622.

Rothkopf, E.Z. (1965). Some theoretical and experimental approaches to problems in written instruction. In J.D. Krumboltz (Ed.), *Learning and the Educational Process*. Chicago: Rand McNally.

Rundus, D. (1971). Analysis of rehearsal processes in free recall. *Journal of Experimental Psychology*, 89, 63-77.

Spitzer, H.F. (1939). Studies in retention. *Journal of Educational Psychology*, 30, 641-656.

Thios, S.J., and D'Agostino, P.R. (1976). Effects of repetition as a function of study-phase retrieval. *Journal of Verbal Learning and Verbal Behavior*, 15, 529-536.

Whitten, W.B. II, and Bjork, R.A. (1977). Learning from tests: Effects of spacing. *Journal of Verbal Learning and Verbal Behavior*, 16, 465-478.

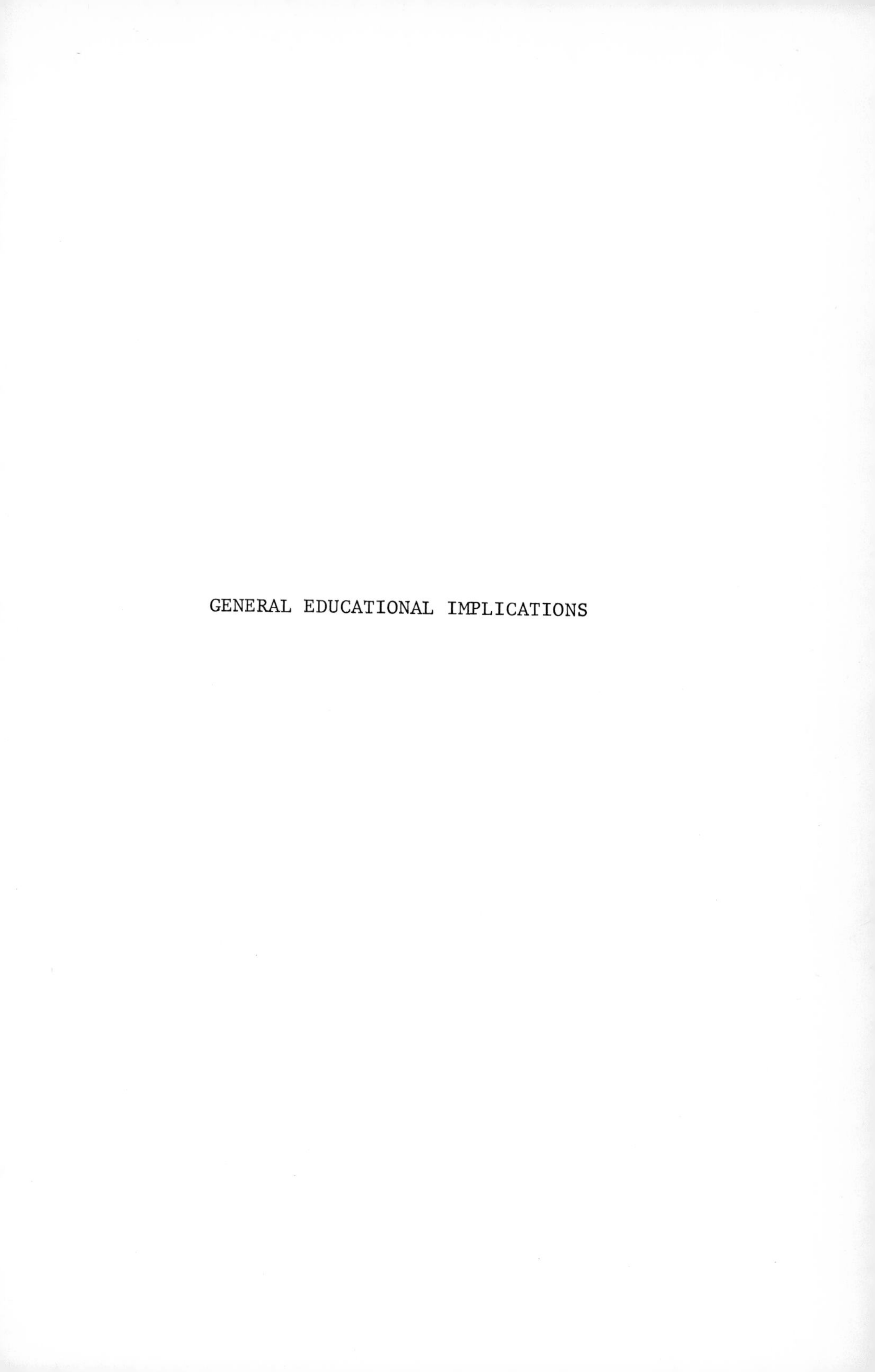

GENERAL EDUCATIONAL IMPLICATIONS

THE COMPREHENSION AND MEMORY OF SIMILES AS A FUNCTION OF CONTEXT

Neal E. A. Kroll, Raymond W. Berrian, and Alan F. Kreisler
University of California, Davis, CA. 95616 U.S.A.

The present experiment systematically varied the contexts of a series of similes to study the effect of 6 different types of contexts on (*a*) the speed of comprehension of the simile, and (*b*) the memory of the simile. The memory of these similes was further studied as a function of the type of recall cue and the relationship of that cue to the previous context. Contexts related to the Subjects of "Good Similes" generally resulted in slower classification times and more errors, but better recall, than did contexts related to their Predicates. The opposite tended to be true for "Bad Similes."

I. INTRODUCTION

The comprehension of figurative language has been shown to be a serious problem for "semantic marker" theories of linguistic meaning. Psychological theories have been open to similar criticisms(*e.g.*, Pollio, Barlow, Fine, & Pollio, 1977). Since there is growing evidence that the processes required for the understanding of figurative language are similar to the processes required for the understanding of any novel sentence, a development of a comprehensive theory of sentence comprehension may require a much more complete understanding of the processes involved in figurative language than is currently available. Until recently, most of the research on this topic has involved the comprehension of isolated (or context-free) figurative statements and, thus, probably bears little relationship to normal comprehension processes. Recently, Ortony (*e.g.*, Ortony, Schallert, Reynolds, & Antos, in press) has begun to compare the comprehension of figurative and literal sentences within a context. However, the actual role of the context has yet to be studied in detail.

In the present experiment, brief (one sentence) contexts were given to the subjects immediately preceding the presentation of the simile. Subjects were instructed to judge the communication value (Good *vs.* Bad) of the simile as a figurative statement, regardless of its possible value as a literal statement. In contrast to Ortony's experiment, subjects were instructed to ignore the context sentence, which was often irrelevant or even misleading. Pilot work had convinced us that, with any less extreme instructions regarding the context, subjects routinely would misconstrue the task, judging as "good" only those similes whose context literalized them. The question now was, in what ways and to what degree would the context play a role when subjects were not specifically looking for a coherent sentence pair?

II. METHOD

A. *Subjects*

Twenty undergraduates participated individually and received credit in an introductory psychology course. The data from 3 of these subjects were discarded because of excessive errors and abnormally long decision times.

B. *Materials*

The authors, with the help of numerous colleagues, developed a number of similes and selected 72 that seemed to be reasonably straight-forward, without being at the level of a cliché (*e.g.*, "Her lectures were like an electric storm."). Another 72 similes were constructed which were deliberately obscure and unlikely (*e.g.*, "The meat loaf was like a flashlight."). The former will be referred to as "Good Similes," the latter as "Bad Similes." Context sentences were constructed for all similes. In half of the context sentences, the Subject of the context sentence was also the Subject of the simile. In the other half, the Subject of the context sentence was the Predicate of the simile. For Good Similes, the context sentences were further divided into Relevant, Irrelevant, and Misleading contexts. For example, the simile "The refugees were like windblown leaves." could be introduced by a Relevant context dealing with the Predicate ("Windblown leaves fly aimlessly."), by an Irrelevant context dealing with the Subject ("The refugees arrived by boat."), by a Misleading context dealing with the Predicate ("Windblown leaves were numerous."), *etc*. Relevant contexts refer to the relationship between Subject and Predicate expressed in the simile, Irrelevant contexts refer to a property of the Subject or Predicate not normally shared by the other, and Misleading contexts refer to a property that could be shared by the Subject and Predicate of the simile, but not to the relationship expressed in the simile. Each subject saw only one context sentence per simile, but had an equal number of each of the 6 types over the 72 Good Similes and the Good Similes were introduced by different contexts across subjects.

The Bad Similes could not, naturally, be introduced by Relevant contexts (since they had no real message), but were introduced by either Irrelevant or Misleading contexts dealing with either the Subject or Predicate of the Simile. For example, the Misleading context dealing with the Subject of the Bad Simile "His beard was like a table." was "His beard was brown." Since the present experiment focuses on the comprehension of Good Similes, context sentences were not varied over subjects for the Bad Similes.

C. Procedure

The subjects were told that they would be shown pairs of sentences back-projected onto the small screen in front of them. The first sentence of each pair was shown for 3 sec., during which time it was read aloud by the subject. The second sentence of the pair followed 1 sec. later and was not read aloud. Rather, subjects decided as rapidly as possible if the second sentence represented "a reasonably clear metaphoric communication" and indicated their choice by pressing one of two keys in front of them. Since pilot work had shown that some people interpret this task as a challenge to see if they can rationalize even the most bizarre simile, while others prefer to play it safe and classify all but the most obvious similes as Bad Similes, subjects were told that these similes had been carefully studied and classified by three experts and that the task was to learn the classification criteria used by the experts. Whenever the subject misclassified the simile, the experimenter stopped the timers and discussed the subject's reasons for the choice. With this new procedure, most of the errors were conservative ones (classifying Good Similes as Bad) and most of these were self-correcting, *i.e.*, the subject would say that they now saw it as soon as the experimenter stopped the timers. The following examples were given to the subject in the instructions:
First sentence: "The totem pole was made out of wood."
Second sentence: "The arrow was like a totem pole."
Answer: Bad Simile--even though both are made out of wood and both are possible Indian artifacts, this would be a literal communication and there is no readily discernible metaphoric communication in the second sentence.
First sentence: "His personality was very pleasant."
Second sentence: "His personality was like an anchor."
Answer: Good Simile--this sentence is a meaningful metaphor, indicating that his personality was a liability to him. Note that in this case the first sentence was somewhat misleading in that a pleasant personality would probably not be "an anchor." However, the decision is to be made on the second sentence *by itself*.

The first 24 trials of the series were not scored so as to help reduce the number of error classifications (and the resulting disruptions) during the actual experiment and also to allow the subject to approach an asymptotic decision speed prior to scored trials. Subjects were not informed of this distinction and these 24 "practice trials" were not differentiated. This left 60 Good Similes (10 with each of the 6 types of contexts) and 60 Bad Similes that were actually scored.

After a subject had completed all 144 trials, they were given booklets consisting of lists of cue sentences, one cue sentence for each of the Good Similes in the scored trials, one for each of 16 of the Bad Similes in the scored trials, in addition to starting with six cue sentences from the "practice trials." The subjects were told that they should use each cue sentence to help them to recall one of the similes. They were told that sometimes the cue sentence would be the context sentence that they had seen for that simile, but not always. In fact, the cue sentence was the same as the context sentence for all practice similes and all Bad Similes cued in the second phase, but only for half of the Good Similes. The other Good Similes were cued by sentences that had been used as context sentences for other subjects. The subjects were allowed to work through the booklets at their own pace.

III. RESULTS

The decision times for the correctly classified similes were averaged for each subject as a function of the type of preceding context sentence. The mean decision times, averaged over subjects, are presented on the top of Fig. 1. If the preceding context sentence deals with the Subject of the simile, the classification time of a Good Simile is longer than if the context sentence deals with the Predicate, 2.87 *vs.* 2.66 sec., $t(16) = 4.616$, but just the opposite is the case for Bad Similes, 2.56 *vs.* 2.77 sec., $t(16) = 3.280$. Within the Good Similes, comparisons of individual pairs of types of contexts found only the Subject/Misleading and Predicate/Misleading to differ significantly, $t(16) = 3.818$. We are currently nearing completion of an extension of this experiment with some changes in the similes and a different form of memory testing. In the extension, we are finding the same pattern of increasing decision times over Relevant, Irrelevant, and Misleading contexts in the Subject context conditions, but the Predicate context conditions appear to all result in the same decision time, which is approximately the same as the Subject/Relevant condition. The pattern for Bad Similes remains the same.

The percentages of misclassifications for the various conditions are presented on the bottom of Fig. 1. Subjects made almost no misclassifications of the Bad Similes, but for Good Similes, Subject related contexts resulted in more misclassifications than did Predicate related contexts, 29.0% *vs.* 19.2% $t(16) = 3.915$.

The mean percentages of similes recalled, of those that had been correctly classified, are presented in Fig. 2. The recall of those similes cued with the same sentence previously used as a context sentence for a particular subject are presented at the top. With Good Similes, the Subject related cues resulted in better recall than the Predicate related cues, but the difference failed to reach significance, 50.1% *vs.* 40.9%, $t(16) = 1.937$. In comparing individual points, the Subject/

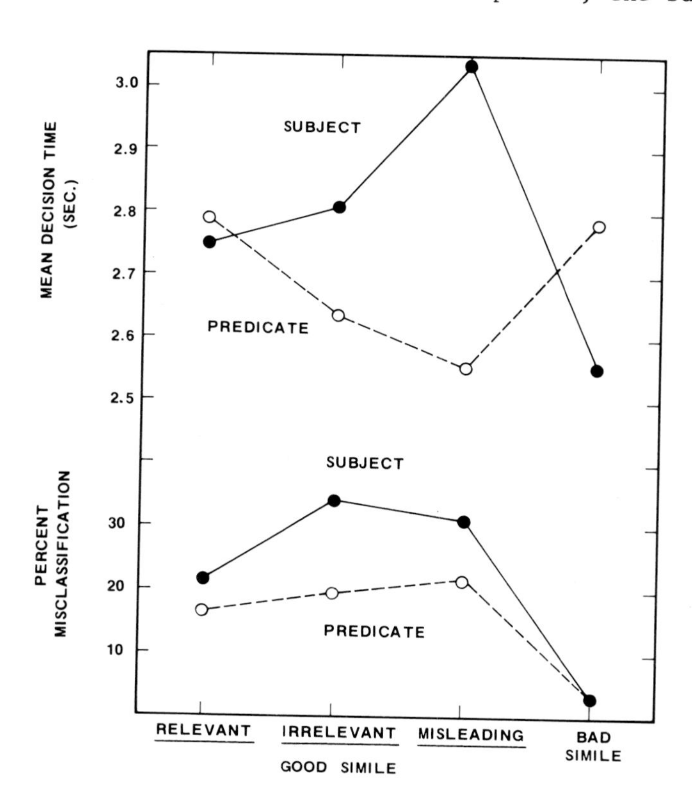

Fig. 1 TOP: Mean decision time, in seconds, of correctly classified similes as a function of context sentence. BOTTOM: Mean percentage of misclassifications as a function of context sentence.

Relevant cue resulted in a greater percentage of recall than did the Subject/Irrelevant, $t(16) = 2.574$, and the Predicate/Irrelevant cue resulted in a lower recall percentage than either Predicate/Relevant, $t(16) = 2.647$ or Predicate/Misleading, $t(16) = 2.400$. While the tendency with Good Similes was for Subject cues to result in better recall, the opposite was true for Bad Similes, $t(16) = 2.861$, resulting in a significant interaction of Good/Bad Similes by Subject/Predicate Recall Cue, $t(16) = 4.269$. For those 11 subjects who made at least two classification errors in each of the Subject and Predicate context conditions of the Good Similes, the average recall of misclassified similes was 39.0% and 34.7%, respectively.

The recall of those similes cued with different sentences than those previously used as context sentences for the subject are presented at the bottom of Fig. 2. (Note that this was only tested with the Good Similes.) Here the Predicate cue appears to aid recall better than does the Subject cue. While this difference is not significant, $t(16) = 1.965$, the

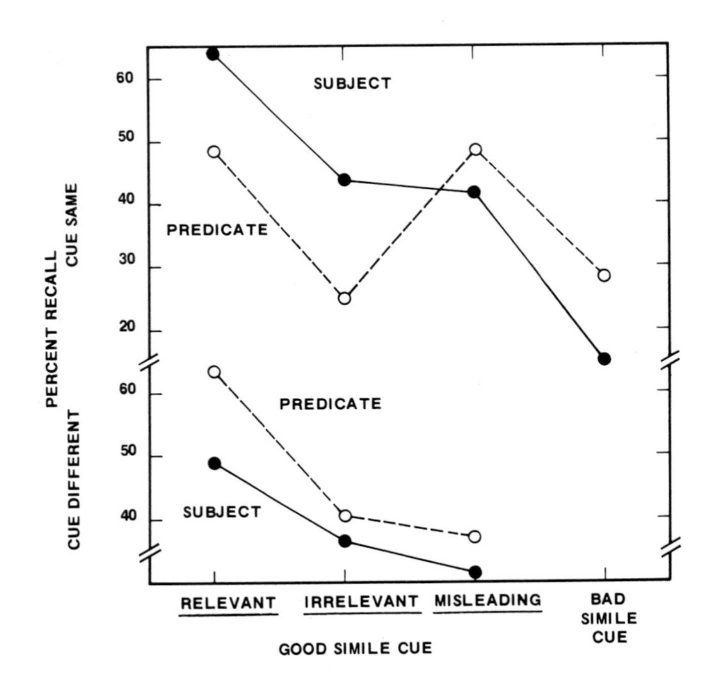

Fig. 2 Mean percentage of similes recalled, of those that had been correctly classified, as a function of cue sentence. TOP: Cue and context sentences identical. BOTTOM: Cue and context sentences different.

interaction between Same/Different Cue by Subject/Predicate Cue is significant, $t(16) = 3.114$.

IV. DISCUSSION

The recall data (Fig. 2) is quite similar to that found by Verbrugge and McCarrell (1977), *i.e.*, the Relevant cue sentence, which is a statement of the implicit resemblance (the Ground) of the simile, is the best recall cue for the simile. The present results go beyond those of Verbrugge and McCarrell in showing that this is true even when the initial context for the statement was misleading and should tend to obscure the Ground.

While much of the recent work on the understanding of figurative statements has focused upon describing what people derive from the figurative statement, our major motivation was to focus on how these interpretations are derived. In this, regard, the recall data from those tests where the cue sentence was different from the context sentence (Fig. 2, bottom) suggest that cues dealing with the Predicate of the simile result in better recall, probably because the predicate of a sentence tends to convey the majority of the information of the simile. (*e.g.*, See Hornby, 1972, and his discussion of the Prague School. Note that we are assuming that, for the simple declarative sentences used as contexts, cues, and similes in this experiment, the psychological Subject and Predicate are the same as the logical ones.) To understand why the Subject cues should result in better recall than the predicate cues when the cue sentences are identical to the context sentences (Fig. 2, top), we must examine the data from the decision times and the decision misclassifications (Fig. 1).

When attempting to interpret the decision time results, it would probably be best to keep in mind the pattern of significant results and the results of the replication study now under way. Then one finds that the relevancy variable (Relevant *vs.* Irrelevant *vs.* Misleading) and the simile-value variable (Good *vs.* Bad) are virtually ineffective when the context sentence has the Predicate of the simile as its own Subject. On the other hand, these variables have very large effects on decision times when the context and simile sentences share Subjects: the Subject/Relevant context being at the same level as the Predicate contexts, the Subject/Irrelevant being somewhat slower, the Subject/Misleading being much slower, and the Subject contexts for the Bad Similes being much faster. One way of understanding this pattern, at least for simple declarative sentences, would be as follows: Rather than the two domains of a sentence being tied together by a mediator (*e.g.*, Pollio, 1974), the

Subject is seen as limiting the possible range of meanings of the Predicate, which in turn is the part of the sentence that actually conveys new information which acts back upon the Subject, elaborating it. In the present experiment, if a context sentence is a Predicate type, we have a pair of sentences of the type $Y_1 = Z$. $X = Y_2$., and the Subject of the Simile (X), being different from the Subject of the context (Y_1), sets up a different set of possibilities and the subject finds it relatively easy to judge the simile independently from the context and/or to treat Y_2 as relatively independent from Y_1. However, if the context sentence is a Subject type, we have $X_1 = Z$. $X_2 = Y$. and the Subject of the simile (X_2), which helps to define its Predicate (Y), already has its own range of meanings defined from the previous usage (X_1) which the subject apparently has difficulty ignoring. Thus Irrelevant and Misleading contexts make it more difficult to see that a particular $X_2 = Y$. is a Good Simile, and make it easier to reject other $X_2 = Y$. as Bad Similes. The same general pattern is found with the error data if one adds the subjects' conservative bias, making the error rates extremely low in the Bad Simile conditions. Note that while we, like the Prague School, see the major new information being introduced by the Predicate, we are assuming that the Subject plays a major role in how the Predicate will be interpreted.

REFERENCES

Hornby, P. A. (1972). The psychological Subject and Predicate. *Cognitive Psychology*. 3, 632-642.

Ortony, A., Schallert, D. L., Reynolds, R. E., & Antos, S. J. (in press). Interpreting metaphors and idioms: Some effects of context on comprehension. *Psychological Bulletin*.

Pollio, H. R. (1974). *The psychology of symbolic activity*. Addison-Wesley, Reading, Mass.

Pollio, H. R., Barlow, J. M., Fine, H. J., & Pollio, M. R. (1977). *Psychology and the Poetics of Growth*. Erlbaum, Hillsdale, N. J.

Verbrugge, R. R., & McCarrell, N. S. (1977). Metaphoric comprehension: Studies in reminding and resembling. *Cognitive Psychology*. 9, 494-533.

LEVELS OF PROCESSING, STUDY PROCESSES AND FACTUAL RECALL

J.B. Biggs
Faculty of Education, University of Newcastle
Shortland, N.S.W., 2308, Australia

ABSTRACT

While the levels of processing (LOP) model appears potentially fruitful for educational applications, certain difficulties need to be met; measuring coding depth and spread, the question of what-is-learned, and individual differences. Recall of poem and prose material was used here under two encoding conditions; time on task, structural complexity and length of *S*s' responses, and individual study strategies were recorded. Depth and spread measures were not related to immediate or long term recall, but conditions and study strategies suggesting nonelaborative coding were. In its present form, the LOP model does not yet appear useful for educational applications.

INTRODUCTION

A common learning situation, in both school and laboratory, involves reception learning from a finite display of information, followed by immediate and/or delayed recall.

The levels of processing (LOP) model (Craik & Lockhart, 1972; Craik & Tulving, 1975) would appear to be fruitful for deriving educational applications in this context. Marton (1976), citing the LOP model, distinguished "deep level" and "surface level" processing in university students on the basis of introspective reports after a learning event, and showed that students categorised as deep processors were academically more successful than surface level processors.

Marton's findings are encouraging, but not crucial for LOP theory. To say, as do Craik and Tulving (op.cit.; p292), that "subjects remember not what was 'out there', but what they *did* during encoding", implies a confusion between the *process* of memorising and *what it was* that the student should remember; the latter is usually the concern of educators. For example, if students are instructed to learn specific details in a connected prose passage, one would expect a different outcome than if they were instructed to learn meanings. However, because depth of coding is defined in terms of meaning (Craik, 1973), details would be expected to be recalled *better* under instructions for meaningful learning than instructions to learn detail. Marton's experiments showed only that meaningful learning was superior with deeper than with surface coding. The question of retention of detail has yet to be examined.

The application of the LOP model to practical contexts raises other problems:

1. The absence of an independent measure of LOP (Baddeley, 1978; Eysenck, 1978). This problem is particularly pertinent in the *semantic* domain. While Craik has provided evidence for his hypothesis across physical, pattern recognition and semantic domains, as Baddeley says elsewhere (1976; p168, fn): "I know of no good evidence for deeper levels of processing within the semantic domain leading to better retention." Since Craik *et al*.(1975) distinguish between *depth* and *spread*, both or either might be used to refer to the elaborateness of coding, as investigated below.

2. Shallow encoding can be shown to lead to durable retention (Baddeley, 1978; Eysenck, op.cit.).

3. The LOP model says nothing about change, and especially developmental change, in memory processes; and it needs to pay more attention to ecological validity, a point which is particularly important in the context of educative learning (Reese, 1976).

4. Individual differences, apart from developmental differences, might be expected to affect retention; e.g. differences in learning styles or study strategies.

The present paper is an attempt to consider some of these aspects of the LOP model, and to test them in the context of undergraduate learning.

Elaborateness of Coding

The writer has been involved in the development of a taxonomy for assessing the complexity of structure of student learning (Collis & Biggs, 1976). This work originated in applying Piaget's stages to different school subjects, but it rapidly became apparent that we were dealing with the structure of *o*bserved *l*earning *o*utcomes (hence the SOLO Taxonomy), that happened to be isomorphic to, but distinct from, the Piagetian stages. The SOLO Taxonomy most readily applies to the paradigm, earlier referred to, where a finite display of information is presented, such as a piece of prose, a poem, or other symbolic information as nominal stimulus, and the subject is to respond in terms of the functional stimulus. Five hierarchically organised SOLO levels are distinguished:

1. Pre-structural. The response has no logical relationship to the display, being based upon an irrelevancy, tautology, or inability to comprehend.

2. Uni-structural. The response contains one relevant structure or aspect from the display but misses others that are relevant and that might modify or contradict the conclusion. Closure is rapid and oversimplified.

3. Multi-structural. The response contains several aspects, but selects only those that additively cohere with the conclusion; contradictory data are overlooked.

4. Relational. Most or all of the data are comprehended and utilised; conflicts are resolved by the use of a relating concept that is taken directly from the display and its immediate context, so that a firm but comprehensive conclusion results.

5. Extended abstract. All the data are accepted, but the context is transcended by reference to abstract general principles, which may even question the context. Non-given examples or conclusions are referred to, and closure is often withheld or qualified as a result.

Further details of this taxonomy may be found in Biggs (1978). The present point is that SOLO levels, being hierarchical with respect to the content to be learned, meet the requirements of *depth* of coding within the semantic domain (cf. Reese, op.cit; also Craik *et al.*, 1975). *Spread* of coding within a level, may reasonably be operationalised by taking the number of words a subject uses to justify his encoding, since the number of coded features is likely to be reflected in the number of words used.

Individual differences in coding strategy

Learning complex semantic material is likely to be marked by individual differences, and these appear to have been ignored in previous LOP research. Biggs (in press) has described three dimensions in study processes in tertiary students. These dimensions contain a cognitive (strategic) and an affective (motivational) component:

1. Instrumental: motivated by fear of failure and pragmatism, with a minimax strategy of narrowing the learning target to isolated facts and details and rote learning them.

2. Internalising: motivated intrinsically, with a strategy of reading widely and integrating with meaningful previous learnings.

3. Achieving: motivated by need-achieving and competition, with a strategy organizing work modules systematically to obtain maximum grades.

These three dimensions are measured by the writer's Study Process Questionnaire (SPQ) (Biggs, op.cit.). These strategies could affect recall in one or both of two ways. First, directly through LOP, in that a set to learn facts and details would appear nonelaborative, and likely to lead to surface processing; while integrating new with previously learned meanings over a wide range of material, would seem to lead to deep level processing. A set to achieve would be likely to lead to context-dependent processing; deep or shallow, as the student perceives it to be required. Second, strategy deployment may be independent of LOP, as suggested by Eysenck (1978), at encoding as well as at retrieval.

RATIONALE FOR THE PRESENT STUDY AND METHOD

The aim of the present study was to test the LOP model in the learning and retention of poems (Experiment 1) and prose material (Experiment 2) with undergraduate Education students. In Experiment 1, 30 *S*s were given two short poems to study ("Man in the Ocelot Suit" by Brookhouse, and "Spring and Fall" by Hopkins). Students were then asked: "What does this poem mean to you?", to obtain SOLO levels, and then to write out as much of each poem as they could remember. The number of correct words recalled was recorded, as was the time taken by each student for the whole task.

In Experiment 2, the SPQ was administered to another class of 60 undergraduates, and two tasks with instructions. The stimulus materials were two abstracts (750 word and 600 word; taken from *Psychology Today*) of educational experiments, referred to here as "Third Wave" and "Day Care". Half the group were instructed to read the first abstract for meaning (relating purpose of the experiment to evidence, procedures and conclusions) and the second abstract for fact (concentrating on facts and experimental detail); the other half of the group had the order of instructions reversed. An instruction after each experiment was then given to elicit a response for SOLO classification, followed by a list of highly factual questions about each experiment. The factual questions were repeated a week later to test for retention.

The data were inter-correlated; and a number of analyses of variance were carried out.

RESULTS

1. *Relationships between depth and spread of coding and recall*

Table 1 gives the correlations between SOLO level (depth of coding) and SOLO length (spread of coding), time on task (as related to depth of coding (Craik, 1973)), and the number of recalled words for the poems.

	SOLO Man	SOLO Spring	L SOLO Man	L SOLO Spring	N Man	N Spring
SOLO Man	1.00	.12	.71**	.07	*.02*	.21
SOLO Spring	.12	1.00	.31	.70**	.02	*.03*
L SOLO Man	.71**	.31	1.00	.44**	*.05*	.38?
L SOLO Spring	.07	.70**	.44**	1.00	.08	*.14*
Time	.41*	.09	.64**	.57**	*.04*	*.37?*

? = P <.10; * = P <.05; ** = P <.01

Table 1 Correlations between depth (SOLO) and spread (L SOLO) of coding and verbatim recall of poetry (N = 24)

Both length and level of SOLO intercorrelate significantly, as they mostly do with time taken: such consistency indicates some sort of commonality with respect to the various aspects of coding elaborateness. The italicised *r*s in the two right columns are critical for the theory, but none is significant.

Similar correlations between length and level of SOLO, time, and immediate and delayed recall of factual detail in the Third Wave and Day Care tasks were calculated. Again, however, none of the critical correlations between measures of elaborateness of coding and recall were significant; neither was SOLO length with recall *within* level.

2. Depth of coding, study strategies and conditions of learning

Three sets of ANOVAs were carried out on each of Third Wave and Day Care data: Study strategy x SOLO level x Condition (Fact/Meaning) x Occasions (rept. meas.) on factual recall, where the study strategy factors were each of the instrumental, internalizing and achieving scores split at the median. There were no significant effects on the Third Wave data (apart from Occasions) but with the instrumental and achieving strategies as independent variables the following effects (apart from Occasions, which was highly significant) were obtained (see Table 2):

1. Instrumental ($F = 4.83$; d.f. 1,35, $P < .05$)
   Instrumental x Conditions ($F = 7.86$; d.f.1,35; $P < .01$)

Instrum.	Cond.	Occ. 1	Occ. 2
High	Fact	11.32	8.38
	Mean	6.62	4.44
Low	Fact	7.27	4.43
	Mean	7.50	5.28

2. Achievement x Occasions ($F = 5.03$; d.f.1,35; $P < .05$)

Achiev.	Occ. 1	Occ. 2
High	8.97	4.84
Low	7.36	4.70

Table 2 Significant effects and interactions from ANOVAs

The Instrumental x Conditions interaction shows (Table 2) that those students prone to using a rote learning type of strategy tend to recall more facts under conditions encouraging factual recall and less facts under meaningful conditions. This pattern is also evident on long term recall; neither is evident for students not prone to this study strategy. This finding was not mitigated in any way by depth of coding, as assessed by SOLO level, which was non-significant either as a main effect or in interaction.

The achieving strategy showed a significant interaction with Occasions: those prone to using achieving strategies recalled more facts immediately, but not after a lapse of one week.

DISCUSSION OF RESULTS

On the measures of elaborateness of coding used here, it seems that recall of poetry and of prose accounts of details of experiments have nothing to do with elaborateness of coding expressed either in terms of depth or spread. There are several possible explanations for this disappointing finding:

1. SOLO level and SOLO length do not tap what is meant by coding depth, spread or elaborateness. However, when an *S* explains the two experiments, or what a poem means to him, it seems inconceivable, in light of Craik's (1973) definition of depth in terms of meaning, that *none* of complexity of response structure or length of explanation, or even time of processing (*op.cit*), relates to depth or elaboratness of coding. One can only ask what *would* provide such a measure?

2. The *S*s here were fairly sophisticated undergraduates, with consequent restriction of variance. It is possible that in the ecology of tertiary education, differences in LOP could be so slight as to be over-ridden by other factors. It might well be in fact that LOP is a fruitful concept across domains, but is relatively uninfluential within the semantic domain; even given that the SOLO levels to the poems represented the full range from 1 to 5.

3. The effects of LOP relative to strategies is brought out in the fact that individual differences in study strategies, particularly in interaction with instructions for learning, did produce differences in recall. The instrumental (rote learning) orientation under factual conditions is one that is hardly likely to be conducive to "deep" or "elaborate" coding; yet it is precisely that combination that led to best recall both immediately and long term (see Table 2). Surface coding can thus produce durable retention; possibly because of strategy deployment. Eysenck (1978) suggests that in retrieval, LOP affects item search but not strategy selection. The same point might be made at input; the strategy used might be quite independent of LOP, and produce results contrary to those expected on the LOP model. This does not invalidate the latter so much as suggest its incompleteness.

In sum, it would appear that while the LOP model might effectively predict retention across fairly gross domains -- such as physical, pattern recognition and semantic -- it is ineffectual in predicting effects within the semantic domain using sophisticated subjects, i.e. within the area that educators are most concerned. It may well be that further refinements can be made to the model so that the "one grand theory" can fit educational events. In the meantime, however, it would appear that the study of learning conditions, particularly in interaction with individual differences such as student study processes, will provide a more useful framework for studying educative learning. The question of whether LOP or some other kind of model of semantic memory will have educational applications must remain in abeyance.

REFERENCES

Baddeley, A.D. (1976) *The psychology of memory.* Basic Books, New York.

Baddeley, A.D. (1978) The trouble with levels: A reexamination of Craik and Lockhart's framework for memory research. *Psychological Review,* 85, 139-152.

Biggs, J.B. (1978) The relationship between developmental level and the quality of school learning. In: *Toward a Theory of Psychological development within the Piagetian framework.* (S. & C. Modgil eds.), National Foundation for Educational Research, Slough, Bucks.

Biggs, J.B. (in press) Individual and group differences in study processes. *British Journal of Educational Psychology.*

Collis, K.F. & Biggs, J.B. (Nov.1976) Classroom examples of cognitive development phenomena. Paper presented to the Annual Conference, Australian Association for Research in Education, Brisbane.

Craik, F.I.M. (1973) A 'Levels of Analysis' view of memory. In: *Communication and Affect: Language and Thought* (P. Pliner, L. Krames, & T.M. Alloway eds.) Academic Press, London.

Craik, F.I.M. & Lockhart, R.S. (1972) Levels of processing: A framework for memory research. *Journal of Verbal Learning and Verbal Behavior.* 11, 671-684.

Craik, F.I.M. & Tulving. E. (1975) Depth of processing and the retention of words in episodic memory. *Journal of Experimental Psychology,* 104, 268-294.

Eysenck, M.W. (1978) Levels of processing: A critique. *British Journal of Psychology,* 69, 157-169.

Marton, F. (1976) What does it take to learn? Some implications of an alternative view of learning. In: *Strategies for Research and Development in Higher Education* (N. Entwistle, ed.), Swets and Zeitzlinger, Amsterdam.

Reese, H.W. (1976) Models of memory development. *Human Development,* 19, 291-303.

MEETING THE READER'S INTERESTS - WHO SHOULD CARE?

August Flammer, André Schläfli, and Beat Keller
University of Fribourg,
Fribourg, Switzerland.

ABSTRACT

A sample of adult readers was divided into a group with a standard reading to recall instruction (C), a group that was to focus on an aspect that went against the individual interest profiles (E2b), a group whose focus assignments favoured the interest profiles (E2a), and a group that had the freedom to chose the focus of greatest interest (E1a). Learning outcomes were greatest for E1a, followed by E2a, E2b, and C. The results were interpreted as additive effects of three factors: (i) having a focus while reading, (ii) match with individual interests, and (iii) S's own decision-making.

INTRODUCTION

Learning from text depends heavily on what the learner already knows before he reads a given text. No text actually says everything that a reader takes from it. Understanding any text presupposes a great deal of "world knowledge" which helps the reader infer what was said "between the lines".

Recent research has demonstrated that the mere possession of the relevant "world knowledge" does not guarantee its actual use in the inference process. It has to be "activated" or "foregrounded"; one way to do this is by providing titles. Several experiments have demonstrated that the immediate and the delayed recall of semantic units are enhanced by titles (Dooling and Lachman, 1971; Dooling and Mullet, 1973). In general terms these ideas have been discussed recently with the concept of the "schema" (e.g. Norman et àl., 1975).

If an author wants his text to be optimally (i.e. with

least distortion) understood and assimilated, he cannot soley rely on his pointing to the relevant schemata or the building up of these schemata by earlier parts of his text. The experiment to be reported here was started with the following assumption. Not only does a reader bring some activated schemata to the reading process, but he often sticks to them and resists abandoning them. Even if the author intends to hint at some schema, this may actually elicit a different one in the reader because of some idiosyncrasies of the reader's knowledge (Ausubel, 1968) or because of personal preferences or interests. Furthermore, a potentially interesting theme may not be of as much actual interest to a reader if prescribed by the author (or a teacher, etc.). If this is true, readers should be allowed or encouraged to choose the sequence of their own reading as much as the texts permit.

The present investigation aimed to find out whether the reader's decision-making does something more than the optimal, but prescribed, match between the current personal interests and the information to be learned from a text. All Ss had to read the same prose material, but had to focus their attention on different aspects of the content. For some Ss the aspects were prescribed, other Ss were allowed to choose. An independent evaluation of the individual interest profiles allowed a distinction between the Ss who got (or chose) an aspect to focus on that was their interest and the Ss whose main interest was not identical to the prescribed (or chosen) focus. The hypothesis was that the mere fact of having a focus while reading would raise the respective learning outcome (compared to a control reading group); that the interest match would contribute further; and that the active decision-making would prove to be an additional positive factor.

METHOD

Subjects. Fifty-eight first-year students of the University of Fribourg and 38 last-year students of the Teachers' College of Fribourg participated in the experiment. According to several criteria these two groups did not differ significantly in the data reported here. They will therefore be combined in the presentation.

Reading material. Fifteen page-long texts on Australian Aborigines were elaborated. One text was made up on each of five central themes (kinship, initiation rituals, ceremonies, totems, immortal beings) and one on each of the ten pairwise combinations of these five themes.

The texts were revised by ten experts (graduate students in ethnology). After the revision, the expert group was asked to determine a list of keywords to be used as a subject index. They proposed 35 keywords. Thereafter they had to rank them according to their importance in the complete set of the 15 texts. The experimenter then dropped the 20 keywords with the lowest average ranks. The following presentation will restrict itself to the remaining 15 keywords.

Finally the texts were revised, when necessary, in order to have at least six and at the most eight different keywords appear in each text; the total number of keywords that appeared in each text was manipulated so as to lie between 20 and 24 per text. Three key concepts that were fairly different from each other but nevertheless appeared in every text as keywords were defined as "aspects". These were: economy, society, and theory of life.

Recognition tests as dependent measures. 45 true-false test items were constructed. The test sentences were paraphrases of one or more sentences in the text. Each text contained relevant information for three items, one for each "aspect". Thus 15 items were constructed for each of the three aspects.

Cognitive structure as dependent measure. Each member of the expert group was given the aspect "economy" and asked to choose out of the set of 15 keywords those eight that had most to do with this aspect. Thereafter they were to rank the eight keywords. This procedure will be called "keyword ranking for aspects". The ranks were summed over all experts in order to get the average ranking. This was taken as the experts' cognitive structure. The same was done with the other two aspects.

This keyword ranking for aspects was also done with each S, yielding the Ss' cognitive structures. A relatedness coefficient (RC; Garskof and Houston, 1963) was calculated between the experts' and each S's cognitive structure in order to get a measure of the cognitive structure deviation for each S. The higher the RCs were, the smaller the deviations were said to be.

Procedure. First, Ss had to read the five texts corresponding to the five themes in order to get a minimal acquaintance with the material. They were told that this reading should allow them to tell the E afterwards how interesting they found the texts.

After this, the 15 keywords were given, out of which the Ss had to choose eight which they personally felt most interested in. Then they were to rank these eight keywords according to their personal interest priority (i.e., "keyword ranking for interest").

Ss were instructed that the main experiment was to begin. They were confronted with the "aspects" and did the keyword ranking for aspects the same way as the experts (cognitive structure). Then the Ss were told that they would be able to read ten more texts on which they would be tested afterwards for comprehension and retention of a certain aspect.

Twenty-seven Ss (E1) were allowed to determine this aspect themselves, choosing one out of the three. Forty-three Ss (E2) were randomly prescribed one of the three aspects. For further 26 Ss (C-control) no aspect was defined.

The reading was paced but individually sequenced, the Ss being allowed to choose the texts based on the texts' titles. After this reading, the cognitive structure test (keyword ranking for aspects) was repeated, and finally the recognition tests were administered. All this was done within one experimental session of 95 minutes.

RESULTS

Four groups were compared that differed on three factors: (i) S's own decision-making, (ii) interest match, and (iii) focus (Table 1). Group E1 (S's own decision) was reduced to E1a by eliminating those Ss (E1b) who did not choose the aspect that matched their previously shown main interest. This was done by calculating the RC between the keyword ranking for interest and the keyword ranking for each aspect

Table 1: Conditions to be compared

Group	Factors		
	S's own decision	Interest match	Focus
E1a	x	x	x
E2a	o	x	x
E2b	o	o	x
C	o	o	o

as the respective S had given it. E1a contains those Ss for whom the RC with the chosen aspect was the highest among all three. For 21 out of 27 Ss, this was the case; the remaining 6 were too small a group to be studied further.

Group E2 was split into E2a and E2b. E2a contained those Ss to whom an "aspect" was prescribed that randomly matched their previously measured interest priority, and E2b contained the remaining Ss (highest RC for another aspect). Thirteen Ss belonged to E2a and 30 Ss to E2b.

It should be kept in mind that no direct interest ranking of the aspects was ever made by Ss, this in order to avoid choices in E1 that were guided by mere memory of such a ranking, and also in order to avoid frustration in E2b. The contention here that an aspect choice or prescription matched the S's interest is based on his keyword ranking for interest and his own keyword ranking for each aspect.

Overall recognition. Recognition as measured by the whole set of the 45 recognition items was best for E1a, followed by E2a, then E2b, then C (Tab 2). These means differ significantly from one another ($F_{3,86}=4.00$; $p \simeq .01$). While the difference between the means of each adjacent group do not statistically differ, the linear regression on the group order is significant ($r = -.33$; $p < 0.1$).

Intention vs. incidental recognition. The recognition test contained 15 items for each aspect. Thus, those 15 items were said to measure intentional recognition for a given S, which corresponded to the aspect this S had chosen or, in E2a and E2b, that was allocated to this S. The other 30 items measured incidental learning. This distinction is not applicable to the control group.

While the values for incidental learning were slightly, but not significantly lower than those for intentional

Table 2: Overall recognition

Group	n	$\bar{x}$	p for difference
E1a	21	33.62	
			0.14
E2a	13	32.10	
			0.32
E2b	30	31.10	
			0.82
C	26	30.90	

learning, the same general trend over the groups was found for both, intentional and incidental learning (E1a best, followed by E2a and E2b).

Overall cognitive structure. Relatedness coefficients (RCs) were calculated between the mean experts' keyword ranking for aspects and each S's keyword ranking for aspects, each before and after the reading of the ten texts. The size of these RCs was taken as similarity of the S's and the experts' cognitive structure. Reading the texts should result in higher RCs. Thus, RC was taken as another measure of the learning outcome.

Table 3: Mean relatedness between S's and experts' overall cognitive structure

Group	Economy		Society		Theory of life	
	Pre	Post	Pre	Post	Pre	Post
E1a	.74	.78	.74	.83	.80	.87
E2a	.76	.76	.74	.78	.81	.81
E2b	.72	.80	.71	.75	.78	.84
C	.73	.72	.72	.74	.79	.82
r for linear trend (p)	-.06 (>.05)	-.16 (>.05)	-.11 (>.05)	-.32 (<.01)	-.06 (>.05)	-.11 (>.05)
F for partial regre-ssion (p)		2.10 (>.05)		8.71 (<.01)		0.77 (>.05)

Table 3 shows that there is a very slight and unexpected, but statistically unsignificant decrease of the preexperimental RCs from E1a over E2a and E2b to C. The decrease of the postexperimental RCs is more marked, but only in one case is it statistically significant. This case, the society aspect, happens to have been the most attractive for the Ss and also the most frequently chosen one in Ela. It may be that the accommodation of the cognitive structure as measured depends even more than simple information recognition on both information intake and interest.

Cognitive structure after intentional and incidental learning. In order to find out whether the strong RC trend in one case above was due to the larger portion of intentional learning Ss the same analysis was done separately for the intentional and the incidental case.

The regression on the group order was indeed generally more marked in the intentional case than in the incidental one. Yet the only significant partial regression showed up for intentional learning of the society aspect.

DISCUSSION

Empirical support has been found for the additive effects of three different conditions in learning from text: having a focus or thematic aspect to attend to with priority, coincidence of this focus with current personal interests, and freedom to choose the focus by one-self. Actually, the data is statistically significant only for the general trend over the given a priori order of factor addition, the single differences being in the expected direction but not sufficiently high to reach statistical reliability with the chosen sample size. Thus, a replication of the study is desirable. The difference between intentional and incidental learning was not large enough either to be secured against statistical error. A special keyword ranking procedure to measure the structuration of the knowledge did yield results consistent with the recognition measured, but was apparently not reliable enough to reach statistical significance.

Should the results be replicable, it is psychologically and educationally relevant to note that having a focus of attention can raise the retention of textual information, and of all the information, not only the one within the focus. This finding is opposed to the general one on the selective effect of pre-text questions (Anderson & Biddle, 1975; Rothkopf, 1976). This is probably due to the fact that the aspects our subjects had to focus on were more general than the questions normally used in that research.

Another important finding is that the effect of providing a focusing task interacts with the current interests of the reader. These are not readily replaceable.

Finally it is noteworthy that, other conditions held unchanged, the actual choosing or decision-making by the learning subject outweighs the prescription condition in terms of learning outcome. For the psychologist, the distinctive elements of the information processing remain to be investigated; for the educator, our results could point to a potential basic limitation of all prescriptive teaching, be it "individualized" or not (Flammer et al., 1976, 1977).

REFERENCES

Anderson, R.C. and Biddle, W.B. (1975). On asking people questions about what they are reading. In: *The psychology of learning and motivation*. Vol. 9. (G.H. Bower, ed.), 1-47. Academic, New York.

Ausubel, D.P. (1968). *Educational psychology: a cognitive view*. Holt, Rinehart, and Winston, New York.

Dooling, D. and Lachman, R. (1971). Effects of comprehension on the retention of prose. *Journal of Experimental Psychology*. 88, 216-222.

Dooling, D. and Mullet, R. (1973). Locus of thematic effects in retention of prose. *Journal of Experimental Psychology*. 97, 404-406.

Flammer, A., Büchel, F. and Gutmann, W. (1976). Wissensstruktur und Wahl von Informationstexten. *Zeitschrift für experimentelle und angewandte Psychologie*. 23, 30-44.

Flammer, A. and Gutmann, W. (1977). Das Prinzip der Subsidiarität in der pädagogischen Diagnostik. In: *Diagnose von Lernprozessen*. (H.-K. Garten, ed.), 88-96. Westermann, Braunschweig.

Garskof, B. and Houston, J. (1963). Measurement of Verbal relatedness. An idiographic approach. *Psychological Review*. 70, 277-288.

Norman, A.D., Rumelhart, D.E. and the LNR Research Group. (1975). *Explorations in cognition*. Freeman, San Francisco.

Rothkopf, E.Z. (1976). Writing to teach and reading to learn: A perspective on the Psychology of written instructuion. *Seventy-fifth yearbook of the National Society for the study of the Education*. 91-129. University of Chicago Press, Chicago.

BRAIN DAMAGE AND CLINICAL MEASUREMENT

NEUROPSYCHOLOGICAL RETRAINING PARADIGMS AS A TOOL TO STUDY HUMAN MEMORY

Narinder Kapur

Division of Psychiatry, Clinical Research Centre, Watford Road, Harrow, Middlesex, U.K.

It is suggested that the degree of relationship between memory processes can be assessed by examining one process before and after changes have been introduced in the other process by specific retraining techniques. An aphasic patient who could only spontaneously analyse verbal material at the acoustic level, as defined by performance on an odd-word-out task, was successfully trained to use semantic encoding strategies, but no parallel change occurred in his verbal memory performance. This finding is interpreted as constraining the range of viable hypotheses relating spontaneous verbal encoding strategies to verbal memory capacity. Other possible applications of neuropsychological retraining paradigms in memory research are discussed.

Traditionally, behavioural investigations of neurological patients and experimental studies of normal subjects have been run in parallel without much interaction between the two. Recent years, however, have seen a healthy cross-fertilization of data and concepts (e.g. Baddeley and Warrington, 1970; Cermak and Reale, 1978). One of the aims of the present paper is to suggest that a certain area of clinical neuropsychology, that concerned with the retraining of brain-damaged patients, may be able to offer evidence of value to experimental psychologists. More specifically, we would propose that it is possible to evaluate the degree of relationship between psychological processes by monitoring one process before and after changes have been brought about in the other process as a result of therapeutic intervention. Clinical neuropsychology offers a useful vehicle for adopting such an approach since brain-damaged patients often present with coexisting neuropsychological deficits rather than isolated dysfunctions.

Recent developments in the analysis of human memory in normal subjects (Luek, Cicala and McLaughlin, 1976) and in brain-damaged patients with specific memory impairments (Cermak and Butters, 1976) have highlighted types of encoding strategies used to analyse verbal material. An encoding strategy task which can indicate a subject's spontaneous level of analysis of verbal material is one where the odd word has to be selected from triads such as "repair-bend-mend". Choice of the word "bend" would indicate use of a semantic strategy, whereas if a subject chooses the word "repair" he is adopting a visual-acoustic strategy. We encountered an aphasic patient who consistently used a non-semantic strategy on this task. This patient showed no evidence of an amnesic syndrome but displayed subtle deficits on a short-term memory test in which he was required to retain phonemic or semantic features of verbal information. We attempted to examine the relationship between encoding and memory processes by giving our patient a period of intensive retraining in the use of semantic encoding strategies and at the same time monitoring his verbal memory, using tests designed to reflect aphasic patients' retention of phonemic and semantic information (Cermak and Moreines, 1976).

Case History

N.G., who was born in 1928 and is right-handed, was a professional worker before being admitted to hospital in December, 1974 on account of a brain haemorrhage associated with an aneurysm in the left middle cerebral artery. Since an initial operation to control the source of bleeding, his condition has been characterized by a marked expressive aphasia combined with a right-sided hemianopia and sensory impairment. Apart from this, no other major neurological abnormalities have been noted. Psychometric investigations in early 1976 showed a performance IQ of 87, and impairments in reading, writing, left-right orientation, simple calculations and comprehension of complex propositional commands. These were still present at the time of the present investigations which took place approximately two years after the onset of his illness. His speech was generally nonfluent and agrammatic. In addition, he had difficulty in repetition, and could seldom reliably repeat more than 3-4 items. In spite of these difficulties, he was able to use his limited linguistic repertoire to live relatively independently and to communicate in clinical settings. He was always well oriented for time and place, fully aware of current events, and at no stage showed evidence of an amnesic syndrome. For example, on the Rey-Osterreith nonverbal memory test his performance was 61% recall after 45 minutes, much better than that of Korsakoff patients, who are usually unable to recall any part of the original figure.

Pretraining Encoding and Memory Performance

N.G. was presented with each of 18 word triads of the type "hide-ride-conceal". Words were displayed in large upper-case letters and the order of words within triads was randomised to ensure that the use of a particular encoding strategy was unrelated to the position of words on the cards. N.G. was told to pick the "odd word out" and was given no form of feedback after responses. Visual mode of presentation was mainly used in view of N.G.'s repetition difficulty. To allow for any oral reading impairment which might affect performance on the encoding task, the words in each triad were read aloud by the examiner on each presentation and N.G. pointed to the appropriate word. In the case of all 18 triads, N.G. used a visual-acoustic strategy. When the test was repeated two days later using purely auditory presentation, N.G. used an acoustic strategy on 17 triads. Three weeks later, his performance (using visual presentation as described above) was essentially unchanged. Further evidence confirmed the indication in N.G.'s encoding performance that he was impaired in the semantic processing of verbal information. If he was asked, after a response on one of the encoding trials, whether there was any way (other than the visual-acoustic one he had chosen) in which the task could be performed, he was unable to indicate the possibility of a strategy based on semantic relationships between items. A further test was carried out to ascertain the extent to which N.G. was aware of the meaning of words in the triads. Twenty-seven pairs of words were constructed from the 18 triads (13 synonymous and 14 unrelated pairs of words) and were presented using the visual *cum* auditory mode described above. When asked to indicate whether the words in each pair were of the same or different meaning, N.G. made 12/13 correct positive and 8/14 correct negative responses. He appeared therefore to have a "fuzzy" understanding of the meaning of some words, seeming to have a rather low criterion before indicating that two words were of the same meaning.

N.G. also showed a certain "concreteness" in his interpretation of proverbs. For example, when told the proverb "Strike while the iron's hot" and asked to indicate which of two words - "warmth" or "opportunity" - was related to the meaning of the sentence, he chose the word "warmth". Finally, he had some difficulty in giving dual meanings to homonyms such as "sea/see". He was often only able to offer the more concrete of the two possible meanings after hearing the word. Although the above set of evidence did suggest that there were severe limitations in his semantic processing ability, N.G. did not appear to have the agnosic difficulties present in the patients described by Warrington (1975). For example, on the Peabody Picture Vocabulary Test (PPVT), he performed correctly on 95 of the first 100 items compared to a mean of 63.7 by the patients in her study. His good performance on this test was used as a basis for a retraining program aimed at modifying his verbal encoding strategies.

Turning to N.G.'s pretraining memory performance, we used a memory task, developed by Cermak and Moreines (1976), which can be easily administered to aphasic patients. Subjects are asked to detect a repeating word in a list spoken aloud to them, a rhyming word, or a word which is of the same semantic category. We gave N.G. these memory tests, keeping as close as possible to the method adopted by Cermak and Moreines (1976) in Experiment I of their paper. Words were spoken by the examiner at the rate of one word every two seconds. On the repetition form of the test, N.G. was correct on all 12 lists. In the rhyming condition, he scored 4/12 and in the semantic condition he scored 2/12. His performance on the latter two list types was much poorer than that of a group of five matched control patients (mean age = 50.2 years) who scored 8.8/12 and 7.5/12 in the rhyming and semantic conditions respectively.

Training

An attempt was made to train N.G. to use semantic encoding strategies. The training was based on two main principles -
(1) To use those intact functions, such as processing of pictorial information, to assist recovery of those functions which were impaired
(2) To implement the retraining within a "shaping" paradigm such that easy and more difficult tasks were hierarchically ordered.

A training trial essentially consisted of matching words from a word triad to one of four pictures. N.G. was shown one of the pages of the PPVT and, at the same time, a card on which were written three words. Two of these words were semantically associated with one of the pictures and two of the words rhymed with each other, i.e. the triads were similar in construction to those used in the encoding strategy test. An example of materials used on a training trial is the triad "travel-thrive-drive" in conjunction with page one of the PPVT which depicts line drawings of a brush, table, doll and car. After indicating for each word whether it matched any of the pictures, N.G. was asked to select the "odd word out" from the triad. He was not given any explicit instructions on how to do this, but he always used a strategy based on the semantic relationships between words. Using this procedure, 40 training trials were given on day one (the day following the last administration of the encoding strategy test), 30 trials on day two, and a final 30 trials on day three. The sets of pictures used for training were those on pages 1-100 of the PPVT. Each training session was administered twice, once with and then once without pictorial cues.

On day four, the encoding strategy test was readministered to N.G. He responded to 14 triads using a semantic strategy and to the remaining four using a visual-acoustic strategy. On the memory tests, however, his performance was essentially the same as before: in the repetition condition,

N.G. scored 10/12, in the rhyming condition 4/12, and in the semantic condition 1/12.

In view of the fact that most of the training had been based on visual presentation of the training series of word triads, whereas the memory tests were presented aurally, a further series of 100 training trials were administered over days six, seven and eight. This time pictures were matched to word triads spoken by the examiner. On day nine, N.G. was again given the encoding strategy test, using purely auditory presentation. As before, none of the triads on this test overlapped with the ones used in training. On this occasion, however, to guard against possible practise effects from previous testing, the order of words within a triad and the order of triads were in a different random sequence than used on earlier tests. N.G. used a semantic strategy on most triads (15/18). On the memory tests, his performance was still largely unchanged: 9/12 in the repetition condition, 3/12 in the rhyming condition, and 1/12 in the semantic condition.

Discussion

The present retraining study indicated that although our aphasic patient could be trained to use semantic verbal encoding strategies, there was no parallel improvement in his ability to retain verbal information compared to before training, when his spontaneous verbal encoding was at a visual-acoustic level. Thus, making our patient more aware of the semantic characteristics of words did not appear to affect his verbal memory. Our findings do not completely exclude the possibility of causal relationships between verbal encoding and memory processes - e.g. within the area of semantic processing, certain types of semantic strategies may be more effective in improving retention of verbal information. The evidence from the present study does rule out the viability of those hypotheses which postulate a simple relationship between semantic versus nonsemantic processing strategy and the retention of verbal information (cf. Nelson and Vining, 1978).

The type of paradigm used here could be extended to examine other issues in memory research. For example, the distinction between episodic and semantic memory, originally proposed by Tulving (1972) and given neuropsychological support by Warrington (1975), could be examined by giving patients, who have defective semantic memory, extensive practice in semantic classification and other similar tasks. By monitoring verbal and pictorial memory performance before and after such training, it would be possible to provide critical evidence on the functional independence of episodic and semantic memory systems.

Another issue which could be fruitfully examined is the relationship between rehearsal processes and memory. It has been shown (Cermak, Naus and Reale, 1976) that those patients who rehearse in a rote fashion at the single word level have poorer verbal memory performance than control subjects who use more elaborate rehearsal strategies. However, this evidence is insufficient to prove that there is a *causal* relationship between rehearsal strategies and verbal retention. We would suggest that if such patients are trained to use more sophisticated rehearsal strategies, where groups of (contextually or semantically) associated words are rehearsed together, then the role of rehearsal processes in memory could be evaluated by monitoring verbal memory performance, pre- and post-training, for material such as word lists.

It is beyond the scope of the present paper to discuss in detail possible applications of neuropsychological retraining paradigms in other areas of cognitive psychology/neuropsychology. However, it is clear that some such applications may be viable - e.g. some light could be shed on the issue concerning the relationship between auditory perception and language comprehension (Tallal and Newcombe, 1978) by taking selected patients with difficulties in phoneme discrimination and monitoring their language comprehension in parallel with a training program aimed at ameliorating their perceptual deficits.

We have so far stressed the theoretical, as opposed to the practical benefits which might accrue from the use of neuropsychological retraining paradigms with brain-damaged patients. Traditionally, both clinical neuropsychologists and experimental psychologists have tended to shy away from the development of therapeutic procedures applicable to neurological patients. This reluctance has often been based on the belief, sometimes well-grounded, that therapeutic intervention at the neuropsychological level cannot, in itself, offer both significant and durable improvement in any functionally meaningful area of the patient's overall condition. Perhaps such a reluctance may be partly overcome by the prospect that neuropsychological retraining studies may be able to offer information of theoretical as well as of practical value.

ACKNOWLEDGEMENTS

Part of this work was carried out at the Maudsley Hospital, London. I am grateful to the following for assistance in various respects: F. Benson, A. Buffery, R. Cawley, C. Frith and G. Powell.

REFERENCES

Baddeley, A.D. and Warrington, E.K. (1970). Amnesia and the distinction between long- and short-term memory. *Journal of Verbal Learning and Verbal Behaviour*. 9, 176-189.

Cermak, L.S. and Butters, N. (1976). The role of language in the memory disorders of brain-damaged patients. *Annals of the New York Academy of Sciences*. 280, 857-867.

Cermak, L.S. and Moreines, J. (1976). Verbal retention deficits in aphasic and amnesic patients. *Brain and Language*. 3, 16-27.

Cermak, L.S., Naus, M.J. and Reale, L. (1976). Rehearsal strategies of alcoholic Korsakoff patients. *Brain and Language*. 3, 375-385.

Cermak, L.S. and Reale, L. (1978). Depth of processing and retention of words by alcoholic Korsakoff patients. *Journal of Experimental Psychology: Human Learning and Memory*. 4, 165-174.

Luek, S.P., Cicala, G.A. and McGlaughlin, J.P. (1976). Spontaneous categorizers retain more than spontaneous alphabetizers. *Memory and Cognition*. 4, 476-482.

Nelson, T.O. and Vining, S.K. (1978). Effect of semantic versus structural processing on long-term retention. *Journal of Experimental Psychology: Human Learning and Memory*. 4, 198-209.

Tallal, P. and Newcombe, F. (1978). Impairment of auditory perception and language comprehension in dysphasia. *Brain and Language*. 5, 13-24.

Tulving, E. (1972). Episodic and semantic memory. In: *Organization of Memory*. (E. Tulving and W. Donaldson eds). Academic Press, New York.

Warrington, E.K. (1975). The selective impairment of semantic memory. *Quarterly Journal of Experimental Psychology*. 27, 635-657.

THE EFFECTS OF CLOSED HEAD INJURY UPON MEMORY

J.T.E. Richardson
Brunel University, Uxbridge, Middlesex, England

1. INTRODUCTION

Closed head injury is a common outcome of industrial, domestic, and recreational accidents, and especially of accidents on the roads. Moreover, it is a condition with which memory dysfunction is frequently associated. One might therefore expect that an investigation of the psychological sequelae of closed head injury would provide valuable information concerning memory function, and would help in the empirical evaluation of theories of human memory. Equally, the application of the methods and models of experimental psychology to this clinical condition is likely to further our understanding of closed head injury, and to assist in the development of effective therapeutic programmes for dealing with its long-term sequelae.

2. CLINICAL CONSIDERATIONS

(a) *Epidemiology*

Approximately 140,000 patients are admitted to hospitals in England and Wales each year with a diagnosis reflecting head injury (Field, 1976). It has been suggested that four times as many patients are seen in accident and emergency departments but are sent home (Jennett, 1976). This represents an enormous amount of potential material for understanding the neurological basis of psychological function. However, very few patients develop complications requiring surgical intervention, and most are discharged within a few days.

(b) *Dynamics*

The physical effects of a blow to the head can be resolved into two components: an axial, linear translation of the skull relative to the brain, and a rotation of the brain within the skull. These components appear to give rise to quite different sorts of damage (Ommaya and Gennarelli, 1974).

Blow to the head
↓
RESOLVED
↓
Rotating brain
within skull
↓
lacerations to
frontal + temporal
lobe

In t... nent produces contusions a... e brain at the
site of i... racranial pressure
lead to d... ed to the site of
trauma. ... trecoup" lesions
are likel... e site of impact
in many ... nt of the brain
within t... d contusions in
the regi... damage to both
the front... opathological
evidence s... show the greatest
damage whe... 1942; Gurdjian,
Webster, a... ement is likely
to produce... locations.

Rotat... kely to produce
surface le... avulsion of the veins leaving the upper borders of the cerebral hemispheres and by compounding the effects of linear movement (Jamieson, 1971, pp. 32-33). However, rotation of the brain is more important because it sets up shearing forces which produce diffuse effects within the brain. The most common effect of these forces is an immediate loss or disturbance of consciousness known as concussion.

(c) *Clinical signs*

There is a regular sequence of stages in recovery from concussion (Parkinson, 1977). Concussion itself is characterized by somatic immobility and lack of response to external stimuli. This is followed by a period of somatic mobility in which movements are inadequate, ineffective, and sometimes inappropriate. The next stage is one of normal mobility which is accompanied by impaired cognitive function, and the final stage is that of complete recovery.

From the psychological point of view, it is perhaps more interesting that a characteristic of head injury is an inability to recall events experienced immediately prior to the injury and immediately following the cessation of coma. The length of these periods of retrograde and anterograde amnesia is proportional to the duration of coma, and all three time intervals are regarded by clinicians as indicators of the severity of injury and as predictors of the eventual outcome.

Following Russell (1932), it is customary to distinguish between cases of "severe" and "minor" head injury, according to whether the period of anterograde amnesia exceeds 24 hours. Cases of severe head injury are likely to require surgical intervention; however, the vast majority of admissions to British hospitals are cases of minor head injury.

(d) *Sequelae*

The outcome of closed head injury may vary from complete recovery to death. Severe brain damage may produce a variety of intellectual, neurological, and psychiatric deficits, depending upon the amount of tissue destroyed (Lishman, 1973). Psychometric measurement shows a generalized impairment of cognitive ability, but this often returns to normal levels over a period of several months (Mandleberg and Brooks, 1975).

While most cases of minor head injury have no long-term sequelae, a proportion (variously estimated at up to one-third: Editorial, 1973) present with the so-called post-concussional syndrome, involving complaints of headache, dizziness, anxiety, irritability, poor concentration, depression, and fatigue. This condition is still poorly understood, but there is general agreement that it represents a neurotic reaction to the short-term organic consequences of head injury (e.g. Editorial, 1973; Elia, 1974; Lidvall, Linderoth, and Norlin, 1974).

3. EMPIRICAL EVIDENCE

(a) *Methodological considerations*

It is readily appreciated that the failure to demonstrate reduced performance in a clinical sample does not guarantee that the patients are free from impairment; it may simply be that the test employed was not a valid measure of the relevant skill. It is however less easily appreciated that the demonstration of reduced performance is itself of limited value in understanding the nature of the impairment, since it does not distinguish between selective and generalized deficits (Maher, 1974). Thus, studies which have demonstrated a generalized impairment of cognitive, linguistic, and memory function (e.g. Brooks, 1972; Groher, 1977; Thomsen, 1977) must be regarded as having limited usefulness for understanding the consequences of closed head injury.

A rather different problem with previous research is that the tests employed have often been chosen on an *ad hoc* basis with little attempt to ensure their appropriateness in terms of psychological theories of memory function. While certain psychometric scales may have a respectable clinical history, they may be somewhat different from the tasks investigated in laboratory research. Accordingly, the use of such tests will only permit a more detailed description of the clinical sample, and it will not be possible to give a theoretical interpretation of the findings. In order to relate the performance of clinical patients to psychological theories of memory function, it is necessary to employ techniques and procedures which have been extensively used in experimental research with normal subjects (*cf.* Brooks, 1975).

(b) *Memory function during anterograde amnesia*

Despite the fact that the immediate post-traumatic period presents with an obvious memory impairment, there has been little research on the nature of this deficit. When compared with a control group of accident victims, Fodor (1972) found that patients tested soon after head injury were impaired in the recall of related stimulus material when tested after a short delay. There was no relationship between severity of neurological symptoms and memory performance. However, in this study performance in immediate recall was subject to a ceiling effect, and performance in delayed recall on unrelated stimulus material was subject to a floor effect; consequently, further research is needed to support Fodor's conclusions.

(c) *Memory function following severe head injury*

Most of the experimental research on memory performance beyond the period of anterograde amnesia has been concerned with cases of severe head injury. Such patients manifest a generalized impairment of function, observable in free recall, recognition memory, and paired-associate learning, with both pictorial and verbal material, and with both unrelated words and connected narrative (Brooks, 1972, 1974, 1975, 1976; Levin, Grossman, and Kelly, 1976). The duration of anterograde amnesia predicts the degree of impairment (Brooks, 1972, 1974, 1976; Levin *et al.*,1976; Parker and Serrats, 1976), and the presence of neurological signs indicative of brain-stem involvement is also important (Levin *et al.*,1976).

(d) *Memory function following minor head injury*

Early research suggested that even minor head injury may yield a disturbance of memory function beyond the period of anterograde amnesia (Conkey, 1938; Ruesch, 1944). However, there has been little systematic investigation of this idea. I have recently found this disturbance to be specific to concrete material; there was no sign of an impairment in the recall of abstract material in a sample of 40 cases of minor head injury (Richardson, in preparation). The difference between the recall of concrete words and the recall of abstract words varied inversely with the duration of anterograde amnesia

4. THEORETICAL INTERPRETATION

So far, I have considered the evidence on the effects of closed head injury in relation to the period of anterograde amnesia and the severity of injury. The various sets of evidence have been related to different theoretical frameworks for discussing human memory.

(a) *Organization and memory*

A variety of psychological models of memory converge on the idea that organizational factors are important in determining recall performance. Fodor (1972) interpreted her findings on memory during anterograde amnesia in terms of this idea, and concluded that closed head injury yielded a reduced capacity for using organizational structure in the material to be remembered. This implies that head-injured patients are impaired not in the ability to register information in memory, but in the ability to retrieve information at the time of recall. That anterograde amnesia involves a retrieval problem is supported by evidence (admittedly tentative) that it may be alleviated by the administration of various drugs (Oliveros, Jandali, Timsit-Berthier, Remy, Benghezal, Audibert, and Moeglen, 1978; Russell and Nathan, 1946) and by hypnosis (Milos, 1975).

(b) *Primary and secondary memory*

The two-store theory proposed by Waugh and Norman (1965) has recently been criticized on empirical, methodological, and heuristic grounds (Baddeley and Hitch, 1974; Craik and Lockhart, 1972; Watkins, 1974). However, the appropriate response to these criticisms is not to abandon the model, but to insist that its application to a given situation be supported by the use of several different techniques for evaluating the contribution of the two hypothesized components of total performance.

Brooks (1975) has presented a variety of findings to support the conclusion that the continuing memory impairment found after severe head injury is a selective deficit in the person's ability to store information in secondary or long-term memory. First, his subjects showed an impairment in free recall, but not in their span of immediate memory. This was replicated by Brooks (1976) in a later study, but Thomsen (1977) found a significant impairment on memory span following severe head injury. Second, the impairment in free recall was more pronounced when recall was delayed for 20 sec by an irrelevant activity. Third, with immediate testing, head-injured and control patients diverged mainly on early and middle serial positions. This has been found by other researchers (Parker and Serrats, 1976). Fourth, when long- and short-term components of immediate free recall were quantified, the groups differed on the former, but not on the latter. Finally, when extra-experimental intrusions were classified as similar to the items to be remembered in either acoustic or semantic terms, the groups differed in terms of the number of semantic confusions, but not in the number of acoustic confusions.

Brooks argued that severe head injury affected storage into long-term memory rather than retrieval from long-term memory, since his patients produced fewer prior-list intrusions than the controls. However, Thomsen's (1977) patients showed a greater tendency to produce intrusions from previous tests into their recall, and so Brooks' conclusion must be regarded as equivocal at present. Nevertheless, it appears that the two-store model is a useful basis for investigating memory function following severe head injury.

(c) *Mental imagery*

Laboratory research has shown that mental imagery is an important factor in human learning and memory. Moreover, a number of recent studies have suggested that one can often give a plausible account of memory impairment resulting from neurological damage as a deficit of imaginal encoding (Baddeley and Warrington, 1973; Jones, 1974; Richardson, in press).

In studying patients admitted to hospital following minor head injury, I have found a specific deficit in their recall of concrete material (Richardson, in preparation). This may be interpreted as a selective impairment in the use of mental imagery as a form of elaborative encoding in long-term memory. This is an interesting conclusion, since it conflicts directly with a common clinical assumption, that neurological damage leads to an impairment in abstract thinking (Goldstein, 1948). It appears that the results obtained with cases of minor head injury do not generalize to severe head injury, which produces a deficit on both concrete and abstract items (Thomsen, 1977).

5. CONCLUSIONS

Our understanding of the psychological consequences of closed head injury is still very primitive. This is scarcely for want of an adequate number of cases, since vast numbers of patients are admitted to our hospitals each year. I suggest that research on this clinical population will provide valuable information on human memory and its neurological basis.

REFERENCES

Baddeley, A.D. and Hitch, G. (1974). Working Memory. In: *The Psychology of Learning and Motivation: Advances in Research and Theory*. Vol 8. (G H Bower ed), pp. 47-90. Academic Press, New York.

Baddeley, A.D. and Warrington, E.K.(1973). Memory Coding and Amnesia. *Neuropsychologia*. 11, 159-165.

Brooks, D.N. (1972). Memory and Head Injury. *Journal of Nervous and Mental Disease*. 155, 350-355.

Brooks, D.N. (1974). Recognition Memory, and Head Injury. *Journal of Neurology, Neurosurgery, and Psychiatry*. 37, 794-801.

Brooks, D.N. (1975). Long and Short Term Memory in Head Injured Patients. *Cortex*. 11, 329-340.

Brooks, D.N. (1976). Wechsler Memory Scale Performance and Its Relationship to Brain Damage after Severe Closed Head Injury. *Journal of Neurology, Neurosurgery, and Psychiatry*. 39, 593-601.

Conkey, R.C. (1938). Psychological Changes Associated with Head Injuries. *Archives of Psychology*. 33, No. 232.

Courville, C.B. (1942). Coup-Contrecoup Mechanism of Cranio-Cerebral Injuries. *Archives of Surgery*. 45, 19-43.

Craik, F.I.M. and Lockhart, R.S. (1972). Levels of Processing: A Framework for Memory Research. *Journal of Verbal Learning and Verbal Behavior*. 11, 671-684.

Editorial (1973). The Psychiatric Sequelae of Head Injury. *Medical Journal of Australia*. 2, 873-874.

Elia, J. (1974). Cranial Injuries and the Post Concussion Syndrome. *Medical Trial Techniques Quarterly*. 21, 127-161.

Field, J. (1976). *Epidemiology of Head Injuries in England and Wales*. Department of Health and Social Security, London.

Fodor, I.E. (1972). Impairment of Memory Functions After Acute Head Injury. *Journal of Neurology, Neurosurgery, and Psychiatry*. 35, 818-824.

Goldstein, K. (1948). *Language and Language Disturbances*. Grune and Stratton, New York.

Groher, M. (1977). Language and Memory Disorders Following Closed Head Trauma. *Journal of Speech and Hearing Research*. 20, 212-223.

Gurdjian, E.S., Webster, J.E. and Arnkoff, H. (1943). Acute Cranio-Cerebral Trauma. *Surgery*. 13, 333-353.

Jamieson, K.G. (1971). *A First Notebook of Head Injury*. 2nd edn. Butterworths, London.

Jennett, B. (1976). Assessment of the Severity of Head Injury. *Journal of Neurology, Neurosurgery, and Psychiatry*. 39, 647-655.

Jones, M.K. (1974). Imagery as a Mnemonic Aid after Left Tem-

poral Lobectomy. *Neuropsychologia*. 12, 21-30.
Levin, H.S., Grossman, R.G. and Kelly, P. (1976). Short-term Recognition Memory in Relation to Severity of Head Injury. *Cortex*. 12, 175-182.
Lidvall, H.F., Linderoth, B. and Norlin, B. (1974). Causes of the Post-Concussional Syndrome. *Acta Neurologica Scandinavica*. 50 (Supplement 56).
Lishman, W.A. (1973). The Psychiatric Sequelae of Head Injury: A Review. *Psychological Medicine*. 3, 304-318.
Maher, B.A. (1974). Editorial. *Journal of Consulting and Clinical Psychology*. 42, 1-3.
Mandleberg, I.A. and Brooks, D.N. (1975). Cognitive Recovery after Severe Head Injury: I. Serial Testing on the Wechsler Adult Intelligence Scale. *Journal of Neurology, Neurosurgery, and Psychiatry*. 38, 1121-1126.
Milos, R. (1975). Hypnotic Exploration of Amnesia after Cerebral Injuries. *International Journal of Clinical and Experimental Hypnosis*. 23, 103-110.
Oliveros, J.C., Jandali, M.K., Timsit-Berthier, M., Remy, R., Benghezal, A., Audibert, A. and Moeglen, J.M. (1978). Vasopressin in Amnesia. *Lancet*. 1, 41-42.
Ommaya, A.K. and Gennarelli, T.A. (1974). Cerebral Concussion and Traumatic Unconsciousness. *Brain*. 97, 633-654.
Parker, S.A. and Serrats, A.F. (1976). Memory Recovery after Traumatic Coma. *Acta Neurochirurgica*. 34, 71-77.
Parkinson, D. (1977). Concussion. *Mayo Clinical Proceedings*. 52, 492-496.
Richardson, J.T.E. (in press). Memory and Intelligence Following Spontaneously Arrested Congenital Hydrocephalus. *British Journal of Social and Clinical Psychology*.
Richardson, J.T.E. (in preparation). Mental Imagery, Human Memory, and the Effects of Closed Head Injury.
Ruesch, J. (1944). Intellectual Impairment in Head Injuries. *American Journal of Psychiatry*. 100, 480-496.
Russell, W.R. (1932). Cerebral Involvement in Head Injury. *Brain*. 55, 549-603.
Russell, W.R. and Nathan, P.W. (1946). Traumatic Amnesia. *Brain*. 69, 280-301.
Thomsen, I.V. (1977). Verbal Learning in Aphasic and Non-Aphasic Patients with Severe Head Injuries. *Scandinavian Journal of Rehabilitation Medicine*. 9, 73-77.
Watkins, M.J. (1974). Concept and Measurement of Primary Memory. *Psychological Bulletin*. 81, 695-711.
Waugh, N.C. and Norman, D.A. (1965). Primary Memory. *Psychological Review*. 72, 89-104.

IS AMNESIA REMEDIABLE?

Edgar Miller
Addenbrooke's Hospital
Cambridge, England

Memory impairments are extremely handicapping to those who suffer them. As yet there seems to be no possibility of a general therapeutic procedure that will enhance memory. On the other hand amnesia is never absolute and it is possible to identify ways in which the adverse consequences of memory impairments might be ameliorated. This paper presents a selective discussion of amnesia from the point of view of drawing conclusions as to how existing knowledge might be used to reduce the effects of amnesia.

INTRODUCTION

Disturbances in memory are very common and occur in a wide range of clinical conditions that affect the brain. It requires very little imagination to realise that memory disorders can be extremely handicapping to those who suffer them. Despite the frequency of memory problems and their potential impact on everyday life, most psychological research into amnesia has been characterised by two things. Firstly it has concentrated heavily upon the more spectacular but less common forms of amnesia such as the Korsakoff's syndrome. Secondly experimental work has focussed on the problems of elucidating the nature of the memory impairments and has almost totally neglected the practical problem of what might be done to help those who are afflicted.

To some extent these biases are understandable. The rarer forms of amnesia are of particular interest because they are often more severe and the amnesic picture is not complicated by too many other psychological deficits. Many of those concerned with research into amnesia come with a strong background and interest in experimental psychology and with a concern for normal memory processes as well. It is thus natural to see the study of amnesia as a means towards understanding memory processes in general rather than a means of working towards providing help for those who suffer from amnesia.

It is in no way the purpose of this presentation to deny the value of studying the rarer forms of amnesia in order to answer scientific questions. This work is both legitimate and useful in its own right. What is deplored is the almost total neglect by psychologists of the practical problems that people face in trying to live with amnesic symptoms. This requires research which is directed towards rather different goals and which is much more biased towards the commoner forms of memory disorder.

In the absence of any extensive worthwhile literature on the remediation of memory disorders this paper will necessarily be somewhat speculative. After considering the goals of intervention in memory disorders it will present a highly selective and tentative discussion of some issues surrounding amnesia. This is in an attempt to draw conclusions as to how clinical psychologists might set about making a start on the problem of relieving amnesic symptoms. Some of the very few reported attempts to improve the memory performance of amnesic patients will also be referred to.

WHAT IS A REASONABLE GOAL?

In terms of very general principles there are two possible goals in helping people with memory problems. The first can be referred to as restitution and has the aim of trying to improve the memory process itself so that it returns to something approaching its premorbid state. This will have the effect of improving the individual's functioning over a wide range of situations that have been affected by memory loss. The second goal is much less ambitious and consists of amelioration. Given that the patient has a memory impairment it is possible to look for ways of reducing its impact on his life even though the efficiency of the memory process itself may remain unchanged.

The problem of achieving restitution of memory functioning is immense. In the present state of knowledge the possibility of discovering any psychological means of doing this is extremely remote. Drugs are suggested from time to time but the history of work in this field is not encouraging. An example is cyclandelate which gave quite promising early results in cases of arteriosclerotic dementia (e.g. Fine, Lewis, Villa-Landa and Blakemore, 1970) which have not stood up to subsequent investigation (Davies, Hamilton, Hendrickson, Levy and Post, 1977).

For the present restitution does not appear to be a reasonable goal for therapeutic endeavour and it is necessary to fall back on amelioration.

THE AMELIORATION OF AMNESIC SYMPTOMS

In practice any amelioration which reduces the impact of a memory disturbance in a way that is significant for the everyday life of the afflicted individual is likely to depend upon two things. The first is that amnesia is never absolute. Some capacity to acquire and retain information will still remain even though efficiency is markedly reduced. This residual memory function allows some room for manoevre. Secondly it will be necessary to identify specific situations with which the patient cannot cope adequately because of poor memory and which make an important contribution to his well being. Efforts towards amelioration are likely to be carried out in the context of specific problems in living because any beneficial effects are unlikely to generalise to unrelated situations. Fortunately it not infrequently happens that patients with memory problems, such as after a severe head injury, could improve their independence and quality of life if only they could manage certain specific things. These would then become the target for any intervention.

In principle there seem to be two basic ways in which memory impairments might be ameliorated. The first is by altering the environment so that the demands placed upon memory in order to deal satisfactorily with a given situation are reduced. The second is by making the maximum and most efficient use of the patient's residual memory capacity. Some brief comments and examples will be given for each of these two approaches.

Reducing memory load

Although this seems to be a very logical and obvious approach the idea of manipulating the environment to reduce memory load has attracted very little interest, at least in the clinical setting. Nevertheless this is a commonly used strategy in everyday life. An example is the housewife who keeps a list in the kitchen on which she writes those articles of foodstuffs which she needs to purchase on her next visit to the supermarket. This is one way of reducing the memory load involved in shopping.

This general approach could be used in working with memory impaired patients and the clinician occasionally encounters a patient with a fading memory who has coped initially by making increased use of lists and other aids to memory. Just how this approach might work out in practice will obviously depend upon the particular problem situations encountered by the individual patient and the opportunities that they offer for appropriate manipulation. This writer can recall no specific relevant example in the literature on amnesia although interesting possibilities can be found elsewhere. Newman and Scantlebury (1964) used a teaching machine as a means of getting unskilled but normal subjects to carry out a technically complex industrial task involving electronic equipment (the repair of amplifiers). The whole test and repair sequence was broken down into a series of small but relatively simple steps. Each of these was set out on a separate frame of the teaching machine programme. The subject carried out what the frame told him to do and pressed the appropriate response button. This led to the next frame, or in some cases a remedial frame to correct a mistake indicated by the response.to the previous frame. This programme proved effective in getting domestic cleaning staff to find and rectify quite complicated faults. Amongst other things such a programme provides an external memory store of what needs to be done in the situation and similar devices could be used to help memory impaired patients carry out industrial and other tasks.

Making effective use of residual capacity

The fact that the patient may be amnesic does not mean that there is a total loss of all ability to acquire and retain information. If a key situation (or situations) can be identified whose mastery is prevented because of amnesia then it may be possible to teach the patient to cope effectively. Learning will be very slow and for this reason it is essential that this be achieved by the most efficient method. The literature on normal memory is rich with regard to variables known to have an effect on learning and retention. In addition to exploiting this work on normal memory there are also some indications in the experimental literature on amnesia as to variables that might be particularly significant in patients with memory disorder but which may not be quite so critical with normals.

A common concern in recent research into normal memory has been the use of imagery. It has been repeatedly shown (e.g. Atwood, 1971; Paivio, 1969) that the use of visual imagery can enhance recall. Lewinsohn, Danaher and Kikel (1977) studied a small group of brain injured patients with memory difficulties on a paired associate learning task and a "face-name" task which required the subject to learn names to go with faces shown by photographs. The experimental subjects were inferior to normal controls on tests of retention but their performance benefited to the same degree as the controls by training in the use of imagery. Glasgow, Zeiss, Barrera and Lewinsohn (1977) describe a single case study involving a young adult who had a marked difficulty in remembering the names of people he encountered following a head injury sustained in a road traffic accident. Although there were some initial difficulties with the technique Glasgow *et al* report that the use of visual imagery did help their patient remember the names of people

The factors that will enhance recall in amnesic subjects are not necessarily the same as those that will affect normal subjects given comparable conditions for learning and recall. Warrington and Weiskrantz (1970) showed that the presentation of "partial information" at the time of recall (e.g. the initial letters of the words to be recalled) had a beneficial effect on the recall of subjects with severe amnesia which was not present in normal controls. Similar results have been found by Miller (1975) in presenile dementia and by Squire, Wetzel and Slater (1978) in the period of anterograde amnesia that follows the administration of E.C.T. This "partial information effect" seems to be only found in normals when the trace is particularly weak (Squire *et al*. 1978; Woods and Piercy, 1974).

Since the partial information effect seems to occur in memory disorders as a result of a wide range of causes and is quite powerful in the experimental conditions under which it has been studied it could lead to a very useful technique for clinical application. Jaffe and Katz (1975) have given a rather anecdotal account of the use of partial information cueing in a patient with Korsakoff's syndrome. Even after spending a long period of time in hospital the patient had failed to acquire the names of any of the hospital personnel with whom he came into regular contact. He was then given a name and asked to recall it with the initial letters of the name given as a cue. This cue was gradually faded. With this type of training the patient learned to use the names of several members of staff within a relatively short period.

This type of work is only in the earliest stages of development. It certainly cannot be claimed that any technique has emerged that has yet been demonstrated to have effects that can make an appreciable difference to an amnesic patient's rehabilitation. Nevertheless some interesting possibilities are being opened up. What is required is an increase in the quality and quantity of clinical studies aimed at the amelioration of memory problems. A shift in emphasis in more fundamental research from studies which look for differences between amnesic patients and normals to those which compare groups of memory disordered subjects under different conditions of learning and retention would increase the identification of variables whose effects might be worth manipulating in clinical studies.

CONCLUSIONS

The title given to this paper was "Is memory remediable?" In the present state of knowledge the answer to this question is probably "no" given that by "remediable" would normally be meant the achivement of some definite improvement in the memory process itself. Fortunately this does not mean that nothing can be done to help those with memory impairments. Some kind of amelioration is still possible and the first, tentative steps towards the development of suitable techniques are now being made.

REFERENCES

Atwood, G. (1971). An experimental study of visual imagination and memory. *Cognitive Psychology*, 2, 290-299.

Davies, G., Hamilton, S., Hendrickson, E., Levy, R. and Post, F. (1977). The effect of cyclandelate in depressed and demented patients: a controlled study in psychogeriatric patients. *Age and Ageing*, 6, 156-162.

Fine, E.W., Lewis, D., Villa-Landa, I. and Blakemore, C.B. (1970). The effect of cyclandelate on mental function in patients with arteriosclerotic brain disease. *British Journal of Psychiatry*, 117, 157-161.

Glasgow, R.E., Zeiss, R.A., Barrera, M. and Lewinsohn, P.M. (1977). Case studies on remediating memory deficits in brain-damaged individuals. *Journal of Clinical Psychology*, 33, 1049-1054.

Jaffe, P.G. and Katz, A.N. (1975). Attenuating anterograde amnesia in Korsakoff's psychosis. *Journal of Abnormal Psychology*, 84, 559-562.

Lewinsohn, P.M., Danaher, B.G. and Kikel, S. (1977). Visual imagery as a mnemonic aid for brain-injured persons. *Journal of Consulting and Clinical Psychology*, 45, 717-723.

Miller, E. (1975). Impaired recall and the memory disturbance in presenile dementia. *British Journal of Social and Clinical Psychology*, 14, 73-79.

Newman, E.A. and Scantlebury, R.A. (1964). Teaching Machines as Intelligence Amplifiers. *National Physical Laboratory Report Auto* 31, London.

Paivio, A. (1969). Mental imagery in learning and memory. *Psychological Review*, 76, 241-263.

Squire, L.R., Wetzel, C.D. and Slater P.C. (1978). Anterograde amnesia following ECT: an analysis of the beneficial effects of partial information. *Neuropsychologia*, 16, 339-348.

Warrington, E.K. and Weiskrantz, L. (1970). Amnesic syndrome: consolidation or retrieval? *Nature*, 228, 628-630.

Woods, R.T. and Piercy, M. (1974). A similarity between amnesic memory and normal forgetting. *Neuropsychologia*, 12, 437-445.

MUST AMNESIA BE CAUSED BY EITHER ENCODING OR RETRIEVAL DISORDERS?

A.R. Mayes, P.R. Meudell and D. Neary
University of Manchester, Manchester, M13 9PL, England

Alcoholic amnesics were compared with matched controls on cumulative free recall, cued recall and recognition for word lists learnt normally and with 'high'- or 'low'-level orienting tasks. Normals actually benefitted more from the 'high'-level condition than the amnesics and both groups cued equally well. These results are inconsistent with the semantic encoding and retrieval deficit hypotheses of amnesia. Interpretation of the 'low'-level and recognition data was confounded by floor effects and design imbalances. Nevertheless the recognition error pattern was similar for both groups, confirming the implications of the recall data.

INTRODUCTION

Two hypotheses about the nature of memory breakdown in amnesia are currently influential. The first states that amnesia is caused by deficient *spontaneous* encoding of the semantic aspects of information although the ability to encode in this way is intact. The second states that amnesia arises from a retrieval deficiency. Several versions of this view have not been clearly distinguished (Piercy, 1977) but a commonly accepted form is that amnesics have excessive difficulty coping with interference from irrelevant material during retrieval. Weiskrantz and Warrington (1975) have supported this hypothesis extensively. Critical to this view is the finding that amnesics cued so well when given the first three letters of target words that they approached normal levels of performance.

Part of the evidence for the encoding deficit hypothesis comes from experiments (Butters & Cermak, 1975) which found that amnesics showed release from PI with alphanumeric but not taxonomic shift and a tendency to make more non semantic recognition errors than controls.

The above studies are correlative, but a critical prediction of the hypothesis is that the amnesic deficit should be abolished or certainly markedly reduced if patients are forced to encode material semantically. Although Cermak and Reale (1978) have shown that amnesics recognize words better after performing a semantic as compared to either rhyming or graphemic orienting tasks, this effect only occurs with very easy recognition conditions and is no greater than seen in normals. Further, interpretation is made harder because a learning condition is not included in the study. If the hypothesis is correct amnesics should gain much more than normals from the semantic task compared to the learning condition.Similarly, they should be less impaired by the 'low'-level orienting tasks. To test these predictions we have compared amnesic and normal memory for words following learning or a condition in which subjects remember words identified from their definitions. This 'Socratic' condition was adapted from a study of Erdelyi, Buschke and Finkelstein (1977), in which subjects,allowed multiple free recall attempts,showed greater cumulative word recall in the 'Socratic' condition than after learning. In our study cueing was given after the final recall trial to test the retrieval deficit notion that amnesics gain greatly from cues relative to controls. A 'low'-level orienting condition was subseqently introduced in which subjects counted the number of letters and colours contained in multi-coloured words. This task was intended to decrease the degree of semantic processing performed by subjects.

METHOD

Subjects

The amnesics consisted of 7 male alcoholic Korsakoff patients (mean age, 56.0) with mean WAIS full scale 99, mean WAIS vocabulary of 10.9 and a mean Wechsler memory score of 77. Two control groups of similar age and socioeconomic background to the amnesics were chosen (Group 1, mean age 55.7, mean WAIS vocabulary score of 10.4: Group 2, mean age 56.0, mean WAIS vocabulary score 11.0).

Task

Subjects were asked to remember 6 lists of 15 common nouns

under 3 conditions with 1 word/10 secs. Two lists were required to be learned, 2 lists ('Socratic') were presented as spoken riddles for which Ss generated and remembered solutions and 2 lists ('low'-level) comprised words with multi-coloured letters, the Ss naming the words and stating the difference between the number of letters and colours in each word. After list presentation Ss sorted cards into red and black for 30 secs and then recalled the words in a 90 sec period. Three more 90 sec recall periods were then given - each S thus making 4 recalls for each list. After free recall Ss were given either the first 3 letters of each word ('acoustic' cue) or a 'semantic' cue comprising a part of the 'Socratic' definition insufficient by itself to identify the cued word. Subjects were given a forced choice recognition test approximately 2 weeks after recall.

Material

The 7 lists were presented in 3 forms. For 'Learn' the words were printed in red on cards. For 'Low-Level' the words were printed in several colours with fewer colours than letters. For the 'Socratic' condition Ss were read a riddle, e.g. "It's a wooden plank suspended from 2 chains used for children's amusement. What is it?" If the S did not respond "swing" quickly, an additional hint was given - these were rarely needed. 'Acoustic' and 'semantic' cues were read to Ss. A 4 choice visually presented recognition test was employed consisting of the target word, an 'acoustic' distractor beginning with the same 3 letters as the target, a 'semantic' distractor and an 'irrelevant' distractor beginning with the same 3 letters as the 'semantic' distractor (position of words on cards was random). To see if Ss chose words in a non random fashion, in the absence of mnemonic information, 42 further recognition cards were produced - none of these words had been seen before.

Design and Procedure

The design of the study was complicated because of the way it evolved historically. Four of the amnesic patients were tested on the first 4 lists with the learning and 'Socratic' conditions in a balanced 4x4 Latin Square with each cue condition being tested with each learning condition. Two 'low'-level lists were then given to the 4 patients with cue condition and order of testing counter balanced. Three other patients were tested in the same way as the first 3 in all conditions. The first matched control group was tested in an identical way to the patient group. The second control group was introduced to assay any list effects from the 'low'-level lists. The 7 Ss fitted into a 7x7 Latin Square with lists, learning conditions and order of testing completely balanced (a dummy 7th list was introduced to achieve the balanced design). Approximately 1 test was given each day for each S in each group.

Subjects knew their memory would be tested on the words in all conditions but with the 'low'-level lists they were told it was more important to perform the assigned task quickly and accurately. This latter task was paced by the experimenter and the next word was always presented even when the task had not been completed in 10 secs. On less than 10 occasions did the Ss fail to get the Socratic riddle correct within 10 secs and they were then told the answer.

Subjects were encouraged to produce as many words as possible during the 4 free recall sessions and were also to produce apposite responses to cues. Guessing was allowed both in free recall and in response to cues, the S selecting a single response if necessary. Recognition was tested in 1 continuous session with cards in their list order but with 7 pseudo-recognition cards randomly assigned to each list except the dummy 7th list.

RESULTS

Since the comparisons between the two control groups revealed no significant list effects of any kind with any of the measures, the rest of the analysis concerns the comparison of the amnesic group with its matched control group.

These results are shown in Table 1. The ANOVA reveals a group effect ($p < 0.001$) confirming the severity of the amnesics' memory problem. It also shows an effect of learning conditions ($p < 0.001$) and an interaction between learning conditions and groups ($p < 0.001$). Further analysis indicates that the controls recall more words than the amnesics under each learning condition ($p < 0.01$ in each case). There is also a significant tendency ($p < 0.01$) for both groups to do worse on the 'low'-level compared to the learning condition although the 'Socratic' condition does not produce an improvement. There is, however, a significant tendency for the control group to benefit more from the 'Socratic' condition ($p < 0.01$). Finally, this group is also disadvantaged to a greater extent by the 'low'-level condition ($p < 0.005$). This last tendency is almost certainly caused by a floor effect in the amnesic group's 'low'-level scores, half of which are zero.

	'Socratic'	Learn	'Low'
Amnesics	1.36	2.21	1.07
Controls	7.57	7.07	2.64

Table 1. Cumulative free recall for each learning condition

Table 2 suggests and the ANOVA confirms that both groups benefit equally from the cueing under all learning conditions and with both kinds of cue. There is a non-significant tendency for the amnesics to benefit more than the controls from semantic cues but this tendency is probably exaggerated by a ceiling effect for the control subjects in the 'Socratic' condition. 'Acoustic' cues were more effective than 'Semantic' in the learn and 'low'-level conditions ($p < 0.001$), although as expected, for the 'Socratic' condition, the 'Semantic' cues were more effective than the 'acoustic' cues ($p < 0.001$). For the 'low'-level condition there was a weak and insignificant tendency towards the opposite pattern of cueing efficacy.

	'Semantic' cues			'Acoustic' cues		
	'Socratic'	Learn	'Low'	'Socratic'	Learn	'Low'
Amnesics	7.29	2.57	1.71	4.14	4.00	4.57
Controls	5.86	1.29	1.29	4.14	4.57	4.57

Table 2. Cued minus cumulative free recall scores

The ANOVA shows that the control group recognizes the learnt words better at one fortnight ($p < 0.05$), that there is a main effect of learning conditions ($p < 0.01$) and an interaction between these and groups ($p < 0.05$). Inspection of Table 3 suggests and further analysis confirms that across groups recognition is worse in the 'low'-level than the other two conditions ($p < 0.001$ for both) which are equivalent. The control group, however, mirroring the free recall results, shows greater benefit from the 'Socratic' relative to the learning condition in its recognition scores ($p < 0.025$) and a greater disadvantage following the 'low'-level learning condition ($p < 0.01$). This last result is probably caused again by a floor effect with the amnesic recognition scores, over one third of the scores being at chance (estimated at a guessing rate of 0.25).

Table 4 shows the overall error pattern of the two groups and the ANOVA confirms that they show similar patterns of error. There is a main effect of error type ($p < 0.01$) which further analysis shows reflects the presence of fewer irrelevant than the other two types of error ($p < 0.025$ for both)

	'Socratic'	Learn	'Low'
Amnesics	6.79	7.00	5.64
Controls	12.71	11.64	7.86

Table 3. Correct recognition for each learning condition

which are equivalent. A recognition error interaction with learning conditions ($p < 0.01$) is shown by further analysis to be a consequence of a shift to more acoustic and fewer semantic errors in the 'low'-level compared to the other two

	'Semantic'	'Acoustic'	'Irrelevant'
Amnesics	6.33	6.05	4.57
Controls	3.76	2.81	1.91

Table 4. Type of recognition errors for each group

learning conditions (both at $p < 0.01$) and a tendency towards more semantic than acoustic errors in the 'higher'-level conditions. Both amnesics and controls show a similar slight preference with the pseudo-recognition items for semantically related words (chosen 58% of the time).

DISCUSSION

The data raise a number of problems for both semantic encoding and retrieval deficit hypotheses. In its strong form the first predicts the 'Socratic' task will bring amnesic cumulative free recall up to the level of normal subjects. In a weak form it predicts that they will benefit more from forced semantic encoding. Neither of these effects occurs. A modified form of the hypothesis might argue that similar processing failures occur at encoding and retrieval in which case the same predictions should be made for the effects of cueing. These predictions are not met, however, and despite a ceiling effect normals benefit a similar amount with semantic cueing as the amnesics. Furthermore, the amnesics benefit at least as much as the normals from semantic cueing under all learning conditions which suggests that they encode such information at least as much as normals. Neither kind of cue gives a differential advantage to the amnesics under any learning condition. This result does not conform with the prediction of the retrieval deficit hypothesis which in its strong form requires cueing to abolish the amnesic deficit and in a weaker form predicts a differential improvement in amnesics.

Although normals show a trend towards improvement with the 'Socratic' condition this doesn't achieve significance. They do also show a trend towards greater improvement in cumulative free recall over trials in the 'Socratic' condition as noted by Erdelyi *et al.*(1977). It seems likely that if allowed more time they would have further improved their cumulative free recall score. Several volunteered the information that they had subsequently remembered extra words from the Socratic condition. The amnesics' failure to benefit as much as normals from this learning condition is intriguing. Successful performance of the task may have disrupted their normal learning performance to a greater extent than in normals. There is evidence that amnesic cognitive processing is slow relative to matched controls (Cermak, Butters and Moreines, 1974). Further, the Erdelyi effect is a reminiscence phenomenon which is likely to be absent in individuals who are impaired in laying down memories.

Interpretation of the data from the 'low'-level condition and the recognition measures is difficult because of the occurrence of floor effects and incomplete matching of amnesic and control groups. Unlike the 'Socratic' task the accuracy of performance of the 'low'-level task was not fully assessed. It disturbed recall and recognition relative to the learning condition. It was, however, unclear how it affected information processing although recognition in this condition was associated with relatively more'acoustic' errors and there was an insignificant trend favouring the efficacy of 'acoustic'cues relative to 'semantic' ones compared with the learning condition. Nevertheless to establish that the apparently greater disadvantage of the normals in the shift to the 'low'-level condition is an artefact, the study needs to be repeated *equating* the recall and recognition levels of the amnesic and normal subjects following the learning condition, either by prolonging the latters' retention interval or giving the amnesics greater learning exposure. We feel that this procedure should be generally adopted in studies of amnesic memory to avoid not only floor and ceiling effects, but any artefactual effects that may arise consequent to different levels of retention.

The proportionately equivalent dominance of 'semantic' recognition errors for both groups in the 'higher'-level learning conditions, which is matched by the slight preference for semantically related words in the pseudo-recognition items is open to two interpretations, neither favourable to the modified form of the encoding deficit hypothesis. The first interpretation which is consistent for the change in error pattern for the 'low'-level condition is that the two groups' error pattern reflects their encoding of semantic attributes. The second interpretation, compatible with the first, is that amnesics take a normal degree of notice of semantic features during retrieval.

In conclusion, the pattern of these results presents a serious problem for both current major hypotheses about amnesia. The poor memory of at least some amnesics is unlikely to be caused by superficial encoding or disturbed retrieval processes. We feel that it is more probable that abnormal physiological activities concomitant with and consequent to learning may cause the disorder.

ACKNOWLEDGEMENTS

We would like to thank Barbara Politynska for research assistance and Fran Street for secretarial assistance.

REFERENCES

Butters, N. and Cermak, L. (1975). Some analyses of amnesic syndromes in brain-damaged patients. In: *The Hippocampus*. Vol.2 (R. Isaacson and K Pribram, eds), pp 377-409, Plenum, New York.

Cermak, L.S., Butters, N. and Moreines, J. (1974) Some analyses of the verbal encoding deficit of alcoholic Korsakoff patients. *Brain and Language*, 1, 141-150.

Cermak, L.S., and Reale, L. (1978) Depth of processing and retention of words by alcoholic Korsakoff patients. *Journal of Experimental Psychology: Human Learning and Memory*, 4. 165-174.

Erdelyi, M., Buschke, H. and Finkelstein, S. (1977) Hypermnesia for Socratic stimuli: The growth of recall for an internally generated memory list abstracted from a series of riddles. *Memory and Cognition*, 5, 283-286.

Piercy, M.F. (1977) Experimental studies of the organic amnesic syndrome. In: *Amnesia* (C. Whitty, and O. Zangwill, eds), pp 1-51. Butterworths. London.

Weiskrantz, L. and Warrington, E.K. (1975) The problem of the amnesic syndrome in man and animals. In: *The Hippocampus* Vol.2. (R. Isaacson and K. Pribram, eds), pp 411-441, Plenum, New York.

ASSESSMENT AND REMEDIATION OF MEMORY DEFICITS IN BRAIN-INJURED PATIENTS

J. Grafman, B. A.
C. G. Matthews, Ph.D.
Neuropsychology Laboratory
Clinical Science Center
University of Wisconsin-Madison 53706

INTRODUCTION

One of the most frequent and debilitating deficits to occur following head injury, stroke and other central nervous system insults is loss of memory. In recent years numerous studies have experimentally investigated memory function in neurologically impaired individuals.(Buschke and Fuld, [illegible] 1976). Studies such as these [illegible] s is not a global deficit, [illegible] of memory loss interact [illegible] n and are dependent upon the i[illegible] lness of the stimulus mater[illegible] alled or recognized (Butt[illegible], 1970; Cermak and Butte[illegible] o adapt these experimenta[illegible] nical settings. Not only [illegible] generalizability of resul[illegible] ental groups, but it could [illegible] aking decisions regarding cogni[illegible] and vocational recommendatio[illegible]

BACKG[illegible]

S[illegible] the Wechsler Memory Scal[illegible] unsatisfactory for the rang[illegible] e. Thus, we have developed and are in the process of norming a comprehensive clinical memory examination which will incorporate certain tests and norms now in use. This test battery is based on current theories regarding human information processing. Our model identifies memory as a three-component system containing a sensory information store, a short term store and a long term

store (Broadbent, 1970; Craik and Watkins, 1973; Kintsch, 1977). Information in short term store has a phonemic representation, while information in long term store is generally semantic in property (Neisser, 1967). Information that is associative and can be coded with reference to a prior fund of knowledge achieves a greater depth and intensity of processing according to its relative semantic complexity (Lockhart, Craik and Jacoby, 1976).
The greater this depth of processing, the better retained and the more easily recalled the information. The stimulus information processed in this manner may be of a linguistic or visuospatial nature. Both may be processed in parallel traces and are differentially available as mediator and memory code (Pavio, 1969, 1975). Visual imagery when used as a mediator generally shows superior performance on recall and recognition tasks (Atwood, 1971; Pavio, 1975, Pavio, Yuille and Madigan, 1968).

This view of memory is reasonably consistent with knowledge of hemispheric brain function. In order to encode stimuli in an episodic or meaningful way from short term store into long term store, it is necessary to have at least one functioning hippocampus (although, with only one working hippocampus, certain kinds of information loss are inevitable. Recent evidence indicates that bilateral damage to any part of the "Papez Circuit" will disrupt the encoding process (Drachman and Leavitt, 1974; Butters and Cermak, 1975). It should be noted that Warrington and her collaborators consider the essential deficit one of decoding as opposed to the encoding hypothesis put forward by Cermak's group (Piercy, 1978). A "deeper" or more complex level of processing is completed in the cerebral hemispheres. Selective cortical areas provide specialization of processing (Moscovitch, 1976; Russell, 1971). The right hemisphere is involved to a greater degree with visuospatial information while the left hemisphere attends primarily to information of a linguistic or temporal nature (DeRenzi, 1968; Reitan and Davison, 1974). Specific kinds of modality processing may be identified dependent on local cortical regions. The medial and superior temporal gyri are responsible for acoustic and phonemic identification and integration (linguistic or non-linguistic). The parietal and inferior temporal region is responsible for visual-linguistic and visuospatial perception and memory, and, in addition, provides for meaning and elaboration of basic sensory information. The frontal lobe is involved with intention and production of thought and elaboration of concepts which may result in the ability to produce and perceive metaphors, plans that include time specifications, etc. Callosal lesions produce a disconnection of memories between the right and left hemispheres as so aptly described by Sperry (1974). This deficit is most apparent when stimulus input can be restricted to one hemisphere as in tachistoscopic split field presentations. The accumulated evidence in the split-brain research implicates callosal as well as intra-hemispheric white matter tracts as being responsible for the transmission of memory traces which result in the integration of sensory information and motor behavior between various cortical and subcortical regions.

WISCONSIN NEURO-MEMORY BATTERY

Based on these theoretical concepts, we proceeded to formulate and construct a series of tests which we believe are sensitive to disruption of the various components in our model. This test battery generates a profile to indicate a particular patient's strengths and weaknesses for memorial functioning, plus an appropriate strategy for remediation. The Wisconsin Memory Battery consists of the following tests:

1) Word Fluency Test (Borkowski, Benton and Spreen (1967).
2) Token Test (DeRenzi and Vignolo, 1962).
3) Perceptual Screening Test.
4) Benton Visual Retention Test (Benton, 1974)
5) Test of Facial Recognition (Benton, Van Allen, K de S Hamsher and Levin, 1975).
6) Recurring Figures Test (Kimura, 1963).
7) 7/24 Test (adapted from Barbizet and Cany, 1968).
8. Visual Sequential Coding
9) Digit Span (WAIS).
10) 8 Word List (auditory administration)
11) Word List (auditory administration)
12) Word List (visual administration)
13) 8 Paired Associates (high and low value)
14) Sentences (auditory presention/verbal response)
15) Sentences (visual presentation/verbal response)
16) 8 Word List
17) Story Recall
18) Tactual Performance Test
19) Television Program Questionnaire (Squire and Slater, 1975).
20) Famous Faces (Warrington and Silberstein, 1971).
21) Famous Events (Warrington and Sanders, 1971).

Complete administration time is estimated to be six hours. The test is given on two consecutive days. Test administration sequence is counterbalanced so that the patient does not receive more than two verbal tests consecutively. (Description of and rationale for each of the 21 tests were included in the hand out given to conference participants and is available upon request from the authors).

REMEDIATION

Very few attempts have been made to fully assess memory in brain-injured individuals in conjunction with retraining. More notable efforts have been made with geriatric populations (Treat and Reese, 1976; Meichenbaum, 1974). At a recent American Psychological Association convention (San Francisco-1977), a symposium was convened to discuss intervention techniques with elderly individuals and to indicate future directions this research should take. Symposium participants noted that as with brain injured individuals, many aging people suffer memory deficits that go untreated (Hulicka, 1966). The research summarized by the symposium participants suggested that the basic problem is one of encoding and inefficient organization of material, and that when subjects with these kinds of deficiencies are treated within an intervention program, they are able to achieve significant improvement as quantified by psychometric evaluation. These intervention programs use many of the strategies that are taught in popular paperbacks of the "How to improve your memory" variety.

Patten (1972) has adapted these techniques to a brain-injured population and reported considerable success. In his study he used a peg system to facilitate recall of paired associates in a learning task. Subjects were required to learn a list of 10 numbered peg words and related images. For example, the first peg word was tea and the associated image was teacup. Once the peg system was mastered, the images could be used to remember and later identify a list of random words. In another study, Jones (1974) used three lists of paired associates in a standard learning task. Subjects were patients with right, left and bilateral temporal lobe lesions, plus a control group. On the first list, patient recall was tested without imagery instructions. The second list was read after imagery instructions including visual stimuli prompts. The third list instructed the patients to generate their own mnemonics or imagery for the task. With the exception of the bilateral group, all other groups increased their recall performance when they used imagery mediation (either experimenter or subject generated). While it is encouraging that reorganization of encoding strategies can improve retention and recall; there are several problems with studies such as those just described. The study by Patten and those by Lewinsohn (1977) are essentially case studies that lack suitable controls. Jones showed only an initial improvement in memory, as do the aging studies, with the degree of long-term improvement as yet unknown. Despite these methodological problems and long-term recovery uncertainties, we are encouraged by these initial findings and see no compelling reason why this kind of intervention program should not be expanded to, and systematically tested with a large population of brain-injured individuals.

WISCONSIN PROGRAM

Patients accepted for our memory retraining program are 18 years of age or older, having suffered a stroke or head injury with a memory deficit as the oustanding complaint. The clinical assessment of our standard neuropsychological test battery must result in a positive identification of the memory deficit as the patient's most prominent area of impairment. In addition, at least one of the following examinations must yield positive findings of brain injury: The clinical neurological examination, the electroencephalogram or the computer axial tomography scan. Thus, our patients are pre-tested on the complete Wisconsin neuropsychological test battery (Reitan and Davison, 1974) _and_ on the Wisconsin neuro-memory battery.

Following completion of the test batteries, the patient's test score profile is used to plan a specific remediation program. This program will use material that is familiar, interesting, and appropriate to the patient's previous and current intellectual status. Specific techniques we use include mnemonics (Bower, 1970), imagery (Pavio, 1969), mediation, and strategic organization and elaboration. Training tasks will include verbal or visuospatial material from such standardized sources as the Gates-Mckillop Reading Diagnostic tests (1978) and illustrations or photographs from magazines. Additional examples of various kinds of memory retraining materials and strategies to be employed are described by Lewinsohn and coworkers (1977).

Our retraining program is administered over a 3 month period with three 1-hour sessions per week. At the end of three months, the patients are retested on the neuropsychology and neuro-memory test batteries to obtain comparison scores. Patients are again retested at six months post-baseline (3 months following cessation of training). This provides a measure of the post-training status and stability of memory processes.

The program for memory retraining just described is relatively new. We now have enrolled several head injury and stroke victims from the University of Wisconsin-Madison Clinical Sciences Center. While the results of our psychometric and memory testing are still too sparse to report at this time, we are encouraged by early training gains achieved. Several of our patients who previously were chronically disabled due to severe memory disorders are now attempting to maintain part-time jobs and are doing quite well. This functional gain is correlated with advancement in retraining steps, but we have not yet analyzed post-training test results. In order to experimentally ascertain the reliability of the program, we will shortly undertake a larger study which will contain control groups receiving sham treatments, as well as single subjects serving as their own controls.

DISCUSSION

For memory retraining as well as recovery from aphasia, an important theoretical question is what determines recovery. Certainly numerous variables may be important: 1) locus of lesion; 2) length and type of lesion; 3) age, sex and education of subject; 4) psychological status, i.e. is the patient depressed or confused?; 5) linguistic or perceptual deficits- how do they contribute to the memory deficit?; 6) drug status; 7) type of testing; a) stimulus used, b) response mode, c)reaction time, d) interstimulus-response interval, e) distractors, f) experimental design.

The rationale used for selecting an appropriate strategy for remediation has not at present been formalized or specified. At this stage in our program, we emphasize all strategies equally. We expect to find, and are finding in the case of lateralized lesions that patients perform better with those strategies that presumably are governed by the more intact cortical and subcortical information processing systems. An exception to this would be the severe head injury patient who shows a more generalized memory loss with no trend in strategy preference yet emerging.

CONCLUSION

The significance of memory assessment and remediation in general is that it will allow us to more accurately delineate the effect of a pathological process on a particular cognitive function and its relationship to other cognitive functions, and by inference, to the brain structures associated with specific performance deficits. The significance of a memory retraining program resides in the fact that while the various mnemonic and other memory remediation devices described (above) have been shown to be useful in improving memory for normals and the elderly, neither the efficacy of these techniques nor the difficulty of learning to use them has been systematically studied in the brain injured.

REFERENCES

1) Atwood, G. (1971), An experimental study of visual imagination and memory. *Cognitive Psychology*, 2, 290-299.
2) Barbizet, J. (1970), *Human Memory and its pathology.* W. H. Freeman and Company, 7, 44-54.
3) Barbizet, J. and Cany, E. (1968) Clinical and psychometrical study of a patient with memory disturbances. *International Journal of Neurology*, 1, 44-54.
4) Benton, A. L. (1974), *The Revised Visual Retention Test: Fourth edition*, Psychological Corporation, New York.
5) Benton, A. L., Van Allen, H. W., Hamsher, Kde Levin, H. S. (1975), *Test of Facial Recognition, Form SL*, University of Iowa Hospitals.
6) Borkowski, J. G., Benton, A. L. and Spreen, O. (1967), Work fluency and brain damage. *Neuropsychologia*, 5, 135-140.
7) Bower, G. H. (1970a), Organizational factors in memory. *Cognitive Psychology*, 1, 18-46.
8) Broadbent, D. E. (1970), Psychological aspects of short-term memory. *Proceedings of the Royal Society of London*, 175, 333-350.
9) Buschke, H. and Fuld, P. A. (1974), Evaluating storage, retention, and retrieval in disordered memory and learning. *Neurology*, 24, 1019-1025.
10) Butters, N. and Cermak, L. (1975), Some analyses of amnesic syndromes in brain-damaged patients. *The Hippocampus*, Vol. 2, 377-409. Ed. by Issacson, R. and Pribram, K.
11) Butters, N., Samuels, I., Goodglass, H. and Brody, B. (1970), Short-term visual and auditory memory disorders after parietal and frontal lobe damage. *Cortex*, 440-459.
12) Cermak, L. S. and Butters, N. (1976), The role of language in the memory disorders of brain-damaged patients. *Annals of the New York Academy of Sciences*, 280, 857-867.

13) Craik, F. I. M. and Watkins, M. J. (1973), The role of rehearsal in short-term memory. *Journal of Verbal Learning and Verbal Behavior*, 12, 599-607.

14) De Renzi, E. (1968), Nonverbal memory and hemispheric side of lesion. *Neuropsychologia*, 6, 181-189.

15) De Renzi, E. and Vignolo, L. A. (1962), The token test: A sensitive test to detect receptive disturbances in aphasics. *Brain*, 85, 665-678.

16) Drachman, D. A. and Leavitt, J. (1974), Human memory and the cholinergic system. *Archives of Neurology*, 30, 113-121.

17) Gates, A. I. and McKillop, A. S. (1978), Gates-McKillop Reading Diagnostic Tests. Western Psychological Services.

18) Hulicka, I. M. (1966) Age differences in Wechsler Memory Scale scores. *The Journal of Genetic Psychology*, 109, 135-145.

19) Jones, M. K. (1974), Imagery as a mnemonic aid after left temporal lobectomy: contrast between material-specific and generalized memory disorders. *Neuropsychologia*, 12, 21-30.

20) Kimura, D. (1963), Right temporal-lobe damage. *Archives of Neurology*, 8, 264.

21) Kintsch, W. (1977), *Memory and Cognition*, John Wiley and Sons.

22) Lewinsohn, P. M., Glasgow, R. E., Barrera, M., Danaher, B. G., Alperson, J., McCarty, D. L., Sullivan, J. M., Zeiss, R. A., Nyland, J. and Rodrigues, M. R. P. (1977a), *Assessment and treatment of patients with memory deficits: initial study*, University of Oregon.

23) Lockhart, R. S., Craik, F. I. M. and Jacoby, L. L. (1976). Depth of processing in recognition and recall: some aspects of a general memory system. *Recognition and Recall*, (Ed) Brown, J., London: Wiley

24) Luria, A. R. (1976), *The Neuropsychology of Memory*, (Eds) Winston, V. H. and Sons, Washington, D. C.

25) Meichenbaum, D. (1974), Self-instructional strategy training: a cognitive prothesis for the aged. *Human Development*, 17, 273-280.

26) Moscovitch, M. (February 1976), *Differential effects of unilateral temporal and frontal lobe damage on memory performance*. Presented to the International Neuropsychological Society, Toronto, Canada.

27) Neisser, U. (1967), *Cognitive Psychology*, Prentice Hall, Inc.

28) Paivio, A. (1969), Mental imagery in associative learning and memory. *Psychological Review*, 76, 241-263.

29) Paivio, A. (1975), Imagery in recall and recognition. In *Recall and Recognition*, J. Brown (Ed.), John Wiley and Sons.

30) Paivio, A., Yuille, J. C. and Madigan, S. A. (1968), Concreteness, imagery, and meaningfulness values for 925 nouns. *Journal of Experiemntal Psychology Monograph Supplement*, 76, 1-25.

31) Patten, B. M. (1972), The ancient art of memory: usefulness in treatment. *Archives of Neurology*, 26, 25-31.

32) Piercy, M. (1978), Experimental studies of the organic amnesic syndrome in Whitty, C. M. and Zangwill, D. L. *Amnesia*, Butterworth, London

33) Reitan, R. M. and Davison, L. A. (1974) *Clinical Neuropsychology: Current status and applications*. (Ed) V. H. Winston and Sons.

34) Russell, W. R. (1971), *The Traumatic Amnesias*. London: Oxford University Press.

35) Sperry, R. W. (1974), Lateral specialization in the surgically separated hemispheres In Schmitt, F. O. and Worden, F. G. *The Neurosciences: Third Study Program*, M. I. T. press, Cambridge.

36) Squire, L. R. and Slater, P. C. (1975), Forgetting in very long-term memory as assessed by an improved questionnaire technique. *Journal of Experimental Psychology*, 104, 50-54.

37) Treat, N. J. and Reese, H. W. (1976), Age, pacing, and imagery in paired-associate learning. *Developmental Psychology*, 12, 119-124.

38) Warrington, E. K. and Sanders, H. I. (1971), The fate of old memories. *Quarterly Journal of Experimental Psychology*, 23, 432-442.

39) Warrington, E. K. and Silberstein, M. (1971), A questionnaire technique for investigating very long term memory. *Quarterly Journal of Experimental Psychology*, 22, 508-512.

40) Wechsler, D. and Stone, C. (1945), Wechsler Memory Scale. *Psychological Corporation*, New York.

MEMORY LOSS IN THE AGING BLIND

J. G. Gilbert

352 Mt. Prospect Avenue
Newark, New Jersey
U.S.A.

ABSTRACT

Loss of memory is one of the most frequent complaints of older persons. Memory, however, is a multi-faceted function, the separate facets of which decline differently, so that in speaking of "memory loss" in the aging we must specify what kind of memory is lost. Because of their belief in sensory compensation, some have thought that auditory memory in the blind might be superior to that of their sighted brethren In the present study this has not been found to be the case with the elderly blind who show patterns and degrees of memory decline similar to those of elderly sighted persons.

INTRODUCTION

Learning ability and memory have long been recognized as suffering marked deficits during the aging process. Although as with all mental functions, individuals differ in the rate of decline, it is evident that all those who live long enough will show some decline in memory.

Memory, however, is a complex function. It is not a unitary function but one which bears many facets, each of which may have a different rate of decline (Gilbert & Levee 1971). For example, old persons often remember incidents from their childhood but forget what they had for breakfast or the newspaper article they have just read. In testing the memory of older persons it will be found that immediate rote memory or initial concentration, such as that found in the repetition of digits, shows relatively little loss whereas the ability to form new associations, to integrate new data, and to retain newly learned material suffer severe loss. Also, visual memory seems to decline more rapidly than auditory memory, incidental memory than planned recall, and non-verbal than verbal memory. Botwinick (1967) in his comprehensive summary of the research findings on learning and memory in the aging, shows clearly the complexity of this function and the need to measure its different aspects.

Whether the cause of memory loss be due to failure in acquisition, retrieval, consolidation, or storage, or a combination of these is uncertain, but it is generally considered to have a physiological basis in the functioning of the organism's nervous systerm (Glickman 1961, Deutsch 1962). Efforts to improve this functioning by chemical means, such as magnesium pemoline (Gilbert, Donnelly, Zimmer, & Kubis, 1973), amphetamines, caffeine, etc., have generally proved ineffective. Mnemonic devices and the imagery associations taught by the popular "memory specialists" have often proved effective for a particular situation but have usually proved ineffective for general memory functioning. However, it has always been known that the more a function is used the better it operates and that the more something is practiced the better it is learned or remembered. Because of this, many have assumed that blind persons who, due to their lack of vision, must make more use of their other sense modalities, will therefore develop greater proficiency in these senses than sighted persons. For example, Hartwell (1959) found blind children to be superior to sighted children and acquired blind superior to both sighted and congenitally blind in tactile recognition of simple geometric forms and recognition of complex tactile problems. Also Klimasiński (1976) believes that there is a possibility that blind people experience a compensation based on an increased capacity in the touch sensory register. In contrast to this, Axelrod (1959) found that sighted children performed better than blind children, and later blinded children better than early blinded children in both auditory and tactile perception. Also, in a study of tactile perception in young and older sighted and blind adults (Gilbert & Catalano, 1964) no reliable difference was found between young or old sighted and blind, but superiority of young sighted and blind over old sighted and blind.

It has been pointed out (Worden, 1976) that while the older population in the United States is increasing rapidly, the older blind are increasing faster than the old as a whole. Since 50% of the blind are over 60 years of age, it is obvious that as much as possible must be learned about these people in order to help them to achieve independent, satisfying lives. Unfortunately, most of the research on the blind seems to concentrate on children to the neglect of the older segment of the population. It is particularly important to know whether there is compensation in the auditory learning and memory fields in order to know what can be expected of these older blind persons and what can be done to help them.

In one study of blind children (Gilbert & Rubin, 1965) it was observed that they performed reliably better on digit span than on any other tests, but since no tests of meaningful verbal memory were given, it could not be determined whether this superiority held in the meaningful aspects of memory. No report could be found of any comprehensive or controlled study of the auditory memory and learning ability of older blind persons.

The purpose of this study was to determine the learning ability and memory of older blind subjects compared to that of young sighted persons and of sighted persons of their own age group. It was also desired to determine whether there are sex differences in memory among older blind subjects, and whether there is a difference in learning ability between the newly blinded and the early blinded.

METHOD

Fifty-two blind subjects, 25 men and 27 women, between the ages of 60 and 84, mean age 69.7 were used in this study. A person was considered blind if he had not only been declared legally blind but also was unable to see well enough to read with any kind of correctional lens. Sixteen subjects had been blind five years or less, 36 had been blind from six years to a lifetime. Causes of blindness varied but no accurate data on causes could be obtained because many did not know the cause of their blindness. However, known causes included diabetes, cataract, glaucoma, congenital blindness, arteriosclerotic disease of the retina, and optic nerve atrophy. The subjects were volunteers who were either actively working in various capacities or enjoying the recreational facilities of a day center. No institutionalized persons were used in the study.

Each subject was first given the vocabulary of the Wechsler Adult Intelligence Scale and then Form A of the Guild Memory Scale. The Guild Memory Scale measures various facets of short term memory. It consists of six tests: pooled results of immediate recall of two paragraphs similar to short newspaper articles; delayed recall or retention of these paragraphs after intervening tests; initial recall of ten paired associates; retention of these paired associates after intervening tests; repetition of digits forward and reversed; and memory for designs (omitted with this group because Ss could not see the designs). The Guild Memory Scale has two forms, A and B. It was standardized on 834 subjects between the ages of 20 and 75 years. The basic standardization group consisted of 400 subjects between the ages of 20 and 34 years with more than 100 subjects in each of the following age groups: 35-49, 50-59, 60-75 years. The vocabulary sub-test of the Wechsler Adult Intelligence Scale was used as a control for the intellectual level of each subject and scaled scores determined for each vocabulary level of the basic standardization group. In order to find the loss of the upper age groups on each of the memory tests, the raw score of each subject of the standardization group was first subtracted from the mean raw score for his vocabulary level and the differences averaged. Then each older person's raw score was subtracted from the mean score of the basic standardization group for his vocabulary level. The same procedure was followed with the blind subjects in this study.

RESULTS

Table I shows the mean losses of the older blind group on the five memory tests and compares them to the mean scores of the standardization group.

TABLE I

	Standardization Group-Age 20-34 400 subjects		Aging Blind Group-Age 60-84 52 subjects			
	Means[a]	S.D.	Means[a]	S.D.	Loss	t
In. Rec. Para.	+.04	1.61	-1.64	1.79	-1.68	6.46**
Ret. Par.	-.02	1.97	-3.19	3.72	-3.17	5.98**
Digits F.&R.	+.02	1.48	-0.60	1.87	-0.62	2.30*
Paired Assoc.	-.06	1.36	-2.12	1.59	-2.06	8.58**
Ret. Par. Assoc.	+.06	1.52	-2.27	1.99	-2.33	8.03**

*$p < .05$ **$p < .001$
[a] Rep. mean diff. of each individual's score from the standard established for his voc. level for ages 20-34 yrs.

From this table it can be seen that the aging blind group shows a significant loss on all memory tests. However, it must be noted that the loss on repetition of digits is considerably less than the loss on all other memory tests. Thus, it would seem that the learning difficulty of the older blind subjects lies not so much in difficulty in concentrating long enough to receive the new impressions basic to the learning of new material, but in the formation and retention of new associations and the integration and retention of new, meaningful data.

In order to determine whether there is a difference between older sighted and older blind subjects of the same age, the 103 sighted persons between the ages of 60 and 75 and the blind persons between the ages of 60 and 75 were compared. Table II shows the results of these comparisons.

TABLE II

	Sighted Age 60-75 103 subjects		Blind Age 60-75 41 subjects			
	Means[a]	S.D.	Means[a]	S.D.	D	t
In. Rec. Par.	-1.94	2.18	-1.62	2.05	.32	.82
Ret. Par.	-2.83	2.39	-2.94	2.41	.11	.25
Digits F.&R.	-0.39	1.71	-0.64	2.23	.25	.64
Paired Assoc.	-1.50	1.66	-2.14	1.68	.64	2.06*
Ret. Par. Assoc.	-1.79	1.86	-2.29	2.12	.50	1.25

*$p < .05$

[a]Rep. mean diff. of each individual's score from the standard established for his voc. level for ages 20-34 yrs.

From this Table it can readily be seen that there is great similarity between the performances of the older sighted and the older blind subjects in tests of memory with no indication of superiority of the blind group over the sighted group on any of the tests. The only test in which there is a significant difference is in the paired associates test or in the formation of new associations, and this difference is in favor of the sighted group.

An attempt was also made to determine whether there might be a difference in memory between those who were newly blind (five years or less) and those who were blind six years to a lifetime. Although the number of the newly blind was small (16), there was no indication of any significant difference between the two groups on any of the tests.

Since there have been conflicting reports concerning sex differences in memory with sighted subjects, male and female subjects in this aging blind group were compared. Again, no significant difference was found on any of the memory tests, although the females performed slightly better than the males on each of the five memory tests.

DISCUSSION

The results of this study confirm the findings of previous investigations showing a decline in memory among older subjects. Results also show that this decline occurs in older blind as well as in older sighted subjects. This finding is in contrast to the often expressed notion of compensation and also to the findings of Hartwell (1959) and Klimasiński (1976) and in support of the finding of Axelrod (1959) and of Gilbert and Catalano (1964). Many (often the blind themselves) have expressed the opinion that because they depend upon and must constantly use their memories, blind persons develop and maintain their memories better than sighted persons, but the results on this test have not shown this to be the case.

Further discounting the concept of compensation in the blind and indicating that decline in memory is the usual accompaniment of aging and something which affects most older persons, sighted or blind, is the fact that there is such a similarity in memory on these tests between a group of older sighted and older blind subjects of the same age. The only reliable difference found on any of the tests was in the initial recall of paired associates. The reason for this is not certain but there is the possibility that there is an element of abstraction in the recall of paired associates. The subject is not required simply to recall something which has been read to him but is called upon to abstract elements from each of the words given him to form an entirely new association, often an association which runs counter to old, well formed associations. If this is the reason for the greater difficulty the blind experience in paired associates, it confirms the findings of Rubin (1964) that blind adults experience difficulty in abstracting.

Although the blind individuals who took this test were, on the whole, persons of average intelligence, there were a few extremely bright subjects. These subjects showed relatively little decline in any aspect of memory and performed almost as well as the young sighted subjects.

Practically, this study shows that older blind persons are able to learn and remember as well as older sighted subjects and therefore are eligible for rehabilitation training the same as the sighted, if they are motivated to receive this training. Many, if they wish, can learn to function in remunerative jobs and others can learn to function effectively in their homes and everyday lives.

SUMMARY

This has been a study of memory in the aging blind. Fifty-two subjects between the ages of 60 and 84 (average age 69.7) were given first the vocabulary sub-test of the Wechsler Adult Intelligence Scale and then the Guild Memory Test. The WAIS showed the group to be average in intelligence (vocabulary 10.7). Scores of the memory test were then compared with the scores of the standardization group of 400 subjects between the ages of 20 and 34 years.

Reliable differences in favor of the young sighted group were found in immediate meaningful verbal memory (paragraphs), retention of paragraphs, immediate rote memory (digit span), initial recall of paired associates, and retention of paired associates. Performances on digit span, however, showed much less loss than performances on other memory tests.

When compared with a sighted group of similar age (60-75), there was a reliable difference only in initial recall of paired associates, and this difference was in favor of the sighted group.

There were no reliable differences between the newly blinded (five years or less) and the long blinded (six years to a lifetime).

There were no reliable sex differences on any of the memory tests.

Results show that normal older blind subjects who are so motivated are as well able to benefit from rehabilitation as older sighted subjects.

REFERENCES

Axelrod, S. (1959). Effects of early blindness: Performances of blind and signed children on tactile and auditory tasks. American Foundation for the Blind, *Research Society*, *No. 7*.

Botwinick, J. (1967). *Cognitive Processes in Maturity and Old Age*. Springer Publishing Company, New York.

Deutsch, J. A. (1962). Higher nervous function: The physiological basis of memory. *Annual Review of Physiology*, 24, 259-286.

Gilbert, J. G. and Catalano, F. L. (1964). Age differences in stereognosis among sighted and blind subjects. *Journal of Gerontology*, 19, 1, 88-91.

Gilbert, J. G. and Rubin, E. J. (1965). Evaluating the intellect of blind children. *The New Outlook for the Blind*. September issue.

Gilbert, J. G, Levee, R. F. and Catalano, F. L. (1968). A preliminary report on a new memory scale. *Perceptual and Motor Skills*, 27, 277-278.

Gilbert, J. G. and Levee, R. F. (1971). Patterns of declining memory. *Journal of Gerontology*, 26, 1, 70-75.

Gilbert, J. G., Donnelly, K., Zimmer, L. E., and Kubis, J. F. (1973). Effect of magnesium pemoline and methylphenidate on memory improvement and mood in normal aging subjects. *International Journal of Aging and Human Development*, 4, 35-51.

Glickman, S. E. (1961). Perseverative neural processes and consolidation of the memory trace. *Psychological Bulletin*, 58, 218-233.

Hartwell, Y. (1959). Perception tactile des formes et organization spatiale tactile. *J. Psychol. Norm. Path.*

Klimasiński, K. (1976). Sensory compensation in the Blind. *Przeglad Psychologiczny*, 19, 379-388.

Rubin, E. J. (1964). Abstract functioning in the blind. American Foundation for the Blind, *Research Series No. 11.*

Wechsler, D. (1955). *Wechsler Adult Intelligence Scale Manual*. Psychological Corporation, New York.

Worden, H. W. (1976). Aging and blindness. *New Outlook for the Blind*. 70, 433-437.

THE CLINICAL ASSESSMENT OF MEMORY - A REVIEW

Moyra Williams
MRC Applied Psychology Unit, 15 Chaucer Road, Cambridge, England

INTRODUCTION

There are three main reasons for assessing memory in clinical populations; (1) to help in diagnosis; (2) to monitor changes in the patient's condition; (3) to provide the patient himself with some insight into his difficulties in order that he may overcome them. While the first of these is undoubtedly the commonest reason for assessment, the tests used are frequently criticised.

DIAGNOSTIC PATTERNS OF BREAKDOWN

Memory is not a single entity, and in clinical conditions it may break down in at least six different ways: (1) in the recall of remote events, (2) in the recall of recent events, (3) in the recall of contexts of experience, (4) in the acquisition of new patterns of behaviour, (5) in the performance of acquired skills, and (6) in the sense of familiarity with repeated experiences. In different clinical conditions, each of these may be affected differently as shown in Table 1.

Table 1 is, of course, only schematic, and a rough guide. To say a person is "unable to recall recent events" is too vague. For example, how recent is "recent"? Most subjects suffering from organic amnesia can recall strings of words or numbers immediately after hearing them (as in Digit Span tests) without difficulty. It is only after delays of a few minutes especially if these are filled with other forms of mental activity (Luria, 1971), that they forget. Again in the case of remote memories, what is a person expected to remember? The recognition and naming of former politicians produce variable results (Sanders and Warrington, 1971; Marslen-Wilson and Teuber, 1975) depending on the way the tests are constructed, while Squire and his associates (see Squire, Slater and Chace, 1975) find that in different clinical conditions, different aspects of remote memory may be affected.

Table 1

Showing the general pattern of memory breakdown in different diagnostic groups.

Diagnostic Category	1	2	3	4	5	6
General Cerebral Deterior'n	±	-	-	-	-	-
Toxic States	+	±	±	-	+	±
Depression	±	+	+	-	+	+
Anxiety	-	+	+	-	+	+
Organic Amnesia	+	-	-	-	+	-

Key: + Preserved ± Possibly affected - Always affected

Column 1 = Recall Remote
" 2 = Recall Recent
" 3 = Recall Context
Column 4 = New Learning
" 5 = Acquired Skill
" 6 = Familiarity

There is a wide-spread but erroneous belief that all disorders of cerebral structure and function cause impairment of memory, especially in the delayed recall of recent events. However, this is not so. Using a measurement of delayed recall based on free and prompted responses (where the higher the score the worse the performance, Williams, 1968), Fig. 1 shows that only subjects with cortical lesions perform worse than normal and psychiatric patients. Those with subcortical cerebral lesions perform within the normal limits.

The general overall pattern of breakdown is not the only factor distinguishing the different diagnostic groups.

There are also important differences between the manner of breakdown and in the conditions which influence performance in the different clinical states. For example, in most patients, as in the normal population, recall is assisted by the presence of prompts or cues. However, the effect of these is not the same in all patients. In seniles, the giving of a prompt may impede recall of its target, by distracting the subject into a new area of thought; while in anxiety and fugue states the prompt may increase rather than decrease the resistence to recall of a repressed item (Owen and Williams, 1978).

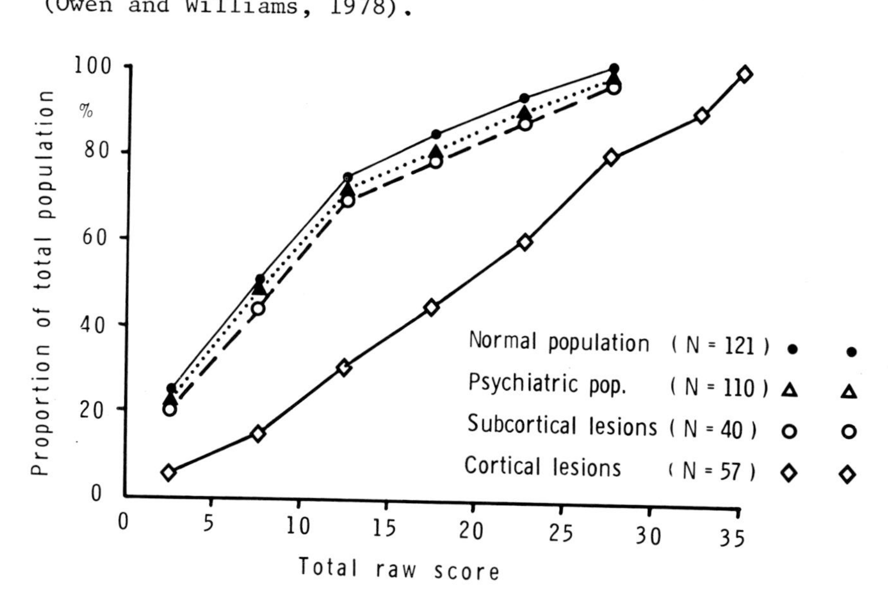

Fig. 1 Showing the proportion of the total population in different diagnostic groups below each score on Williams (1968) Delayed Recall Test.

In the clinical field, two characteristics of forgetting are frequently seen which seldom occur in normal people, but have important diagnostic and theoretical implications. These are *Retrograde Amnesia (R.A.)* and the *Loss of Familiarity*.

RETROGRADE AMNESIA

R.A., the forgetting of past events which had been adequately registered, may be sudden and bounded by sharp cut-off points as after concussional head injuries, or blurred and extensive as in the degenerative diseases. The forgotten incidents are usually determined by time (the closer their proximity to the cerebral insult, the more likely they are to be forgotten) except in psychiatric illnesses where emotional factors predominate. However, time and emotional involvement cannot be completely separated, for even in the organic amnesias, some episodes or events may be recalled because of their emotional significance in otherwise blank periods, (Russell 1959; Williams and Zangwill, 1952).

Another feature of R.A. is its recoverability or shrinkage. This often occurs spontaneously but may be assisted by conversations or by returning to the physical environment in which the events occurred. This again raises points of theoretical interest regarding its causation - i.e. is R.A. due to a failure of consolidation or retrieval?

The assessment of R.A. is usually based on its duration in time, and is regarded as a measure of severity of the causation agent. In the case of head injuries (and clinically induced loss of consciousness in anaesthesia or E.C.T.) the longer the R.A. after full recovery, the more severe the cerebral damage is believed to be (Russell, 1959). Hence, length of R.A. is an important measure. However,accurate means of measuring it, and norms against which performance should be compared are not easily available (Squire, Chace and Slater, 1976). Indeed, in normal people, the ability to describe and detail events leading up to a particular moment in time dependsvery largely on the events following them (Williams, 1969).

LOSS OF FAMILIARITY

This aspect of organic amnesia, although it has been recognised for years, has only come under experimental study quite recently. Claparède's and Bonhoeffer's observations of its occurrence in real-life situations have been described by McCurdy (1926), who stressed the fact that patients were often able to modify their behaviour in the light of experience despite being quite unable to recall the experiences leading to the modifications. In the laboratory, it is most often seen in the subject's ability to "guess" the correct target while at the same time denying any recollection of being asked to remember it.

In normal people, familiarity has two aspects. If shown

a picture of a Table, there is (1) a general sense of familiarity ("I know what this is; it's a picture of something called a Table") equivalent to Tulving's Semantic Memory, and (2) familiarity with the specific event ("Yes, that's the picture you told me to remember") or Tulving's Episodic Memory.

The two are related to some extent in normal people, but to a much greater extent in the classical organic amnesias. For example, targets consisting of high frequency (common) words are more often recognised than those of low frequency (rare) ones (Huppert and Piercy, 1976). Moreover high probability cues (such as, for a picture of a cart, the cue "Put the horse before the ----") arouses recognition of the target more often than low probability ones ("A goods vehicle"). However there is a snag here, for it is not only the true targets which carry a sense of familiarity; the high false positive rate to common words and to responses aroused by high probability cues, suggests that any highly aroused target - whether the arousal is due to frequency of past usage or to present cueing - will be treated as familiar (Owen and Williams, 1978).

This suggests that whereas in normal people, background (or semantic) memory depends on past experience, and incidental (or episodic) depends on the recall of context, amnesic patients rely only on the threshold of the target itself, whether this threshold is due to past arousal (frequency) or to the present situation (high probability cueing).

The part played by language in the recognition process has been much debated. Butters and Cermak (1975) have argued on the basis of many experiments that it is because amnesic patients do not encode data semantically that they have difficulty in recall and recognition, but what exactly they mean by this I am not sure. Amnesic patients, like normal people, do remember words better than visual impressions. In an experiment conducted by Owen and myself (Owen and Williams, 1976), the subjects were shown a target such as that at the top of Fig. 2, and then on the recognition test were offered two alternatives neither of which was identical with the original, but one of which had its picture and the other its name. The majority of amnesics, like normals, picked out the verbal rather than the visual item as the one which had been shown to them (see Table 2).

It may be, however, that although amnesic patients remember words better than pictures, they still do not *store* them or use them for recall in the same way. In normal people, a cue relevant to the homonym of a target is very effective in eliciting recall of the target itself, but in amnesics this is not so. For instance, Hewitt (1978) showed his subjects pictures of objects with common homonyms (e.g. a tennis ball), and found that the cue ("Cinderella did go to the ---- after all" was just as effective in eliciting recall of the picture as the cue "His backhand stroke made the ---- spin". In amnesics, however, his homonym cues only elicited recognition of the target in 50% of cases.

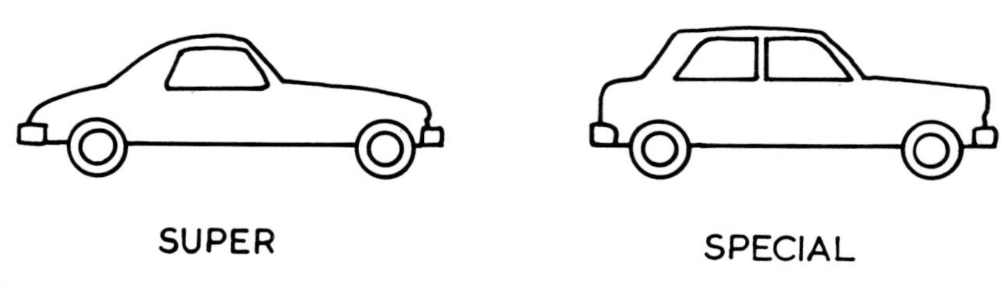

Fig. 2 An example of the Target and Recognition choices used in an Experiment on Familiarity.

Table 2

The number of responses in each category made by subjects on the choice recognition test, using the stimuli in Fig. 2.

Subjects	N	Total possible	Correct	Don't Know	Word	Picture
Controls	6	24	13	1	9	1
Korsakov	6	24	-	3	16	5
Demented	6	24	-	7	8	9

Whether this is due to storage (i.e. in normal people, all the different meanings of a word are stored together as in a dictionary, but in amnesics they are not), or to retrieval (i.e. in normals, the arousal of one word spreads to its neighbours lowering their threshold to recall, but in amnesics such a spread is absent-the "Premature Closure" of Talland, 1965) - or whether indeed some different explanation is demanded, it is still, in my opinion, too early to say.

CONCLUSIONS

The study of clinical mental disorders has often been undertaken in the hope that it would throw light on normal mental processes, and indeed by highlighting the defects which may occur in memorizing there has been every reason to believe that some insight may be gained into normal memory mechanisms (Piercy, 1977). However the main conclusion that seems to come from clinical studies is the infinite variety of ways that past experiences may regulate present behaviour; and to lump these all together under a single heading - Memory - is confusing. To talk of Memory Impairment as if it can all be attributed to a single defect (that of encoding, storage or retrieval) is not very helpful. It is much more useful to describe what a patient can do and to determine the variables affecting his behaviour in different conditions- and the present author believes that it is from such an approach that future advances will come.

REFERENCES

Butters, N. and Cermak, L.A. (1975). The memory of disorders of alcoholic patients with Korsakov Syndrome. *Annals of the New York Academy of Science*, 233, 61-75.

Hewitt, K. (1978). Thesis presented to Cambridge University for PhD.

Huppert, F.A. and Piercy, M.F. (1976). Recognition memory in amnesic patients. *Cortex*, 12, 3-20.

Luria, A.R. (1971). Memory disturbances in local brain lesions. *Neuropsychologia*, 9, 367-378.

McCurdy, J.T. (1926). *Common Principles in Psychology and Physiology*. Cambridge University Press, London.

Marslen-Wilson, W.D. and Teuber, H-L (1975). Memory for remote events in anterograde amnesia: Recognition of public figures from newsphotographs. *Neuropsychologia*, 13, 353-364.

Owen, G.M. and Williams, M. (1976). Words versus picture recognition in amnesic and aphasic patients. *Neuropsychologia*, 15, 351-354.

Owen, G.M. and Williams, M. (1978). Factors affecting the sense of familiarity. *(in preparation)*.

Piercy, M.F. (1977). Experimental studies of the organic amnesic syndrome. In: *Amnesia*. (C.W.M. Whitty and O.L. Zangwill eds), (2nd Edition), Butterworths, London.

Russell, W.R. (1959). *Brain, Memory and Learning*. Clarendon Press, Oxford.

Sanders, H.I. and Warrington, E.K. (1971). Memory for remote events in amnesic patients. *Brain*, 94, 661.

Squire, L.R., Slater, P.C. and Chace, P.M. (1975). Retrograde amnesia, *Science*, 187, 77-79.

Squire, L.R., Chace, P.M. and Slater, P.C. (1976). Retrograde Amnesia following E.C.T. *Nature*, 260, 5554.

Talland, G.A. (1965). *Deranged Memory*. Academic Press, New York.

Williams, M. (1968). The measurement of memory in clinical practice. *British Journal of Social and Clinical Psychology*, 7, 19-34.

Williams, M. (1969). Traumatic retrograde amnesia and normal forgetting. In: *The Pathology of Memory*. (G.A. Talland and N.C. Waugh eds), Academic Press, New York.

Williams, M. and Zangwill, O.L. (1952). Retrograde amnesia following head injury. *Journal of Neurology, Neurosurgery and Psychiatry*. 15, 54.

DRUGS AND MEMORY

DRUGS AND MEMORY: A BRIEF REVIEW

Stuart J. Dimond
Department of Psychology,
University College Cardiff
Wales, U.K.

This review shows that the subject of drugs and memory as a topic is something that has come of age and that its achievements although recent are now substantial. The idea is expressed that intellectual function can be modified through the effect that drugs have upon the brain and nervous system, and the technology for this is seen as a major advance in drug research with important clinical implications. This report concentrates on agents which disturb memory, agents which inhibit it as well as on substances which enhance memory performance and the clinical applications of this are discussed.

A few years ago such a session as this would not have been possible for at that time virtually nothing was known about the effects of drugs on learning and memory. Recently, however, there has been a considerable expansion in the number of papers published in the area. Numbers of publications do not necessarily indicate progress, but they do show the significance which is attached to subject matter by the total world population of research workers. It is interesting therefore to look at the number of publications in the area indicated by Index Medicus.

During the late 60s the number of publications remained relatively steady, at under 60, and then in the 70s and continuing to the present time we see a major interest in this area with steadily increasing numbers of publications. In 1978, these were well over 100.

The emphasis of much recent research in the behavioural sciences has been placed on the study of those techniques by which behaviour can be manipulated and changed for the solution of essentially practical problems.

This manipulation has come to be called psychotechnology. We discuss today a particular area of psychotechnology where behaviour is changed and modified by direct interference with the physical processes of the brain.

The psychotechnology we consider of course is one widely used and employed for the modification and change of human conduct and that is in the use of drugs which have their effect largely upon the brain and nervous system. In one sense of course this is no new thing. Each society seems to have possessed its own substances for intoxicating and blotting out the mind, whether this be Betel nuts, Cocaine, Alcohol or Marijhuana. The widespread use of Alcohol in our own society is an example where sanction has been given to the use of a drug known to radically change mental action and behaviour through its use, and of course it is known that in states of severe alcoholism much of the fabric of the patient's memory is completely destroyed.

We have also witnessed another revolution, instituted this time by the medical profession itself, in the use of drugs to modify behaviour through the effect that they have upon the brain and nervous system. As we all know the worldwide consumption of tranquilizers, antidepressants and stimulants reaches staggering proportions and is likely to increase. Chemical therapy of the emotions, the alleviation of anxiety, the treatment of nervousness can be regarded as one of the miracles of the 20th Century because of the relief from suffering which it brings. The pharmacological control of behaviour which this implies although widespread has been quietly accepted but society still has to give its explicit consent to the revolution which has taken place in its midst with regard to how far the conduct and mental functioning of man may or should be changed as the result of pharmacological control.

In line with the technological approach adopted here I think we have to regard memory as a very precious resource indeed both for the individual who has his own memories to sustain and for society at large which is dependent on the effective memory functioning of its individuals. We must therefore look very carefully at those ingested agents or features of our chemical environment capable of destroying or disturbing memory and disrupting behaviour as a consquence.

There are a number of drugs which have important effects on memory of a deleterious kind. Many drugs of course will have adverse effects not necessarily because of any target affinity for the mechanisms of memory themselves but rather for the intoxicating quality they introduce into mental life during the acute stages. This is probably so with the hallucinogens (Pugiliese, 1973). Marijhuana may have more direct effects. Disturbances of memory and thought were reported for its use as early as 1932 by Beringer. One of the commonly reported characteristics of marihuana intoxication is difficulty in performing tasks that require the accurate retrieval of information recently stored in memory (Tinklenberg and Darley 1976). It has been reported subsequently to impair the formation of new learning in man although equally it appears to leave learning already accomplished very much intact. Consequently it is commonly suggested that it impairs short term memory (Abel 1975). Clearly the acute effects which result from the intoxication have consequences which are often of considerable practical importance and smoking marihuana in socially used dosages causes significant deterioration on simulated instrument flying tests for at least two hours afterwards even in experienced pilots (Blaire et al. 1976).

Alcohol is another commonly used substance which has deteriorative effects upon the memory process. Although short term memory may be preserved intact and an absence of intellectual loss there may in chronic alcoholism be a severe kind of amnesia - that of the Korsakoff type - where there exists a gross impairment of long-term memory (Warrington 1973). Of course this is a severe chronic condition. Most of the other effects of alcohol appear to follow from the general intoxicating effect of the drug as it works at that moment.

We have seen that memory can be influenced by various agents affecting brain functions. Among these the general anaesthetics have to be counted (Porter 1972). Some anaesthetics have more effects than others. Even low concentrations have been shown to disturb psychological functions which involve memory (Adam 1973). Of course most anaesthetic gases are administered in much higher quantities. Concern with the effects of the anaesthetic gases on memory includes not only the ephemeral effects but also the possible long-term effects due to these drugs. Laboratory studies show that even in dosages which do not produce unconsciousness low concentrations will impair the retrieval of verbal material learned under the drug influence, whereas slightly higher concentrations prevent long-term registration with no apparent recovery. Many patients particularly those occupying intellectually demanding positions complain about a loss of verbal competence where they may have greater difficulty in expressing ideas, in writing and in searching for words, and this may last for days, weeks or even longer after an operation.

Adam (1973) showed that very low concentrations of fluroxene and halothane affected verbal memory selectively. To have a loss of memory for the events leading up to surgery could in fact be advantageous because it reduces some of the traumatic aspect, but of course a memory problem even if temporary after surgery could place the patient at a disadvantage and would certainly not help the process of recovery. The question of the possible effects on people who work with anaesthetics also needs investigation.

We are now more sensitive to the devastating effects which some environmental pollutants can have. In most instances severe neurological disturbance or physical degeneration as for example that associated with methyl mercury poisoning follow after a period where the only visible symptoms are those of psychological disturbance often indicated in memory performance. Clearly the effects of environmental pollutants on psychological function is something which needs investigation particularly as these effects appear early on and appear to signal the severe consequences which can follow. I believe that this is something with which the behavioural scientist should be much more actively concerned particularly as concerns ordinary everyday pollutants such as car-exhaust fumes and so on.

There are a number of drugs which have been deliberately exploited because they inhibit the formation of memories. These are usually specific and selective blocking agents such as Puromycin (Agranoff 1967), Acetoxycycloheximide and cycloheximide (Agranoff 1967), Actinomycin D (Barondes and Jarvik 1964) and 8-Azaguanine (Dingman and Sporn 1971). The use of these substances is reviewed by Rahwan (1971). It should be pointed out however that these drugs have almost always been employed as tools in scientific research almost invariably with animals and so far they await practical application for this purpose. Nevertheless it seems to me that a potential is growing to block or to prevent the consolidation of memories and that this could be used in the clinic to alleviate the distress of the person who experiences a terrible trauma and who may have to live with the memory of that trauma for considerable periods of time. I could see many advantages for that person in having the memory erased or at least softened. The other side to this technological approach to drug use is to see what can be done about learning and memory problems through the use of drugs. My own interest in this lies in the studies of a Nootropic drug Piracetam (UCB 6215) which we found to facilitate verbal learning in normal university students (Dimond 1977) and also some tactual learning in schizophrenic patients (Dimond 1978). This raises the question of whether learning and memory improvements can be produced in the perfectly normal person and whether capacities here can be increased, but most importantly the technology of drug use is devoted to those instances where severe memory or learning problems are quite disabling.

A number of drugs have been reported to improve learning and memory performance. Amongst these are Glutamic Acid (McGaugh and Petrinovitch 1965), Ribaminol (Glasky and Simon 1968), Magnesium Pemoline (Cyclert) (Plotnikoff 1973), Tricyanoaminopropene (Daniels 1967). Vitamin B.12 (Rahwan 1971), Piracetam (Wolthius 1971, Mindus 1975, Dimond and Brouwers 1976). A recent report in Science (Vol.201 p.275) from the National Institute of Mental Health in Washington reported two experiments which show that injections of arecholine enabled a group of 24 year old volunteers to learn lists of words (vegetables, cities, fruits) substantially quicker than without such injections. Recently Vasopressin (Legros et al. 1978) has been reported to facilitate memory in aged patients. This is an interesting finding because Vasopressin is a hormone produced by the pituitary gland at the base of the brain and studies in amnesia suggest that this hormone may work on the mechanism of memory to induce a recovery from amnesia. Much of this work is of recent origin and some of it is not unequivocal in that negative reports as well as positive occur in the literature. I believe the picture at present is congruent with the idea that substances are capable of modifying learning performance and inducing upward changes in performance. This to me seems to be a remarkable development, but the substances themselves are capable of doing this only with certain limits and we await the development of powerfully acting substances.

REFERENCES

Abel, E.L. (1975) Marihuana, learning and memory. *International Review of Neurobiology*, 18, 329-56.

Adam, N. (1973) Effects of general anaesthetics on memory functions in man. *Journal of Comparative Physiological Psychology*, 83, 294.

Adam, N. (1976) Effects of general anaesthetics on search in memory in man. *T.I.T. Journal of Life Sciences*, 6,29-34.

Agranoff, B.W. (1967) Memory and protein synthesis. *Scientific American*, 216, 115-122.

Barondes, S.H. and Jarvik, M.E. (1964) The influence of Actinomycin D on Brain RNA Synthesis and on memory. *Journal of Neurochemistry*, 11, 187-195.

Blaine, J.D., Meacham, M.P., Janowsky, D.S., Schoor, M. and Bozzetti, L.P. (1976) Marihuana smoking and simulated flying performance. Chap. in *The Pharmacology of Marihuana*. Ed. M.C. Brande and S. Szoura. Raven Press. New York.

Daniels, D. (1967) The effect of TCAP on acquisition of discrimination learning in the rat. *Psychonomic Science*, 7, 5-6.

Dimond, S.J. (1977) Drugs to improve learning in man. Implications and neuropsychological analysis. Chap. in *The Neuropsychology of Learning Disorders*. Ed. R. M. Knights and D. J. Bakker. University Park Press, Baltimore.

Dimond, S.J. (1978) *Introducing Neuropsychology*.C.C. Thomas. Springfield. Illinois.

Dimond, S.J. (1978) Disconnection and psychopathology. Chap. in *Hemisphere asymmetry of function and psychopathology*. Ed. J. Gruzelier and P. Flor-Henry. (In press).

Dimond, S.J. and Brouwers, E.Y.M. (1976) Increase in the power of memory in normal man through the use of drugs. *Psychopharmacology*, 49, 307-309.

Dingman, W., and Sporn, M.B. (1961) The incorporation of 8-Azaguanine into Rat Brain RNA and its effect on maze learning by the rat: an enquiry into the biochemical basis of memory. *Journal of Psychiatric Research*, 1, 1 - 10.

Glasky, A.J. and Simon, L.N. (1968) Ribaminol, a memory drug. *American Profession of Pharmacology*, 34/1, 29.

Imam, A. (1970) Incidental learning: a study of developmental trends. University of Wales Library, Cardiff. Ph.D. Thesis.

Legros, J.J. et al. (1978) Influence of vasopressin on learning and memory (letter). *Lancet*,1 (8054), 41-42.

McGaugh, J.L. (1968) Psychopharmacology. A review of progress. 1957-1967. Washington D.C. U.S.P.H.S. publication no. 1836.

McGaugh, J.L. and Petrinovich, L.F. (1965) Effects of drugs on learning and memory. Chap. in *International review of Neurobiology, Vol. 8*. Eds. C.C. Pfeiffer and J.R. Smythies. Academic Press, New York.

Mindus, P. et al. (1975) Does piracetam counteract the ECT induced memory dysfunctions in depressed patients. *Acta Psychiatric Scandanivica*, 51, (5), 319-26.

Plotnikoff, N.P. (1973) Pemoline enhancement of maze performance in young rats. *Behavioral Biology*, 9, 117-21.

Porter, A.L. (1972) An analytic review of the effects of non-hydrogen bonding anaesthetics on memory processing. *Behavioral Biology*, 7, 291, 309.

Pugliese, A.C. (1973) The effects of drugs on learning and memory. *The International Journal of the Addictions*, 8(4), pp. 643-656.

Rahwan, R.G. (1971) The biochemical and pharmacological basis of learning and memory. *Agents and Actions*, 2, 87-102.

Signoret, J.L. and Whiteley, A. (1978) Choline influence on learning and forgetting in human amnestic syndromes. Paper presented to the European Brain and Behavior Society. London July, 1978.

Tinklenberg, J.R. and Darley, C.F. (1976) A model of marihuana's cognitive effects. Chap. in *The Pharmacology of Marihuana*. Ed. M.C. Braude and S. Szana. Raven Press, New York.

Wolthius, O.L. (1971) Experiments with UCB 6215, a drug which enhances acquisition in rats. Its effects compared with those of methamphetamine. *European Journal of Pharmacology*, 16, 283-297.

Vojtechovsky, M. and Safratova, V. (1970) The effects of some psychotropic drugs on memory consolidation in man. *Activinas Nervosas Super, (Praha)*, 13, 2.

Warrington, E.K. (1973) The nature and significance of Neurophysiological Deficits associated with alcoholism. Chap. in *Alcohol, Drugs and Brain Damage*. Ed. James G. Rankin, Addiction Research Foundation of Ontario.

NOOTROPIC DRUGS AND MEMORY

C. Giurgea
Neuropharmacological Research Department,
UCB, Brussels, Belgium
S.J. Sara
Center for Experimental and Comparative Psychology,
University of Louvain, Pellenberg, Belgium

Pharmacological agents have been widely used over the past few decades in an attempt to unravel the biological mystery of how a living organism conserves information about the environment and response contingencies for use in organizing subsequent behavior. In the case where the site of action and/or biochemical effect of a substance is well established, the substance can be used as a tool for understanding the physiological substrates of the psychological process in question. In this way, the manipulation of neurotransmitters by agents which are known to accelerate syntheses, block re-uptake or otherwise modulate the activity of the system, can provide information concerning the role of these systems in learning and memory. There are, however, instances in which empirical evidence shows that a psychoactive drug whose mechanism of action is not necessarily well understood, appears to have an effect on memory.

To ascertain that behavioural effects of a pharmacological agent are indeed on learning and memory is a complex task, and this is true for both positive and negative effects, in the clinic and in the laboratory. The presence or absence of a "trace" must necessarily be estimated through a behaving organism whose level of motivation is manipulated by the experimenter through food or water deprivation, or by administration of some painful stimulus, or in the case of human investigations, through verbal remarks. The performance is evaluated in terms of latency of response, rate of response, trials to criterion. Such behavior is essentially and directly dependent upon a memory "trace" and its availability (retrieval), but the performance of the learned task is also a function of motivational state, reactivity to stress (anxiety), locomotor activity, reaction time, perceptual capacity. It is well known that all psychoactive drugs influence these processes in varying degrees. For example, animals treated with benzodiazepines and chlorpromazine are less responsive to painful shock, so it is not surprising that they have difficulty in learning a shock escape or avoidance task. It is difficult, if not impossible, to determine if this performance deficit is due to this motivational variable or to some direct effect of the drug on memory processes. Psychostimulant drugs in small doses have been reported to facilitate learning and memory. But here again, the distinction between a memory effect and a performance effect has not always been clearly defined by the experimental procedure. Motor facilitation or hyperactivity induced by stimulant drugs could account for the differences in response latencies or rate. In line with this analysis, it is trivial to note that most of the drugs which have been reported to impair learning have been of a sedative kind, while those showing facilitation have been analeptic drugs (see Essman, 1971 for review). The present paper deals with nootropic drugs, which modulate memory without being either sedative or stimulant.

MEMORY AS CNS PLASTICITY

Konorski (1967) poses the problem of memory as one of functional plasticity of the cerebral cortex. This plasticity is regarded as a fundamental property of higher nervous functioning. For Konorski, the study of plasticity *is* the study of memory, and the problem is conceptualized in purely physiological terms. Such questions as the nature of the morphological expression of this plasticity, the mechanism by which these modifications occur, and the factors which influence the rate of plastic change, should be fundamental questions in neurophysiological research. Konorski considers that differences between species or between individuals within a species with regard to learning ability are really differences in plasticity. Plasticity of the nervous system is weakened by illness, brain damage, fatigue, ageing. Many clinical situations involve deficits of plasticity and produce an amnesic syndrome. These include cerebral vascular accidents, cerebral hypoxia, epilepsy, alcoholism, lesions of the temporal lobe-hippocampal region of the brain, ageing. Although pharmacological treatment of these syndromes has not been very successful in the clinic, the creation of animal models of these dysfunctions has shown that there is a good deal of lability in memory processes.

LABILITY OF MEMORY IN ANIMALS

There are several ways of inducing memory deficits

experimentally in animals. The most widely used technique is by far the one trial inhibitory avoidance response followed by electroconvulsive shock, which produces a reliable retrograde amnesia. Amnesia induced in this way is preventable or reversible by increasing the level of vigilance of the animal by injection of strychnine immediately before the retention test (Sara & Remacle, 1977). Using the same inhibitory avoidance task, we have recently shown that poor performance due to undertraining can be reversed in the same way that ECS induced amnesia can.

A third technique in manipulating animal memory is simple spontaneous forgetting. Surprisingly, there is little literature on long term retention in animals in the experimental psychology literature, perhaps due to the fact that a well learned classically conditioned or operant response is highly resistant to the passage of time, as both Pavlov and Skinner have remarked. We have recently developed a complex spatial discrimination task - appetitive maze learning - within which reliable forgetting can be demonstrated. This "forgetting" seems, however, to be a retrieval failure, rather than a trace decay, because the forgetting can be alleviated by either a pre-test reminder or by stimulation of the reticular formation (Sara, Deweer and Hars, 1977). Thus memory is labile, particularly memory retrieval, in three different situations where there is an experimentally induced deficiency.

NOOTROPIC DRUGS AND VIGILANCE

A pharmacological agent which acts selectively on cortical plasticity without directly affecting motivation, locomotor activity or perception, would be an invaluable tool in memory study. The nootropic group, represented mainly by piracetam, has been reported by several authors to facilitate memory in a clinical situation, in normal human subjects and in infra human subjects in laboratory experiments (see Giurgea and Salama, 1977 for review).

These drugs have none of the usual analeptic effects and appear to act directly on cerebral plasticity or what is called integrative activity of the brain. Furthermore, we have presented arguments elsewhere supporting the suggestion that the action of the drug is specifically telencephalic and increases cortical vigilance (Giurgea, 1976). The concept of vigilance or arousal has been used rather loosely in both psychology and physiology. These terms refer to the same concept as cortical tonus in the Pavlovian school and this would seem to be an important element in the regulation of the rate of plastic changes in the nervous system. Probably the best electrophysiological expression of cortical tonus is present in the EEG as modulation of the alpha rhythm, which can be seen as a waxing and waning wave of 8-10 cps with an occipital pre-dominance. As Adrian has pointed out, a good alpha rhythm is an expression of cortical wakefulness which underlies mental activity.

Bente (1977) has recently reported that a group of aged hospitalized patients, treated chronically with piracetam showed a shift in EEG spectrum with a clear increase in the power spectrum of alpha frequency accompanied by a decrease in the delta and theta bands. Such an observation, along with the fact that the drug has none of the usual analeptic properties, suggests that there is a direct and selective action on telencephalic vigilance and perhaps on plasticity as the term is used by Konorski.

NOOTROPIC DRUGS AND MEMORY RETRIEVAL IN ANIMALS: RECENT RESULTS

The results which we are reporting here indicate that the nootropic drug piracetam and its analog etiracetam, are capable of reversing memory deficits particularly (but not necessarily exclusively) at the retrieval level of information processing. In these studies we have used several of the preparations described above, in which there is a memory deficit which has already been shown by other techniques to be a reversible amnesia. We define a retrieval effect in relation to the experimental procedure. All subjects receive the same treatment during training and are then divided into equivalent matched groups; drug treatment is administered 30 min. prior to retention test. Any effect is considered to be on the retrieval processes.

GENERAL METHOD

Subjects in all experiments were young Sprague Dawley or Wistar rats, weighing between 150 and 250 g, either raised in our laboratory or purchased from a commercial supplier. They were housed in groups of 6-7 on a twelve hour light dark cycle. Animals were trained and divided into matched groups according to their training performance; drugs were always administered 30 min. prior to the retention test.

Inhibitory Avoidance Experiments

Experimental Amnesia. Animals were trained on a one trial step through inhibitory avoidance task, followed by ECS.

Retention tests occurred at 24h after training and animals were retested at 30 min. intervals. Rats treated with piracetam had a faster recovery of memory than a control group. In fact, there is no memory deficit even on the first test (Sara and David-Remacle, 1974). We have recently seen similar effect with etiracetam, an ethylated piracetam derivative. As can be seen in Fig. 1, those animals treated with 50 mg/kg (s.c.) of the drug avoid significantly better on the retnetion test than saline treated animals.

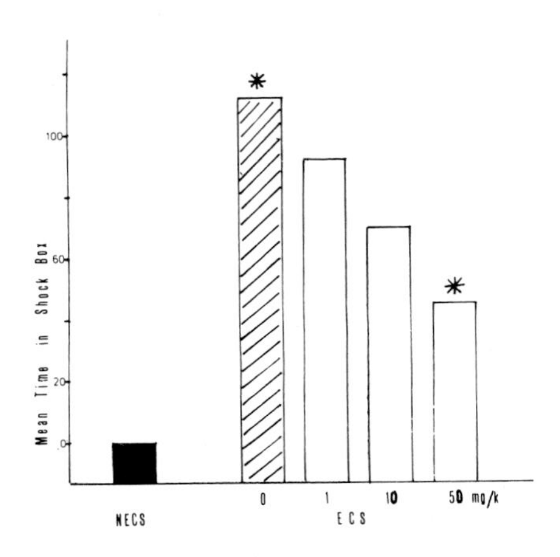

Fig. 1 Etiracetam reversal of ECS-induced amnesia. Note that all non ECS control rats (black bar) avoid the shock compartment 24h after training. Rats submitted to ECS after training show amnesia (striped bar). Rats treated with etiracetam (50 mg/kg s.c.), 30 min. prior to retention test, show significant reversal of the amnesia ($U=40$; $n=12, 12$; $p < .05$). There is no significant effect of 1 mg/kg or 0 mg/kg. Similar results have been reported with piracetam (Sara and David-Remacle, 1974).

Undertraining. Using a similar training paradigm, retention can be impaired by adding a delay of reinforcement. Animals injected with etiracetam, 30 min. before retention test, show significantly better avoidance. Piracetam does not have a significant effect in this situation (see Fig. 2).

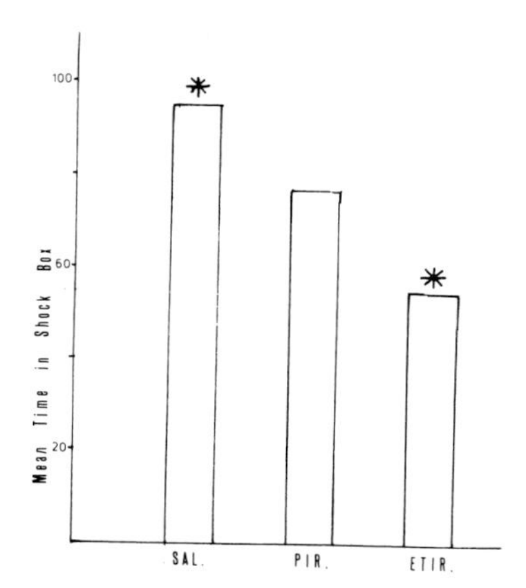

Fig. 2 Etiracetam facilitation of retrieval after undertraining. Animals are trained with a 90-180 sec. delay of reinforcement. Saline treated rats fail to avoid 24h after training; pretest treatment with etiracetam significantly facilitates retrieval. (U=208, n=24, 24; p<.05). There is no effect of piracetam.

Forgetting

We have recently discovered that spontaneous forgetting can be alleviated by pretest injection of a nootropic drug. By spontaneous forgetting we mean the performance decrement seen after a long training-to-test interval in the absence of any experimental physiological, chemical or environmental manipulation. The nature and causes of forgetting have long been of interest to experimental psychologists, especially the question to what extent forgetting is due to trace decay and to what extent to retrieval failure. However, there are few data available concerning forgetting in nonhuman species from which to derive a paradigm for a psychphysiological or psychopharmacological approach.

Operant Conditioning. In our first attempt at such an approach we used a simple bar press response for water reinforcement. Rats were shaped just to a point where they emitted five unassisted responses within five minutes. After a three week training-to-test interval, there was some loss as seen through latency to emit the first response. Once the response is re-established;however, the rate of responding increases as if there had been no interruption suggesting that the memory deficit was a retrieval failure. If piracetam is administered immediately before the retention test, we observe a significantly lower latency to respond (Sara,

David, Weyers, Giurgea, 1978). This effect was also seen with etiracetam in a subsequent experiment where the effect was also evident on the number of responses emitted during the first retention session. On subsequent sessions there were no differences between saline and drug-treated animals, thus ruling out the possibility that etiracetam-treated animals respond more because they are thirstier or more active (unpublished results). It must be said, however, that this operant conditioning paradigm shows relatively inconsistent levels of forgetting from one experiment to another with the same training conditions and the same training-to-test interval, especially in terms of the number of responses on the first retention test.

K maze. Recently we have been working with a behavioral paradigm in which a more robust and reliable forgetting can be demonstrated. Animals are trained in a modified K-maze consisting of 6 successive binary choices. After one trial per day for five days, rats show a relatively stable performance when measured either by time to run the maze or by errors. With a three week training-to-test interval, reliable forgetting can be seen, both for time and errors. Injection of etiracetam (50 mg/kg s.c.), 30 min. before retention test, alleviates forgetting. Rats treated with this drug make fewer errors and run the maze faster than saline treated animals (Fig. 3). It is important to note that without this long training-to-test interval and the subsequent deficit in maze performance, there is no effect of the pretrial drug treatment. Thus, the conclusion that the drug acts on memory retrieval. Piracetam is inactive in this test.

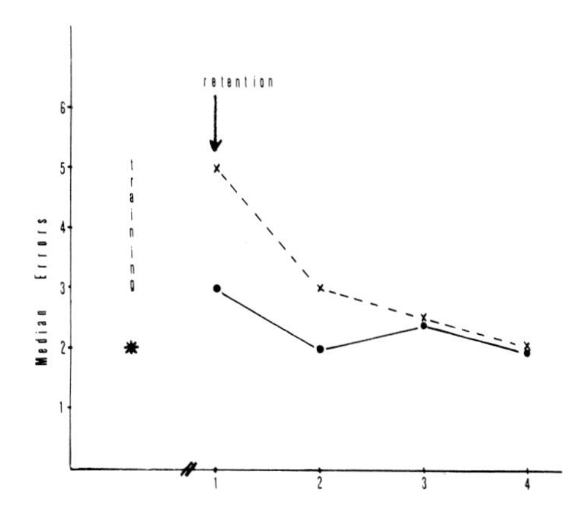

Fig. 3 Median errors at the last training trial for all subjects (*) and at testing and retraining for matched saline (x) and etiracetam (•) groups. Training-to-test interval is 25 days, with 24h interval between retraining sessions. Animals are injected daily during retraining. The difference between groups is significant only at the first (retrieval) test (U=21, n=11, 12; p <.02, two tailed). A similar patter of results was obtained when run time was used as the retention measure.

FINAL REMARKS

Memory retrieval is implied through the organized adaptive behavior of the subject in the test situation. This kind of behavioral organization must necessarily involve an integration of the incoming information available in the environment, endogenous information relating to homeostasis, and previously acquired information represented in the nervous system of the organism - information concerning response contingencies, etc. It is this integrative activity, probably a largely telencephalic function, that is facilitated by the increase of vigilance afforded by nootropic drug treatment.

Meyer and Meyer (1977) have argued strongly that many clinical amnesic syndromes should be treated as retrieval failures. They base their position on the extensive work on recovery of memory after cortical damage in rats and cats. These investigators argue that since persistent memory deficits in animal preparations can be reversed through amphetamine treatment prior to exposure to the test situation, then similar deficits in humans must be reversible, i.e. must be retrieval deficits. The work of Warrington and Weiskrantz (1970) lends clinical support to the position of Meyer and

Meyer. These authors have shown that many amnesic patients are able to remember if the memory is appropriately tapped, thus leading to the conclusion that the patient suffers from retrieval dysfunction. Moreover, Milner (1972) now regards the question of the nature of memory deficits in brain lesioned patients as an open one, after years of supposing that her amnesic patients suffered from storage failure.

These results from the clinic and from the laboratory firmly establish the clinical interest of a drug which has a direct effect on the integrative activity involved in memory retrieval. Given these recent results in laboratory animals, we reaffirm our position concerning the telencephalic functional selectivity of nootropic drugs (Giurgea, 1975; Giurgea and Salama, 1977). The position of nootropic and related drugs, such as the centrally acting neuropeptides, in the classiciation of psychotropic drugs, has not yet been generally agreed upon and would appear to deserve further consideration.

REFERENCES

Bente, D. (1977) Vigilanz: Psychophysiologische Aspekte. *83. Kongress, Wiesbaden*, 4, 17-21. Ed. B. Schlegel, J.F. Bergmann-Verlag, Munchen (in press).

Essman, W.B. (1971) Drug Effects and Learning and Memory Processes. *Advancement in Pharmacological Chemotherapy*, 9, 241-330.

Giurgea, C. (1976) Piracetam: Nootropic pharmacology of neurointegrative activity. *Current Developments in Psychopharmacology*. Chapter IX, Vol. 3, 223-273. (Spectrum Publ.)

Giurgea, C. and Salama, M. (1977) Nootropic Drugs. *Progress in Neuro-Psychopharmacology*, Vol. 1, 235-247.

Konorski, J. (1967) *Integrative Activity of the Brain*. The University of Chicago Press.

Meyer, D.R. and Meyer P.M. (1977) Dynamics and bases of recoveries of functions after injuries to the cerebral cortex. *Physiological Psychology*, 5, 133-165.

Milner, B. (1972) Disorders of Learning and Memory after Temporal Lobe Lesions in Man. *Clinical Neurosurgery*, 19, 421-446.

Sara, S.J. and David-Remacle, M. (1974) Recovery from Electroconvulsive Shock-induced Amnesia by Exposure to the Training Environment: Pharmacological Enhancement by Piracetam. *Psychopharmacologia*, 36, 59-66.

Sara, S.J. and David-Remacle, M. (1977) Strychnine-induced Passive Avoidance Facilitation: A Retreival Effect. *Behavioral Biology*, 19, 465-475.

Sara, S.J., David-Remacle, M., Weyers, M. and Giurgea, C. (1978) Piracetam facilitates retrieval but does not impair extinction of bar pressing in rats. *Psychopharmacology* (in press).

Sara, S.J., Deweer, B. and Hars, B. (1977) Reticular stimulation facilitates retrieval of memory after an extended training-to-test interval. *Abstracts of the Society for Neurosciences, Annual Meeting*.

Warrington, E.K. and Weiskrantz, L. (1970) Amnesic Syndrome: Consolidation or Retrieval? *Nature* (London), 228, 628-630.

SOME PRACTICAL ASPECTS OF DRUGS AND MEMORY IN THE ELDERLY

Per Mindus, MD
Department of Psychiatry
The Karolinska Hospital
S-104 01 Stockholm, Sweden

Abstract: Two Swedish studies are used to illustrate practical psycho-social consequences of reduced mental faculties in the elderly. A curvilinear relationship between alertness and memory functions is discussed in view of clinical practice. After a short review of the literature, some practical problems in clinical trials with tentative memory drugs in the elderly are outlined and a study on mental functions with Piracetam in normally aging volunteers is reviewed. Also, a recent negative study on young, healthy volunteers is reported for comparisons. Some limitations to the practical use of future "memory drugs" are discussed as well as interesting examples of such drugs based on endogenously produced substances ("endomnesics"), e.g. neuropeptides.

INTRODUCTION

Many years of intensive memory research have contributed little to the practical management of memory impairment in the elderly. Yet, this is a formidable problem both quantitatively and qualitatively. Aging individuals are increasing in numbers in the western countries. It is well known that certain cognitive functions are impaired in the elderly. Particularly, memory functions, perceptuo-motor speed and the capacity to solve new problems seem to decline. In our achievement-oriented society, the psycho-social consequences of reduced mental (and physical) ability are obvious. Two studies from my own country, Sweden, may illustrate the practical situation of the aging person in an industrialized country. Marke and Nyman (Helander 1976) reported an increase in subjectively rated anxiety with increasing age in a large group of Swedish males. Particularly, the level of anxiety increased in the ages between 66 and 70, i.e. at retirement. A cross-sectional study comprising every third 70-year old inhabitant of Gothenburg, the second largest city in Sweden, was made by Svanborg (1977). The study showed that anxiety and nervousness were common in the group and that 1/3 of the 70-year old women studied regularly used sedative and hypnotic drugs. Every sixth of the probands did not communicate daily with other persons and 70% never visited their neighbours. It appears that many aging individuals lead a life of splendid isolation, which is not "splendid",but rather constitutes a situation of sensory deprivation. They often suffer from reduced alertness, vitality, depressed mood and complain of impaired memory function. This, in turn, tends to impair their psycho-social activity and a vicious circle may be induced (see Kuypers and Bengtsson 1973, Lehmann 1975).

AROUSAL, ANXIETY AND MEMORY FUNCTIONS

The mechanisms behind the decline in memory performance of aging individuals are not clear. Reduced alertness has been related to this decrement (Cronholm and Schalling 1976). However, Eisdorfer (1970) observed a high activation of the autonomous nervous system in aging persons in learning situations. The administration of betablockers reduced this activation and improved mental performance. In brief, there are indications that the decrement in mental performance in the elderly may be related to either a too high or a too low level of arousal or vigilance. The relationship between arousal, anxiety and mental performance has hypothetically been described as curvilinear (Hare 1970). In patients assumed to have a too high level of arousal, the administration of sedatives may reduce anxiety and improve performance, e.g. memory functions. But in states of suboptimally low levels of arousal, sedatives may induce more anxiety and further decrement in memory function. In clinical practice, aging persons suffering from insomnia are often treated with barbiturates. Some of them, paradoxically, may develop confusion and further insomnia. It is a common clinical observation that the administration of coffee may induce sleep in these patients. The point which I wish to emphasize is that in practice, pharmacotherapy with sedative and hypnotic drugs is based on the assumption that the subject's level of arousal is high. However, this may not always be the case. On the contrary, one may speculate that alertness is lowered in many aging persons with dysmnesia. Therefore drugs which increase the arousal and improve memory functions seem to be most rational in such subjects.

REVIEW OF THE LITERATURE

As regards drugs with central stimulant properties, the literature on studies of such drugs in geriatric patients was reviewed by Lehmann and Ban (1975). In 16 controlled and comparative studies on the effects of Pentylenetrazole, the most thoroughly studied of the stimulants, only five produced some clearly favourable results. Methyl phenidate is another psychostimulant. In five uncontrolled clinical studies in geriatric patients favourable results were reported, while one uncontrolled and one comparative study did not observe any beneficial effects of the drug. However, in a recent controlled study by Kaplitz (1975) of methyl phenidate in 44 apathetic and withdrawn geriatric patients, significant effects were recorded in several parameters rated by independent observers. No side-effects were reported. Coffee does not seem to have been evaluated in systematic clinical trials. Summing up, controlled clinical studies with psychostimulants are few, and the results are inconsistent.

SOME PRACTICAL ASPECTS OF RESEARCH INTO MEMORY DRUGS

As regards the practical pharmacological management of his elderly patients with dysmnesia, the clinician will have to rely on researchers providing suitable compounds. Unfortunately, research in geriatric psychopharmacology has almost exclusively concerned the development of antipsychotic and sedative pharmaceuticals. In comparison, little attention has been paid to research into memory improving substances. This is remarkable when one considers the access to appropriate animal models: aging rats are plentiful - rats with e.g. guilt feelings or delusions are not. Although animal experiments with tentative "memory pills" may seem promising, preliminary clinical trials may give negative or vague results. In some cases this has to do not only with characteristics of the compounds tested, but also with the designs of the clinical trials. This leads us to some practical aspects of clinical research on "memory drugs". The group of subjects studied should be as homogenous as possible in respect of sex, socio-economic status, education, diagnosis, duration of illness, degree of pathology, chronological, and - if it were possible to determine - biological age. The subjects' clinical conditions should not be too severe: institutionalized, bed-ridden patients may therefore be unsuitable for this kind of clinical trials. Geriatric populations often are heterogenous in these respects. A drug may have beneficial effects in one, but not in another subgroup and the net drug effect will be nil. Intra-individual comparisons with balanced "cross-over" may be used to reduce inter-group of inter-individual variations. Of course, drug effects must be estimated with reliable and validated methods. At the Department of Psychiatry, the Karolinska Hospital, Stockholm, we have tried to develop such methods. As a practical example of clinical research on drugs and memory in the elderly, I will report briefly on a study with Piracetam (1-acetamide-2-pyrrolidone, Nootrop^{R}).

PIRACETAM

Piracetam has been shown to improve learning and memorizing in young and aging rats. It also exerts a protection against the effects on learning of hypoxia and electro-convulsive shocks (Giurgea and Mouravieff-Lesuisse 1972, Sara and Lefevre 1972). In man, controlled clinical studies have shown effects of the drug on states of fatigue, lack of vitality and other symptoms related to aging (inter al. Stegink 1972, Kretschmar and Kretschmar 1976). Other authors have not been able to confirm these results (inter al. Dencker and Lindberg 1977, Gustafson et al. 1977). This may have to do with differences in material, method and dosage. The mechanisms of action of Piracetam are not clear. According to Giurgea (1973), the drug increases the ATP/ADP ratio in the brain. It is assumed that this ratio decreases with age. The drug does not have central stimulant properties as judged from biochemical studies in rat (Nybäck et al. 1978).

INFLUENCE OF PIRACETAM ON NORMALLY AGING VOLUNTEERS

We studied the effects of the drug in 18 healthy, normally aging individual with the median age of 56 years (Mindus et al. 1976). They all reported a certain but constant impairment of their memory and concentration abilities. Intra-individual comparisons of their performance with Piracetam and a placebo was made with double-blind, balanced cross-over technique. Performance was evaluated with self-ratings, two independent observers' ratings, a verbal memory test and manual and computerized perceptuo-motor tests which have been shown to be sensitive to drug-induced variations in perceptuo-motor functions. In their present forms they have high test-retest reliabilities. In brief, the subjects did significantly better on a majority of the tests when on Piracetam. This was in agreement with the observers' ratings. The results are summarized in the Table I. However, even if significant statistical differences were obtained, the effects in individual cases were sometimes small. Continued research may perhaps provide us with more potent drugs.

Self-ratings	non-significant
Psychologist's ratings	$p < .05$
Psychiatrist's ratings	$p < .05$
The Bourdon-Wiersma test	$p < .001$
The Digit Symbol test	$p < .001$
The Spoke test	$p < .05$
The KS Memory test	non-significant
The Reaction time test	$p < .10$
Critical flicker fusion (asc)	non-significant
Critical flicker fusion (dsc)	$p < .05$
The Krakau visual acuity test	$p < .05$

Table 1. Results of ratings and tests of 18 normally aging volunteeers when on Piracetam as compared to a placebo. (From Mindus et al. 1976)

INFLUENCE OF PIRACETAM IN YOUNG VOLUNTEERS

Researchers in gerontology and geriatrics often make use of comparisons between aging and younger populations. Therefore it may be of some interest to report here briefly on the effects of Piracetam in the young, healthy individual. Dimond and Brouwers, in their interesting study (1976), recorded statistically significant improvement of verbal learning in eight students of psychology in comparison to eight students receiving a placebo. However, the authors noted no significant effects of the drug on a non-verbal test. In order to elucidate this further we studied the effects of Piracetam on 24 young military subjects (non-smokers) undergoing highly qualified military training (Mindus et al., in preparation). Self-and two independent observers' ratings, computerized analyses (SPA) of their EEG's and manual and computerized tests like those above were given. In addition, Elithorn's maze, a new Nonsense Syllable memory test and a Digit Span test were administered with an on-line minicomputer. No statistically significant improvement of performance on tests were obtained with Piracetam. One of the two observers (P.M.), however, rated subjects as highly significantly more alert, vigilant , etc.when on Piracetam than on placebo. Also, the SPA revealed statistically significant differences in the EEG's, but the effect pattern was variable and difficult to interpret. In summary, one may conclude that the drug has different effects in the normally aging and in the young healthy subjects, at least when effects are estimated with our methods.

The discrepancy between the above results and those reported by Dimond and Brouwers (1976) may be related to differences in material and method (e.g. intra-v.s. inter-individual comparisons, the use of verbal v.s. non-verbal tests, smoking habits of subjects, etc.). The authors discuss a selective effect of Piracetam on verbal memory. With respect, I do not believe in such a selectiveness in a simple compound like Piracetam, which probably readily penetrates into the cells. It may well have a generalized effect not only within the central nervous system, but also on extra-cerebral cells. A support for this assumption is the observation by Sheth (1975, pc), that the walking pain threshold of a patient with angina pectoris varied with the repeated single-blind administration of Piracetam, placebo, Piracetam, placebo etc.

PRACTICAL USE

Even if clinical trials indicate that a compound improves memory functions in the elderly, this does not guarantee its practical usefulness. Of many practical aspects (side-effects, drug regimen compliance, interaction with other drugs taken by "polydrug" aging persons etc), I wish to point at a few general aspects that sometimes seem to be forgotten: 1. The drug must be packed in bottles that may be opened by individuals with reduced hand strength and motility - a practical problem for many aging persons. 2. The drug must be easy to take (swallow). 3. The drug regimen must be simple. 4. Prepacked medication boxes (Dosett[R]) indicating next dose are useful to prevent overdosage due to automatism and forgetfulness. They should also be equipped with symbols for persons with reduced vision.

Let us presume that memory researchers have provided the clinicians with a drug which possesses all these virtues. Then another practical problem arises. How do clinicians know which patients are likely to benefit from the drug? Here we must turn to the psychologists to ask them to provide us with simple screening methods.

Finally, let me conclude this review of some practical aspects on drugs and memory in the elderly with a theoretical speculation. Matthies and co-workers (1973) have shown that the RNA precursor orotic acid, which is probably synthesized in the brain, is of importance to memory functions. Recently, a beneficial effect of thiaminedisulfide monoorotate on human memory was reported (Szirmai et al. 1977). Also, de Wied and collaborators demonstrated the effects on animal learning and memory of ACTH-like substances and of vasopressin analogues (de Wied et al. 1975, de Wied 1977). Recently, a beneficial influence of vasopressin on learning and memory in humans was reported (Legros et al., Oliveros et al., 1978). It appears that the administration of certain substances postulated to be produced in the brain may be useful in the treatment of dysmnesias. The concept of endogenous "memory substances", which I would call "endomnesics", is very appealing.

REFERENCES

Cronholm, B. and Schalling, D. (1976) Cognitive decline with aging, and working capacity. *Proceedings of a symposium on Society, Stress and Disease. Stockholm.*

Dencker, S.J., and Lindberg, D. (1977) A double-blind study of Piracetam in the treatment of Senile Dementia. *Nord, Psykiat. Tidskr.*, 31, 48-52.

Dimond, S.J. and Brouwers, E.Y.M. (1976) Increase in the power of human memory in normal man through the use of drugs. *Psychopharmacology*, 49, 307-309.

Eisdorfer, C. (1970) Improvement of learning in the aged by modification of autonomic nervous system activity. *Science*, 170, 1327-1329.

Giurgea, C.E. and Mouravieff-Lesuisse, F. (1972) Effet facilitateur du piracetam sur un apprentissage répétif chez le rat. *Journal of Pharmacology*, 3, 17-30.

Giurgea, C.E. (1973) The "nootropic" approach to the integrative activity of the brain. *Condition. Reflex*, 8, 108-115.

Gustafson, L., Risberg, J., Johansson, M., Fransson, H. and Maximilian, V.A. (1977) Effects of Piracetam on regional cerebral blood flow and mental functions in patients with organic dementia. *Psychopharmacology*, 56, 115-118.

Hare, R.D. (1970) *Psychopathy. Theory and Research.* Wiley, New York.

Helander, J. (1976) Hygiene conditions at work and the problem of premature aging. *Proceedings of a symposium on Society, Stress and Diseased, Stockholm.*

Kretschmar, J.H. and Kretschmar, C. (1976) On the dose-effects relationship in the therapy with Piracetam. *Drug Research*, 26, 1158-1159.

Kuypers, J.S. and Bengtsson, V.L. (1973) Social breakdown and competence - a model of normal aging. *Human Development*, 16, 181-201.

Legros, J.J., Gilot, P., Weron, X., Claessens, J., Adam, A., Moeglin, J.A., Audiberg, A. and Berchier, P. (1978) Influence of vasopressin on learning and memory. *Lancet*, 1, 41-42.

Lehmann, H.E. (1975) Rational pharmacotherapy in geropsychiatry. *Proceeding of the 10th International Congress of Gerontology, Jerusalem.*

Matthies, H. (1973) Biochemical regulation of synaptic connectivity. In Zippel, H.P. (Ed.) *Memory and transfer of information.* Plenum Press, New York and London.

Mindus, P., Cronholm, B., Levander, S.E and Schalling, D. (1976) Piracetam-induced improvement of mental performance. *Acta Psychiatry, Scandinavia,* 54, 150-160.

Mindus, P. and Schalling, D. (1977) The use of non-sedative drugs in the elderly. *Proceeding of the IV Congress of the International College of Psychosomatic Medicine,Kyoto.*

Nyback, H., Wiesel, F-A. and Skett, P. (1978) Effects of Piracetam in brain monoamine metabolism and serum prolactin levels in rat. Submitted to *Psychopharmacology.*

Oliveros, J.C., Jandali, M.K., Timsit-Berthier, M., Remy, R. Audiberg, A. and Moeglin, J.M. (1978) Vasopressin in amnesia. *Lancet,* 1, 42.

Sara, S.J. and Lefevre, D.(1972) Hypoxia-induced amnesia in one-trial learning and pharmacological protection by Piracetam. *Psychopharmacologia (Berl.)* 25, 32-40.

Sheth, P. (1975) *Personal communication.*

Stegink, A.J. (1972) The clinical use of Piracetam, a new nootropic drug. *Drug Research,* 22, 975-977.

Svanborg, A. (1977) Seventy-year-old people in Gothenburg. A population study in an industrialized Swedish city. II General presentation of social and medical condition. *Acta Medicine, Scandinavian Supplement,* 611, 5-37.

Szirmai, E., Klosa, J., Srebo, Z. and McGuigan, F.J. (1977) The influence of Thiaminedisulfide Monoorotate on the Human Memory. *Drug Research,* 27 (11), 12, 2414-2416.

deWied, D., Bohus, B. and Van Wimersma-Greidanus, T.B.(1975) The significance of vasopressin for pituitary ACTH release in conditioned emotional situation. *Symposium of the International Society of Psycho-neuroendocrinology, Visegrad.*

de Wied, D. (1977) Behavioural effects of neuropeptides related to ACTH, MSH and beta-LPH. In: Kriger DR, Ganong, W.F. (Eds.) *ACTH and related peptides: Structure, Regulation and Action. Annals of the New York Academy of Science,* 297, 263-274.

DRUGS AND MEMORY : METHODOLOGICAL ISSUES AND DATA

Dylan M. Jones
Department of Applied Psychology
UWIST, Cardiff
Malcolm J. Lewis and T.L. Brian Spriggs
Department of Pharmacology,
Welsh National School of Medicine, Cardiff.

This paper critically evaluates three approaches to the study of drug-induced changes in retention : (a) retrospective analysis, (b) performance on a wide range of psychological tasks, and (c) comparisons between performance in various memory paradigms. Data from two experiments involving the effects of benzodiazepines (diazepam and nitrazepam) and an anticholinergic drug (hyoscine) on retention are used to illustrate the latter two approaches. These drugs appear to act by having a deleterious effect on primary memory. It is claimed that the absence of an adequate task taxonomy encompassing both memory and non-memory tasks makes such conclusions about functional deficits at best tentative.

INTRODUCTION

This paper outlines two exploratory experiments involving the action of benzodiazepines (diazepam and nitrazepam) and an anticholinergic drug (hyoscine) on memory of healthy adult subjects. Apart from an exposition of what we believe to be the mode of action of these drugs, we hope to raise several methodological issues in relation to the study of the effects of drugs on memory. This account will therefore forego a detailed analysis of the data in an attempt to illustrate methodological issues with relevant empirical testimony (for a detailed account of these experiments see : Jones, Lewis and Spriggs, 1978; Jones, Jones, Lewis and Spriggs, in preparation).

At the outset it should be understood that the object of study is a clear and unambiguous account of drug-induced changes in memory rather than a generalized change in performance. There are three main methods which can be employed to converge on this aim. The first is a retrospective analysis of the sensitivity of various tasks, representing a range of psychological function, to the drug. This approach is typified by McNair's (1973) compilation of the performance effects of anti-anxiety drugs. He listed the results of ninety-seven studies eventually classing the tasks employed into those of high, average, low or indeterminate sensitivity. Not only were the levels of task sensitivity disappointingly low, but the analysis did not reveal any readily distinguishable psychological factors which differentiated sensitive from non-sensitive tasks. For instance, the learning of paired-associates was a highly sensitive task, while the learning of nonsense syllables was an insensitive one. Obviously, without any intra-experimental confirmation of these effects and a more explicit psychological account of the differences between these tasks any conclusions must be considered tentative. Any approach of this sort will founder on the inevitable insufficiency of experiments involving a particular task. In McNair's case tasks of high or low sensitivity were represented by fewer studies than those of average sensitivity.

The second approach is illustrated by our first experiment; that of employing a battery of psychological tasks representing both memory and non-memory tasks with a view to localizing a drug-induced effect to one particular faculty. The third approach, which follows from the second, is a comparison of different types of memory tasks. This method should allow the localization at a particular stage or level of processing of the drug's action. This last system is illustrated by our second experiment.

EXPERIMENT 1.

This study investigated the effects of a clinically typical dose of diazepam (5 mg) on a range of tasks. As in both our studies the design employed independent groups of subjects, each subject randomly assigned to treatments. Three groups were assembled, viz. placebo, control, and drug groups. Treatments were administered orally under double-blind conditions. Five tasks were used in all : an auditory vigilance task - involving the detection of infrequent signals consisting of three successive odd and uneven digits in an hour long session, with digits presented at a rate of one per second; a visual search task: searching for a few letters among many, lasting fifteen minutes; a mental arithmetic task requiring three-by-two digit multiplication, for fifteen minutes; and finally, a short term memory task involving the recall of auditorily presented nine digit strings.

There were no significant effects of diazepam on vigilance (correct detections and commission errors) or mental arithmetic (attempts and errors). However, visual search did show an effect of drug, with the number of letters being 22.53% fewer in the drug condition than in the placebo condition ($t = 3.73$; d.f. = 50; $p < 0.01$). Short term memory for digits was also significantly influenced by the drug. This effect took the form of a drug by serial position interaction ($F = 1.65$; d.f. = 16,600 $p < 0.05$). The diazepam group showed more errors in the early and, more particularly, the medial serial positions than both the placebo and control groups.

What can we deduce about the characteristics of drug sensitive tasks? In this first study no single characteristic seems to differentiate sensitive from insensitive tasks. For example, mental arithmetic was insensitive to the action of the drug yet it contains elements of self-pacing and short-term memory which were characteristics of the two sensitive tasks. Similarly the vigilance task was paced like short-term memory, but it was insensitive. These examples highlight the difficulty of inferring faculty from task. There is a danger of falling into a nominalist trap whereby labels attached to tasks are taken to be exclusive descriptors of the underlying mode of action. From these data it seems likely that a combination of factors, rather than single characteristics of tasks, may be responsible from the drug-induced deficits. The finding that diazepam impairs the performance of several tasks may imply that a common combination of task-demand characteristics rather than one particular faculty is affected.

EXPERIMENT 2.

This study exemplifies the third method outlined above, that of comparing the action of drugs on a range of memory tasks. Like the comparison of memory and non-memory tasks this approach is plagued by an absence of consensus about what makes the tasks different. In other words, there is no adequate task taxonomy available.

We attempted to further investigate the anti-memory effect found in experiment 1 by employing two memory tasks with one involving the free recall of categorizable lists (c.f.Bousfield, 1953) and, as before, a task involving short term memory for digits. It was hoped that the study would replicate our earlier finding with digit span and allow us to explore the possibility that drugs influence the higher-order organization involved in categorical recall. In addition, we compared the action of two drugs, nitrazepam and hyoscine, against a placebo group. This was done with a view to differentiating these two drugs, with their different pharmacological actions, in psychological terms.

Both hyoscine and nitrazepam have been shown to produce anti-memory effects. Recent evidence indicates that these effects may arise out of different pharmacological actions. Hyoscine appears to act centrally on cholinergic mechanisms: Ghoneim and Mewaldt (1977) found that physostigmine acted in an antagonistic fashion to the effects of hyoscine on memory but no antagonistic effects were found between physostigmine and a diazepam-induced memory deficit. Latterly, Costa, Guidotti, Mao and Suria (1975) have suggested that the action of diazepam is GABA-ergic.

Nitrazepam (5 mg), hyoscine (hyoscine hydrobromide, 0.3 mg) and placebo (lactose) treatments were administered orally under double-blind conditions. Figure 1 shows that both hyoscine and nitrazepam produced deleterious effects on digit retention. This effect took the form of a drug by serial position interaction ($F = 1.88$; d.f. = 16,784, $p < 0.05$). Notice that both drugs produce roughly equivalent effects in both extent and location. Most striking is the absence of any effect in recency. Performance on early items in serial lists of this sort is generally considered to be a result of the action of primary memory. It appears from these data that these drugs influence the action of this store. The recency portion of the auditory serial position curve has been ascribed to the action of Precategorical Acoustic Storage (PAS). Crowder and Morton (1969) envisage that PAS is the auditory analogue of the visual buffer outlined by Sperling (1960). These present data indicate that the action of PAS is not influenced by either hyoscine or nitrazepam.

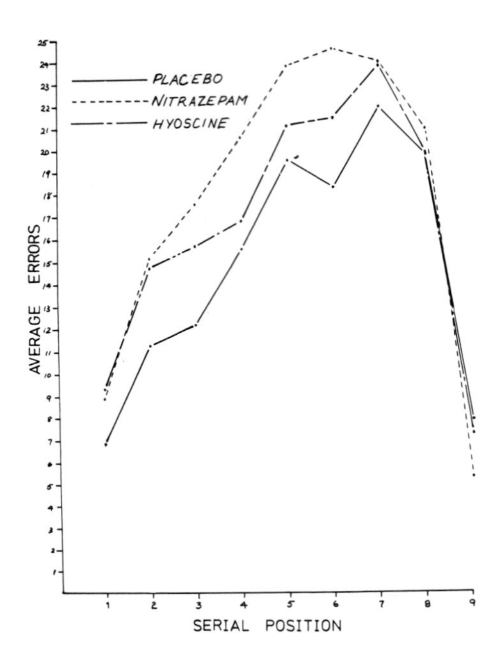

Fig. I. Serial position curves for nitrazepam, hyoscine, and placebo groups.

In the category clustering task five lists of thirty items were presented. Within each list there were six randomly inserted instances of each of five categories drawn from the Battig and Montague (1969) norms. There was no effect of drugs on the number of items recalled ($F = 1.07$; d.f. = 2.99, $p > 0.05$). Clustering was assessed using two computed scores: the C - score of Dalymple-Alford (1970) and the BDD-score of Bousfield and Bousfield (1966). Neither scoring technique showed any main effect of drug (C - scores arc-sin transformed: $F = 0.54$; d.f. = 2.99; $p > 0.05$). These data from the second study suggest that while nitrazepam and hyoscine have differing pharmacological actions their psychological action may be identical and task specific.

GENERAL DISCUSSION

The presence of an effect with digit retention and the absence of an effect with category clustering might be put down to a number of sources. For example the tasks were presented in different modalities. However experiment 1 showed that a visual task (namely visual search) is capable of showing an effect of benzodiazepines. Moreover an auditory vigilance task containing a short-term memory component failed to show an effect in experiment 1. Another distinguishing feature between the tasks in experiment 2 was the use of order cues : recall for digit strings was ordered whereas the clustering task required free recall. Indeed in the latter task the very antithesis of serial ordering was necessary since items were drawn from disparate portions of the list in the assemblage of cohesive clusters. In view of these differences one possible explanation about the particular form of the results is that these centrally depressant drugs reduce the use of availability of order cues. Thus serial recall of digits would be deleteriously affected but categorical recall would be undisturbed by the drugs. However this view presupposes that in normal circumstances order cues do not in fact impair categorical recall.

In conclusion, we advocate that before the action of any drug can be labelled 'anti-memory' a clear distinction should be made between the effects of the drug upon performance and its effects on retention. It may be the high loading of intrinsic knowledge of failure, so characteristic of memory, that is the mediating factor rather than retention *per se* (see Jones, 1979 for a discussion of these issues).

REFERENCES

Battig, W.F. and Montague, W.E. (1969). Category norms for verbal items in 56 verbal categories. *Journal of Experimental Psychology (Monograph)*. 80, part 2, 1 6 45.

Bousfield, W.A. (1953). The occurrence of clustering in recall of randomly arranged associates. *Journal of General Psychology*. 49, 229-240.

Bousfield, A.K. and Bousfield, W.A. (1966). Measurement of clustering and sequential constancies in repeated free recall. *Psychological Reports*. 19, 935-942.

Costa, E., Guidotti, A., Mao, C.C., and Suria, A. (1975). New concepts on the mechanism of action of benzodiazepines. *Life Sciences*. 17, 167-168.

Crowder, R.G. and Morton, J. (1969). Precategorical acoustic storage. *Perception and Psychophysics*. 5, 365-373

Dalrymple-Alford, E.C. (1970). The measurement of clustering in free recall. *Psychological Bulletin*. 1, 32-34

Ghoneim, M.M. and Mewaldt, S.P. (1977). Studies on human memory : The interactions of diazepam, acopalamine and physostigmine. *Psychopharmacology*. 52, 1 - 6.

Jones, D.M. (1979). Stress,arousal and memory. In :Applied Problems in Memory. (M.M. Gruneberg and P.E. Morris, eds), Academic Press : London (in press).

Jones, D.M., Lewis, M.J. and Spriggs, T.L.B. (1978). Effects of low doses of diazepam on human performance in group administered tasks. *British Journal of Clinical Pharmacology*. (in press).

Jones, D.M., Jones, M.E.L., Lewis, M.J. and Spriggs, T.L.B. (1979). Drugs and memory : effects of low doses of nitrazepam and hyoscine on retention. *British Journal of Clinical Pharmacology* (in preparation).

Sperling, G. (1960). The information available in brief visual presentations. *Psychological Monographs*. (Whole No. 11).

McNair, D.M. (1973). Antianxiety drugs and human performance. *Archives of General Psychiatry*. 29, 611 - 617.

INDEX OF CONTRIBUTORS

SUBJECT INDEX